A History of Esthetics

A History of
ESTHETICS

REVISED AND ENLARGED

by *Katharine Everett Gilbert*

Late Professor of Philosophy in Duke University

and *Helmut Kuhn*

Professor of Philosophy in
the University of Erlangen

GREENWOOD PRESS, PUBLISHERS
WESTPORT, CONNECTICUT

The Library of Congress has catalogued this publication as follows:

Library of Congress Cataloging in Publication Data

Gilbert, Katharine (Everett) 1886-1952.
   A history of esthetics.

   Includes bibliographies.
   1. Aesthetics--History. I. Kuhn, Helmut, 1899-
joint author. II. Title.
[BH81.G5 1972]   111.8'5   76-163548
ISBN 0-8371-6207-6

111.85
G465h
1972

Copyright 1939; Copyright 1953 by Indiana University Press

Originally published in 1954
by Indiana University Press, Bloomington

Reprinted with the permission
of Indiana University Press

First Greenwood Reprinting 1972

Library of Congress Catalogue Card Number 76-163548

ISBN 0-8371-6207-6

Printed in the United States of America

"Aesthetic reflection . . . . has always been most vital when most historical"

BOSANQUET

PREFACE TO SECOND EDITION

FOR THIS second edition a new final chapter, entirely displacing that in the first, has been written by Mrs. Gilbert; Mr. Kuhn has no responsibility for the present form of the work. Minor corrections and revisions have been made throughout. Mrs. Gilbert is greatly indebted to Dr. Freda L. Townsend and Dr. Rosa Lee Walston for thoughtful and painstaking assistance in the preparation of this edition.

PREFACE

THIS BOOK is designed for those University students of the various arts and for all other curious souls who are possessed with a more than common desire to know what esthetic terms mean. What is here written is based, not on absolute definitions of those terms nor on any fixed philosophical system, but on a theory of the best way to satisfy that desire. He who can go to the fountainhead will not fetch his drink from the water pitchers, Leonardo da Vinci said. This book aims in a sense to lead the more than commonly curious to the fountainheads. But fountainheads in philosophy are not located definitely, as the analogy might suggest, on some map of the streams and centers of culture. If they were, an anthology of sources might have been furnished, and so the task completed. Of course one may get a little way along in the process of understanding by reading what Heraclitus said about poets, St. Thomas about beauty, and Helmholtz about music. But to learn what any man, or any number of men, thought about esthetic questions, will not of itself slake philosophical thirst. The slowly developed conclusions of the thinkers of the world must always be transfused into the intellectual circulatory system of the inquirer to become appeasing truth. Even this is not enough. The mere transfusion of the lifeblood of master spirits into receptive minds is not yet truth. Though the situation is too static, too mechanical, when the inquirer's mind is simply exposed to a series of classic utterances, there is too much pure flux in the mere circulation of current of ideas, the turning and returning of a stream piped between source and seeker. A radical transubstantiation into element of mind for all the participating members of the situation must take place before there can be genuine progress toward understanding what esthetic terms mean.

An interpretation of this radical transubstantiation should begin to suggest the nature of this book to anyone who wishes to know. Those who wrote it, like their proposed readers, were possessed with a more than common desire to know what art and beauty mean. They therefore asked many of those who in centuries past had reflected on these terms what relevant ideas they had been able to develop. The answers were received into minds that questioned once again, because already in a measure furnished. After thousands of years of accumulated opinion on the nature of art and beauty, the mind of an inquirer today, however eager, cannot be an empty room. However strong the intention of clearing the mind of obstructing preconceptions, the pride and mass of twenty-five hundred years of argument and reflection will stir within one and make its stand. Even while listening to the ancients, there will be the impulse on the part of the modern to say with the humanist Giovanni Pico and the pioneer Bacon: We are the true ancients of the world and on the shoulders of those who have gone before. Why then should we altogether conform our conceptions to those of the inexperienced and youthful in the world's history?

Soon the dialogue between the writers and the sources began to grow more subtle and complicated. The first dialogue seemed as time went on to be supplanted by a second, and in the new one the parties and platforms were less definitely located. Moreover, the new one had a fascinating, but at the same time baffling, way of suspending itself in a middle sphere halfway between the historical documents and the writers. And the questions and answers, the claims and retorts, passing between the two main interlocutory parties yielded now and then and more and more to a dialogue between the giants themselves. With that, the writers of this history resumed their attitude of listening. Instead of answering back they fancied themselves hearing something, and hearing not so much direct question and answer among the members of the tradition as these reverend sources engaging closely with each other, extenuating their various errors, explaining at some length the connotation of their terms and definitions, trying little by little to make an in-

tellectual design out of what began as debate—and all this philosophical process happening not 'out there,' rather within the
writers' heads, or if not quite housed within, then taking place on
some tenuous spiritual platform projected ethereally out from the
writers' own minds in the direction of the historical interlocutors.

For example, early in the business the writers listened to the
words of Plato and Aristotle on the subject of the art of rhetoric.
First Plato said: Rhetoric is not an art; it is a knack. Aristotle countered: Rhetoric is an art whose method and parts I can and will
set out. Plato then defended himself: I myself dealt with the
structure of good speeches in the *Phaedrus*, but in the *Gorgias*
I showed the other sort of speech-making which you have
neglected. Then as to the listening writers the plot of the dialogue
began to thicken, the over-againstness of the historical figures,
Plato and Aristotle, began to disappear, the resisting intellectual
substance of each of the speakers began to melt into coöperating
emphases and stages in a development, and the life of history, a
greater thing than any man or any document, began to take up all
persons present: Plato, Aristotle, and the inquiring writers, into
itself, making them functions and organs of its sustaining spirit.
Another instance: as an untreated source St. Augustine told the
curious authors of this book who were possessed with the passion
to know what art and beauty mean: Number, weight, and measure
are beautiful, as dispositions of the living God who is the Father
of Beauty. And again as untreated source William Blake said to
them: "Bring out number, weight, and measure in a year of death."
In this case the authors had a contradiction to interpret, not as in
the case of Plato and Aristotle, by exploring further the writings
and experiences of a master and pupil, but by sympathetically entering into the determining animus of widely sundered ages. Behind St. Augustine was a decaying Pythagoreanism baptized and
given second birth by Christianity. Behind William Blake was
weariness of mathematical science and thirst for exuberance and
flowing energy. So all the way along interpreting context and
source material had thus to be bound together to make sense out of
the conceptions of art and beauty proposed by the thinkers of the
various periods. The esthetic abstractions in the idealistic German

movement of the early nineteenth century became less forbiddingly abstract, took on indeed an altogether more becoming complexion, when the same abstract terms—absolute, unity, synthesis—were found in the unoffending love-letter literature of the time. Effluences of courtships endeared the metaphysical Higher Unities!

What then do art and beauty mean? After submitting to the discipline of history the authors must say: Their meaning is not within the four corners of any one or two propositions, but is that fullness of significance which distills from the long-sustained process of all the definings. Who today would say where beauty lies? It is neither in Athens nor Strassburg, but in all the places where there has been an objective counterpart of an authentic esthetic feeling. The meaning of art and the meaning of beauty are similarly within the dialectic of the whole manifold of philosophical systems and styles.

ACKNOWLEDGMENTS

The authors wish to express their gratitude for various types of assistance. The Graham Kenan Fellowship in Philosophy under the directorship of Professor Horace Williams of the University of North Carolina made possible the first years of study leading toward this book and helped again the final year. The Research Council of Duke University granted aid toward it for five years. Dr. Clara W. Crane rendered invaluable assistance in searching and making records from many sources. Professor Clarence Thorpe of the University of Michigan permitted the authors the privilege of an examination of a manuscript on the esthetics of Hobbes; Professor George A. Morgan of Duke University, of a manuscript on Nietzsche. Professors George F. Thomas and Stephen A. Emery of the University of North Carolina read and made helpful suggestions concerning parts of the manuscript of this book. The authors also wish to acknowledge the special generosity of Dr. Marion Crane Carroll, and Dr. Edgar Wind of the Warburg Institute. Mr. Arthur Dowling of Duke University has attended to innumerable details. *The Philosophical Review* is here thanked for permitting the use of about seven pages of Mrs. Gilbert's article entitled "Aesthetic Imitation and Imitators in Aristotle" of November, 1936.

Mrs. Gilbert labored on this book for some years before Mr. Kuhn became her collaborator. Mrs. Gilbert is in the main responsible for chapters two to twelve with the exception of the second half of chapters ten and eleven; also chapter thirteen and the second half of chapter fourteen. The rest are for the most part the work of Mr. Kuhn. But there is much of each author in the other's portion.

––––––––––

The brief book-lists at the end of the chapters are not offered as bibliographies but as first aids to students using this book and needing other types of general information on the periods and writers discussed. No standard text by the important individual authors is given in these supplementary lists, as the notes consist largely in references to such works. So far as was possible the lists have been restricted to include only works in English.

K. E. G.

H. K.

November, 1939

TABLE OF CONTENTS

mony and symmetry dominate number. – Ugliness a failure of esthetic response. – Secret accord between subject and object. – Aquinas echoes Augustine. – Shining form; shaped effulgence. – Clarity. – Material aspect of light. – The Ladder of Beauty. – Esthetics and religion. – Likeness and difference of Creator and created. – The created as shell of truth. – Symbol. – Manifold meanings. – Reversed substantiality of spirit and flesh. – Beauty and imagination mediate between one and many. – Augustine's reasoned defense of beauty. – Remote symbols. – Time in beauty. – The veil sometimes approaches independence. – No 'fine art' in Middle Ages. – But servile arts approach fineness. – Art as making. – Beauty may inform art but does not lie within it.

CHAPTER VI

Renaissance (1300-1600) 162

How new a birth was the Renaissance? – The mirror. – The veil. – From craft to profession. – The Renaissance, complete and complex. – Art elevated by demonstrating its godliness. – But the new secular spirit requires intellectuality also. – Labor: what is hard to do is pleasant in achievement. – Mental equipment of the artist. – The artist as philosopher and critic. – The importance of learning. – Art is nature at one remove. – Rôle of mathematics. – Mystical strain. – The dignity of man. – Poetry as imitation. – Ancients the 'fountain' for literary waterdrawers. – Art's moral and metaphysical import. – Beauty as concealed nature. – Sidney: the poet as improver of what is. – Art no longer cosmic energy but human power. – Harmony deepens its meaning. – Design: rationalized intuition of harmony. – Poetic enthusiasm. – Fracastoro: the enhancement of nature. – Nature as stimulus to creation rather than subject for copying. – The problem of pleasure. – Beauty as expedition of sensory function. – Secularization brings rationality and individuality. – Classics fallible to spirit of modernity. – Castelvetro: delight and novelty as poetic ends. – Dürer on genius. – Poetry as pure fiction. – Rebellion in criticism.

CHAPTER VII

The Seventeenth Century and the Neo-Classic Regime to 1750 201

Reason in philosophy, rules in art. – Democritus supplants Aristotle. – Ambiguity of imagination in Bacon. – Descartes: beauty is equable stimulation. – Demonstration final even for beauty. – Hobbes: the mind is matter in motion. – Fancy, however, is purposive, quasi-rational, synoptic. – Hobbes' esthetic psychology between two worlds. – Synthesis left for the critics. – Moral aim fundamental. – 'Invention' and its sources. – Deep meaning of 'verum' in verisimilitude. – Reason and

CHAPTER VIII

The Eighteenth Century British School 233

CHAPTER IX

The Eighteenth Century in Italy and France   268

CHAPTER X

German Rationalism and the New Art Criticism   289

CHAPTER XI

Classical German Esthetics: Kant, Goethe, Humboldt, Schiller   321

tion. – Goethe both a subject for esthetics and a teacher of it. – Harmony of intellect and imagination in Goethe. – Imagination anticipates reality. The artist master and slave of nature. – The creative emulation of artist and nature. – Love creates beauty. – Humboldt's esthetics part of a universal anthropology. – The dialectic of creation and appreciation. – Schiller the moralist sympathetic to Kant, Schiller the poet critical. – The synthetic function of Schiller's theory. – "All poets are nature or seek nature." – The corruption of mankind and the problem of an esthetic education. – The play-drive responsible for artistic creativeness. – An esthetic ideal of human perfection.

Contents

CHAPTER XIV

Absolute Idealism: Fichte, Schelling, Hegel

Esthetics as center of philosophical development. – Intellectual and esthetic intuition. – Esthetics within Schelling's system of 'Absolute Idealism.' – Art manifests eternal forms within the 'reflected' world. – Affinity of art and organic nature. – Schelling's system of arts. – Greek mythology as artistic creation. It reveals philosophy of nature. – Speculative history of art. – Hegel's dialectical reconciliation of contrasts. – Nature creeps up toward beauty, but only art achieves it. – The formal principles qualify rather than constitute beauty. – The best material for art: the Divine in human shape. – Oriental symbolism the forecourt of art. – Perfection reached in Classic art. – Art eclipsed by Christian spiritualism. Romantic art and its disintegration in Romantic irony. – The system of arts corresponds to the history of art. – Poetry—the universal art. – Limits of the dialectical reconciliation.

CHAPTER XV

Dualistic Idealism: Solger, Schleiermacher, Schopenhauer

Art, through irony, reveals ideal world. – Solger's 'irony' not identical with Romantic irony. – Schleiermacher's *via media* between construction and experience. – First definition: art is expression. – Second definition: art an imaginative play. – Unity of the two proposed definitions. – Schopenhauer's metaphysical paradox: blind striving supplants reason. – Hedonistic Pessimism. – Salvation through Platonic-esthetic contemplation. – System of arts reflects hierarchy of Ideas. – Music reveals Will itself. – Estheticism anticipated.

CHAPTER XVI

Society and the Artist

Art's place within the new society. – French Idealism under German influence. – Saint-Simon: the artist in the triumvirate of reform. – Comte: art is conditioned by the present and prepares the future society. – Taine: art is a product of its environment. – Naturalism—the new democratic art. – The artist comes home to earth. Zola: the poet as experimentalist. – Guyau: the principle of art is life. – Art for Art's Sake Movement—disillusioned Romanticism. – Worship of

of Croce's simplification: Has he purified art at the expense of the
art-object's physical reality? — Collingwood, at first a Crocean, turns
to an interpretation of art's new ways. — *The Waste Land*, our age's
healing revelation. — Santayana, complement to Croce, makes art
spring from physical nature and accident but at times ascend to symbolic wisdom. — About 1925 begins the dominance of theories of the
symbol. — Ernst Cassirer, a pioneer. — Contributions to the theory of
symbols by the Warburg Institute. — Susanne Langer's theory of the
symbolism of music: unconsummated symbol of the inner life. —
Semantic analysis of I. A. Richards: evocative function of poetical
signs, projectile adjectives. — Empson on ambiguity. — Esthetic pluralism in semantics. — The rational and logical outside semantics.—
Popularity of interpretation through psychoanalytical symbols. — Bodkin on archetypes; Nahm on presuppositions. — The Neo-Thomist
roots symbolic function in Divine activity; the Oriental in metaphysical correspondences.—From doctrine of symbols to various psychological trends. — Instinct the basis of artist's creative power. —The
good Gestalt is the physiognomy of a whole. — Types and temperaments. — Variety of artistic temperaments; classifications of Evans
and Read, following Jung and Dilthey. — Herbert Read on importance
of art for society. Need to recover trust of feeling and intuition. —
Support of Bergson and Whitehead. — The new architects and designers have a theory of communal human values. — Lewis Mumford's
organic social philosophy balanced by respect for the individual. —
John Dewey's social philosophy flowers in esthetics.— Achievements
of his followers. — Lalo's relativistic esthetics is social and modelled
on musical polyphony. — Many historical researches and translations;
fewer general systems. — Phenomenological esthetics of Moritz Geiger.
— Studies in recent esthetics. —Journals.

A History of Esthetics

CHAPTER I

Beginnings

THE THREE following quotations from Xenophanes and Heraclitus point truly to the intellectual situation from which esthetics sprang:

"Homer and Hesiod have imputed to the gods all that is blame and shame for men: stealth, adultery and mutual fraud." [1]

"The poet errs in saying: 'Would that strife might perish from among gods and men.' For there would be no harmony without high and low, no animals without the opposition of female and male." [2]

"Most men's teacher is Hesiod. He is the wisest they think—he who does not even know day and night. They are one." [3]

These sayings, among the earliest references to art in the philosophy of the western world, suggest that esthetics was born in a quarrel rather than in any pure act of understanding. When, at the height of Greek speculation in the fourth century B.C., Plato refers to "the ancient quarrel of poetry and philosophy" [4]—a quarrel in which he even in his day felt compelled to take part—he is speaking of an actual clash between two groups of Greeks in the sixth and fifth centuries B.C. Poets and philosophers both claimed exclusive possession of the fount of wisdom. Devotion to wisdom and truth is always the meaning of philosophy, but in the period to which Plato refers it had been the meaning of poetry too. For

---

[1] Xenophanes. Cf. Hermann Diels, *Die Fragmente der Vorsokratiker*, 5th edition, 21 B, 11.

[2] Heraclitus. Cf. Diels, 22 A, 22. We slightly changed the form by quoting Aristotle's indirect report ("Heraclitus blames the poet . . .") as Heraclitus' direct saying.

[3] Heraclitus. Cf. Diels, 22 B, 27.

[4] *Republic*, 607b.

I

the great epics of Greece furnished more than simple esthetic
delight, and the spell they cast was more than musical. They played
a part in Greek life comparable to that of the Bible in the Christian
era. The myths which were their raw material both taught and
formed the popular mind. It was against this combination of myth
and poetry, embodying an ancient and reverend outlook on life
and interpretation of the nature of things, that the philosophers of
the Greek Enlightenment, the Cosmologists and Sophists, had to
assert their claims. Thus poetry appeared upon the horizon of
philosophy not as a subject of investigation but as a rival.

Apart from their interest as beginnings, the polemical remarks
of Heraclitus quoted above are important as shadows cast before
of an antagonism that in various forms was to persist through the
centuries. The time has never come when there were no poets with
the urge to prophesy or with the vocation of wise man. In 1821
Shelley wrote that poets combined the functions of prophet and
legislator, and the struggle between the poet and philosopher in
Nietzsche is even closer to our own day. So long as poets as well
as philosophers try to give a true interpretation of life as a whole,
the active forces producing the original dispute will always remain alive. Thus the irritation of the early philosophers against
the great poets of their people may mean something deeper than
the bare signal accompanying the birth-throes of a new form of
intellectual activity. Whether the poets are blamed by the philosophers for feigned wisdom or obvious ignorance, or whether—
as has often happened in the history of esthetics—they are praised
for clothing in apt imagery divine truth, in either case the common
claim of ability to disclose what life really is holds within itself a
motive to jealousy and mutual recrimination. It is then easy to
understand why Protagoras suggested that perhaps Homer and
Orpheus were really Sophists who were concealing their true profession through fear of spiteful persecution. And on the other
hand by hinting that great Homer was a Sophist in disguise
Protagoras was able to borrow a little of the glamor of the poet's
name to improve his own somewhat ambiguous reputation as a
Sophist.[5]

---

[5] Plato, *Protagoras*, 316d.

But this first encounter of poets with philosophers in their competition for the name and fame of wise man and teacher is not yet esthetics. Esthetics proper begins to take shape for us when we attend to the whole body of philosophical reflection at this period. The place and outlines of the early meditations on the nature of art and beauty were determined by the total plan of archaic philosophy. This being true, esthetics shared in the three major philosophical enterprises of dawning Greek speculation: (1) cosmology, or theory of the structure of the Universe; (2) psychology; and (3) theory of purposive human activity (Techne). Within these wider spheres, the narrower emerging esthetics developed a metaphysics of beauty, a doctrine of the soul's response to beautiful phenomena, and a theory of the process by which beautiful things are created.

What was involved in the notion of 'World' which the early cosmologists created? Two things. First, an all-embracing order; second, a special point of view and attitude toward this order on the part of the thinker. The cosmologist began by searching for a Unique Principle which should bind together all possible objects within his horizon of contemplation and show them as related expressions of a fundamental law. The objects so subjected to the ordering mind could be high or low, dignified or humble: heavenly bodies circling in their orbits, or the pig "bathing in the mire," for this latter situation exemplifies the pervasive law of the mingling of contraries such as the pure and the impure.[6] Another humble instance is the soul drenching its native fire in the wet of wine.[7] This illustrates the broad law of the degradation of elements when they pass from a higher to a lower plane. For the thought of these cosmologists nothing remained apart from the total scheme. The coherence of all things was to them a necessary condition of the very existence of a world. Human nature with its moral laws and ideals was from this point of view continuous with the behavior of the elements and the growth of plants. The way conceptions were loosely stretched to embrace at once man-made procedure and simple natural process stands out in the cosmologist's notion of the

[6] Diels, 22 B, 37.
[7] *Ibid.*, 117.

rhythm of life in the universe. At bottom, he said, the universe is a combination of opposites: light and dark, hot and cold, dry and wet. Now one partner in this combination will prevail and now again the pendulum will swing in favor of the opposite. The world lives and moves by this endless alternation. The circular movement set up by the oscillation makes the world's end and the world's beginning meet, and thus the compensation of elements becomes the ultimate rhythm of all things. No wonder that a sphere was the geometrical form chosen by the early cosmologists to represent the nature of the universe as a whole.

The outlines of this doctrine of rhythm were obviously drawn from that fundamental periodicity that divides day from night, the year into summer and winter, and perhaps the larger units of an aeon into successive evolution and decay. Cosmological doctrine connects this basic periodicity with the rhythms of vegetable and animal life, with growth, a time of flowering and decline, with youth and old age, birth and death. Indeed human life itself takes part in the same rise and fall with its alternation and balance of joy and pain, happiness and misfortune, grandeur and misery.[8] The grand rhythm which rules the different spheres of experience leads the philosopher to assume one supreme principle, one substance—let the name be what it will—some god-like Being sustaining itself in poise amid the restless flux and reflux of opposing phenomena.

The second element involved in the cosmologist's doctrine of the world was his special attitude or angle of vision. He not only as philosopher distanced the object of his contemplation; he arrogated to himself an aristocratic position in his method of handling his subject-matter. Keenly aware of the narrowness and unsteadiness of the popular outlook, he saw it as a normal part of the limits and shiftings of human existence itself. He was alive to the fact that his claim to comprehensive knowledge of the world as one self-sufficient reality would have to collapse if he could not rise above the fluctuating illusory experience of the "blind masses." In so far as he was successful in his subordination of common human weakness he believed himself entitled to be called an observer

---

[8] Cf. Werner Jaeger, "Solons Eunomie," *Sitzungsberichte der Preussischen Akademie, Phil.-histor. Klasse,* 1926.

of things, and a decipherer of that nature "which loves to hide." [9]
Thus, though objective, he did not rise above a specifically human
point of view. What he actually did was to reach a higher level
within the human sphere, the level of the ruler. A representation of
Pythagoras on a coin from Samos symbolizes this characteristic
of the philosopher's attitude. The philosopher is portrayed pointing with his right hand to a globe in front of him and holding a
scepter in his left. Though this coin was made long after the time of
Pythagoras, it hits off with peculiar sureness that combination of
royal power and universal knowledge to which the ancient philosophers aspired. Philosophical impartiality here implies less the
indifference of a pure intellect than the superiority of a ruler
and legislator. The dispassionate and severe posture reflects the
judge rather than the intellectual inquirer.[10]

The anthropomorphic Cosmos just outlined was particularly ESTHETICS AS AN
apt for furnishing a metaphysical basis to esthetics. For a general OUTGROWTH OF
theory of the world which puts man and nature into intimate rela- COSMOLOGY.
tions with each other, and which judges the world in the light of
human procedures and values, makes a happy background for the
specific science of beauty and art. The reason for this is that the
theory of beauty and art has on its own part an innate tendency
toward this same anthropomorphism. There are many examples
both early and late of a carrying over of favorable cosmological
notions into esthetics or near-esthetics. For example, the sphere,
for Pythagoras, was not only the shape of the universe; it was also,
according to a Pythagorean pronouncement, the most beautiful
among all solid figures as the circle is among the planes.[11] The
beautiful, according to Democritus, is the object of divine reason.[12]
Though the word 'beautiful' as employed in these early fragments
probably does not imply a pure esthetic value, the divergence in
meaning does not do away with the force of the underlying argument. What really counts is the fact that whenever a later esthetic

---

[9] Diels, 22 B, 123.
[10] Cf. the reproduction of the coin on the title-page of Diels, Vol. I.
[11] Diels, 58 C, 3 (pp. 463, 24f).
[12] *Ibid.*, 68 B, 112.

doctrine tried to trace the source of beauty in the universe at large, whenever, in other words, a metaphysic of beauty was attempted, this early type of cosmology was sure to be reinstated. The idea of the microcosm, the notion that the structure of the universe can be reflected on a smaller scale in some particular phenomenon, has always been a favorite in the history of esthetics. It was Democritus (*c.* 460 B.C.) who first applied the term microcosm to man.[13] Even the famous doctrine of art as the imitation of nature lies in germ in these early cosmologies, if we take imitation in its liberal and true meaning, not as the duplication of isolated things, but as the active attempt to participate in a superior perfection. "We must be good or imitate those that are good," said Democritus.[14] Probably a supplementary influence causing the idea of imitation to be applied to the relationship between human art and nature, was the experience of medical science with its demand for close observation of nature and nature's ways.

The attempt of the historian of esthetics to trace the roots of his science in ancient cosmology is like that of the historian of the analogous discipline of ethics. The writer on ethics cannot be sure that the famous idea of a "life according to nature," apparently suggested in a fragment of Heraclitus,[15] really means thus early what it does in the later doctrines of the Stoics. But of this he can be sure: the Stoic doctrine, whenever it appears, is closely linked with the type of cosmology, the source and model of which was drafted centuries before in Ionia. Similarly the historian of esthetics may only go so far as to maintain that the conditions making possible a certain type of esthetic doctrine were fixed in early cosmology. The ancient frame-work became effective through Plato's *Timaeus*—the dialogue that welded the archaic conception to Plato's own Idealism and that became one of the great lesson-books for medieval and modern philosophers. The history of esthetics demonstrates the weight and power of the cosmological tradition. If a metaphysical account is to be given of the human susceptibility to beauty, the world must be interpreted

---

[13] Diels, 68 B, 34.
[14] *Ibid.*, 68 B, 39.
[15] *Ibid.*, 22 B, 112.

as naturally responsive to the emotional demands of human nature.
Precisely this intimate congruity with the human being constitutes
a marked feature of the Universe in archaic cosmology. For these
thinkers, as for the artist, the cosmos is a living being: "All things
are full of gods." [16]

Early psychology was the complement of early cosmology.
The closeness of outlook of the two follows immediately from the
human traits imputed to the world as a whole at this date. The
soul of man was easily duplicated in a Soul of the World when
the very structure of things was made to turn on man's functions
and demands. The immortal godlike Being of the World must
be animated by the same principle of life that bestows on man
growth, locomotion, and the faculty of knowledge. Knowledge,
or perception, on this view, is possible because the organ of knowledge is an abridgement of the world itself. Since "like knows
like," the soul must consist of a mixture of all the elements. It is
true that another group of Pre-Socratic thinkers taught that "the
opposite knows the opposite." But in spite of the surface contradiction, these theories have a common basis. Both look on knowledge as a feature of the interaction of Universe and Soul. On this
basis, Democritus developed his theory of inspiration: A select and
enraptured soul, receiving the effluences of a divine substance, gives
birth to the poetic vision.[17]

COSMOS AND PSYCHE: NASCENT IDEAS OF A PSYCHOLOGY OF BEAUTY.

Whatever the truth or falsity of anthropomorphism in general, at least in the sphere of esthetics the actual correspondence
between subject and object, laid down by the early philosophers
as a cosmological principle, can be freely affirmed. Here first
and beyond question the real import and bearing of the general
hypothesis is revealed. We should not be able to perceive and
appreciate a statue or a poem, if the emotional qualities of the
work of art did not answer to analogous feelings in us. Thus the
early speculators reported a vision of the world which in some
respects is a necessary attribute of an artist's vision. Did then the
pioneers of western philosophy confuse cognitive and esthetic

[16] Aristotle, *De Anima*, 411a, 7.
[17] A. Delatte, *Les conceptions de l'enthousiasme chez les philosophes présocra-
tiques*, 1934.

A History of Esthetics

experience? Or did they, in this very dawn of reflective thought, lay hold on a feature which, though common to all kinds of experience, is brought into sharper relief by the 'esthetic' activity?

PYTHAGOREANISM—
A FIRST EXAMPLE
OF AN ESTHETIC
DOCTRINE.

Pythagoreanism furnishes the best example of a comprehensive philosophy built on the human model. In the Pythagorean principle, "Number are the whole Heavens," [18] the reduction of the world to order and affinity to mind reached its extreme limit. The members of this school were probably led to their generalization by observing how far mathematics could go in expressing the nature of astronomical phenomena. But for them as for all the others, what happened in Heaven was to be sought again on earth. The same Principle that ruled Nature had to be discovered in human life. In the processes of the crafts they found number, ratio, and proportion again incarnated. Number entered still more deeply for them into their religious code. The Pythagorean Order is said to have taught its members how to conduct their lives holily and abstemiously and to purify their souls in preparation for their immortal destiny. Though reliable records fail us, we are certain that these religious brothers fashioned the rhythm of their daily walk on those harmonious proportions which they believed to reign in Heaven and to command the revolutions of the stars.

Thus, although the various strains of thought mentioned earlier moved toward and prepared the ground for a true philosophy of art and beauty, the effectual gathering together of these strains and the actual delivery of the new spiritual child came with Pythagoras. The process of connecting a general theory of the world and mind, on the one hand, and of art, on the other, took place in this way. The general hypothesis that number is the substance of reality finds its most available demonstration in music. So the metaphysical assumptions of these thinkers led them to inquire into the nature and mutual relations of musical sounds, and to try to express these relations in numerical proportions. This study of the mathematical basis of music developed in two directions. It led to the creation of the science of acoustics by Archytas, the leading Pythagorean in Plato's time. Archytas recognized that

---

[18] Aristotle, *Metaphysics*, 986a, 17.

all musical sounds are caused by motions following one another at certain intervals, and that sound heard is high or low according to the length of the intervals. "If a thing is tuned too high, we lower the tension, so reducing the vibration and lowering the pitch. It follows that a tone consists of parts, which must be related in numerical proportion." [19]

The second development had moral and cosmic meaning. The older original band of Pythagoreans cared less for the scientific exactness of their statements than for the metaphysical and ethical import of their ideas. It was these members who created that wider theory of music containing the concept of the 'music of the spheres,' with all its overtones of human significance. According to this doctrine human music—first among pleasure-giving arts—is essentially an imitation. Its model is the harmony obtaining among the celestial bodies. These, in their far-reaching revolutions, not only are the chief facts in the natural scheme—the true cosmos behind the superficial phenomena of nature—but at the same time they best embody mathematical law. The pitch of the notes in this heavenly harmony is "determined by the velocities of the heavenly bodies, and these in turn by their distances, which are in the same ratio as the consonant intervals of the octave." [20] This Pythagorean cosmos is a kind of divine music box: the stars, arranged at harmonious distances from each other, run their courses with predetermined speed, and the ether stirred by their motion gives out the most powerful of all melodies. To the human ear, however, this unparalleled tune is sheer silence. As a man born and living on the coast finally ceases to hear the uninterrupted noise of the waves breaking on the shore, so for similar reasons our ears cannot detect the harmony of the spheres.

This hypothesis of music made by the stars and planets is the evidence of an esthetic element in the early cosmologies. And in this case also there is a parallel doctrine of the soul, an elementary psychology. The soul for the Pythagorean thinker is a harmony, or rather an attunement, based on numerical proportion. Such an interpretation of the psyche explains our peculiar pleasure in

[19] F. M. Cornford, *Plato's Cosmology*, 1937, 322.
[20] J. Burnet, *Early Greek Philosophy*, 4th ed., 306.

music. According to the principle 'like knows like' the soul responds joyfully to the harmonious vibrations that affect and move kindred elements out among the circling worlds. The soul's attunement may be compared to the concord of the strings of the lyre. As the lyre will get out of tune when touched by an unskilful hand, so the harmonious disposition of the soul will be sensitive to mishandling. But this sensitiveness is balanced by a capacity for improvement in response to musical treatment. For music, itself an imitation and vehicle of divine melody, can tune the soul to that eternal harmony which it is the musician's task to bring from heaven to earth. It is the function of music to imprint upon the soul the hall-mark of its divine origin.

Within the frame of this metaphysical-psychological doctrine, it is easy to see that the rotating heavens, as the model for imitation, might be replaced by Soul. And if music may be regarded as an imitation of the individual instead of the heavenly soul, the diversity of tunes and musical modes can be accounted for. They will then answer to the different ethical dispositions and temperaments. The Pythagorean doctrine of musical *ethos*, or character, distinguished two types: the harsh and bracing tunes expressing a manly and war-like disposition, and the sweet and languid modes, characteristic of a gentler temper. Since these tunes have the power to produce in others the mood or attitude they express, music comes to be an invaluable instrument for modifying character and soothing mental suffering. With the help of music rough and passionate natures can be attuned to a milder rhythm, or despondent listlessness disciplined into brisk activity. All this went bodily into the later esthetics of Plato.[21]

SOPHISTIC CRITI- CISM AND GREEK DEMOCRACY.

Besides those early philosophies of the world and of the soul, which converged and bore valuable fruit in Pythagoreanism, there was a third set of ideas pregnant for the future of esthetics. This third intellectual tendency began to mold a theory of the nature of artistic production. It was thanks to the Sophists that the 'craft' —an exercise of skill guided largely by practice and tradition—was

---

[21] H. Abert, *Die Lehre vom Ethos in der griechischen Musik*, 1899, §2; "Die Stellung der Musik in der antiken Kultur," *Die Antike*, II, 136ff.

elevated into the 'art'—a methodical, teachable procedure. To understand how the Sophists were able to bring about this important innovation requires brief attention to their general social and intellectual significance, and especially to the instrument, oratory, by means of which they accomplished their ends.

The sophistic movement, beginning in the first half of the fifth century B.C. with the labors of Protagoras, Hippias, and Gorgias, and brought to fulfilment by Socrates, had both a destructive and a constructive aspect. The Sophists attacked the main fortresses of archaic wisdom, the old comprehensive scheme of the world-structure and theory of Being. They attacked along with this the social distinction it implied between the discerning philosophical aristocrat and the 'blind masses.' Protagoras taught that common experience open to all men at all times and places, however much despised by the cosmologists, is the only knowledge there is. No knowledge is possible, he said, concerning the existence and nature of the gods. All truth is whatever the individual, "the measure of what is and is not," perceives and takes for truth.[22] Neither is there any absolute goodness. The good is the useful; moreover, the useful according to the current opinion of the citizens. Thus Protagoras took the part of common sense and the man on the street against the claim of the superior individual. A parallel shaft of sophistic criticism destroyed the privileged position of the idea of 'timeless being,' sole property of an intellectual group set apart and above the common herd.

Thus the work of the Sophists was closely connected with the rise of Greek democracy, and on its constructive side helped the emergence of the rank and file toward political control. In most cases the Sophist himself belonged to the common people and owed his influence and fame not to birth or rank, but to his efficiency and native gifts. His success depended upon the protection of the great and the applause of the multitude, whom he led by appealing to rudimentary instincts. Thus he was the minor brother of the great democratic leaders of his time. He did not build up for himself a vague notion of the 'many.' He knew them

---

[22] Diels, 80 B, 1.

at first hand and how to deal with them, for they were his audience.

The intellectual place of the Sophist and his mission in Greek society would naturally affect his choice of words and the way he put his sentences together. Pushed forward by the practical aspects of his vocation he did much for the development of the new art of rhetoric. If one desires, not to teach some unknown truth, but to guide and persuade large numbers of people, one's arguments have to conform to the opinions of the hearers and those opinions have to be arranged in such a way that the conclusions aimed at seem to follow automatically. Thus the speaker, imperceptibly molding the mind of his audience in accordance with his own practical ends, gives the audience the impression that he is only the mouthpiece of its own most cherished convictions. A kind of bargain is struck; the speaker buys the consent of his audience at the price of his apparent conformity to the prevailing outlook. But he alone is aware of this exchange.

SOPHISTIC RHETORIC AND THE IDEA OF ART.

The important rôle played by the Sophists in the history of esthetics rests, then, on the way in which they remodeled the whole conception of 'technique'—that is, of conscious human production—through the influence that spread from their transmutation of the special craft of the orator. In their concern with this practical process, they were definitely groping after basic intellectual principles. Now, though rhetoric has in common with all pleasure-giving arts the objective of enjoyment, by its orientation toward the intellect it differs in the means of procuring that enjoyment. The swayers of the mob observed the effects of their words with something of the scientist's precision, comparing actual effects with intended ones. They adjusted means to ends, invented rules that the facts would sustain, and finally set up a causal connection between artistic instruments and envisaged results. The larger amount of conscious deliberation in rhetoric as compared with the majority of the skilled crafts practised in Athens at this time enabled the sophistic orators to substitute a semblance of law and science for rules of thumb. They enlarged the meaning of technical activity to include the use of reckoning and the deliberate pursuit of ends. In rhetoric the productive gift is normally combined with a tendency to argue. This makes another bond between the craft of the rhetorician and the idea of conscious method. For all these reasons is it any wonder that rules and general statements which apply in essence if not in particular form to other arts were first discovered in the field of rhetoric? Is it any wonder that sophistic rhetoric furnishes us the outlines of a type and a first example in the history of artistic technique?

In a famous passage of the *Phaedrus,* Plato compares the organization of a speech with that of a living body.[23] This comparison was used later with reference to other arts, and it appears in the *Poetics* of Aristotle and of Horace. The observations sustaining the familiar formulas came from the Sophists. They were the first to reflect upon the characteristics of different types of composition, the relation of part to whole, the proper sequence of topics, effective elocution, rules to be observed on the one hand in long speeches, and on the other in disputes made up of brief statements and short replies. It is common knowledge that these observations and prescriptions licensed many tricks, and that there was a tendency in Sophistry to secure an effect at any price. But there is plenty of evidence that these abuses were outnumbered by acute and realistic observations preparing the way for a sound theory of art. The Sophists deserve credit for devoting attention not to achieved objects of beauty, but to the process of their creation and to the psychological response. They were the first to raise productive activity to the plane of self-conscious reflection. And in esthetics the question: What is beauty? will always be accompanied by the other question: How are beautiful things created? The Sophists were pioneers in seeking the solution of the second problem.

Another alteration made by the Sophists in the general significance of the term 'art' has to do with its economic relations and position in public life. In a society which held that the noble leisure of the well-bred gentleman was the only dignified kind of life, the employment of skill to earn one's living put the 'artist' of whatever kind or degree—physician, sculptor, carpenter—among the lower orders. What determined social status was whether a

---

[23] 264c.

man studied and labored for his own pleasure and self-fulfilment
or whether he used his ability in a professional way for economic
ends. If he chose the second alternative, he was classed with the
commoners; and along with all working people was excluded from
the noble and free pleasures of privileged citizens.

The Sophists, upstarts and revolutionaries as most of them were,
had to defend their reputation and influence against the ban laid
on the 'banausos,' the professional worker and bread-winner. They
travelled around from city to city professing to teach political
wisdom. And the records have it that they demandèd fairly large
fees for their public lectures. But while thus accepting the humil-
iating implications of a worker for daily bread, they were able at
the same time to associate this part of the meaning of craftsmanship not only with the notion of high skill but even with that of
intellectually guided activity.

SOCRATES—A
SOPHIST AND THE
NATURAL ENEMY
OF THE SOPHISTS.
It is, however, hard to imagine how philosophy could have
profited by the new ideas and attitudes embodied in the Sophistic
movement, if it had not been assisted by the man who may be regarded as the greatest of the Sophists and, at the same time, their
natural enemy. Point for point, Socrates' teaching corresponds to
that of his brother-sophists.[24] Though he does not take part in
the criticism directed against the early cosmology and ontology,
his way of thinking presupposes the results of this critical work.
More than any other of his contemporaries, he neglected all questions referring to cosmological facts, as he thought them irrelevant
to his particular inquiry. For Socrates, man is no longer a being
that has to study the Heavens in order to understand himself. His
attention is entirely absorbed by human life as it is shown in human
intercourse, revealing its true purpose in the living word, used
in conversation and dispute as the instrument for the common
quest of truth. The problem on which these conversations centered
was verbally the same that the Sophists before him had pretended
to treat and solve: the problem of political virtue. In his inquiry
he also availed himself, even much more definitely than his pred-

---

[24] Cf. Helmut Kuhn, *Sokrates. Ein Versuch über den Ursprung der Meta-
physik*, Berlin, 1934.

ecessors, of the idea of art as the general scheme of rational activity. What distinguishes him from the Sophists is that he took all this seriously. The simple fact that a man ventured to do in absolute sincerity and full consciousness what the typical Sophist did only half-consciously and half-heartedly, with even a note of frivolity, reversed the whole position of sophistic thought and resulted in ideas which appear to be the strict contradiction of sophistic relativism and empiricism.

Socrates like any Sophist found the man of his time bereft of the security that the idea of the Universe had bestowed on the early thinkers and that went with traditional morality and inherited customs. This man was wide-awake to the joys of intellectual life, keenly apprehensive of new ideas but at the same time an easy prey to intellectual quackery. Instead of taking advantage of this peculiar situation as the Sophists had done, Socrates recognized the outstanding opportunity it offered. The traditional standard of life had lost its validity, and minds of a sharper intelligence and more delicate sensibility were feeling the edge of the question: What are we to do? With these men Socrates discussed the typical sophistic problems. He asked questions about 'goodness' and 'political virtue.' But Socrates' questions were real questions. Simply and seriously he desired to know (and he desired his interlocutors to know with him) what goodness, in personal life and in the life of the community, really is, and he firmly believed that the knowledge acquired would be capable of guiding human life. The participants in these conversations were not pupils paying for their lessons but friends and fellow-citizens, men beset by the same anxiety for the righteousness of their conduct as was felt by Socrates. Like the Sophists, he knew how to arouse profound emotions in his hearers, not by humoring them with rhetorical tricks nor by playing on their sensibility, but by appealing to conscience and pointing out the issue at stake.

In his conversations Socrates also availed himself of the idea of art. In doing so, however, he did not intend to frame his expositions artistically by rules which might guarantee their effectiveness. In talking about shoe-makers, carpenters and saddlers, he wished to present a surprisingly simple idea. The shoe-maker ap- SOCRATES' NOTION OF ART.

parently possesses the art of making shoes and this art implies a twofold knowledge: first, of the end embodied in the intended product (determined, in this case, by the particular demand of foot-gear); second, of the appropriate means. Just so the medical art comprises first the knowledge of health as of its purported end or Good, second the knowledge of medical treatment as the means of the attainment of the Good. Now if we raise the question as to the nature of virtue, or if we ask: What is good?, we attempt to discover the 'royal art' of living well. The product of such an art would be a morally perfect life. This art would be based upon the knowledge primarily of a supreme end or the 'Good in itself' and, in the second place, of 'good actions' as the means leading to the proposed aim. Socrates never pretended to possess such an art. But he demonstrated, by his life and by his influence on his friends, that the earnest endeavor to grasp it is, in the limits of human weakness and ignorance, itself an achievement. In not assuming wisdom, Socrates established Philosophy in the literal sense of the word: as a craving for wisdom and as the methodical process towards it. We shall encounter these thoughts again at the heart of Platonism.

Socrates insisted upon the discrimination of end from means, laying thus the foundation of the rational analysis of art as worked out by Plato and Aristotle. Again, he drew a sharp line between an absolute or supreme end, and the ends that are ends only with regard to a group of subordinate acts, but means when regarded in themselves and with respect to their place and function in life. The latter distinction corresponds to that between arts which are concerned with a particular function within life, and arts concerned with human life as a whole. It is obvious that all the manual arts or crafts including medical art (for life in the biological sense is not the whole of life) fall under the first head. The ideal achievement within the second class would be wisdom; the approximate performance is philosophy. The philosopher, in setting the craftsman's strictly methodical and successful work as a model for his own labor, will not forget the limits within which his model is valid. He knows well that it ranks in a lower class and thus his admiration for handicraft will be tempered by some irony. On the other hand, he will find rivals in his own sphere and it will be his special concern to define the philosopher's attitude toward these competitors professing like himself the supreme art. There is, in the first place, the Sophist pretending to teach political virtue. But on close investigation he proves to be a mere artisan and money-maker in a sphere where the principle of craftsmanship, always confined to the attainment of relative ends, has lost its applicability. Therefore he is a bad artist in respect to his craftsmanship and he is a charlatan and fraud in his pretended wisdom. The politician is the second competitor. According to Greek habits of thinking, it lies with him to frame the life of the community as a whole. On this point, the conclusion that Plato drew later on became inevitable: the philosopher is the only true politician. But there is still a third claimant left: the poet. He does not, like the Sophist and the political leader, dabble in the management of practical affairs. In leaving things as they are, his activity seems comparatively innocuous. But he too is concerned with life as a whole. He portrays it and he is bound to assess its values and set a model for practical imitation. With regard to this third applicant only two alternatives are open and Socrates' greatest pupil lingered over the choice. Either the philosopher, who has already usurped the ruler's throne, must proceed now to take to poetry as to an additional task, or he has to acknowledge the poet's claim and concede him an inspired wisdom.

In establishing philosophy as the art of discourse and knowledge, Socrates distinguished the definition as the end of the process of research and the induction as its means. Before him, essential qualities of beautiful objects were described, important features of the esthetic phenomenon visualized, outlines of a virgin field of research fixed. It is the way of the beginner in philosophy, to start research by collecting beautiful things and describing their properties. The philosophic research of the master is from its very beginning directed toward the definitive question as to what 'beautiful' in itself means. It was Socrates who raised this problem and taught his disciples how to proceed toward the solution.

SUPPLEMENTARY READING

F. M. Cornford, *From Religion to Philosophy. A Study in the Origins of Western Speculation*, 1912.

John Burnet, *Greek Philosophy*, Part 1, 1914.

Werner Jaeger, *Paideia. The Ideals of Greek Culture*, tr. by Gilbert Highet, 1939.

P. M. Schuhl, *Essai sur la formation de la pensée grecque*, 1934.

CHAPTER II

Plato

THE TERMS 'art' and 'fine arts' did not exist for Plato in the sense in which we use them today any more than they did in the period before him. But the ideas which we express by those terms began to come into being and to receive definition in the ferment of Plato's thought. So they might be called, if we adopted a phrase of Bacon's, migratory or traveling instances of conceptions. Bacon said that the migration or journey of a thing to be defined from one state to another or from non-existence into existence, as, for example, the birth of white color out of transparency in the roughening of the surface of the sea, furnishes a favorable situation for scientific analysis.[1]

Let us start then with the term 'art.' One method Plato uses to define art is to trace its origin. This origin being obscure, he sometimes playfully covers it with the myth of Prometheus. The prehuman animals, the story goes, were supplied by the gods with furs and hairy skin for protection against the cold, and with claws to secure prey for food and for fighting enemies. But the human creature, in this primeval distribution, was a forgotten man. Prometheus, then, in concern for bedless, naked, defenseless man, stole fire from Heaven and the arts of weaving and metal-working from Athena and Hephaestus.[2] Thus the Greek myth hints that 'art' came into the world as skills and resources by which man could meet his first needs when bare 'nature' was not enough. In

ART AS SKILL; PROMETHEAN ORIGIN.

---

[1] *Novum Organum*, The Second Book of Aphorisms, XXIII.

[2] *Protagoras*, 320d–322. See also *Statesman*, 274c. All the passages from Plato are given in the translations of the Loeb Classical Library unless there is indication otherwise.

this imaginative picture of cultural origins art equals what man adds to nature through his specifically human intelligence in order to succeed in the struggle for existence. It is nature, altered or wrought for man's comfort and convenience. Though this fable of the beginnings of art, in its context in the *Protagoras*, is a Sophist's device to advance a thesis, the conception of art as the exercise of human skill represents, as we have noted in the previous chapter, the ordinary Greek view of the time.

STANDARD OF THE MEAN FROM PY- THAGORAS.

But another aspect of art is often presented by Plato as fundamental, especially in the later dialogues. The founder of this second part of art is also referred to as "a Prometheus." [3] This second Prometheus, the historical Pythagoras, was not only one of the founders of arithmetic and geometry, but through the investigations he started, the fosterer of the use of measurement in the service of the simple practical skills. Man was thus enabled not only to build and weave and till, but to weave and till and build efficiently. He learned to count and weigh his instruments and materials, so that his command over nature, and his ability to satisfy his wants, were much greater than in the pre-mathematical era. Literate experience succeeded to illiterate.

Plato calls this second "better road" for art a gift of the gods and says that it descended from heaven accompanied by "a gleaming fire." By all the literary devices of which he is master he surrounds the unfolding of the deeper significance of this Pythagorean way with the atmosphere of a too little appreciated importance. "Through it," he declares, "all the inventions of art have been brought to light." [4] It has always been by observance of the "standard of the mean," which is at the heart of the method, that all the works of artists have succeeded in being "good and beautiful." [5] What variant of mathematical procedure does Plato thus single out as the parent of all discovery, excellence, and beauty in the arts? Not mathematical manipulation for its own sake, not the abstract measurement that is concerned with the infinite addition, subtraction, multiplication, and division of neutral units, but

---

[3] *Philebus*, 16c.
[4] *Ibid.*
[5] *Statesman*, 284b.

measurement that respects the end in view on the concrete occasion of measurement. The true art of dialectic, the extreme development of the better way, differs from futile mathematical disputation in diligently seeking a thing's "whole number" instead of allowing computation to leap unreflectively from unity to infinity.[6] One does not measure off cloth for the mere delight of setting in motion "the greater and the less" or "the one and the many," but for determining the right amount of cloth for a garment. There is a comparison of the great and the small with a mean or ideal standard, Plato says; and it is this calculation with reference to a desired end or sought good that makes all the difference between fruitful, effective art and haphazard treatment.[7]

Plato's drift is that with the progress of civilization art becomes a scientifically controlled operation on nature by man for a foreseen good. Art is thus defined not alone by its contrast with nature and accident but by its infusion of precise knowledge and envisaged good. The variant of the mathematical method which Plato associates with art makes art goal-seeking, and so takes it out of the class of mathematical processes as we commonly think of them. Once art receives into itself the particular kind of calculation that revolves around a standard or good, it is committed to the measurement of the various goods in relation to each other. The spirit of Pythagoras let loose in art will not stop. Or perhaps one had better say: In Platonism, Pythagoras transcends himself; his ideas sea-change themselves into something rich and strange. A profound doctrine of the art of human good and of contemplative wisdom is distilled by Plato out of arithmetic and geometry. But this change goes on by very gradual stages. The weft, we say, returning to our humble example, is measured in the light of the garment desired. But with reference to what good does one measure the value of clothes? The size and shape of the bit and shuttle must be determined by the user of the bit or shuttle, for he best knows its value and its nature at work.[8] This is Plato's first answer in simple practical terms. The master of any art is the one who

ART AS WISDOM AND SCIENCE.

---

[6] *Phil.*, 16e.
[7] *Ibid.*, 17.
[8] *Republic*, Bk. X, 601c.

best knows the function of its products. But who shall judge the relative utility of the various values? Generalship has to do with matters of war and peace. But who knows when it is better to make war? [9] A physician has the art to cure. But when is it better to cure? Who professes that supreme art by training in which one learns to weigh and count all the human functions and ends on some common scale? He would be a royal artist, a kingly keeper of weights and measures.[10] Plato's main quest in all his thinking is the intellectual determination of the nature of this royal art. He concludes that its practitioner is the philosopher-king. For the philosopher spends all his days in learning what goods are true goods, what are the intrinsic values in terms of which all the ends of all the other arts are measured. [11] When this student of 'goods' is also the guardian of a state, he directs the several functions of the crafts and professions for the best of each and for the whole, and he distributes rewards according to needs and deserts. He reckons at their right value goods of property, such as houses and garments, goods of the body, such as health and beauty, and goods of the soul, such as wisdom, temperance, and justice. Thus the attempt to redefine art leads Plato to compare ordinary techniques such as agriculture, medicine, and weaving, but most of all the crafts of the poet and politician, with a ruling and presiding art, this latter to involve measurement and science plus engagement with the good. He fuses the idea of function with the idea of exact classification and division, and an ideal at once of wisdom and of practical virtue takes shape in his mind.

It is obvious that Plato's many-stranded reasoning about art moves in a region remote from the esthetic arts of our present-day connotation. But it does not follow that Plato's royal art and arts connected with pleasure and beauty go on roads that never cross. It is true that when Plato brings together his ideal of the royal art and the various pleasure-producing functions and image-

---

[9] *Statesman*, 305.

[10] *Ibid.*, 305c, d.

[11] *Republic*, Bk. VI, 505. Plato develops his conception of the philosopher-king notably in *Republic*, V, VI, and VII; *Statesman; Alcibiades* I.

making activities: poetry and music, painting and sculpture, the
rhetorical, culinary and costuming arts,[12] these go away from the
presence of the other; [13] or, to use another Platonic metaphor, the
two types will not mingle in the same cup.[14] But it is precisely
after watching in the movement of the Dialogues the reactions of
these various functions to each other, whether repugnances or
affinities, that the outline of Plato's esthetic theory succeeds in
standing out before our minds.

The position of poetry and music—the two were one for the
Greeks—among the image-making arts is what interests Plato
most. The reason for this has already been suggested in the first
chapter. It lies in the persisting rivalry of poets and philosophers
as purveyors of wisdom. In order to decide whether poetry is a
real art or not, Plato examines critically the current view of the
poet's function.[15] When in the Dialogues a philosophical investigation is going forward, one notices that a poet's way or view is very
likely to stand in dramatic interest second only to the philosopher's
own. For the poets "are our fathers, as it were, and conductors
in wisdom," [16] Plato makes Socrates say when he takes a fresh
start in defining friendship. To the ordinary Greek of the time,
as has already been suggested, Homer's poems were not mere
exciting tales told vividly and rhythmically, and suspended aloof
from fact in a world of make-believe. They were manuals of
divinity, war, and statecraft. For Plato's uncritical contemporary,
the truth about the gods and the future life was in Homer, Hesiod,
and the dramatists, or it was nowhere. There existed for his religious
guidance no Sacred Scripture in a class by itself, and no order of
learned theologians to codify dogma. One learned the behavior
of divine beings and the pleasure of the gods from the great poets.
When, as Homer relates, Zeus discoursed with Hera, his lady, or
Ares smote Athena, real things happened in the objective order

POETS PURVEY WIS-
DOM.

---

[12] *Gorgias,* 464, 465.

[13] *Phaedo,* 106.

[14] *Philebus,* 61c.

[15] For a discussion of this problem from the standpoint of literary criticism
see Allan H. Gilbert, "Did Plato Banish the Poets or the Critics?" *Studies in
Philology,* January, 1939.

[16] *Lysis,* 214a.

of the universe, not merely motions in a poet's brain. And Homer could teach more than theology. He was assumed to be master of the art of generalship and versed in the ways of the human heart and of social intercourse. Upon this conception of Homer, the poet, as at the same time teacher, artist, and scientist, Plato often trained his engine of analysis.

IS IT REAL WIS-
DOM?
He asks, for example: How expert is Homer on the nature of the gods? Homer pictures them quarreling, lying, and hard-hearted.[17] Now the philosopher, whose views must always have a rational basis, is constrained to associate the idea of the god-like with attributes of goodness, truth, and beneficence.[18] The philosopher's inference must be that Homer fails to understand the nature of the gods concerning whom he is supposed to be an authority.

Then there is the question of the poet's knowledge of war-fare and statecraft. Let us put a question to Homer, Plato says. If you are wise, Homer, in questions of private and public good, where have you deposited the tangible results of your wisdom? Did you ever devise any good code of laws or frame any constitu-tion? Is there any war on record which was brought to a success-ful conclusion by your assistance? Surely a man wise in these weighty matters would choose to leave behind him definite evidence of the power of his learning. From you, however, we have noth-ing of the sort.[19]

THEY KNOW NOT
WHAT THEY DO.
Plato constantly suggests that the poet is not what he has always been taken to be. From the early *Apology* and *Ion* all the way through to the *Laws* of his old age, Plato presses the point that poets compose on subjects they do not understand. In the *Apology*, Socrates tells, half humorously but with a serious undercurrent of meaning, of his cross-examination of a group of poets with a view to finding out how wise they were and how well they under-stood their own words. "Taking up the poems of theirs that seemed to me to have been most carefully elaborated by them, I asked them what they meant, that I might at the same time learn some-

---

[17] *Republic*, Bk. II, 377, 378.
[18] *Ibid.*, Bk. II, 379.
[19] *Ibid.*, Bk. X, 599–600.

thing from them. Now I am ashamed to tell you the truth, gentlemen; but still it must be told. For there was hardly a man present,
one might say, who would not speak better than they about the
poems they themselves had composed." Plato then expresses his
belief that poetry is inartistic and unscientific: "I presently recog-
nised this, that what they composed they composed not by wisdom,
but by nature and because they were inspired, like the prophets
and givers of oracles; for these also say many fine things, but
know none of the things they say." [20]

In the *Ion* there is the same withholding of the traditional
acknowledgment that poets are the sages and teachers of men.
Emphasizing the blindness both of poets, and the dramatic interpreters of poets, Plato compares their action to the unconscious
force of the magnet. Though prize winner in the elocutionists'
Olympic, Ion has no discrimination about poets, nor can he talk
about his hero, Homer's, themes when he loses his literal cue.
His 'science' is no better than that of a good parrot. He no more
understands the why and whither of his so-called art than the
magnetized ring understands why it attracts iron, or the load-
stone its secret influence. And for that matter, great Homer himself is but another magnetic ring one degree nearer the source of
magnetic influence. "All the good epic poets utter all those fine
poems not from art but as inspired and possessed, and the good
lyric poets likewise. . . . Seeing then that it is not by art that they
compose and utter so many fine things about the deeds of men—
as you do about Homer—but by a divine dispensation, each is able
only to compose that to which the Muse has stirred him . . . for
not by art do they utter these things but by divine influence." [21]
Men "of the poetic turn," having no understanding, yet succeed
in many a great word,[22] Plato says again, in no spirit of harsh
censure, but meaning that they are inspired by the gods rather
than guided by science in what they do. In another context with
somewhat sharper satire he says that they are forsooth in a charm-

[20] *Apology*, 22c.
[21] *Ion*, 534.
[22] *Meno*, 99.

ing state of mind about their own creations.[23] In the *Laws*, Plato's
last work, the unwisdom of poetry is explicitly declared, the reason
for it assigned, and a comparison of the wisdom of a true artist
set over against it. Everybody knows, the Athenian stranger is
made to say, that when a poet is composing he is not in his senses.
He is the mere creature of the uprush of inspiration in his soul.
This irrational spring which accounts for the nature of his product
compels him "often to contradict himself, when he creates characters of contradictory moods; and he knows not which of these
contradictory utterances is true." There immediately follows the
contrasted picture of the true artist's obligation to scientific truth.
The true artist is the just lawgiver, the philosophical king. "It
is not possible for the lawgiver in his law thus to compose two
statements about a single matter. . . . He must always publish
one single statement about one matter." [24] Now while Plato here
as in the other passages cited partly explains the poet's failure by
a reference to his divine frenzy, he also furnishes a definition of
the poet's art. This definition recurs, and in one of the most important passages for esthetics in the whole Platonic *corpus* is submitted to careful analysis.

IMITATION
FRAUGHT WITH UN-
WISDOM.

Plato says in the midst of the passage just referred to that the
poet's "art consists in imitation." In the *Timaeus* he refers to poets
as "the imitative tribe." [25] At the beginning of Book X of the
Republic a critical return is made upon this linkage of poets with
imitation and a thorough-going examination of the whole idea of
imitation called for. Concern with the notion leads in the end to
its subtle subdivisions in the late dialogue, the *Sophist*. And after
all no less serious treatment would justify the legislators' banishment
of the poets from the ideal city, or their sharp restriction, the
policy recommended both in the *Republic* and the *Laws* as necessary for the communal health.[26] 'Imitation' thus becomes a second
instance of a migratory term in Plato. To understand this concept, which is in some one of its forms at the root of the poet's

---

[23] *Republic*, Bk. X, 602.
[24] *Laws*, 719, C, D.
[25] *Timaeus*, 19, D.
[26] *Republic*, Bk. III, 401; Bk. X, 605, 607; *Laws*, Bk. VII, 801.

incompetence, we must recall, Plato suggests, our most comprehensive scheme of the nature of all being.[27] In this scheme there are three levels: the highest contains the 'Ideas' or 'forms' of things; the second the actualities of the physical and practical world; and the third the shadows and reflections of these actual objects and facts. It is not necessary for the purposes of esthetics to discuss the various interpretations of the 'Ideas' that inhabit the highest realm of being. What is sun-clear in regard to Plato's exposition is his belief that for any class of objects we like, there is only one 'Idea' and that that one is stable, real, and true. The 'Idea' answers to the true definition of the thing. It is also clear that increasing distance from the top-level implies ever more lack of unity, reality, and truth. Now it is the wisdom of the philosopher-king, who is also the royal artist, to understand and contemplate the unitary, true, and real. Craftsmen and all kinds of men of affairs deal with the things of the second order. They make couches and chairs, ships, coats, wars, policies and enactments. At the third remove, poets and painters make images of the things that are on the second level. The number of images that can be made is, of course, infinite, and images are not bound to have any consistent logical relation to each other. It is this contrast between commitment to a single consistent, criticized view and unlimited freedom to make a picture from any angle or present a matter in any way that troubles the soul of Plato. For him the ideal artist like the good citizen must be single-minded and consistent: "To do one's own business and not to be a busybody is justice." [28] The poet can hardly so be.[29] Even the craftsmen and men of affairs on the second level of being do not possess critical definitions of their acts and purposes. The ordinary doer or worker, absorbed in his obvious task, Plato tells us, does not understand the ultimate utility of his art, its limits, and relations, but moves within the bounded circle of his special function. Only the dialectician-artist of the good life, private and public, who has labored at the 'Ideas,' names, and definitions of beings and actions, will always

[27] *Republic*, Bk. X, 596, 597
[28] *Ibid.*, Bk. IV, 433.
[29] *Laws*, Bk. IV, 719.

place functions correctly.[30] Socrates jokingly and yet accurately describes himself in the *Gorgias* as one who always says the same things about the same subjects.[31] Imitators of imitators, who never really think and define, will inevitably be intellectually innocent and wavering in their representations. Inconsistency is, then, only one side of imitation, as poets imitate.

ART NO LESS, NO MORE THAN A MIRROR.

Plato brings into relief his distrust of the imitative clan of poets, and also of the painters, whom in this respect he classes with the poets, by a comparison of the works of these artists with the reflections of a mirror. By a glass turned round and round "you will speedily produce the sun and all the things in the sky, and speedily the earth and yourself, and the other animals and implements and plants."[32] This is the sort of maker or imitator the painter is. Indeed it is a good joke to call our artist-mirror a maker at all.[33] The revolving mirror illustrates the inconsistency and senseless irrationality of poetry and painting by the infinite number and variety of the things it can imitate. As all things indifferently are doubled by the looking-glass, so the mimicking artist is a versatile fellow who can put on a show of the outside of anything because he understands nothing in terms of its fixing definition or idea. The less depth, the more breadth. Our universal genius has an adaptable gift for taking off the bare look of things. Lysippus, a sculptor in the more refined manner of Plato's day, boasted that he had carved men as they appeared, whereas the older sculptors had only carved men as they were.[34] The analogous artist in paint can give a plausible impression of the sea, earth, heaven, and gods, and all other things; "moreover, he makes them all quickly and sells them for very little."[35] But unfortunately the reason why the imitative arts can present everything is that they neglect the whole for the shadow. Plato feels that on such grounds the poet and

---

[30] *Republic*, Bk. IV, 443, 444.
[31] *Gorgias*, 491.
[32] *Republic*, Bk. X, 596e.
[33] *Sophist*, 234.
[34] *The Elder Pliny's Chapters on the History of Art*, 65; ed. Jex-Blake and Sellers, p. 53.
[35] *Phaedrus*, 248.

painter must be graded low among human beings. In the *Phaedrus* the types of human being are arranged in ten classes in order of worth. The imitators are put sixth.[36]

Plato doubtless had in mind as a particular instance of bad imitative art the new school of illusionistic painting coming into favor in his time, practised by Apollodorus, Zeuxis, and Parrhasius, in which perspective and variations in tone were used to give the complete semblance of the outer world. The 'shadow,' said by Plato in the passage quoted above to be preferred to the 'whole,' was the technical term used to describe these new-fangled painters: they were called 'shadow-painters.' Those who used light and shadow to communicate the universal appearances of things sacrificed, to Plato's mind, the honest though limited truths of art as presented for instance by Polygnotus: measure, form, relation. They pretended a painterly omniscience. As Plato carries forward his discussion of imitative painters in *Republic* X, it occurs to the reader that perhaps he was thinking of such a special group. He says that the painter of a couch not only copies the actual couch that some carpenter has made, but "touches or lays hold of only a small part of the object," [37] because he takes up a special angle of vision, from the side or from the front or from some other point. Plato thought of a real couch as embodying objective proportions of length, breadth, height, and thickness, the same for all men; so that the neglect of these scientific facts in the interests of individual vision struck him as a sort of shamming. Plato may even have had an actual vase-painting in mind, for there is extant a representation of Dionysus lying on a couch in front of a temple, done in the new illusionistic manner of Aristarchus and Apollodorus.[38]

Analogous contemporary movements in the other arts probably gave special poignancy to Plato's censure of artistic imitation. **INCONSISTENCY AND INNOVATION.** Timotheus, one of the chief innovators in musical technique in Plato's time, not only increased the number of strings of the lyre

[36] *Sophist*, 234.
[37] *Republic*, Bk. X, 598b.
[38] R. G. Steven, "Plato and the Art of His Time," *The Classical Quarterly*, Vol. XXVII, 1933, p. 150.

to eleven or twelve, but indulged in "immoderate imitative realism." For example, his colorful reproduction of the loud laments of Semele, while in labor during the birth of Dionysus, brought down upon him the public reprimand of the Spartan Senate.[39] Whenever imitation is condemned, the inconsistent manifold it implies is condemned with it. True Being, correct definition, is one; second or third-hand Being is many and lawless. In an exactly parallel way, the contemporary movements in art were characterized at once by illusionism and by unbridled innovation. When Plato said that "the overseers of our state . . . must throughout be watchful against innovations in music . . . fearing when anyone says that that song is most regarded among men 'which hovers newest on the singer's lips' " [40] one may wonder whether he had in mind the boast of this same Timotheus who said: "I do not sing what men have sung in time past. In novelty is power. . . . Far from us be the Muse of the old days." [41] Or was he perhaps thinking of the wilful ways of Philoxenus as they appeared to the admiring contemplation of a dramatic character in a play by Antiphanes: "Certainly Philoxenus is the first of poets. He has terms that are his alone, words wholly new, and that constantly. As for melodies, with what art he can vary and modulate. He is truly a god among men; he knows true music." [42] Musicians of the day were altering scales and instruments according to their mood, and dramatists and other poets extravagantly creating rhythms and devices in the experimental development of their craft. Phrynis mixed hexameters and free lyric verses and made a lyre sound like a trumpet. Plutarch, in giving the history of music, thus speaks of the days before Phrynis: "In the early times it was not permitted to musicians, as it now is, to introduce mutations in melody or rhythm at pleasure. The Nome, which they employed, having its appropriate pitch and measure, to these they were required to adhere without change." [43] There is a spirited

---

[39] Croiset, A. & M., *Histoire de la Littérature Grecque*, Vol. III, p. 34.
[40] *Republic*, Bk. IV, 424.
[41] Croiset, *op. cit.*, Vol. III, p. 639.
[42] *Ibid.*, Vol. III, p. 460.
[43] Plutarch, Περὶ μουσικῆς, trans. Bromley, 1822, p. 17.

description in a drama by Pherecrates of the apparent wildness
and confusion of the dithyrambic poet Cinesias, whom Plato ac-
cuses of caring only for popularity. His mingling of extravagant
fancies with the evolutions of the chorus produces a kind of
dizziness, says Pherecrates. It is as when watching the maneuvers
of soldiers one suddenly sees at the right those who one instant
before were at the left.[44]

We said that the poet's right to be called an artist stood or fell
in Plato's opinion with the outcome of his competition with an
undoubted artist. In this competition the poet on the whole failed
because he was not wise in that complete sense which Plato required. And in his failure the poet dragged down to a lower level
with him other craftsmen who pursued a similar course of uncritical imitation. It was inevitable that Plato should also associate
with this group of men whom he was testing for knowledge those
who were the natural enemies of his hero Socrates as professing
teachers of wisdom: the Sophists. For the Sophists produced a
superficial imitation of the true art of justice and wisdom. The
kinship between the Sophists and Euripides, for example, was
very close. The sophistic doctrine which made reason the servant
of the desires and passions is nowhere better illustrated than in
Euripides' plays. "We know the good and we recognize it, but
we are unable to stand by it," says Phaedra.[45] Like Antiphon the
Sophist, Phaedra's nurse appeals to the law of nature, as older
and stronger than human law or human reason.[46] Plato also was
interested in the resemblance of Sophistry to the new shadow-
painting. In discussing the Sophists' view that to appear just is
better than to be just ("If I am unjust and have procured myself
a reputation for justice, a godlike life is promised") Plato makes
a direct allusion to the new painters' style. If he follows the Sophists,
he says, he must draw about himself a shadow-outline of virtue to
be the front and show of his house. Behind this false façade done in
the new Agatharcan manner, he will trail behind him the shifty

SOPHISTS ALSO
SLAVES OF AP-
PEARANCE.

---

[44] Croiset, *op. cit.*, Vol. III, p. 634.
[45] *Hippolytus*, 380f. References to Sophistry pervade the play.
[46] *Ibid.*, 459ff.

fox.[47] Because of the philosophical character of Plato's conception of the royal art, the Sophists, the pretending professors of philosophy, made up for him the paradigm of a kind of artistic mimicry. There were other groups that Plato from time to time put for similar reasons in the same class. The rhetoricians, who sham the art of sound speech; cooks, who simulate the art of dieting; costumers and tailors, who do the same with the art of making the body appear well, are obvious brethren of dramatic impersonators, realistic painters, and sophistic reasoners.[48] All of them produce an agreeable external show through blindly copying the bare outward form of a truth, ideal, or object.

ALL IMITATION IS
SECOND-RATE.

A careful reader of the earlier Dialogues will not miss noting that for Plato there are imitations and imitations. Although Plato may let it be said without any immediately qualifying adjective that poetry and painting are by nature imitations, the context will usually show that imitation is after all a wide term, these arts that peculiarly interest the critic of shadow-painting forming only one class under it. In the later Dialogues, particularly in the *Sophist*, the logical problem of the proper subdividing of the concept 'imitation' is explicitly faced. The earlier ideas on the subject are now cut and neatly arranged. At the very end of the *Sophist*, a kind of extenuation is offered for the lack of strict scientific classification of these terms at any earlier date. Where can we find a name, the chief speaker asks, for the ultimate species in this sectioning of art and imitation? He adds: "No doubt it is hard to find one, because the ancients, it would seem, suffered from a certain laziness and lack of discrimination with regard to the divisions with the result that there is a serious shortage of names." [49]

This laziness, then, is now overcome, and we are told in a discourse at once pedantically exact and yet full of humor the place of imitative painters among other types of imitator. The process of sectioning and sub-sectioning so far as it can interest us proceeds as follows. There are two kinds of making: divine and human.

---

[47] *Republic*, Bk. II, 365c.

[48] *Gorgias*, 464–66; *Phaedrus*, 261d–268.

[49] *Sophist*, 267d. Trans. from F. M. Cornford, *Plato's Theory of Knowledge*. Harcourt, Brace, 1935, pp. 329–30.

The divine maker produces two kinds of things: real things—animals, plants, earth, air, fire, and water; and in the second place, reproductions of these originals—dream-images, "and in daylight all those naturally produced semblances which we call 'shadow' when dark patches interrupt the light," [50] or reflections when appearing on polished, bright surfaces. Paired off with these divine products are two sets of human ones: real things, such as houses; and in the second place, the likeness of these artifacts—the painting of a house, "as it were a man-made dream for waking eyes." [51] The second class of human products is now in its turn bisected. There are images that are like, and images that only appear to be like. The first group contains the faithful copies of the originals, the second, phantasms in which some sort of falsity lurks. We pause here to notice Plato's application of this bisection to painting. He mentions first a kind of painting that is a successful imitation of the original, corresponding to it in length, breadth, depth, and color, even though as 'imitation' belonging to a distinct order of existence; secondly, the many distorting special views of the original. It is this second class of paintings which occupied his attention in *Republic* X [52] although it was not there so searchingly defined. And it is this class of semblance or phantasm which interests him now, because he is on the way to the lair of the Sophist, and the arrows point toward fantastic rather than true likeness-making. As the logical bisecting goes on, semblance-making is subdivided, and true likeness-making left hanging. Phantasms may be produced either by tools, as in sculpture and painting, or by human impersonation. The human mimic again is two. He is either a deliberate actor with a full understanding of his part, or he is a pretender to the character he puts forward. When this pretence to character is insincere, we have the Sophist and very near him the demagogue. A little earlier in the conversation [53] the chief speaker refers to the then common phenomenon of the distortion of large figures for the sake of beauty of effect. He calls the

BUT FANTASTIC IMITATION IS BAD.

---

[50] *Ibid.*, 226b, c; trans. Cornford, *op. cit.*, p. 327.
[51] *Ibid.*, p. 328.
[52] 589.
[53] *Sophist*, 236.

adaptation of the composition to a particular point of sight, the abandonment of truth and the recourse to fantastic art. Plato, we should infer from such passages, would have sided with Alcamenes and against Phidias in the competition which, as the legend goes, Phidias won because he allowed for the distance from the spectator of his statue when it should be put in place. Alcamenes, the loser, carved his statue, according to the principles advocated by Plato, with regard only to mathematical rightness and regardless of any point of sight.[54]

CORRECTNESS.

In the second book of the *Laws*,[55] when an Athenian is defending to a Spartan the nobler music of the peace-loving state, the attributes of accurate imagery are again named. The rightness of an imitation, the Athenian says, lies in the reproduction of the quality and proportions of the original. The similarity between the two terms in the situation must be both quantitative and qualitative. Applying the case to painting, the Athenian explains that the portrait of a man must show the members of the body in their correct number and exact relation to each other, and that, throughout, the colors and shapes of model and replica should correspond. Before any other excellences of a work of art are judged, the connoisseur must pass on this truth or correctness of the painting. The correctness has to do with general intention, not alone with mechanical parallelism. In other words, Plato has here in mind his modification of the Pythagorean conception of measurement by the reference to a function or meaning. "A man who is to make no mistake of judgment about a particular production must, in every case, understand what that production is. If he does not understand what it is, that is, what it is meant for, or of what it is in fact an image, it will be a long time before he will discern the rightness or wrongness in the artist's purpose." [56]

REASONABLE AND
IRRATIONAL PLEAS-
URE.

But in this passage in the *Laws* the contrast between correct and distorted imitation is only one feature of the inquiry into the

---

[54] J. Overbeck, *Die antiken Schriftquellen zur Geschichte der bildenden Künste bei den Griechen*, 1868, No. 772.

[55] 666ff.

[56] *Ibid.*, Bk. II, 668, trans. from A. E. Taylor, *The Laws of Plato*, Dent, 1934, p. 47.

meaning of imitative art. That good artists and judges of art will concern themselves with 'truth' is laid down as a kind of minimum requirement, and attention is centered on another opposition. There are certain products of the image-making art which have no value, furnish no utility, no good, beyond a mere accompanying pleasure. There's a gusto and savor, everyone knows, which attends necessary and useful actions and processes, such as eating or learning. Such pleasure is a concomitant good. But that an activity should yield only pleasure is not good. Nothing solid or serious is then offered for appraisal. Never should we use the criterion of pleasure to measure the worth of a function when any other is available. Plato uses the word 'play' to characterize the products of the various arts of imitation when harmless pleasure is their only value.[57] He often makes a connection between phantasms, distorted imagery, and play or jest.[58]

Drama and music and dancing are, like sophistry, he says, properly forms of entertainment and jugglery.[59] "Imitations created by the use of painting and music, solely for our pleasure"[60] belong on the ornamental side of existence. And in the *Sophist* the question is put: "Is there any more artistic or charming kind of joke than the imitative kind?"[61] Magic and jugglery are akin to painting, for children and simple persons enjoy being taken in by the semblance of reality given in both instances. Rhetoric is a habit of "producing a kind of gratification and pleasure,"[62] or, again, it is a catering to undisciplined appetite. Plato contrasts sharply those practical activities which are serious, important, and useful—the arts of the physician and statesman, for example—which are based on science and have a rational and worthy end in view, even if not the royal end, with those other activities which are amusing, recreational, and useless or worse—flute, lyre, and harp-playing accompanied by singing, and all poetry and

---

[57] *Ibid.*, Bk. II, 667.
[58] *Republic*, Bk. X, 602b; *Statesman*, 288.
[59] *Sophist*, 235b.
[60] *Statesman*, 288c.
[61] *Sophist*, 234b.
[62] *Gorgias*, 462c.

oratory—which have no other aim but to afford gratification.[63] This second class of 'arts' is addressed, he says, to a "public compounded of children and women and men and slaves as well as free" [64] indiscriminately, and the practitioners amuse the people as if they were children, and neglect their true welfare.[65] Plato gives Cinesias as an example.

ART'S CHARMS
DANGEROUS. Plato's definition of certain arts as fantastic imitations may be amended then by saying that these playful mimickings excite irrational pleasure. "Mimetic art . . . is an inferior thing cohabiting with inferior," [66] sentimental efficacy. The revolving mirror of poetry and painting always possesses the positive attribute of glamor or natural magic. "The most recent historian of ancient painting, E. Pfuhl, employs in speaking of Apollodorus a word which means magical evocation." [67] And Apollodorus as an illusionistic painter seems to represent the group of artists most disturbing to Plato's mind. Homer, the pretender to knowledge, deprived of his music and rhythm would not be a serious concern to the practical philosopher, but Homer's imitations plus the charm of his verse excite the soul and steal the heart.[68] The world of fine art is differentiated not only by being a "shadow of some other" fabricated by a blind weaver, but by possessing that peculiar kinship with and power over the emotions which a sensuous pattern inevitably claims. Beauty is by nature a "mighty spell," a "bloom"; [69] poetry is a "honeyed muse." [70] In its more sinister aspects it may be a sorcery or drug-dispensing art.

UNCONTROLLED
PLEASURE BECOMES
UNCONTROLLABLE. The natural connection of a certain class of arts with pleasure is for Plato a cause of the gravest concern. Since impure pleasure is so closely connected with art that it forms part of its definition, a complete analysis of art will include an analysis of pleasure. Plato makes this analysis in the *Gorgias*, *Philebus*, and *Timaeus*.

---

[63] *E.g. Gorgias*, 501.
[64] *Ibid.*, 502d.
[65] *Ibid.*, 502e.
[66] *Republic*, Bk. X, 603b.
[67] P. M. Schuhl, *Platon et l'Art de son Temps*, 1933, p. 23.
[68] *Republic*, Bk. X, 601.
[69] *Loc. cit.*
[70] *Ibid.*, Bk. X, 607.

Pleasure when uncontrolled by wisdom or the good, he says, wakens, nourishes, and strengthens men's lower impulses and withers and starves the highest part.[71] What more particularly does this mean? The pleasures here in question turn our lives into a game of see-saw: we are at one moment high with gratification, at the next low with the ending of the last pleasure and the craving for a new one; and this process of up and down is repeated without limit. The pursuit of impermanent delights makes us, then, like leaky vessels or sieves,[72] that are no sooner filled than they are empty. We become infected by an abnormal thirst and infinite discontent, for the more thrills we get, the more we want. We become one with the "restlessness men miscall delight." In our weakness we often crave a "good cry." [73] Imitation for imitation's sake goes with emotion for emotion's sake, and there is a minimum of truth and substance in both.

For research of gratification not only splits up our existence longitudinally, so that like waves we ever rise and fall, but it introduces tension into the single moments of our existence. Piquant contrast and a simultaneous tension between pleasure and pain are part of the agreeable excitement of witnessing a tragedy. In witnessing tragedies, people enjoy their very weeping.[74] The ridiculous in the same way is a complex of the pain of spite and the pleasure of laughter.[75] The greater complexity of such states of mind means a corresponding unclearness. The soul is relatively turbid as it is thus pulled in two directions at the same moment, and hysteria, if not mild madness, is the consequence. Socrates asks Ion, the declaimer, if he is in his right mind when he recites. "Are you carried out of yourself, and does your soul in an ecstasy suppose herself to be among the scenes you are describing?" [76] And Ion replies: "I will tell you without reserve. When I relate a tale of woe, my eyes are filled with tears; and when it is of fear

PLEASURE IS TURBID, A DRAIN ON REASON.

---

[71] *Ibid.*, Bk. X, 605.
[72] *Gorgias*, 493–94.
[73] *Republic*, Bk. X, 606.
[74] *Philebus*, 48.
[75] *Ibid.*, 50.
[76] *Ion*, 535b.

or awe, my hair stands on end with terror and my heart leaps." [77]
If on one side pleasurable function is insatiable and turbid, on the
other it withers and starves the reasonable and temperate part of
human nature as fast as the appetite for excitement is nourished.
For pleasure is preoccupying. It produces forgetfulness and neglect
of the main business of life. The turbidity of enthusiasm or
hysterical pleasure prevents reason, the "calculating principle,"
from estimating things as they really are. "Pleasure is the greatest
of impostors." [78] It makes small things look big, and big small,
so that it militates against the virtue of truthfulness, which is the
perfection of our faculty of reason. The glamor of the stage again
beguiles us into a false estimate of what is admirable or amusing.
We should blush to be guilty of such clownishness and buffoonery
as we can swallow with gusto when we are only spectators. [79] The
pleasures of most art are not only at war with reason and truth, but
also with poise and self-control.

ACTION'S PLEASUR-
ABLE BLOOM NOT
WHOLLY BAD.

But this 'pleasure' or 'glamor' which accompanies human process
and product is not for Plato unambiguously evil. Often his words
taken from isolated passages might convince us that it is so. But
like the terms 'art' and 'imitation,' the term 'pleasure' and the
related words implying the charm of the image-making functions
cover a wide area of application. The import of pleasure is in its
turn sensitive to the use made of the word and the company it
keeps. It can even be pure and absolute, when a spectator enjoys
the contemplation of abstract geometric forms, as the circle and
the straight line, pure tones or colors, and odors. [80] The better
possibilities for pleasure are brought out in the passage in the *Laws*
from which we diverged some little time back in order to develop
the more sinister side of pleasant feeling. The whole case for
pleasure is here brought to trial. The Athenian interlocutor both
commends pleasure: "I actually go myself with the current
opinion so far as this: the standard by which music should be
judged is the pleasure it gives"; [81] and condemns it: "It is commonly

---

[77] *Loc. cit.*, c.   [80] *Philebus*, 51b, c.
[78] *Philebus*, 65c.   [81] *Laws*, Bk. II, 658, trans. Taylor.
[79] *Republic*, Bk. X, 606c.

said that the standard of rightness in music is its pleasure-giving effect. That, however, is an intolerable sentiment, in fact, 'tis a piece of flat blasphemy." [82] If these two statements, both of which represent aspects of Plato's thought, can be reconciled, the case concerning pleasure will be set out in its full meaning.

When Plato through the Athenian declares that he accepts the criterion of pleasure for music, he immediately adds: But not just anybody's pleasure. He then unfolds at once the inherent affinity of music for the soul. This affinity is in part suggested by the conception of music as imitation. The choric art, of which music forms a part, is a "mimic presentation of manners, with all variety of action and circumstance, enacted by performers who depend on characterization and impersonation." [83] But the repugnance or congeniality between music and soul is really the attraction or repulsion of two elements within a single whole rather than of two distinct entities. Music conceived in abstraction from the moral temper it presents is in fact music with the soul of music gone. Plato's notion is better conveyed by saying that music partakes of soul than by saying that it imitates soul. A man listening to music finds himself again, so to speak, in the music. And so it follows that when either because of native bent or training a man's character possesses a certain habit or tone, his appetite can be satisfied with nothing in music but its musical kin. That the very medium and essence of music is psychic so that psychological terms applied to music are not metaphors, but literal qualifications, is brought out by a turn in the dialogue.

The Athenian is pursuing home the determining attributes of good music. Wouldn't a man of courage and a coward assume different attitudes and 'sing different tunes' in the presence of the same danger? he asks. The interlocutor not only assents, but will even add a little to the description. They would probably betray their soul-difference even in the color of the cheek. Now the Athenian replies to this amendment that when one wishes to apply critical terms taken from such a human source to music, one may not borrow from this phenomenon of turning pale or the reverse,

MUSIC PARTAKES OF SOUL.

---

[82] *Ibid.*, Bk. II, 655, trans. Taylor.   [83] *Ibid.*, Bk. II, 655, trans. Taylor.

because music is not in its substance a phenomenon with color. It is in its substance a bearer of figure and melody; so that the attitude assumed by a human body and the oral expression of a man in danger would furnish characterizations immediately appropriate to music. The Athenian adds a stricture on the contemporary musical-critics. The leaders of choruses have not been punctilious in this matter, but have spoken of brilliantly-colored music.[84] Terms of value applied to any art should respect the art's medium.

Since, then, it is of the essence of music to express dispositions of the soul, the ultimate goodness of music may be referred to this moral and mental criterion. Good music is what expresses a good temper. The pleasure that good men feel will be the touchstone of excellence. Plato draws this out humorously with a fable. In order to be perfectly sure that it is not just anybody's pleasure that may determine taste, nor the pleasure of the majority, but that it is the pleasure of the best men, let us fancy a competition in simple pleasure-giving. The prize is to go to the man who can entertain the spectators best. A call to a festival would probably bring out a reciter of Homer, a tragedian, a performer of comedies, and "I should not be surprised if one of them [the performers] thought his best chance of the prize was to exhibit a puppet-show." [85] When the votes are cast, the tiny children will vote for the puppet-show; the big boys for the comedy; most people probably, including cultivated women and youths, for the tragedy; whereas the old men would probably vote in favor of the renderer of an epic from the great tradition. Now only one of these groups can be right. So the question returns for settlement to the qualification of the groups. It is the old men who are best-educated and most noble of soul. It is therefore their judgment that should be taken. [86]

Pleasure is then allowed to remain the criterion of the image-making arts by Plato after it has undergone modulation into the key of character. One breaks up music and finds in it an essence of moral temper. One passes in review moral tempers. One finds

---

[84] *Laws*, Bk. II, 654–55.
[85] *Ibid.*, Bk. II, 658, trans. Taylor.
[86] *Loc. cit.*

that the best moral temper is the justest and wisest. One returns with this discovery to the original unbroken whole of music entitled to say: The goodness of music waits upon the ethical inquiry into the goodness of men. Pleasure remolded into what pleasure ought to be, pleasure welded to goodness, can settle esthetic as well as moral disputes. The theory of Plato is one "which declines to separate the pleasant from the just." [87]

This doctrine of the inherence of soul in music is of primary importance in Plato's esthetics not only because it largely settles for him the problem of a standard of taste, but also because it is the basis of his famous and elaborately developed application of esthetic ideas to education. One can either break up music and find the attributes of a mental disposition within; or one can move in the opposite direction and apply the whole pattern of all the musical arts to the malleable substance of the soul of a child. In the first case the mental temper—courage, justice, or wisdom— is the crystal discovered within. In the other, the developed art might be compared to a royal seal that is to be stamped upon spiritual wax. Plato conceived of the learning-process in children as involving a larger measure of immediate and unconscious absorption of form and habit, and less of the conscious acquisition of ideas and facts than we do today. In the program of education he recommended in the *Republic* and in the *Laws* he leaned heavily on this possibility of the unconscious assimilation of manners and taste, on the impressibility of a young spirit in the presence of a general spiritual quality. "Imitations if continued from youth far into life, settle down into habits and [second] nature, in the body, the speech, and the thought," [88] he says. Plato is here calling attention to the way formal habits of comely behavior may be introduced early and remain a lifetime. "Rhythm and harmony find their way to the inmost soul, and take strongest hold on it." [89] He is telling us that the instruction of youth is not like packing boots into a trunk, but more like putting animals to pasture; for it implies the child's assimilation of vital and formative nutriment.

MUSIC'S POWER MAY SHAPE SOULS.

[87] *Laws*, Bk. II, 663.
[88] *Republic*, Bk. III, 395d.
[89] *Ibid.*, Bk. III, 401d.

The body and soul grow by what they feed on. "It is . . . inevitable that a man should grow like whatever he enjoys, whether good or bad, even though he may be ashamed to approve it." [90] (We often observe how quickly children acquire the accent of a locality, or the 'lilt' of a foreign language.) In order that there should be an education of the taste and imagination of children in this natural subconscious way, Plato makes certain strict prohibitions, and equally strict prescriptions. Half the children's time and attention is to be devoted to dancing, singing, and hearing popular myths.

POETRY MUST BE PRUNED.
Plato's theory of the process of learning, then, underlies his recommendations of changes in the poetry to be taught to young Athenians. Songs "are really spells for the souls," [91] he says, and art being magic, and youthful minds being plastic, and a state existing for the creation of generous souls and bodies, certain courses must be pruned or deleted. First, we must ask the responsible leaders in the state to prepare an expurgated edition of Homer, for Homer is the staple of diet in imaginative literature. Now we know that what is good is always self-sufficient, balanced, and single in essence.[92] Therefore, the representations of divine and heroic beings in Homer must conform to our best conception of what is admirable. It is obnoxious and misleading to picture the inhabitants of Olympus as hysterical and shifting, or subject to external or accidental pressure. "Then we shall request Homer and the other poets not to portray Achilles, the son of a goddess, as lying now on his side, and then again on his back, and again on his face, and then rising up and drifting distraught on the shore of the waste unharvested ocean, nor as clutching with both hands the sooty dust and strewing it over his head, nor as weeping and lamenting in the measure and manner attributed to him by the poet." [93] We must also take out the lines in which Zeus is said to dispense good and evil indifferently, for what in strict usage can be called divine is never neutral, but always good and

[90] *Laws*, Bk. II, 656, trans. Taylor.
[91] *Ibid.*, Bk. II, 659 and 33a, trans. Taylor.
[92] *Republic*, Bk. II, 380–81.
[93] *Ibid.*, Bk. III, 388b.

the source of goodness.[94] Again Hades must be described as a place fit for divine beings and one to which noble and generous souls will rejoice to go; not, therefore, as in the unabridged Homer, full of grim and squalid mansions, or like a cavern full of bats.[95]

Not only, according to Plato, should the Homeric myths be cleared and straightened so as to represent ethical feeling to the children right-side-up, and to be assimilated by their minds in true proportions, but the formal molds of poetry and music should be regulated in the light of philosophical definition. The patterning of the elements in arts is as important as the content. Rhythms and melodies and plastic relations may, through their mere swing and shape, relax and split up the centrality and unity of the organism. As we saw, they may tend to produce mixed pleasures, and mixed pleasures tend to pull about and loosen the bonds of the human soul. So the Lydian style in music, which is relaxingly sweet,[96] and the complex styles, which break up the order and unity of the spirit, are forbidden. Plato fears the influence of excessive variety of effects, flutes and "instruments of many strings or whose compass includes all the harmonies," [97] and program music of the frankly imitative type, because they accent the part at the expense of the perfect whole, they stimulate through novelty and surprise, instead of knitting into a close, transparent weft. Rather than forming the growing constitution into which it passes, such music disintegrates it. Plato thinks that too composite and colorful a style in music, poetry, or dancing is like rich and highly-spiced food for the body—it leads to indigestion and weakness. Elaborately embroidered patterns, natural actors who can fit themselves into any character, emotional emergency, situation, or histrionic cliché, will find no place in Plato's materials for elementary training. Music and dancing are to be of two types: the Phrygian, war-like and nerving; and the Dorian, sobering and tempering.[98] Simple metres in poetry, and simple literary

SENSUOUS PATTERNS WHOLESOMELY SIMPLE.

---

[94] *Ibid.*, Bk. II, 379.
[95] *Ibid.*, Bk. III, 386–87.
[96] *Ibid.*, Bk. III, 398–99.
[97] *Ibid.*, Bk. III, 399c.
[98] *Ibid.*, Bk. III, 399.

designs—the narrative and heroic, and not the dramatic—are enjoined.[99]

Thus wise statesmen will recognize and use the magic of art toward the production of good citizenship, Plato thought. Over against Plato's proscription of drama must be set his prescription, even as early as when he wrote the *Republic*, of a planned beautiful environment for children, an environment consisting of gracious buildings, gardens, vases, and urns, and embroidered garments.[100] These taste-forming sights are to coöperate with equally taste-forming sounds: martial music, which will get the children's very hearts, and inspire them to valorous deeds; and balancing the stimulant to courage there are to be sober choirs of peace singing praises to the gods, making the growing generation orderly, just, and reverent. Taken together these helpful art-forms may be called the winds of fair works blowing gently upon impressionable sensibilities.[101] Just as iron is tempered and improved by the fire so the passions are softened and made useful by the proper application of harmonies.[102]

Such are the social potentialities of art in the hands of wise governors. If Plato's expulsion of the poets from his model city is an offense to our present feeling, his faith in the practical efficacy of the art he enjoins may easily be an equal shock. It is what Plato loves and admires and confides in that he chastens. When he says that songs are spells he thinks more of the good in them than the evil. As Plato grows older, he recognizes more and more that art is the specific for shaping emotion, and that pleasures and pains, thus molded to good ends, are the indispensable allies of reason. In the *Phaedrus* Plato makes reason a charioteer who rules his steeds; later in the *Laws* he makes reason a weak cord which cannot draw the human puppet in the right way without the coöperating force of pleasure-cords.[103]

---

[99] *Republic*, Bk. III, 392.
[100] *Ibid.*, Bk. III, 401.
[101] *Loc. cit.*
[102] *Laws*, Bk. II, 671.
[103] This theme is developed in E. Wind, "Untersuchungen über die Platonische Kunstphilosophie," *Zeitschrift für Ästhetik und allgemeine Kunstwissenschaft*, XXVI, 1932.

Though we have seen that pleasure is allowed by Plato to become the standard of taste and the leading-string of youth, when
it is the pleasure of a noble soul, still we must never lose sight of
Plato's constant disparagement of the multitude's identification
of good and pleasure in comparison with "the finer spirits'"
identification of good and knowledge or intelligence.[104] What is
the exact nature of the finer spirits' intelligible goodness which
is the alterative and restorative of pleasure? To inquire into the
nature of this goodness is to study the last slippery concept that is
fundamental to Plato's esthetics. Straight through that conversation in the second book of the *Laws* when the Athenian is pressing
closer and closer to the real goodness of music—whether he is
speaking of the nobility of the song or its fitness and decorum—
its final excellence is always expressed by some form of the Greek
word *kalos*. To this term we must now attend. Though often
translated 'beautiful,' it no more coincides with the idea conveyed
in English by that word than does *techné* or *mimesis* mean straight-
away our 'art' or 'imitation.' The more recent translators have in
many cases used the English term 'good' where the earlier ones
use 'beautiful,' and the words 'fair' and 'noble' and 'fine' are frequently employed. The concept behind the word was definite,
however rich, in Plato's philosophizing, but it was the intellectual
product of much analysis and speculation. For the ordinary undisciplined mind the various sides of the idea of *to kalon* have to
be adumbrated by the use of first this and then that adjective, and
Plato himself employs a whole dialogue and important sections
of others for its elucidation. Not only does he need much space
for it, but also many analogies and dialectical processes before he
can feel that its nature stands forth.

The early dialogue, the *Hippias Major*, which is wholly concerned with the analysis of *to kalon*, is a sort of rehearsal for the
later more constructive and powerful presentations of the same
idea in the *Symposium* and the *Republic*. All sorts of naïve and
commonplace conceptions concerning beauty are exposed and
cleared away. For example, the stupid and conceited Hippias

---

[104] *Republic*, Bk. VI, 505b.

confuses the abstract idea with the example: beauty is a beautiful maiden or horse.[105] Socrates stands over against him constantly in insisting that *to kalon* must be so defined as to be that predicate which fits all attributions of beauty. The term must explain the fineness of maidens, horses, musical instruments, and pottery. When Socrates so states his logical demand as to suggest the idea of the essential attribute of the thing to be defined,[106] Hippias characteristically drops this notion to the material plane, and asserts that gold is that which, added to a thing, brings beauty. Gold then must be our universal predicate and form.[107] Socrates shows the limitations of this crude definition. What is beautiful must be so everywhere and to everyone, he reiterates.[108] Whereupon Hippias has a fresh inspiration. Everywhere and to everyone it is beautiful to be healthy and wealthy, honored by the Greeks, enjoy a long life, have a fine funeral, and be survived by your children.[109] Such a sum of fine things must surely equal the universality in beauty which Socrates demands. Socrates quickly retorts that for Achilles and his grandfather Aiakos and many divine beings, not long life and burial at the hands of children, but death was obviously the beautiful thing.[110] Hippias then makes a further blunder by identifying the beautiful with what appears beautiful, as in the case of shrewdly selected vestments which set off one's person.[111] Socrates points out how intolerable is the state of affairs which such a conception of the beautiful would cover. There would be an outer show, fine but false; an underlying reality, unfine, and leading to a false impression. It is true that in the case of the beautiful, the appearance and the reality are well known to differ. But will one then choose as 'beauty itself' the fine exterior?[112]

NOT SUCCESSFUL FUNCTIONING NOR PLEASURE.

Socrates then tries his own hand at definition and builds toward, without reaching, the conception that the later Dialogues make

---

[105] *Hippias Major*, 287e, 288b-c.
[106] *Ibid.*, 289b.
[107] *Ibid.*, 289e.
[108] *Ibid.*, 291d.
[109] *Ibid.*, 291e.
[110] *Ibid.*, 292e–293.
[111] *Ibid.*, 294.
[112] *Loc. cit.*

overt. That is beautiful which can do its particular work well, he suggests; so may not beauty be successful functioning? [113] This, again, however, he finds must be amended because none of us would be willing to praise as noble the competence to do harm. Perhaps the beautiful is the beneficial. Here is a hint of the Platonic thesis that beauty is goodness. This definition comes to grief because of the distinction between productive power and product. If beauty is the cause of goodness, goodness and beauty differ as father and son or author and work. So the beautiful must differ from the good, that is to say, it must be non-good—an intolerable conclusion.[114] Recourse is then had to pleasure as the defining term of beauty. Would it be possible to define beauty as that which makes us feel joy through hearing and sight? [115] The problem such a definition raises is partly that of the limitation of the noble and fine to the sensuous, partly the adjustment of pleasure as such to the differentiation of the two channels, vision and hearing.

What Hippias scornfully calls the "scrapings and shavings" [116] of this early dialogue on beauty are made into an impressive intellectual structure by later discourses. Near the end of the *Symposium*, after Plato has eloquently portrayed what Beauty Itself is and the manner of life which most nearly touches this ideal, he adds almost as if looking back at Hippias's jejune proposals: "This [the very essence of beauty] when once beheld, will outshine your gold and your vesture, your beautiful boys and striplings." [117] In these more adequate dialogues the essence of beauty is used as one name for what a philosopher spends his life in seeking. And what the philosopher spends his life in seeking is, in Plato's eyes, what all men, if the divine part in them could be fully brought alive, would necessarily desire. "When it comes to the good nobody is content with the possession of the appearance but all men seek the reality." [118] The goodness of a thing is for Plato

"KALOS" IS WHAT PHILOSOPHER SEEKS.

---

[113] *Ibid.*, 295c-d.
[114] *Ibid.*, 296c-e.
[115] *Ibid.*, 297e.
[116] *Ibid.*, 304.
[117] *Symposium*, 211b.
[118] *Republic*, Bk. VI, 505d.

the basis of its existence. All beings, animate or inanimate, *are* in proportion to their participation in the Good. The intellectual pursuit of the Good, philosophy, is the specifically human mode of this universal craving after essential, incorruptible Being. But as man is a compound of body and soul, leaning both ways, the significance of his striving is ambiguous with regard to its place in nature. Philosophy is the severance of the soul from her bodily habitation, and hence may be described as dying in life. On the other hand, it is the flowering of life itself, a sublimation of that divine power which in the animal kingdom impels male to female, fills the human lover's heart with longing and enthusiasm, inspires the holy host of Theban youths with invincible courage and

ITS DYNAMIC SIDE IS EROS. breathes in the poet's song, moving his hearers to tears—it is Eros. Philosophy, this latest invention of the human spirit, the youngest of the arts, stands revealed as "the oldest and noblest of the gods." Plato makes Socrates say in so many words that love is a philosopher.[119] Both endure the pangs of violent passion; both, if good fortune attends the course of their passionate courtship and labor, consummate all in the bliss of communion and the bringing to birth of offspring. Both the native endowment for love and for philosophy include propensive vigor and sensitiveness to grace of form. The early love-situation so inevitably embraces in itself the admired object, the perceived form acknowledged as beautiful, that beauty and love are genuine counterparts.[120] The dynamic of Eros is set in motion by the perception of loveliness; "for when it meets the ugly it coils itself close in a sullen dismay." [121]

THE LADDER OF BEAUTY. Out of this beginning the philosophic road emerges. For the philosopher in earnest with his calling follows the beautiful object of his affections as it mounts before him.[122] The main interest for Plato in love specifically philosophic is the ascent of the way, the ladder of beauty: dialectic. The first step up is the universalizing of beauty. The lover "must remark how the beauty attached to this and that body is cognate to that which is attached to any other,

---

[119] *Symposium*, 204b.
[120] *Ibid.*, 204d.
[121] *Ibid.*, 206d.
[122] *Ibid.*, 210-11.

and that if he means to pursue beauty in form, it is gross folly not to regard as one and the same the beauty belonging to all." [123] The fair body of his beloved becomes part and instance of a world of physical beauty. The next step involves the change from body to soul. Even a slight measure of mental grace will come to outweigh in his estimation a great deal of personal beauty. From insight into the higher beauty of spirit, the lover will proceed to the beauty of customs and laws; from thence, to the beauty of learning and the sciences. He now nears his journey's end.

The Beauty that lies at the end gives meaning to all the lower beauties. But in itself, it is beheld only by those who can persevere on the common human road far beyond common human will or capacity. Those who have great courage, power or memory, and understanding, and hold fast to the end, have suddenly revealed to them "a wondrous vision." [124] Plato conceives of this vision as if it were the mystic fulfilment of a rite. The attained Beauty Absolute is not strictly susceptible of description in normal terms, because it is beyond being and knowledge. But ordinary words may furnish intimations of its nature. Still more one may be made to realize it by the statement of the contrasts between it and what ordinary opinion calls beautiful.

First, Beauty Itself is stable.[125] The many beauties come into being and pass out again. No concrete object, either physical or spiritual, which we might praise by calling it beautiful, could satisfy the test of Beauty's permanence. Bodies and ornaments, laws, customs, and sciences, however good, fine, or appropriate, are limited and perishable. The contrast for Plato between the Ideas or essences and the particular existences or instances always implies the opposition between an unchanging one and the changing many.

BEAUTY IS IMPERISHABLE.

In the case of the Idea of Beauty, however, its steady fixedness of character has a special significance for the growing soul. Our most intimate need is to prolong and stabilize our good and what

---

[123] *Ibid.*, 210b.
[124] *Ibid.*, 210e.
[125] *Ibid.*, 211.

we essentially are.[126] This instinctive demand, Eros operative in us, appears dimly before our everyday consciousness as the longing for immortal life; and the longing for immortality makes itself felt in us as the urge to beget children; for through the generations that spring from our loins we picture ourselves as undying types. Now Beauty is conceived by Plato as the presiding genius of procreation,[127] for only when the desire to produce is favored by the presence of beauty does it get in play. So the instinct to bear children, or, if we are nobler beings, to leave behind us intellectual children—poems or the constitutions of states—is our participation in the principle of the one perduring beauty.[128] Plato believes, however, that so long as the desire to attain to the One Beauty is envisaged as satisfied by the production of entities other than our own selves, there is imperfection tainting the love. The lower physical cravings demand the physical evidence of new persons; the somewhat higher cravings of our spirited part demand actions and motions and entities parallel in excellence to their soul-quality, brave deeds or useful objects; but the reason, the divine part in us, also wishes to be established, and wrought, so to speak, into enduring bronze. Here a pregnant truth appears. The will of the divine part in us to maintain itself can only be represented as the coming home of the soul to itself, and the soul's final appreciation of its own intrinsic nature.[129] In its final meaning, then, Beauty as the goddess of childbirth [130] fosters our re-creation of ourselves in the image of divinity. We are helped to disengage the imperishable element residing in us through all the transmigrations and pilgrimages of the soul, and through union with essence to ensure its power to abide and resist all change.

IT IS THE REALI-
ZATION OF THE
DIVINITY IN US.

UNIFORM MOTION
IS BEST.
One way of stating the contrast between an Ideal One and the many copies is to say that the first is immovable and the second moving.[131] Therefore, the influence of Beauty Itself upon the soul may be expressed in terms of motion, as may the genesis of human

---

126 *Symposium*, 206, 207c-d.
127 *Ibid.*, 206d.
128 *Ibid.*, 209.
129 *Republic*, Bk. VII, 518; *Charmides*, 165.
130 *Symposium*, 206b.
131 *Timaeus*, 28.

art. Plato repeats, in a story-telling mood, the common saying that the arts of dance and song mark the passage from brutish raging and roaring and irregular childish leaping and skipping to the rhythmic movements ordained and led by Apollo and the Muses at the great festivals.[132] Though to be at rest is on Plato's view better than to exhibit any kind of motion, there is also a great difference in the excellence of kinds of motion. Order in motion is an imitation of the stable. Passing in review the ten kinds of motion,[133] Plato indicates that movement confined to one place about a center, like that of a well-turned cartwheel, or a well-made globe, is the best. This regular and uniform motion in one compass about a center is the movement of wisdom. Absolute Beauty itself being self-same has the tendency to set up self-same or regular and rhythmical motion in the soul, in so far as the soul is able to take on this kind of motion. All that is beneficent and wise is, for Plato, a meeting of like with like, congeniality, or self-relation; circular motion thus belongs to this class.[134] But only the intelligible part of the soul is able to move steadily round on its own axis. Plato has an explanation of how the disciplining of irregular and disorderly motions into the good order of self-returning movement in the intelligence is accomplished.

The heavenly bodies which are lesser gods move in circles, and our creator has so made us that we have a means of learning to mimic star-motion. The end and use, justification and interpretation of sight and hearing lie here, and we are able to understand why in the *Hippias Major* Socrates rejected the definition of the beautiful as the "pleasant to sight and hearing" as incomplete. "The god invented and gave us vision in order that we might observe the circuits of intelligence in the heaven and profit by them for the revolutions of our own thought, which are akin to them, though ours be troubled and they are unperturbed; and that, by learning to know them and acquiring the power to compute them rightly according to nature, we might reproduce the

SENSES AIDS TO HARMONY.

---

[132] *Laws*, Bk. II, 653, 654.
[133] *Ibid.*, Bk. X, 893, 894.
[134] *Ibid.*, Bk. VIII, 837; *Lysis*, 221, 222.

perfectly unerring revolutions of the god and reduce to settled order the wandering motions in ourselves." [135] The same argument is then given for the existence of hearing: "Of sound and hearing once more the same account may be given: they are a gift from heaven for the same intent and purpose. For not only was speech appointed to this same intent, to which it contributes in the largest measure, but also all that part of Music that is serviceable with respect to the hearing of sound is given for the sake of harmony; and harmony, whose motions are akin to the revolutions of the soul within us, has been given by the Muses to him whose commerce with them is guided by intelligence, not for the sake of irrational pleasure (which is now thought to be its utility), but as an ally against the inward discord that has come into the revolution of the soul, to bring it into order and consonance with itself. Rhythm also was a succor bestowed upon us by the same hands to the same intent, because in the most part of us our condition is lacking in measure and poor in grace." [136]

BEAUTY THE
MEANING OF SIGHT
AND HEARING FOR
THE SOUL.

While pulling to pieces the definition of beauty as the pleasant to sight and hearing, Socrates called attention to the need of some underlying common principle that should show why what is pleasant to sight is also pleasant to hearing, and why what is pleasant in general, when not restricted to the two channels of sight and hearing, may not be identified with the beautiful. [137] What he was urging was that an Idea or unifying concept cannot be simply expressed in terms of the separate senses because these are not bound together in any unity. He now suggests that beauty may be identified with what might be called the intelligible of sight and hearing: the function which they serve in the economy of the soul. The same sublimation of the sensuous joys of color and tone into the pure realm of intellectual form and relation is made in the *Republic*. Plato is outlining the proper education of the philosopher. The philosopher through his education must be made to mount that very ladder toward beauty, self-same and

---

[135] *Timaeus*, 47b-c, trans. Cornford: *Plato's Cosmology*, Kegan Paul, 1937, p. 158.

[136] *Ibid.*, 47b-c, trans. Cornford.

[137] *Hippias Major*, 298–303.

eternal, which was the theme of the *Symposium*. He must study astronomy, but not linger with the gorgeous "blazonry of the heavens"; [138] and when he studies musical harmony, he must not be drawn hither and thither as common theatre-goers are, by the lure of novel musical forms.[139] The right use of the "natural indwelling intelligence of the soul" draws the lover of wisdom and beauty away from the "sparks that paint the sky"—"decorations on a visible surface"—and away from the blows of the plectrum and the fine discrimination of delicate intervals to the eternal laws of number engraved in these images.[140] And these laws of number are expressions of the single Idea of the Good and Fair.

But though the One Beauty is always contemplated rather than actually beheld in physical vision for Plato, he continually reminds us of the analogy between light and beauty. The glory of wisdom is not seen by mortal eyes. But the best physical parallel to the Ideal Goal of Being is the sun.[141] The Idea of Good, Beauty, is the reality that gives truth to the objects of knowledge and the power of knowing to the knower, just as light is the author and cause of the coming together of the fire in the eye with the fire that colors objects. In the *Phaedrus* Plato refines his treatment of the relation of light to Ideas up to the point of assigning the Idea of Beauty a special place connected with human vision. Beauty is at once the loveliest and the most clearly seen of all the Forms; for Beauty shines through the clearest of our senses—sight.[142] Wisdom itself would be dangerously and terribly lovely, if she could be seen. Plato of course does not mean to imply that, after all, Beauty is sensuous. Beauty, like Wisdom, is supersensible. Still, beauty 'takes off,' as it were, through the power of the eye to see color and light. The close connection established by Plato between light and spiritual beauty had an important development, as we shall see, in Neo-Platonism and the theological esthetics of the Middle Ages.

BEAUTY AND LIGHT.

---

[138] *Republic*, Bk. VII, 529c-e.
[139] *Ibid.*, Bk. V, 475d.
[140] *Ibid.*, Bk. VII, 531–31c.
[141] *Ibid.*, Bk. VI, 508.
[142] *Phaedrus*, 250d.

MEASURE AND PRO-
PORTION.

The dissatisfaction indicated in the *Hippias Major* with the definition of the beautiful as the appropriate [143] also gets its positive ground in the later dialogues. Beauty itself as absolutely undivided [144] cannot have parts, so cannot fit nicely together, and therefore cannot be the harmony of any physical object. At the same time the perfect unity of the Heavenly Paradigm can ordain among earthly compound beauties such unity and fitness as is possible to them. This results in the requirement of harmony or decorum in music, painting, drama [145] rhetoric, as well as in the nobler arts of political and private virtue. A good speech is like an animal skilfully carved at the joints, so that the natural articulation of the creature is respected,[146] Plato says. Good taste demands of the choric art that tune, diction, and actor shall fit the sentiment conveyed and the reigning tone of the whole. The true Muse would never permit senseless jumbles of feminine strain with masculine words, slavish rhythms with freeman gestures, or animal noises with human myth.[147] "Measure and proportion are everywhere identified with beauty." [148]

DID PLATO WRITE
NO ESTHETICS?

"With beauty and virtue," not with beauty alone, this concluding passage of the *Philebus* reads. And the sentence before reads: "So now the power of the good has taken refuge in the nature of the beautiful." In the *Hippias Major*, mere appropriateness and utility were rejected in favor of beneficence as a definition of beauty; not any end, but only a moral end, will serve. To us as students of Plato it has been obvious for some time that 'Beauty Itself,' as Plato defines it, is the goodness of a life devoted to justice united with the wisdom of a philosopher's understanding.

Throughout this chapter the reasons have clearly appeared why Plato may be said to have written an anti-esthetic rather than an esthetic. Those who declare that his philosophy has little or no connection with modern ideas on art and beauty are impressed

---

[143] *Hippias Major*, 293e–94.
[144] *Symposium*, 211.
[145] *Republic*, Bk. III, 401–402; 396–98.
[146] *Phaedrus*, 264c.
[147] *Laws*, Bk. II, 669–70.
[148] *Philebus*, 64e.

with the moral and intellectual content in his 'beauty,' with the astonishing extension of his term 'art' to shoe-making on one side and dialectic on the other, and with the ascetic tendencies in his doctrine of imagery and pleasure. But though Plato's esthetic ideas are far from ours, they bear an interesting and important relation to ours. There are those who will even say that Plato's ideas on these subjects compose *in toto* a useful criticism and amendment of our own. What it all comes to is that Plato makes no separate kingdom for what we today call esthetic concepts. It is, therefore, as true to say, it would seem, that he wrote nothing but an esthetics, as to say that he wrote none. For his thoughts about the fair and seemly, and of patterned charming forms in diverse media, overflow all his inquiries. This happens without injury to the sharpness of his logical divisions. He cuts otherwise than we; and he joins together otherwise.

OR WAS IT ALL ES-
THETICS?

By way of gathering in our results let us notice the 'tumbling back and forth' in Plato of esthetic experience in the narrower sense and a general theory of values. The poet, we are told, is an artist because his power is enthusiasm rather than conscious craftsmanship or wisdom. The poet and the philosopher are therefore two instead of one as in the traditional view. But this distinction will not hold absolutely. For the philosopher, whose soaring art of dialectic inspired by a vision of fair wisdom is the paradigm of all the arts and sciences, is not an authentic artist unless he is moved by love. Moreover, he must love with the divine part of him. If this be so, then he, like the poet, is god-controlled, enthusiastic.[149]

IF ART IS POOR
PHILOSOPHY, PHI-
LOSOPHY IS EXCEL-
LENT ART.

Once more, poets and painters are not only mimics, but imitators on the third and lowest level of being—therefore, on still another ground, at a great distance from philosophers whose love is true being and whose proper place in the state, royal. But this apparent distinction no more holds than the first. Philosophers are also imitators of sorts. The very philosophical ascent toward wisdom and truth requires imitation, that is, participation in the real being, rated harshly by the standard of independent kinghood.

---

[149] *Phaedrus*, 249e.

For the skilful artificer of justice and virtue in the state must keep looking at his perfect model, like a good painter whose eyes move often away from the surface of his tablet to the source of his design.[150] Thus the highest class of men known to Plato, the lovers of wisdom, must be interpreted in terms of these apparently despised ones—the painters. The sculptor is but a common workman—not to be thought of as fine or noble or wise for a moment. And yet when the harmonious beauty of the philosopher-king's product, the well-organized state, requires an adequate symbol, the symbol is found in the duly proportioned and colored statue, of which no part has too much or too little.[151]

The Muses are often associated by Plato with the irresponsible joy-caterers of an effete civilization. Yet philosophy itself is music.[152] The music that Socrates makes in his life and speech is above the poems of Homer, but Socrates must borrow in one sense the apparel of Homer. For his achievement must be presented under the metaphor of music and poetry.

The dramatists are expelled by Plato from his ideal city. Sometimes his low estimate of them embodies itself in satire. At the very end of the *Symposium*, Plato describes in a concise skit how Agathon, a writer of tragedies, and Aristophanes, a writer of comedies, were still sitting with Socrates over their cups at dawn after the previous night's banquet. One can only think of Socrates in this connection as the chief participant in a supreme tragedy and the main actor in the drama of the Dialogues, a drama with a double meaning. He is the bearer of the deeply earnest intent as well as the centre of the comic show. The two practitioners of the art of literary phantasms were feebly following the argument of the enduring and alert Socrates. Socrates was saying that "the fully skilled tragedian should be a comedian as well"—presumably because neither one rightly knows what he is about. Agathon and Aristophanes "began to nod," then fell asleep, and Socrates put them to bed. This humorously and yet profoundly exemplifies Plato's view of the place of dramatic art on the scale of the func-

---

[150] *Republic*, Bk. VI, 501–501b.
[151] *Ibid.*, Bk. IV, 420.
[152] *Phaedo*, 61.

tions.[153] Still it is possible to say that for Plato drama is expelled
and ridiculed in the interests of a higher drama. When the
Athenian of the *Laws* is making clear that the good political constitution is far better than any stage-play, one can hardly tell
whether dramatic poetry owes more for its evaluation to the conception of a good kingdom or the good kingdom to theory of
tragedy. "We ourselves," the citizens are made to say, "to the
best of our ability are the authors of a tragedy at once superlatively
fair and good; at least, all our polity is framed as a representation
of the fairest and best life, which is, in reality, as we assert, the
truest tragedy. Thus we are composers of the same things as
yourselves, rivals of yours as artists and actors of the fairest
drama." [154] The state is a living form, pregnant with tensions; but
measured and ruled by order and insight.

Plato has many severe censures to pass on the art of words.
Rhetorical speeches often do nothing but flatter the wild beast in
us,[155] he teaches. The more serious works, he writes in the seventh
epistle, are never precipitated into words at all. They "abide in
the fairest region," *i.e.* in the head, where thoughts still communicate only with themselves.[156] The same idea is expressed at
the end of the long analysis of rhetoric in the *Phaedrus*. Legitimate literary art is "the living and breathing word of him who
knows, of which the written word may justly be called the
image." [157] Socrates says: "He who thinks . . . that he has left
behind him any art in writing, and he who receives it in the belief
that anything in writing will be clear and certain, will be an
utterly simple person. . . . Writing . . . has this strange quality
and is very like painting; for the creatures of painting stand like
living beings, but if one asks them a question, they preserve a
solemn silence." [158] Thus first and last Plato puts esthetic experience in its place, often in a low place. But he also often colors

---

[153] *Symposium*, 223d.

[154] *Laws*, Bk. VII, 817d. Cf. Hans-Georg Gadamer, *Plato und die Dichter*,
Frankfurt a. M., 1934.

[155] *Republic*, Bk. IX, 571, 572; *Phaedrus*, 272e; *Gorgias*, 454.

[156] *Epistle*, 7:334c.

[157] *Phaedrus*, 276.

[158] *Ibid.*, 275c–d.

the higher places of mathematics and dialectic with hues borrowed from esthetic experience. Only so can he make his imitation faithful to the thing imitated.

SUPPLEMENTARY READING

Mortimer J. Adler, *Art and Prudence*, New York, 1937, Ch. I.

R. G. Collingwood, "Plato's Philosophy of Art," *Mind*, 34 (1925), pp. 154–172.

Allan H. Gilbert, *Literary Criticism from Plato to Dryden*, New York, 1939.

W. C. Green, *Plato's View of Poetry* (Harvard Studies, I, 29), 1918.

G. M. A. Grube, *Plato's Thought*, London, 1935, Ch. VI.

R. L. Nettleship, *The Theory of Education in the Republic of Plato*, Chicago, 1906.

Erwin Panofsky, *Idea*, Leipzig and Berlin, 1924.

Constantin Ritter, *The Essence of Plato's Philosophy*, New York, 1933.

P. M. Schuhl, *Platon et l'Art de son Temps*, Paris, 1933.

Mary Swindler, *Ancient Painting*, London, 1929.

A. E. Taylor, *Plato*, London, 1922.

George Saintsbury, *A History of Criticism*, 3 Vols., Edinburgh and London, 1934, Vol. I, Bk. I, Ch. II.

Lionello Venturi, *History of Art Criticism*, New York, 1936, Ch. II.

CHAPTER III

Aristotle

MOST of the esthetic topics discussed by Aristotle had already been discussed by Plato. For instance, Aristotle's *Poetics* begins with the general principle that the arts of poetry and music with their subdivisions of epic, tragedy, comedy, lyric, and flute and lyre-playing are species of imitation.[1] But that the pleasure-giving arts are imitations is a commonplace in Plato, and Plato anticipated most of Aristotle's sub-divisions and principles of division.[2] Again, probably the most widely known single phrase in the *Poetics* occurs at the end of the definition of a tragedy. Aristotle there says that tragedy must contain "incidents arousing pity and fear, wherewith to accomplish its catharsis of such emotions."[3] A library of commentary and argument has been written in the effort to explain what the tragic purgation of pity and fear through pity and fear is, and the name of Aristotle has been traditionally attached to the conception. Yet Plato had already in the *Laws* prescribed music and the dance as a medicine for fear. "Frights are due to a poor condition of soul. So whenever one applies an external shaking to affections of this kind, the external motion thus applied overpowers the internal motion of fear and frenzy, and by thus overpowering it, it brings about a manifest calm in the soul."[4] In a sense, then, the Aristotelian doctrine of fine art as a cathartic is the development of a Platonic one. Again, in the

ARISTOTLE A HEAVY BORROWER FROM PLATO.

---

[1] *Poetics*, 1447a. The translations from Aristotle are from the Oxford edition, W. D. Ross, editor.
[2] *Republic*, Bk. III, 394b–c.
[3] *Poetics*, 1449b.
[4] *Laws*, Bk. VII, 790–91.

59

Politics Aristotle inquires into the educational uses of music and the other arts; [5] but Plato had labored with passionate insistence upon the importance of music and dancing and poetry in children's education. [6] Aristotle emphasizes the importance for virtue of learning to like and to dislike rightly, [7] but Plato had already said the same. [8] It seems clear that Aristotle was a liberal borrower of Plato's esthetic ideas.

BUT SCIENTIFIC   And yet when Aristotle's debt is fully admitted, it remains true
ANALYSIS HIS OWN.   that to read him is to pass suddenly into a different intellectual climate from that of Platonism. In reading the *Symposium* and *Phaedrus* we learn about art through art; in reading the *Poetics* and *Politics* we learn about art through science. The atmosphere that pervades and carries the esthetic theory in Plato's case is full of color, light, and story, and the lively drama of actual discussion. There are banquets and flute-girls, drinking and jesting, chariots, and the fine meadows of the plains of heaven. There is irony, myth, and the intellectual tournament. In Aristotle there is only careful cool analysis. But the difference of external literary form is only the surface-reflection of the different ways in which the problems of esthetics presented themselves to the two men. In reading Plato our interest centers in the problem of the apparent contradiction between his love of beauty and his rejection of poetry. Both the love and the rejection are so emphatic and so warm that the tension between the opposed attitudes is felt as intolerable and probably as invalid. In reading Aristotle, we find no such contradiction and therefore feel no such pressure toward reconciliation. The reconciliation has indeed been accomplished, partly already within the long movement of Plato's own thought and partly in the passage from Plato to Aristotle, and Aristotle is therefore in a position to begin quietly, within poetry itself, drawing distinctions between technically successful and inept, early and late forms of the poetical art; and he is in a position to carry his dissection of material into refined issues.

---

[5] *Book* VIII.
[6] *Republic*, Bks. II and III; *Laws*, Bks. II and VII.
[7] *Nicomachean Ethics*, Bk. II, 1104b.
[8] *Laws*, Bk. II, 653–53e, 659d.

There will be, then, no gross novelty in the esthetic material dealt with in this chapter, but a new temperament will break up old shapes into new forms and will manifest at times stout independence. Indeed, Aristotle's sober physician-like temper of diagnosis, patient devotion to detail, insatiable curiosity regarding subtle likenesses and differences, and his submission of conception to the test of perception sometimes mislead us into thinking that teacher and pupil had nothing in common.

In spite of our valid insistence on the fundamental likeness between Plato and Aristotle, the first thing we must note is a difference. Aristotle does not leave us blindly to guess how his own conception of 'art' stands related to Plato's. He explicitly attaches his own conception of the origin of craftsmanship to a rebuttal of Plato's story of its Promethean origin. "Much in error . . . are they," he says, obviously intending Plato's story, "who say that the construction of man is not only faulty, but inferior to that of all other animals, seeing that he is, as they point out, barefooted, naked, and without weapon of which to avail himself." [9] The brutes are in reality the inferiors, for they have only one weapon apiece, whereas man has his hand—a tool for making other tools.[10] Because of this precious possession man is that animal best equipped for warlike attack and defense; "for the hand is talon, hoof, and horn as well. So too it is spear, and sword, and whatsoever other weapon or instrument you please; for all these can it be from its power of grasping and holding them all." [11] As for clothing, man is indeed obliged to make his own sandals. But then animals are reduced to sleeping with their sandals on.[12] Thus Aristotle rejects the imputation of niggardliness to Nature, implied in the myth of Prometheus repeated by Plato to picture the beginnings of human artistry.

Aristotle thought of Nature as prudent and just. He bids us observe how rightly Nature orders the generation of all things in proper gradations.[13] Man is her noblest son, and it would be a contradiction of Nature's essential habit to bestow less on the

ORIGIN NOT PROMETHEUS BUT HUMAN HAND.

---

[9] *De Partibus Animalium*, 687a.
[10] *Loc. cit.*
[11] *Ibid.*, 687b.

[12] *De Part. An.*, 687a.
[13] *De Gen. An.*, 733a.

animal that "alone stands erect, in accordance with his godlike nature and essence," [14] than on the quadrupeds, who bend themselves toward the earth. That widely useful tool, the hand, which Nature, in her discriminating wisdom, has given to her favorite is the source of man's capacity to invent the many crafts. Thus for Aristotle's thought craftsmanship (*techné*) begins as handiness coupled with the impulse to imitate the giver of the hand. For in the exercise of his native resourcefulness, man copies Nature's ways.[15] The transcendent element in Plato's philosophy makes art for him spring from a contest with Nature plus the following up of an impulse toward divinity. Aristotle confines his admission of transcendent elements within close limits. He stresses the beauty and order within Nature. No fiery sparks from heaven, no arduous ascent toward timeless beauty, but the more modest inventive imitation of the habits of the natural mother yields art for Aristotle. Though in the end art for Aristotle completes what Nature has begun,[16] this process of going beyond the model can only take place after long schooling according to the model. When Art goes to school to Nature what does she find?

NATURE DYNAMIC AND PURPOSIVE.
    Aristotle's 'nature' was energy working toward a goal.[17] He thought of all things as dynamic and purposive. While we today commonly think of the world as made up of independent objects, many of them lifeless, he thought of it as composed of processes or makings that had a good reason for being just what they were. Movement is part of the very definition of all plants and animals and of even such details of vegetation as leaf, root, and bark,[18] he said. Happiness is not a fixed state of mind, but an activity;[19] the soul not a precious spiritual essence, but a principle of life;[20] the physical elements not atoms nor definite kinds of substance, but tensions between contraries.[21] All things, he said, are either com-

---

[14] *De Part. An.*, 686a.
[15] *Physics*, 194a; *Meteorology*, 381b; *De Mundo*, 396b.
[16] *Phys.*, 199a.
[17] *De Gen. An.*, 717a.
[18] *Metaphysica*, 1026a.
[19] *Nic. Eth.*, 1097b.
[20] *De Anima*, 413.
[21] *Phys.*, 188a.

ing-to-be or passing-away; and Nature orders all the comings and goings like a good housekeeper.

As nature was primarily for Aristotle a vital process working its way out into and up through natural products, the developing and producing, coming-to-be and passing-away of things according to a plan, so art was for him a doing and shaping, a movement set up in some medium by the soul and hand of the artist. For Nature and art, Aristotle says, are the two main initiating forces in the world.[22] The difference is that nature has her principle of motion within herself, while "from art proceed the things of which the form is in the soul of the artist." [23] The working of the natural elements, heat and cold, makes iron hard or soft; but the well-designed movement of a tool makes the sword.[24] "All art is concerned with coming-into-being, *i.e.*, with contriving and considering how something may come into being.[25] Art has to do with the making of things made. The arts are among the principles or sources of motion and change.[26] But in art the beginning and end of the motion pass over into the things to be made from the human contriver; in nature they lie immanent.

Art, then, is human making in the image of divine making, for art emulates the processes of nature, and God is the prime mover of nature. Though less in degree, Phidias' wisdom is parallel to the wisdom of the philosopher whose concern is with the divine ultimate principle of the universe, and whose ways are themselves godlike.[27] Nature furnishes the law by which a man begets his child, and an architect draws houses out of stones on an analogous plan.[28] The carpenter builds his house by setting up a movement in tools, which movement then puts form into wood, as the male element shapes the female element when a child is begotten.[29] Indeed, Nature produces according to a constantly repeated pat-

ART EMULATES NA-
TURE; IT IS PAT-
TERNED ENERGY.

---

[22] *Meta.*, 1032a.
[23] *Ibid.*
[24] *De Gen. An.*, 734b, 735a.
[25] *Nic. Eth.*, 1140a.
[26] *Meta.*, 1013a.
[27] *Nic. Eth.*, 1141a.
[28] *Meta.*, 1034a.
[29] *Gen. An.*, 730b.

tern illustrated most clearly in biological process, the development of form out of matter, or the maturation of the complete individual out of the shapeless germ. Aristotle compares 'form' or 'fulfilment' to being awake, and 'matter' or 'potentiality' to being asleep. Or actually performing an act is 'form' and merely being able to perform the act is 'matter.' [30] Nature works then by urging all things to realize their capacities to the full, and the soul of the artist plants that same drive toward self-completion within some 'matter.' A bronze bowl issues from the metal on the same essential plan as the plant grows from the seed or the animal from the sperm.[31]

This being Aristotle's view of art in general, it is not surprising to find what we call the fine arts for him not a sum of art-objects lying inert in a museum or mere shows for a spectator, but patterned energy. His approach to art was the biologist's.

Our next task then is to trace the way in which the concept of 'imitation' as applied to the imitative arts of music and poetry was affected by his primary concern with organic process. The ideal of art which Plato brought as a test to all image-makings and pleasure-producings was his rudimentary one of skill modified into nobility by the ideas of exact measurement and the concept of the good. For by compounding technique, measurement, and the Idea of the Good he produced his concept of the royal art. The components of Aristotle's standard for the arts are not so heterogeneous. He combined the notion of original human ingenuity: resourcefulness, handiness, with that of the ultimate product of natural process: a perfect animal. When Aristotle confronts poetry and music with his organic and functional ideal for art, there is no active incompatibility as there was in Plato's case. Imitative art easily slips into place as one developing function among many; a specific kind of producing. And the results are the normal, though fair, products of humanly assisted growth and generation. "Imitation in the sense in which Aristotle applies the word to poetry is . . . seen to be equivalent to producing or

---

[30] *Meta.*, 1048a, b.
[31] *Ibid.*, 1032a–b, 1033a.

creating according to a true idea which forms part of the definition of art in general." [32]

We must first follow the development of the general function of imitation; for imitation becomes a high form of art, and worthy of being called "creating according to a true idea" only after a long process of development. Aristotle tells us that "the general origin of poetry was due to two causes, each of them part of human nature. Imitation is natural to man from childhood, one of his advantages over the lower animals being this, that he is the most imitative creature in the world." [33] In tracing art back to its beginnings in primitive functions, Aristotle is only carrying out his normal genetic program. Both in ethics and theory of knowledge he looks for the origins. The moral virtues can come into being only after a long training of the natural impulses. Courage, liberality, and friendliness are not genuinely activities in accordance with right reason until after the instincts to fight and to give and to love have for a long time been trimmed and shaped by teachers and law-makers. Knowledge too is a late development. First comes simple sense-experience. If the sensation can persist or 'make a stand,' and not be carried away in a meaningless flux of animal responses, we have what Aristotle calls the presence of the earliest universal in the soul. But if the sensation dies as soon as it is born, and there appears no nisus toward memory nor the accumulation of skill, then the indispensable germ of human knowledge is lacking. The sensation must be remembered; the memory must become meaningful for common experience; common experience must be rationalized by the arts and sciences; the arts and sciences must be integrated by the all-embracing wisdom of philosophy. [34]

Although the material on the development of the function of imitation is not massed in one place as is this discussion of growth in knowledge, it may be assembled from various places and is like and in part coincident with the other. To compare the growth of imitation thus with the growth of knowledge throws peculiar light

GENETIC METHOD APPLIED TO KNOWLEDGE.

THE PARALLEL EVO-LUTION OF ART OUT OF INSTINCT.

---

[32] S. H. Butcher, *Aristotle's Theory of Poetry and Fine Art*, p. 153.
[33] *Poetics*, 1448b.
[34] *Posterior Analytics*, 99b, 100a.

on imitation; for imitation as art not only copies nature's movement, which is the primary physical fact, but emulates the knowledge process which is the final actuality of things. Just as human intelligence does not begin to function until an elementary power to universalize, to transcend the particular event, arrives in the soul, so in imitative art a first condition is some sort of combination of the parts into a whole. "The beautiful differ from those who are not beautiful and works of art from realities in that in them the scattered elements are combined." [35] However, corresponding to the sensations as pre-logical elements in knowledge, there are pre-technical elements which antedate artistic combination but are necessary to its existence. Such would be the colors in painting, the separate notes of the scale in music, words with their properties of clearness and meaningfulness in poetry and rhetoric, incidents of suffering, of reversal of fortune, of discovery, of identity, furnished by the history of individuals and nations and serving as grist for the tragedian, and the particular thoughts and feelings of men, used as material by all literary composers.

SIMPLE HARMO- The raw matter of art begins to be organized when reason
NIES. combines these elements in certain proportions. The first stand of a universal in knowledge is matched, as we have said, by a first stand of combination in art. Such would be the agreeable complementariness of colors in painting and the harmonious relations of tones in music. The Aristotelian author of *De Mundo* writes: "It may perhaps be that nature has a liking for contraries and evolves harmony out of them and not out of similarities. . . . The arts apparently imitate nature in this respect. The art of painting by mingling in the picture the elements of white and black, yellow and red, achieves representations which correspond to the original object. Music too, mingling together notes, high and low, short and prolonged, attains to a single harmony amid different voices; while writing, mingling vowels and consonants, composes of them all its art." [36] Other examples for the arts would be the ornament of metaphor which is a "sign of genius, since a good metaphor implies an intuitive perception of the similarity in

[35] *Politics*, 1342.
[36] 396b.

dissimilars"; [37] again, the degree of kinship in the parties to a deed of horror; and the direction of a movement from happiness to misery or misery to happiness in a play. These are all simple threads of connection with an affective quality; and they mark the first stage of the weaving of elements into beautiful wholes.

The next step in the growth of knowledge after persistence in memory is called 'learning by experience.' A doctor, for instance, has this grade of knowledge when he can name the nature of an illness though he does not possess any general scientific principles concerning it. It is acute perception without full understanding. Though experience is less excellent than science in respect to the amount of rationality embodied in it, it sometimes surpasses the higher types in its immediate utility. A doctor who through empirical knack, through responsiveness to the character of the disease immediately before him, can cure this particular sick man, may be better for the moment than his superiors in scientific medicine.[38] The esthetic analogue to this empirical faculty would apparently be illustrated by the immediate responsiveness of the soul to the soul-mood in music. A simple arc of stimulus and response seems to bind together the sensitive hearer and the tune. No inference is necessary. The nature of the tune is felt at once. Aristotle declares musical modes to be the most imitative of all forms. "Why do rhythms and tunes, which after all are only voice, resemble moral characters, whereas savours do not, nor yet colors and odours? Is it because they are movements, as actions also are?" [39] He means that the resemblance of music to moral states is more direct than the resemblance of a picture or statue to an emotional content. "Rhythm and melody supply imitations of anger and gentleness, and also of courage and temperance, and of all the qualities contrary to these, and of the other qualities of character. Experience proves this. For we experience the effect

ANALOGUE OF EX-
PERIENCE IN ART.

---

[37] *Poetics*, 1459a.

[38] *Meta.*, 981a.

[39] *Problems*, XIX, 29, 919b. Cf. Marget's "face was changed both in colour and shape by the unknown terrible thing that lived in her brain. Her voice was changed, in the same way, and it was her voice Kit dreaded most, because *his ear had the straighter run to his soul*." Constance Holme, *Beautiful End*, 1935, p. 116. Italics mine.

upon our soul of hearing them." [40] "The Hypophrygian mode has a character of action (hence in the *Geryone* the march-forth and arming are composed in this mode); and the Hypodorian is magnificent and steadfast. . . . The Phrygian is exciting and orgiastic." [41] Music's rendering of character is not as rich in universal significance as tragedy's imitation of a complete and serious action, for tragedy presents the destinies of a group of human beings; but it is more effortless. There is, as it were, an underground passage connecting the mobile energy of the soul and the mobile energy of music that gives the one quick access to the other.

Aristotle says that the esthetic experience of enjoying the likeness in a portrait is also on this level of learning or experiencing. "The reason of the delight in seeing the picture is that one is at the same time learning—gathering the meaning of things, *e.g.* that the man there is so-and-so." [42] But the imitation of a portrait is not as immediate as the imitation of a tune, and the pleasure of detecting the resemblance is therefore perhaps as keen, but certainly more roundabout. In taking in the whole sense of a picture, we do not respond intuitively to a stimulus, but we draw an inference, and feel a semblance of the scholar's delight when new light breaks in on the mind. For, says Aristotle, while shapes copy character, they exhibit rather the symptoms or deposits of a mental habit than the mental habit itself.[43] It is the body of man that the portrait must render, and bodies are molded by passion but are not the very stuff of passion. The pleasure of learning occurs in this case when a pattern of line or color has achieved such unity that we recognize not only the class of thing intended (man) but the member of the class (so-and-so). We enjoy palpating the essential soul beneath the outward show of bodily figure. We have "gathered the meaning" in that we have discovered an identity of character connecting a flesh-and-blood person and well-composed pigment. Right use of complementary color helps representation, Aristotle says. But representation arrives when the significant

---

[40] *Pol.*, 1340a.
[41] *Prob.*, 922b.
[42] *Poet.*, 1448b.
[43] *Pol.*, 1340a.

object shines through the point or line, and the logical label of a name can be attached to the whole. "The most beautiful colors laid on without order (that is without coöperation toward a single end) will not give one the same pleasure as a single black-and-white sketch of a portrait." [44]

The function of imitation reaches its goal and produces, so to speak, a perfect animal when its issue is a good tragedy. For while music and painting and sculpture imitate character, and are meaningful wholes, the 'true idea' according to which they are produced is not as rich and strong as the unity of plot. Degree of universality measures honorableness for Aristotle- both in intellectual knowledge and in imitative art. Order and symmetry, the disposing of parts toward a single end, are present in all imitation; but the tragic plot, with its greater compass and yet greater compactness, shows esthetic order at its maximum. Within its combining force it holds together more parts [45] and more varied media of representation than other art forms. It has six organic constituents: plot, character, thought, diction, music, and spectacle. [46] The arts of instrumental music and dancing lack tragedy's logical thought with verbal expression. The plastic and pictorial arts lack both logical speech and music. The epic and rhetorical discourse lack spectacle and music, and are thinner and looser in texture. From one point of view rhetoric is a subsidiary art—part of the dramatist's equipment. For when Aristotle comes to the constituent of 'thought' in tragedy, he refers his readers to his *Rhetoric*. [47] Aristotle compares the organic unity of a musical mode to a political community with its articulation into ruling and subject part. [48] He might have com-

ORGANISM OF TRAGEDY LIKE LOGIC OF SCIENCE.

---

[44] *Poet.*, 1450a, b.

[45] Cf. Pirandello, *Six Characters in Search of an Author:* "The Manager: 'Ah, just *your part.* But, if you will pardon me, there are other parts than yours: his (indicating the father) and hers (indicating the mother). On the stage you can't have a character becoming too prominent and overshadowing all the others. The thing is to pack them all into a neat little framework and then act what is actable. I am aware of the fact that everyone has his own interior life which he wants very much to put forward. But the difficulty lies in this fact: to set out just as much as is necessary to the stage.'"

[46] *Poet.*, 1450a.

[47] *Ibid.*, 1456a.

[48] *Pol.*, 1254a.

pared a tragedy to an empire with political communities as its
members; for melodies are but parts of plays. Or, since characters
and thoughts are also but parts of plays, he might have compared
tragedy to an organism of organisms.

The unity of action in a well-contrived tragedy corresponds to
and foreshadows the full-blown rationality of science in the world
of intellect. Indeed, Aristotle in one place calls tragedy 'philosophical.' [49] The superiority of science (and the art which is equivalent
to the scientific control of nature) over experience is not only its
generality, its stretch and compass, but its explanation of why
things come to pass. "Knowledge and understanding belong to art
rather than experience, and we suppose artists to be wiser than men
of experience . . . ; and this because the former know the cause,
but the latter do not. For men of experience know that the thing
is so, while the others know the 'why' and the cause." [50] Now it is
the function of a plot to exhibit the 'why' of human destiny. And
the more convincingly the causal sequence is given, the better the
plot. "The only events of which absolute necessity can be predi-
cated are those which form part of a recurrent series," [51] Aristotle
says, and the virtue of a tragedy is for him the exhibition of misery
or happiness as necessary, as something that under the circumstances had to be, as part of a series that might recur because illustrative of law. "The poet's function is to describe, not the thing
which has happened, but a kind of thing that might happen, *i.e.*,
what is possible as being probable or necessary." [52] The most ambitious poet will imitate an 'action' which is a continuous curve of
destiny absorbing and sweeping forward by the law of its movement all particular events and individual persons, as a line resolves
points. "In a play . . . they do not act in order to portray the
Characters; they include the Characters for the sake of the action
. . . a tragedy is impossible, without action, but there may be one
without Characters." [53] A good tragedian will sketch in a system

---

[49] *Poet.*, 1451b.
[50] *Meta.*, 981a.
[51] *De Gen. et Corr.*, II, 27.
[52] *Poet.*, 1451a.
[53] *Ibid.*, 1450a.

of men and things as the pattern of their interaction brings weal or woe: the diagram of a king's rise and fall, the bonds that tie men to tragic deaths, the sacred obligation to avenge a murdered father or daughter, the doom hanging over a royal line, or the need for the fulfilment of an oracle's prophecy. In the development of the characters and speeches of a tragedy the logic of the necessary rules over all; marvels, discoveries, reversals, choruses, must all seem links in the fateful chain. Aristotle often uses the work of Sophocles as illustrative of the firm logic he requires. A revelation of identity is best when it occurs in the natural course of the plot and not through artifices of signs and necklaces, Aristotle says, and instances the *Oedipus Tyrannus.*[54] "The Chorus too should . . . be an integral part of the whole, and take a share in the action —that which it has in Sophocles rather than in Euripides." [55]

Art is always a less perfect system than philosophy for Aristotle, but the kind and amount of unity required by him for a good tragedy (with its several incidents so closely connected that the transposal or withdrawal of any one of them will disjoin or dislocate the whole)[56] makes it a close parallel. All works of art which have plots or stories for their soul are 'living organisms,' but the tragedy is more concentrated than the epic, and so is a superior type of imitation. But of the epic, also, it holds that the plot must be a living whole.[57] The degree of coherence differs, but the kind of organization is the same as in tragedy—a single theme with clear start, development, and conclusion. That Homer achieved a quasi-dramatic unity in his epics is the reason he stands first in his class. The improvisations that were the ancestors of tragedy and comedy, hymns, panegyrics, and lampoons, were imitations of character and passion, and had, so to speak, amoebic souls, but they grew rather than were contrived. The spirit of reverence or of revelry conveyed by them was scarcely the result of fully self-conscious art. They were more properly on the stage of 'experience.'

---

[54] *Poet.*, 1455a.
[55] *Ibid.*, 1456a.
[56] *Ibid.*, 1451a.
[57] *Ibid.*, 1459a.

By thus comparing the artistic function of imitation not only to biological process but to the intellectual function—as indeed Aristotle himself leads us to do—we have watched the development of the universal element in art from a slight two-term relationship to its complete realization in the embodied logic of a tragic plot as well as in the perfect animal. For imitation, like everything else in Aristotle, has matter and form. In *Republic* X Plato treats imitation not as an expanding but as a highly diminished function, because he is disturbed by the contemporary illusionism. As the Platonic 'Idea' passes downward through the employment of the craftsman to that of the imitator, it progressively narrows its compass. A painter of a bed only copies the space-and-time bed that some carpenter has made, and gives only a special view of the bed, either oblique or direct, according to the angle of vision.[58] Thus in Plato we have the attenuation of a universal in art to the limit of individual vision, while in Aristotle the universal is itself present in art, and tragedy is called "more philosophic and of graver import than history." [59]

Aristotle named a second cause of poetry besides the instinct to imitate. What the second cause is cannot be made out because the paragraph in which the two are given is obscurely arranged.[60] Some commentators think it is "the sense of harmony and rhythm" mentioned at the end of the paragraph. But we have just observed that the first cause of poetry, the instinct to imitate, when in full flower, becomes essentially this suggested second cause. For an organic whole is an embodied harmony. And rhythm is the principle of order, and the best order is necessary order. We delight in rhythm because it regularizes and numbers motion,[61] Aristotle says. It is tempting to write a gloss on the cryptic paragraph about the two causes of poetry, when one has in mind the full range of imitation from its potentiality in instinct to its actuality in plot-creation. Can it be that the two causes of poetry are imitation at its least (the earliest universal in the soul of art—the matter)

---

[58] *Sophist*, 598.
[59] *Poet.*, 1451b.
[60] *Ibid.*, 1448b.
[61] *Prob.*, 920b.

and imitation at its greatest (developed sense of the nature of a whole—the form)? One can fancy that Aristotle's thought moved thus: The liking to reproduce starts the doubling of reality in drama and painting. But to make or see a resemblance between imitation and thing imitated is to single out the unity in the duality. To single out unity in variety is to discover essence. To discover essence is to be intelligent. The highest product of intelligence is form. And form is symmetry and order and definiteness, which are essential attributes of beauty or harmony. This, however, is of course not Aristotle's own formulation. He simply enumerates two causes in human nature that account for poetry. These two are either the instinct to imitate and the love of harmony, or the instinct to imitate and the pleasure commonly taken in detecting likenesses. He notes the fact that people enjoy the clever imitation of such things as dead bodies or fish and toads, which are repulsive in real life. Whatever was Aristotle's train of thought, he has stated the two main sources of art in this short passage: the liking for slices of life given in semblance, and the love of design.

In a sense artistic production through imitation reaches its fruition in the beautiful shapes it makes. For it is then the expression of feeling in accordance with right reason. But this end of art has a further end in its effect on beholders. Functions telescope in Aristotle. The form of the creative artist becomes the matter of pleasure of the sensitive spectator, and as we shall see, this pleasure, though a form, becomes the material of the educating statesman. The energy released into a song or play by the genius of the maker does not cease when it satisfies all the canons of sound workmanship and beautiful shape. It sets up a new energy—an emotional activity in those who receive the beautiful shapes into plastic souls. If the plot of a tragedy is, as Aristotle says, its soul and first principle, the pleasure of the spectator is the soul and first principle of the plot. The end of tragedy is for him the peculiar pleasure it causes; by implication the end of comedy is its peculiar pleasure, of epic the same, of music, of sculpture, of painting, each its own pleasure. An inquiry into the nature and value of pleasure for Aristotle is then a necessary part of his esthetics, as it was in the case of Plato.

FORM OF ART IS THE MATTER OF PLEASURE.

Both Plato and Aristotle defined the chief end of man as the exercise of the divine part in him. And both in some sense identified the divine part with reason. But Plato with his more transcendent tendency sometimes interpreted the life of pleasure as brutish and obstructive to reason. Aristotle carefully reviews this doctrine of pleasure and rejects it. Apparently his most considered opinion on the nature of pleasure made it not an independent class of existence but an accent and high light on the function with which it was associated and from which it derived its ethical rating.[62] As such, a function could be wolfish or asinine; the pleasure qualifying its performance could be through a legitimate metonymy called by the same hard name.[63] But Aristotle thought it was a mistake to judge of pleasure in general by its lowest connections and manifestations. Only those who know the pleasures that accompany pure thought and the listening to music and the viewing of sculpture know pleasure at its best and in its essence.[64] For pleasure is carried along by the nisus of nature toward the good; just as nature may turn up "worms and beetles and other ignoble creatures" that belie her general good intention,[65] so pleasure, though fundamentally the ally of reason and nobility, may be the gratification accompanying the lowest impulses. In general pleasure is for Aristotle the symptom of the fulfillment of desire, the consciousness of the fullness of life;[66] and when these are in accordance with right reason, then also pleasure is in accordance with right reason. The pleasantness of imitative art might be called—adapting a phrase of Aristotle's—the bloom on the face of reason. When he says that the final cause of tragedy is to produce pleasure he clearly means that a mental state is aimed at which is reasonable and choiceworthy.

Since pleasures are for Aristotle 'peculiar' to the activities which they intensify and crown, it is obviously necessary to understand the actual functions of imitations in order to understand

---

[62] *Nicomachean Ethics,* 1174b.
[63] *Magna Moralia,* 1205a.
[64] *Nic. Eth.,* 1176a.
[65] *Mag. Mor.,* 1205a.
[66] *Nic. Eth.,* 1175a.

their emotional color. The pleasures in question accompany processes of repletion and purgation, and also uniform, continuous activity. Art's humblest function is to satisfy a want or to relieve a pain, on the analogy of the relief to hunger furnished by food. Sleep, food, drink, and music make "care to cease." [67] Sickness both of soul and body arises out of excess and defect, and when a man's energy is depleted by the day's labor, his power may be restored to normal by the enlivening stimulation of imitative music. As art may thus fill up the empty places in the soul, and increase energy, so it may clear our souls of unhealthy accumulations. The psycho-physical system calls as often for reducing and cathartic potions as for nerving tonics. There are certain emotions which, though wholesome in proper degree, readily become poisons. There are persons who have small resistance to these emotions and fall ill of them with great ease. "Feelings, such as pity and fear, or again, enthusiasm, exist very strongly in some souls, and have more or less influence over all. Some persons fall into a religious frenzy, whom we see as a result of the sacred melodies—when they have used the melodies that excite the soul to mystic frenzy— restored as though they had found healing and purgation. Those who are influenced by pity and fear—and every emotional nature —must have a like experience, and others in so far as each is susceptible to such emotions, and all are in a manner purged and their souls lightened and delighted." [68] Aristotle calls the production of such a catharsis the peculiar pleasure of tragedy.[69] It has been argued, probably over boldly, that in the missing book of the *Poetics* on comedy the final purpose of the lighter sort of drama may have been given as the purgation, perhaps of envy and malice, perhaps of impure pleasure.[70] Not only music, then, but the drama serves humanity by unburdening heavy souls and by inducing the peculiar pleasure of relief.

These are the human uses of the arts of motion for Aristotle. But the mechanism by which these medicinal effects are brought KATHARSIS THE ACTIVITY AND PASSIVITY OF THE SAME FUNCTION.

[67] *Pol.*, 1339a.
[68] *Ibid.*, 1342a.
[69] *Poet.*, 1453b.
[70] Lane Cooper, *An Aristotelian Theory of Comedy*, Ch. IX.

about has been a subject of unending controversy. That the cure is homeopathic Aristotle tells us: pity is evacuated through pity; fear through fear; religious enthusiasm by enthusiasm. How may one understand more in detail the operation of the pleasurable catharsis? There are those who think Aristotle's meaning very simple and obvious. Excessive pity, it runs, is to be driven out by the expulsive force of an exhausting emotional experience. The spectacle of the desolate aged blind Oedipus for example will wear out a sentimental beholder and compel a season of restoring calm. A disturbing force, on this theory, is vanquished by a greater disturbing force of the same kind. Plato, Aristotle's teacher, had said that fear and such psychological ailments, being internal motions, could be remedied by the application of a greater external motion. This explanation taken in its literal simplicity seems as unlikely as certain highly subtle ones that have been offered. Probably Aristotle's meaning lies somewhere between the unmodified physical analogy we have just given and one that would use more extensively his theory of the balance of elements, which might be developed as follows: Aristotle thought of evils in the soul as like diseases in the body. But the body was sick when one of the elements composing it increased to extreme proportions; and the soul was ill when one of its native propensities was indulged to excess. For the body to be well a proper balance between the tendency to heat and the tendency to cold had to be maintained. Generally ill-health resulted from the cold element getting the upper hand, and a cure was effected by applying more heat to 'concoct' the system, and restore the proper bodily temperature. For the development of a moral habit of soul those responsible for the education of youth, teachers and law-makers, were bound to secure behavior that was in accordance with right reason, neither too timid nor too rash, neither too wasteful nor too niggardly. The preservation of the golden mean for the functions of soul and body was the ideal of medicine and of ethics. Indeed, there was less an analogy between the health of soul and of body than an identity. For the soul was not one thing and the body another for Aristotle, but the soul was the fulfilment, realization or form of the body, and what damaged or benefitted the one, damaged or benefitted the other. The soul-body was awry, then, when it was in the literal sense of the word out of balance or out of order.

We understand then that for Aristotle if stage-plays and music were to be therapeutic agencies they were to restore a balanced functioning to a soul-body afflicted with deficiency or excess. They were to insinuate into the organism the principle of the norm, and draw back the disarranged habit to the middle path. Now the universal condition for effectual relationship Aristotle believed to be a general similarity between agent and patient with such difference between the parties to the transaction as made one give and the other receive an influence. Within a common substratum the driving force for change comes from the tension of opposite principles, one operating, the other undergoing an operation.[71] The condition favorable to creative activity throughout the cosmos is not bare like to like—futile repetition—but the mutual adaptation of contrary principles. New living creatures can only be born when male meets female and not when male meets male. A right ratio must adapt two distinct terms to each other. Thus we see that music and drama were to be on Aristotle's view not only passively pleasant but actively moving and soul-transforming; they had to be congenial to the psycho-physical condition that was to be worked on. There had to be such affinity between disease and cure that the diseased part could receive to the maximum the action of the medicine. Pity then was to work on pity, fear on fear, frenzy on frenzy, ill-humor on ill-humor. As the heat of wine quenches the natural heat of the body,[72] so the true pity of the *Oedipus Rex* or the *Oedipus at Colonus* will quench the false pity of unreflective sentimentality.[73] For it is not the same pity that cures and that is the thing to be cured. In Aristotle's constantly reiterated terminology, the medicine is pity's form, and the disease is pity's matter. The form differs from the matter as activity differs from passivity, and true shape from irregularity. What will happen then will be that the active and shapely pity incarnated in the *Oedipus* or in

---

[71] *De Gen. et Cor.*, 323a, 324b.

[72] *Prob.*, 954b.

[73] Richard Burton states that he wrote about melancholy, *The Anatomy of Melancholy*, to cure himself of melancholy.

some well-arranged discourse will work on the indiscriminate excessive pity of weak sentimentalism and will purge off the unhealthy excess. The crude emotion will be molded into the perfect essence. The essence of pity is stated by Aristotle in the definition of it in the *Rhetoric:* "Pity is a feeling of pain caused by the sight of some evil, destructive or painful, which befalls one who does not deserve it, and which we might expect to befall ourselves or some friend of ours, and moreover to befall us soon." [74] Indiscriminate pity is a weakness, for it depresses us whenever the spectacle of impending misfortune presents itself, whether deserved or undeserved.

THEATREGOER'S EMOTION IS SHAPED RATIONAL EMOTION.

Aristotle requires a good tragedy then to throw before us a picture of a man who is undeservedly dashed down by misfortune, but who had a fault which was a partial cause of the catastrophe. He is to be a person *like us* (so that we shall sense the kinship and the probable likeness of fate) but he is better than we are, for his fault is comparatively slight and he errs in kingly manner. The plot must be so managed that pity in its true form shall be displayed. The deed of horror must be enacted between friends and in ignorance of the identity of the persons. The law or science of a pitiful action is in these stipulations. Aristotle does not explicitly connect the unhealthy condition of pity with a derangement of the physical elements in the body. Fear, on the other hand, he says, is accompanied with an excess of cold, as can be observed in the trembling as if from chill of those who are in a state of terror.[75] Warmth and reason then must be supplied by the application of the pleasures of a fearful tragic spectacle. The paralyzing, disorganizing fear that depletes one's energy and takes away the happiness of mind and health of body must be brought under the sway of the fear that is reasonable. And the fear of the inevitable consequences of wrong-doing, witting or unwitting, is rational. But when we understand why calamity comes upon erring humanity, and no longer tremble at it as at a blind demonic force striking wildly on the just and the unjust, we are restored to a vital calm in the presence of inevitable law. Nothing gives peace so quickly as adequate explanation. And the perfect logic of the perfect plot,

---

[74] *Rhetoric,* 1385b.
[75] *Prob.,* 948a, b.

Aristotle shows, always tells the 'why' of the dire events. Thus is the pain of baffled unmotived fear transformed into the pleasure of a fear that understands itself and its causes. In a similar fashion, we may suppose, Aristotle believes that enthusiasm will act upon enthusiasm and, perhaps, the spirit of comedy upon the reveller.

The peculiar pleasures that accompany attendance at dramatic performances are colored then by the return of the reign of an emotion that is proportioned and ordered, after pity and fear had introduced disarray into the mental economy. Music achieves its pleasure also in part through purgation. The Phrygian mode is naturally passionate. When played on the flute, which as an instrument has a passionate *timbre*, the combination takes hold of minds turbulent with ecstasy and cures them so that they seem to have been purged by some drug.[76] In general, melodies and rhythms have such affinity for human souls that their grip is quick and strong, and whatever they do to change our mental state, they do more powerfully than the other arts. Lydian airs wrap us softly and sadly; the Dorian keep us stable.[77] Because of the peculiar intimacy and directness of music's effects, all those who would influence character must understand its action. While music relaxes, and purges, it has a still higher use.

The third type of pleasure that art can furnish—one which Aristotle connects particularly with music—is that of rational enjoyment. The noblest use of music is to fill our leisure with an activity that has all the qualities that something intrinsically good possesses.[78] Whatever is intrinsically good is complete and rational. It has form and sweetness, and is not subject to growth and decay. All the labor that we engage in during our lifetime is for the sake of enjoying at last pure sustained orderly pleasure. Philosophical reflection and pleasures of sight and hearing are qualified to satisfy this supreme test. As the act of seeing is entire at any moment, and is not increased or improved by continuing longer, so pleasures of mental cultivation, the pleasures of a well-spent leisure, are whole and complete, and are not added to by any continuance.[79] Boys and vulgar persons cannot understand or feel them. The

RATIONAL ENJOY-
MENT OF INTRINSIC
GOODS.

---

[76] *Pol.*, 1342a–b.
[77] *Ibid.*, 1340b.
[78] *Ibid.*, 1338a.
[79] *Nic. Eth.*, X, 5–7 and *Pol.*, 1339a.

pleasures of the visual arts are according to Aristotle the least
stirring, because they are not developed out of the medium of
motion—succession of sounds in time—as are the musical and literary
arts. But though the temporal arts are more expressive, imitative
of moral disposition,[80] and effectual for changing the souls of men,
it would seem to be implied that pleasures of statues and portraits
furnish the more divine pleasure. For divine activity does not
involve motion.[81] God's enjoyment is activity without change or
passive ingredient. Now the activity of thought in man comes
nearest to being of this sort,[82] but sight is that one among the
external senses which is nearest the serene element of thought.[83]
When Aristotle selects an example of an artist to compare with the
divine fashioner of the universe, it is not Sophocles nor Olympus
that he chooses, but Phidias the sculptor. Aristotle also expressly
warns his readers that the common association of beauty only with
motion is wrong. The beautiful, he says, is found also in motionless
things.[84] Mathematics is distinctly enlightening on esthetic problems, he goes on to say, because this science demonstrates in a
special degree the nature of order, symmetry, and definiteness,
which are the chief forms of beauty.

STATESMAN'S AND
EDUCATOR'S ART
ONLY ONE GOOD IN
ITSELF.

Art achieves its purpose, then, when it gives pleasure, and the
pleasure varies according to the character of the art and the taste
and age of the audience. But even the pleasure of rational enjoyment, which is the highest art can furnish, is not an end in itself.
No good that imitative art can furnish can be an end in itself, because the imitative arts are instrumental arts. The most authoritative art, that which can truly be called the master art, is the ethical
and political, Plato's royal art of the philosopher-king. Not until
we consider the ethical and social uses of the fine arts do we come
to a full stop. The statesman, then, takes the pleasurable effects
that music and dancing, poetry and painting produce and adopts
them as tools for the molding of character.

---

[80] *Pol.*, 1340a.
[81] *Meta.*, 1074b.
[82] *Nic. Eth.*, 1177a–b.
[83] *Ibid.*, Book X, Ch. 3. See Welldone, 325.
[84] *Meta.*, 1078a.

While statesmen are concerned to regulate the work and play of the whole body of citizens in the best way, their chief responsibility is the education of the young. Aristotle inquires, therefore, whether music (for that is the most powerful of the arts) can be used to train children toward virtue.[85] The goal of education is to make human beings love, hate, and rejoice rightly, for if men's wills can be made to agree with the dictates of reason, they will do spontaneously what they ought. The natural sweetness of music then can be used to attract children toward virtuous habits. Each musical mode has its ethical character. Let the suitable mode be applied to the soft substance of a young soul, and the child will absorb the steadfastness, courage, or gentleness from the pattern of the music into his own flesh and bone. Music is thus literally a formal discipline in Aristotle's eyes. "Even in mere melodies there is an imitation of character, for the musical modes differ essentially from one another, and those who hear them are differently affected by each. Some of them make men sad and grave . . . others enfeeble the mind, . . . another, again, produces a moderate and settled temper. . . . The same principles apply to rhythms; some have a character of rest, others of motion, and of these latter again, some have a more vulgar, others a nobler movement. Enough has been said to show that music has a power of forming the character, and should therefore be introduced into the education of the young. . . . There seems to be in us a sort of affinity to musical modes and rhythms, which makes some philosophers say that the soul is a tuning, others, that it possesses tuning."[86] The statesman will of course avail himself of the other pleasurable effects of music, its power to purge and to relax, and to fill nobly the leisure of the best class of citizens. He holds these rewards in his hands as devices for building the good city.

Aristotle thus emerges from his long consideration of the imitative arts, particularly music and poetry, near the place where Plato takes his stand. The royal art of the statesman is for both the ultimate authority in the disposing and regulating of the ministry to pleasure. Aristotle is slower than Plato in passing

ARISTOTLE GENTLER THAN HIS MASTER ON RHETORIC.

---

[85] *Pol.*, 1340a–b.
[86] *Loc. cit.*

adverse moral judgment on popular amusements and more aware of the plurality of approximate ends that charming and moving performances may serve. He seems even at times to think of training in skill as serving a purely esthetic end. Children are to be taught to draw in his best state, for example, not only for utilitarian ends, but in order to be cultivated purchasers of art-treasures and better judges of the human form.[87] And the amount of instruction in music given to free-born children is governed partly by simple respect for the dignity of the person. Children are to learn enough music to become intelligent critics, but not enough to become public performers for the diversion of others.[88] Still the dignity of these respected children is associated in Aristotle's mind, as in Plato's, with their ultimate place and function in the government of the city-state. A crucial test for the relation of Aristotle's theory of art to Plato's is a comparison of their attitudes toward rhetoric. Plato, in the *Gorgias*, evolved the conception of rhetoric as an irresponsible mockery of the art of justice, the statesman's supreme art. Rhetoric is not a real art at all, Socrates is made to say, but a gift for clever man-handling, in a word, a technique of flattery.[89] The other side of the same intransigent idealism appears in the *Phaedrus* where Plato conducts the true art of speech away from physical sounds and above written symbols into the ethereal medium of pure spiritual intercourse. Aristotle's *Rhetoric* has been called "an expanded *Phaedrus*," [90] and how much he owes to Plato's notions and distinctions can be discovered by comparing the two treatments carefully. But here as always Aristotle is more moderate and analytical. Also, by confining his attention to the constructive side of the matter, he gives a different tone to his whole treatment.

Aristotle rests much of his case for rhetoric's redemption to art from the obloquy of Sophistic flattery on its closeness to logic. The body of a good speech, he claims, is an enthymeme, that is, a popular kind of syllogism. The orator's premise may not be too

---

[87] *Pol.*, 1338b.

[88] *Ibid.*, 1340b, 1341a.

[89] 463.

[90] Thompson, Introduction to the *Phaedrus*, p. xx, cited by J. H. Frisse, Introduction to Aristotle's *Rhetoric*, p. xxi.

deep nor too meticulously developed into its consequences; but the orator does rely on a syllogism—that kind of syllogism that deals with human action and leads to choice.[91] One could even call the rhetorical argument an expanded maxim,[92] for the sagacious speaker draws his premises from ideas and sayings that are widely current. Examples are: Do not nourish immortal wrath, for you are mortal; again: A mortal should have mortal, not immortal thoughts.[93] Aristotle remarks shrewdly that hearers are pleased with maxims that are nothing more than generalizations of their own pet views. So a man who has bad children or bad neighbors gives ready assent to a speech that leads off with a general remark on the discomfort of having neighbors and the stupidity of begetting children.[94]

Though this rough and ready form of syllogism is the substance of rhetoric as the plot is the soul of tragedy,[95] there are two other kinds of 'proof' which the good speaker must know how to avail himself of: proof from his own character which must appear sensible, virtuous, and benevolent; and proof from the emotional tendencies in the audience—the mental winds which carry conviction, whatever may be the true facts and reasons in the case. Aristotle devotes a long section of the *Rhetoric* to the analysis of anger, friendliness, pity, fear, shame, etc.; to the influence of age on emotion, whether hot and generous youth, crabbed age, or the prime of life;[96] and to the typical occasions and situations of emotions.[97] For example, men tend to resent most the depreciation of those things which they personally most esteem; they are angrier at injuries from friends than enemies, because expectation is overturned, and at bad treatment from inferiors because this seems to be contempt.[98]

Finally, Aristotle discusses style and delivery as important and neglected instruments in the orator's hands. "It is not sufficient to

---

[91] *Rhetoric*, 1394a.
[92] 1394b.
[93] *Ibid.*
[94] 1395b.
[95] 1354a.
[96] 1377b.
[97] Bk. II, Chs. i–xviii.
[98] 1379a–b.

know what one ought to say, but one must also know how to say it." [99]   A public speaker should be rhythmic in his utterances, but avoid the obtrusiveness of metre.[100] The pitch and volume of the voice should suit the theme. The words and phrasing of the prose discourse, however artistically devised, should be set in a lower and more relaxed key than in poetry. Though the orator should avoid heavy or foreign words, he should keep to the golden mean of clearness and appropriateness, and never descend to banality.[101] Even a debater's jests should reflect the gentleman.[102] Sensitiveness to the emotional color of the audience and the subject-matter helps the speaker's style; for the audience will respond with sympathy to what is feelingly given to them. "The hearer always sympathizes with one who speaks emotionally, even though he really says nothing." [103]   Though Aristotle's dissection of the speaker's art is thus sometimes tinged with reserved irony, his penetration to the causes and conditions of an orator's persuasive power is on the whole a masterpiece of humanistic science.

EUPLASTICITY EX-
ALTED IN ARIS-
TOTLE.
On one further point Aristotle carries on the labors of Plato. And once more Aristotle seems to be refuting Plato, but comes nearer fulfilling him. He suggests that as a psychological type the poets belong not below tradesmen and gymnasts, as Plato had once declared,[104] but in the highest class along with philosophers and statesmen. In the *Poetics* Aristotle mentions briefly the personal qualifications necessary to the poet, and in the *Problems*,[105] we find this temperament and bodily make-up assigned to philosophers, statesmen, and all gifted souls. Poetry, Aristotle says, demands a man with a special gift for it. He must be able to visualize well. The dramatist must even be able to feel himself into the experiences he is portraying. He must not only be able to see the scenes he is describing as if they were before his very eyes; his body must go through the very motions that the human drama shaping itself in

---

[99] 1403b.
[100] 1408b.
[101] 1404a–b.
[102] 1419b.
[103] 1408a.
[104] *Phaedrus*, 248.
[105] 953a.

his fancy requires.[106] This is the type of writer whose story will be convincing. He must live the life of his brain-children as he works. The man with the innate capacity for taking on shape is the born genius. But it is this very euplasticity characteristic of the 'tribe of imitators' which degrades them in Plato's estimation. 'Clever multiform gentlemen' can do everything, and are nothing. Their magical assumption of any part, their facile aping of gesture, look, and manner are carried through, it seemed to him, at the expense of unity and consistency of character. Plato admired steadfastness of purpose and singleness of function; in his ideal state, one man played one part only. Therefore this bewildering chameleon, whose colors came with the changing occasions and who could easily assimilate himself to alien molds, never seemed to settle himself to any definable employment or form, was unsuited for engaging in the program of a well-ordered city. He was, indeed, two removes from the philosopher and truth.

But for Aristotle that malleability which characterized the poet characterized in a sense the philosopher also. The philosopher is surely devoted to the truth of being. But how does one learn the truth of being? To be highly intelligent is to adapt oneself with infinitely graduated responsiveness to the peculiar character of stimuli. The soul in knowing must somehow be all the things it knows, just as the dramatist in engendering plays must be his *dramatis personae*. As the hand is the tool of tools,[107] so is the mind the form or place of forms.[108] The gift and greatness of poet and philosopher is then equally this impressionability, this actual lack of resisting unassimilable substance. Aristotle thus interpreted as a virtue that which struck Plato as the dissipation and prostitution of power.

Aristotle presses back high gifts of both these classes to a source in their bodily make-up, the melancholic temperament. The predominance of the nimble, wine-like black bile in their systems makes them excitable, moody, restless in sleep, and with a tendency toward mental derangement. He who has black bile in proper

---

[106] *Poet.*, 1455a–b.
[107] *De Part. An.*, 687.
[108] *De Anima*, 429a.

ratio in his body is a genius; in extreme proportions, is mad. Aristotle mentions Empedocles, Plato, and Socrates among philosophers as atrabilious, and "most of the poets." [109]

Plato often enlarged upon the distance separating philosophers from imitative artists; Aristotle groups them together. Plato had contrasted the philosopher as a spectator of universal truths with the painter who depicts singular aspects of singular things. Aristotle claims that universals are the concern of both. Plato thinks it a poet's shame that he readily assumes a multitude of shapes and the philosopher's glory that he is single-minded. Aristotle makes them both in their own way infinitely plastic. And yet in the *Phaedrus* itself in which Plato places poets and imitators in so humble a class, he may be said to have anticipated Aristotle's grouping of the poets with the philosophers as melancholics. For Plato's doctrine of "possession and madness" which "takes hold upon a gentle and pure soul, arouses it and inspires it to songs and other poetry," [110] has much in common with the melancholic temperament of the physician's son. Black bile is erotic and unbalancing in tendency, but it is also, Aristotle declares, the fire that warms the genius of all gifted souls.

SUPPLEMENTARY READING

Mortimer J. Adler, *Art and Prudence*, Ch. II.
S. H. Butcher, *Aristotle's Theory of Poetry and Fine Art*, 4th ed., London, 1932.
Lane Cooper, *The Poetics of Aristotle, Its Meaning and Influence*, Boston, 1923.
Lane Cooper, *An Aristotelian Theory of Comedy*, New York, 1922.
F. M. Cornford, *The Origin of Attic Comedy*, London, 1914.
Allan H. Gilbert, *Literary Criticism from Plato to Dryden*. (Contains a new translation of the *Poetics*.)
A. E. Haigh, *The Tragic Drama of the Greeks*, Oxford, 1896.
R. P. McKeon, "Literary Criticism and the Concept of Imitation in Antiquity," *Modern Philology*, August, 1936.
W. D. Ross, *Aristotle*, London, 1923.
George Saintsbury, *History of Criticism*, Vol. I, Bk. I, Ch. III.

[109] *Prob.*, 953a.
[110] *Phaedrus*, 245.

CHAPTER IV

From Aristotle through Plotinus

AFTER ARISTOTLE (d. 322 B.C.) the next name of first MUCH INTEREST IN
magnitude in esthetics is Plotinus (204–269 A.D.). What ART.
then of those five centuries and more that flowed between?
The lack of great theories was certainly not due to any neglect of
the place of art in human life during the Alexandrian and Roman
periods. On the contrary these were among the chief periods in
the history of western civilization for the creation and appreciation of works of art. The production of fine buildings, pictures,
and statues went on at a pace befitting the expansion and growing
wealth of Rome. Plutarch remarks concerning Domitian that
merely to see a single colonnade in his palace, or one of his baths,
or a concubine's apartment would elicit the exclamation: " 'Tis
not pious nor nobly ambitious that thou art; thou art diseased; thy
mania is to build; like the famous Midas, thou desirest that everything become gold and stone at thy touch." [1] On the side of the
literary arts the splendor of the Augustan Age is proverbial.
Moreover the creative artists during these centuries were fertile in
adaptation and invention. They originated certain forms: the
pastoral, the novel, and the satire, and they pushed the arch [2]
and the love-lyric on to a new expressiveness; they devised architectural complexes which matched in materials and plan the
mental habits of those powerful ones who swayed the Empire; [3]

---

[1] *Lives*, I, ed. Loeb, Vol. I, p. 543.
[2] "Every product of Egyptian, Oriental, and Greek architecture appears as
child's play by the side of the fully developed Roman arch." Franz Wickhoff,
Roman Art, trans. Strong, London, 1900, p. 17.
[3] Vitruvius, *De Architectura*, I, 2, 8, ed. Loeb, Vol. I, p. 23.

finally they developed the sculptured relief toward illusionism as in the continuous narrative reliefs on the arch of Titus and the column of Trajan, and the portrait toward realism. The passion for making beautiful things was no greater than that for knowing about them. The more solid aspect of the desire to know about art appears in the long list of erudite works, the editions of the Homeric text, technical treatises, histories, grammars, catalogues, and books of criticism; the more superficial is illustrated by the declamations about paintings of the last Sophists, and the type of dinner-talk reported by Athenaeus in which one passed lightly and knowingly from styles of music to styles of cookery. It was in this period that Horace wrote his *Art of Poetry*, Vitruvius his manual for architects, Aristoxenus his hand-book on music; and Quintilian his directions for the training of orators, to mention only four works that became authoritative for centuries of practice. With the productivity and learning went a new feeling for beauty, the appreciation of objects of virtu as such, apart from their moral or intellectual associations. In the refined and elegant atmosphere of the Republic and the age of Augustus even a philosopher might be a collector and dilettant. In Cicero's letters to Atticus (beginning 69 B.C.) there is free and familiar expression of enthusiasm for "figures of Hermes in Pentelic marble with bronze heads" which he has "fallen in love with" from the mere description, and an importuning of Atticus to buy for him well-covers, and bas-reliefs to insert in the stucco-walls of his hall. Atticus is bidden to send anything else of the kind that would suit Cicero's colonnade and gymnasium—"the more the merrier"—for Cicero's love of such things passes, he fears, the bounds of decorum.[4] His references to his library reveal a man of exquisite taste as much as a man of learning. His library, he says, "seems to have acquired a soul" since two library-slaves have bound and affixed parchment title-slips to his books.[5]

BUT LACK OF SPEC-   The reason for the lack of important esthetic theory lay not,
ULATIVE POWER.   then, in the absence of artistic production, erudition, or sensitiveness, but in the absence of range of speculative power. For the

---

[4] *Letters to Atticus*, Bk. I, Letter viii, ed. Loeb, Vol. I, p. 21.
[5] *Ibid.*, Bk. IV, Letter iva; Vol. I, p. 281; Bk. IV, Letter viii, Vol. I, p. 293.

genius of Rome, the theory of arts was brought close to practice and on the whole cut loose from large abstract ideas, from relation to the 'probable and necessary' as in Aristotle, from intuited essence and love of the divine as in Plato. The new preoccupation with art was of other sorts: one confiscated it; collected it; hired a single servant-artist or thousands of slaves to bring it into being; or one composed epigrams and flowery speeches in praise of it and so showed oneself off in its presence; one classified, sub-classified, analyzed, recorded its history, even its actual letters and syllables; one told off its points and knew a vast deal about it; one varied its form and dissected its parts. But not between Plato and Plotinus was the problem of its value on an ultimate scale of measurement pressed home, nor that final curiosity satisfied which does not rest short of finding beauty's real place, as distinguished from its logical compartment, on a map of reality. Esthetic goods were cherished that did not appeal to the broad-sweeping and through-searching Plato and Plotinus: elegant living, detailed information, cosmopolitan acquaintance, a precise technical vocabulary, new approaches in criticism, the systematization and popularization of facts and rules relating to art, accurate texts and the preservation of manuscripts. The esthetic character of the period has been epitomized in the saying that there was "dispersive pressure of humane culture" rather than "depth of inspiration." [6]

And yet in spite of the lack of any first-rate systematic esthetic theory between Aristotle and Plotinus, a brief account must be given of the interval. In the first place, there were many new distinctions drawn and interesting philosophical suggestions of limited scope: for example, concerning the poetical and rhetorical imagination, and concerning esthetic qualities such as sublimity and grace, which are partly due to the contribution of the beholder and which cannot therefore be identified with classical organic wholeness. Both the beauty of artistic form in and for itself and the beauty of external nature were consciously acknowledged. And there were an indefinite number of illuminating *aperçus,* such as those that praise the value of esthetic reserve. For example, in

PERIOD RICH IN SUGGESTIVENESS.

---

[6] B. Bosanquet, *History of Aesthetic,* p. 86.

regard to literary composition Theophrastus wrote: "Not all points should be punctiliously and tediously elaborated, but something should be left to the comprehension and inference of the hearer." [7] And in regard to painters Pliny wrote in the same vein that Apelles of Kos surpassed Protogenes "in knowing when to take his hand from a picture, a memorable saying, showing that too much care may often be hurtful." [8] Here is an almost romantic appreciation of the beauty of the unfinished and suggestive—of the sketch—in contrast to the reposeful self-sufficiency of the complete product. But in the second place—and this is the main thing—what happened to the esthetic consciousness between Plato and Neo-platonism made a difference to the form in which Plato's theory of beauty could rise again from the dead. Plotinus himself humbly estimated his own function as little more than interpreter of his ancient master. The fortunate philosophers of antiquity discovered Truth, he taught, and those of later times have simply the obligation of rediscovery and of bringing to vivid consciousness. "These teachings are, therefore, no novelties, no inventions of today, but long since stated . . . , our doctrine here is the explanation of an earlier and can show the antiquity of those opinions on the testimony of Plato himself." [9] But this self-estimate of Plotinus is only half-true. The esthetics of Plotinus, resembling on the one hand the theory of the pursuit of Beauty in the *Symposium* and *Phaedrus* of Plato, on the other, contradicted both Platonic and Aristotelian doctrine on two major points: that art is imitation, and that the excellence of art is a harmonious disposition of parts.

MEANING OF THE TIME FOR UNDER-STANDING PLO-TINUS.

The capacity of Plotinus materially to deepen the philosophy of art in two places was not altogether original genius. In his new anti-Platonic theses he gathered into broad theory special tendencies in criticism and psychology in the centuries between himself and Plato: the tendencies to respect and examine the energy of the soul in transport and imagination, and to acknowledge the beauty of

---

[7] Quoted by Demetrius, *On Style*, 222, ed. Loeb, p. 439.

[8] *The Elder Pliny's Chapters on the History of Art*, ed. Jex-Blake and Sellers, Bk. XXXV, p. 121, §80.

[9] *Enneads*, V, I, 10; trans. Stephen MacKenna, London and Boston, The Medici Society, 1926, Vol. IV, p. 12.

esthetic units. It is an interesting fact that Plotinus was assisted in and prepared for his important restrictions on Platonic esthetics, not so much by gradual approximations in philosophy itself, as by accumulations of minute critical explorations which seem of themselves philosophically slight. Moreover, in so far as Plotinus was an exegete of the old doctrine of Plato, that is, in so far as he recalled in fresh phrases to his listeners the ladder of love in Plato's *Symposium* upon which the spiritually-minded are to climb to the Single Sea of Beauty above the beauties of earth, the historical situation throws light on the development of the mysticism in Plotinus' hands. He lived on easy terms with the religious mysteries of purification flourishing in Rome and Alexandria at the beginning of the Christian era. For Plotinus was not a mere system-weaver; he was a practical teacher in the busy heart of a complex, stirring world. His method of teaching, moreover, was not to impose a succession of propositions, but to encourage questions and discussion from listeners who differed with him. It is small wonder then that his writings reflect the changed face of affairs and contain a more exclusive and single-hearted mysticism and asceticism than is to be found in Platonism. Indeed, it is easy to see what effect the mere extent and force of the sensuous luxury of the passing Roman civilization would have on one who, like Plotinus, had accepted the vocation of recalling men from the Circe of sense-gratification to the true home of the spirit 'over yonder.' Even the serious work of relating scholarship to art and the refined feeling of connoisseurs, while it might unconsciously influence him, would seem to him an unfortunate dispersion of interest toward the unreal material detail of beauty. Just in proportion, then, as men knew more about art and cared more about its simple self, the asceticism of Plotinus had a larger subject of protest, more mass to push against, than did Plato's more tempered asceticism. It is necessary, therefore, at least to suggest the minor aspects of changing taste and scholarly industry during the Graeco-Roman period in order to understand the conditions under which Plotinus wrote.

The varieties and degrees of the new esthetic interests might be taken at a glance by means of twin images of concentric circles: in the center of one the discriminating observer and lover of fine objects of art; in the first and smallest circle, moving out from this center toward the darkness of vulgar covetousness and exhibitionism, the chatterer and eulogist; in the next larger circle the ultra-fastidious and merely sensuous esthete; then the collectors, and finally, the Emperors and Conquerors, who gathered curios while they devastated and who were builders of palaces and magnificent patrons of art. One might suggest in the image the thinning out of the intellectual appraisal of the worth and meaning of art; in the center, critics of various degrees of speculative power who approached in their interests the philosopher of beauty himself; then the grammarians and writers of technical treatises; last, the philologists and textualists and recorders and distinguishers of manners and styles.

THEOPHRASTUS GIVES DETAIL RATHER THAN PENETRATION.

The change toward pettiness and pedantry began with Aristotle's own pupils. By comparing the work of Theophrastus and Aristoxenus with that of Aristotle we can see clearly something of the shift in interest which was to characterize the whole period. Theophrastus, who followed Aristotle as head of the Peripatetic school, wrote on many of the same subjects as his teacher, and his doctrine was much the same. Both wrote on metaphysics, ethics, and psychology, and both added notably to the existing stock of detailed scientific knowledge—Aristotle in the field of zoology, Theophrastus in botany and mineralogy. Both men wrote on esthetic subjects. Balancing Aristotle's *Poetics, Rhetoric*, and chapters on music, are the treatises *On Comedy, On the Ridiculous, On Music, On Enthusiasm, On Style*, a *Poetics*, and a *Harmonics* by Theophrastus.[10] But the most famous work of Theophrastus, and the one with which his name is primarily associated, is *The Characters*. This gallery of vivid portraits of human types is the crucial work for understanding the relation of Theophrastus to his predecessor. At first glance these pleasantly ironical sketches, full of sensuous imagery, seem to owe nothing to Aristotle. But it has been convincingly argued that the novelty of the *Characters* is more apparent than real. Aristotle inserted portraits, a memorable one of the Magnanimous Man, in his *Nicomachean Ethics*. And in

---

[10] J. W. H. Atkins, *Literary Criticism in Antiquity*, Cambridge Univ. Press, 1934, Vol. I, p. 155.

the *Rhetoric* the descriptions of the Ages of Man are colorful, and the part treating of human emotions concrete and extended. The *Characters* of Theophrastus, the claim is made, were similarly intended to point off rhetorical and ethical doctrine. But to this parallel a leading English student of Theophrastus replies that "to every special characteristic of the Magnanimous Man Aristotle sub-joins, as usual, a statement of the principle on which it depends." [11] His case against the parallel between Aristotle and Theophrastus rests chiefly, however, on the different spirit of the sketches them-selves, whatever the setting in Theophrastus may originally have been. "No one would object to philosophical truths receiving humorous illustration. But when a delineation of character has been so worked up that every sentence is a point or a witticism, its fitness to illustrate general truths is spoilt by the interest of its details. A writer whose first object was to show by examples how certain principles work, would do ill if he set before the imagination a mass of particulars so humorous that the thought of principles must at least be undermost." [12] Theophrastus may have intended his stories to point morals; but when one reads and savors the stories, one cannot doubt that whatever their supposed utility, they would always themselves 'steal the show.' The author of the portraits liked his creations as an artist likes such things; he lingered over turns and tricks of speech and dress because his lively fancy enjoyed the colorful pattern of the human drama. His attention went, in a word, to details and surfaces rather than to principles and systems as with Aristotle. Aristotle's portrait of the Magnificent Man is a marginal illustration on the ethical doctrine of the Golden Mean; the Golden Mean is the expression of reason; reason, in its turn, part of the ultimate constitution of things. In Aristotle's theory of tragedy, again, character is made subordinate to plot—a segment of action—and action is related to logical necessity. The master always demanded the beginning, middle, and end—the reasonable order sustaining person, passion, or incident; while for Theo-phrastus, apparently, these details justify themselves.

Whether in his lost *Poetics*, Theophrastus put more stress on the GREATER TECHNI-CALITY.

[11] *The Characters of Theophrastus*, ed. Jebb-Sandys, 1909, introduction, p. xv.
[12] *Ibid.*, Introduction, p. xiii.

element of character portrayal than on that of plot, we do not know; but we do know that he was responsible for increased attention to the word as an esthetic unit in the art of rhetoric. Beside this accent on the discrete verbal element, he refined on and elaborated the desirable qualities of style. Whereas Aristotle had named two: clearness and propriety, Theophrastus named four, for he added correctness and ornateness, and in treating of ornateness, he emphasized the help given by figures of speech.[13] In respect to music, he followed Aristotle in relating musical modes to mental states; but whereas Aristotle had linked modes with total ethical character, Theophrastus connected them with the passions only.[14] These items about the ideas of Theophrastus are but straws, but they show which way the wind was beginning to blow: toward greater refinement of technical analysis, toward image instead of idea, and away from the ardors of metaphysics. Aristotle himself christened his successor "Theophrastus," *i.e.*, "he of the graceful style," and accused him of interpreting what he had been taught "with an excess of clearness." [15]

ARISTOXENUS' IN-
NOVATIONS IN
MUSIC AND THE-
ORY.

A second member of Aristotle's group of followers, Aristoxenus, did no less than accomplish a revolution in the philosophy of music.[16] He rejected both the musical theory of Pythagoras, that music is at bottom a physico-mathematics, and the theory at the opposite pole, that it is without a law—a mere knack of the ear. The "marvellous order" [17] of musical notes has as its final court of appeal man's ear working in conjunction with man's intellect, he taught; and the essence of a musical note is not the length of chord required to sound it, but its clearly felt and apprehended dynamic relation to other notes.[18] With this conception of the limits and criteria of music Aristoxenus founded his new system of harmony or musical modes. His system ran counter to the prevailing taste, a taste unfortunately addicted, he felt, to the sweetness of chromatic

---

[13] Atkins, *op. cit.*, Vol. I, pp. 157, 158.
[14] Plutarch, *Quaestionum convivialium libri* IX, I, 5, 2.
[15] Diogenes Laertius, *Lives of Eminent Philosophers*, V, Ch. 2; ed. Loeb, Vol. I, p. 485.
[16] *The Harmonics of Aristoxenus*, ed. H. S. Macran, Oxford, 1902, p. 87.
[17] *Ibid.*, p. 196.
[18] *Ibid.*, p. 193.

music. Aristoxenus believed that there was an affinity between certain musical modes and moral states, as Aristotle and Plato had taught. But he warned his readers that it is possible to exaggerate this relationship.[19] He called attention to the qualification in his own statement of the connection: "in so far as musical art can improve the moral character." [20] The work of Aristoxenus is a good example of a contribution to esthetics from within the arts. For his energy went mainly to technical matters, but his sound musicianship enabled him to pronounce justly, though briefly, on the wider nature and relations of his art.

The Aristotelian school did not continue to exist in philosophical loneliness during the centuries that followed the death of the founder. Zeno, first of the Stoics, emigrated to Athens within a few years of that event, and Epicurus had gone thither about fourteen years earlier. As the Peripatetic school waned, Stoicism and Epicureanism gathered strength, and in the second century A.D., the former school could boast the adherence of a Roman Emperor, Marcus Aurelius. The Stoic contribution to esthetics consisted largely in detailed technical discriminations in grammar and rhetoric. Materialists in their view of the nature of things, they declared the utterance and sound of a word to be merely the reverse side of a thought; reasonable speech is nothing but articulated sound. They therefore occupied themselves at length with the bodily side of the thinking process, marked off parts of speech, studied the vowels and consonants, and in so doing prepared the way for the rhetorician Dionysius of Halicarnassus, who in the second century A.D. elaborated a theory of beautiful patterns of rhythms and sounds determined by the smallest verbal elements. Several Stoics wrote treatises *On Voice;* Diogenes wrote on *Language;* Antipater *On Words and Their Meaning.* They pointed out five virtues of literary style: faultlessness in the employment of the Greek language, lucidity, economy, fitness, and a distinguished manner free from colloquialisms.[21] We also owe to the Stoics a diligent cultivation of the allegorical method of interpreting re-

STOIC MATERIALISTIC ESTHETIC; RESTRAINT.

---

[19] *Ibid.,* p. 181.
[20] *Ibid.,* p. 188.
[21] Diogenes Laërtius, *Lives,* VII; ed. Loeb, pp. 165–69.

ligious myths. All the gods and goddesses of Homer and Hesiod were explained as physical elements or processes or mental dispositions: Zeus, a divine fire; Athena, prudence; Dionysus, wine; Demeter, fruit, etc. The Epicureans, exponents of a life of pleasure, occupied themselves with poetry. One of their number, Philodemus of Gadara, wrote in the first century before Christ a book *On Poems*, the surviving fragments of which suggest the presence of acute discussions of poetical style and function.[22] Pleasure, however, for the Epicureans denoted undisturbedness rather than positive diversion or action; and in keeping with their ideal of a calm frame of mind there are expressions of indifference regarding the more strenuous aspects of esthetic experience. "Only the wise man will be able to converse correctly about music and poetry, without however actually writing poems himself."[23] The "wise man," it would seem, however, need not have found composition incompatible with his even frame, if the saying of Epicurus could have been trusted, that "writing is no trouble."[24] Lucretius, whose *On the Nature of Things* is the great literary monument of the Epicurean school, makes a realistic suggestion as to the origin of vocal and instrumental music. Men formed flutes and pipes in imitation of the hollow reeds through which they heard the zephyrs whistle; and they learned to sing by mimicking the liquid notes of birds.[25] A materialistic explanation of the difference between pleasant and unpleasant sensations was offered: the first are due to the impact of smooth caressing particles, the second to that of rough ones.[26] That esthetic theorizing became cooler, more minute, more scientifically analytical and realistic in the post-Aristotelian period, is thus borne out by a consideration of the thoughts on art among the Stoics and Epicureans.

HISTORICAL CON-
SCIOUSNESS.

Another concern with art which had been only a slight moment in Aristotle's organic philosophical treatment began to occupy more attention soon after him. Aristotle had introduced

[22] Atkins, *op. cit.*, II, pp. 54ff.
[23] Diogenes Laërtius, *Lives*, X; ed. Loeb, p. 647.
[24] Dionysius of Halicarnassus, *On Literary Composition*, ed. Roberts, p. 282.
[25] v, 1379–83; ed. Loeb, p. 439.
[26] *Ibid.*, ii, 551, 623; pp. 287, 293.

an almost parenthetical passage in his *Poetics* [27] on the history of the drama from its origin in ritualistic improvisations to its culmination in Euripides, as he had devoted an analogous section of his *Metaphysics* to the history of philosophy before him. But the master's eye had been mainly fixed on the structure and function of drama in its full flowering. How it arrived at this perfection he had investigated only as contributing to the knowledge of the type. For tragedy he had noted the change in the number of actors from one to two by Aeschylus, the addition of a third by Sophocles. He was more interested in the plan and use of the poem when finished and in the climax of the development in Sophocles, *Oedipus Rex*, than in the events of the process. But very soon after him the past career of the arts began to be treasured for its own sake. The history of literature was not first written as a continuous narrative, but developed out of various historical tendencies: the establishment of lists or canons of the best writers in the various kinds; the realization that Homer must be understood in the light of his own epoch and his own language, and again that the example Polybius had set (210–125 B.C.) in treating the social and political development of the Graeco-Roman world between 250 and 150 B.C. could be well followed in the history of oratory and poetry.[28] The Alexandrian canon of epic, iambic, tragic, comic, elegiac, and lyric poets seems to have begun with Aristophanes of Byzantium (c. 257–180 B.C.);[29] and Aristarchus (217–145 B.C.) of the same Alexandrian school seems to have started the interpretation of a literary text out of the conditions of civilization appropriate to it.[30] He said that a poet must be interpreted from himself and what really pertains to him. A further critical interest showed in that the lists of poets and orators increasingly received additions of technical comments, so that epithets calculated to epitomize the writer's style became affixed to the names. In reviewing the orators, for example, Quintilian speaks of the force and compactness of Demosthenes' language and his muscular style, of the more fleshy and less muscular style of Aeschines, of Lysias' likeness to a clear spring rather

---

[27] 1448b–1449b.
[28] Atkins, *op. cit.*, Vol. I, p. 185.
[29] *Ibid.*, p. 191.
[30] *Ibid.*, pp. 188–89.

than a mighty river; while the neat and polished manner of
Isocrates suited him, he adds, rather to the fencing-school than to
the battle-field.[31] Such lists were not confined to historical surveys,
but became common in the writings of critics and connoisseurs,
with the increasing attention to technical procedure and virtuosity.
One showed one's nicety of discrimination by attaching the right
single epithet to each name: "Isocrates possessed sweetness, Lysias
delicacy, Hyperides pointedness, Aeschines sound, and Demosthenes
energy . . . Africanus had weight, Laelius smoothness, Galba
asperity, Carbo something of fluency and harmony." [32] The lists
had a tendency to harden into triplets and perhaps decades, showing the tendency to formalism implicit in them. Like Aristotle,
but without his freedom of handling, critics named styles that
were at two extremes, and then a mixed one, a mean between the
two. Of oratorical manners, one was described as full but not
swollen, another as plain but nerveless, and a third as a combination of the virtues of the others.[33]

COMPARISON OF
STYLES.

Also soon after Aristotle there began with Xenocrates of
Sikyon the recording of the history of painting and sculpture and
the comparison of styles largely for their own sake.[34] The better
known account of artists and their works and manners in Pliny's
Natural History (c. 50 A.D.), and the writings of other learned
men on art, as those of Varro and Antigonus, trace back to this
scholar of the third century B.C. Indeed, Duris of Samos, a pupil
of Theophrastus, wrote a book of this type.[35] Xenocrates' history
consisted of brief statements about a large number of silver-
chasers, workers in bronze, painters, and sculptors. Their chief
works were named and an estimate given of their characteristic
styles and merits. Sometimes in these histories the names of the
artists occurred in a series showing how, step by step, the conquest of some technical problem in art took place. For instance,

---

[31] *Institutes of Oratory*, Bk. X, 1, 76–80; ed. Loeb, Vol. IV, pp. 44f.
[32] Cicero, *De Oratore*, Bk. III, Ch. VII, ed. Bohn, p. 339.
[33] *History of Classical Scholarship*, J. E. S. Sandys, Vol. I, p. 131.
[34] *The Elder Pliny's Chapters on the History of Art*, ed. Jex-Blake and
Sellers, pp. xviff.
[35] *Ibid.*, p. xlvi.

there is the famous list of the five great sculptors who advanced steadily in the solution of the problems of symmetry and realism: Phidias, the suggestive pioneer; Polycletus next, who developed interest by learning to shift the figure's weight to one leg; then Myron, a more diligent observer of symmetry and a "multiplier of truth," but still archaic; Pythagoras, the fourth, interested in the realism of details—hair, veins, and sinews; finally Lysippus, who made his figures slimmer, his details finer,—the inventor of a new canon, and the author of the suggestive comment that he represented men as they appeared, whereas other artists had represented them as they were.[36] There is in Pliny a parallel account of the development of the technique of painting from its simple beginnings in mere outline to perfect realism and the full glory of color. First, he said, came simple line drawing; then the outline filled in with plain red color; then the inspiration of Eumarus to distinguish between the sexes by using the white for the flesh of women, "thus marking the first stage in the progress from monochrome to polychrome painting"; next the discovery of foreshortening and of the importance of the articulation of the body and of drapery, by Kimon of Kleonae; portraiture with Panaenus; facial movement and the movement of the body under drapery with Polygnotus; then the first great fruition of the painter's art in Apollodorus, who "opened the gates of art" by discovering the importance for realism of light and shade.[37]

Aristotelian esthetic theory was like the amoeba, which splits up on maturing, the parts then carrying on a life of their own. The topics of diction, musical modes, dramatic characterization, and the historical development of literary types, all formed parts of the original esthetic body. But in the post-Aristotelian times these topics interested thinkers in and for themselves. For a race of philosophers was substituted a race of specialists in technical matters. The gain for understanding how artistic effects were produced was very great. For example, the analysis by Dionysius of Halicarnassus of the sources of literary charm, a model of thoroughness, though not original, goes to the length of examin-

INDEPENDENT LIFE OF ARISTOTELIAN FRAGMENTS.

[36] *Ibid.*, p. xvii.
[37] *Ibid.*, pp. 101–107, Bk. XXXV, Secs. 56–62.

ing the agreeable or disagreeable effects of single syllables and even letters. He arranged the vowels in a series to show the decrease in musical capacity from the round and open 'a' to the thin 'i'; and he showed that there is rhythm even in a single word, if the word has more than one syllable. He proved from examples how Homer had produced exquisite effects by the humble verbal material that any farmer or sailor could have furnished him, exercising his skill in the subtly varied and musical order he gave to simple elements.[38]

MANUALS.   Aristotle's *Poetics* had been written to a certain extent as a manual for the guidance of young practitioners in the art of poetry. In the Augustan age Horace wrote his famous manual: *The Art of Poetry*. When we compare the two we can feel that philosophy, logical relation to first principles, is precisely the pervasive ingredient in the earlier work, and that another temper and interest, that of a conversational literary epistle, has taken its place in the later one. Scholarly industry has been able to show that this change in the method of dealing with poetry did not come about suddenly. Already in the works of the post-grammarians, Neoptolemus of Parium and Philodemus of Gadara, a model for the division of the subject into three principal topics had been set up, and a zeal for formal analysis exhibited.[39] Horace follows, then, the orthodox Hellenistic order of treatment: first, the subject-matter, next the form; finally the poet himself. The order in Horace is not obvious, and it is easy for the theory to remain in the reader's mind as a series of discrete pronouncements. Unity in plan and consistency in characterization are recommended by Horace as they were by Aristotle. But Horace does not base his directions upon a metaphysic of matter and form or a logic of the probable and necessary. He sets down maxims and counsels based on culture, good sense, and delicate feeling. The would-be poet must study the Greek models day and night,[40] must not publish

---

[38] Dionysius of Halicarnassus, *On Literary Composition*, Ch. 14, ed. Roberts, pp. 136–50.

[39] The important work has been done by C. Jensen, in his *Philodemos über die Gedichte*, Fünftes Buch, 1923.

[40] ii, 268, 269.

too soon,[41] must not introduce arbitrary ornament.[42] His aim must be to please, to profit, or both.[43] The dramatic poet must have five acts and no more;[44] he must never have a fourth actor.[45] Horace furnishes a good set of rules, memorably phrased, but hardly any principles; and where principles occur they are borrowed from other sources. Vitruvius wrote his manual for architects in the reign of Augustus, and Quintilian his *Institutes of Oratory* near the end of the first century. These manuals are erudite and orderly; they illustrate how information about art was being industriously stored and disseminated. They also illustrate the shift of interest from reasoning about art to information, and from causes to facts.

Cicero (106–43 B.C.), dating approximately half-way between Aristotle and Plotinus and being one of the most philosophically-minded of those appearing in the interval, illustrates in his complex, eclectic thinking, the losses and gains of the age. Even though the greatness of his models and the spaciousness of his ideas link him with the great Greek philosophers, there is in him, even so, a different direction of attention, more care for the way things *seem* to the listener, and more concession to practical needs than in those of the great age. Through the mouth of Crassus in the dialogue *On the Orator*, addressed to Brutus, he takes issue with the simple single-mindedness of Socrates, who, he says, taught men to think of the matter and let the manner take care of itself. One must take care of the matter, Cicero agrees, but also of the method of presentation. "If a speaker understand a subject ever so well, but is ignorant how to form and polish his speech, he cannot express himself eloquently even about what he does understand."[46] In enumerating the things a good orator should know, Cicero emphasizes the importance of a knowledge of life and manners, and sets aside as of but little moment the obscurities of physics and the subtleties of logic. By right method, by the art of getting up a subject for an occasion, the artist in the spoken

CICERO HAD STRENGTH AND WEAKNESS OF HIS AGE.

---

[41] ii, 388–89.
[42] i, 15.
[43] ii, 333–34.
[44] i, 189.
[45] i, 192.
[46] *On the Character of the Orator*, Bk. I, Ch. XIV, ed. Bohn, p. 159.

word shall appear to know even more than the one who, as expert, has taught him.[47] The urbane man of letters in Cicero likes to discuss the "form, and, as it were, the complexion of eloquence." [48] Thoughts cannot be made "to shine without the light of language." [49] "A certain intellectual grace must . . . be extracted from every kind of refinement, with which, as with salt, every oration must be seasoned." [50] In an age which saw the addition of thirty-three new esthetic terms to make possible refined criticism of stylistic quality, Cicero was one of the main contributors to the technical fund. He coined many terms, transferring to literature qualities primarily moral or physiological.[51] In such ways Cicero enforced his opinion that the 'how' is 'all in all.'

But Cicero always looks both ways. The 'how' for him follows the 'what' and the 'when.' His seriousness and tolerant breadth keep him constantly aware of the importance of knowledge and of familiarity with the best traditions. He passes also beyond the cultivated conservative's view of the knowledge and discipline necessary for a good orator, and outlines an ideal. The ambitious orator must fix his attention not on any empirical model, but upon an exalted pattern lodged in his own soul. He must imitate this inner form, even as Phidias copied an imagined ideal form rather than an actual model when he carved his Zeus or his Athena.[52] This acknowledgment of the part played by the artist's own imagination in producing a work of art sets Cicero apart from and above the Roman purveyors of rules. But Cicero's treatment of the artist's imagination was not profound. One finds the same suggestion of an inward model in Vitruvius: There is this difference "between the architect and the layman; that the layman cannot understand what is in hand unless he sees it already done; the architect, when once he has formed his plan, has a definite idea how it will turn out in respect to grace, convenience, and pro-

---

[47] *Ad Brutum*, Bk. I, Chap. XII, p. 156; Ch. XV, p. 160.
[48] *De Oratore*, XXXIV, Bohn, p. 182.
[49] *Ibid.*, Bk. III, Chap. VI, p. 338.
[50] *Ibid.*, Bk. I, Chap. XXXIV, p. 182.
[51] Sandys, *op. cit.*, Vol. I, p. 191; G. Saintsbury, *History of Literary Criticism*, Vol. I, p. 220.
[52] *Ad Brutum*, Par. 2.

priety." [53] And Cicero himself speaks coolly of the non-existence of the ideal orator, suggests to his correspondent that there may be errors in the picture he (Cicero) has drawn, and that he is therefore subject to correction. Not only is Cicero cool about the concept, but the treatment of it is not fresh or adequate. A pre-existent psychological image, so definite that the artist's sole task is to reproduce it point for point, is not an 'ideal' in any very valuable sense. For Plato and Aristotle, and later again for Plotinus, an 'ideal' in the individual consciousness springs from a metaphysical source above commonplace reality. Of such a divine origin Cicero gives no hint. Cicero's contribution to esthetics lies, then, not in any one place, but in the wealth and justice of many ideas. His universal appreciativeness appears in his statement that there is no compartment of style for the perfect orator, because the perfect orator will speak in whatever style the case may demand. One of the most original esthetic suggestions of Cicero's is his distinction of beauty into masculine and feminine types, dignity and grace.[54] Distinctions using both these terms, but applying more narrowly to style within the arts, had been made. Cicero's advance consisted in making the distinction general.

As in Cicero, so typically in Graeco-Roman times one must PLUTARCH ON UG-
seek for the progress of esthetics in separate items. In his work LINESS.
on *How to Study Poetry*, Plutarch of Chaeronea (50–100 A.D.) emphasizes a problem suggested in Aristotle's *Poetics:* does ugliness preserve its ugly nature when it enters art. Can that which is ugly in reality become beautiful in an imitation? He answers that it cannot. But he adds that the element of dexterity involved in a deceptive imitation is, on the other hand, admirable, and the thing made thus receives a certain reflected glory from the virtuosity of the maker.[55] Plutarch moves forward in that he tries to solve as a problem what Aristotle merely presents as an esthetic situation. But the level of his solution betrays itself when he remarks that real ugliness becomes acceptable in imagery as the squeaking pig or

---

[53] Vitruvius, *De Architectura*, VI, 8, ed. Loeb, p. 59.

[54] *De Officiis*, I, 1, 36; see also *De Oratore*, 3, 25.

[55] Plutarch's *Moralia:* "How to Study Poetry," 17f., ed. Loeb, *Moralia*, Vol. I, pp. 93ff.

creaking windlass achieves fascination in ventriloquism, and the
dead body of Jocasta attractiveness in Silanion's silver and bronze
imitation. Plutarch's whole philosophical position is elementary.
In discussing whether boys may safely read the fictions of the
poets, he answers that they may on condition that they are warned
to emulate the morally good examples set down by the poets and
to beware the evil ones.[56] The philosophy of art seems to move for
the time being on the surface of thought, as the criticism of art
tends to move on the sensuous surface of the phenomenon.

LONGINUS: GREAT STYLE SPRINGS FROM ARTIST'S GREATNESS. In literary critics of the magnitude of Cicero, Horace, and
Dionysius of Halicarnassus, the tendency for attention to shift
from the inner drift to outer vesture never goes to extremes, for
the serious bent and high gifts of the authors prevent the taste for
superficial brilliance. But that the tide of technical interest was
setting in toward externals appears from the eloquent protest of
Longinus, writer of the treatise usually called *On the Sublime*
in the first century A.D. He seems as he writes to be recalling poets
and orators from the outside to the inside of literature. He seems,
indeed, almost to be taking the side of Socrates against Cicero.
And he is actually taking the side of Plato against Cecilius, the be-
littler of Plato.[57] He defends the case of greatness of soul against
correctness of form and a pleasing exterior. Slips and irregularities,
he says, are inevitable in those who accept the highest challenge.
But the suffrage of the ages, "so long as the waters run and the
trees grow tall," goes to those objects in both nature and letters
which are cast on a large mold rather than to those which are
scrupulously finished and balanced by rules of art.[58] The naked
compact beauty of God's words at the Creation: "Let there be
light," [59] and of Sappho's fierce expressions of love bear the stamp
of inner inspiration, and transport us to ecstasy; [60] while the careful phrases and images of more conscious artists may persuade and

---

[56] *Loc. cit.*
[57] *Literary Criticism, Plato to Dryden,* ed. A. H. Gilbert, New York, 1940,
Longinus, "On Literary Excellence," Part I, Sec. 1.
[58] *Ibid.,* Part IV, Sec. 36.
[59] *Ibid.,* Part II, Sec. 9.
[60] *Ibid.,* Part II, Sec. 10.

flatter us, but fail of the highest effect.[61] Beautiful words are the light of the mind, indeed. But the eminence and excellence of language, which carries away all ages and classes of men, and stays stamped on the memory—catholic and abiding beauty—is the note that rings from a great mind. Beautiful words and all the other devices of style "charm us and dispose us for the majestic, the worthy, the excellent . . . and wholly master our minds." [62] But the potency of literary style springs from something deeper than technical rules and analysis—from passion, rather, and from the preoccupation of the author with things beyond the pale of the actual world, with infinity, the ocean, the stars, the spurting flames of Etna.[63] Authentic sublimity, always spiritual, induces ecstasy in the listener. The hearer becomes like a horse, prancing or rearing. He fancies himself the producer of what he hears.[64] Certainly a step toward Plotinus is taken in the emphasis in Longinus on ecstasy and on the fitness of the great soul to the great object. But his treatise seems to be the product of enthusiasm, for the ideas do not constitute a reasoned system. Longinus seems rather to give the series of marks of the high style, some of them valid, some of them scarcely so, than to deduce the nature of his subject from a primary cause. He belongs among the epoch-making literary critics rather than among the philosophers. But he is an important figure in the Graeco-Roman dialectic of external technical appreciation and criticism versus inward feeling, tact, imagination, ecstasy; of art degenerating into artificiality versus a nature almost identified with the irrational and supernatural.

The call back to Nature was not theory alone in these days. NATURE AND RE-
Christ and the Stoics summoned men to an appreciation of the ALISM.
beauty of the lilies of the field, more beautiful than Solomon in all his glory, to the charm of the gaping of ripe figs, the bending of an ear of corn, or the foam of a boar. As early as the third century B.C. the Stoic Chrysippus had instanced the beauty of the

---

[61] *Ibid.*, Part IV, Sec. 30.
[62] *Ibid.*, Part V, Sec. 39.
[63] *Ibid.*, Part IV, Sec. 35.
[64] *Ibid.*, Part I, Sec. 7.

peacock's tail as proof that beauty is one of Nature's goods. The motive grew to religio-lyric intensity in the writings of the Church Fathers. In arguing that there is matter of delight in Nature's mere accessories and appendages, that "in olives that are ready to fall their very approach to over-ripeness gives a peculiar beauty to the fruit," Marcus Aurelius is explicitly setting the artificial beauty of 'imitations' against the natural beauty of ripe fruits and the features of animals. A man of sensibility "will look on the actual gaping jaws of wild beasts with no less pleasure than the representations of them by limners and modellers." [65] The tiger in the painter's shop represented to him presumably the widespread actively pursued cult of dilettantism and connoisseurship among the followers of the Roman court. For his predecessors at the head of the Empire had led a willing, luxury-loving aristocracy into extravagances of collecting such 'imitations.'

The call back to Nature from art, and to spirit from material things, recurs in a beat and rhythm, in conjunction with the contrary tendencies in the maturing and then ageing Empire. Beginning with Alexander, conquering generals and rulers had set the example of collecting and exhibiting to an admiring people the beautiful objects of art plundered from Greece and Syria, India and Egypt. The kings of Pergamum and Syracuse, the generals of the Republic, and succeeding emperors plundered and purchased, collected and built, until Mummius is said to have filled Rome with sculpture, and Augustus to have found Rome of brick and left her of marble. Nero himself learned to paint and model and was one of the greatest collectors of antiquity. Two of his statues are said to be as fine as any to be found anywhere. The Flavian emperors gathered an artistic court about them and collected and built with Augustan splendor. Under the favor of royal patronage, rich and novel modes of representing groups in relief were invented and effects of illusion made possible by a new sense of spatial bonds of eye-glance. Parallel to the illusionism that developed in group sculpture was that of portrait sculpture. The Roman emperors multiplied themselves manyfold in busts and

---

[65] *The Communings with Himself*, Bk. III, Ch. 2, ed. Loeb, p. 47.

paintings, and in the time of Nero even the gladiators and their attendants had their realistic likenesses exhibited on the public colonnades. Much virtuosity was displayed in the rendering of the peculiar individuality and specific look of the subject—a virtuosity commemorated earlier by Pliny in the saying that Apelles made so perfect a likeness that a reader of character could tell from it how long a sitter had lived or was likely to live.[66] There was the same zeal for getting the very life of an object in art in painters of common scenes. A certain Piraicus earned the title of painter of odds and ends because he depicted barber's shops, cobblers' stalls, asses, eatables and similar subjects, and he was matched by another, Studius, who did harbors and fish-ponds, figures coming up to country houses on donkeys or in carriages, staggering porters, bargaining women, and "other scenes of like vivacity and infinite humor." [67] Literary invention was fertile: Plautus and Terence developed the interest in everyday family life and manners; the romantic novel arrived with Apuleius' *Golden Ass,* and idyllic poetry and epigrams and lyrics met the varied tastes of the time.

But the swing toward realism and petty virtuosity was con- CHRYSOSTOM: AR-stantly balanced by some mystic theory of the ways of genius. TIST'S VISION WAITS ON THE The psychology of genius received two slight increments shortly FASHIONING. before Plotinus, both relating to the way in which the gods are represented in the highest art. As if in reply to the teaching of Cicero that an ideal image lies ready-formed in the artist's mind, his task being merely to transfer the image to some material medium, Dion Chrysostom (50–117 A.D.) contends that the divine ideal does not exist in clear shape until an artist has finished the process of making a statue or poem containing his version of the god. The god waits upon genius for delivery from chaos, so to speak. Dion Chrysostom further justifies the use of the human rather than the animal form for the depiction of divinity. Painters and sculptors cannot, he says, depict the gods' spiritual properties directly. Wisdom and reason are as such neither tangible nor visible. Therefore, artists take the natural carriers of God-like

[66] Pliny, *op. cit.,* XXXV, 88, ed. Jex-Blake and Sellers, pp. 125–27.
[67] *Ibid.,* XXXV, 112, pp. 145–47.

reason and wisdom, that is, the human form, thus using the closest symbol for what they would represent.[68] Philostratus, a contemporary of Plotinus, gives in his *Life of Apollonius of Tyana*, a comparison between imitation and imagination. A debate is going on: should the gods be represented as animals or as human beings? The Greek champion of the human aspect claims that Phidias was guided in his choice by imagination, "a more cunning craftsman than imitation. For imitation will fashion what it has seen, but imagination goes on to what it has not seen, which it will assume as the standard of reality; and imitation is often baffled by awe, but imagination by nothing, for it rises unawed to the height of its own ideal. If you have envisaged the character of Zeus, you must see him with the firmament and the seasons and the stars, as Phidias strove to in this statue; and if you are to fashion Athene, you must have in your mind strategy and counsel and the arts, and how she sprang from Zeus himself." [69]

PROMISE OF SPECULATION; DECAY OF APPRECIATION.

Although up to the very time of Plotinus certain conceptions were deepening as if in preparation for his speculative achievement—as, for instance, in the idea of imagination as formative and as combining sentiment with intelligence—the practical appreciation of art in criticism and connoisseurship reached a low ebb. From the days of Theophrastus, and even in Plato himself, we have illuminating portraits of affected fops who collect foreign curios and decorate their houses and persons with fantastic draperies. Indeed the history of literature would support the belief that the genus esthete has always been with us. But there is a growing bitterness and detail, a more elaborate satire, in the portraits during and after the first century A.D. Persius, a Roman Stoic of the first century, sketches the poet who, got up sprucely with a new toga and a birthday ring, tickles his audience by panting out verses and rolling wanton eyes. "Alas, for our national character, when old men become caterers to indecent ears," he makes one of his speakers say.[70] The satire of Lucian (2nd century A.D.) informs us of the exhibitionist impulse of professional speakers in his time

---

[68] Oration XII, *De Dei Cognitione.*
[69] Bk. VI, Ch. XIX, ed. Loeb, Vol. II, pp. 77–81.
[70] *Persius,* Satire I, ll. 13–23.

who liked to compete with painting and architecture in arousing sentiment and making a scene live. As Alexander longed to swim in the Cydnus, says the speaker in "The Hall," "so will a man of taste, finding himself in a large, brilliant, and gay hall, long to compose speeches in it . . . to seek repute and gain glory in it, to fill it with his voice and . . . to become part and parcel of its beauty." A mere philistine would simply cast his eyes about, crane at the ceiling, and gesticulate. But a man of culture will collect an audience and wax eloquent. "To me, at least, it seems, that a splendid hall excites the speaker's fancy and stirs it to speech, as if he were somehow prompted by what he sees. No doubt something of beauty flows through the eyes into the soul, and then fashions into the likeness of itself the words that it sends out. . . . The frescoes of the walls, the beauty of their colors, and the vividness, exactitude, and truth—each detail might well be compared with the face of spring and with a flowery field, except that those things fade and wither and change and cast their beauty, while this is spring eternal, field unfading, bloom undying. Naught but the eye touches it and culls the sweetness of what it sees." The speaker concludes by saying that he has been drawn to this hall to speak as if by a magic wheel or a Siren; "for," he says, "I had no slight hope that even if my phrases were homely before, they would seem beautiful if adorned, so to speak, in fine clothing." [71] Lucian recurs again and again to the affectation of dilettantism in his time; for example, in his *Zeuxis*, he compares the research of novelty whether in literature or sculpture to the tricks of the conjuror.[72] Preciosity in language, exhibitionism in rhetoric, a loosening of appreciation not only from thought and feeling, but from the very subject of the speech, are all prone to herald a strong reaction. The extraordinary picture, for instance, which Athenaeus gives us, about the beginning of the third century A.D., of a banquet in which luxury and research of elegance and erudition swamp all sense of proportion or contact with reality, can be set beside a picture from Cyprian of the desolation of the world in the same

---

[71] Ed. Loeb, Vol. I, pp. 177ff.
[72] "Zeuxis and Antiochus," ed. Loeb, Vol. II, p. 95.

age.[73] In the *Deipnosophists* of Athenaeus, the dramatic characters seek always the word, the story, the history, the critical observation that should accompany the arrival of the fish, the boar, the wine, the flutes. When the ham and chicken are served, a learned discussion of the word 'tender' follows. When wine is brought in, someone tells the funniest story of antiquity about a drunken revel, or another, in a more serious vein, tells the fine differences of various flavors of wine, the proper age at which to begin drinking, the effects and relations of wine. A dictionary of cookery is matched with the actual bringing in of silver and gold platters of all the kinds of fish that ocean and lake afford. A whole little esthetic of music surrounds the occasion of the hearing of a water-organ or the listening to songs. Talk turns on the moral effects of music, instruments simple and complex, songs, regular and irregular. A life of pleasure and luxury, common and popular in that day, is compared with the simpler life of the old days. The pleasure-loving Tyrian host feels that life begins with the appearance of refinement and lordly pleasure; but the Cynic guest takes a more critical view of the devotion to silver goblets and alabaster boxes, unguents and aphrodisiacs, cheese-cakes and almonds.

The lectures of Plotinus were delivered in Rome a few years after Athenaeus had painted this luxurious banquet scene with its sensuous details of glitter of gold and jewels, playing of flutes, and full gamut of savors. At such a moment the words of the philosopher strike the ear almost like an antiphonal, for his burden is a summons away from the pleasures of sense to union with the Ineffable One. His summons is, as it were, from the table of carnal delicacies to the symbolic heavenly table of religious communion. The tastes and interests which Athenaeus sums up both for his own time and the preceding centuries seem to be related through contrast to the characteristic note of the *Enneads* of Plotinus, which are as necessary for understanding him as is the far-gone thought of Plato which Plotinus believed himself to be reviving. The earnest call to conversion from sensuous living, in its intensity and perva-

---

[73] *Ad Donatum.*

siveness, strikes one as a direct response to the caressing of sensuousness in Athenaeus or the emptiness of criticism in Callistratus.

Plotinus begins his treatment of beauty on the level of the PLOTINUS REJECTS conventional opinion at his time. Beauty is addressed, he says, HARMONY. chiefly to sight and hearing, and includes combinations of words and all kinds of music. It includes also kinds of conduct and character. If this is the extension of the term, what, he inquires, is the intension, or essence. There are signs even here at the beginning, of the surface-scorning definition he will ultimately give. "The same bodies," he says, "appear sometimes beautiful, sometimes not; so that there is a good deal between being body and being beautiful." [74] The conventional definition: Beauty is harmony, will not do. It is both too narrow and too wide. It is too narrow because single, uncombined things like lightning, gold, a musical tone, and moral acts are beautiful. The very Intellectual Principle itself, which is supremely beautiful, is "essentially the solitary." Moreover, beauty in the aggregate demands beauty in the detail. It is too wide because a perfectly articulated system of ideas may be false and ugly, though exhibiting the quality of harmony in a high degree.[75] In other words, a simple quality or entity may be as beautiful as classic harmony; and harmony, again, may exist without involving at the same time any beauty. The traditional concept of beauty obviously needs revision.

Plotinus follows up the preliminary esthetic skirmish by a BEAUTY THAT more serious engagement with the whole problem of beauty. We WHICH IS LOVED mean by beauty in the last resort, he says, what we love. The ON PERCEPTION. principle that bestows beauty on material things "is something perceived . . . at the first glance, something the soul names as from an ancient knowledge and, recognizing, welcomes it, and enters into unison with it." [76] The philosophy of beauty, then, must investigate this psychological fact, this yearning of the human spirit for what is sympathetic to it, its passage out of itself to find what is like it, and the joy that crowns success. In identifying the beautiful with the object of desire, Plotinus repeats the theme

---

[74] *Enneads*, I, 6, 1; MacKenna trans., Vol. I, pp. 77, 78.
[75] *Ibid.*, I, 6, 1, Vol. I, pp. 78, 19.
[76] *Ibid.*, I, 6, 2, Vol. I, p. 79.

of Plato's *Symposium*. Like Plato, Plotinus teaches that our liking, as we find it lying on the surface of our affective life, is not serious devotion. Our choosing part climbs a ladder to its goal in perfect choice of perfect object. But Plotinus' theory of the wandering from home and return of the restless soul is a more definite and elaborate system of ideas than Plato's. Plotinus asks, why should the soul want something it has not, and why should it find its peace and satisfaction in a certain type of intuitive experience—union with Beauty?

LOVE OF BEAUTY IS METAPHYSICAL HOMESICKNESS.

Plotinus teaches that, as individual and embodied souls here and now, we represent a middle-moment in our complete history. We sprang originally from the Primal Fountain of all Being, the Perfectly Good, the One. This Creative Origin proceeds forth from itself because its character is to act and multiply. But its emanation step by step, from the One, through the Intellectual Principle, then to World-Soul, finally to individuality, involves a lowering of existence, as light raying from the sun becomes dimmer as it departs farther from its burning source. Also the Infinite Energy of the Primal One meets the resistance of dark inert matter, formless Non-Being, as it journeys. Thus a human individual is a being separated from his proper place in the One, which is his true home, and is mixed with alien elements. His restless longing is therefore to return home, to retrace his steps back to where the energy is stronger, the unity clearer, and the elements purer.

This metaphysical pilgrim's progress accounts both for moral and for esthetic experience, then, in the philosophy of Plotinus; and when we long for beauty, we also long for home—for goodness, for God, and for truth. The moment that the concept with which Plotinus intends to replace the abandoned inadequate one of harmony of parts thus acquires its full metaphysical significance it seems simultaneously to become too diffuse to be helpful. If beauty is that with which we ultimately desire to be united, and this again is the Good, the One, the Spring of Being, the solution of the problem is as much ethics as it is esthetics, and rather more an inclusive mysticism than either. But a further search reveals more specific esthetic significance in the doctrine of the One. The thought

of Plotinus plays back and forth between the way a sculptor
or architect creates and Nature creates, or between concrete
natural beauty and Divine Beauty.[77] Art cannot be imitation in the
common sense, Plotinus says, because more comes out from the
hand and brain of the artist than common nature shows. There
is a richer fertility in the soul of a Phidias than can be expressed
in terms of facile copying. "We must recognize that they [the
arts] give no bare reproduction of the thing seen but go back to the
Ideas from which Nature itself derives, and, furthermore, that
much of their work is all their own; they are holders of beauty
and add where nature is lacking. Thus Phidias wrought the Zeus
upon no model among things of sense but by apprehending what
form Zeus must take if he chose to become manifest to sense." [78]
Phidias himself was in possession of beauty, we are told. His
genius is explained not by the commerce between his senses and
the external world, but by the current of creative energy that
flowed into him straight from the underlying ideas or reasons which
the external world itself copies. "The artificer holds (the form
or design) not by his equipment of eyes and hands but by his
participation in his art." [79] The beauty of the statue comes from
the way it has been worked by the workman, rather than from
the simple external facts of relation of parts and color. The stone
block has much in common in general form and color with the
statue which is evoked from it. The difference lies in the life that
the sculptor communicates to the finished product which is lacking in the raw material. The beauty consists not in the stone
but in the form that art confers on stone. The same applies to
architecture. The beauty of a building comes not from shape and
color, if these are taken apart from the formative power of the
architect. What pleases is the accordance between the building
and the Ideal Form operating in the architect's mind and enabling
him to bind and control shapeless matter.[80] For the artist does

MORE SPECIFI-
CALLY, THE BODY-
ING OF IDEA.

[77] *Enneads*, I, 6, 9, Vol. I, p. 88; I, 6, 2 and 3, Vol. I, p. 80f.; V, 7, 3, Vol.
IV, 72.
[78] *Ibid.*, V, 8, 1, Vol. IV, p. 74.
[79] *Ibid.*, V, 8, 1, Vol. IV, p. 73.
[80] *Ibid.*, I, 6, 3, Vol. I, p. 81.

nothing less than call a dead thing to life when he forms it. And ugliness is the obverse: not being mastered by plastic power.[81] Where the Creator of all has not quickened some mass into complete responsiveness; where potentiality has remained unstirred; where there is a dead, unworked area in a picture; or an unresponsive surface in a statue; an unattached, hanging, or monotonous set of notes in a piece of music, there is the foe of beauty, the presence of ugliness, and metaphysical non-being. So we may define the difference between ugly and beautiful faces. It is the life of the soul shining through the bodily parts that makes faces beautiful. Living faces are more beautiful than dead, because there is the light of intelligence in them. Regular features do not ravish us as does the bloom of expression. "Since the one face, constant in symmetry, appears sometimes fair and sometimes not, can we doubt that beauty is something more than symmetry?" [82]

The beauty of color is also form for Plotinus. The splendor of fire "has color primally," and burns the energy of its fierce glory into the dull element of darkness. The pouring in of unembodied light unifies the shapeless dark chaos of non-being in a manner that reaches us as diversity of tint. The original power to bind and organize, passed down into art and genius, causes then the "sweetness of color" as well as the outlines and relations of objects.[83] There is more beauty in the living than in the dead, in color than in darkness; there is more beauty in the creator than in the created. The artist possesses, in the fecundity of his imagination and skill, more reservoirs of esthetic value than are conferred by him on his products. But higher than the level of the creating mind of the artist is the level of the art itself, from which the individual derives his talent. Beauty, Plotinus says, "exists in a far higher state in the art; for it does not come over integrally into the work; that original beauty is not transferred; what comes over is a derivative and a minor . . . everything that reaches outwards is the less for it, strength less strong, heat less hot, every

---

[81] *Enneads*, I, 6, 2, Vol. I, p. 80.

[82] *Ibid.*, I, 6, 1, Vol. I, pp. 78f.

[83] *Ibid.*, I, 6, 3, Vol. I, p. 81. This theory of color is sponsored in modern times by Goethe. Cf. F. Koch, *Goethe und Plotin*, 1925.

power less potent, and so beauty less beautiful . . . every prime cause must be, within itself, more powerful than its effect can be: the musical does not derive from an unmusical source but from music." [84]

The World-Soul again is higher than art because it is not dependent on any force or material from outside, and it does not dispense any force or material to a place outside itself. It is a "Self-indwelling Principle." The productivity of Nature is like the art of the wax-worker, Plotinus says, with this important difference. The wax-workers are limited in that they cannot generate of themselves the colors they use. But Nature is "a thing completely inbound." [85] All that it uses comes from itself and remains with itself. It is "static and intact" so that its making is a brooding contemplation or vision. 'Nature, asked why it brings forth its works, might answer, if it cared to listen and to speak: "It would have been more becoming to put no question but to learn in silence just as I myself am silent. . . . And what is your lesson? This; that whatsoever comes into being is my vision seen in my silence, the vision that belongs to my character who, sprung from vision, am vision-loving and create vision by the vision-seeing faculty within me. The mathematicians from their vision draw their figures: But I draw nothing: I gaze and the figures of the material world take being as if they fell from my contemplation." ' [86]

This for Plotinus is the source and pattern of artistic creation. A product is dead and less than the artist; the artist is a particular man, and less than his art; the art is dependent on an external material medium and so is not self-sufficient; the creative act dominating Nature is alone self-sufficient. Here act and vision are one; color and shape arise together within the process. By a process of self-discipline we can acquire the "only eye that sees the mighty beauty" of the One.[87] We must 'self-gather' into the purity of our being and cut away and smooth and chisel the personality we find at this center, until we have made ourselves a perfect work. Then noth-

ARTIST LESS THAN ART; ART LESS THAN NATURE.

HIS MYSTICISM.

---

[84] *Ibid.*, V, 8, 1, Vol. IV, pp. 73f.
[85] *Ibid.*, III, 8, 2, Vol. II, pp. 120f.
[86] *Ibid.*, III, 8, 4, Vol. II, p. 123.
[87] *Ibid.*, I, 6, 9, Vol. I, p. 88.

ing from without clings to the authentic man, and one has "become very vision." [88] To become very vision means for Plotinus to participate in the kind of creativity that the Soul of Nature carries on, and that is the source of the creative energy of the arts. At the same time this esthetic key of "becoming very vision" in order to understand the workings of genius turns a double lock. It opens the door on the mystic introversion recommended by Plotinus and suggests the source of the sensuous appeal of what purports to be extremely spiritual. A wholly in-gathered observation sees lights and hears music that are a reflex of real light and real music, and that are not corrected by the criticisms of outer contacts. It sometimes seems as if the flight of Plotinus to the 'dear country' 'over yonder' was little more than the re-embracing of this country's music and color in a frame of ecstasy. The delicious troubling of which he writes, the savor and fragrance, transparence and splendor, which are to qualify our experience of the 'One,' Fountain of Form, often seem transported by a change of place rather than of character to the higher level.

Plotinus rejected the crudities of the mystery-cults that surrounded him in Alexandria and Rome, the elaborate pageantry and ceremonial of the rites of Isis and Mithra. These were congenial to what is stupid and gross in man. But an effluence from their splendor seems to have reached the recesses of his thought, even while he explicitly repudiated many of their ideas. Not only have general analogies between Plotinus' expressions and those of these mystery cults been noted, but he apparently had in one passage the exact details of the temple of Isis in the Field of Mars before his mind's eye when he described the process of spiritual purification to which he was exhorting his followers.[89] In a measure, he retained the flavor and essence of sense while casting out its body. A double attitude toward magic also is present in Plotinus. He rejected the common practices of sorcery and astrology. At the same time he insisted that the soul of the world shows its presence everywhere by the affinities and subtle sympathies of things. A kind of sympathetic magic unites man and the stars, even though

---

[88] *Loc. cit.*

[89] *Ibid.*, I; VI, 6, 9, Vol. I, p. 88.

the mummery of astrology is superstition. "The true magic is internal to the All" where "there is much drawing and spell-binding."
Particular instances of ensorcellation, match-making, prayer, musical incantation are but shadows of the primal love and sorcery
given in nature. "If the vibration in a lyre affects another by virtue
of the sympathy existing between them, then certainly in the
All . . . there must be one melodic system." [90] "In such a total,
analogy will make every part a Sign." [91]

Sooner or later Plotinus makes Beauty both transcendent and
immanent, and thus strains to the breaking-point the logical consistency of his system. But what is loss to logic is at least part
gain to esthetics. When one reads in the sections on *Providence* or
Against the Gnostics praises of the beauties of the here and now
one knows that what is beautiful for this philosopher is not only
noble for thought and contemplation, but also pleasant to sight
and hearing. The art in things shows not alone, he says, in grand
features of the universe, but in the cunning workmanship of
animal forms, the grace of leaves, and the lavishness of exquisite
bloom.[92] The glory of the sun always enthralls him. If, as his
adversaries would claim, there is a sun more splendid than the one
we can behold, what a sun that must be! [93] he exclaims. He compares the movement of the All, the pageant of the circling heavenly
bodies and the life of plants and animals, to a great choral procession and the scattered items of ugliness to some turtle that crosses
the way athwart the column.[94]

The influence of the philosophy of Plotinus on later thought—
medieval, Renaissance, and even modern—can hardly be exaggerated. For example, St. Augustine repeats almost verbally the
passage just cited. This influence was due to the combination of
a program of cosmic creation and soul-recall with over-tones of
sensuousness and magic. Dante's *Divine Comedy* embodies St.
Thomas' scholasticism. But whence comes Dante's profuse use

---

[90] *Ibid.*, III, 4, 40, 41, Vol. III, pp. 96f.
[91] *Ibid.*, II, 3, 5, Vol. II, p. 164.
[92] *Ibid.*, III, 2, 13, Vol. II, p. 26.
[93] *Ibid.*, II, 9, 4, Vol. II, p. 220.
[94] *Ibid.*, II, 9, 7, Vol. II, p. 225.

of images of light and sound to express the theological idea? And a vague doctrine of 'sympathy' supplies a needed irrational moment in esthetic theories through many centuries, conspicuously in Leibniz, but more surprisingly, if more slightly, even in a follower of common sense and nature like Hume.

SUPPLEMENTARY READING

Bosanquet, *History of Aesthetic*, London, 1892, Ch. V.

E. Bréhier, *La Philosophie de Plotin*, Paris, 1928.

Murray W. Bundy, "The Theory of Imagination in Classical and Mediaeval Thought," *Univ. Ill. Stud. in Lang. and Lit.*, Vol. XII, nos. 2–3.

F. P. Chambers, *Cycles of Taste*, Cambridge, 1928.

E. R. Dodds, comp. and ed., *Select Passages Illustrative of Neoplatonism*, New York, 1924.

W. R. Inge, *The Philosophy of Plotinus*, London, 1918.

Allan H. Gilbert, *Literary Criticism from Plato to Dryden*.

Saintsbury, *History of Criticism*, Vol. I, Bk. I, Chs. IV, V, VI, Bk. II.

Venturi, *History of Art Criticism*, Ch. II.

E. Krakowski, *Une Philosophie de l'Amour et de la Beauté. L'Esthétique de Plotin et son Influence*, Paris, 1929.

CHAPTER V

Medieval Esthetics

W HAT was the fate of esthetics in the early Christian DID MEDIEVAL SPIRITUAL TONE CRUSH OUT ESTHETICS? era?" inquires a recent writer on the history of taste. He answers: "A new people were procreated and, like the Heracleidae of old, were founders of a new culture. For them there was at first no esthetics. . . . Comparatively barbarous, they had no use for the finesses of the ancient civilization. . . . Churches were built on the plan of the basilica, replete with Pagan types of carving, fresco, and mosaic. . . . But the old sophisticated esthetics was gone. . . . Only a few of the Eastern saints and scholars cultivated spasmodically the old esthetics without disloyalty to a good conscience; but they were exceptional. The stark Christianity of the Iconoclastic controversy finally put an end even to these lingering esthetic remnants. . . . The very Gospels, in their one and only mention of the beauty of architecture, seemed to convey the reproof of Christ, a reproof symbolic of the mood and temper of the centuries to follow. . . . Early Christianity unconditionally renounced Fine Art as Fine Art. . . . In effect, esthetics had been so completely crushed out, by the pressure of the Christian moral resistance, that its history had need to begin again from the beginning. . . . A notice of self-conscious formal beauty never disturbs the innocence of medieval documents. . . . The few 'artistic' documents, such as those of Villars de Honnecourt, were late in date and even then are disappointing. They are chiefly technical note-books, occasionally enlivened by a religious exhortation. They are now famed and consulted because of the complete absence of anything more informative. . . . Passages in the *Summa Theologica* of St. Thomas Aquinas have definitions of

Beauty and Goodness and indeed of 'beautiful things' . . . borrowed from Aristotle. . . . There is a long distance between this
anemic Aristotelianism and the full-blooded esthetics which was
to mark the Renaissance. Probably the nearest approach to a
doctrine of Beauty in the Middle Ages was the Neo-Platonic
treatises of Dionysius the Areopagite, *On Divine Names*, which
achieved so extraordinary a popularity in all the learned circles of
Europe. It represented Beauty as one of the Divine Names, but
ipso facto that Beauty had no more to do with esthetic Beauty than
Plato's idea of moral Beauty aforetime. . . . The Middle Ages
must be recognized as an era when formal beauty in Fine Art,
a self-conscious thought or act, did not exist." [1] This denial of an
esthetic consciousness to the Middle Ages seems at first sight
plausible. The classical German historians of esthetics leaped from
Plotinus to the eighteenth century,[2] and a recent historian gives
four pages out of three hundred and nineteen to medieval thought
on the subject.[3] Moreover, the reasons assigned in the quoted
passage seem right: that esthetics was crushed out by 'the Christian moral resistance,' and also that the nearest approach to a
philosophy of beauty in the Middle Ages, made by Dionysius the
Areopagite, confused beauty with a divine attribute. It is true
that some degree of moral resistance to some form of art or beauty
meets one on the pages of the Church writers early and late. In
the second and third centuries of our era when Christianity was
fighting at close quarters with Paganism, and when the beginnings
of ascetic monasticism were sending thousands to a sordid life
in the desert, Pagan art was associated in Christian thought with
Pagan heresy. Sculpture savored of idolatrous and wicked Emperor worship; the theater suggested sensuality and brutality.
Tertullian in the second century said that the arts of the theater
were patronized by the "yoke-devils" of passion and lust, Bacchus
and Venus.[4] St. Jerome reported that he was scourged till black

---

[1] F. P. Chambers, *Cycles of Taste*, pp. 108–16.
[2] *E.g.*, Max Schasler, *Kritische Geschichte der Aesthetik*, Berlin, 1872, p. 253
[3] Benedetto Croce, *Aesthetic*, trans. Ainslie, 2d ed., London, Macmillan, 1929,
pp. 174–79.
[4] *De Spectaculis*, X, Loeb, p. 250.

and blue by the angels before the Judge of Heaven because he loved Cicero too much;[5] St. Mary of Egypt felt remorse over the songs of her childhood that would float back; St. Basil writes on the wickedness of laughter, saying that seems to be the one bodily passion that Christ never experienced.[6] The mystic strain that sprang from one side of Augustinism and reached its climax in the twelfth century was also strongly ascetic. St. Bernard tried to make himself unobservant of the beauty of nature for Christ's sake. And St. Francis wrote that God had chosen him to tread under foot the beauty of the world so that men might know that every grace comes from God.[7] He started to throw down with his own hands a great house which had been built for his followers, saying that a cell with walls of mud and dab was all that he could countenance.[8] St. Augustine, the 'exemplar of the Middle Ages,' grew increasingly intolerant of life's amenities as he grew older. He then called dramatic utterances 'smoke and wind,'[9] satisfaction in musical harmony for its own sake a vulgar delight,[10] performances on the stage voluptuous madness, love of it filthy scab[11] and vanity.[12] He dwelt on the lewdness of classical theatrical entertainment.[13] He lamented that the sons of men go down the "stream of hell" when they are only following the example of the gods as portrayed in Homer and the Roman playwrights.[14] He contrasted the pure Christian pity which seeks to do away with pain and want with the impure pity of the theater. In the theater, he said, we sentimentally enjoy our counterfeit sympathy and sorrow, and care more for sinful lovers and spectacular villains than for

---

[5] *Nicene and Post-Nicene Fathers*, 2d Ser., V: VI, p. 35, St. Jerome, Letter XXII.

[6] *The Ascetic Works of St. Basil*, trans. W. K. L. Clarke, London, 1925, S.P.C.K., p. 180, Longer Rules, XVII.

[7] *Little Flowers*, IX.

[8] *The Mirror of Perfection*, at the Sign of the Phoenix, Longacre, 1900, VII, p. 13.

[9] *Confessions*, Bk. I, Ch. XVII, Loeb ed., p. 51.

[10] *Nicene . . . Fathers*, 1st Ser., V: II, p. 252, *City of God*, Bk. XVII, Ch. XIV.

[11] *Confessions*, Bk. III, Ch. II, Loeb ed., p. 105.

[12] *Ibid.*, Bk. IV, Ch. I, 147.

[13] *City of God*, II, 8, p. 27; II, 27, p. 41.

[14] *Confessions*, Bk. II, Ch. XVI, pp. 52-53.

the robbed and the poor of real life.[15] At times his asceticism even went to the length of condemning serious 'liberal' studies. The Bible contains the only 'liberating' literature, he argued; and those who are devoted to the so-called liberal arts are more enslaved than 'free.[16] The Bible should take the place in men's concern of impious poetic myths, proud oratorical lies, and the subtleties of philosophy. St. Thomas drew analogies from the mechanical arts, as most theological writers did, but he does not discourse on secular fine art.

ART A LIAR WHO ROBS WHOLESOME QUALITIES FROM EXPERIENCE.

On the whole, the early Christian moral resistance echoed Plato's two main objections to art in the tenth book of his *Republic*. As Plato had said that the unreal imaginative character of painting and poetry placed these arts at two removes from 'the king and from truth,' so the Christian thinkers derived the image-making, dissembling arts—especially the arts of the theater—from the Devil, the "liar from the beginning." Tertullian wrote: "The Author of truth loves no falsehood; all that is feigned is adultery in His sight. The man who counterfeits voice, sex or age, who makes a show of false love and hate, false sighs and tears, He will not approve, for He condemns all hypocrisy. In His law He denounces that man as accursed who shall go dressed in woman's clothes; what then will be His judgment upon the pantomime who is trained to play the woman?"[17] Plato's second main objection to the imitative arts in *Republic* X is their tendency to water the passions and make the less stable part of human nature prevail over the rational virtues. The connection of the fine arts with the passions was in the same way an offence to the Christians. The Christians prized not so much the rational virtues as the habit of gentleness. The fruits of the Spirit are love, joy, peace, meekness, temperance, long-suffering, kindness. Christians found the opposite emotional habit in the Pagan secular arts. In his youth as a close student of the classics, St. Augustine had learned to declaim and to feel inwardly the Homeric passages where heathen passions were brought into vivid relief: the wailing of Aeneas over

---

[15] *Confessions*, Bk. III, Ch. II, Loeb ed., pp. 60, 61.
[16] *Nicene . . . Fathers*, 1st Ser., Vol. I, Letter 101, A.D. 409.
[17] *De Spectaculis*, XXIII, Loeb ed., p. 287.

the death of Dido, the anger of Juno, the lasciviousness of Jupiter. After his conversion he deplored the acquaintance with the passions which he had thus gained.[18] As the Church associated gentle feelings with the white dove of peace, so the black crow became for it the symbol of the more brutish psychological habits. The Church thus shaped to its peculiar set of ideas an old Roman superstition. The crasser, wilder passions were gradually identified with the Greek gods; their source was claimed to be the hellish vapors of the Delphian cave, and a sinister, demoniacal connotation was established not only for heathen poetry but for poetry in general.[19] The vices which the men of the Middle Ages linked with art: hypocrisy, sensuality, violence, seemed to them the more dangerous, as they had in earlier times to Plato, because of the accompanying seductive charm. "Poets are pernicious, for because of the sweetness of their modulations, souls fall from grace," said Lactantius. Art appeared to the Churchman in the guise of a Siren engaged in drawing men off from the narrow way of righteousness; and in proportion to its power to attract was the obligation heavier to make no terms. One of the best-known expressions of this stern rebuttal of the seductive charm of the Muses in the Medieval period is from Boethius: he makes philosophy, true consolation of troubled spirits, rebuke the Muses as unholy maidens, offering "sweet poison" instead of a true remedy, and as killing the fruitful seed of reason with the unfruitful thorns of the passions.[20]

The accumulation of instances like these, mostly from the writings of the Church Fathers, lends color to the contention that there was no esthetics in the Middle Ages on account of the prevailing moral censoriousness. In the scheme of values, righteousness was not only supreme, but at times it seemed icily solitary. Little room was then left in the cultural program for the pleasure-giving arts when the consuming interest was in the glorification of God and preparation for Heaven. Already in early manhood

---

[18] *Confessions*, Bk. I, Ch. XIII, Loeb ed., pp. 39–43.

[19] K. Borinski, *Die Antike in Poetik und Kunsttheorie*, Leipzig, 1914, pp. 13, 14.

[20] *Consolations of Philosophy*, I, I; Loeb ed., pp. 131–33.

St. Augustine thanked God that he had put behind the trivialities and puerilities of the study of profane literature which had beguiled his youth. On account of this moralistic strain in Augustine, it has been thought small loss to the history of esthetics that his early treatise, *On the Fitting and the Beautiful,*[21] has perished. On the whole it can be claimed that this severely practical Augustinian temper was the typical temper of the philosophical Middle Ages. It said in effect: Life is earnest business; reflection should be committed to serious things; there is room neither in life nor in reflection for anything but the study of righteousness.

BEAUTY AS A NAME OF GOD.
The second ground given for the absence of esthetics in the Middle Ages was the confusion of beauty with a name of God. "That Beauty had no more to do with aesthetic Beauty than Plato's idea of moral Beauty aforetime," we are told.[22] The comparison is just. In the end medieval philosophy has about as much to do with esthetics as Plato's. But on the other hand that is no small amount. Initially it is true that the presence of a theory of beauty in the midst of Christian theology seems unlikely. The problems of creation and redemption are on the face of them far removed from those of artistic style; and works of art are particular entities formed from sensuous media, whereas God is Spirit and his Providence is universal. For the Christian philosopher, nothing was wholly and unconditionally real but God alone. God was the ultimate subject of every judgment. Matter, the sense-organs, the local habitation of beauty, and the apparatus of its first apprehension by man, therefore, were in the strict sense illusory. The mass of marble that must coöperate with the sculptor's preconception of a beautiful figure; the trumpet's blare and the lyre's vibration, gold and the resplendent color of pictures, though assigned a place among the orders of experienced phenomena, were allowed after all only a feeble and flickering mode of existence. For from the eternal way of estimating things, they were but vestiges and traces, carnal fictions, insubstantial shadows, farthest away of all things from the source of being. God, who created all things, was the standard by which amount of reality was measured, and

---

[21] *Confessions,* Bk. IV, Chs. XIV–XV, pp. 189, 191.
[22] Chambers, *op. cit.,* p. 116.

He is ineffable, imponderable, invisible. Quantity and authenticity of reality were, then, regarded as proportionate to quantity and authenticity of divinity. The paradox was accepted that the more sensuous, the less real; the more intelligible, good, and Deiform, the more real. Thus a doctrine hostile to simple perception and unfavorable to the appreciation of art took hold of men's minds.

The doctrine that reality is spiritual was connected by early Christian philosophers with an historic event, cardinal in their faith: the resurrection of Jesus. They believed that when Christ rose from the dead, he gathered up into that single act the universal conquest of body, and the meaning of things henceforth became spiritual. This extreme metaphysical idealism had varying fortunes in the history of creeds and the fixing of heresies. Its extreme application was the iconoclastic movement of the eighth and ninth centuries. The theory of this movement was that a spiritual religion is debased by the attempt to make it intelligible to the outward eye; that the presence of puppets and grinning figures in niches is essentially idolatry; and that those who have by the grace of God penetrated to the first and constitutive principles of things should always live in the ideal world.

Certainly in so far as utterances and movements like those just given are characteristic of medieval philosophy, esthetic theory might seem to be excluded from its pages. But a further search among the writings of the Churchmen complicates the matter. The recalcitrant human nature of the Fathers and their not infrequent acquaintance with classic literature and philosophy led them to find ingenious reasons for the defense of those arts and beauties which at other times their consciences compelled them to repudiate. These thinkers were in the center of a conflict, like men between the virtues and the vices, or the immortal soul between the angels and devils, in medieval picture and story. For example, St. Augustine did not rest with the simple assertion that poetry and painting are luxurious lying. By an involved dialectic he removed the sting of the abusive description, and found in poetic fiction a kind of truth. Falsehood he defined as dissembling resemblance: "the false is.that which pretends to be that which it is not; or tends to be that which it is not." Falsehood in general

AUGUSTINE: ART'S DECEPTION NOT REAL DECEPTION.

divides into (*a*) deceptions brought about by nature; and (*b*) deceptions brought about by living beings. The deceptions brought
about by living beings subdivide into (*a*) practical and deliberate
deceptions, and (*b*) deceptions from the motive of amusement.
Under this last head he placed poetry, comedy, wit, mimes.
Though in a sense false, and so subject to the condemnation of the
Church, these artistic fictions were then presented as relatively
innocent. But Augustine attributed to them not only agreeableness
and innocence, but also a paradoxical kind of honesty. Works of
art, he says, tend to be something which they yet cannot fully be. A
painted man cannot be the complete human being toward which
its nature seems to move, and comedies cannot be the persons in
action which they mimic, and which they try in one sense to
'realize.' But the will of the inventor of these fictions is bent on
a truth to which the deceptive show is a necessary instrument.
The will of the inventor makes the actor Roscius, one must admit,
a false Hecuba; but on the other hand, the inventor's will makes
of him a true tragic actor, and this was his primary intention.
From these considerations St. Augustine draws the inference that
a work of art is true just by its particular species of falsehood, and
that the artist cannot be true to himself and fulfill his purpose unless in a sense he is a maker of lies. He who is not a false Hector
cannot be a true tragic actor. Again, the image of a horse is not
true unless it is a false horse, and a man's reflection in a mirror must
be false man to be true image.[23] Thus is St. Augustine driven by
the force of moral resistance to reflect further on the nature of
artistic fiction. In another passage, he draws a clear distinction between the lie believed, such as the heresy of the Manicheans, and
the 'willing suspension of unbelief' in the reading of tales and
verses. "Medea flying, although I chanted sometimes, yet I maintained not the truth of; and though I heard it sung, I believed it
not: but these phantasies [the Manichean heresies] I thoroughly
believed." [24]

---

[23] *Soliloquies*, Bk. II. See K. Svoboda, *L'Esthétique de St. Augustin et ses
Sources*, Brno, 1933, pp. 50, 51. The entire treatment of St. Augustine is greatly
indebted to this scholarly study.

[24] *Confessions*, Bk. III, Ch. VI, Loeb ed., p. 119.

The same complex situation exists in regard to art's kinship with emotion. At times the sensuously moving properties of some of the arts were defended by the Churchmen. The cruel and lustful passions were naturally always condemned wherever found, in art or outside it. But the stirring of the passions was useful to the preachers of a militant doctrine by the same token that in other places it was harmful: for passion means seduction and potency. Thus eloquence was an art assiduously studied and practiced by the early Churchmen. The Christian teacher should have eloquence, St. Augustine taught, "to awe, to melt, to enliven, and to rouse." He should not be "sluggish and frigid and somnolent." [25] He must know how to "conciliate the hostile, to rouse the careless." [26] The artistic devices of rhetoric add drawing power to the sermon's true doctrine. Thus the good end purified the passionate medium, and esthetic elements such as rhetorical balance, contrast and metaphor, hyperbole and other figures of speech, were sheltered by the Church. St. Augustine even furnishes general justification of the place of charm in life, and said: "As we must often swallow wholesome bitters, so we must always avoid unwholesome sweets. But what is better than wholesome sweetness or sweet wholesomeness?" [27] Here morality does not drive out esthetic value: rather the two are treated as complementary goods.

Once more, the meaning of Beauty as Divine Name is not quite simple. It is true that the domination of theology forces the traditional feeling for beauty to speak a new language. It is always true that the challenge of a new authority forces problems into the light. For example, in so far as early Christianity interpreted matter and the body as evil and outside the Providence of God, the sensible and material properties of art were not tolerated. But the question was forced: Exactly what is this condemned matter? Is it a shadow? Has it a shape? Is it penetrable? When the Manicheans began to make of matter a substantial principle which they placed in darkness, or unordered motion, over against

---

[25] *Nicene . . . Fathers*, 1st Ser., V: II, *On Christian Doctrine*, trans. Shaw, Bk. IV, Ch. II, p. 575.

[26] *Ibid.*, Bk. IV, Ch. IV, p. 576.

[27] *Ibid.*, Bk. II, Ch. V, p. 577.

A History of Esthetics

light, the good and orderly, the contest with this heresy moved
Christians to welcome the material and sensuous phenomena of the
Universe once more into the fold of the Divinely governed. The
Manichean heretic made God the bare contour of his world, so
occupied was he with matter as independent evil substance.
Tertullian replied: Let matter receive greater honor—under the
form of Christ's cross![28] There is small wonder that a Father who
was taken with the beauty of roses, and even of "one flower of the
hedge-row, one shell of any sea . . . one feather of a moor-fowl"
should wish to find some theological justification,—even though
an austere one—for putting matter among the good things.[29] So
it became heresy to deny a place in God's kingdom to matter.
If the body is made a vessel separate from and contrary to the
soul, argued Cyrill of Jerusalem, then the desecration of the body
follows easily.[30] Far from being limited by an evil matter, the
inclusive nature of Divinity was asserted to reach even so far as
BUT MATTER somehow to redeem the bad will and the ugly object. But to in-
MUST NOT COME clude too much in 'divinity' is dangerous for Christian thought also.
TOO CLOSE TO If the exclusion of matter, ugliness, and evil from God's dominion
GOD. limits his power, and is a heresy, there is also the danger that an
all-embracing inclusiveness for God will obliterate the distinctive
characteristics of evil and ugliness. The problem then becomes
urgent to define precisely the meaning and relationship of these
doubtful elements. For esthetics the problem is: Under what
categories can the beauty of fine art and of nature be thought, so
as to keep them humble enough in relation to Divine Truth, and
yet distinctive enough for the expression of their characteristic
qualities?

THIS PROBLEM   Esthetics was neither crushed out in the Middle Ages by the
NEITHER CRUSHED Christian moral resistance nor confounded to its perdition by
OUT NOR CON- theology. It was not a simple case of opposition between medieval
FUSED. thought and esthetics, but of taking new distinctions, subtilizing
relationships, and extenuating values which seemed at first alien to
the new world-outlook. The apologists for art ingeniously 'spoiled

---

[28] K. Borinski, *op. cit.*, p. 71.
[29] Tertullian, Loeb ed. Introduction, p. xvi.
[30] K. Borinski, *op. cit.*, p. 70.

the Egyptians' for their own purposes, that is, converted to their own purposes the culture of Pagan antiquity, and so, to an extent, retained the classic arts under the protection of the church, though in strange garments. Vergil was saved because he seemed to have prophesied the coming of Christ, the Homeric characters and tales because they supplied a useful store of examples and symbols for the illustration of religious truth, Vitruvius because he taught men how to build the new churches. Plato, Aristotle, and Plotinus supplied the logical distinctions and a cosmology which could be sanctified by being put to holy uses. Cicero taught eloquence for the preachers.

But the Middle Ages not only borrowed from ancient art and thought for the defence of its new esthetics; they invented new philosophical tools. It goes without saying that there was great variety of thought in the Middle Ages on esthetic questions as on questions of theology. The old notion that intellects were at that time in a strait-jacket, and that artistic symbols were rigorously codified, has had to be relaxed and modified in the light of a larger number of varied facts. But the ideas here presented, first of all from St. Augustine, secondarily from St. Thomas, with addition and illumination from Dante, the Scholastic poet, and from Dionysius the Areopagite and the mystics, give the direction of the main current.

St. Augustine (354–430), following Cicero whose definition had become a platitude, defined beauty as "proportion of the parts, together with a certain agreeableness of color." [31] Other medieval definitions vary only slightly the way of conceiving the formal harmony. Albertus Magnus defined beauty as "elegant commensurability"; Bonaventura, as "numerable equality"; [32] St. Thomas, as involving the three conditions of integrity, proportion, and brightness. [33] Wherever the medieval philosophers found these qualities and relations, there they found their beauty, whether in the whole spectacle of the Universe, in man, in buildings, or in songs;

---

[31] *Nicene . . . Fathers*, 1st Ser., V: II; *City of God*, Bk. XXII, Ch. XIX, p. 497.
[32] *Works*, Quaracchi ed., I, 544.
[33] *Summa Theologica*, Part I, Question 39, art. 8, trans. Dominican Fathers, 2d ed., London, 1921, p. 147.

in a word, whether in objects natural or artificial, or in the total scheme of things. Beauty did not imply for them any special connection with the fine arts. It implied abstractly a pleasing relationship among terms, and the terms could be spiritual or material, moral or physical, artistic or natural, limited or vast. To test medieval sensitivity to beauty by the attitude toward the arts is to cut the cord between esthetics and beauty. For the arts became disciplines, even 'astringents' in the Middle Ages, and pleasure was only to a limited degree connected with artistic enjoyment.

WORLD'S HAR-
MONY SIGN OF
DIVINE ORIGIN.

Though the conception of beauty as harmony came in principle from Plato and Aristotle—for St. Thomas' formulation simply summarizes the qualities that Aristotle specifies as characterizing a good tragedy or statue, and the common formula which St. Augustine repeats *verbatim* from Cicero was new in nothing but the set form of the phrase—the definition was fertilized by union with medieval philosophy. In this way it won a new accent and rose to fresh applications. The harmony that pleases human beings in nature and in artificial objects is not really, so it was said, an attribute of these things as independent entities, but a reflection into them of their divine origin. God, as the Creator of all, has set his seal upon his works. Now the Creator is one. His simplicity and unity are absolute. But when God seals his works, he has to give them, or they strive to show, the best possible imitation of this oneness. The creature world is everywhere multiple and divisible. In emulating the Oneness of God, it achieves unity in variety, or harmony. The reason, then, that harmony, concinnity, and order in physical objects are beautiful, is that harmony is the highest degree of God-like Oneness that the secular world can achieve. The universe, a defective image of God, imitates in its variety and plurality God's simplicity and simple perfection.

AUGUSTINE'S 'NEO-
PYTHAGOREANISM.'

The relation of the Divine One to the earthly Many, which thus gives birth to the harmony of beauty, is taken sometimes in an abstract mathematical sense, and sometimes more freely. The dialogue of Plato which most influenced Christian medieval thought was the *Timaeus*, which describes the creation of the world out of geometrical seeds: isosceles and scalene right-angled triangles. It also explains earthly and stellar motions by an elaborate mathematical doctrine. The dominance of this Dialogue in later thought tended to produce a belief in an almost magical efficacy of number. In St. Augustine the influence appears in his making number the essence of things—in a kind of Christian Pythagoreanism. Number and abstract formal arrangement are the principles that make the world go well when they are baptized, so to speak, in the evangelical font, and they turn the world finally into a congenial music for the soul. Number makes the world what it is, and each object the specific entity that is it; it furnishes a way of human salvation and of intellectual understanding. Above the spirit of the artist is Number Eternal in Wisdom.[34] The essence of both beauty and existence is in number.[35] The esthetic principle of beauty as formal harmony becomes thus also the principle of cosmology, practical religion, and human apprehension.

By setting numbers to work God created the world out of nothing. St. Augustine's description of the way the process developed, beginning with the Primordial One, sounds like an arithmetical incantation: "Number begins with one. It is beautiful by equality and resemblance, it is joined by order . . . . [Everything was formed] from the beginning by means [therefore] of a form which is equal to it and like, thanks to the richness of this beauty by which, through the dearest love, are united the One and the One, proceeding from the One." [36] This formal principle combining unity, equality, resemblance, and order, is transmitted from the supreme beauty by fixed stages down the scale of existence. The rational number of the angels transmitted the divine law to earth. On earth the existence of the human body followed from its number-harmony and from imitating the stars and angels. The human body has among its parts a concord without which it could not exist, created by Him who has the key to that concord.[37] The members of animals, to which the creative impulse next descends, possess an obvious numerical equality, being balanced on the two sides of the body. Plants grow by the time-rhythms proper to their

[34] *De Libro Arbitrio*, Bk. II; see Svoboda, *op. cit.*, p. 94.
[35] *De Ordine*, Bk. II; see Svoboda, p. 28.
[36] *De Musica*, Bk. VI, 56; see Svoboda, pp. 86, 87.
[37] See also *City of God*, Bk. XXII, Ch. 27.

seeds. The earth, lowliest among the elements, is neatly numbered, balanced, and ordered. For it makes a wonderful progress from the number one to the number four: from the initial point to length, to breadth, to height. In respect to the three dimensions, length, breadth, and height, earth has equality; in respect to the four quantities, it has proportion; for the length is to the point as the breadth is to the length and as the height is to the breadth. Also the spherical form of the earth witnesses to its perfect Source in the Father of Forms. The water, like the earth, tends toward unity, and is even more beautiful because the parts of water are more alike, and the quantity of resemblance is therefore greater. Yet more beautiful are the air and the firmament, for similar formal reasons.[38]

NUMBER AS PRIN-
CIPLE OF SPIRIT-
UAL DEVELOP-
MENT.
St. Augustine also uses number-harmony to explain the law of the soul's itinerary to God. How, he inquires, is the human soul which longs to rest in contemplation of the Divine Beauty, to travel back to the Single Spirit from which it has been separated by birth in the body? For the supreme good is *Monas*, or the spirit deprived of the division incident to sex and discord, Augustine declared; and vice is *Dyas*, indefeasible Two-ness, or the failure to submit to the power of the One. The return can be accomplished by grasping at the formal essence of things seen and heard until Form itself, that is, pure spirituality, at last arrives. The spiritual Reason, best part and guide of the soul, seeks the non-sensuous realm as alone congenial to it. Reason finds the congenial Essences by extracting progressively the more and more abstract measurable aspects of objects until united with Measure Clear and Bare. "The reason, turning to the domain of sight, that is, to the earth and sky, noticed that in the world it is beauty that pleases the sight; in beauty, figures; in figures, measures; in measures, numbers." She discovers that all the arts and sciences are ordained by number, that she, reason, is herself the number by which all things are reckoned, or rather that number is where she desires to go.[39] When the soul shall have been ordered by the arts, when it shall have made itself harmonious and beautiful, then only shall it dare to contemplate God. Then it will discover the beauty by the

---

[38] *De Musica*, Bk. VI; see Svoboda, *op. cit.*, pp. 87, 88.
[39] *De Ordine*, Bk. II; see Svoboda, *op. cit.*, pp. 27, 28.

imitation of which all things are beautiful and in comparison with which all things are ugly.[40] Thus St. Augustine teaches that to spiritualize oneself is to formalize oneself. The way to salvation and truth leads to order and number. And order and number are defining traits of beauty.

The formal principle of beauty as the many-in-one determines for St. Augustine the most beautiful geometrical figure. He says an equilateral triangle is more beautiful than a scalene, because the scalene contains less equality. But the triangle in general equality connects sides and angles, while in the square, equality connects identities: that is sides with sides, and angles with angles. So the square generally possesses more equality than the triangle and is to be preferred from the esthetic standpoint. But even a square is tainted with slight irregularity, for the sides differ from the angles, and the lines joining the center to the angles are not equal to the lines joining the center to the middle of the sides. Hence the circle, which has the greatest measure of equality, surpasses in beauty the other figures.[41]

MATHEMATICS AS ESTHETIC RULE.

In St. Augustine's references to the esthetic relations of architectural elements, the geometrical spirit seems equally to reign. One feels the absence in him of such delicacy of feeling and closeness to the phenomenon of beauty as one finds in Cicero's sudden appreciation of the dignity of his paved portico and colonnade, or in his fastidiousness about the stuccoing of a ceiling. It almost seems that, for St. Augustine, capacity to count and measure equips one to be a connoisseur of buildings. Witness his theory of windows, doors, and arches: "One is shocked at any unnecessary inequality in the parts of fabricated things. One is not content, for instance, if a house has one door on the side and another almost in the middle but not quite. On the contrary, one is satisfied if there is a window in the middle of a wall and a window at each side of it at the same distance from the middle." This, he says, is admirable *ratio*—reasonableness—in architecture.[42] In another passage, he imagines an architect explaining the agreeableness of the perfect

---

[40] *Loc. cit.*
[41] *De Quantitate Animae;* see Svoboda, *op. cit.*, pp. 59, 60.
[42] *De Ordine*, Bk. II; see Svoboda, *op. cit.*, p. 25.

balance of equal arches thus: "It pleases because it is beautiful, and it is beautiful because the parts are like and are brought by a certain bond to a single harmony." [43]

BUT FEELING NOT ABSENT.

In his theories of eloquence and of music, St. Augustine at times expresses his feeling for the sensuous exterior of the esthetic phenomenon, and so relaxes his use of the mathematical standard. This was doubtless partly the result of greater first-hand experience on his part. In his young manhood he was himself a teacher of rhetoric, a professional interpreter of poetry, and he was by temperament an artist in words. He often consulted immediate intuition in the choice of lovely words and rhythms. The word 'Artaxerxes' wounds the ear, he says; the word 'Euryalus' soothes it. [44] He uses the same test of the sense of hearing for the selection of one line of verse in preference to another. He even speaks of the advantages in some cases of the criterion of immediate experience. "Men of quick intellect and glowing temperament find it easier to become eloquent by reading and listening to eloquent speakers than by following rules." [45]

Yet this concession to the rôle of feeling and perception in esthetic experience on the part of Augustine, is, even in the case of the arts of sound, much overbalanced in his theory by mathematical demonstrations of types of rhythm and their relative value. Music, whether vocal or instrumental, he defines as the science of good modulation. Rational motions, those which can be expressed in terms of the simplest mathematical relationships, he judges preferable to irrational ones. A one-to-one relationship he holds best of all. But 'connumerable' relationships, those in which the smaller of two numbers divides into the larger without remainder, as $2 : 4$, and those with a common divisor, he regards as excellent. [46] In the end the intoxicated manipulation of arithmetical relations drowns the appeal to experience, as in the following demonstration that the first four numbers constitute the most beautiful musical progressions. The proportion $1 : 2 :: 2 : 3$ includes the first number

---

[43] *De Vera Religione;* Svoboda, *op. cit.,* p. 107.

[44] *De Dialectica;* Svoboda, *op. cit.,* p. 57.

[45] *Nicene . . . Fathers,* 1st Ser., Vol. II; *On Christian Doctrine,* Bk. IV, Ch. 3.

[46] *De Musica;* Svoboda, *op. cit.,* p. 67.

of all, the first number that is an organic whole having beginning, middle, and end—3—and the first number that is an arithmetical square—4 (in the sense that four terms are needed for its expression). And the sum of the first four numbers is 10, the basis of the whole system of enumeration.[47] Thus at times the appeal to number is more fantastic than rational. Mathematical relationship may illustrate not the principle of esthetic order but the vagaries of irrational symbolism, as when a baptismal font is made octagonal to signify the eight parts of a regenerated man: four sides for the four humors of the body; three sides for the three spiritual parts: soul, heart, and mind; and one side for the part newly born through Christ. The number seven, again, sometimes becomes less a part of an ideal system of order than a magic word: there are seven ages, seven virtues, seven capital sins, seven requests in the Pater Noster, seven planets, seven tones in the scale.

But the many illustrations of the exaggeration and distortion of the central principle of harmony and symmetry do not invalidate the position of that principle itself. What answers in the end to the esthetic ideal of elegance and order is not the extreme application of it by means of number-mysticism, but the symmetrical patterns projected by poets and philosophers now on to nature as a whole and now on to the miniature reflections of cosmic harmony in natural bodies and artificial products. The world becomes God's poem.[48] Or God becomes an architect who is not dependent on materials outside himself, as an earthly architect is. Or God may become a sculptor: "If a work of Phidias proclaims itself through harmony and right proportions without any signature, how much more true is this of the world as the masterpiece of the highest of sculptors!" [49] The whole universe, celestial and terrestrial, becomes stylized as a double hierarchy. According to Dionysius the Areopagite everything in heaven and earth was balanced and harmoniously graduated. The 'perfections, orders, and degrees' of heaven were the seraphim, cherubim, thrones,

HARMONY AND SYMMETRY DOMINATE NUMBER.

---

[47] *Ibid.*, p. 70.
[48] *Nicene . . . Fathers*, 1st Ser., Vol. II; *City of God*, Bk. XI, Ch. 18, p. 215.
[49] Athanasius, *Oratio contra gentes*, Ch. 35; Migne, *Greek Fathers*, 25, 69. Cited by Borinski, *op. cit.*, p. 69.

dominions, virtues, powers, principalities, archangels, and angels. Without break the ladder descends through the classes of existence on earth.[50] The Franciscan poetry reflects the scheme: Brother John of Verna "was one night so lifted up and rapt in God that he beheld in Him, the Creator, all created things in heaven and on earth, and all their perfections and degrees and their several orders. And then he perceived clearly how every created thing was related to its Creator . . . "[51] It is the basis of Dante's *Divine Comedy:*

> All things, whate'er they be, an order have
> Among themselves; and form this order is,
> Which makes the Universe resemble God.[52]

The same double hierarchy forms the basis of the decoration in ceilings and vaults, as in the Baptistery at Florence and the Brizi Chapel at Orvieto.

The gracious, partitioned formality of the mystic universe has its counterpart in the formality of medieval poetry, music, and architecture. In Dante's *Divine Comedy* there are three parts, thirty-four canticles in the Inferno and thirty-three in each of the other two parts, and nine circles in Hell, nine levels in Purgatory, and ten Heavens in Paradise. The metrical hymn was added by St. Ambrose (340–397) to the psalms and canticles which had before him composed the entire musical service of the Church; so that the element of measure and beat came to rank as an ordering principle along with melody. The schema of the medieval cathedral façade was a persistent if not an absolute uniformity: orientation to the west; a tympanum with Christ in Judgment and the blessed on one side balancing the damned on the other; twelve apostles matching twelve prophets, and the four evangelists matching the four major prophets. Though there is abundance of variety and spontaneity in medieval productions, the idea of symmetry and balance dominates all. The medieval mind liked to find correspondences and parallels, harmonies, chords rich and slight, that

---

[50] *The Celestial Hierarchy; The Ecclesiastical Hierarchy.*
[51] *The Little Flowers of St. Francis,* LII, trans. T. Okey.
[52] *Paradiso,* I, 104.

made of the world at large, of natural bodies, and of the work of man's hands, an imitation of Divine Unity. St. Augustine recommended for particular study the marvels of proportion and relationship in the human body—and so out of the presuppositions of his religious mysticism forecast that which would actually be fulfilled by the naturalistic interests of Leonardo and Michelangelo.[53] But his mind was not yet set on harmonies in the natural world as effects of natural causes; rather the accords which he saw everywhere reflected a mystical source. The three principles—measure, number, and weight, or as sometimes stated, mode, form, and order, —at the basis both of existence and of beauty, answer to the three persons of the Holy Trinity.[54] The perfectly drawn circle, iambi and octaves, balanced statues and balanced windows, all mimicked for him the form of God, the most beautiful of all forms.[55]

Augustine's general argument, as so far represented, is then that the universe proceeds by order, for God loves order and is the author of it. All things are created according to measure and are therefore in harmony in the One. How can such a theory account for the patent facts of ugliness? Augustine is prepared for this objection to his vision of cosmic beauty. There is no absolute ugliness, he says. But there are objects which, relatively to others which are more completely organized and symmetrical, lack form. Ugliness is only comparative deformity. But Augustine says the mutual fitness and harmony of things cannot be perceived by souls which are not attuned to it. Rightly attuned souls will (*a*) look at all things in their contexts; (*b*) patiently discover the ingenuity of adjustment of parts in creatures which at first glance seem repulsive; and (*c*) appreciate the rôle played by contrast and gradation in the manifestation of harmony. (*a*) Nothing can bear the test of an isolating examination, for things were made to be seen in combination and are only apprehended for what they are when seen in their natural setting. For example, sin, when punished, becomes part of the beauty of justice. Augustine compares the spectators who, because they are disagreeably impressed by a

UGLINESS A FAIL-URE OF ESTHETIC RESPONSE.

---

[53] Borinski, *op. cit.*, pp. 59, 60.
[54] *Nicene . . . Fathers*, 1st Ser., Vol. III, p. 154; Bk. XI, Ch. XI.
[55] *De Ordine*, I, 18; II, 2, 11, 21f.

single object, complain that the whole universe is defective, to the man who looks at one stone in a mosaic and, instead of seeing the part it plays in the whole pattern, blames the artist for poor workmanship. He enforces his point by other comparisons. "It seems to us that many things in the Universe are confused, but we should not comprehend the beauty of a house if we were placed in the corner like a statue. In the same way, a soldier does not understand the order of an army, and in a poem a syllable endowed with life and feeling would not understand the beauty of the entire poem, a beauty which it itself helped to create." (*b*) Augustine seeks to sustain his argument for the esthetic perfection of the world by calling attention to the subtle contrivances revealed in the bodies of such tiny and ignoble creatures as the flea. (*c*) But his most important and expanded argument is based on the emphasis given to harmony by contrast. Just as in a speech antitheses are pleasing, and a cock-fight is diverting, so the beauty of things results from distinction and variety. Poets love to use solecisms and barbarisms to 'season' their poetry. The consonance of sweet music is made sweeter by the agreement of different voices, and a good play needs clowns and villains to make the heroes show their quality.[56] Already Plotinus had said: "Take away the low characters and the power of the drama is gone; they are part and parcel of it." Thus Augustine locates ugliness for the most part in the untrained eye of the beholder and not in the nature of things. In so far as ugliness is objective for him, it means a lesser degree of beauty.

SECRET ACCORD BE-
TWEEN SUBJECT
AND OBJECT.
 The proper proportions which constitute beauty in the object must be matched by a parallel proportionateness in the subject, if the experience of beauty is to be consummated. Right ratio must connect the spectator of beauty with the spectacle, as well as the parts of the things seen among themselves. For correspondence between stimulus and response makes a sensation welcome to the sentient observer. In his earliest treatise, *On the Fitting and the Beautiful*, Augustine had asked himself why we are drawn to beauty, why beauty and love, as Plato had already said in his *Symposium*, are correlative terms. The gracious aspect which attracts us turns

---

[56] *De Ordine*; Svoboda, *op. cit.*, pp. 20, 21.

out upon examination to be the wholeness or unity of what is seen or heard. The soul loves to receive sensations which agree with it and rejects sensations unsuitable and harmful. The drawing together of sense and object is due to a secret accord or mutual adaptation of the two terms to each other. Now the senses, in so far as they are ordered by their mistress, reason, are wholes and adapted to wholes. Therefore the senses of sight and hearing which furnish us experience in more rational and integral form than the lower senses are distinguished by Augustine as the 'higher,' 'esthetic' senses. One can touch and taste things only partially; but mostly in sight, and next in hearing, one grasps what is present in its total frame and meaning. We speak of *sensibilia* of taste, touch, smell as reasonable only with reference to their utility,—*e.g.* a reasonable medicine. Such experiences have no intrinsic reasonableness. The pleasures of sight and hearing are also in part the pleasures of that right ratio—that golden mean between extremes—which makes the stimulus fit the organ in quantity or degree, as well as in quality or kind. For instance, one avoids excessive obscurity and excessive brilliance, and sounds that are either too strong or too weak.[57] That accord with the perceiving which is conditioned by 'oneness' in the stimulus is facilitated by symmetry in the thing seen, and by rhythm in the thing heard. For there is a certain parity that comes through sensible rhythms in spoken or sung verse, and an equipoise is felt in the contemplation of a balanced façade. Reason shines through sense in the agreement of parts, by consonance, by symmetry in a building, by measures in poetry and music. Augustine calls the esthetic form of visual objects 'beauty' and of auditory objects 'suavity.' [58]

In its general outlines St. Thomas's theory of beauty is very close to that of St. Augustine. It has been suggested that St. Thomas is to St. Augustine as Aristotle is to Plato. The implication is that both in Greece and the Middle Ages the later thinker dealt with goodness and beauty for man, and not with beauty and goodness in the abstract, and that the later thinkers were more lenient toward

AQUINAS ECHOES AUGUSTINE.

---

[57] *De Ordine*, II, 30–33, see Svoboda, *op. cit.*, pp. 25, 92; *De libero arbitrio*, II, 16–19, see Svoboda, *op. cit.*, p. 92.

[58] *De Ordine*, *loc. cit.*; see Svoboda, *op. cit.*, pp. 25, 92.

the human hunger for recreation and the place of art as food for the hunger.[59] It is true that St. Augustine became more and more ascetic as he grew older. But just as Aristotle, with all his more constructive and analytical bent, hardly put forward a single esthetic notion which was not already present in a Platonic conversation, so the more elaborate system and tolerant attitude of St. Thomas was founded on concepts and theories which St. Augustine either early or late had set down. Beauty, said St. Thomas, is that which, having been seen, pleases (*quod visum placet*).[60] He relates the pleasing to the organ of sight by means of fit proportion. The identification of beauty with form, which is St. Augustine's principal esthetic thesis, follows at once. Beauty feeds the sense with something orderly, and only the orderly senses, sight and hearing, can assimilate to themselves order and measure. Beauty is different from goodness in that for the esthetic experience contemplation is enough; for the practical utilities including the good, appetite must be satisfied. Referring to Aristotle's classification of kinds of causes, St. Thomas says that beauty is really a formal cause.[61] Not only St. Augustine and St. Thomas, the two greatest philosophers the Christian church produced in the Middle Ages, but in their train all the other teachers and preachers, put form first in explaining beauty.[62]

St. Thomas suggests that the act of knowing is made easier by the presence of the order that beauty is. St. Augustine suggests that the act of making is made easier by the rhythmic movement that characterizes the artist at work. For artists have numbers as guiding principles in their labor. They manipulate hands and tools in the light of the numbers they carry in their souls. Their inner reason keeps a reckoning of the celestial numbers and this is their criterion. All their members rise and fall in figures, that is, rhythmically. The dance comes into being when movement has

---

[59] Cf. Mortimer J. Adler, *Art and Prudence*, Longmans, Green, 1937, p. 80: "We shall find in the writings of St. Thomas the rift which can occur in Christianity because of the difference between Plato and Aristotle." The whole book is a valuable exposition of Thomistic esthetics.

[60] *Summa Theologica*, II, xxvii, i.

[61] *Ibid.*, I, v, iv.

[62] See, for example, St. Francis' canticle: *Our Lord Christ*.

no other end but pleasure. But all artists whether they work in the spatial or temporal arts aim at 'good form' in both execution and product. "Above the spirit of the artist is number eternal, in Wisdom." [63] Many musicians are instinctively rhythmical in their movements and singing. Like the nightingale, they follow the laws of number through bodily imitation and habit, not through clear mathematical understanding.

Form then remains the first note of beauty, and its dominance is not materially threatened by the existence of limited areas of deformity. There issues from the same divine source and coöperates —in the end coalesces—with the energy of form a second esthetic principle: light or splendor. St. Augustine speaks of beauty as the splendor of order, or of truth; Albertus Magnus defines it as the splendor of form shining on the proportioned parts of matter; [64] and St. Thomas calls effulgence the third property of beauty after integrity and due proportion or consonance. [65] The brilliancy of the beautiful as St. Thomas intends it means "the shining forth of the *form* of a thing, either of a work of art or nature . . . in such a manner that it is presented to the mind with all the fullness and richness of its perfection and order." Words meaning light—*claritas, splendor, resplendentia, fulgor, lux, lumen, illumino, lucidus, illustro*—are almost as common in medieval theological writing as words meaning form.

The simplest interpretation of beauty as splendor is the pleasantness of bright color or lustre. And this obvious meaning is to the very end part of the philosophical meaning. St. Thomas himself at times interprets it so: "Effulgence: so bright colored objects are said to be beautiful." [66] And 'sweetness of color' was commonly added to 'congruence of parts' in the conventional definition of beauty. It is easy to think of the gold and lapis blue in the mosaics and illuminations of manuscripts as concrete examples of this esthetic splendor, as one thinks of the logic of cathedrals and the structure of canticles as illustrating the meaning of esthetic form.

SHINING FORM; SHAPED EFFULGENCE.

---

[63] *De libero arbitrio*, II, see Svoboda, *op. cit.*, pp. 93, 94.
[64] *Opus de Pulchro et Bono*.
[65] *Summa Theologica*.
[66] *Ibid.*, 1, quest. 39, answer 8.

But there is more behind. The lure of bright color and the glitter of gold are only the surface symbols of the full force of splendor. To realize the full force one must know that within and behind sensuous light the mystics saw a light not located, more brilliant than the sun, and within this light another light, 'The Living Light Itself,' the sight of which made sadness and pain vanish.[67] One must be aware also that the conception of God as this Living Light itself came to Augustine and Bonaventura, Erigena and St. Francis, laden with a complex religious and philosophical history. The idea of God as Light goes back to the Semetic *Bel*, the Egyptian *Ra*, and the Iranian *Ahura Mazda*, who were partly the sun and stars and partly the beneficent functions of light, the giving of life and knowledge, 'the universal largesse of the sun.' In Plato the sun is compared to the supreme Idea of the Good. As the sun is the Father of Generation and Visibility in the world of Becoming, so the Idea of the Good is the Source of Being and Truth in the intelligible kingdom. St. Augustine felt the influence of both the Iranian strain which identified physical light immediately with the source of being and goodness, and also the Platonic strain, especially as it came to him through Plotinus, in which a clear distinction was made between spiritual and physical light. Instead of the Plotinian theory of concentric circles of being with a fountain of light at the center and darkness at the outer rim, St. Augustine thought of the creation of the world as proceeding through the power of the Trinity, but in both cases the Source overflows with light.

In the *Celestial Hierarchy* by the Pseudo-Dionysius there is a notable passage in which the author inquires why the writers of the Holy Scriptures preferred the description of fire for holy things beyond any other comparison. He instances the wheels of fire and living creatures of fire in Ezekiel, and rivers of fire and thrones of fire. He then examines 'sensible fire' to learn why it should be the favorite type of Divinity. Fire, he says, is in everything and can pass through everything without losing its own character. By fire being in all things is meant presumably that everything has the

---

[67] St. Hildegarde; quoted in Charles Singer, *Studies in the History and Method of Science*, Oxford, 1917, p. 55.

capacity to be illuminated and burned. Yet this fiery capacity is normally hidden. So God is everywhere, but He is invisible. Then follows a lyrical celebration of the energy and majesty of fire, the upshot of which seems to be that, like God, fire can conquer all other things, but is itself above all influence or need.[68] By the more orthodox Church writers the first two persons of the Trinity were often conceived of as two brightnesses and opposing, but coeval parents, or two lights in one as impossible of separation as the sun and its radiance. If, by an impossible act, one could separate the Son from the Father, one would identify the Splendor of the Trinity with the Second Person. For the Second Person is Divinity declaring itself, streaming forth, and disposing and allotting place and rank. Christ is the necessary forth-flashing of the Godhead, the verb in the Celestial grammar; and in this procession of the Unity out of itself both its radiancy and its formative action appear. "I am that supreme and fiery force that sends forth all the sparks of life. Death hath no part in me, yet do I allot it, wherefore I am girt about with wisdom as with wings. I am that living and fiery essence of the divine substance that glows in the beauty of the fields. I shine in the water, I burn in the sun and the moon and the stars," [69] said St. Hildegarde. Dante gathered up the conception of the Trinity as a three-fold light at the climax of the *Paradiso* in an immortal image. The Lofty Light appeared to him under the form of three rings

> of three fold color and of one content
> and one, as Rainbow is by Rainbow, seemed
> reflected by the other, while the third
> like a Fire breathed equally from both.[70]

The Triune Creator of the world, conceived as light, does not merely dazzle and intoxicate his creatures. But he does do that. St. Augustine confesses that his weak and throbbing sense was beaten back by the radiance of God. But God as light determines the metaphysical place and rank of classes of beings, and reveals

---

[68] Ch. XV, Sec. II; Migne: Series Graeca, Tom. 3, Cols. 328–29.
[69] Singer, *op. cit.*, p. 33.
[70] *Paradiso*, XXXIII, 116–21 (trans. Langdon).

truth. Splendor is not a merely sensuous efflux, but a formative and informative energy. *Forma est lumen purum.*[71] Light and form are identified because light is the finest and highest of substances, the most excellent of elements, as form is the end to which any given thing aspires. So as in the system of forms the one rises above the other, each lower kind striving to take its mold and nature from that next above, until God crowns all, the Form of Forms; so earth, water, air, fire constitute a hierarchy that builds upward toward pure spiritual essence in the Empyrean. In any one of the elements—for example, in water—the upper brighter layers are superior in value, for the fierier, brighter, and lighter a thing, the nobler it is. The angels in the Christian scheme are the successors of the stars in earlier belief; both alike are celestial fires and pure intelligences, and both are carriers forth of divine effulgence, only less in glory than the Intelligible Light of the Divine Word itself.

CLARITY.   A third esthetic function, which again unites with a function of esthetic *form*, is performed by medieval Splendor. First we saw that light charms the senses; then, that, as the radiant energy of the Creator, it shapes, orders, and models the universe of beings. But more than this, light makes knowing easy beyond even what correspondence can yield. The truth of our knowledge, Augustine says, depends on illumination by the Sun of our Soul. The clarity of the beautiful is "a property of things in virtue of which the objective elements of their beauty—order, harmony, proportion—manifest themselves with clearness and arouse in the intelligence a facile and plenary contemplation." [72] The pleasures of cognition flow not only from the relations of parts within the object, but from luminousness. By its clarity the nature of an object goes out as it were to meet the knower half-way, and clothes the whole experience with a superadded excellence, which, upon being seen, pleases. When St. Thomas defines beauty he seems to emphasize

---

[71] The whole topic of the philosophical meaning of light is elaborated· in C. Baeumker, "Witelo, Ein Philosoph und Naturforscher des XIIIten Jahrhunderts," *Vorträge zur Geschichte der Philosophie des Mittelalters*, Münster, 1908, Bd. III, Heft 2, p. 351.

[72] Maurice de Wulf, *Philosophy and Civilization in the Middle Ages*, Princeton, 1922, p. 28.

the immediacy of its apprehension. There is no waiting for analysis, no labor of proof. Sight is enough. "Clarity," it has been well said, "is for beauty what evidence is for truth." [73] The light of beauty might be called the radio-activity of the element of form, for corresponding form in the object and subject of knowledge we have already seen to be the condition of esthetic cognition. But "clarity," says Duns Scotus, "is a certain refulgence," and adds, "over and above light and color, self manifestation. So we speak of clear light or clear truth or clear intellection, that is, manifest light, truth, or intellection, and as manifest, so perfect." [74]

Light as the speeder and helper of cognition is not merely a spiritual agency. It is the subtlest of material elements, fire. A physical theory of pleasant cognition supports the metaphysical theory of the refulgence of manifest truth. Basil had early said that the reason we admire the simple beauty of the sun, or gold, or the evening star, is that these things are adapted to our sight. For our eyes are informed with a luminous matter, a fire, that on the principle of like to like, makes kind meeting with the fires in nature. The eyes being the noblest of the sense-organs, and fire being the purest and finest of the material constituents of the universe, the pleasure of beholding shining things is simply demonstrated. But light or fire is also the medium on which rational relationships easily glide past the portals of the senses to the reason within. As Christ was called both the Light of the world and the Logos ruling the world, so any transaction resting on the notion of light rests also at one level further down upon the idea of reasonable relationship.

MATERIAL ASPECT OF LIGHT.

The importance and the complexity of the medieval conception of light can be seen from an example. In explaining the nature of the popular speech which he wishes to make the literary language of Italy, Dante names four attributes of an ideal vulgar tongue. [75] The first attribute he names is illustriousness. And having laid the mark down as the first requirement, he proceeds to explain what the epithet 'illustrious' means. He says that to be illustrious means

---

[73] *Ibid.*, p. 29.
[74] Liber IV, *Sententiae*.
[75] *De Vulgari Eloquentia*, I, XVII.

to shine forth illuminating and illuminated. He then says that men are illustrious when being set in high places they illuminate others by their justice and clarity. Or having been made illustrious by good discipline, they shine forth by conferring similar good discipline on others. He then applies his ideas to the vulgar tongue, and shows how, being illuminated itself through a process of purification and through its own eminence, it sheds honor and glory on those who use it. The "sweetness of its glory," he says, makes him put behind him even the bitterness of his own exile. The splendor of a language then implies for Dante eminence and good form; then the outgoing of these virtues on others in sweetness, honor, and glory.

THE LADDER OF
BEAUTY.

Form and light, blending in the idea of actively shaping form, are the two chief marks of beauty for medieval thinkers. Wherever these marks are set, there beauty appears. But the energy of their presence varies greatly; and although an illustrious language or a balanced façade is esthetically pleasing, beauty appears in its purity nearer its source. "The sky is beautiful. But invisible creation is more beautiful still." Above the beauty of buildings and speech, waves and hilltops, is incorporeal beauty, accessible only to the intellectual part of man. God is the "unique and unfalsified Beauty." [76] If one wishes to be acquainted with beauty in its clearest manifestation, one abandons the charms of nature and art for the Eternal Wisdom. How then is one to pass from thin, imperfect beauty to perfect, undoubted beauty? By climbing up the ladder of the degrees of beauty, which raises one from mere sense-impressions finally to reasons and divine blessedness. Augustine names the rounds of the ladder in different ways, but the significance of the different stages lies on the surface. They are called: bodily animation, sense, art, virtue, tranquillity, the entrance, observation. Or again they are named thus: of the body, through the body, about the body, toward the soul, in the soul, toward God, with God. Still differently expressed they become: what·is beautiful from another part, through another thing, about another thing, near the beautiful, in the beautiful, toward beauty, and with

---

[76] *Nicene . . . Fathers*, 1st Ser., Vol. I, p. 542; St. Augustine, *Soliloquies*, Bk. I, Sec. 14.

beauty.[77] In every case the lowest round means the beauty of an almost unformed, external physical stimulus; the progression carries the spectator toward beauties more unified, moral, and inward, toward the consummation in which beauty means union with God's unity and assimilation with his Form.

Thus the dividing line between esthetics and religion seems to be wiped out, and the judgment of the art critics who say there is no esthetics in the Middle Ages appears once more to be justified. But this could be a true judgment only if the relation between the lowest rung of the ladder and the top were one of exclusion. Not only is it not true that our obligation to climb toward the vision of God—in at least a part of medieval thought—excludes our enjoyment of the sensuous beginnings, but a theory grows up binding the extremes of highest and lowest beauty together. Christian theology joined its strength to the already existing popular tendency toward symbolism, and thus made rational and defensible an artistic habit that was one of the most striking and characteristic features of poetry and architecture in the Middle Ages. Theology so adapted its austerity toward what is "of the body, through the body, and about the body" as to prove a relationship of positive attraction instead of negative repulsion between "in the body" and "in the soul, toward God, and with God." The problem is to understand the various elements in this mitigation of asceticism to positive employment of sense media.

ESTHETICS AND RELIGION.

The first element is the Christian doctrine of God's creation. What God made, he caused to be like himself. However little we may today assert a necessary analogy between effect and cause, we can understand the medieval notion of the resemblance between created and Creator by certain obvious facts. An animal or plant gives birth to an animal or plant of the same species, fire breeds fire, and movement, movement.[78] For the medieval mind, created things were images or intimations of God; and therefore if God is beautiful, all his works are somehow beautiful. But the Christian doctrine of creation is nicely balanced between the pantheistic absorption of things into divinity by the recognition of God-likeness everywhere

LIKENESS AND DIFFERENCE OF CREATOR AND CREATED.

---

[77] *De Quantitate Animae*, 70–9. Svoboda, *op. cit.*, p. 63.
[78] E. Gilson, *The Spirit of Medieval Philosophy*, London, 1936, p. 95.

and the theory of God's sublime aloofness and distinction from all that is finite. Things are like Him, and therefore must be beautiful; but they have capacity only to be, in a strictly limited degree, reflections of Him. Thus we saw that, while all things would like to be Ones in imitation of the absolute Unity of God, they can only succeed in being harmonies, because they are made up of parts and are excluded from that seamless indivisibility which can characterize God. In a similar way, things cannot be true mirrors of God, but will be sometimes only faint 'shadows' of Him, because they are too much weighted with the grossness of matter to be clear, distinct reflectors. A form often does not harmonize with the intention of an art because the material element is deaf in responding.[79] Created beauty is thus often referred to as the beauty of the image or the shadow or the intimation. These terms aim at defining that middle region occupied by phenomenal forms between full resemblance and full opposition.

THE CREATED AS
SHELL OF TRUTH.
The second element in the recovery of sensuous beauty under the protection of Christian theology is the modification of the idea of simple resemblance between created and Creator into that of outside covering and inside truth. Instead of being mirrors of Divinity things may be curtains, screens, or cloaks of Divinity. An outer wrapping may come closer to the thing itself, as its external phase, than a separate copy. This interpretation of the relationship between God's beauty and sensuous beauty absorbs and is colored by certain already existing intellectual practices which used the same idea of the inner-outer relationship. For example the Typology of the Early Alexandrine Fathers redeemed for Christianity the sayings of the prophets and wise men of the Old Testament by elaborately drawing out the parallels between the literature of the two dispensations. Jewish doctrine was found to be the inadequate external anticipation of the internal Christian fulfilment. But the words of Moses and the prophets, though hulls, so to speak, of the words of Christ, were holy hulls, and not far from the truth of the Kingdom of Love. The allegorizing of classic myth—the borrowing of classic shapes for Christian

---

[79] Dante, *Div. Com.*, Paradiso, İ, ll. 127–29.

ideas—was a usage depending on the same interpretation of the relation between Christianity and what is outside Christianity. The classic cloak was put on the new body: *e.g.*, an angel was drawn in the shape of classic Victory; Amor and Psyche used as types of God's love and the human soul; Orpheus as well as Moses taken as the type or inadequate symbol of Christ.

The actual word 'symbol' passed into the service of Christian SYMBOL. and artistic theory from an earlier literal employment meaning a mark or sign of recognition. The Apostles' Creed was the external label of an internal faith and was called the Christians' symbol. The symbol, therefore, became the visible sign and emblem of the invisible inward tendency of the soul. The idea of the veil or covering then easily found expression in the word 'symbol' and a sensuously-appearing symbol came to mean something no farther away from the heart of Divine Wisdom, than the outside is from the inside, or the veil from what is behind the veil.

The third element in the assimilation of sensuous show to inner MANIFOLD MEAN-
INGS. truth is the refinement of the sensuous show into manifold meanings, all of which are 'true' of a given document. Clement of Alexandria had already in the second century distinguished the four possible meanings of a writing: the literal, moral, anagogical, and mystical. These are the very four that Dante in the thirteenth century claims for the interpretation of his *Divine Comedy*. "For the clarity of what is to be said, one must realize that the meaning of this work (the *Commedia*) is not simple, but is rather to be called *polysemos*, that is having many meanings. The first meaning is the one obtained through the letter; the second is the one obtained through the things signified by the letter. The first is called literal, the second allegorical or moral or anagogical. In order that this manner of treatment may appear more clearly, it may be applied to the following verses: 'When Israel went out of Egypt, the house of Jacob from a people of strange language, Judah was his sanctuary and Israel his dominion.' For if we look to the letter alone, the departure of the children of Israel from Egypt in the time of Moses is indicated to us; if to the allegory, our redemption accomplished by Christ is indicated to us; if to the moral sense, the conversion of the soul from the woe and misery of sin to a state of grace is indicated to us; if to the anagogical sense, the departure of the consecrated soul from the slavery of this corruption to the liberty of eternal glory is indicated." [80] But the meanings did not need to be four. The sense of divine utterances is manifold and infinite, says Erigena, even as in one and the same feather of the peacock we behold a marvellous and beautiful variety of colors. Not only can the meanings be many, but an outward show that appears simple is often the richest in hidden significances. In his Prologue to his explanation of the Song of Mary, Hugo of St. Victor says that the worst obstacle to the interpretation of Scripture is that the simplest-seeming passages are really the most pregnant. When the letter seems to offer no difficulty, as in the case of Mary's song, there we may be sure an idea is adumbrated that is well-nigh beyond the power of terrestrial minds. [81]

REVERSED SUBSTAN-   Thus everything that met the senses of the medieval man,
TIALITY OF SPIRIT   whether in the living book of nature or in the written book of the
AND FLESH.   Bible or in the pictures and forms sculptured on the churches, became

all allegory
Of Jesus Christ the Son of Mary
. . . all divinity.

Though the interpretations varied, and though already the clever profane mocked at sign language, on the whole the ordinary phenomena presented to sense and feeling became names written in water, dream-children, phantoms floating by. The imagination which holds in the back cell of the brain the store-house of sense-impressions is analogous to water, said Isaac of Stella (d. 1169). [82] The things seen and heard and passed in daily walks borrowed whatever they had of essential character from an unseen and unheard source, and were, contrary to the vulgar opinion, themselves more frail and passing than their ineffable model. The medieval man, then, worked this miracle of conversion. He melted

---

[80] *Epistle to Can Grande,* trans. Gilbert, *Literary Criticism, Plato to Dryden,* (*Epistola decima*), 1940, p. 202.
[81] Migne, Series Latina, Tom. 175, p. 414.
[82] Bundy, *op. cit.,* p. 207.

the sensible world into the ghostly, and raised the ideal into the solid.

St. Francis turned his inspired gaze on nature and animals and found the law of piety written therein. In the rivulets flowed the Trinity, and in the lion, ox, and eagle breathed the evangels. Flowers and fruiting trees were used in the decoration of churches to represent the fruits of good works. Snails symbolized the emergence of our Lord from the tomb; the dove meant the Holy Spirit; butterflies, cranes, peacocks, salamanders, swans, the nut, the rose, the pansy, daisy, marigold, all had their sacred, mystic meaning. The glassy illusory quality thus attributed to the creature world by the peculiar accent of medieval symbolism seemed to fertilize it for the imagination. Medieval thought absorbed an earlier Oriental fancy for monsters—monsters with four heads, eagles with two, bird- and fish-women, centaurs, griffins, unicorns—which the poor world of fact cannot yield. So also the twelve stones of the apocalypse added their lustre to those fetched from common earth or ocean.

Beauty, then, that strictly taken belongs only to God as a Divine Name, was let down from heaven to earth by means of a cosmic cord of symbolism. The imagination was referred to sometimes as a little boat that plied between the celestial and earthly spheres.[83] Though the essence of beauty remained spiritual, it pierced its outer sensuous shell and in a measure sanctified it. The world of color, sound, and shape earned restoration to favor in theological esthetics by the assistance it could give in pointing, reflecting, and vivifying religious teaching. Or better: the Divine Name was allowed to poise midway between pure spirit and gross matter in symbolic suggestion. For the churchmen who reflected on these matters were always drawn in two directions. On the one hand their vocational consciences told them that there was some overflowing from the "fountain of truest beauty" in the "outward form of all things," and that there was testimony of Divinity in the "interchanges of day and night, . . . the revolution of years, . . . the fall and return of leaves to trees, the

BEAUTY AND IM-
AGINATION MEDI-
ATE BETWEEN ONE
AND MANY.

---

[83] For example, by Synesius. See Bundy, *op. cit.*, p. 149.

boundless power of seeds, the beauty of light, the varieties of colors, sounds, tastes, and scents." [84] And on the other hand, they were aware that according to the theory of their religion "the external eyes see marble and gold; the internal eye sees wisdom and justice." [85] It is 'within' that the daughter of the king is resplendent. St. Augustine thus recognized, and undoubtedly felt the temptation in himself, that he who passes to the truth by way of the symbol may pause by the wayside with the symbol itself. "Alas for those who love, instead of you, your beckonings, and stray among the traces." [86] One may be decoyed by the charm of the creature instead of 'tending to the something else' symbolized by it. For the beauty of things may be referred to their ultimate meaning according to either of two methods: as picture or as image. [87] If one admires the world as an image of God, then one has a well-disposed eye; but if one lingers in the beauty of the picture itself, then one has a bleared eye, and is like the bat or owl which sees best in shadow and lives in darkness. Our model should be the attitude toward music of the Sweet Singer of Israel. David was a man skilled in songs, who dearly loved musical harmony, "not with a vulgar delight, but with a believing disposition, and by it served his God, who is the true God, by the mystical representation of a great thing. For the rational and well-ordered concord of diverse sounds in harmonious variety suggests the compact unity of the well-ordered City." [88] It is not the symbols, but the love of the symbols, that soils us. Lingering and dallying with sensation, not its existence or proper employment, is the menace to religion.

AUGUSTINE'S REA-SONED DEFENSE OF BEAUTY.

But however firmly the teachers of the Church insisted on the direction in which symbols must point, it was inevitable that once sensuous shows were given a foothold in God's kingdom, appreciation of them for their own sake should begin to creep back

---

[84] St. Augustine, "On the Profit of Believing," *Nicene . . . Fathers*, 1st Ser., Vol. III, pp. 363, 364.

[85] Psalms 45, 13.

[86] St. Augustine, *On the Free Will*, Ch. XVI, 43.

[87] St. Bonaventura, *Commentary on the Four Books of Sentences of Peter Lombard*, Commentary on Bk. I. Distinction III, Part I, Question 11, Conclusion.

[88] *Nicene . . . Fathers*, Vol. II, p. 352; *City of God*, Bk. XVII, Ch. 14.

in. Traces of this slipping back to a pure estheticism may be noted from the very beginnings of the Middle Ages. St. Augustine was temperamentally responsive to light, 'the queen of colors,' and to the suavity of singing. He has difficulty in reining in his attention to the beauty of the Ancient of Days because of the beguilement of color and music. He makes acute observation on the shifting of color on wave-surface as he looks out over the mountains at Casciago, and, remembering how his feelings themselves chanted when touched at the time of his conversion by melody and rhythm, he is tolerant of the outer forms of music.[89] It is not surprising then to find St. Augustine wrestling with the problem of the value of the sensuous charm itself, and trying to give a reasonable defense of it. "Why is it, I ask, that if anyone says there are holy and just men whose life and conversation the Church of Christ uses as a means of redeeming those who come to it from all kinds of super-stitions, and making them through their imitation of good men members of its own body . . . how is it, I say, that if a man says this, he does not please his hearer so much as when he draws the same meaning from that passage in Canticles, where it is said of the Church, when it is being praised under the figure of a beautiful woman: 'Thy teeth are like a flock of sheep that are shorn, which came up from the washing, whereof everyone bears twins, and none is barren among them?' Does the hearer learn anything more than when he listens to the same thought expressed in the plainest language, without the help of this figure? And yet I don't know why, I feel greater pleasure in contemplating holy men, when I view them as the teeth of the Church, tearing men away from their errors, and bringing them into the church's body, with all their harshness softened down, just as if they had been torn off and masticated by the teeth. It is with the greatest pleasure too that I recognize them under the figure of sheep that have been shorn, laying down the burdens of this world like fleeces, and coming up from the washing, *i.e.*, from baptism, and all bearing twins, *i.e.*, the twin commandments of love, and none among them barren in that holy fruit. But why I view them with greater

---

[89] *Confessions*, Ch. XXXIII, *Loeb*, Vol. II, p. 167.

delight under that aspect than if no such figure were drawn from the sacred books, though the fact would remain the same, is another question, and one very difficult to answer. Nobody, however, has any doubt about the facts, both that it is pleasanter in some cases to have knowledge communicated through figures, and that what is attended with difficulty in the seeking gives greater pleasure in the finding." [90] Here as in so many places Augustine devises an ingenious apology for surface-pleasantness. The enigmas of Scripture, he says, banish ennui; and by the obstacle they offer to our apprehension force our respect.[91] This idea was to trickle down through the centuries until in Abbé Dubos in the eighteenth century it was destined to become the basis of a striking system. In another passage, dealing with the same problem, Augustine gives the same explanation a little more subtly. Why, he inquires, are we more moved by allegories and images than by plain words? He offers an explanation that reminds us of Plato's theory of the origin of art: that animals like motion.[92] We have to move mentally from riddle to answer, from picture presented to the imagination to spiritual truth, and the mental excursion, as such, is pleasing to us. As a torch burns more brightly when in motion, so our emotions flame joyously when thought is active.

REMOTE SYMBOLS.   What is only hinted by St. Augustine is developed into an ingenious theory by the Pseudo-Dionysius. He confronts himself with the problem of the value of remote symbols, such as the use of the image of a worm to express the nature of Christ. This verges, we feel, toward an absurd and pernicious representation of what is holy, he says. But such condemnation of the use of dissimilar and incongruous symbols for holy things, such as the lion, panther, leopard, and rushing bear, is thoughtless. If we take thought we shall see that the shock of the incongruity of such symbols goads our minds to unravel the mystery of their meaning better than the use of more cognate, and seemingly adequate symbols, such as Word, Essence, Light. All symbols fall far short of a true in-

---

[90] *Nicene . . . Fathers,* 1st Ser., Vol. II, p. 537; *On Christian Doctrine,* II: VI, 7.
[91] *Ad Consentium Contra Mendacium;* Svoboda, p. 166.
[92] *Nicene . . . Fathers,* 1st Ser., Vol. I; *Epistle* 55, Ch. XI, Sec. 21.

dication. It is therefore a more appropriate use of symbols to make the discrepancy palpable, than to gloss over the function of a symbol by using comparisons that approach adequacy.[93]

St. Augustine ingeniously found ways to defend musical semblance, as well as rhetorical devices. The body of music, though it is not reasonable and articulate like intelligent speech, yet has the sweetness of its linkages, Augustine says. The *art* of music is timeless; but the *phenomenon* of music extends itself through time, and is dependent on our grasp in one instant of past, present, and future. It is thus the child of Jupiter and Memory,[94] as the Greek myth teaches. As Jupiter's offspring, music needs no defense to religion; for she is in so far numerous, measurable, and one-like. But "also to things falling away and succeeding a certain temporal beauty in its kind belongs, so that neither these things that die, or cease to be what they were, degrade and disturb the fashion and appearance and order of the universal creation; as a speech well-composed is assuredly beautiful, although in it syllables and sounds rush past as it were in being born and dying."[95] The transience of music, he says again, is not ugly. Verse is beautiful in its kind even if we cannot pronounce two syllables at once and the charm is caused by the carrying over of one syllable to another.

TIME IN BEAUTY.

We have already noticed how St. Augustine early in life defended fiction and theatrical impersonation, calling attention to the esthetic purpose involved. Truth, he had said in his early writing, is like Proteus—multiform.[96] Philosophy must not scorn poetry, for poems can express truth under a figure.[97] But there are other writers and other conceptions that mark the tension between adumbration of divinity, and lingering with the show. The word 'symbol' we have noticed meant a covering, screen, or veil. The veil had a tendency to become an independent esthetic cate-

THE VEIL SOMETIMES APPROACHES INDEPENDENCE.

---

[93] *On the Heavenly Hierarchy*, Ch. II, "That Divine and Heavenly Things Are Appropriately Revealed, Even Through Dissimilar Symbols." Migne: Series Graeca, Tom. 3, Cols.

[94] *De Ordine*, II, 41; Svoboda, p. 27.

[95] *Against the Manicheans; Nicene . . . Fathers,* 1st Ser., Vol. I, p. 353.

[96] *Contra Academicus*, III, 1, 13; Svoboda, p. 20.

[97] *Ibid.*, III, 1, 7; Svoboda, *loc. cit.*

gory, instead of adhering strictly to its task of forming the outside of Christian wisdom. There was not steady adherence to the concealment by the veil; the veil could be simply the entrance or outer approach; it could be allurement to what was within. There was a stumbling back and forth between these ideas. A veil finally became, in Renaissance thought, the esthetic property of *delicatesse*, and there are hints preparatory to this change in the attitude of the mystics toward the veiling symbol. Hugo of St. Victor says that the external and visible sign, which veils the idea from the mystic's intelligence, excites his activity and awakens by its presence his sleeping soul. Roused from the slumber in which she was plunged, the soul fixes her gaze upon this transparent veil, which the truth illumines, and tries to contemplate it more at her ease in its beauty and brilliance.[98]

Thus, however much Christian thought in the Middle Ages strove to stigmatize beautiful appearing, as belonging to the world, the flesh, and the devil, inexpugnable humanity prevented complete suppression. The Church wished to impress the masses of the people, and rhetoric with the music and embroidery of fair speech was its instrument. But not only did it use rhetorical device and music's sweetness to entice the crass multitude toward the vision of divine truth; the Church's voice came through ecclesiastics who felt the lure of sense themselves. For their own emotional fulfilment as well as for their practical success they conceived the appeal of sense in ways that would excuse and justify it to religion. Thus the appeal of sense, aided by the common humanity of bishops and mystics, from time to time got out of hand. The image and the symbol then interested men for their own sakes and because of their own nature.

NO 'FINE ART' IN   What applies to the whole realm of sense-appearance applies to
MIDDLE AGES.   the arts. Esthetics does not lie for the Middle Ages in a theory of the arts any more than in a theory of play or semblance. Poetry and painting in our sense were little esteemed; the making of armor and the masonry of cathedrals and castles were more important. The word 'art' taken simply, in the Middle Ages, had

---

[98] Hugonin, "Essai sur la Fondation de l'Ecole de Saint-Victor de Paris," in Migne, *Series Latina*, Tom. 175, p. 70.

nothing to do with esthetics. The general concept of art for the period was one quoted by Cleanthes from Quintilian: "Art is methodical efficiency." Or more literally: "Art is capacity, working by a way, that is, by order." [99] The seven liberal arts were established by the canon of Martianus Capella as Grammar, Rhetoric, Dialectic; Music, Arithmetic, Geometry, and Astronomy. There is no mention of poetry or painting here, and in fact poetry was sometimes treated as a pendant to logic, or rhetoric. The Dutch Meistersingers called themselves rhetoricians, because poetry was only a 'secondary rhetoric,' and since Aristotle had said that men could not think logically without framing imagery, poetry was sometimes made a propaedeutic to logic.[100] Painters were often classed with saddlers, because saddles were painted in that time, and there is record of the court-painter of Edward II receiving a bonus because he danced on the table and made the king laugh heartily—a plain enough indication where his chief function lay.[101]

Esthetic qualities did not then attach to the arts through the setting apart of any such class as 'fine' in our modern sense. Nevertheless, that scientific skill which was art for the medieval mind led in another fashion toward beauty. Whenever any matter, whether the shoe-maker's or the sculptor's, was reduced to form by the operation of a trained and rational workman, it became beautiful. Sounds that have no measure or rhythm, that do not suggest the unity of an ideal numerical order, are not 'fine' sounds; they have no beauty. The arts of rhetoric and music work the raw material of voice and instrument into figures and beats, and in this way serve esthetic purposes. Architecture, though a servile art like sculpture and painting, serves an esthetic purpose when arches and doors and windows are disposed symmetrically.

BUT SERVILE ARTS APPROACH FINENESS.

The mechanical or servile arts are those which require for their operations an unyielding basis of matter. When something is left over from the operation, something that can be shown and felt, then form has been baffled in its attempt to transmute and govern matter, and the exercise involved in the art is not suitable to free-

---

[99] Borinski, *op. cit.*, p. 30.
[100] Borinski, *op. cit.*, p. 33.
[101] G. G. Coulton, *Art and the Reformation*, Oxford, 1925, p. 74.

men. "Now the mechanical arts are so called from the word *moechor* (to commit adultery)," writes St. Antonio of Florence, "for in them man's intellect is as it were adulterated, since it is created principally for the understanding of spiritual things, and in these mechanical arts it is occupied with material (*factibilia*) things. There are seven such arts: wool, construction, navigation, agriculture, hunting, medicine, and the theater. . . ." [102] Hugo of St. Victor gives the same derivation for the word mechanical in connection with art. The followers of these arts, he says, must borrow their material from nature, whereas the devotees of the liberal arts are properly called 'free' either because they require liberty of mind for their thinking, or because the normal practitioners are noblemen. [103]

ART AS MAKING.   Sometimes the mechanical arts were called the poetical arts because they involved the making of some material thing, such as a house, or bench, or dish, and they then were distinguished from the theoretical and practical arts that had been discussed by Aristotle. In this classification painting becomes a form of poetry, because a painting is a thing made and left visible to the senses after manufacture. St. Augustine grouped the practical arts, whose end is an action and not a work, with the poetical arts, and called them both mechanical as not leading to or working in the medium of spirit. But beauty can reach down below 'liberality' in the arts and commute to loveliness all those products and those actions which exhibit the energy of formative power. Like Plotinus, Augustine taught that the art in the artist is a part of the super-intelligible realm, and is nobler than his product. And like Aristotle he says that artists create according to a form carried in their souls. The new Christian element is the interpretation of the 'form' and the 'art' as gifts of God, and as making artists godlike in what they see and do. The art of the maker consists in a certain state of the spirit, a possession of numbers which as it were beat time like an orchestral leader, for the shaping of the images and the motions of the muscles. The artist sees within the inner light put there by God, and the effects of this light are extrinsicated by him into

[102] Coulton, *op. cit.*, pp. 83, 84.
[103] *Loc. cit.*

wood or stone or string or stretched skin. The light and number by which the artist works are an immortal part in him. The intention of the artist, though it moves his members and the wood or stone, is itself immovable, and is outside the flux of time. God is the artist of nature, and the human artist follows in his ways, looking at the pattern that eternal Wisdom implants in him, except that he is limited by the conditions of his material medium, as God the All-Powerful is not. Unlike God, the Creator, then, the artist produces bodies with bodies according to the idea in his soul; while God makes form with form.

For esthetics in the Middle Ages the arts were not the cases of beauty, from which a general definition of beauty might be framed. The opposite was true. The general properties of beauty were given, and the arts as wholes, or in examples, showed properties entitling them to the epithet beautiful. Certain of the poetical, mechanical, or 'adulterate' arts—sculpture, architecture, painting, etc.—correspond most closely to our present-day concept of the 'fine' arts, and claim to our way of thinking kinship with beauty; but this was not true for the Middle Ages. The 'liberal' arts, being more spiritual, more strictly numbered and ordered, were nearer the esthetic ideal. But there was a third group of arts closer even yet to the goal of beauty. These were the theological arts concerned with man's supernatural faculties. The disciplines that put methodical efficiency into the parts that man shares with God were the ones most impregnated with light and form, as closer to the source. "And the soul of man which is endowed with the nobility of the highest faculty, *viz.* reason, participates in the divine nature under the aspect of everlasting intelligence. For the soul in the supreme faculty is so much ennobled and so completely divested of matter that the divine light streams into it as into an angel, and hence man is called by philosophers a divine animal." [104] Pleasure and luxury, ornament and utility, were, in this cast of thought, what made things unbeautiful. St. Bernardino of Siena was of such a persuasion: "Artificers of ornaments sin when they invent superfluous and curious things; wherefore St. Chrysostom saith,

BEAUTY MAY IN-FORM ART BUT DOES NOT LIE WITHIN IT.

---

[104] Dante, *Convivio*, III, II, 14, trans. Jackson, Oxford, 1909, p. 131.

'we must cut away much from the art of shoemakers and weavers. . . .' As to those who practice elaborate church music, St. Bernardino quotes from Canon Law: 'such a singer-minister exasperates God with his morals while he delights the people with his voice.' " [105] St. Augustine had drawn a fundamental distinction between the useful and necessary arts and the superfluous arts.

Thus the participation of any art in esthetic value is for the medieval theory a matter of proportion. There is an art which is standard for all the various arts, as there is a supreme beauty which confers esthetic excellence on particular beauties. The supreme art is the art of contemplation in which the soul sees God only on the inner mirror of the mind. In this Plotinian conception of the oneness of mirrored and mirroring, through an ingathering of spirit to its essential function, the ideal is given for the arts of shoemaker and musician alike. Their productions and numerousness must copy the simple unity of blessed contemplation; their effectuality must copy its perfect absence of self-interest and release into divine generosity; their contamination by physical medium must yield to the transformation of matter and darkness into form and light. Any art can borrow some of the efficacy of the highest art, and in so far forth, it is an art which tends to give pleasure, fruition or blessedness, contentment of spirit and self-sufficing well-being. Then the Muses of the arts become one with the Christian Virtues.

SUPPLEMENTARY READING

Adler, *Art and Prudence*.
Bosanquet, *History of Aesthetic*, Ch. VII.
Bundy, "The Theory of Imagination in Classical and Mediaeval Thought," *Univ. Ill. Stud. Lang. Lit.*, Vol. XII, nos. 2–3.
L. Callahan, *A Theory of Aesthetic According to the Principles of St. Thomas Aquinas*, Washington, 1927.
G. G. Coulton, ed. and trans., *Life in the Middle Ages*, Cambridge, 1928.

---

[105] *Works*, ed. de la Haye, Vol. I, p. 161; Vol. III, p. 160; quoted in Coulton, *op. cit.*, p. 85.

C. A. Dinsmore, *Aids to the Study of Dante*, Boston, 1903.

Etienne Gilson, *The Spirit of Mediaeval Philosophy*, London, 1936.

C. H. Grandgent, *Dante*, New York, 1916.

W. P. Ker, *The Dark Ages*, New York, 1904.

Jacques Maritain, *Art and Scholasticism*, New York, 1930.

Saintsbury, *History of Criticism*, Vol. I, Bk. III, Chs. I, II.

Karl Svoboda, *L'Esthétique de St. Augustin et ses Sources*, Brno, 1933.

Venturi, *History of Art Criticism*, Ch. III.

Maurice de Wulf, *History of Mediaeval Philosophy*, trans. Messenger, London, 1925.

CHAPTER VI

Renaissance (1300–1600)

HOW NEW A BIRTH
WAS THE RENAIS-
SANCE?

B Y THOSE who view history dramatically and see only its high lights and deep shadows the Renaissance is seen as the glorious restoration to humanity of the esthetic consciousness which the ascetic Middle Ages had suppressed. For them Petrarch, 'the first modern man,' stands as a herald of light in contrast to St. Augustine, 'the exemplar of the Middle Ages,' who stood at the threshold of the Dark Time. They picture to themselves Petrarch collecting medals and coins among the Roman ruins, lamenting over the departure of ancient classical beauty, and chanting in rapture the verses of the Homer he could not yet translate; Brunelleschi making drawings of every recoverable architectural detail in order to restore the 'good old manner' of simple gracious balanced building; Giotto drawing sheep in the open air instead of blindly following ecclesiastical prescription; and with this awakened sensitiveness to the art of a lost golden age and to the charm of natural forms immediately given to sense they compare Gregory's deliberate destruction of pagan temples and palaces, the disgusting courting of squalor by the Egyptian hermits, and Boethius' conception of the Muses as cruel and deceptive Sirens.

THE MIRROR.   Now up to a certain point the student of the history of esthetics might support this artificial contrast of the Renaissance with the Middle Ages by noting, with judicious selection of examples, the change in application of certain figures of speech, favored in both epochs, but focussing different attitudes toward beauty. For the medieval man the natural world is a mirror, the shapes and figures on churches and manuscripts mirrors, and an encyclopedia of knowledge was called a *Speculum*. But what were these mirrors

for? What did they reflect? They reflected the perfection contained in God's abysmal being. Nature, the Living Book, and the
Bible, the Written Book, were both 'true mystical mirrors of the
highest wisdom.' But when the figure of the looking-glass comes
into the employ of the modern man, how does it work? In the
time of the Medicis, Maximilian II, and Elizabeth of England the
written word is thought of not so much as mysteriously adumbrating
the secrets of Deity as holding the mirror up to common life and
nature. It is used not so often to vivify the relation between a
natural and supernatural, or a visible and invisible realm, as to
make clear the function of some secular art—painting or poetry.
Attention is shifting from the way the divine word overflows into
a mirroring medium to the thought of painting or poetry as a
'lively adumbration of things.' In speaking of the technical activity
of the painter, Alberti asks: What should painting be called except
the holding of a mirror up to the original as in art?[1] Leonardo
often makes use of the analogy in a thoroughly practical way:
"When you want to see if your picture corresponds throughout
with the objects you have drawn from nature, take a mirror. . . .
You should take the mirror for your guide—that is to say a flat
mirror—because on its surface the objects appear in many respects
as in a painting. Thus you see, in a painting done on a flat surface,
objects which appear in relief. . . . The picture has one plane
surface. . . . The picture is intangible, in so far as that which
appears round and prominent cannot be grasped in the hands. . . .
You, who have in your colors far stronger lights and shades than
those in the mirror, can certainly, if you compose your picture
well, make that also look like a natural scene reflected in a large
mirror."[2] Again: "You ought to represent nature as seen in your
looking-glass, when you look at it with one eye only."[3] Elsewhere he compares the mirror to the mind of the painter rather

---

[1] Behn, *Leone Battista Alberti als Kunstphilosoph*, Strassburg, 1911, p. 13;
Janitschek, *Kleinere Kunsttheoretische Schriften*, Vienna, 1877, p. 93.

[2] *The Literary Works of Leonardo da Vinci*, ed. Richter, 2 Vols., London,
1883, Vol. I, pp. 264, 265. #529.

[3] Leonardo da Vinci, *A Treatise on Painting*, trans. Rigaud, London, 1802,
p. 200. #350.

than to the painting itself. But in this connection also the mirror is to reflect nature and not supernature. "The mind of the painter must be like unto a mirror, which ever takes the color of the object it reflects, and contains as many images as there are objects before it. Therefore realize, O Painter, that thou canst not succeed unless thou art the universal master of imitating by thy art every variety of nature's forms." [4] Again: The painter "above all . . . should keep his mind as clear as the surface of a mirror, which becomes changed to as many different colors as are those of the objects within it." [5] And: "A painter ought to study universal nature, and reason much within himself on all he sees, making use of the most excellent parts that compose the species of every object before him. His mind will by this method be like a mirror, reflecting truly every object placed before it, and become, as it were, a second nature." [6] And in Dürer we find the familiar comparison: "Every form brought before our vision falleth upon it as upon a mirror." [7] In the same spirit George Puttenham in his *The Arte of English Poesie* (1589) protests in a long passage against "construing to the worst side" the word "phantastical" or "imaginative" as applied to a poet. The imagining brain is like a mirror, he says, and mirrors are fitted out with different kinds of glasses according to their quality. The mirror or imagination of a true poet is "illuminated with the brightest irradiations of knowledge and of the verities and due proportion of things . . . this sort of phantasy . . . is to the sound and true judgment of man most needful." He classes poets, because of the "passing clear glass or mirror" which they carry, not with the light-headed, "as has become the fashion with gentlemen and princes," but with those who are "meet for all manner of functions, civil and martial." [8]

---

[4] Leonardo da Vinci, *Thoughts on Art and Life*, trans. Baring, Boston, 1906, p. 102. #47.

[5] *The Notebooks of Leonardo da Vinci*, arranged and translated by Edward McCurdy, 2 Vols., New York, 1938, Vol. II, p. 278.

[6] *Treatise on Painting*, p. 206. #360.

[7] *The Literary Remains of Albrecht Dürer*, ed. Conway, Cambridge, 1889, p. 177.

[8] *Elizabethan Critical Essays*, ed. Gregory Smith, 2 Vols., Oxford, 1904, Vol. II, p. 19.

The tendency toward secularization might be illustrated further in the change in application of the figure of the veil. For the medieval mind true being lies hidden within a veil or symbol, and that true being is occult and spiritual. Olympiodorus (late sixth century) compares the imagination to a concealing veil: The veil of phantasy interferes with true apprehension and is, so to speak, the vesture of clogging desire. That is why we speak of phantasy with the flowing robes. Calypso, who bewitched the companions of Ulysses, was an embodiment of deluding phantasy; and we need rightness of reason to see through the veil, as Ulysses needed the antidote of a magic herb.[9] Gilbert of Holland (d. 1172) distrusts the veil of imagination also.[10] Medieval poets referred to the fictitious product of the imagination, allegorical poetry, as a veil covering truth. Dante speaks of the transparency of his allegory as the thinness of the veil.[11] Boccaccio, whose scheme of thought is still medieval, uses the general figure of a veil or sheath twenty-four times in his *Genealogy of the Gods* to signify the obscuring cover of poetical form.[12] This typical medieval figure of the veil is used, of course, by the mystically-minded not only in immediately post-medieval days, but always. Peter Sterry says that God is seen through the veil of his created world dimly, "as the sun in a morning mist." And in the nineteenth century Shelley sings of the painted veil of life.

Contrast with this the attitude toward the 'veil' of Giordano Bruno (1548–1600), true son of the Awakening. Calling himself the Excubitor, Awakener of sleeping minds, he cries: "Lo! here is one who has swept the air, pierced the heavens, sped by the stars, and passed beyond the bounds of the world. The key of his diligent curiosity has opened to the view of every sense and every power of reason such closets of truth as can be opened by us. He

---

[9] Olympiodorus, *In Plat. Phaed. Comm.*, ed. Norvin, Leipzig, pp. 34, 35, 38; cited by Bundy, "The Theory of the Imagination in Classical and Medieval Thought," *Univ. Ill. Studies in Language and Literature*, Vol. XII, p. 144.

[10] Gillebertus Abbas, *In Cantica Sermo*, XLV; cited by Bundy, *op. cit.*, p. 210.

[11] Dante Alighieri, *La Divina Commedia*, "Purgatorio," VIII, ll. 20, 21.

[12] *Boccaccio on Poetry*, ed. Charles Osgood, Princeton, 1930. See index, under "poetry, veil of fiction," p. 211; also note 8, p. 157, for a summary of the subject.

has stripped nature of her robe and veil." [13] And again: "The Nolan has given freedom to the Human spirit and made its knowledge free. It was suffocating in the close air of a narrow prison-house, whence, but only through chinks, it gazed at far-off stars. Its wings were clipped, so that it was unable to cleave the veiling cloud." [14] In other words, that 'truth of things' which for the medieval man was 'adorned with beautiful veils' of charming music and fable, the modern man by the aid of reason and science views and touches directly.

FROM CRAFT TO PROFESSION.

Though passages like these do show a movement toward freedom and the open air which was gradually altering men's attitudes toward life and art, they represent this movement too much by contrast. There was no sudden substitution of nature and reason for mysticism and authority. Another change was brewing, a more self-conscious and definite alteration: the graduation of painting and poetry from the class of humble crafts to that of liberal professions. This change is illustrated by Alberti's (1404–1472) essay on painting, written, as he declared, to raise this art above its lowly status of craft to a position of defender and exponent of contemporary thought. [15] The opinion of Michelangelo's father and uncles, who thought themselves disgraced because the youthful member of the family preferred to draw rather than pursue the normal literary curriculum, typifies the attitude that was to pass away. Late in life Michelangelo wrote to his brother Lionardo not to let the priest address letters to him any more as *Michelangelo scultore*, because this epithet placed him with the keepers of craftshops. He no longer took orders under such a title, but was addressed simply as Michelanguolo Buonarroti. [16]

THE RENAISSANCE, COMPLETE AND COMPLEX.

But though a new attitude toward the arts of poetry, painting, and sculpture—the assignment of them to the liberal arts—and a new confidence in human powers, and belief in the observation of

---

[13] E. A. Singer, "Giordano Bruno," in *University Lectures*, Univ. of Pa., Philadelphia, 1914–15, p. 437.

[14] Giordano Bruno, *Cena*, Dialogue IV; cited by William Boulting, *Giordano Bruno*, London, 1914, p. 125.

[15] Janitschek, *op. cit.*, p. xxix.

[16] *Michelangelo*, trans. and ed. R. W. Carden, London, 1913, p. 234. Letter of May 2, 1548.

physical nature, gradually arrived as the Renaissance itself matured, no esthetic right-about-face occurred with military suddenness and precision in the fourteenth century. Rather is it true that the Renaissance was to the end wandering between two worlds, one, not dead, but declining; the other, not powerless to be born, but as yet embryonic. Indeed one of the chief notes of the whole period is its complexity and completeness of intention, its not abandoning old forms even while forging new ones. Thus though there are examples of bitter war-fare between the priests, who guarded the theological ideal of divine wisdom and beauty, and the adherents of the new learning and art, medieval piety lived on, not only in reformers and preachers like Savonarola, but also in the new generation of poets and painters: Petrarch and Boccaccio, Alberti and Dürer. The Bible did not cease to be an authority because classical authorities were gaining in prestige. The very arguments of St. Augustine himself were used by the new Humanists, who felt obliged to defend their arts of poetry and painting to those who succeeded St. Augustine as trustees of religion and morality; and Petrarch wrote out his confession to his dead but chosen and vividly imagined spiritual mentor St. Augustine.[17] One of the stock objections to poetry was that it was a texture of lies. St. Augustine had defended the 'lying' of fiction and the illusions of the theater on the ground of acknowledged convention. An actor to be a true actor must be a fictitious personage, he said.[18] Boccaccio echoes this defense, saying that poets are not liars since they do not intend to deceive. Their free handling of historical record injures no one; it is the accepted method of the poetical process.[19] Boccaccio also echoes Augustine's defense of rhetorical figure in the Scriptures, and of passionate appeal in sacred oratory.[20] What is figurative or allegorical is pleasanter because the "difficult involutions" challenge effort;[21] and it "exercises the mind of the learned with its hidden truth."[22] Poetry's "fervid expression" tends to

---

[17] J. H. Robinson and H. W. Rolfe, *Petrarch*, New York, 1898, p. 93.
[18] See Chapter V, p. 155, note 1.
[19] Osgood, *op. cit.*, pp. 62, 63; XIV, 13.
[20] *Ibid.*, pp. 49, 50; XIV, 9.
[21] *Ibid.*, pp. 61, 62; XIV, 12.
[22] *Ibid.*, p. 51; XIV, 9.

"awake the idle, stimulate the dull . . . and subdue the criminal" [23]
as the eloquence of the preacher, according to St. Augustine, has as
its end to melt and arouse.[24]

ART ELEVATED BY
DEMONSTRATING
ITS GODLINESS.

But echoes of and references to the Church Fathers in the
new defenders of the arts of poetry are less important than the
common claim that poetry is noble because it is a kind of theology,
or because theology is a kind of poetry, or because poetry comes
from the "bosom of God." [25] A worldly mind might conceivably
borrow arguments from the Holy Fathers, and put them, by ingenious transposition, to worldly ends; precisely as the Church
Fathers were taught by Augustine to "spoil the Egyptians" [26] of
literary riches with which to vanquish the Egyptians, *i.e.* heretics.
But the continuity between Petrarch and Boccaccio, together with
the long line of Italian and English critics inspired by them, and
the medieval apologists for the sacred sciences, was not in reality
one of the letter but of the spirit. Petrarch wrote to his brother
Gherardo: "Poetry is very far from being opposed to theology.
. . . One may almost say that theology actually is poetry, poetry
concerning God. To call Christ now a lion, now a lamb, now a
worm, what pray is that if not poetical? And you will find thousands of such things in the Scriptures, so very many that I cannot attempt to enumerate them. What indeed are the parables of
our Savior in the Gospels, but words whose sound is foreign to
their sense, or allegories, to use the technical term? But allegory
is the very warp and woof of all poetry." [27] Petrarch proceeds to
argue that the Psalms are poetry, and that the Church Fathers
took his view of the matter; moreover, that the Fathers themselves
employed the poetical form. "Do not look askance then, dear
brother, upon a practice which you see has been approved by
saintly men whom Christ has loved. Consider the underlying
meaning alone, and if that is sound and true, accept it gladly, no
matter what the outward form may be. To praise a feast set forth

---

[23] Osgood, *op. cit.*, pp. 39, 40; XIV, 7.
[24] See Chapter V, p. 156, note 2.
[25] Osgood, *op. cit.*, p. 41, XIV, 7.
[26] See Chapter V, p. 159.
[27] Robinson and Rolfe, *op. cit.*, pp. 261, 262.

in earthen vessels but despise it when it is served in gold is too much like madness or hypocrisy." [28] If this citation seems unfair because it is addressed to a member of a clerical order, who would naturally be moved only by arguments for poetry which emphasized its moral and religious character, others in a long train from Boccaccio down might be given which present poetry as sister to theology, as inclusive of the Bible, and as a pleasant way to a moral end. Poetry's task is "to set men's thoughts on things of Heaven." [29] To condemn poetry is to condemn the method of Christ and the substance of the Old Testament; poetry is useful because "it lures away noble souls from those foundering under moral disease." [30] Parnassus lures us to the truth, writes Tasso, as sugar smeared on the cup's brim persuades the child to drink a wholesome medicine.[31] Sir Philip Sidney (1554–1586), who carried the Italian manner of Defense of Poetry into England, and set a model for a multitude of "defenses," calls poetry "virtue-breeding delightfulness," and "medicine of cherries." [32]

Far from breaking, then, with the medieval scheme of values which put the service of God highest, the Renaissance treatment of the fine arts knew only one first step in the way to exalt them, *viz.*, that of making them also instruments in God's service, and partakers of his Wisdom. It is sometimes said that the chief characteristic of Renaissance esthetic was not the recognition of the arts, but the association of the arts with beauty. But association of the arts with beauty had to pass through the stage of borrowing the splendor of God's countenance. To the early Renaissance thinkers as to the medieval churchmen, supreme excellence emanated from God, and the road to the emancipation of the arts was through a demonstration first of all of qualities which should bring technical performance of the arts close to the source of Goodness. This is as true of the early painters as it is of the writers

[28] *Ibid.*, pp. 264, 265.

[29] Osgood, *op. cit.*, p. 39, XIV, 6.

[30] *Ibid.*, p. 78, XIV, 16.

[31] Torquato Tasso, *Gerusalemme Liberata*, I, 3. (Trans. Wiffen, London, 1893, p. 2.) The argument is directly or indirectly borrowed from Lucretius, *De rer. nat.*, I, 936ff.

[32] *Sidney's Apologie for Poetrie*, ed. Collins, Oxford, 1907, pp. 26, 27.

on poetry. For Alberti and Leonardo, the painter must be a kind of priest,[33] and piety and virtue were regularly thought of as part of the necessary equipment of the would-be painter. Painting itself was called divine; and the effect of both the study of the painter's art and the sympathetic observation of his products was to lead men to the love of God.[34] Leonardo repeats the saying of Dante that "in art we may be said to be grandsons unto God." [35] Alberti argues for painting that it "has represented the Objects of the Worship of Mankind; by which means it has been a very Great Help to Piety." [36]

BUT THE NEW SECULAR SPIRIT RE-QUIRES INTELLEC-TUALITY ALSO.

The arrival of the secular spirit in the Renaissance came about, then, neither suddenly, nor by a general repudiation of the godly aim of art. It arrived rather by the slow encroachment upon the religious spirit of the claims of science and classical learning which were becoming now increasingly important for artists. The poet and painter clearly saw that they must rehabilitate themselves among the professions by acquiring wide and detailed knowledge, and by exhibiting that power through method, that skill through a way, which was Quintilian's conception of art in general.[37] They sought to win respect through the possession of the intellectual as well as the moral virtues. Painting "is a music and a melody which only intellect can understand," Michelangelo said.[38] The acquisition of various kinds of knowledge, both the general culture of a philosopher and the thorough understanding of the technical problems of the craftsman, was looked to for the raising of the poet's or painter's dignity. Promotion should come partly by associating him with the learned, and partly by marking him

LABOR: WHAT IS HARD TO DO IS PLEASANT IN ACHIEVEMENT.

off as a person who had overcome great difficulties. It was not an original idea with the Renaissance that what is laborious in the doing is excellent in the achieving. St. Augustine had explained the value of abstruse Biblical imagery by the pleasure we take

---

[33] J. Wolff, *Leonardo da Vinci als Ästhetiker*, Jena, 1901, p. 142.

[34] *The Notebooks of Leonardo da Vinci*, Vol. II, p. 229.

[35] *Ibid.*, Vol. II, p. 228.

[36] *The Architecture of Leon Battista Alberti. In Ten Books. Of Painting. In Three Books. Of Statuary. In One Book.*, trans. Leoni, London, 1755, p. 251.

[37] See Chapter V, p. 157, note 99.

[38] De Hollanda, *op. cit.*, p. 16.

in overcoming difficulties,[39] and the idea occurs earlier in the classical writers. Today we would, I think, reason in the opposite direction, and say that hard work is made valuable by being applied to ends already shown to be worth the effort. But it became axiomatic in the Renaissance that value attaches to a vast expenditure of labor as such. "The appreciation of art is the appreciation of difficulties overcome; a picture holds its spectators by its apparent artifice." [40] Here the labor involved, the scientific knowledge required, has become the very definition of art. "The artistic is that in the invention of which the artist suffers labor and exercises his genius greatly; and the inartistic, that in the invention of which he does not employ much subtlety of genius, as the inartistic of itself is capable of being seen by an ordinary wit." [41] The same praise of labor occurs in the sayings of the plastic artists. For example, Michelangelo is reported as saying that the skill of a great painter is shown in the matching of his fear with his understanding. The ignorance of "others appears in the presumptuous boldness with which they exercise their unskilful art." [42] In the frequent competitions as to which of the arts, painting or sculpture, painting or poetry, is the greatest, the argument of the difficulty of the one or the other plays its important rôle. Alberti uses it, for example, in his exaltation of painting over poetry.[43] The painter's genius is supreme because his medium is the most difficult.

The kinds of arduous knowledge required of the artists who are to be worthy of a newly-won social esteem, and of fame, stretch from philosophical understanding of cosmic laws, the laws of morality and the laws of motion, to competency in such technical matters as draughtsmanship, rhetorical ornament, and metre. There is some tendency for admiration to fix upon the more outward shows of the inward wisdom and the arduous labor. Although, for example, Boccaccio insists on the allegorical character of poetry

---

[39] See Chapter V, p. 154.

[40] Castelvetro, *Poetica d'Aristotele*, p. 350. Cited by Charlton, *Castelvetro's Theory of Poetry*, Manchester, 1913, p. 28.

[41] *Loc. cit.*

[42] De Hollanda, *op. cit.*, pp. 70, 71.

[43] Behn, *op. cit.*, p. 60.

("It veils truth in a fair and fitting garment of fiction") he forces a fancied etymology of the word *poetry* to give him as its essential meaning "speech which is exquisitely wrought," *exquisita locutio*.[44] With all his piety he belongs to a new age in devoting a larger share of attention to the adornment of interwoven words, the pleasantness of the rind of the fable. But pleasure abandoned freely to the show is not the general result of the secularization of interest. Only in the case of the few bold heretics is the connection cut during the Renaissance between the scientific understanding of an objective order and the scientific power to display that object in a suitable medium. On the whole there is a parallelism maintained between a true philosophical content intellectually mastered and a skilful and pleasing rendering of the content. This maintenance of a parallel order of sciences, one of content and one of form, is a far more intellectual and self-conscious attitude toward art than the medieval cherishing of a symbol mainly for its pointing toward a mystic union with God. But it leads to the seventeenth and eighteenth century Neo-Classical desire to make art the expression of reason rather than to the present conception of art as the expression of beauty.

MENTAL EQUIP-
MENT OF THE
ARTIST.

The ascent of poet and painter from common workman, mere story-teller, or idle prattler to equality with the theologian and philosopher was due primarily, then, to his increase in literary and technical knowledge. His education had to be thorough and liberal. A real poet must possess a knowledge of grammar, rhetoric, and at least the principles of the other traditional arts, both moral and natural, Boccaccio says. Moreover he must command a strong and abundant vocabulary, be familiar with archaeological remains, and know both history and geography.[45] And Du Bellay (1524–1560) addresses the would-be poet as "one instructed in all the good arts and sciences, principally natural and mathematical, versed in all kinds of good authors, Greek and Latin, not ignorant of the 'parties' and 'offices' of human life." [46] Indeed it was a

---

[44] Osgood, *op. cit.*, pp. 39, 40, 42, XIV, 7.
[45] *Ibid.*, p. 40, XIV, 7.
[46] Du Bellay, *La Défense et l'Illustration de la Langue Française*, Paris, 1903, p. 31.

commonplace among the early Italian defenders of the art of poetry (it is in Scaliger and Minturno, for example)[47] to prescribe solid erudition as a prerequisite for creative literary work. Castelvetro, who on a number of important points delighted in contradicting the common views of the apologists for poetry, is on the question of a liberal education less heretic than he seems. He does indeed insist that poetry is to be distinguished by its aim of giving pleasure from science which aims at truth.[48] But he will not tolerate the Platonic doctrine that the source of poetry is divine madness.[49] For it is through conscious artistry, through hard study and not through irrational genius, that poetry comes into being.[50] He will not even admit that Plato himself seriously meant to assert so unintellectual a spring for the origin of poetry.[51]

We also find frequent references to the strenuousness and stretch of a painter's education. The artist must be a "good man well-versed in good literature. He must know geometry, and he must know poetry and oratory, which will furnish him with much matter."[52] "Painting requires a . . . full and strenuous education, careful, systematic," conscientious.[53] A painter is so precious a member of society that care for his upbringing should begin, according to Dürer, at birth. He must be nurtured in learning from the first—kept eager to learn and not vexed. He must know how to read and write and speak Latin. Dürer suggests that the early studies of a painter-child may be severe enough to injure his health. If there is danger of melancholy from this source, he must be "enticed therefrom by merry music to the pleasuring of his blood."[54]

The artist's function, then, is so noble and arduous that nothing less than universal knowledge can serve as a basis for his work. THE ARTIST AS PHILOSOPHER AND CRITIC.

[47] J. E. Spingarn, *A History of Literary Criticism in the Renaissance*, New York, 1908, p. 43.

[48] Castelvetro, *Poetica d'Aristotele*, pp. 29, 586, trans. Gilbert; cited by Charlton, *op. cit.*, p. 42, notes 1 and 2.

[49] *Ibid.*, pp. 67, 511; Gilbert, pp. 310-311; cited by Charlton, *op. cit.*, p. 22, notes 2 and 3.

[50] *Ibid.*, p. 67; Gilbert, *loc. cit.*; Charlton, p. 22, note 3.

[51] *Ibid.*, p. 65; Gilbert, *loc. cit.*; Charlton, pp. 20, 21, note 1.

[52] Janitschek, *op. cit.*, pp. 143, 145.

[53] *Ibid.*, pp. xxv, xxvi.

[54] Quoted by T. S. Moore, *Albrecht Dürer*, New York, 1905, p. 328.

He is not usually envisaged as a being of sentiment or genius over against one who scientifically understands. The title to which he aspires is not 'imagist' but philosopher, that is, lover of wisdom, and interpreter of the forms and causes of things. In defending poetry Boccaccio meets the charge that poets are merely apes of philosophers by replying that "they should be reckoned of the very number of the philosophers." [55] Do not these fools who debase poetry know that Vergil was a philosopher, a poet from whom "the sap of philosophy runs pure"? [56] The critics are careful to point out the different roads travelled by philosophy and poetry, the one being the road of the syllogism and a plain prose style, the other being the road of contemplation and adorning veils of semblance. Also "it is the philosopher's business to dispute in the lecture-room but a poet's to sing in solitude." [57] But these distinctions, however important, do not do away with the underlying agreement in a common knowledge of the secret springs of things. "I could never thinke the study of *Wisdome* confin'd only to the philosopher," [58] writes Ben Jonson (1573 (?)–1637), epitomizing the growing critical attitude; for one who can successfully feign wisdom, has it. Painting is philosophy, Leonardo declares; for it subtly speculates on movement and form. The expressiveness and varieties of movement, and the *truth* of all the natural species, "seas and plains, trees, animals, plants, and flowers," are her theme. "And this is true knowledge." [59] "If poetry treats of moral philosophy, painting has to do with natural philosophy; if the one describes the workings of the mind, the other considers what the mind effects by movements of the body." [60] Because the artist not only steadily regards nature with his eyes, but "reasons much within himself on all he sees," [61] there issues finally from his personality as a whole a criticism of nature, rather than a photograph

---

[55] Osgood, *op. cit.*, p. 79, XIV, 17.

[56] *Ibid.*, p. 52, XIV, 10; p. 79, XIV, 17.

[57] *Ibid.*, p. 79, XIV, 17.

[58] *Critical Essays of the Seventeenth Century*, ed. Spingarn, 3 Vols., Oxford, 1908, Vol. I, p. 28.

[59] *Literary Works*, §652.

[60] *The Notebooks of Leonardo da Vinci*, Vol. II, p. 228.

[61] Leonardo da Vinci, *A Treatise on Painting*, p. 206.

of it. "The painter is by necessity constrained to amalgamate his mind with the very mind of nature and to be the interpreter between nature and art, making with art a commentary on the causes of nature's manifestations which are the inevitable results of its laws." [62]

In his coveted title of philosopher the Renaissance artist shows his double nature: his medieval respect for theology and the wide secular wisdom which speculates on the subtle reasons for things combined with his modern respect for special knowledge. No sharp line divides the functions of the new philosophical painter or poet as a rival of the Divine Artist on the one hand, and as student of mathematics, perspective, and philosophy on the other. The industry by which artists hope to trace out God's secrets is a diligence in the observation of fishes and gesticulating groups on street-corners, the gestures of the deaf-and-dumb, dissection of corpses, measuring off the proportions of horses, and tracing objects through veils at various distances; or again commenting on Aristotle's or Horace's *Poetics* and showing how each truth laid down is illustrated by Vergil or Homer, learning types of character from the classic models of Lucretia, Cato, Achilles, Ulysses, or finding 'fables' in classic myths. The excellent laboriousness which was to make painting, sculpture, and poetry liberal and fit for freemen was thus magnificently inclusive. It constrained the liberal artists to emulate God by the perfection of their doing, and at the same time to master the use of hand and eye, to absorb the classical *corpus*, and to exhibit in sensuous proofs this manifold learning. THE IMPORTANCE OF LEARNING.

The Renaissance artist's study of nature and the medieval craftsman's use of symbolism do not then represent opposed attitudes. It is indeed through a kind of passionate attention to the coloring and shape of individual natural objects and unwearied practice in drawing them that the artist hopes to gain wisdom. But the artist's ambition does not end with the correct copy. He does not understand the nature that he is imitating to be an assemblage of independent entities, nor as exhausted by its outward show. ART IS NATURE AT ONE REMOVE.

---

[62] *Thoughts on Art and Life*, p. 98. #38.

There are, it is true, statements by the great Italians which would seem to justify the narrow goal of bare reduplication as the purpose of their art. "That painting is the most commendable which has the greatest conformity to what is meant to be imitated. This kind of comparison will often put to shame a certain description of painters, who pretend they can mend the works of Nature." [63] Again: "One painter ought never to imitate the manner of any other; because in that case he cannot be called the child of Nature, but the grandchild. It is always best to have recourse to Nature, which is replete with such abundance of objects, than to the production of other masters, who learnt everything from her." [64] The same praise of freedom in contrast with the bondage of rules and masters is more pithily expressed in the passage: "He who can go to the fountain does not go to the water-vessel." [65] Leonardo also claims a superiority of the art of painting over the art of poetry because of its greater proximity to nature. Painting is for him a 'truer' thing than poetry, which uses signs and not direct images as its material.[66] For Dürer too, "Art standeth firmly fixed in nature, and whoso can read her forth thence, he only possesseth her. . . . The more closely thy work abideth in life, so much the better will it appear; and this is true." [67]

Isolated passages like these, and Vasari's 'talkative rather than generative' descriptions of the phenomena of illusion in Italian painting: Giotto's fly, the spectacles on Ghirlandaio's bishop, Pollaiuolo's quail, Filippo's snake hole, and Bonsignori's dog, might persuade the reader for the moment that Renaissance naturalism meant blind mimicry and that speculative philosophy had little part in it. But this was not so. Exercise of all the mental faculties from memory to the contemplation of God's order was called in to make and interpret rightly the copy of a natural form. The more thoughtful the naturalists became, the more they fused their artistic ideal with the exacting one of essential form and harmonious

---

[63] Leonardo da Vinci, *A Treatise on Painting*, p. 201, Ch. CCCLI.
[64] *Ibid.*, p. 203, Ch. CCCLXIV.
[65] *Thoughts on Art and Life*, p. 110. #60.
[66] *The Notebooks of Leonardo da Vinci*, Vol. II, pp. 227ff.
[67] *Literary Remains*, p. 247.

design. Nature is to them no copy-book model but a complex of laws or a hidden essence to be 'read forth.'

The use of the senses in exact observation was then for the Renaissance painters only a beginning of an artist's method. The motion of a man's arm or the color of a fish's fin entered into the science of the painter through its subjection to mathematical or anatomical discipline. Out of a union of special departments of knowledge, perspective, anatomy, psychology, applied to the data of sense, is to arise a total philosophical treatment of nature which will enable the artist to compose a second nature, thus following after God's way and partaking in his perfection.

That mathematics should be enlisted to aid the truth of painting during the fifteenth and sixteenth centuries is no wonder, when we think of the part it was playing in the reorganization of the sciences. The words of Dürer concerning his first sight of a treatise by Jacopo of Venice on human proportions symbolize the interest in and hope of painters from mathematical treatment of their subject: "He showed me the figures of a man and woman, which he had drawn according to a canon of proportions; and now I would rather be shown what he meant . . . than behold a new kingdom. If I had it (his canon), I would put it into print in his honour." [68] The way Dürer actually honored him was by undertaking a journey to Italy to learn the new science of proportions, by then regarding himself as called to teach and disseminate the new learning, especially in Germany where he felt that artists lacked science, but also, in so far as he could, in the whole world, and finally by composing a treatise *On Proportion*. In this study he made a scale composed of six hundred parts. He also treated of the proportions of horses and buildings and of the mathematical science of perspective.

A book on the nature of perspective had been written by Alberti before the work of Dürer. In 1509 was published *De Divina Proportione* by Luca Pacioli, in which was anticipated the law of the golden section, experimentally established by Zeising in the middle of the nineteenth century. Another very

RÔLE OF MATHE-
MATICS.

---

[68] Brit. Mus. MS: Vol. II. 43; cited by Conway, *Literary Remains*.

influential tractate on proportion written at this time was by Piero della Francesca. The union of art with mathematics in Italy showed the fusion of the new confidence in measurement and mechanism with a mystical Pythagoreanism. Federigo Zuccaro (1539–1609) matched the height of figures in terms of head-lengths with kinds of dignity and divinity: seven head-lengths for Cybele and the Sybils; eight for Juno and the Madonna; nine for Diana. Lomazzo curiously mingled a theory of proportions with the ancient doctrine of humors and of celestial influences: Raphael, he said, had a scheme of proportions inspired by Venus; Michelangelo, one inspired by Saturn.[69] Leonardo gives perspective a prominent place among the knowledges that a painter must have, if he is not to sail "without a rudder or compass." "Practice must always be founded on sound theory, and to this Perspective is the guide."[70] And he tried to match proportions in painting with musical relationships.

MYSTICAL STRAIN.   Anatomical dissection was also a laboratory aid to the artists in converting the raw natural material of their profession into science. Raphael and Dürer used the scalpel, and Michelangelo carried his investigations so far that he became ambitious to write a learned treatise on the anatomical basis of human movement. Leonardo's work on anatomy survives in the form of many important drawings, by which he made substantial additions to the science of anatomy. His sketch-books may occasionally be found as part of the equipment of medical schools. In Michelangelo's brain there was no warfare between scientific empiricism and reverence for the classics. He laid open the torso with his dissecting instrument like any medical student. But the clayey house he thus handled and observed was to him at the same time a model in symmetry and proportion for the architect's house. And this property of the human body Michelangelo had been taught by Vitruvius. "Wherefore it is very certain that architectural members ought to follow the same rule as the members of the human body," he wrote to Cardinal Rodolfo Pio of Carpi. "He that has not mastered, or does not master, the human figure,

---

[69] Schlosser, *Die Kunstliteratur*, Vienna, 1924, p. 398.
[70] *Literary Works*, Vol. I, p. 18. #19.

and in especial its anatomy, can never comprehend it." [71] But over and above his anatomical interest and his respect for the classical tradition, Michelangelo had a fundamental feeling for the dignity of man. As a member of Lorenzo dei Medici's Platonic Academy he was associated with a group of men of almost universal power and learning. In the spirit of this philosophical and cultivated body, Michelangelo mingled reverence for divine things with a lively sense of the nobility and capacity of a human being. A comrade of his in the Academy was that erudite and knightly Pico della Mirandola, who composed a lofty oration in praise of the dignity and greatness of man—man the God-like, the center and bond of the world and interpreter of nature. Michelangelo thought likewise of this highest creature in God's universe as the noblest subject for a painter. "That work of painting will be most noble and excellent which copies the noblest object. . . . And who is so barbarous as not to understand that the foot of man is nobler than his shoes, and his skin nobler than that of the sheep with which he is clothed." [72]

What mathematical and anatomical science render as reasonable and precise representations, must be turned into permanent possessions of the spirit and into mental habits or discourses. Speaking in terms of the brain-anatomy of that day, one would say that the impressions received by the senses and combined by the common sense, must then be stored in the forward cell of the brain over which memory presides. Leonardo advises the student of painting to use his leisure time in conning over his collection of studies, and in memorizing and evaluating them. There, on winter evenings, "all the drawings from the nude which you have made in the summer should be brought together, and you should make a choice from among them of the best limbs and bodies, and practise at these, and learn them by heart." [73] He thus enjoins the commutation of them into ideal possessions. "The mind of the painter should continually transmute the figure of the notable objects which come before him into so many discourses, and imprint them

---

[71] *Michelangelo,* trans. Carden, p. 315.
[72] De Hollanda, *op. cit.,* pp. 69, 70.
[73] *The Notebooks of Leonardo da Vinci,* Vol. II, p. 260.

on his memory, and classify them and deduce rules from them, taking the place, the circumstances, the light and shade into consideration." [74]

Thus the naturalism of the Renaissance painters, their zeal to apprehend perfectly the object that was before them, widened and deepened into the creation of intellectual records. Their fresh enthusiasm over the fountain-head of Nature was not naïve. Their painting was itself a kind of commentary on nature, just as the versions of Plato and Aristotle, published by the Humanists of the time, were interpretations of their great originals. When Michelangelo declares that Flemish painting is hardly to be called a proper art, one reason he assigns is that the Flemings concern themselves with exact duplication of the external shows of meadows, bridges, rivers, woven stuffs, etc., and that they do this "without reason or art." [75] What he himself intends to do is not only rational in that it is grounded in anatomy, but also in that it claims perfection by its imitation of God's way of creating the world.

A study of the early Renaissance doctrine of poetry to search out its philosophical significance yields an analogous picture. On the whole the art of painting was thought to be the philosophy of movement or of physical nature, and the art of literature, the philosophy of morals. One of the diversions of the day was disputation as to the merits of these two arts. But however much the painter might claim for himself greater universality or superior closeness to nature, and the *littérateur,* superior intellectuality, their two arts only parted after a common start as supplementary mirrorings. "Painting is dumb poetry, poetry a speaking picture." In the earliest important *Defense of Poetry,* that of Boccaccio, which was at many points the model for most of those written for the next two hundred years, the author treats his art as a general ape of nature, thus bringing poetry very close to what painting aimed to be. "The epithet [ape of nature] might be less irritating [than ape of philosophers], since the poet tries with all his powers to set forth in noble verse the effects, either of Nature herself, or of her eternal and unalterable operation . . . the forms, habits, dis-

---

[74] *Thoughts on Art and Life,* pp. 115, 116. #68.
[75] De Hollanda, *op. cit.,* pp. 15, 16.

course, and actions of all animate things, the courses of heaven and the stars, the shattering force of the winds, the roar and crackling of flames, the thunder of the waves, high mountains and shady groves, and rivers in their courses . . . so vividly set forth that the very objects will seem actually present in . . . the written poem." [76] This wide interpretation of what poetry was to imitate dominated criticism before the influence of Aristotle's *Poetics* began to be felt through translations into the vernacular about the middle of the sixteenth century. [77] From this time, starting with Castelvetro, Italian critics were to wrestle with the precise limitations and definitions of Aristotle's dictum: Poetry is the imitation of the actions, passions, and character of men. The problem was: How does such a definition distinguish poetry from history, which is obviously a record of human behavior; from moral philosophy, which also puts into words, and so copies, the same subject matter; from painting, which in the historical genre, is clearly an imitation of men's actions, passions, and characters?

The Renaissance literary critics also had their fountain-head of the character, actions, and passions of men to which they resorted for models of imitative writing, analogous to the fountain-head, nature, which Leonardo recommends to painters. [78] The newly translated classic poets, and above all Vergil, were their well-spring of moral imagery. If this does not seem to connote immediate observation of men's actions, passions, and characters, it must be remembered that Aeneas and Dido were alive and fresh to Minturno and Vida almost beyond our power of realization. In 1527 Vida declares that unhappy are they

ANCIENTS THE "FOUNTAIN" FOR LITERARY WATER-DRAWERS.

> Who with fond rashness trust themselves too much . . .
> Who scorn those great examples to obey,
> Nor follow where the ancients point the way.

And he goes on to prophesy

> The fate of all his works prevents his own.
> Himself his moldering monument survives,

---

[76] Osgood, *op. cit.*, pp. 79–80. XIV, 17.
[77] Charlton, *op. cit.*, p. 13.
[78] *Thoughts on Art and Life*, p. 110.

And sees his labors perish while he lives;
His fame is more contracted than his span,
And the frail author dies before the man.[79]

The characters and events portrayed in the *Aeneid* were nature seen by a clearer, more penetrating vision than the Renaissance man, intoxicated with admiration for the newly recovered classical antiquity, would have conceived it possible for his unaided eyes to compass. When the Humanists wished to observe how life moved in its original perfection, they did not trust their capacity to select from the passing show around them, but they read in the ancients, 'who knew how.'

But just as the painters' references to the relation of their art to nature seem on first inspection to imply more naïve correspondence than their fuller, more reflective statements support, so the writers on poetry often mean by literary imitation of the actions, manners, and morals of men, a thing more ordered and straightened by method than the isolated term might seem to suggest. The *Poetics* of Aristotle and Horace became the literary instruments parallel to the sciences of anatomy, perspective, and proportion, by which the raw data of vision were converted into properly designed forms for the great Italian painters. But there was a flickering unsteadiness of meaning in the word 'imitation' in both arts.[80] The poets were required to be 'verisimilar'; and often an actual historical happening, or the introduction of stage device, was recommended as the best way to guarantee the seeming truth to nature. For example, Castelvetro recommended the use of verse on the stage because the voice can be raised in poetical declamation more easily than in ordinary prose discourse, and so stimulate emotional states.[81]

The technical knowledge of the art of poetry absorbed from Aristotle and Horace turned poets and critics into 'moral philosophers.' But the word philosophy meant more than technical knowledge. The poet was to be a teacher of virtue and instructor in

---

[79] Vida, *De Poeta*, Book III; trans. Pitt in *The Art of Poetry*, ed. Albert S. Cook, Boston, 1892, pp. 133, 134.

[80] Spingarn, *op. cit.*, pp. 37ff.

[81] Castelvetro, *La Poetica d'Aristotele*, p. 30.

civic righteousness. The reading of poets, it was believed, conduces to righteousness. Their works are full of exquisite and candid monitions and teachings, of moving and enticing illustrations of the virtues, of images of brave heroes, chaste heroines, loyal followers, and just empires.

The most inclusive definition of the arts made them either a perfecting of nature or an emulation of God's creative activity. For the orthodox strain of thought imitation was the essence of any art. Simple imitation was expanded into imitation of nature, this again into imitation of the art of God. A poet is another God, said Scaliger boldly, for he can create what ought to be.[82] Nature was envisaged as hidden behind or under the visible show. Cennino Cennini says: "For painting we must be endowed with both imagination and skill in the hand, to discover unseen things concealed beneath the obscurity of natural objects and to arrest them with the hand, presenting to the sight that which did not before appear to exist." [83] But the search for this secret law or method was fraught with religious significance. It was the search for God's habits, and these by hypothesis are perfect. Dürer wrote that men have lost the traces of divine beauty through Adam's fall, as they have lost their other original virtues. "The Creator fashioned men once for all as they must be, and I hold that the perfection of form and beauty is contained in the sum of all men." The artist must find the traces of the lost perfect form.[84]

ART'S MORAL AND METAPHYSICAL IMPORT.

Thus the demand for truth of representation, pushed to its conclusion, means the demand for *beautiful* representation. For a copy of God's methods of creating would reflect something of the beauty of those methods. Dürer (1471–1528) teaches with much vigor that, though the vestiges of Divine Beauty in nature are very difficult to find, it is the part of every good man to lend a hand. He confesses: "What beauty is I know not." "I know not certainly what the ultimate measure of true beauty is, and can-

BEAUTY AS CONCEALED NATURE.

---

[82] Scaliger, *Poetics*, Book I, Ch. I; cited by F. M. Padelford, *The Great Critics*, ed. Smith and Parks, New York, 1932, p. 113.

[83] *The Book of the Art of Cennino Cennini*, trans. Herringham, London, 1899, p. 4.

[84] *Literary Remains*, p. 166.

not describe it aright." [85] "There liveth . . . no man upon earth
who could give a final judgment upon what the perfect figure
of a man is; God only knoweth that." [86] But he adds that perhaps
mathematics will help. It is worth trying. "Because now we cannot altogether attain unto perfection, shall we therefore wholly
cease from our learning? By no means . . . if so be that thus
[mathematically] we may draw forth a part of the beauty given
unto us and come so much nearer to the perfect end." [87] Beauty
as art "stands firmly fixed in nature" for Dürer, and nature in God.
Therefore an artist must study God through science and observation, for only by such submission—which entails imitation—shall
a man ever be able to make a beautiful figure. "He who can tear
her out of nature, he has her." [88] Michelangelo sometimes conceived of art as the removal of the external masses that concealed
an internal beautiful form. [89] His carving was an art of removing
or cutting away from the block of stone what concealed the beautiful statue within. In such strains of thought, clearly a heritage
of piety, the 'perfection' of artistic work connoted the discovery of
an ideal order or essence already present by God's grace in the
existent order, and the artist acknowledges himself a follower or
finder, rather than primarily a maker or inventor. In so far then
as beauty is but concealed nature, the imitation of nature is as
much the road to beauty as to verisimilitude and life-likeness, and
painters pursue an ideal while transcribing the given.

Alberti keeps imitation of nature and beauty apart most of the
time, but occasionally shows their mutual implications for one another. He taught that beauty is to be approached through nature;
but though accurate and close observation was necessary, those
things must be taken from her which will "lead the spirit of the
beholder far beyond the thing he looks at." [90] Although the
painter is to go to school to nature, this does not in the least prevent

---

[85] Dürer, *op. cit.*, pp. 179, 244, 245.

[86] *Ibid.*, p. 179.

[87] *Ibid.*, p. 245.

[88] Wölfflin, *Die Kunst Albrecht Dürers*, Munich, 1926, p. 369.

[89] *Michelangelo*, ed. Carden, p. 251.

[90] Janitschek, *Leone Battista Albertis kunsttheoretische Schriften*, Vienna, 1877, p. 150.

his representation of perfect things. For Beauty, though at rest with herself, is also poured out through all nature. For Alberti's thinking there is an identity between imitating nature and imitating the Source, the single original unity and beauty, out of which nature springs.

Those who wrote on the theory of poetry rested their critical observations on a similar vague philosophy of the relation of beauty to art. One variant on the theme of art as imitation of inner truth as well as purveyor of beauty, is Sir Philip Sidney's picture of the peerless poet. He "goeth hand in hand with Nature," but "groweth in effect another Nature." [91] Sidney argues that the whole system of the liberal arts has nature for its object and submits to her. The poet alone is able to pass beyond and over all the works of nature, because the Heavenly Maker made him in his turn a maker. "Nature never set forth the earth in so rich tapestry as divers poets have done, neither with pleasant rivers, fruitful trees, sweet-smelling flowers, nor whatsoever else may make the too much loved earth more lovely." [92] The poet creates the ideal lover Theagines, the ideal friend Pylades, the ideal soldier Orlando, the ideal prince Cyrus. The "erected wit" of the poet makes us know what perfection is. He is the author of the architectonic art, the one that rules all the others, because what astronomers, historians, and moral philosophers present in unfruitful and unconnected particulars or "wordish descriptions" and "bare rules," the poet presents in a perfect picture which can strike, pierce, and possess the soul more than philosophy, and is more liberal of perfect patterns than history "with its bare 'was.'" Having everything from Dante's Heaven to Dante's Hell under the authority of his pen, he devises a Nature above Nature. And this is not a castle in the air, even though its medium is "imitation or fiction," because the ideal characters of a poet's making generate of the kind. The poet "bestows a Cyrus on the world to make many Cyruses." [93] The moral aim of poetry is here conceived not as divorcing poetry from reality, but as increasing the quantity of

SIDNEY: THE POET AS IMPROVER OF WHAT IS.

---

[91] Sidney, *op. cit.*, p. 8.
[92] *Loc. cit.*
[93] *Op. cit.*, p. 9.

moral reality. The perfection of artistic work means a raising on top of obvious nature, by divine aid, a new power and glory.

ART NO LONGER COSMIC ENERGY BUT HUMAN POWER.

The artist's invention has subtly shifted from finding what is already there, though hidden, to selecting or creating or fashioning a mental image by human strength alone. Dürer and Fracastoro (1483–1553) both insist on the energy of art, impersonally conceived, to produce beautiful form. Dürer says it is art and not man that works the magic of art; [94] Fracastoro, that it is art and not God which inspires the frenzy of genius. "God is not the cause, but music itself, full of a sort of great, exalting wonder which makes the pulse beat with the rhythm as if stirred by some violent frenzy, and takes away self-possession, and rouses one to ecstasy." [95] Fracastoro goes on to say that poets are called divine because they are touched with this divine madness. But he insists on the gradual evolution of the art from human origins. In this period the line between the human contribution and the divine infusion in the composition of genius was lightly drawn and shifting in its position.

Not God's giving so much as man's choosing came to be the cause of beauty. Giotto initiated a new era in the history of painting not alone because he went to nature instead of blindly reflecting studio-formulas, but also because he went to nature with his human power of determination. He selected out of nature "the brightest parts, from her best and loveliest features." The freedom of the human will shines out here not as a moral postulate, but as a necessary basis of artistic achievement. Be on the watch to take the best parts of many beautiful faces, was a common dictum.

HARMONY DEEPENS ITS MEANING.

Now to choose is to enter into a situation with the capacity that marks man as man. But to choose the brightest and loveliest features out of nature's infinite offerings was for art-theorists only the first step in the humanization of the product. Out of what he chose he set out to make a harmony. Harmony, we know, has been the accepted synonym for beauty or for the artist's goal through all the ages of a philosophy of art. But only the general

---

[94] *Literary Remains*, p. 247.
[95] Girolamo Fracastoro, *Naugerius, sive de Poetica Dialogus*, trans. Kelso, p. 65.

term has remained the same. Harmony meant for the medieval man, it will be remembered, the maximum of human emulation of Divine Oneness. The Creative World, doomed by its character from the beginning to be manifold, raises itself into harmony, a "well-ordered city," a choir of agreeing voices, by its effort to be as much as possible like the simple Unity of God. In our own time, harmony is still an esthetic rubric. But psychology rather than theology is now the queen of sciences. So esthetic harmony is today sometimes defined as harmony of impulses: synaesthesis. It is then our task to note what the man-produced harmony of a good painting or poem signified to Alberti, Dürer, or Leonardo. Harmony meant complete agreement of the different parts of the art object with each other and with the whole. What the wit and hand of man, his contrivance and invention, were to confer on the elected natural elements, was depth and completeness of organization. Various words and formulas were employed to convey the notion of utter togetherness: ratio, proportion, concinnity, correspondence, composition. A mathematical canon was one of the devices used to turn a man, a woman, a child, a horse, a building, or a statue into an agreeing whole. But rules and compasses and ingenious schemes of hundreds of measured analogous lines and areas contributed only what quantitative relatedness can to organic integrity. The 'use and office' of each part was taken into consideration so that a single emotional effect might characterize the work. If in a painting you are representing a dead man he must seem "all dead to the very Nails," and "the Living, all alive." [96] Alberti reports a much admired "piece of History" painted by Meleager. In the corpse "every Thing [seemed] sunk and languid"; but not only in the corpse. The pall-bearers "seemed at the same Time to mourn and labor with every Limb." [97] Decency and correspondence forbade incongruities, such as a figure "full of Juice" with a "scraggy Hand," or a large man in a very small house as if "cooped up in a Cupboard." [98] The members must be answerable, then, to each other, not alone in mathe-

---

[96] Alberti, *op. cit.*, p. 257.
[97] *Ibid.*, pp. 256, 257.
[98] *Ibid.*, p. 257.

matical ratio, size, and order, but in color, function, dignity, and
"whatever else may conduce to Beauty and Harmony." [99] Harmony
spreads itself. Harmony involves breadth of view to cover all the
aspects of a work. It also involves depth of analysis to ensure that
all levels of the complete entity are organized. "The parts of a
History are Bodies; the parts of the Body are the Members; the
parts of the members are Superficies." [100] That in the superficies
"the lovely Lights [should] sink away into sweet Shades" is as
necessary as that all the bodies should be correspondent to the
action.[101]

DESIGN: RATIONAL-
IZED INTUITION OF
HARMONY.

The harmony that flows out of man's selection from nature
and adjustment of part to part in the whole becomes incorporated
for Renaissance art as an ideal into the art of design. This art of
design, parent and fountain of the three arts of architecture, sculpture, and painting, is shaped like an arc. In characterizing this
art, erected on the ideal of harmony, Vasari reflects Michelangelo.
Design comes out of experience and passes back into experience.
For it is forged in the intellect out of the siftings of many particular experiences to make a single standard of the excellent. "It
is like a form or idea of all the objects in nature, most marvellous
in what it compasses, for not only in the bodies of men and
animals, but also in plants, in buildings, in sculpture and in painting, design is cognizant of the proportions of the whole to the
parts and of the parts to each other and to the whole. . . . From
this knowledge there arises a certain conception and judgment." [102]
And then this archetype or pattern, harmonious and single, trans-
lates itself, through the pencil or crayon, into visible actuality.

Design is a science: an abstraction or arrangement of the things
found in nature; it is also a force by dint of which new bodies are
made by man incorporating the just and delight-breeding relationships nature has furnished. By the efficacy of design man can
build a "neat-handsome structure instead of a nasty ill-contrived

[99] Alberti, *op. cit.*, p. 256.
[100] *Loc. cit.*
[101] *Ibid.*, p. 257.
[102] Vasari, *On Technique*, trans. Maclehose, ed. G. B. Brown, London, 1907,
p. 205. Ch. I, #74. "Of Painting."

hole." But his neat-handsome structure, if the architect were a Renaissance disciple of Vitruvius, derived its proportions from the proportions of the natural human body. From human body to artist's brain; in artist's brain the elicitation of essential ratios; from rational schema to comprehensive method and skill [art]; from art to hand, and from hand to the chipping, polishing, arranging, and piling of blocks of stone to make a palace.

But the great power of this art of design sometimes led the increasingly self-confident artist beyond the given dimensions of the human body. Choice and arrangement became independent of the natural source. However much Michelangelo may have rooted his skill in dissections of the human body, "he would make his figures of nine, ten, and even twelve heads long, for no other purpose than the research of a certain grace in putting the parts together, which is not to be found in the natural form, and would say that the artist must have his measuring tools, not in the hand but in the eye, because the hand but operates; it is the eye that judges." [103] The appeal here in the deliberate alteration and distortion of nature for greater grace is from one human engine to another, not from man to God, nor even from man to nature.

The tendency of the art of design to become a rich and widely-branching growth is illustrated by Dürer's "Words of Difference." Dürer held up as standard a canon of an ideal figure similar to Alberti's, but in the third of his *Four Books of Human Proportion* he teaches the young German artist how to modulate freely from the fundamental key. It may stand in a man's will, Dürer says, to depart from the golden norm toward the "large, long, small, stout, broad, thick, narrow, thin, young, old, fat, lean, pretty, ugly, hard, soft, and so forth," [104] and this may be done through conscious skill and method also. The wise artist has many strings to his bow, even though he has among them a single best. He should be ready with patterns for men of various characters and temperaments. "By their bodily proportions it can be shown, in the case of all families of men, which are of fiery, watery, or earthy temperament; for

[103] J. A. Symonds, *The Life of Michelangelo Buonarroti*, 2 Vols., New York, 1925, Vol. I, pp. 204, 205.

[104] *The Literary Remains of Albrecht Dürer*, p. 241.

the power of art . . . mastereth every work." [105] Fascinated as he is by the new Italian system, which reduces all the complexity of natural fact to science, Dürer yet never forgets that art stands fixed in nature and that nature never repeats herself. The canon held. Yet inconsistently, the incompatibility of standards of beauty held also. "Beauty is so put together in men and so uncertain is our judgment about it, that we may perhaps find two men both beautiful and fair to look upon, and yet neither resembleth the other, in measure or kind, in any single point or part." [106] The art of designing let down from heaven to earth began to sail on broad, far seas.

POETIC ENTHUSI-
ASM.

For the art of poetry the steady march toward human freedom through selection, rejection, and a synthesizing enthusiasm is summarized by Fracastoro: The poet first "began to modulate sounds, to select the musical, and reject the unmusical, or slur them as much as possible, to delight especially in metaphors, to give attention to sonority and smoothness, and in short to all the other beauties of language. Then he proposed to consider feet and metres, to make verses and to see what was appropriate for each idea. For subject-matter he desired to select as far as possible only the beautiful and excellent, and to ascribe to it only beautiful and admirable qualities. If these were lacking he proposed to form them through metaphors, to search for digressions, and comparisons, to omit none of the other devices which make for excellence of speech, arrangement, transitions, figures, and other ornaments not in use today. As soon as he had joined all the beauties of language and subject and had spoken them, he felt a certain wonderful and almost divine harmony steal into him, to which no other was equal. And then he observed that he was, as it were, carried out of himself. He could not contain himself, but raved like those who take part in the mysteries of Bacchus and Cybele when the pipes are blown and the drums re-echo." [107]

---

[105] *The Literary Remains of Albrecht Dürer*, p. 248.
[106] *Loc. cit.*
[107] Girolamo Fracastoro, *Naugerius, sive De Poetica Dialogus*, trans. Kelso in *Univ. of Ill. Studies in Language and Literature*, Urbana, 1924, Vol. IX, No. 3, p. 65.

In the dialogue *Naugerius* in which Fracastoro tries to capture again the many-sidedness and suspense of a Socratic dialogue, the various possible ends of the poet are passed in review, with a halt amid music and cheering by the on-lookers at the suggestion that poetry's end is, as Aristotle says, to imitate the universal and not the particular. This Aristotelian universal is converted subtly by Fracastoro into Plato's Idea of the Beautiful: a single and absolute essence. "The poet is like the painter who does not wish to represent this or that particular man as he is with his many defects, but who, having contemplated the universal and supremely beautiful idea of his creator, makes things as they ought to be." [108] But Fracastoro's "ought to be" does not fade out of sight into a spiritual vision, but is illustrated through the ornaments of Vergil. It would be enough for a common man to say: "or where there is a grove." But Vergil, who had evidently contemplated the supreme Idea, had the wit to paint a wood with added beauties:

FRACASTORO: THE ENHANCEMENT OF NATURE.

NATURE AS STIMU-LUS TO CREATION RATHER THAN SUB-JECT FOR COPYING.

> Or where some grove,
> Dark with thick oaks lies in sacred shadow.

The poet is versed in the sciences and can teach them. But when he presents agriculture or navigation or philosophy, the material is brought to us "alive, perfected, and adorned," and not "rude" and "bare." For example, "If some philosopher, using unadorned language, should teach that some mind pervades the universe, I should fall in love with this idea as being a noble idea. But if this same philosopher should tell me the same thing in poetic fashion, and should say:

> Know first, the heaven, the earth, the main,
> The moon's pale orb, the starry train
> Are nourished by a soul,
> A bright intelligence, which darts
> Its influence through the several parts
> And animates the whole.

"If, I say, he presents the same thing to me in this way, I shall not only love but be struck with wonder, and I shall feel a divine

---

[108] Fracastoro, *op. cit.*, p. 60.

something has entered into my soul." [109] Typical of the Renaissance in his attempt to grasp at various inconsistent ideals imperfectly worked out, Fracastoro finds it possible to describe a poet's decorative additions both as a development of the original material and as rhetorical devices.

Fracastoro's literary theory thus gives certain evidences of the growing Humanism. In this Humanism the ideal of the artist, the perfect picture or 'fore-conceit' which he has in his mind of the work to be done, allows interference with nature in the interests of beauty. Once feeling his own strength, the artist is started on a road which makes him substitute human reason for divine nature, and human pleasure for virtue and piety. More and more attention was given to the embroidering of the veil, to the balancing of periods, and to the introducing of conceits, to Euphuism, to twisting the columns and billowing the surfaces, to the play and effectiveness of the outward show itself—to the baroque. Ultimately bold spirits were to say that the only thing to be considered in a work of art was the pleasure it gives. Its truth, its power to teach, its balancing of its own wit with nature's efficacy were to be thrust back to let stand in accented isolation the one end of pleasure.

THE PROBLEM OF PLEASURE.

But the meaning of pleasure baffled the critics of the Renaissance as much as the meaning of harmony. Whose pleasure is to be considered? And why should pleasure be a criterion of beauty? These questions pressed for answer in the minds of the more thoughtful ones. They answered uncertainly, now appealing to the taste of the majority of men as the best criterion, now saying that a painter alone can trust his pleasure as true judgment of art, now frankly saying that agreeableness, like beauty, is a riddle. A painter alone can judge of paintings, said Dürer. But he added: "Anyone *may* give thee counsel." Even nitwits may happen to say something useful. [110] And Leonardo said even more humbly: "A painter should welcome criticism from everyone. For though a man may not be a painter he may have a true conception of the form of another man." [111] And Alberti found art wandering, not when it threw off

---

[109] Fracastoro, *op. cit.*, p. 60.
[110] Dürer, *op. cit.*, p. 180.
[111] "Trattato." ♯ 137.

tradition, but when it ceased to aim at the pleasure of all the people.

The theory of Aristotle, that a proportion subsists between sense and the object of sense, was at this time revived to explain how beauty and pleasure are related. Proportionateness may constitute beauty not only within the frame of the work but may bind the spectator congenially to what he views. Dürer thought pleasure must be abandoned as an esthetic criterion in favor of the golden mean. But this ideal of the golden mean may be converted into a relation, a subject-object relation, as well as merely require the avoidance of the too much and the too little.

We find the ideal of proportionateness turned in this direction in the early seventeenth century by Descartes (1596–1650). He also, like Dürer, had asserted the criterion of beauty to be a variable one, and to be decided practically by the generality of pleasure. But for the mathematical philosopher this variable has its constant. Speaking in general, he says, neither the beautiful nor the agreeable means anything but the relation of our judgment to an object.[112] He then refers for elaboration to his *Compendium on Music,* where he explains why one sound is more agreeable than another. Delectation, he says, "requires a certain proportion of the object to the sense. . . . Among objects of the sense, that is not most grateful to the mind, which is most easily perceived by the sense; not that, on the contrary, which is with the most difficulty apprehended; but that which is perceived not so easily, as that natural desire, whereby the senses are carried toward their proper objects, is not thereby totally fulfilled; nor yet so difficult as that the sense is thereby tired." [113] The harmony of beauty here signifies not a proportion of lines or masses or members, but of stimulus and response.[114]

Though neither in the orthodox esthetic opinion of the Renais-

BEAUTY AS EXPEDI-TION OF SENSORY FUNCTION.

---

[112] *Oeuvres de Descartes,* ed. Adam and Tannery, 11 Vols., Paris, 1902, Vol. I, pp. 132–34.

[113] *Ibid.,* Vol. X, p. 92; Eng. trans., London, 1653, p. 3.

[114] Cf.
                                      the mind
           Is indissociable from what it contemplates,
           As thirst and generous wine are to a man that drinketh
           Nor kenneth whether his pleasure is more in his desire
           Or in the savor of the rich grape that allays it.
                  Robert Bridges, *Testament of Beauty.*

sance, nor in the attempts at reflection by individual artists or critics, is there a theatrical change from medieval philosophy, yet insensibly all along the line, here a little and there a little, by making the beauty of form ever more and more the beauty that hard-won science can furnish, the beauty of light the distinction or 'meed of praise' that art can confer on great men, the beauty of a symbol the delicate embroidery and pleasing relationships in the outward cover, a new spirit enters esthetics. An almost religious devotion to the authority of the newly recovered classics, Plato, Aristotle, Horace, Vergil, helps to mediate and lubricate the change.

SECULARIZATION BRINGS RATIONALITY AND INDIVIDUALITY.

An intellectual and Pagan authority, however imposing, is likely to sit upon the mind of man otherwise than a religious authority. For when man relates himself to what man has made, discussion is always possible. So grounds and reasons were drawn whole from Plato and Aristotle, but at the same time the habit of reasoning was drawn from the same arsenal. Plato himself furnishes the best example of the self-destructive energy that can be fetched from a rational authority. The Defenses of Poetry which were written by the hundred, and which appealed for some of their weight to Plato, were found, to the mild consternation of the discoverers, to be anti-Platonic. Though the metaphysical doctrine of beauty which justified carnal fictions and secular poetry was indeed largely abstracted from the Dialogues, Plato himself was even so a 'poet-whipper.' He drove the tribe of imitators, though garland-crowned, from his ideal commonwealth. This paradox was the final knotty problem which worried and tested these 'defenders.' Plato became their 'sweet enemy.' Sidney's stout independence in the solution of this difficulty represents the independence of a whole group, and no unique defiance. It was the expression of a period which put all authorities, no matter how sweet or high, below the authority of man's own judgment. "If Plato," Sidney said, "will defile the fountain out of which his flowing streams have proceeded, let us boldly examine with what reasons he did it." [115] He decided that Plato condemned the abuse rather than the essence of poetry, and that even the dispraise must be viewed in the context of Plato's writings taken as a whole. Why should the tenth book of the

---

[115] Sidney, *op. cit.*, p. 44.

Republic overpower the sense of the *Phaedrus* and the *Symposium?*

This wrestling with Plato by means of material from Plato is CLASSICS FALLIBLE only one example of the emancipated attitude toward the classic TO SPIRIT OF MO-that shines forth more and more clearly in the Renaissance. And DERNITY. yet, here again, the indication of something new in esthetic theory, and the pointing to a definite revival of classical learning as the cause, is partly fallacious. For Boccaccio bent Plato to his own uses as an apologist of poetry before Marsilio Ficino (1433–1499) had become the transmitter through translations of Plato's main ideas to Lorenzo's Platonic Academy; and Boccaccio's roots go straight back to Augustine and Lactantius. To the objection to poetry, echoed from the Christian Fathers, that Plato himself exiled the poets from his ideal republic, Boccaccio replies that "only the poets who wrote ill things" were driven out. "I cannot think that Homer was exiled." [116] But the notes of defiance to religious authority, and even classical authority, thickened in the sixteenth century. In 1536, Peter Ramus (1515–1572) successfully defended the thesis at the University of Paris that "the utterances, one and all, of Aristotle, are false, and vain imaginations." [117] To be sure, Ramus represented the minority, his works were suppressed by royal mandate, and he was exiled again and again. Still, he had his following, and his tone of defiance had already been voiced and was to increase rather than decrease. A split in the ranks of the Aristotelians was a notable kind of protestantism in those times. On September 19, 1512, Giovanni Pico had already written with a more inclusive spirit of self-sufficient modernity to the literary critic, Bembo: "We are greater than the ancients in my opinion." And he continues, in Professor Bullock's paraphrase: "If they were greater than we, how can we hope to straddle into their stride? If (as Pico believes) we are greater, shall we not ludicrously waddle, when we narrow our stride to theirs? Rhetorical style should change with changing years." [118] In 1543 Ortensio Landi ridiculed Italian subserviency to "that vile beast Aristotle." [119]

---

[116] Osgood, *op. cit.*, p. 89. XIV, 19.

[117] Spingarn, *op. cit.*, p. 137.

[118] Bullock, "The Precept of Plagiarism in the Cinquecento," *Modern Philology*, Vol. XXV, No. 3, February, 1928.

[119] Spingarn, *op. cit.*, p. 164.

That 'bold examination' with which Sidney confronted his sweet enemy Plato, Ramus, 'the master of those who know,' and Pico, classical authority in general, was carried forward in the mind of the Renaissance to particular problems regarding poetry, art, and imagination. Though the orthodoxy of the time provided a set of rational definitions as to the end, instrument, essence, model, and materials of the arts, and though it assumed a moral purpose as a justification of art, and a supermundane origin of it, there was a lively heterodoxy which promised a new orientation, perhaps still rather distant.

CASTELVETRO: DE-
LIGHT AND NOV-
ELTY AS POETIC
ENDS.

The radical reaction against the moral purpose of poetry is expressed succinctly by Castelvetro: "What do beginning, middle, and end matter in a poem provided it delights?" [120] And Bernardo Tasso (1493-1569) confesses: "I have spent most of my efforts in attempting to please, as it seems to me this is more necessary and also more difficult to attain; for we found by experience that many poets may instruct and benefit us very much, but certainly give us very little delight." [121] Castelvetro's assertion that pleasure and not instruction or virtue is the aim of poetry is the most extreme that we find in theories of poetry at this time, and represents the pervasive heterodoxy of his whole theory of poetry. The poet must not confuse his business with that of philosophy, natural science, or satire, because what is required of him is "to delight and to recreate the minds of the crude multitude and of the common people." [122] Let the poet leave hidden truth to philosophers and scientists, who are far removed from poetry. His obedience to the rules of art, his occasional faults shall all be forgiven, if he caters to the popular demand for pleasure. Castelvetro forces Aristotle to teach this doctrine of his, as Plato was often converted from his literal statement to his Renaissance interpretation. As Plato, so it was said, did not in good earnest mean to banish poets, so Aristotle, it was alleged, did not mean to state that purgation

---

[120] *Poetica d'Aristotele*, p. 158. As Englished by Saintsbury, *History of Criticism*, Vol. II, p. 87.

[121] Spingarn, *op. cit.*, p. 55.

[122] Castelvetro, *op. cit.*, p. 29; trans. Gilbert, p. 307; cited by Charlton, *op. cit.*, p. 60.

of pity and fear was the end of poetry.[123] The pleasure of the mob is to be produced by the poet's introduction of the marvellous and by the industry with which he overcomes difficulties. As Castelvetro insists more exclusively on the end of pleasure than most of his contemporaries, so he insists on the novelty of the poet's work. He is not to copy the ancients, because he would not then invent. Invention becomes with him not the discovery of something hid in nature or classic writing, but something made up by the poet himself. He insists on a strict interpretation of the poet as a maker or creator. The painter copies; the poet "makes something quite original, entirely different from what has been done up to that day." [124]

DÜRER ON GENIUS.

The free rebellious note in the writings of the "most acute Castelvetro" has often been remarked. Not so often noted have been the utterances of Dürer still earlier in the century pointing out the unaccountability and inexhaustibility of the artist's genius. Though Dürer burned with the desire to furnish German painters with Italian science and models, he was aware that no amount of favorable nurture could take the place of nature. Much practice of the hand, and the acquisition of the arts of measurement are worth while only for one who has a "natural turn." The "natural turn" of the painter means an imagination teeming with figures, a fertility so rich and spontaneous that if he were to live hundreds of years he could every day produce a form never seen or even thought of before. God certainly gives certain men great gifts! This wonderful gift may show itself best, contrary to the vulgar opinion, in a little rough sketch. In half a day, if the genial fit is on, he may surpass what another takes a year for. One so endowed is not of his age. His work frequently has no parallel for centuries earlier or later.

POETRY AS PURE FICTION.

Dürer would never have cut off human genius from divine inspiration or cultivation through study. So the teeming wayward fancy, for him, still owed its debt to God and to study of nature and mathematics. There was, however, a tendency in literary criticism at this time to sever cleanly the bonds between poetry and nature

---

[123] *Ibid.*, p. 275; trans. Gilbert, pp. 315-316; cited by Charlton, *op. cit.*, p. 66.
[124] *Ibid.*, p. 68; cited by Charlton, *op. cit.*, p. 35.

and poetry and classical models. Certain ones declared the substance of poetry to be pure fiction. This interpretation contravened the orthodox doctrine that poetry is imitation of the universal. That is, the inventive genius of the poet is occupied in figuring forth the Platonic ideas, the patterns laid up in heaven of a more excellent goodness and heroic citizenry. This interpretation of imitation as copying, even though it were the penetration to God's secret law or Aristotle's universal, solemnized and fettered the performance of the poet in some degree. The rational analysis of the meaning of the term 'imitation' which the intellectual energy of the literary criticism of the Renaissance precipitated, issued finally in the suggestion that 'imitation' is imagination or fancy in the modern sense. For example, at the very beginning of the fifteenth century Lionardo Bruni explains that we receive no moral impression from poetry because we realize it is "fictitious." [125] And about the middle of the century Battista Guarini explains that we are not shocked by the sad or wicked elements of poetry as we would be in "real life" because in poetry we are concerned solely with the artist's success or unsuccess in fitting his persons and actions well together. "We criticize the artist, not the moralist," [126] he says. And how far is it from Sidney's observation—an echo of Minturno's "*Numquam ne fallit, qui omnia confingit*" [127]—that "for the poet, he nothing affirmeth, and therefore never lieth," to the observation that he affirms nothing, and therefore never makes moral judgments of any sort? Pallavicino (1607–1667) asks whether it is reasonable to suppose that the eager press of people who rob themselves of sleep to witness the staging of romances take for literal truth what they see and hear. Do they suppose the figure of Fortune is a real woman? And that rocks actually become horses? [128] Poetry exists for one end, and one alone, he says: to fill our minds with fresh and splendid visions. Though these esthetic visions convey no scientific truth, humanity has prized their makers above the professors of

---

[125] Spingarn, *op. cit.*, p. 10.
[126] *Loc. cit.*
[127] Antonio Sebastiano Minturno, *De Poeta*, 1559, p. 68.
[128] *Antologia Storica della Critica Letteraria Italiana*, ed. Andreoli, Vol. I, p. 263.

all other arts. No other book is guarded as is a book of poetry. No other intellectual type is called divine.[129]

Lively heterodoxy in criticism went farther. In the declaration of independence of artistic criticism, trenchant notes were struck by speculative philosophers. Apostle of freedom of thought in science and religion, Giordano Bruno was also a believer in freedom of poetical expression. He said: There are as many species of poet as there are of human sentiment. Stupid pedants have restricted the kinds to those who wear the laurel or the myrtle, but there are white-wine poets who wear the vine-leaf; bacchanalians who wear the ivy; singers of law and sacrifice who wear the olive; of agriculture, who wear the poplar, elm, and corn; and there are a jolly, homely sort who "buckle on [a] wreath composed of salad, sausage, and the pepper-caster." [130] Similarly, censorious enslavers of genius have measured poetical excellence by conformity to 'the rules.' "Know for certain, my brother, that such as these are beasts." [131] Poetry is not born in rules, but rules in poetry. True poets are recognized not by an intellectual yard-stick but by their singing. The Rules of Aristotle are useful only to apes; and the critics who stipulate so much and such and such metaphors, invocations, singleness of fable, absence of prologue or epilogue "are no other than worms," "that know not how to do anything well, but are born only to gnaw and befoul the studies and labours of others." [132] The rebellion of Francesco Patrizzi against the Aristotelian code was less flaming and more systematic. In *Della Poetica* (1586) he claimed that Aristotle's critical rule had too narrow a basis and was confused and obscure. He proposed a substitute which he based on the whole development of literature to his time.[133]

REBELLION IN CRITICISM.

---

[129] *Ibid.*, Vol. I, pp. 263, 264.
[130] Giordano Bruno, "A Discourse of Poets," in *Library of the World's Best Literature*, Vol. V, p. 2617.
[131] *Ibid.*, p. 2616.
[132] *Loc. cit.*
[133] Spingarn, *op. cit.*, pp. 165, 166.

SUPPLEMENTARY READING

Bosanquet, *History of Aesthetic*, Ch. VII.
Allan H. Gilbert, *Literary Criticism from Plato to Dryden.*
Erwin Panofsky, *Idea*, pp. 23–38.
Saintsbury, *History of Criticism*, Vol. II, Bk. IV.
Gregory Smith, ed., *Elizabethan Critical Essays*, 2 Vols., Oxford, 1904.
J. E. Spingarn, *History of Literary Criticism in the Renaissance*, New York, 1899.
Venturi, *History of Art Criticism*, Ch. IV.
K. Vossler, *Poetische Theorien in der italienischen Frührenaissance*, Berlin, 1900.

CHAPTER VII

The Seventeenth Century and the Neo-Classic Regime to 1750

REASON IN PHILOS-OPHY, RULES IN ART.

THE REIGN of reason which flourished in France in the seventeenth century and continued there and in England in the eighteenth is typified in philosophy by Descartes (1596–1650). Descartes marvelled that Philosophy had languished so long in unfruitfulness from neglect of the mathematical model of reasoning, and he resolved for his own part to accept no idea as true which did not force itself upon his reason with the same self-evidence he found in the intuition of his own existence or which could not be deduced from axioms and fundamental certainties by secure logical chains.[1] On the critical and creative side the age is exemplified in Corneille (1609–1684), the first martyr to the ideal of rigid rule among creative dramatists, who took up his cross willingly and so furnished all poets with an heroic example.[2] In three critical prefaces: "On the Function and Parts of the Dramatic Poem"; "On Tragedy"; and "On the Three Unities" he undertook to show that the theater could only be raised to good form, elegance, and order by strict adherence to the Aristotelian rules. The close connection between Descartes' ideal of clear and distinct thinking and the ideal of order, finish, and coherence for art in such writers as Corneille, Racine, and Boileau has been noted: "The literary seventeenth century realized at every point the Cartesian esthetics of which Descartes did not write the first

---

[1] *Oeuvres de Descartes,* ed. Adam and Tannery, 11 Vols., Paris, 1902, Vol. VI, pp. 8, 18, 32, 33.

[2] Karl Borinski, *Die Antike in Poetik und Kunsttheorie,* 2 Vols., Leipzig, 1914, Vol. II, p. 163.

word." [3] The formulation of scientific method in the arts, and the appeal to Aristotle had been going on in Italy for more than a century. One of the characteristic features of the Renaissance there had been the defenses and rivalries of poetry, painting, and sculpture and the plundering of Aristotle, Horace, Plato, and Vitruvius for conceptions, patterns, and arguments. The French critics went beyond the Italians in dry lucidity, analytical distinctness, and self-consciousness about method, but the broad outlines of their thought were the same and reflected a common origin.

DEMOCRITUS SUP-   It is true that the philosophy of the seventeenth century paral-
PLANTS ARISTOTLE. leled the rising Neo-Classicism in art. But philosophers on the whole turned against the Aristotelian spirit from which art drew its fresh inspiration. Their Greek philosopher was Democritus rather than Aristotle or Plato. They applied reason to politics, psychology, optics, physics, to general method and metaphysics and in this their kinship was with Copernicus and Galileo, Kepler and Newton. On the whole it may be said that the French dramatists and critics created the new rational manner for their age and country without the help of philosophy, and even in the face of the condescension of philosophy. Occupied with learning and the new mathematical science, philosophers did not follow sympathetically the changes going forward in the literary or artistic world. Indeed, their eyes on the free irregular forms of an earlier period, and failing for the most part to modify their traditional conception of the sinister properties of the fancy, they even accented the contrast between the spheres of philosophy and art. The more philosophy succeeded in strengthening and straightening itself according to the new scientific method, in turning all things into matter and motion with Hobbes, or in making the processes of spirit automatic and mechanical with Spinoza, the more it repudiated the waywardness and colorfulness of imagery. One might compare the case of philosophy to that of a lady who would win her lover's favor by abuse of her rival; so did philosophy seem to court favor with mathematics by disparaging references to poetry and fancy's visions. The relations of the kingdoms of philosophical reason and

---

[3] Emile Krantz, *L'Esthétique de Descartes*, Paris, 1882, p. iii. The whole book is an elaboration of this thesis.

of the imagination began to be defined by a set of antitheses: the one versus the many; the certain versus the fleeting and inconstant; the even mirror of Nature versus the crooked; objective order and truth versus the expression of personal disposition and accidental circumstance. The great philosophers of the period, Descartes, Spinoza, Leibniz, Bacon, Locke, and Pascal, were men of good sense and practical interests, some of them of marked scientific gifts; but their well reined-in thoughts were on guard against the fatuousness of ranging sympathy and pleasing personal conceits. Locke (1632–1704) is perhaps the most grudging of all in his references to the work of wit and fancy: "I confess," he writes, "in discourses where we seek rather pleasure and delight than information and improvement . . . , ornaments . . . can scarce pass for faults. But yet if we would speak of things as they are, we must allow that all the arts of rhetoric, besides order and clearness, all the artificial and figurative applications of words eloquence hath invented, are for nothing else but to insinuate wrong ideas, move the passions, and thereby mislead the judgment, and so indeed are perfect cheats." [4] The fancy he compares to a court-dresser, who is out with his "colors, appearances, and resemblances" to catch the unwary and divert them from truth; and eloquence he compares to a reigning beauty concerning whose charms all men prefer to be deceived. The culture and taste of Leibniz (1646–1716) fitted him for more catholic sympathies; yet in the frank mood of correspondence we find him speaking as a representative of philosophical rationalism: "I am glad indeed that Dryden received a thousand pounds sterling for his Vergil, but I wish that Halley could have had four times as much, and Newton, ten." [5] In other words the value of poetry to science is in the ratio of about one to seven. In another letter he makes his judgment of relative values equally clear: "I am sorry about the loss by fire of the Holbein paintings in Whitehall. Yet I feel after all a little like the Czar of Russia who told me that he more admired certain pretty machines

---

[4] *Locke's Philosophical Works*, ed. St. John, 2 Vols., London, 1913, Vol. II, p. 112. "An Essay Concerning Human Understanding," Bk. III, Ch. 10, #34.

[5] Leibniz, *Die Philosophischen Schriften*, ed. Gerhardt, 7 Vols., Berlin, 1890, Vol. III, p. 222.

than all the beautiful paintings he had been shown in the King's palace." [6]

The typical philosophical superciliousness toward the products of the imagination broke down at points, and in places where one might little expect it, as in the appreciation of poetry and fancy by Hobbes, the thoroughgoing materialist. But on the whole the creative imagination and its works were only appreciated by the philosophers when the imagination was interpreted in such a way as to make it continuous with the understanding. The art-critics during this period had more philosophy in them than philosophers had art-sensitiveness. For this very reason the esthetic fragments in Bacon, Descartes, Hobbes, and Leibniz, though groping and ambiguous, are peculiarly interesting.

AMBIGUITY OF IM-
AGINATION IN
BACON.

Bacon (1561–1626) divides the intellectual globe into three parts and assigns a faculty of the mind to each: memory to history; the imagination to poetry; reason to philosophy.[7] In discussing the province of poetry, he appears at first sight to do full justice to the independence of a poet's fancy and the height of his invention. "If the matter be attentively considered, a sound argument may be drawn from Poesy, to show that there is agreeable to the spirit of man, a more perfect order and a more beautiful variety than it can anywhere find in nature. . . . Whence it may be fairly thought to partake somewhat of a divine nature; because it raises the mind and carries it aloft, accommodating the shows of things to the desires of the mind, not [like reason and history] buckling and bowing down the mind to the nature of things." [8] But Bacon passes from this acknowledgment that poets can build a golden world to place science and philosophy definitely higher. He says: "But we stay too long in the theatre [the abode of poetry]; let us now pass to the palace of the mind, which we are to approach and enter with more reverence and attention." [9] In the next section of the work, which deals with science and philosophy, he begins by calling poetry a "dream of learning," and by saying, not that it

---

[6] Leibniz, *op. cit.*, p. 223.
[7] Bacon, *op. cit.*, Vol. VIII, p. 407.
[8] *Ibid.*, pp. 440, 441. "Of the Advancement of Learning."
[9] *Ibid.*, p. 469.

is divine, but that "it would be thought to have in it something divine." And he frankly announces the greater importance and reality of the coming theme by declaring: "But now it is time for me to awake and rising above the earth, to wing my way through the clear air of Philosophy and the Sciences." [10] Though in naming the faculties of the mind Bacon at one period allows the imagination an equal third place with the memory and the understanding; [11] in another place he leaves only memory and the understanding, and drops imagination to the position of messenger between the other two.[12] He also says twice that the concerns of the imagination are rather a sport or play of the mind than a work or duty.[13] This is not an early anticipation of the definition of art as play. Bacon's typical attitude toward pure plays of the imagination is mild tolerance from above. Ornaments of speech and the treasury of eloquence are fatuous in his estimation. In his essay on "Beauty" Bacon makes strangeness in proportion an indispensable attribute, and ridicules the folly of Dürer's attempt to reduce beauty to a mathematical relationship. But affectation of strangeness or anything adorned or swelling is strictly forbidden in the ordering of Solomon's house in the *New Atlantis* "under pain of ignominy and fines." [14] Of the three kinds of poetry—narrative, dramatic, and parabolic—the last, used by religion and availing itself of symbols and allegories, is to his mind the best. Bacon, then, belongs with the new age of science. What positive appreciation of poetry he expresses is in the spirit of the century that was receding, a century in which the arts were glorified not as free devisers of fair forms but as ingratiating expressions of scientific truths or moral ideals.

Though Descartes attempted to define beauty, wrote a treatise on music, and testified more than once to the majesty or sweetness of literary style, the interesting esthetic fragments in his writings are an episode and complication in the total body of his rationalistic

DESCARTES: BEAUTY IS EQUABLE STIMULATION.

---

[10] *Ibid.*, p. 470.
[11] *Ibid.*, Vol. VIII, p. 407.
[12] *Ibid.*, Vol. IX, p. 61.
[13] *Ibid.*, Vol. IX, p. 62; Vol. X, p. 404.
[14] *Ibid.*, Vol. V, p. 409, "New Atlantis."

philosophy rather than a major contribution to esthetic theory. In his *Discourse on Method* he speaks of the incomparable power and beauty of eloquence and the ravishing delicacy and sweetness of poetry. Still, like Bacon, he wakes up from his state of dreamy fascination and enters "with more reverence and attention" the palace of mathematical science and of the new philosophy which is to be founded on the model of mathematical clarity and distinctness.[15] In several letters he expresses admiration for the vigor, purity, and harmony of Jean Louis Balzac's way of writing. Once he even goes so far as to say that "the really important pronouncements are in the writings of poets rather than of philosophers." The reason is that poets have written with "the ecstasy and power of imagination." [16] In this connection he records a dream in which he was offered the choice of a dictionary, symbolizing the encyclopedia of the sciences, or a collection of the works of the poets. He chose the second. In poets, he says, in spite of certain follies, there is gravity and sensitiveness, and greater capacity to kindle the sparks of wisdom in men than there is in philosophers.[17] But however much he might acknowledge at odd moments the sweetness and kindling power of the arts, his abiding admiration was for chains of reason-coercing deductions. Descartes' esthetic norm, as we gather it from his *Correspondence*, *Compendium of Music*, and *Treatise on the Passions*, swings back ultimately to a mathematical and logical ideal, although it makes a circuit through individual psychology and the agitation of the nerves. In response to a request from Father Mersennes for a definition of beauty, he wrote in 1630 that beauty was in much the same case as preference for one sound over another. Both were relative to the varying individual judgment. What makes one dance, makes another weep, because esthetic preference depends much on casual association. If one chanced never to have heard a *gaillarde* except in periods of affliction, the rhythm and pattern would become indissolubly united with painful emotion.[18] In this letter and often in his cor-

---

15 Descartes, *op. cit.*, Vol. VI, pp. 6, 7.
16 *Ibid.*, Vol. X, p. 217.
17 *Ibid.*, pp. 182–84.
18 *Ibid.*, Vol. I, pp. 132–34.

respondence Descartes comes back to the ideas expressed in his *Compendium of Music* of 1618, drawing on it and enlarging on it as something close to his interests and in agreement with his mature conviction. In the *Compendium*, beauty is allied with agreeableness, and agreeableness is congeniality, or adaptation of stimulus to response. The human voice is the most agreeable of sounds "because it holds the greatest conformity to our spirits," [19] and among human voices a friend's is the most sympathetic. The general tendency of musical rhythms again is to set up an affection or passion in the soul similar to that of the music: a slow measure excites gentle and sluggish feelings, such as languor or sadness, and a nimble and swift measure, nimble and sprightly passions, such as joy or anger. Thus any given motion in an esthetic stimulus tends to elicit its counterpart among the motions of the soul. The natural law of 'like to like' is used roughly to explain the effects of music and preferences in sound.[20]

But this vague Empedoclean law is shifted by Descartes toward the ideal of the golden mean. That sensation or arrangement, interval or rhythm, pleases which neither bores nor fatigues.[21] The extremes to be avoided in esthetic experience are those of the confusing, implicated figure, laborious and tiring, on the one hand, and of monotony and unfulfilled desire on the other. The noise of thunder or the splendor of the sun is displeasing because out of proportion to its sensory-receptor. The "mother in the Astrolabe" is displeasing because "too implicate a figure" for the natural activity of sight.[22] If one consults Descartes' treatment of the passions of the soul and his directions for regulating the mind in order to obtain a better understanding of this esthetic idea, one finds that passions and sentiments are good which minister to well-being, preserve health, protect from danger, and exercise without straining.[23] Physiology thus explains what mathematics analyzes and proves. Descartes' pronouncement in favor of simple ratios in

---

[19] *Ibid.*, Vol. X, p. 90; *Renatus Des-Cartes Excellent Compendium of Musick*, translated by A Person of Honour, London, 1653, p. 1.

[20] *Ibid.*, Vol. X, pp. 91, 92; pp. 2, 3.

[21] *Ibid.*, Vol. X, p. 92; p. 3.

[22] *Ibid.*, Vol. X, p. 91; p. 2.

[23] *Ibid.*, Vol. XI, p. 383.

musical intervals, fifths and twelfths, and two-part or three-part time, and his condemnation of artificial counterpoint and acrostics in retrograde verses have reference to his theory of bodily motions. Esthetic experience begins in sensation; sensation starts an agitation of the nerves; this agitation, preserved in the measure and combined in the proportions which stabilize the organism as a whole, is pleasurable and beneficial. It is because gentle exercise is always good for the nerves that the contemplation of painful emotions on the stage is valuable, even though pain in actor tends to waken pain in beholder. We receive no harm from the spectacle; and stimulation as such brings pleasure.

DEMONSTRATION
FINAL EVEN FOR
BEAUTY.

But ultimately the beauty of certain ratios and proportions in music rests for Descartes on their superior demonstrability in the mathematical sense. Although Descartes says that the man who is most susceptible to passions involving both body and soul can taste the most sweetness in this life,[24] he yet places above the health and comfort brought by adjusted desires, the intellectual joy which results from spiritual activity, and from the voluntary union of the spiritual part of man with what is bodiless. In the end the imagination is treated simply as handmaid to the reason. And the calculations of proportions that make the substance of the musical *Compendium* have to do for the most part with arithmetical analogies, not with the analogy of sound to sense. Descartes definitely repudiates appeal to the sense of hearing in music as compared with trust in its well-assured demonstrations.[25] He says he finds the arguments of the musicians who deny the proportions of consonances too absurd to answer. It is, he says, as if one should argue against the system of mathematical proportions in architecture because the eye fails to grasp a thousandth part of their exactitude.[26] The diagrams in the *Compendium* by which Descartes graphically sets forth the order and connection of tones and intervals are then scarcely more than an illustration of his rational ideal for all knowledge. All matters to be studied, he taught, are to be analyzed into their simplest elements, and the ideas obtained placed in a series of in-

---

[24] Descartes, *op. cit.*, Vol. XI, p. 488. "Les Passions de l'Âme," Article CCXII.
[25] *Ibid.*, Vol. I, pp. 227, 228.
[26] *Ibid.*, p. 286.

creasing complexity in order that the mind may march with un-failing security from one self-evident truth to the next. For we should busy ourselves about nothing that offers less certitude than arithmetic and geometry.[27]

At the same time that Descartes was objecting to the puzzle-like character of fugues, Hobbes (1588–1679) was objecting to the "ambitious obscurity of expressing more than is perfectly con-ceived" in poetry, and lines that some called strong, but that he set down as "no better than riddles." [28] Descartes wrote his book on music, on the whole a mere second-hand text-book, following the theory of Zarlino and without many original ideas. Hobbes on the other hand wrote two pieces of literary criticism: an answer to Davenant's Preface to *Gondibert* and a preface to his own trans-lation of Homer, which together have won him the estimate that his "esthetic is consistent and logical throughout, the first of its kind in English literature." [29]

Hobbes was, indeed, the first Englishman to wrestle by means of intellectual tools with the conception of the creative fancy. He states his dissatisfaction with the current and traditional theory of the passions and affections, and his own ambition to be the first to speak sense in this matter. In talking about mental processes, he complains, people use many words and make nothing under-stood. They say "the senses receive the species of things, and de-liver them to the common sense; and the common sense delivers them over to the fancy, and the fancy to the memory, and the memory to the judgment, like handing of things from one to another." [30] The logical mind of Hobbes rebelled against this picture of men-tal life as a toy-exchange of goods by little business-men in the brain. His own account of the fancy only half emerges from al-legory and tradition, but his attempt to draw the "wild ranging" of the poet within the neat scheme of his mechanical philosophy

HOBBES: THE MIND IS MATTER IN MO-TION.

---

[27] *Ibid.*, pp. 362–66.
[28] *Critical Essays of the Seventeenth Century*, Vol. II, p. 63. "Answer to the Preface to Gondibert."
[29] Spingarn, "Jacobean and Caroline Criticism," *Cambridge History of Eng-lish Literature*, New York, 1911, Vol. VII, Ch. 2, p. 302.
[30] *The English Works of Thomas Hobbes*, ed. Molesworth, 11 Vols., London, 1839, Vol. III, p. 10. "Leviathan," I, ii.

is a boldly interesting attempt to combine and reconcile apparent incompatibles.

In trying to introduce order into the psychological chaos, Hobbes leaned on the presupposition of his whole philosophy that in reality nothing exists but matter and motion, and that all philosophy is ideally nothing but addition and subtraction. A sensation is a motion received from without; our formation of an image from the sensation is a counter-pressure or motion outwards. The memory is a store-house of the residues of motions. In the mixture of memory with new impressions, the old adheres to the new. The loss of vivacity in what is the dying swing of the original motion turns images into instances of mental decay: passive, pale, and expiring vibrations. Motions within us can be added, subtracted, multiplied, and divided. The romancer, actor, or dramatist "compoundeth the image of his own person with the image of the actions of another man, as when a man imagines himself a Hercules or Alexander." [31] Nothing new arises in the mind when no new vibrations are started by the impact of an outer object, "unless we choose to call that new which is compounded of old ones [vibrations], such as a chimera, a golden mountain, and the like." [32] Dreams result from mixed motions within the organism. A steady motion, or strong original impression, can become a ruling and controlling motion or passion. Motions go in 'trains' and thus compose connected thinking or fancying.

How, then, with so mechanical a view of the operations of the mind, is it possible that Hobbes did constructive and original work on the nature of the poet's fancy? One answer is that he magnified the office of the fancy rather by fragmentarily attributing to it functions which his basic mechanism can hardly carry, and which echoed the traditional allegorizing of the mind's faculty, than by a theory of mind to which an appreciative view of the creative imagination is really congenial. At various times Hobbes draws within the province of fancy the motive force of the passions, the ordering faculty of judgment and philosophy, and the native elevation and speed of a gifted temperament.

---

[31] *The English Works of Thomas Hobbes, op. cit.,* p. 6.
[32] *Ibid.,* Vol. I, p. 400. "Elements of Philosophy," IV, xxv.

As the mind's builder with images, fancy works well, Hobbes says, when it aims at some clearly envisaged goal. In this sense fancy includes the passion and desire which make a mind active and keep it from being commonplace and dull. Mental dynamics thus, for fancy, becomes a part of mental architectonics. All quickness and steadiness of the mind's motion follow from the passionate effort toward the end conceived. Fancy again may include delicacy in the relating activity. The man of strong fancy sees similitudes where others see no interesting relationship, and his ranging is quick and sudden as well as piercing. "From thence proceed those grateful similes, metaphors, and other tropes, by which both poets and orators have it in their power to make things please or displease, and show well or ill to others, as they like themselves." [33]

Fancy, again, may include judgment, *i.e.*, intellectual discernment. At times Hobbes holds to a distinction between the fancy as detecting similarities and the judgment as detecting differences, but at other times his tendency to make artistic genius absorb all the functions of mind makes him drop the discrimination.

Like most contemporary writers on the mental faculties Hobbes debates at times the weight to be given to the judgment, held now to be a separate power, in comparison with that to be given the productive imagination. In general, he says, an extravagant fancy cannot redeem a defect in discretion. But in any kind of poetry, though both judgment and fancy are required, "the fancy must be more eminent." [34] The sublimity of a poet rests on his fancy. This fancy is what most readers like in poetry and call fury. In other words, on normal occasions good sense is better than imagination. But poetry cannot submit altogether to this general norm. Enthusiasm is the moving and taking quality in poetry.

In one complex and suggestive passage Hobbes calls the poet's fancy architectural and philosophical. He says that in those cases—fortunate for the poet—in which philosophy has already introduced order and system among the data of experience, fancy finds the substance which she would elaborate ready-prepared, and needs

---

[33] *Ibid.*, Vol. IV, p. 55. "Human Nature."
[34] *Ibid.*, Vol. III, p. 58. "Leviathan," I, viii.

only to "make a swift motion over" this material to be ready to sing and dance. But where philosophy has failed to do her part as she has thus far failed in the case of moral philosophy, there fancy must do both the ordering and arranging, fetch both substance and words, and not omit the adorning and ingratiating.[35] This is a very high estimate of the compass of the poetic faculty. It seems far removed from a view of imagination as a mere machine for retaining or multiplying previous impressions. It implies that fancy not only burns and flies, but thinks and classifies. But even in this supreme moment of Hobbes' esthetic speculation there is less sensitiveness than appears. The philosophy he is talking about and desiderating is computation. He is not really suggesting that poetry can fulfill the high destiny of philosophy. He is saying rather that while philosophy still lags, and mechanical explanation has not yet covered all the territory of being, poetry may function as a *pis aller*. The philosophy that in some measure has prepared smooth ground for the song and dance of poetry is physical science, astronomy and engineering. The moral philosophy that for Hobbes is lacking and which poetry must supply is a mechanics of the passions and affections. Moreover, to define poetry as moral philosophy and painting as physical philosophy was already an old story in the criticism of the arts.

HOBBES' ESTHETIC PSYCHOLOGY BETWEEN TWO WORLDS.

In the end, then, what we have from Hobbes is a striking instance of crossing strains. The classical psychological tradition interweaves with the new mechanical science. For Hobbes all was matter and motion, whether in the mind or not. In his discussion with Descartes, he urges that reason depends on names, names on imagination, "and imagination, as I think, on the motion of the corporeal organs. Thus mind will be nothing but the motions in certain parts of an organic body." [36] The swiftness and piercingness of fancy in its search for the materials of poetry is the tenuity and agility of the vital spirits. Indeed, that admirable unity which Hobbes attributes to the mind and which makes him seem a modern is bought at the price of an uncompromising materialism. The

---

[35] *The English Works of Thomas Hobbes*, Vol. IV, pp. 449, 450. "Answer to the Preface to Gondibert."

[36] *The Philosophical Works of Descartes*, trans. Haldane and Ross, 2 Vols., Cambridge, 1912, Vol. II, p. 65.

fancy can include memory, sense, judgment, and the passions, because all are complexes of motions taking place within the body.

The few friendly moves on the part of the philosophers toward art are the exception rather than the rule in the seventeenth century. For the most part the arts found themselves in a cool, unpropitious philosophical *milieu*. Those who should have been their philosophical interpreters were absorbed in the progress of science. If then art was to walk with the times in this scientific and progressive age, it had to shift for itself. Philosophy gave it little direct help. "The true value of poetry," Rapin wrote in 1673, "is so little known that scarce ever is made a true judgment of it." [37] This true judgment the hundreds of critics in France, carrying out the suggestions of earlier critics in Italy, attempted to furnish. Most of them judged poetry in such a way as quickly to place her on the winning side with the new scientific philosophy. But they achieved this by a remarkable perception. As Thomas Aquinas found it possible to be a good Christian and yet use the pagan philosophy of Aristotle for his rational scheme of Christian doctrine, so the critics drew without intellectual discomfort and with happy results both from Aristotle and from the new mechanical science. None of the professional philosophers of the age except Leibniz was conscious of the possibility of such a fusion of influences. Hobbes and Bacon, though they opened the doors of reason to the messenger of imagination, did not see that Aristotle, to whom the poets loved to resort for principles, supplied a better foundation than Democritus for a theory of the fancy, and one quite as easy to combine with the fashionable exact science. Ben Jonson (1573?–1637) observed—what anyone must have been able to see—that in a period of rapidly advancing natural knowledge it would be strange if some of the new knowledge did not enter into the molding of poetical form. And so indeed it came about. The Aristotelian tradition was bowed and buckled to the mental frame of Newton's age. Without losing grip on Aristotle's logic, analysts gave fresh attention to his doctrine of motion; and his theory of efficient causality was accorded equal weight with his theory of

SYNTHESIS LEFT
FOR THE CRITICS.

---

[37] *Monsieur Rapin's Reflections on Aristotle's Treatise of Poesie*, trans. Rymer, London, 1694, p. 10, I.

formal and final causes. In Du Bellay's list of the subjects for study for an aspiring poet natural and mathematical science are mentioned as of chief importance. Diversely colored strands, then, composed the reason and good sense of Neo-Classic art doctrine. Like Descartes, and satisfying the new Cartesian instinct for clarity, Boileau (1636–1711) wrote a poet's Discourse on Method, but he drew his content from Aristotle. Like Hobbes, Le Bossu (1631–1680) wrote a mechanics and dynamics of the passions, linking this with the effects of poetry, but he drew his content from Aristotle.

Hobbes speaks boldly and freshly among the philosophers when he says that imagination and reason must work together for the making of heroic verse. "So far forth as the Fancy of man has traced the ways of true philosophy, so far it hath produced very marvellous effects to the benefit of mankind. But where these precepts [of philosophy] fail . . . there the Architect, Fancy, must take the philosopher's part upon herself . . . not only be the Poet to place and connect, but also the Philosopher, to furnish and square her matter." [38] But though radical for philosophy, the idea of the philosophizing poet or painter was already commonplace in criticism. A saying of Le Bossu reads almost like an illustration of Hobbes' demand that the poet organize his material philosophically, if he does not find it already organized to his hand by philosophy proper: Poetry is analogous to Theology, the science of divine things, because it organizes into genera and species human moral behavior, making it thus easy for man's comprehension, as Theology organizes into species and genera the persons and actions of the Deity.[39] And Hobbes' general declaration that things go well with poetry when fancy traces the ways of philosophy, finds a counterpart, easy to multiply, in the statement by Henry Reynolds that poets and philosophers belong together as "who are or should be both professors of but one and the same learning," [40] though the one group uses verse and the other prose.

---

[38] Hobbes, *op. cit.*, Vol. IV, pp. 449, 450. "Answer to the Preface to Gondibert."

[39] Le Bossu, *Traité du Poème Épique*, Paris, 1708, p. 7.

[40] *Critical Essays of the Seventeenth Century*, ed. Spingarn, 3 Vols., Clarendon Press, Oxford, 1908, Vol. I, p. 153.

But no general kinship between poetry and philosophy was enough for the critical compatriots of Descartes. A crisper fashioning, a drier model, an abandonment of morality's tendency to soar, was wanted for the new theorists of art. In searching out the ultimate properties of matter, Descartes had driven forth one after the other of the humanly interesting attributes: color, fragrance, taste, and so in the end had left his exemplary piece of wax, a bare figure of number and ratio.[41] A parallel impulse moved the critics. They would be the new champions of rational order in the uncouth regions of the fancy. So poetry trussed and laced herself; cried up strict rules and decorum; stiffened and narrowed the unities of time and place; adopted the common language of prose and practical sense. The literary critics alluded freely to the Gothic barbarism of earlier writers, their lack of polish and refinement, their innocence of science and method. Instructions on how to conduct the understanding for "sure marching in this world," "for true knowledge of things as they are," and systems and prescriptions of the laws of tasteful and rational painting and poetry were the popular type of treatise. Dogmas were crystallized and recorded, so that any intelligent man should be able to think, compose, or depict by going to the book. Nature, it was admitted, must give a man genius. But a man would never get far who trusted to native endowment alone without submitting to the discipline of reason and rules. Art must cultivate nature. "Your genius and good star may lift you high," writes Vauquelin de la Fresnaye in 1594. "By its aid you may write works capable of astonishing future generations. But if you wish your work to be perfect you must learn all the rules of art. Moreover these rules are not to be picked up anyhow, but learned methodically." [42] A host of critics emphasized the importance of regular method, but it was Boileau (1636–1711) who fixed the code. He it was who before all others perhaps assimilated poetry to the Cartesian clear and distinct idea. Reason's yoke, he wrote, has falsely been supposed to hinder verse-making. On the contrary, this rational control, far from harming poetry, renders her divine.

---

[41] Descartes, *op. cit.*, Vol. VII, pp. 30–34.
[42] Vauquelin de la Fresnaye, *L'Art Poétique*, ed. Pellissier, Paris, 1885, Bk. II, lines 435–43.

> Love reason, then; and let whate'er you write
> Borrow from her its beauty, force, and light.[43]

The music and the beauty of the words are secondary to the clear thought:

> As your idea's clear, or else obscure,
> The expression follows, perfect or impure;
> What we conceive with ease we can express;
> Words to the motion flow with readiness.[44]

Even in 1746 Batteux is still seeking the clear and distinct idea at the basis of the arts, and wants "to clear away the mists, and establish true precepts." [45]

The codification of the law of poetry began one hundred years later in England; so we find Pope repeating Boileau's doctrine in his *Essay on Criticism.* The great poet Vergil, he writes, fancied for a time that he might dispense with rules and models and go to Nature direct for his inspiration. But a wiser Vergil was soon writing according to a method as strict and rules as confining as if worked out by the organizing mind of Aristotle himself.[46] This 'Art of Poetry,' with its rules of order, was referred to by the French critic Rapin as the "instrument of genius." [47] So genius had its instrument as philosophy had its *Novum Organum.*

The search for a general rational program took place at much the same time and in much the same way in respect to painting. It was declared to be the function of the newly founded French Academy to find rules for painting that were simple, infallible, and mutually illuminating. Earlier painters and theorists had walked too much by observation and habit, and too little by theory. "Their science was in their fingers rather than in their heads." De Piles, "prince of the critics of French painting," carried his zeal for accurate discrimination of the parts of painting—composition, color,

---

[43] Boileau, *L'Art Poétique,* ed. Smith, Cambridge University Press, 1898, "Chant Premier," lines 37–39.
[44] *Ibid.,* "Chant Premier," lines 151–55.
[45] Batteux, *Principes de la Littérature,* 5 Vols., Paris, 1764, Vol. I, pp. xviii, 4.
[46] Pope, *An Essay on Criticism,* Part I, lines 130–39.
[47] Rapin, *op. cit.,* p. 26. XVIII.

design, and expression—and the degree to which the famous painters excelled in these, so far that he drew up a table in which he
gave mathematical values to the attainments of each. It was characteristic of him as a seventeenth century *savant* that he combined
with the use of number to measure artistic skill, insistence on the
value of classic models in sculpture.

'To please according to the rules' was then the ideal of the MORAL AIM FUN-
arts. The rules were arranged in order; the parts were counted DAMENTAL.
and compared. Rule One for poetry was: fix the moral purpose to
be achieved. "Let us remember that we learned from Horace that
we cannot please the greatest number unless we include in our
work a moral purpose." [48] Even before one selected a subject or
fable one selected the end one wished to have in view, "for by
it one regulates the whole work and all its parts." [49] The peerless
poet, thinking of the way he will fashion manners and morals by
his poetry, must be a good man. This stipulation of good character
in the poet tied the Renaissance critic of poetry to the medieval
mystic, and now again ties the Neo-Classical code-writer to his
Renaissance predecessors in criticism. "Because the Muses will not
lodge in a soul if it is not good, holy, and virtuous, you shall be of
good nature, not bad, frowning, or surly; but animated by a noble
spirit, you will permit nothing to enter your mind that is not super-
human and divine. You shall have in the first place conceptions that
are elevated, grand, and beautiful, not trailing on the ground." [50]
So writes Ronsard (1524–1585). An atmosphere of the fear of
God and reverence for the good is to surround and direct the
whole. The next explicit rule, then, following this injunction
of virtue, well-understood and thoroughly traditional, directs the
poet or painter to hunt out a suitable myth or thesis as the subject
of the proposed work. This is called his 'invention,' and means,
not something originated by him, but a congenial literary source
discovered by him in his learned searching of the classic authors.

---

[48] Corneille, *De l'Utilité et des Parties du Poème Dramatique*, 1660, trans. in
European Theories of the Drama, ed. Clark, p. 140.

[49] Le Bossu, *op. cit.*, pp. 37–43.

[50] *Oeuvres Complètes de Ronsard*, 2 Vols., Paris, Bibliothèque de la Pléiade,
Vol. II, p. 998.

Since painting used literary sources at this period, the beginning
of method for both was the same. One must first find the subject
for a picture, and then adapt its central substance to the particular
kind of thing, the particular end in view at the moment. "The
choice of a subject is called good," says Chapelain (1595–1674)
"when it is adapted to the purpose." [51] Chapelain gives an example.
"The choice of the fable of Adonis was good for the new type of
peace-poem because the action occurred in time of peace; it is
simple rather than complicated with intrigue; it is all love; and it
is seasoned with the sweet circumstances of peace and with the
discreet salt of witty conceits." Invention, as the prime material
requisite, means not the bare selection of a theme, but the ordering,
arranging, and designing of that theme: the fresh dressing of it so
as to make it appropriate to the mood and occasion, and though old
yet in a sense new and original. The same principle applies to
painting. One might select for a theme the rape of Europa, but
this invention would then be painted with a French Court environment to make it appropriate to the age in which it was destined to
be exhibited. "The Invention of a Painter consists not in inventing
the subject, but in a capacity of forming in his imagination the
subject in a manner best accommodated to his art, though wholly
borrowed from Poets, Historians, or popular tradition. . . . He
must in a manner recast the whole, and model it in his own imagination." [52]

'INVENTION' AND
ITS SOURCES.

Thus invention, the first part or element of a Neo-Classic poem
or picture, implied reverence for and use of the models of antiquity,
the literary subject, and the design of this matter to place, time,
and circumstance, as well as composition in the narrower sense
of pleasing formal pattern. "Among the particulars of this Art,
the Subject and Design ought to have the first place, because it is,
as it were, the first Production of the Wit; and the Design in a
Poem is what they call the Ordonnance in a Picture. The great
painters only are capable of a great Design in their Draughts, such

---

[51] *La Préface de Chapelain à l'Adonis*, in Festschrift, Heinrich Norf, Halle,
1905, p. 36.
[52] *The Literary Works of Sir Joshua Reynolds*, 2 Vols., London, 1886, Vol. II,
p. 307. "Notes on *The Art of Painting*," Note XII, Verse 109.

as a Raphael, a Julius Romanus, a Poussin, and only great Poets are capable of a great subject in their Poetry."[53]

The shifting of the definition of invention and the Italian influence upon it become still more apparent when this design, taken from antique sources and remodeled, is identified with *verisimilitude*, or imitation of nature. It is the same thing to select properly from the ancient storehouse of sculptured form and fabled story, and to choose judiciously the loveliest of Nature's forms; and both are the first and chief part of art-method or adherence to the rule. At this very moment the founders of modern philosophy were saying that the creative imagination of the artist distorts nature. Imagination, says Bacon, "exceeds the measure of nature, joining at pleasure things which in nature would never have come together and introducing things which in nature would never have come to pass" so making "unlawful matches and divorces of things."[54] While Bacon was saying this, Boileau was saying: "Nothing is beautiful but what is true."[55] And soon Pope was to exhort poets thus:

> First follow Nature, and your Judgment frame
> By her just standard, which is still the same.
> Unerring Nature, still divinely bright,
> One clear, unchang'd and Universal Light.[56]

The rules of poetic art, the first principles of method are, he says, "Nature still, but Nature methodized."[57] The Frenchman Rapin had used almost the same words earlier: "I affirm that these Rules well considered, one shall find them made only to reduce Nature into method, to trace it step by step, and not suffer the least mark of it to escape us. 'Tis only by these rules that the Verisimilitude in Fictions is maintained, which is the Soul of Poesy."[58] Even before the age of reason arrives Taille writes in the Preface to his tragedy *Saul* (1572): "In conclusion, I have not fabricated fabulous histories

---

[53] Rapin, *op. cit.*, pp. 26, 27. XIX.
[54] Bacon, *op. cit.*, VIII, 407, 408; VIII, 439.
[55] Boileau, *Épîtres*, IX.
[56] Pope, *An Essay on Criticism*, Part I, lines 68–72.
[57] *Ibid.*, line 89.
[58] Rapin, *op. cit.*, pp. 17, 18. XII.

here about the madness of an Athamant, an Hercules, a Roland, but
I present histories which truth herself has dictated, and which wear
on their brow their safe-conduct." [59] Emphasis on the importance
of truth for a poet appears again and again in sentences like these:
"The treasuries of poesie cannot be better bestowed than upon the
apparelling of Truth." [60] "The true artificer will not run away
from nature, as he were afraid of her, or depart from life and
the likeness of Truth." [61] "It is of verisimilitude that the poet must
take care." [62]

DEEP MEANING OF
'VERUM' IN VERI-
SIMILITUDE.

But the truth to nature which is enjoined by defenders of
poetry as religiously as by scientific philosophers has to be interpreted. It can no more be 'picked up by the way' than the rules.
When poetical verisimilitude is interpreted, the closeness of theory
of poetry to philosophy becomes even more apparent. In subjecting the mind to the nature of things philosophers were to find out
what were variously called the 'forms' or 'laws' or 'essences' of
things. Not the variously colored and shaped sense-world, as it
casually meets and impresses the first glance of the eye, but the
inward ruling causes that lie behind and explain the order and
connection of these chance phenomena were the philosopher's
concern. And so for a poet or painter, not actual men and actions
with their baffling mixture of good and bad, but types of character and purified logicized fables leading in a way analogous to the
syllogism to a consent of the mind, and to virtuous deeds, composed the true model in nature. Appealing for authority and text
to Aristotle's saying that a good poet imitates things not as they
are but as they ought to be, the neo-Aristotelian critics taught the
writer to picture the moral order of nature, the reasons that
the discerning eye of the mind discovers behind the visible con-
glomeration. For example Chapelain, though a heretic in his preference for epic over the drama, explains clearly the normal attitude
on the relation of poetry to history. When I read histories, he says,

---

[59] Jean de la Taille, *Saul*, Paris, 1598, p. 5.
[60] *Critical Essays of the Seventeenth Century*, ed. Spingarn, Vol. I, p. 186.
Sir William Alexander, "Anacrisis."
[61] *Ibid.*, Vol. I, p. 23. Ben Jonson, "Preface to The Alchemist."
[62] Le Bossu, *op. cit.*, p. 11.

I am not taught that the good are rewarded and the bad punished, for there chance and fortune govern men's lots. But in poetry (a sublime science like philosophy) moral justice always runs true to type. I get no moral profit from reading about Caesar or Pompey. On the other hand, "I see from the reading of poetry, under the accidents which happen to Ulysses and Polyphemus, what is reasonable and what happens in general to all those who act in the same way." I learn not simply about the piety of Aeneas and the wrath of Achilles, but of "piety and what follows and wrath and its effects, so that I know its nature fully." The classic writers, seeing that moral instruction could only be got by changing things to suit their purpose, "banished truth from their Parnassus" and kept the better and more profitable "verisimilitude." If we can believe peoples' stories, the Achilles of Homer and the Aeneas of Vergil were no better, actually, than they should be; but the poets, knowing their business, "proposed under their names" men who behaved as men ought to behave.[63]

From the present-day point of view it would hardly seem that the substitution of Piety-in-General for the concrete individual Aeneas or of Type-of-Wrath for Achilles would make a poem more emotionally effectual. The rubber-stamping of character, the marshalling, restricting, and bleaching of the fable to a correct moral pattern would seem to us today to rob the content of the story of that variety, fullness, and individuality which are necessary for interest and pleasure. But the Neo-Classical theorists interpreted the rational generality of their fables and characters otherwise. Precisely through the exact adjustment by general formula of poetical means to passionate end, they believed they could touch the springs of passion with a scientist's non-wastefulness and foreknowledge. Verisimilitude, another name for 'things-as-they-ought-to-be,' brings nothing to the attention of the spectators "that is not easily judged to be so." And thus the "imagination is captured and lets itself be led by the purpose of the poet." History is not so easily believed in spite of the fact that it is the 'naked truth.' For the 'naked truth' tyrannically forces belief, not through

---

[63] Chapelain, *op. cit.*, p. 38.

its own persuasiveness and reasonableness, but by the arbitrary assertion of the chronologist.

The same doctrine of the universality of Nature occurs in directions for the painters. The painter is to seek out the lovelier forms in Nature's boundless store. "To paint particulars is not to paint nature, it is only to paint circumstances. When the artist has conceived in his imagination the image of perfect beauty, or the abstract idea of forms, he may be said to be admitted into the great council of Nature." [64] But to generalize from Nature directly, *i.e.* from the "sudden and vicious variety of actual forms," is too difficult. The artist is to avail himself of the united powers of all his predecessors, that is, he is to study the antique, and thus come at nature through art.

The rules that follow in the artist's book of directions from these primary ones of right choice of subject, right relation to nature, right moral purpose, are maxims for the purifying of the instrument toward the desired end of the insensible influence on the imagination. The effect to be produced is a medicinal one on men's hearts. Nothing that will cause resistance in the succession of events in the story, nothing that will seem out of key in the disposition of the parts of the picture, nothing that will seem rude or vulgar in word or line is to be allowed, because, as Corneille says, the audience must leave the theatre—or must end the poem or leave the picture—with the mind doubting of nothing and at peace. Skilful judging of all things toward this end is the detail of the discipline of the artist. The colors in a picture must be 'social.' If they seem of their own accord to grow together, there will be the subtle communication of this harmonious relation to the color-receptors in the spectators. The graceful form and the grand air recommended are for the sake of securing acquiescence: the pleasure that is to 'carry' the profit. It is the honey smeared on the cakes containing the tables of the law. Aristotle's doctrine of organic unity in a good poem (nothing can be added nor taken away from the perfect work of art) now becomes interpreted by this more intense and sophisticated age with less freedom and breadth. Since it is

---

[64] Reynolds, *op. cit.*, Vol. II, p. 300. "Notes on *The Art of Painting*," Note III, Verse 51.

necessary that the action be complete, one must also not add anything further, since when the effect has been attained, the listener
desires nothing further and is bored by all the rest. So it is that the
expressions of joy which two lovers show on being reunited after
many obstacles, must be very short, says Corneille. The 'unities of
time and place' are not suggestions, as with Aristotle, but prescriptions, in the spirit of an age of rational science. "The stage on
which [the play] is represented being but one and the same place,
it is unnatural to conceive it many," [65] says Dryden. The new restrictions regarding words suitable to verse, correct rhyming,
proper figures, are all with the end in view of contenting the ear
and eye and transporting the spirit, because in this way the inner
chambers of man's spirit become more readily open, more gra-
ciously hospitable to eternal moral truths.

A typical discussion of the nice adjustment of means to clearly
anticipated mental effects occurs in Le Bossu: "The epic narrative
. . . must also be moving and impassioned, so that it may transport
the mind of the reader, fill it with disquiet, give it joy, throw it
into terror, make it feel again the violence of all the movements,
for all that it knows the subjects are feigned and invented. . . .

LE BOSSU: THE
WRITER'S EMO-
TIONAL ALCHEMY.

"The passions are necessary, then, for great poems; but they
are not all necessary or suitable for all. Comedy has for its share
joy and pleasant surprise. Tragedy on the other hand has terror
and compassion. The epic poem holds as it were a mean which
comprehends all these passions, as we see in the sadness of the
fourth book of the *Aeneid*, and in the plays and diversions of the
fifth. The passion proper to this sort of poem is admiration. It is
less opposed to the passions of the two other species. We admire
with joy the things which surprise us agreeably; we admire with
terror and sadness those which horrify and grieve us.

"Beyond the admiration which in general distinguishes the
Epic poem from the dramatic, each epic has further its own proper
passion which distinguishes it from other epics and which establishes a singular and individual difference between these poems of
the same species. These singular passions are in accordance with

---

[65] *The Prose Works of Dryden*, 4 Vols. London, 1800, Vol. I, Part II, p. 48.

the character of the hero. Anger and terror reign in the Iliad because Achilles is choleric, and 'the most terrible of all men.' The Aeneid is all in passions tender and gentle, because that is the character of Aeneas. . . . We have two more things to say here about the passions: one is the means of making them accepted in the hearer; the other is the means of making them felt. The first concerns disposing hearers to them; the second is not to mingle together several incompatible passions." [66]

Le Bossu continues his discussion by explaining how the proper approach should be made to get the desired reaction. If you want to move an object from its present location to another location, you first go to it, and, so to speak, accept passively its present situation. So in dealing with the audience. You must begin by taking it as it stands—emotionally. If it is tranquil, you must first be tranquil. Only so can you carry it somewhere else. "A man is in a state of repose and tranquillity. You wish by a discourse made for the purpose to induce wrath. You must commence your discourse in a quiet manner; thus you will join him to you. Then, marching with you, so to speak, he will not fail to follow you into those passions toward which you gradually lead him." [67]

Another psychological law for the control of the emotions is to keep them neat. The soul only feels an effect strongly when the effect is disengaged from confusing elements. Never stir up incompatible emotions. If you wish to carry the soul from excitement to tranquillity—to suspend its activity with violence, as in admiration—you can do so by learning the laws of the 'blood and vital spirits.'

Thus the critics studied how to pull the proper wires to get the right reaction. Science was preëminently necessary at this point, for to arouse and control sentiment by representing sentiment

> Thy last, thy noblest task remains untold,
> Passion to paint and sentiment unfold.

The final cause or purpose of the piece 'first in thought and last in execution' became then a subject for careful analysis. In exam-

---

[66] Le Bossu, *op. cit.*, pp. 346–49.
[67] *Ibid.*, p. 349.

ining the passions as results to be obtained by proper compounding and isolating of mental elements, the critics fused their own literary interests, and their obedience to the Aristotelian law, with the current study of the passions. This current had more than one strain. But the characteristic note of them all was the assimilation of mind-process to body-process. This visible and measurable process might be mechanical or chemical. But there was a prevailing demand that the obscure and apparently wandering and sportive phenomena of the spirit should submit to the kind of calculation and regulation which was giving a compass to the ocean-traveler and bringing the orbits of the heavenly bodies into provable mathematical formulae.

Spinoza (1632–1677) represents the extreme mechanistic tendency. He professed the ambition to write as objectively about the emotions of the mind as he would about lines, planes, or solids.[68] Descartes' theory of the passions seemed to Spinoza to admit irrational sequences. But Descartes and Hobbes also wished to make of the passions and actions of the soul merely a more refined clock-work. Psychology translated itself into terms of ratios of rest and motion, disturbance and equilibrium, impression inward and endeavor outward, rise and fall of energy, tracks in the brain worn deeply or lightly, rising vapors and flowing spirits, tubes and fibres.

Though the philosophers prided themselves on the unconditional modernity of their treatment of the mind, their theories were less new than they supposed. They felt the kinship between Harvey's discovery of the circulation of the blood and their theory of a self-maintaining psychical strain. But Spinoza's and Hobbes' views were built on the traditional Aristotelian pattern, little though they acknowledged the authority of Aristotle. It was easier for the literary writers governed by the spirit of 'finesse' to take at once from Aristotle and from Harvey than for those more rigidly governed by geometry. But Aristotle pushed his analysis of mental functions back ultimately to motions and impressions and heat and cold tension. So when Le Bossu described the action of poetry in terms of arrests and progressions, and suspensions, he was neither at odds

DYNAMICS OF PLEASURE BOTH NEW AND TRADITIONAL.

---

[68] *Ethics*, Part III, Introduction.

with the seventeenth century scientific mode nor with the great exemplar Aristotle. And a scarcely broken tradition binds together Cicero's teaching that mere rapidity of agitation makes thought agreeable, and the theory of Dubos in the eighteenth century that the true source of our love of the beautiful is our instinct to be always in motion in order to avoid ennui. When 'wit' and 'fancy' were explained in the new enlightened age by the poetical 'furor,' and the poetical 'furor' was referred to distillations, bubblings, and whirlings, to abundant and varied impressions on the inward mirror of the mind, the typical action of black bile in the melancholic temperament as described by Aristotle was the basis of the view. Doubtless the more scientific among the philosophers wished to depart from the chemical analogies of fermentation in descriptions of mental process. The literary group were less fastidious. They knew from their long series of authorities, Greek, Roman, and Italian, that it was the function of poetry, not only to instruct and please, but to *move* the contemplators. To *move* others, they felt, the genius must himself be in motion, and must create in his artistic instrument the appropriate verisimilar motions. Theories of motion were welcome then both from the camp of Galileo and from the camp of Aristotle. If the imagination is 'lively,' let a property of physical energy be intended; let it be the 'passing' of a very subtle wind, or the speed of spirits that are tenuous and agile. Let wit be flamelike, and judgment be 'cold and heavy.' In so far as terms connoting palpable motions can be used to explain the effects and causes of art, in so far can the whole business be put under rational control.

LEIBNIZ: SCIENCE'S WORLD-PICTURE HALF THE TRUTH.　　What the critics of poetry and painting perceived vaguely and utilized practically—that Aristotle could be followed as an authority and yet science could be in the result—Leibniz perceived intellectually. He thus parted company with the rest of the philosophers of his time. He acknowledged final causes as well as efficient and material causes, whereas the philosophical fashion was to discard 'purpose' as a figment of the mind. Like Hobbes, Leibniz drew into a single scale the various functions of the mind, especially imagination and clear thought. But Hobbes made this scale by supposing more and more complicated mechanisms, the higher the function. Leibniz, putting into seventeenth century dress Aristotle's insight that form is simply matter realized—the purpose simply the explication of the mechanical substructure—wrote: "Nature must always be explained mathematically and mechanically, provided it be kept in mind that the principles of the laws of mechanics and of force do not depend upon mathematical extension alone, but have certain metaphysical causes." [69] The metaphysical causes, then, of the motions in songs, or the motions in the spirit, are not merely previous impacts, endeavors inward or outward, or boiling spirit, according to Leibniz. The ultimate metaphysical causes are in the good purposes or in the delightful order which unfold the meaning of the motions. Leibniz speaks in the typical Neo-Classic fashion of the moving power of poetry and music. They have "unbelievable power to move." By them a man may be "roused to madness . . . be lulled, excited, moved to laughter, tears, to every sort of feeling." [70] What then is the esthetic significance of such effectual imagery for Leibniz? To answer this, one must look both ways from the given pleasing phenomenon, and speak in two distinct languages. The mechanical explanation carries one to the mathematical basis of music. The revelation of the ultimate metaphysical cause carries one to the intuition of the harmony of God's universe. "Music, mathematical in its basis, is intuitive in its emergence." [71] The intuitive emergence of musical harmony is the clear symbol it furnishes of God's best possible plan for the world, his Providence which has created a world in which there is united the greatest possible variety with the greatest possible order. This, we are told, is no vague metaphor. One thing explains another, or is symbolized by it when there is such a constant and regulated relation between the two as holds between an architect's projection in perspective and his finished edifice. [72] Thus though mathematics and living form, sense-pattern

---

[69] Leibniz, *Discourse on Metaphysics, Correspondence with Arnauld, and Monadology*, trans. Montgomery, Chicago, 1927, pp. 135, 136.

[70] Leibniz, *Opera Omnia*, 6 Vols., Geneva, 1768, Vol. 6, p. 306.

[71] Jean Baruzi, *Leibniz, avec de Nombreux Textes Inédits*, Paris, 1900, pp. 102, 103.

[72] Leibniz, *Discourse on Metaphysics*, p. 212.

and reasonable world, nature and grace, are incommensurable, because no exact mathematical relation can be established between
them, there are "seizable practical equivalences." "Just as well-
nigh nothing is pleasanter to the senses of man than harmony in
music, so nothing is pleasanter than the wonderful harmony of
nature, of which music is only a foretaste and small evidence." [73]
Painting and music, he writes again, are fragments of the complete
order, proportion, and harmony of God. "All beauty is an emanation from his light." [74]

TASTE AND REASON
NEITHER IDENTI-
FIED NOR DIVORCED. Leibniz distinguished four grades of knowledge: [75] (1) obscure
and dark knowledge made up of 'little perceptions' such as the
vague congeries of the dream-state or the unrecognized but received sensations of the separate waves beating on the shore; (2)
clear but confused knowledge, in which phenomena, such as colors,
are recognized but are not intellectually defined; (3) distinct
knowledge in which a definition or scientific explanation is possible;
and (4) adequate or intuitive knowledge in which all the marks of
objects are known exhaustively and gathered into a single complete
survey. Now esthetic knowledge is in the main placed on the second level. We feel a something, "I know not what," that arouses
sympathy in us. "Taste as distinguished from understanding consists in confused perceptions of which one cannot adequately render
an account. It is something approaching instinct." [76] "One does
not always detect in what the agreeableness of a thing consists, or
to what sort of perfection in us it ministers, as it is felt by our spirit
rather than our understanding." [77] In passages like this Leibniz
reveals his kinship with Shaftesbury and Hutcheson in England,
who rested the feeling for beauty on a vague propension of the
mind rather than on reason and good sense; with the Swiss literary

---

[73] Leibniz, *Philosophische Werke*, trans. Buchenau, ed. Cassirer, 4 Vols.,
Leipzig, 1906, Vol. II, p. 132.
    [74] Leibniz, *Oeuvres*, ed. Jacques, 2 Vols., Paris, 1842, Vol. II, p. 3. Preface to
"Theodicy."
    [75] *Discourse on Metaphysics*, p. 41, Sec. 24.
    [76] Quoted by Cassirer, *Leibniz' System in seinen wissenschaftlichen Grund-
lagen*, Marburg, 1902, p. 459. (From ed. Gerhardt, Vol. III, pp. 430ff.)
    [77] Quoted by Cassirer, *op. cit.*, p. 462. (From *Opera Philosophica*, ed. Erdmann,
Berlin, 1840.)

critics, Bodmer and Breitinger, who urged attention to the esthetic significance of primitive poetry. But the 'taste' of Leibniz is not an instinct or sympathy that is to be left to its own devices. Rather it is to be formed on the pattern of what reason and tradition have already declared good. The lower and vaguer perceptions always were pregnant for Leibniz with their own rational explanation, so that taste might start as a *Je ne sais quoi,* but it culminated in a moral lesson or a rational demonstration. A pattern of music or painting could never be abstracted from the impulsion of the mind that bore it, tending to carry it on beyond its mere appearance to metaphysical meaning and distinct ratios and proportions. Thus neither the passages in Leibniz in which he teaches that the enjoyment of music is unconscious counting, nor that taste is an instinct, nor that poetry exists to give examples of prudence, can be taken out of their setting. Leibniz constantly modulates and shades a simple abstract idea by suggesting its control by other aspects of the total problem. To rationalism he gives his allegiance in so far as he teaches that mathematics explains feeling and that beauty is an affair of ratios; to the philosophy of instinct he concedes that vague presentiments of pleasure precede complete rational grasp of beauty, and also that rational understanding emerges in the end in intuitive vision; to mysticism, he gives his consent in so far as he believes that an occult sympathy invisibly draws together all the parts of the universe, and makes the mirror of each individual soul reflect the 'grand entire'; to moralism, he grants that art gives pious lessons and should be utilized to give more, so that blessedness and religion may increase among men; but of the opposed doctrine of disinterested pleasure in art, he shows his appreciation: "The contemplation of beautiful things is agreeable in itself, and a . . . picture by Raphael touches him who looks at it with enlightened eyes, though he draws from it no profit." [78]

Leibniz seems to be the most advanced thinker of his era because of his capacity for synthesis. In him certainly were the germs of the thought that made Baumgarten the official founder of Esthetics in 1750. In him is sympathy for Shaftesbury, the

THE NOTE OF RE-BELLION.

---

[78] Quoted by Cassirer, *op. cit.,* p. 467.

founder of the empirical school of British Estheticians in the next century. And he has even been thought to have fragmentarily anticipated Kant. But it is a question whether the more advanced thought appears in thinkers like Leibniz who see all sides, developing none to extreme conclusions, or in narrower but bolder heretics, who perceive a single line of neglected truth, and make the most of it. Among the literary critics of the seventeenth century there were two: the Spaniard Juan de la Cueva (c. 1650–c. 1708) and the Frenchman Ogier, who rebelled against the respect for Aristotle's authority and the drawing up of a fixed body of rules to govern poetical composition. They both argued that different conditions and customs, temporal and national, require different modes of expression. "The taste of nations is different, as well in matters pertaining to the mind as in those of the body, and . . . just as . . . the Spaniards imagine and prefer a type of beauty quite different from that which we prize in France, and just as they desire their sweethearts to have a different figure, and features other than those we desire to see in ours, to such a degree that there are some men who will form an idea of their beauty from the same features that we should consider homely, just so, it must not be doubted that the minds of nations have preferences quite different from one another, and altogether dissimilar feelings for the beauty of intellectual things, such as poetry." [79] Ogier goes into details, explaining that the Aristotelian doctrine of the unity of time, making messengers come in suddenly pat, is far-fetched for a modern stage. The Greeks, he said, kept to uniform models because their stage was religious and therefore conservative, and because popular taste is slow to accept change, and the Greek tragedians were competing for prizes. [80]

SPINOZA'S HISTOR-
ICAL INSIGHTS.

Is there a philosopher of the century who gathers this heretical feeling into a more reflective form? Strangely enough, one can find sympathy for this insistence on the historical interpretation of symbolic form in Spinoza, the philosophical geometer. Spinoza held even more consistently to the geometrical ideal than Descartes,

---

[79] *European Theories of the Drama*, ed. Clark, Cincinnati, 1918, p. 121. Preface to "Tyre and Sidon."

[80] *Ibid.*, pp. 120–22.

and beauty was mentioned by him only to be put in the list of accidental things to which we attach a value because we desire them.[81] And he occupied himself with none of the arts, not even with the mathematical art of music, except in so far as his remarkable discussion of the Bible as literature [82] contained incidentally principles applicable to all literature. And these in an important way it did; but in a form which was not adapted to the consciousness of the period and so was not followed up. Spinoza argues that respect for the Holy Scriptures and loyalty to religion are not lessened but increased by freedom of thought in respect to them.[83] Freedom of thought in respect to the Bible, he maintained, led to the conception of its various parts and symbols as the products of human imaginations, colored by natural temperament, and national and temporal habits of speech and behavior. If a prophet were naturally optimistic, he would write of victories, if a rustic, he would use figures of oxen and cows, if a soldier, of armies, to point his words.[84] The imagination employs a language quite different in form from mathematical reasoning, though its pictures and hieroglyphics are carriers of truth; but the truth of imaginary discourse can only be got at by familiar knowledge of the historical and individual conditions of the writing. If one wishes to know for example what the figure of the wheel in Ezekiel means, one must not speculate *a priori* on the secret wisdom contained in all wheels, but one must examine what the culture and experience of Ezekiel could probably have made it mean to him. Spinoza thus drew as sharp a line between reason and imagination as any one in his century did; but he pointed by the way to the treatment of the many-colored veil woven by the imagination that would neither distort it by making it a mystical message nor destroy it by applying to it the inappropriate standard of mathematics.

---

[81] *Ethics*, Part I, Appendix.

[82] *Tractatus Theologico-Politicus*, 1670. Trans. Elwes, 1909.

[83] The full title of the work is: A Theologico-Political Treatise Containing Certain Discussions Wherein Is Set Forth That Freedom of Thought and Speech Not Only May, Without Prejudice to Piety and the Public Peace, Be Granted; But Also May Not, Without Danger to Piety and the Public Peace, Be Withheld.

[84] *Ibid.*, Chapter II, "Of Prophets."

SUPPLEMENTARY READING

Bosanquet, *History of Aesthetic*, Ch. VIII.

G. N. Clark, *The Seventeenth Century*, Oxford, 1929.

English Critical Essays, 16th–18th Centuries (World's Classics, Oxford
Univ. Press).

Allan H. Gilbert, *Literary Criticism from Plato to Dryden*.

Emile Krantz, *L'Esthétique de Descartes*, Paris, 1882.

I. Langdon, *Milton's Theory of Poetry and Fine Art*, New Haven,
1924.

Mario Praz, *Studies in Seventeenth Century Imagery* (Studies of the
Warburg Institute, Vol. I), London, 1939.

J. E. Spingarn, ed., *Critical Essays of the Seventeenth Century*, 3 Vols.,
Oxford, 1908–1909.

Basil Willey, *The Seventeenth Century Background*, London, 1934.

Saintsbury, *History of Criticism*, Vol. II, Bk. V, Chs. I–IV.

Venturi, *History of Art Criticism*, Ch. V.

CHAPTER VIII

The Eighteenth Century British School

THE SPIRIT of irony for one moment lights up the history BRITISH ESTHETICS of esthetics when it makes John Locke (1632–1710), who BASED ON LOCKE. was of all the great seventeenth century philosophers the most supercilious toward poetry, inspire an entire new esthetic movement. When David Hume said that all the critics after Aristotle had talked much and said little because they failed to direct their taste or sentiment by the accuracy of philosophy, he meant by his eulogistic phrase "the accuracy of philosophy" [1] the new doctrine of associationism, connected with the Lockian 'new way of ideas.' Locke's new way consisted in making the starting-point in any scientific investigation not a general truth of reason but a particular psychological event. To explain meant for a Lockian, whatever more it meant, to point out the historical source of any process in a sense-impression. It was Locke's method that Addison (1672–1719) followed when he wrote his important eleven papers for the *Spectator* on the "Pleasures of the Imagination." [2] And yet perhaps in the end the spirit of irony plays not so much over Locke as over the alleged "accuracy of philosophy" itself. For though it would be a mistake to minimize the influence of Locke on Addison, Hutcheson, Kames, Hume, and Burke, the esthetic systems that grew under their forming hands had a refractory tendency to rejoin, after a short independent journey, the well-worn highroad of seventeenth century reason and Neo-Classic taste. Or perhaps one

---

[1] Hume, *Essays Moral, Political, and Literary*, ed. Green and Grose, 2 Vols., London, 1898, Vol. II, p. 19. "Enquiry Concerning Human Understanding," Part I, Sec. 2.

[2] Addison, *Works*, 3 Vols., New York, 1854, Vol. II, Nos. 411–22.

might even say that the esthetic creed of the new 'inner sense' school inspired by Locke never seriously differed from the creed of the upholders of reason. If, as radical empiricists often say, sense is manifold and reason one, sense individual and particular, reason general and typical, sense inductive, reason deductive, one would expect a theory contrasting with rationalism to grow up on a sensationalistic basis, realistic in tendency and making much of specific variations in personal and national taste. But after allowing for all the variety of utterances and definite notes of rebellion in the new British school against the 'rules,' one is forced to admit that the kinship of the 'taste' they found on inner sense, sentiment, passion, or intuition is more with Boileau's neo-classic rules than

BUT GALLICISM BRINGS IN REASON BY THE BACK DOOR.

with Ogier's relativity of time and place. These writers worked with a new mechanism—the frame of human nature—but they turn out a product that differs surprisingly little from the one that fits Descartes' rationalism. Why did the radical beginning not make a radical ending? In part it was because the practical authority of the French taste which came out of Boileau's age dominated the Great Britain of at least the first half of the eighteenth century. The *Vitruvius Britannicus* furnished the designs for gentlemen's houses; Palladio, Inigo Jones, and Christopher Wren were the great authorities on architecture; Pope's dynasty was supreme in poetry until in the sixth decade its style was challenged by the literary critics, Joseph Warton and Edward Young; Sir Joshua Reynolds, annotator of Du Fresnoy's *Art of Painting*, was the first President of the Royal Academy.

GRACIOUS REASON- ABLENESS IN ALL THE ARTS.

The actual practice of the arts was more rigidly governed by canons of correct taste and presented a spectacle of greater solidarity and conformity than in most other centuries. The artistic atmosphere of the time has been well described by Laurence Binyon. "With all the stirrings under the surface, it [the eighteenth century] presents to us as we look back, the picture of a period perfectly coherent in its aims and tastes. . . . An eighteenth century interior charms us still by the pervasiveness of its atmosphere. Everything in the room, like the room itself, is planned, proportioned, finished with the same research for order, elegance, and grace. There is a suffusion of reasonableness over the whole. Anything either heavy or extravagant would strike an echoing discord. It is the same with architecture as with furniture and the minor arts. And when we come to the more intimate expressiveness of poetry and painting, each of these answers and corroborates the other. No period had more the courage of its taste. Genius, however overpowering, was not to have its excesses and licenses condoned. Neither Shakespeare nor Milton intimidated Dr. Johnson; each must submit to the tribunal of reason. The reign of reasonableness produced once more something of the same system and cohesion which marked the medieval mind." [3]

In part, then, the *content* of esthetic judgment, whatever its mechanism, was taken over from tradition. Philosophy, however "accurate" or however stirred to new ways by fresh blood, is inevitably influenced by the practices of the circumambient culture. Even David Hume (1711–1776) was in many ways conventional. Although he said in the spirit of the new empiricism that the greatest genius, when nature fails him, "throws aside the lyre, and hopes not from the rules of art to reach that divine harmony which must proceed from her inspiration alone," [4] and that the standard of taste arises from the animal frame, he believed, as the classical critics had believed for two centuries and more before him, in the Aristotelian unities of time, place, and action. The difference with him was largely that he had a novel explanation of how the Aristotelian unities worked. The "bond or tye" which holds together a tragedy is for Hume not a necessity of reason, but the association of ideas. Association of ideas through cause and effect explains the unity of dramatic action; the loose association by resemblance explains the unity of such a piece as Ovid's *Metamorphoses*, which needed only the one circumstance of a divinely caused fabulous transformation to tie its parts together; and historians, epic poets, and tragedians all make use of association by contiguity. [5] Hume was a bolder spirit than most of the philosophers of his age and country. He challenged the first place given to plot

EVEN HUME STRAINS HIS EMPIRICISM.

---

[3] Binyon, *English Poetry in Its Relation to Painting and the Other Arts*, 1918, in Proceedings of the British Academy, Vol. VIII, p. 391.

[4] Hume, *op. cit.*, Vol. I, p. 15. "The Epicurean."

[5] *Ibid.*, Vol. II, pp. 17–23. "Enquiry Concerning Human Understanding."

in the Aristotelian rules for tragedy,[6] advocated crossing romantic strains with classic,[7] and said that the difference between history and poetry is rather one of degree than of kind.[8] And yet even his taste for Vergil and Racine,[9] and for elegance and simplicity of style,[10] and his agreement in large measure with classical standards, illustrate the fact that the Lockian school was more interested in pulling Neo-Classic reason to pieces to see what it was made of and how it worked than in disputing its validity. In tracing the esthetic treatises of the British school of this period, one observes again and again that what seemed to be a limited empirical function, a sense or a sentiment, is dilated or bent outwards at need to include a mathematical law, conformity with the dominant moral ideal, or an abstract idea.

SHAFTESBURY'S 'SENSE' REFLECTS PLOTINUS MORE THAN LOCKE.

This loose and expansive texture of the esthetic 'inner sense' was also due partly to the influence of Lord Shaftesbury (1671–1713). On one side Shaftesbury belonged to the new movement, and might even through his influence on Francis Hutcheson (1694–1746), its first clear professional spokesman, be called its initiator. But though Shaftesbury was the first to apply the term 'sense' to value-experience, he was opposed to the doctrine of Locke. He employed the word 'sense' to suggest the immediacy and sureness of the deliverances of our conscience and our taste. This motive, the desire to guarantee the importance and seriousness of our feeling for beauty and goodness by making it congenital with our entire being, was a leading one throughout this whole phase of esthetic history. The mind cannot be without its eye and ear to discern,[11] Shaftesbury said. But his fundamental philosophical sympathy was with Plotinus and Marcus Aurelius, and a sense of harmony connoted for him a spiritual kinship with the harmony of the universe and the 'inner numbers' of a noble life. His inner sense was like Leibniz's sympathy: a magic bond which predetermined

---

[6] *The Critical Review*, April 7, 1759, p. 331.
[7] *Letters*, ed. Grieg, 2 Vols., Oxford, 1932, Vol. I, p. 253. #135, July 2, 1757.
[8] *Essays, loc. cit.*
[9] *Ibid.*, Vol. I, p. 241. "Of Simplicity and Refinement in Writing."
[10] *Ibid., passim.*
[11] Shaftesbury, *Characteristics*, ed. J. M. Robertson, 2 Vols., London, 1900, Vol. I, p. 216. Treatise III, "Advice to an Author," Part III, Sec. 3.

the well-disposed soul to vibrate in unison with the divine harmony.

In a period, then, when the Neo-Platonist Shaftesbury felt so keenly the missionary zeal that he declared that "if anything be stirred, or any studies turned that way [toward correct taste] it must be I that must set the wheel a-going and help to raise the spirit," [12] and separated himself off from the taint of the "physiologist" Locke; and when the gifted architect Vanbrugh failed to receive appreciation of his ability because he neglected the Augustan rules—in such a period it is not strange if reason and morals become in one way and another attached to the esthetic function, even though a new model has been set up in the sense of sight.

Addison begins with the fact of experience closest to actual sensation, "the primary pleasures of the imagination," arising from actually seeing something. He declares that sight is the most perfect and delightful of our senses and that the primary pleasures of the imagination are from visible objects present, and the secondary are from visible objects absent, but recalled. What kinds of things are pleasant to see? he enquires. And he answers: There are "three sources of all the pleasures of our imagination, in our survey of outward objects. . . . What is great. . . . What is new. . . . What is beautiful in our own species . . . (and) in general." [13] As examples of the great, vast, or grand he cites a vast uncultivated desert, huge heaps of mountains, high rocks and precipices, a wide expanse of waters. As examples of the new he cites the surprising elements in the varying spectacle of nature, and imperfections of nature such as monsters. By beauty he means in the first place members of our own race and kind, and in the second place gaiety and variety of colors, symmetry and proportion of parts, arrangement and disposition of bodies, and just mixture and concurrence of all.

At the beginning this seems to be a simple report of elementary esthetic experiences. But Addison goes quickly on to caution us that although he has named physical, external sources of pleasure,

[marginal note:] EXPANSION OF SENSE IN ADDISON: THE GREAT, THE NEW, THE BEAUTIFUL.

[marginal note:] BEAUTY AS GOD'S PRECAUTION AGAINST OUR INDIFFERENCE.

---

[12] *The Life, Unpublished Letters, and Philosophical Regimen of Lord Shaftesbury*, ed. Rand, New York, 1900, pp. 468, 469.

[13] *The Works of Addison*, 3 Vols., New York, 1854, Vol. II, p. 138. "The Spectator," No. 412.

and has seemed to imply that the pleasures of the imagination are direct, not further to be analyzed relations between those objects and ourselves, the state of affairs is not actually so. The sources of pleasure are not, as it had seemed, in an external relationship to us, but altogether in us. Moreover, the significance of these pleasures turns out to be more occult than the disarming descriptive beginning would suggest. Addison says, "There is not perhaps any real beauty or deformity more in one piece of matter than another, because we might have been so made, that whatever now appears loathsome to us, might have shown itself agreeable." [14] What we really like in the great, vast, or grand proves to be the "loving to be filled with an object, or the grasping at anything that is too big for [our] capacity." He says—and his remark is indefinitely repeated by the writers of the period—that our pleasure in the sublime or grand is in the end our uneasiness at any restraint upon our freedom. [15] Again, the new or uncommon pleases us ultimately because it gratifies our curiosity. And the sense of beauty is not a direct intuition of a lovely appearance, but the social instinct of kind. With disarming modesty Addison affirms that in treating of the pleasures of the imagination he can only list what proves agreeable, because he "knows neither the nature of an idea nor the substance of a human soul." [16] But what is it he lists? He lists the various agreeable feelings with their presumed occasions that are either closely or loosely associated with experiences of beauty. How far removed the apparent form of the experience may be from its true meaning for Addison comes out in an illuminating passage. In it he says that ideas excited in us are so different from anything existing in the objects themselves that "our souls are at present delightfully lost and bewildered in a pleasing delusion, and we walk about like the enchanted hero in a romance." [17] It then appears that what we know definitely and rationally is not phenomenal experience, but God's purposes in men. Final causes, Addison says, "lie more bare and open to our observation. The Supreme

---

[14] *The Works of Addison, op. cit.,* Vol. II, p. 139.
[15] *Loc. cit.*
[16] *Ibid.,* Vol. II, p. 140.
[17] *Ibid.,* Vol. II, p. 141.

Author of our being . . . has framed us so that we naturally delight in the great, the new, the beautiful, in our own species, as His nature is great and uncircumscribed, His creation novel and to be sought into curiously, and his purpose that we fill the world of His creation. . . . Finally he has made us find the world in general beautiful so that we cannot behold His works with coldness or indifference." [18]

In discussing the "secondary" pleasures of the imagination, that is, the pleasures "from statuary, painting, description, and music," and in discussing the influence of our enjoyment of art on our feeling for nature, Addison, following Lockian psychology, calls in "that action of the mind which compares . . . ideas." [19] We enjoy an example of art the more resemblance it bears in our opinion to nature and we enjoy nature the more the relationship of resemblance between it and art is borne in upon us. We enjoy statues and portraits as mimicry even when the original is "disagreeable or common or small . . . because of the comparison the mind makes." [20] Furthermore it is a process of reflection or comparison which is at the foundation of our pleasure in tragedy or things terrible or piteous. Our delight is due not to the description of what is terrible, but to the reflection we make on the circumstance. "We are not a little pleased to think we are in no danger," [21] from the object we look upon. To sum up, then, the pleasures of the imagination for Addison, though sensuous in their origin, are moralistic, reflective, and religious in their bearings. To intuit beauty means that we like to feel big, we like change, we like our relatives and kinsmen, and we like to make comparisons. And we like these things because it is God's will, leading us to admire Him and His works.

PLEASURES OF IMAGINATION MORALISTIC, REFLECTIVE, RELIGIOUS.

Shaftesbury is less indirect in arriving at a similar expansion of the sense of beauty into a feeling for preëstablished harmony. Although the inner sense is connected for him with "a certain easiness of sight" which answers to "beauty of composition, unity

EXPANSION OF 'SENSE' IN SHAFTESBURY; HIS PLATONISM.

---

[18] *Ibid.*, Vol. II, pp. 140, 141.
[19] *Ibid.*, Vol. II, p. 145.
[20] *Ibid.*, Vol. II, p. 148.
[21] *Ibid.*, Vol. II, p. 149.

of design, the truth of characters, and the just imitation of Nature," [22] the function of the visual experience is to lead us behind the appearance to its moral counterpart and its divine cause. An author must "carry in his eye the model or exemplar of that natural grace which gives to every action its attractive charm. If he has naturally no eye or ear for these interior numbers, 'tis not likely he should be able to judge . . . of that exterior proportion of symmetry and composition which constitute a legitimate piece. . . . The sense of inward numbers, the knowledge and practice of the social virtues, the familiarity and favor of the moral graces are essential to the character of a deserving artist and just favorite of the muses. Thus are the arts and virtues mutually friends, and thus the science of *virtuosi* and that of virtue itself become in a manner one and the same." [23] Although Shaftesbury's readers were encouraged to develop their sensitiveness to the charms of classical art, they were encouraged still more to "remember ever the garden and groves within." [24] To a young man with whom he corresponded he wrote advice to study "that great and Masterly Hand which has drawn all Things and exhibiteth this great Master-Piece of Nature, this World or Universe." [25] In *Advice to an Author* (1710) the same other-worldliness appears. "Though [the artist's] intention be to please the world, he must nevertheless be, in a manner, above it, and fix his eye upon that consummate grace, that beauty of Nature and that perfection of numbers of which the rest of mankind . . . feel . . . only the effect whilst ignorant of the cause." [26] It is to this unknown Cause that Shaftesbury would like to lead by orderly stages the new race of English *virtuosi*—those fine gentlemen and citizens of the world whom he feels the heavy responsibility of bringing into being. He lays it down that the virtuoso climb an esthetic ladder of forms. He is to learn to love first the lowest order or degree of beauty, "the dead forms . . . which bear a fashion,

[22] Shaftesbury, *Characteristics*, Vol. I, p. 158. Treatise III: "Advice to an Author," Part 2, Sec. 2.

[23] *Ibid.*, Vol. I, pp. 216, 217. Treatise III, Part 3, Sec. 3.

[24] Shaftesbury, *Life, Letters, and Phil. Reg.*, p. 179.

[25] Shaftesbury, *Several Letters Written by a Noble Lord to a Young Man at the University*, London, 1716, p. 30. Letter V.

[26] Shaftesbury, *Characteristics*, Vol. I, p. 214. Treatise III, Part 3, Sec. 3.

and are formed, whether by man or nature. . . . Next, and as the second kind, the forms which form . . . which have intelligence, action, and operation. . . . Here . . . is double beauty . . . , [then] that third order of beauty . . . [which] forms not only such as we call mere forms, but even the forms which form . . . [It is] the principal fountain and source of all beauty—architecture, music, and all which is of human invention," and "that lovely race of mental children," "the notions and principles of fair, just, and honest, with the rest of these ideas." [27] This is an obvious adaptation of Plato's *Symposium*.

Thus Shaftesbury's sense of beauty has little to do with the literal senses, and is rather an all-embracing function. It induces us to pass in esthetic experience from effect to cause, from outer to inner, and from part to whole. If we think some isolated portion of the world is ugly we are always to ask, following Marcus Aurelius, "How stands it in the larger piece?" [28]

Francis Hutcheson, disciple of Shaftesbury, is emphatic on the HUTCHESON'S COM-
appropriateness of the term 'sense' for esthetic experience. The POUND RATIO.
perception of beauty and harmony, he says, is justly called a sense because it involves no intellectual element, no reflection on principles and causes. [29] Also it has no kinship with desire, because desire is a "joy which arises from self-love" upon prospect of advantage. [30] Original beauty is the perception aroused in us by pleasing formal relations, particularly uniformity amid variety. This pleasing proportion is intuited in all sorts of geometrical figures and in animals; also in theorems, metaphysical axioms, and general truths. Hutcheson announces that he has found an important mathematical law determining the presence of beauty in all these places. This law is what he calls the compound ratio between uniformity and variety. "Where the uniformity of bodies is equal, the beauty is as the variety." [31] For example, in geometrical figures (triangles,

---

[27] *Ibid.*, Vol. II, pp. 132–35. Treatise V: "The Moralists, A Philosophical Rhapsody," Part 3, Sec. 2.

[28] Shaftesbury, *Life, Letters, and Phil. Reg.*, p. 59.

[29] Hutcheson, *An Inquiry into the Original of Our Ideas of Beauty and Virtue*, London, 1725, p. 10. Sec. I, Par. 13.

[30] *Ibid.*, p. 11. Sec. I, Par. 15.

[31] *Ibid.*, p. 15. Sec. II, Par. 3.

squares, pentagons, hexagons) where uniformity is furnished by the equality of the sides, the beauty increases within limits, with the increase in the number of sides, that is, with the element of variety. Moving in the opposite direction, Hutcheson calls those figures rude in which there is no unity or resemblance among the parts. The uniformity of parts appears in such regular figures as cylinders, prisms, pyramids, and obelisks. As an example of a theorem that is beautiful on the basis of this compound ratio, Hutcheson cites the forty-seventh proposition of Euclid's first Book of Elements; and among philosophical truths Newton's Law of Gravitation and the Theory of Rights, "whence the greater part of moral duties may be deduced." [32]

Hutcheson claims the right to name the perception of this mathematical relationship 'sense,' because the beauty is felt without understanding the reason for it. Richard Price (1723–1791) later expressed his agreement with Hutcheson on the law, a just balancing of unity with variety, but dissent from him on its location in the inner sense. The measurable relationship, he claimed, exists in the object, whether realized by the mind or not. And it is the intellect, he said, which corresponds, in man's mind, to the beautiful balance in the object. [33] Besides original or absolute beauty which equalled for Hutcheson uniformity and variety, a relative or comparative beauty was recognized. Relative beauty arises from the pleasure we feel in the similarity between a copy and an original, and in the fitness of an instrument to an end. Hutcheson says that an imitation "shall still be beautiful though the original were entirely devoid of it: thus the deformities of old age in a picture, the rudest rocks or mountains in a landskip, if well represented shall have abundant Beauty." [34]

BERKELEY: "THE INNER SENSE'S PROGRESS."

A Platonic dialogue was a suitable literary form to portray the respective claims of 'inner sense' and 'rational understanding' in this period. George Berkeley, Bishop of Cloyne (1685–1753), availed himself of its flexibility and dramatic potency to place Alciphron, 'the Minute Philosopher' and champion of esthetic

---

[32] Hutcheson, *op. cit.*, pp. 27–30. Sec. III, Pars. 2, 4, 5.
[33] *Review of the Principal Questions and Difficulties in Morals*, 1758, p. 105.
[34] Hutcheson, *op. cit.*, pp. 35, 36. Sec. IV, Par. 1.

feeling, organ of the '*je ne sais quoi*,' over against Euphranor, the Platonist, who defends esthetic reason. Alciphron says that beauty is a "fugacious charm" which is felt, and that is all. But what quality is felt? asks Alciphron. Symmetry and proportion, as they please the eye, is the answer. But is beauty just symmetry and proportion, or is it symmetry and proportion in relation to the use of the object in question? The argument develops to show that symmetry and proportion mean one thing in a horse, and another in a chair, and another in dress. Reason and mind thus come walking in to the '*je ne sais quoi*'; for the proportions and relations must be so adjusted that the whole is perfect of its kind; and "a thing is perfect when it answers the end for which it was made." [35] Charm addresses itself ultimately then not to a sense, but to reason through the means of sight. There is lack of beauty in the same way that there is lack of convenience and good sense in the pinched, stiffened, and hooped dress of the fashionable woman, or in the Gothic, succinct, plaited garment and full-bottomed wig of the Magistrate. The dialogue pushes the meaning of reason still further back to its source in the Great Designer and Planner of all. "Forasmuch as without thought there can be no end or design; and without an end there can be no use; and without use, there is no aptitude or fitness of proportion, from whence Beauty springs," [36] without the Divine Providence which sustains all reasonableness in the world there cannot be the first springs of beauty. In these few pages of Berkeley we have what might be nicknamed 'The Inner Sense's Progress,' as it passes, not like Bunyan's pilgrim from the anguish of the flesh to the joys of the heavenly Jerusalem but from sensuous simplicity to intellectual and moral all-inclusiveness.

Lord Kames, Henry Home (1696–1782), begins as a staunch member of the inner sense school by drawing up a scale of the various pleasures derived from mental processes, placing those from the physical senses at the bottom as gross and quickly leading to satiety, those from the intellect at the top as refined,

KAMES'S HIER-ARCHY OF MENTAL PLEASURES.

---

[35] *The Works of George Berkeley*, ed. Fraser, 4 Vols., Oxford, 1901, Vol. II, p. 133. "Alciphron," Dialogue III, 8.
[36] *Ibid.*, Vol. II, p. 138. Dialogue III, 10.

and those from the inner senses in the middle.[37] Sight, he says, is
connected with beauty, hearing with harmony or what is agreeable.
But Kames like most of his school leads us behind the senses, with
much elaboration and finesse, into a realization of the divine purpose
involved in the workings of these senses. Our liking for order,
uniformity, and regularity is a benevolent endowment, because it
contributes to readiness of apprehension;[38] our liking for change
and variety and motion was given to us to make us industrious;[39]
our sense of pleasure in novelty exists in us in order to make us alert
in the avoidance of danger;[40] our liking for tragedy exercises our
benevolent social passions, particularly our sympathy.[41] Kames says
that in esthetic matters we must understand the mechanism of the
feelings, and the organs through which they operate. And in this
we recognize the true follower of Locke. Like Locke he would
found his system on origins given in experience.

HUME: EMOTION
AND SENTIMENT
ARE THE PATHS BY
WHICH BEAUTY
COMES TO US.

In Hume the metaphor involved in the use of the word 'sense'
is more apparent. He is clear that there is nothing supernatural
in the psychological springs of poetry. "[A poet's] fire is not
kindled from heaven. It only runs along the earth."[42] One must
study the fabric and structure of human nature to get at the mental
causes of the arts. He like the others refers to "a certain sense,
which acts without reflection,"[43] and to "some internal sense or
feeling"[44] that pronounces on values. But Hume is little concerned
with the data of literal sight or hearing as ingredients of taste. He
is rather concerned with the sentiment or passion or pleasure involved. "Beauty and worth consist in an agreeable sentiment."[45]
The senses are on the whole mere passive inlets. Hume identifies

---

[37] Home, *Elements of Criticism*, ed. Mills, New York, 1833, pp. 11–13. Introduction.

[38] *Ibid.*, p. 105, Part VII, Ch. 3.

[39] *Ibid.*, p. 127, Part VII, Ch. 5.

[40] *Loc. cit.*, Part VII, Ch. 6.

[41] *Ibid.*, p. 213, Part VII, Ch. 15.

[42] Hume, *Essays*, Vol. I, p. 177. "The Rise and Progress of the Arts and
Sciences."

[43] Hume, *A Treatise of Human Nature*, ed. Selby-Bigge, Oxford, 1888, p. 612.

[44] Hume, *Enquiries Concerning the Human Understanding and Concerning
the Principles of Morals*, ed. Selby-Bigge, Oxford, 1902, p. 173.

[45] *Ibid.*, Vol. I, p. 217. "The Sceptic."

beauty with pleasure, and pleasure with the main-spring of our active existence. "Pleasure and pain . . . are not only necessary attendants of beauty and deformity, but constitute their very essence." [46] Or again, he calls beauty a sentiment or passion in human nature which makes man relish the "graces of a well-proportioned statue or the symmetry of a noble pile." [47] Aware of the close connection between symmetry and proportion and reason, he immediately adds that the fact that we prefer well-proportioned figures does not justify the inference that we use our understanding in making this choice. In other words, he is clear in the main part of his writing that it is the natural, emotional part of our animal frame which accounts for our taste. Indeed he makes a direct comparison between reason and taste, contrasting them sharply: "The former [reason] conveys the knowledge of truth and falsehood: the latter gives the sentiment of beauty and deformity, vice and virtue. The one discovers objects as they really stand in nature, without addition or diminution: The other has a productive faculty, and gilding and staining all natural objects with the colours, borrowed from internal sentiment, raises in a manner a new creation. Reason, being cool and disengaged, is no motive to action . . . Taste, as it gives pleasure or pain, and thereby constitutes happiness or misery, becomes a motive to action. . . ." [48] He makes the difference between the reason and taste concrete by an example: "The mathematician, who took no other pleasure in reading VIRGIL, but that of examining AENEAS's voyage by means of the map, might perfectly understand the meaning of every Latin word . . . ; and consequently might have a distinct idea of the whole poem. He would even have a more distinct idea of it, than they could have who had not studied so exactly the geography of the poem. He knew, therefore, everything in the poem: But he was ignorant of its beauty; because the beauty, properly speaking, lies not in the poem, but in the sentiment or taste of the reader. And where a man has no such delicacy of temper, as to make him feel this sentiment, he must be ignorant of the beauty, tho'

[46] *Treatise*, p. 299.
[47] *Essays*, Vol. I, p. 212. "The Platonist."
[48] *Enquiries*, p. 294.

he be possessed of all the science and understanding of an angel." [49] "The standard of the one [reason], being founded on the nature of things, is eternal and inflexible. . . . The standard of the other—" [50] one looks for the contrast to be carried out. If the one is uniform and objective, the other which he calls 'blind' ought to be allowed to be as multiform, it would seem, as it is indeed allowed to be subjective. But no. Even for the sceptic Hume the standard of taste is fixed by God who arranged the several orders and classes of existence and gave to each its peculiar nature.

TASTE CAN BE ANA-
LYZED AND
TAUGHT.

Taste for all its blindness then is a faculty with an orthodoxy— an orthodoxy that can be analyzed and taught. Hume says that "some species of beauty . . . on their first appearance, command our affection and approbation. . . . But in many orders of beauty, particularly those of the finer arts, it is requisite to employ much reasoning, in order to feel the proper sentiment; and a false relish may frequently be corrected by argument and reflection." [51] These latter species demand the assistance of our intellectual faculties. We have to "pave the way" for the right sentiment. This insistence that right taste be taught is characteristic of the whole school. An internal sense may be molded, for even the external senses may be improved in their quality of functioning by exercise and training. But one queries: When the 'eye' is trained so that it is more discriminating in color and more accurate in the estimation of distances, does not the concept of the eye expand and begin to include the mind that uses the eye as its instrument? Is it, quite strictly, the eye that improves? Be that as it may, for the British Empiricists this inner sense is educable. Shaftesbury felt in himself the holy vocation of educating his countrymen to better taste. "My own designs you know run all on moral emblems and what relates to ancient Roman and Greek history, philosophy, and virtue. Of this the modern painters have but little taste. If anything be stirred, or any studies turned this way, it must be I that must set the wheel a-going and help to raise the spirit. . . . My charges turn wholly, as you see, towards the raising of art and

---

[49] *Essays*, Vol. I, p. 218. "The Sceptic."
[50] *Enquiries*, p. 294.
[51] *Ibid.*, 173.

the improvement of virtue in the living and in posterity to come." [52]

Thus far the intellectual elements introduced into the internal sense, or that have glided back into it from the expelled reason, have been (*a*) determination toward, or affinity for an intellectual object such as a mathematical ratio or a perfect proportion of elements; (*b*) susceptibility to intellectual training and to argument and disputation; and (*c*) the general elasticity of its notion such that it may include the faculty of judgment. This last expansion of the original idea of the inner sense is well illustrated by a statement of Gerard's. He says that judgment must fuse with the internal senses to produce true taste. True taste involves "a quick and accurate perception of things as they really are . . . [the comparing and weighing of] the perceptions and decrees of the senses themselves, [and] ultimate sentence upon the whole." Gerard stated that while judgment is always an essential component of true taste, the proportion of the judging and the sensing functions varies from individual to individual. "One man *feels* what pleases or displeases; the other *knows* what ought to gratify or disgust." [53] He cites Aristotle among the ancients and Le Bossu among the moderns as examples of critics who knew rather than felt what was esthetically right.[54]

There is still another way in which the admission of rationality into the esthetic sentiment takes place for these thinkers. Kames speaks of our relish for order and connection, by which he appears to mean a vague power of influencing trains of images toward logical coherence. He says that we cannot break the automatic constant train of ideas, but that we can select, "attend to some ideas and dismiss others, either by will, or by the present tone of mind." [55] When we so control or direct the natural flow of suggestion within the mind, we are illustrating the truth, says Kames, that "we are framed by nature to relish order and connection." [56]

BEAUTY IS CONQUERED CHAOS.

[52] Shaftesbury, *Life, Letters, Phil. Reg.*, pp. 468, 469.
[53] Gerard, *op. cit.*, pp. 85–92. Sec. II.
[54] *Loc. cit.*
[55] Home, *op. cit.*, p. 20. Ch. 1.
[56] *Ibid.*, p. 22.

Suggestion left to itself produces mere sequences, suggestion directed by this relish produces, over and above sequence, order. Witness our "love" for proceeding in history from cause to effect in a time sequence; in science from particulars to the general, rising from effect to cause. The most striking phrase he uses in this connection is a reference to the "exhilaration" of the analytic method. We like grandeur and elevation, he says. We like them best if they are in harmony with the course of nature. "Hence the singular beauty of smoke ascending in a calm morning." [57]

This relish for order and connection seems to be treated by Kames as an immediate original sentiment of human nature. But the order that supervenes upon the sequence presents itself within that part of the mental machinery called the association of ideas, rather than in that part treated as the primary equipment of organs or passions. Hume also, it will be remembered, showed how all that the Neo-Classic reason demanded under the phrase 'unity of action' can be furnished by the mechanism of the association of ideas. Thus this last modification of the constitution of the frame of nature toward rationality takes place in an ambiguous middle region between the inner senses and the 'constant trains of ideas.' The British Empiricists started out by opposition to reason, and little by little and in various ways allowed the animal frame to absorb reason again, to do its work, and to wear its colors.

BEAUTY AND VIRTUE.

There was need of even less stretching of the original conception of 'inner sense' to make it include a bent toward goodness. Shaftesbury and Berkeley had only to go to their father Plato to find virtue and beauty twin sisters. But it was the general climate of ideas as well as the Platonic influence which led these men to draw no clear line between moral values and esthetic. Grace and proportion of character were rated higher than grace and proportion of material objects; but the two were species of the same genus, and the connoisseur in the one was likely to be a connoisseur in the other. "A taste in the fine arts goes hand in hand with the moral sense to which indeed it is nearly allied," [58] says Kames. Reasoning by rational principles on the fine arts, he says again,

---

[57] Home, *op. cit.*, pp. 22, 23.
[58] *Ibid.*, p. 13. Introduction.

"tends to improve the heart no less than the understanding." [59] "By sweetening and harmonizing the temper it is a strong antidote to the turbulence of passion. . . . Pride and envy, two disgustful passions, find in the constitution no enemy more formidable than a delicate and discerning taste. . . . I insist on it with entire satisfaction, that no occupation attaches a man more to his duty, than that of cultivating a taste in the fine arts: A just relish of what is beautiful, proper, elegant and ornamental in writing or painting, in architecture or in gardening, is a fine preparation for the same just relish of these qualities in character and behavior." [60] In still another place Kames says, epigrammatically, that a love of art keeps a young man from gaming, a middle-aged man from ambition, and an old man from avarice.[61] But perhaps none of the writers was more insistent on the intimate relation between beauty perceptible to the external senses and the beauty of the gardens and groves within than Shaftesbury. "*Feel* Goodness and you will see all Things fair and good," [62] he said.

Hobbes and Mandeville had been teaching that man is naturally selfish, and that any higher, kinder impulses of his nature are secondary, based on custom rather than on nature. Hobbism was so thorough and logical that reply to it in philosophical terms was at first difficult. But Shaftesbury and his followers argued that man's original passionate constitution was more complex than Hobbes had allowed, and that man's 'moral sense,' which inclined him to acts of charity and beneficence, and his 'inner sense,' which drew him toward harmony of sound and beauty of form, were within the congenital mental outfit. Shaftesbury refers in his correspondence to the poisonous views of Hobbes, but declares that Hobbes worked off the poison in his "character and base slavish principles of Government." It was Locke whom he accused of striking the home-blow. For Locke, he said, made order and virtue artificial products "without foundation in our minds." He interprets Locke as teaching that bare custom and the catechism

---

[59] *Ibid.*, p. 15.
[60] *Loc. cit.*
[61] Home, *Elements of Criticism*, 3 Vols., London, 1795, Vol. I, p. 10.
[62] Shaftesbury, *Letters to a Young Man*, p. 32, Letter VI.

teach us all the morality we have. If we should happen to lose our catechism with its arbitary doctrines, then right might be wrong and beauty ugliness, for there is nothing in nature to guarantee the permanent intrinsic character of these qualities. In scoffing at this doctrine of "experience," Shaftesbury satirically inquires whether if mankind lost the catechism that gave the meaning of the "idea of woman" (and what is sought after in women) "we might have no understanding of this . . . and the race of mankind might perish in a sober nation." [63]

LAUGHTER SYM-
PATHETIC, NOT
EGOTISTIC.

His follower Hutcheson furnishes an excellent example of the same insistence on value in his theory of laughter designed as a counterblast to that of Hobbes. "The old notions of Natural Affections and kind Instincts," he writes, ". . . the Decorum and Honestum, are almost banished out of our book of Morals; we must never hear of them in any of our lectures for fear of innate Ideas: all must be interest, and some selfish view: laughter itself must be a joy from the same spring." [64] Hutcheson then goes on to point out cases in which our laughter bears no taint of malice or arrogance: parodies, burlesque allusions. We can enjoy the take-off of Homer's *deus ex machina* in Butler's *Hudibras* without feeling any "eminency in ourselves" to either Homer or Butler. This linking of the sense of the ludicrous with sympathy and benevolence was typical of the new school, who not only wished to prove the esthetic sense immediate and independent of rules, but also to make man a noble animal, and not a selfish brute.

POLITICS AND ART.

There was also emphasis on the moral implication of esthetic experience as 'writ large' in the community and state. When Addison said that the beauty of a spacious horizon is "an image of liberty," [65] he symbolized a connection of ideas that was very dear to the men of this time. "The people are no small parties" to the cause of art, wrote Shaftesbury. As the government, so the

---

[63] Shaftesbury, *Life, Letters, and Phil. Reg.*, p. 404. Letter to Michael Ainsworth, June 3, 1709.

[64] Hutcheson, *Reflections upon Laughter and Remarks upon the Fable of the Bees*, Glasgow, 1750, p. 6. "To Hibernicus."

[65] *Spectator*, 412.

taste. "Nothing is so improving, . . . so congenial to the liberal arts, as that reigning liberty . . . of a people, which . . . makes them freely judge . . . of the products . . . of men, in art and science." [66]

Not only did Shaftesbury make a general and universal connection between the state of a nation and its art, but with an evangelist's zeal he applied this doctrine to the political conditions in England at the moment in which he lived. Writing at the time of the war with France and Spain under Marlborough he said, "If we live to see a peace any way answerable to that generous spirit with which this war was begun and carried on, for our own liberty and that of Europe, . . . increase of knowledge, industry, and sense at home will render . . . Britain the principal seat of the arts; . . ." He thinks he finds justification for his optimism in the course of recent history: The English taste in music was low during the corrupt period of the Restoration, "but when the spirit of the nation was grown more free . . . in an instant we outstripped our neighbours the French, entered into a genius far beyond theirs, and raised ourselves an ear, and judgment, not inferior to the best now in the world." [67]

The influence of Locke on our group of writers gave rise to a tendency not only to base the experience of beauty on a sense whose origin and history could be scientifically traced, but, in the second place, to identify beauty itself with the sensation. What Locke taught concerning the secondary qualities of objects, their color, sweetness, fragrance, was carried over to the tertiary properties of objects, the charm and splendor, the esthetic qualities. If sweetness and bitterness are not in the morsel, but in our sensing, so may the grandeur and harmony be not in the objects, but in our sensing. The chief critic of this Lockian moment in the eighteenth century esthetic is Thomas Reid, the Scotch common-sense philosopher (1710–1796). He says that reason and reflection lead us to distinguish in the case of our outer senses between what is felt in us, and the external cause of that feeling. So in observing beauty, we should do. But contemporary philoso-

REID: THOUGH BEAUTY BE FEELING, SOMETHING MAKES US FEEL.

---

[66] *Second Characters*, ed. Rand, Cambridge, 1914, pp. 22, 23.
[67] *Ibid.*, p. 20. "A Letter Concerning Design."

phers, he says, "resolve all our perceptions into mere feelings or sensations in the person that perceives, without anything corresponding to those feelings in the external object." He then proceeds to censure the looseness of the thinking that leads to this subjectivism. There is "no solid foundation for it when applied to the secondary qualities of body; and the same arguments show equally, that it has no solid foundation when applied to the beauty of objects, or to any of those qualities that are perceived by a good taste." [68] It is true, he admits, that in both the case of color and sweetness it is sometimes difficult to understand precisely what it is in the external body that causes the sensation; and so with beauty. But because some of the causes of our feeling are occult, there is no just ground for inferring that therefore the external cause is lacking. Thus the members of the 'commonsense' school kept esthetic object separate from esthetic subject, and indicated that Locke had been misleading at this point.

But the best-known thinkers of the time said that beauty is, at least in part, an attribute of the sensation itself. Hume was accused of putting the finishing stroke to this false way of converting into an "operation of the sensitive part of our nature" the solid matters of the objective order—even truth itself. [69] But men of the acuteness of Hutcheson and Hume can hardly be said to have picked up verities, either intellectual or esthetic, and simply transferred them from the outside half of the balance to the inside. Even Hutcheson, though he said that beauty means precisely the idea of a mind, and that he could not see how objects could be called beautiful were there no mind gifted with a faculty for perceiving this quality, yet tended to think of beauty as a relation between the perceiver and thing perceived. And with Hume the solution is more complex. There are two clear pronouncements of his that put beauty in the person: it is "certain, that beauty and deformity, more than sweet and bitter, are not qualities in objects, but belong entirely to the sentiment, internal or external." [70] And again: "Were I not afraid of appearing too philosophical, I would

---

[68] Reid, *op. cit.*, p. 516.
[69] *Ibid.*, p. 526.
[70] *Essays*, Vol. I, p. 273.

remind my reader of that famous doctrine, supposed to be fully proved in modern times, that *tastes and colours, and all other sensible qualities, lye not in the bodies,* but merely *in the senses.* The case is the same with beauty and deformity." [71] But in both cases Hume warns against inferring that this locating of beauty within the mind lowers its worth, or cuts away from its solid reality. This placement of the qualities, he says, takes nothing away from their reality; "nor need it give any umbrage to critics. . . . Tho colours were allowed to lye only in the eye, would dyers or painters ever be less regarded and esteemed?" [72] But Hume's problem begins to thicken when he admits that though the qualities lie in the mind, certain qualities in objects "are fitted by nature to produce those particular feelings." [73] The word "fitted" seems both obscure and to beg the question of how the mechanism of esthetic experience works. It seems to evoke a sympathetic magic. And indeed, as we read between the lines and search for the premises of this school we find often that the last principle is some application of a mysterious like-to-like. For Addison, Hume, and Burke, the principal and fundamental esthetic experience is the natural attraction we feel for the beauty of our own *kind*. This is more warm and violent, says Addison, than the beauty we find in form and color in the arts. But what is the beauty of kind, but the magical emotion that cements together a class of beings? Hume traces this back to resemblance. All things in nature, he says, have a natural fondness for the things that are similar to them. The old Empedoclean magic is the last indefinable principle that connects the organism of the perceiver with the perceived "occasion" or apparent "cause" or attendant circumstance in the external world.

SYMPATHETIC MAGIC.

Edmund Burke (1729–1797), who was more radically anti-rational than most of his group in reducing the whole esthetic process to passion, frankly made beauty 'turn on' the social instinct of mankind. He was clear, as very few of his contemporaries were, that if immediacy of operation was desired for the esthetic

BURKE: SENSE OF BEAUTY AS SOCIAL INSTINCT.

---

[71] *Ibid.,* Vol. I, p. 218. "The Sceptic."
[72] *Loc. cit.*
[73] *Ibid.,* Vol. I, p. 273.

function, then an instinct, quite independent of reason, must be trusted to carry through the business. "Beauty," he writes, "demands no assistance from our reasoning; even the will is unconcerned; the appearance of beauty as effectually causes some degree of love in us as the application of ice or fire produces the ideas of heat or cold." [74] He perceives that all those writers who had made beauty consist in order and proportion had really relied on reason rather than an immediate sense. "Every idea of order . . . [is] a creature of the understanding, rather than a primary cause acting on the senses and imagination." [75] As Burke made sublimity turn on our instinct of self-preservation in the face of pain or danger, he made the softer and milder esthetic quality the result of our inborn social sense. "I call beauty a social quality; for where women and men, and not only they, but when other animals give us a sense of joy and pleasure in beholding them . . . they inspire us with sentiments of tenderness and affection toward their persons; we like to have them near us." [76]

Since for him this social instinct equals the whole of our sense of beauty, Burke naturally sub-divides it, making species of the social instinct correspond to species of beauty. These divisions he found to be three: sympathy, which explains our pleasure in tragedy; imitation, which grounds our pleasure in painting, sculpture, and poetry; and ambition or emulation, connected with the sublime.

TRAGEDY MOVES THROUGH SYM-PATHY.

The first species of sympathetic magic was used by Burke to solve the ever-recurring problem of the pleasures of tragedy. "Pity is a passion accompanied with pleasure, because it arises from love and social affection. . . . As our Creator has designed we should be united by the bond of sympathy, He has strengthened that bond by a proportionable delight; and there most where our sympathy is most wanted, in the distresses of others. . . . Delight hinders us from shunning scenes of misery; pain prompts us to relieve those who suffer. . . . And all this antecedent to any rea-

---

[74] Burke, *A Philosophical Inquiry into the Origin of Our Ideas of the Sublime and Beautiful*, London, 1823, p. 127. Part III, Sec. 2.
[75] *Loc. cit.*
[76] *Ibid.*, p. 51. Part I, Sec. 10.

soning, by an instinct that works us to its own purposes without our concurrence." [77]

Burke believed that the age-old problem of the pleasure we take in witnessing tragic spectacles is solved by this natural passion, this inborn drive, toward fellow-feeling. Sympathy makes us take a concern in what other men feel. He draws the inference from this explanation, that where our fellow-beings most vividly need our sympathy, there we feel it most. In an actual spectacle of a fire or a hanging, there is more liveliness, more immediacy and urgency, than in a stage-representation of such things. Therefore it is not to the artistic form of tragedy that we are most drawn by sympathy, but to the real thing. Any audience would leave a play at the news of a hanging in the next square.[78] If, then, the explanation is to be given of tragedy in art as more poignant than tragedy in life, the passion of sympathy needs to be supplemented by some other principle.

Sympathy, for Burke, not only makes us feel with others; it prompts us to copy whatever they do. The tendency to mimic is, he thinks, as natural to us as the tendency to pity. This passion, then, is the basis of the so-called imitative arts. A kind of drive toward imitating others' motions and forms, and the appearances of external objects, is at the bottom of painting, sculpture, and poetry.

PAINTING AND PO-ETRY PLAY UPON IMITATIVE IN-STINCT.

The third species of sympathy that explains esthetic experience is "ambition" or "emulation." We love to think well of ourselves, and any circumstance that stimulates in us a swelling and expansion of our personality is welcome to us. "This swelling is never more perceived, nor operates with more force, than when without danger, we are conversant with terrible objects; the mind always claiming to itself some part of the dignity and importance of the things which it contemplates." [79]

THE SUBLIME AP-PEALS TO SELF-RE-GARD.

In emphasizing the immediacy of the working of these social passions, Burke expressly repudiates all more rational explanations. It would not disturb him that the reader found some suggestion of

NATURAL ELEC-TION.

---

[77] *Ibid.*, pp. 57, 58. Part I, Sec. 14.
[78] *Ibid.*, pp. 58, 59. Part I, Sec. 15.
[79] *Ibid.*, p. 64. Part I, Sec. 17.

a magical natural election in his views. The going forth of the spirit to other spirits and to the world around it by an irresistible natural force, by a magical emanation, or tendency to fuse with a kindred force or form, is exactly what he is proclaiming. The mind in its esthetic experience, he says, is not drawn at once to fine proportion or to perfection or symmetry, but to some ultimate similar.

This recourse to natural election occurs in other writers of the time, though not with the explicitness and systematic development that it does in Burke. Hume, for example, explains our pleasure in the balance of a statue, by the pleasure we take in sympathizing with a well-set-up, strongly standing figure, and our dislike of a lack of balance in painting or sculpture, by the suggestion conveyed to us sympathetically of falling. Here is the same principle of a sympathetic magic attaching us to the objects we contemplate. We feel ourselves somehow at one with the persons and objects represented and their apparent sensations become our real sensations. "A figure which is not justly balanced, is disagreeable; and that because it conveys the ideas of its fall, of harm, and of pain: Which ideas are painful, when by sympathy, they acquire any degree of force or vivacity. Add to this, that the principal part of personal beauty is an air of health and vigor, and such a construction of members as promises strength and activity. This idea of beauty cannot be accounted for but by sympathy." [80]

This appeal to sympathetic magic comes out more clearly in Kames and Gerard, where a doctrine is announced vaguely anticipating the late nineteenth century theory of "empathy." In Part VI of his *Elements of Criticism* Kames entitles a section: "The Resemblance of Emotions to their Causes." He thinks he is the first to have made the observation of this kind of resemblance. He says: "Sluggish motion . . . causes a languid and unpleasant feeling; slow uniform motion a feeling calm and pleasant; and brisk motion, a lively feeling that rouses the spirit and promotes activity. . . ." [81]

The "fitness" or "resemblance" or "sense of kind" which brings

---

[80] *Treatise*, pp. 364, 365.
[81] Home, *op. cit.*, p. 94.

mind and object together in the esthetic experience is explicitly compared by Gerard to the magic of magnetism. "As the magnet selects, from a quantity of matter, the ferruginous particles which happen to be scattered through it, without making an impression on other substances, so imagination, by a similar sympathy equally inexplicable, draws out from the whole compass of nature such ideas as we have occasion for, without attending to any others." [82] "The magical force" of fancy, Gerard says, so orders and disposes the rude, undigested chaos of our first perceptions that genius, seconding her, can readily design a "regular and well-proportioned whole." [83] This same inexplicable sympathy becomes the natural engine not only for binding the percipient to what he pleasurably perceives, but for binding together the parts of a mental or artistic whole. Hume says that the story is the least important part of a poem. What we want is a rapidity of movement and warmth of affection that will raise our sentiments to a certain pitch. Now this is achieved not through the objective unity of a well-designed plot, but through insuring a constant communication of emotions. There must not be any sensible breach or vacuity. The first rule of art is not, as with Aristotle, to invent a well-knit story, but to produce something equably enflamed and lively. The sympathy of one scene must carry the hearer on to the next.

When sympathetic magic becomes the communication of motion, and the emphasis begins to fall for esthetic experience not on the fitness of a thing to a mind, but on *viability*, the unimpeded passage of energy from moment to moment in the enjoyment of a poem, then indeed the mantle of rationalism begins to fall off. And indeed along with overt rationalism, all through the period of the Neo-Classical criticism, one source of esthetic pleasure was said to be the sheer joy of movement. Turning consciously against the followers of Boileau who were in modified ways still insisting on the close connection between art and reason, the French critic L'Abbé Dubos insisted that poetry, painting, and music are good because they banish *ennui*. Our spirits need stirring and changing,

MERE MOTION OF THE MIND GIVES ESTHETIC PLEASURE.

---

[82] Gerard, *op. cit.*, pp. 168, 169.
[83] *Ibid.*, p. 169.

and "the arts of poetry and painting are never more applauded than when they grieve us because in grieving us they stir us." [84]

HOGARTH: VARIETY
IN UNIFORMITY. In Great Britain there was not in the eighteenth century this clean isolation of the charm of mental movement. But Hogarth, the empiricist who with Burke made the most radical break with Neo-Classic theory and taste, gave emotion as such an important place. In William Hogarth (1697–1764), painter and author of *Analysis of Beauty*, we find an esthetician who is in the main and not on one side an esthetic radical. The whole eighteenth century school of taste was satirized by him in a picture he drew of Burlington House with Pope whitewashing it and bespattering the Duke of Chandos' coach. In this sketch Hogarth intended to ridicule all that Academicism that Burlington House stood for as the home of the Royal Academy and the Palladian architecture of Mr. Kent. Besides his objection to organized and orthodox 'taste,' Hogarth complained of the moralistic tone in esthetic writing at that time. He said that those who had written on grace had soon turned "into the broad, and more beaten path of moral beauty." [85] He also objected to the vagueness of his predecessors in esthetic theorizing. In his own construction he proposed to offer a definite, non-moral, non-literary, absolute key to the puzzle of the nature of beauty. Although Hogarth proposes his master-key as an invention of his own, he surrounds it with a grave air of antiquarian sanction by making it a rediscovery of the secret of both Michelangelo's power, and of the greatness of Greek art. He says that Lomazzo tells in his *Treatise on Painting* that Michelangelo instructed a pupil of his "that he should always make a figure pyramidal, serpent-like, and multiplied by one, two, and three." [86] Lomazzo had remarked that in his opinion "the whole mystery of the art consists in this precept." [87] In the plate containing many drawings of objects illustrating his theory, Hogarth includes a torso by Michelangelo which is supposed to embody this 'mystery of the art.' After invoking Michelangelo as a favoring

---

[84] Dubos, *Réflexions Critiques sur la Poésie et sur la Peinture*, Paris, 1719. Part I.
[85] Hogarth, *The Analysis of Beauty*, London, 1772, p. iv. Preface.
[86] *Ibid.*, p. v.
[87] *Ibid.*, p. vi.

muse for his theory, Hogarth goes on to claim the concurrence of the wisest of the Greeks. With much circumstance of names and dates, he reports that he found a reference to 'the great key of knowledge,' the essence of the 'beau ideal,' by which the Greeks had succeeded in beauty beyond other nations. This secret was brought to them by Pythagoras, and was referred to as the 'analogy,' and had a certain mathematical import. But, says Hogarth, in reading eagerly forward to discover concretely what this analogy was, he found his author suddenly retreating into the obscurity of the phrase '*je ne sais quoi.*' The other phrases, 'touching or pathetic unity,' and 'infinite variety of parts' were the only definite hints that Hogarth got concerning the analogy of the Greeks. But he believed that he had read enough to assure himself that his own magical solution was identical with the Pythagorean analogy. He says, "It shall be my business to show it was a key to the thorough knowledge of variety both in form and movement." [88]

The esthetic idea that Hogarth thus introduces is his "precise serpentine line." Many writers on art, he observed, had referred to kinds of beautiful lines, or had made of a well-drawn line the infallible sign of supreme artistic craftsmanship. Dufresnoy and Roger de Piles had recently written that grace depended much on flowing wave-like serpentine lines. But just as the book on the Greek analogy had lapsed into nebulosity when the moment for precise elucidation had come, so these French writers failed to define or depict this linear source of grace. Again appeared the baffling phrase '*je ne sais quoi.*' Hogarth says that although a precise serpentine line is the acme of beauty, winding lines, such as might fall under the description of the French writers, are as often ugly as beautiful. All depends, Hogarth thought, on fixing meticulously the depth of curve and relation of curves in the ideal line. The line of beauty, he says, is composed of two contrasted curves. These curves must not only move in opposite directions, but they must have a mean depth—that is, they must be neither too swelling and turgid nor too slight and dry. [89] He draws a picture

THE LINE OF BEAUTY.

---

[88] *Ibid.*, p. xvi.
[89] *Ibid.*, p. 49.

of seven such 'S' shapes, the depth of curvature varying from the almost straight to the almost circular. The fourth or mean is the chosen one. This being the line of beauty, the precise serpentine line is like it, but still richer. It is such a line as would be formed by a fine wire twisted in a single sweeping curve around a cone, touching the base at one end and the vertex at the other. He compares it to the cone-like motion of flame.

Having given us the key, Hogarth uses it to indicate the beauty of a large number of objects natural and artificial, for example: the line of an iris petal, of various bones in the body, of bells, candles, chairlegs, and corsets, cornucopia, serpents, and horses. Hogarth gives sometimes series and sometimes merely a small group of examples of these objects to illustrate the result of both the use and the omission of the line. Now it is easy to see that Hogarth could apply his principle where there is an obvious outline as in the case of a human profile, but it is less clear how he could solve by its means the problem of beauty in the case of solid forms. He meets this complication by directing that all solid objects shall be regarded as contained in a shell or onion skin, and that the shell or skin shall in its turn be regarded as made up of lines or wires.[90] It is analogous to the thought of a solid as made up of planes, and of a plane as made up of lines, so that the ultimate geometrical element is in all cases the line. There is an interesting example of his versatility in the use of his line-standard in his treatment of color. The true test of successful use of color by a painter is his power to paint flesh, says Hogarth. The painter who would excell in flesh tints, must consider how nature herself builds up the bloom of the flesh-tint in a living being. He then describes how the cuticle, "thin like goldbeater's skin," is so arranged as to show the cutis below, the cutis in its turn revealing an infinite network of tender threads filled with different colored juices. It is then by threads constituting nets, constituting in their turn layers of skin, that nature produces her beautiful colors. The artist should follow suit. He should take the bloom or virgin tints of each primary color and delicately pencil in with vivid lines the areas of the neck and cheeks, and forehead.[91]

---

[90] Hogarth, *op. cit.*, p. 7.   [91] *Ibid.*, Ch. 14.

Not only is color of a texture made up of linear forms, but the sentimental meaning of a picture has the same technical grounds. Plain lines, says Hogarth, make people look foolish and ridiculous. The bulging line of the face and body of Silenus makes him look swinish.[92] Thus with great resourcefulness Hogarth refers aspects of art which would superficially seem to have little to do with line to his cherished standard.

In his theory of the line of beauty Hogarth likes to believe that he has found a sure standard, participating in the eternity and immutability of mathematical principles. It is with the line as a geometric pattern and as claiming finality that his name is usually associated in the history of esthetics. But it is a question whether Hogarth was quite as much interested in the line as a sure geometrical principle, as he was in its embodiment of a maximum of linear *variety*. "Those lines which have most variety in themselves contribute most towards the production of beauty,"[93] he says. An inelegant figure is one composed of unvaried lines. And in enumerating the abstract attributes of beauty: fitness, variety, simplicity, symmetry, distinctness, intricacy, uniformity, and quantity, it is to variety that he gives the palm. "The art of composing well is the art of varying well."[94] In magnifying the esthetic value of variety Hogarth invokes the sanction of great names, as we saw he did originally for his line. He quotes Milton,

> So varied he and of his tortuous train,
> Curl'd many a wanton wreath in sight of Eve,
> To lure her eye.

And from Shakespeare's *Antony and Cleopatra* he quotes with approval:

> Nor custom stale her infinite variety.[95]

Simplicity, he says, without variety is insipid; and symmetry is not beautiful except in so far as it ministers to fitness. For useful objects—chairs and tables—fitness is an important esthetic quality. "When a vessel sails well, the sailors always call her a beauty;

VARIETY THE PRINCIPAL ABSTRACT ATTRIBUTE OF BEAUTY.

---

[92] *Ibid.*, p. 128.
[93] *Ibid.*, p. 39.
[94] *Ibid.*, p. 40.
[95] *Ibid.*, p. xvi.

the two ideas have such a connection." [96] But it is to variety and
intricacy—and to these as causing physical and mental movement—
that Hogarth most often returns. "The active mind is ever bent to
be employed," [97] he says, coming at this point very close to the
chief thought of Dubos. And his serpentine line expresses motion. "The greatest grace and life that a picture can have is that
it expresses Motion: which the Painters call the *Spirit* of a picture.
Now there is no form so fitted to express this motion, as that of the
flame of fire, which according to Aristotle and the other philosophers, is an element most active of all others: because the forme
of the flame thereof is most apt for motion: for it hath a Conus
or sharp pointe wherewith it seemeth to divide the aire, that so
it may ascend to his proper sphere. So that a picture having this
forme will bee most beautiful." [98] There is the pleasure of the eye
in following curves, the pleasure of the hand in making a lively
movement with pen or pencil. Hogarth describes the movement
our eye makes in following a country dance as beguiling. The
windings of the figures lead the eye "a wanton kind of chace." [99]
He ingeniously explains the charm of a face as due to the variety
of its expressions; and the charm of the body as due to the variety
of artful dress and decoration with which satiety is avoided. This
is very close to Dubos' notion that an art most pleases us which
teases us on, and prevents ennui. In the shifts and colors of
costume, Hogarth says, "The mind at every turn resumes its
imaginary pursuits concerning it [the human body]. Thus, if
I may be allowed a simile, the angler chooses not to see the fish
he angles for, until it is fairly caught." [100]

Like many other inventors of magic formulas, Hogarth believed that the adoption of his principle of the serpentine line,
with its various implications, could be of great practical usefulness to actual artists. He said that he thought a new order, or new
orders of architecture could be designed by the aid of his principle.

---

[96] Hogarth, *op. cit.*, p. 14.
[97] *Ibid.*, p. 24.
[98] *Ibid.*, p. vi. Quoted from Lomazzo.
[99] *Ibid.*, p. 25.
[100] *Ibid.*, pp. 36, 37.

"Churches, palaces, hospitals, prisons, common houses, and summer houses might be built more in distinct characters than they are by contriving orders suitable to each." [101] This he suggests as the road to emancipation from Palladio, who, he said, every architect thought at that time he must slavishly follow, whether he were going to build a palace in Lapland or the West Indies.

But Hogarth has been called England's eighteenth century 'false prophet of beauty.' He was in many ways not typical of his time. His ideas seem closer to those of the French critic, Diderot, than to the orthodox views on beauty and the art of painting surrounding him in his own country. Those typical ideas with their unresolved contradiction between a rational and classical content, and an irrational sense-origin, are perfectly embodied in the *Discourses* of Sir Joshua Reynolds. But the balance is heavily weighed toward traditional reason and good sense. Nine-tenths of his thought is on the side of Dufresnoy and De Piles, who meant for French painting what Boileau meant for French poetry; and one-tenth links him with Locke and Hume.

As David Hume defended the traditional doctrine of the Aristotelian unities, but defended them on the basis of a new philosophy of human nature, that of the mechanism of association, so Sir Joshua Reynolds (1723–1792) defends the traditional doctrines of the imitation of ideal beauty, the perfect state of nature, but he also defends this doctrine on the basis of the new philosophy of human nature, having recourse like Hume to the association of ideas.

Reynolds makes the typical classical emphasis on rules. He says it is a "false and vulgar opinion that rules are the fetters of genius: they are fetters only to men of no genius." [102] In laying down in his 'First Discourse' the method for a beginner in the study of painting to take, he says, "I would chiefly recommend that an implicit obedience to the *Rules of Art*, as established by the practise of the great masters, should be exacted from the young student. That those models which have passed through the ap-

REYNOLDS: NO ART WITHOUT RULES.

---

[101] *Ibid.*, p. 45.
[102] *The Literary Works of Sir Joshua Reynolds*, 2 Vols., London, 1852, Vol. I, p. 309.

probation of ages, should be considered by them as perfect and infallible guides; as subjects for their imitation, not their criticism." [103] This insistence on rules and models always involves the exaltation of authority and lack of trust in individual opinion. And this distrust is clearly voiced by Reynolds: "Take the world's opinion rather than your own. You must have no dependence upon your own genius." [104] Again, "It may be laid down as a maxim that he who begins by presuming on his own sense has ended his studies as soon as he has commenced." [105]

ENDURING NATURE, NOT FLUX, IS FOR THE CANVAS.

The familiar idea that the correct rules are founded on nature is present also in Reynolds. In his treatment of color, his exhortation is: "Have recourse to nature herself, who is always at hand, and in comparison of whose true splendor, the best colored pictures are but faint and feeble." [106] And in more general vein he says, "Correct nature by herself." [107] But as would be expected, that nature which is the well-trained artist's model is nature universalized. In his notes on Dufresnoy's *Art of Painting:*

> 'Tis painting's first chief business to explore
> What lovlier forms in nature's boundless store
> Are best to art and ancient taste allied.[108]

Reynolds comments, "There is an absolute necessity for the painter to generalize his notion; to paint particulars is not to paint nature, it is only to paint circumstances. When the artist has conceived in his imagination the image of perfect beauty, or the abstract idea of forms, he may be said to be admitted into the great council of Nature." [109] "Observe the works of nature," he says; but then he adds, "Select; digest; methodize; compare." For him the "whole beauty and grandeur of art consists in being able to get above all singular forms, local customs, particularities, and details of every kind." [110] That 'grand style' which Reynolds admired and sought to introduce as the fashionable manner in England was as remote as possible from the exact imitation of nature associated with the

---

103 Reynolds, *op. cit.,* Vol. I, p. 308.
104 *Ibid.,* Vol. I, p. 322.
105 *Ibid.,* Vol. I, p. 309.
106 *Ibid.,* Vol. I, p. 320.

107 *Ibid.,* Vol. I, p. 333.
108 *Ibid.,* Vol. II, p. 257.
109 *Ibid.,* Vol. II, p. 300.
110 *Ibid.,* Vol. I, p. 333.

Dutch genius. A cat or fiddle painted so finely "that it looks as if you could take it up" does not mean Raphael and Michelangelo.[111] It was these great Italians who "attended only to the invariable, great, and general ideas which are fixed and inherent in universal nature" that Reynolds believed illustrated the ideal attitude of the painter toward nature.[112] Painting, he said, is in the same ratio to the mechanical imitation of nature as poetry is to the detailed record of facts in history.[113]

How close Reynolds' theory of the generalized imitation of nature approaches to Dr. Johnson's (1709–1784) theory of poetry can be seen from the following quotation from *Rasselas:* "The business of a poet is to examine, not the individual, but the species; to remark general properties and large appearances; he does not number the streaks of the tulip, or describe the different shades of the verdure of the forest."

This road to the ideal imitation of nature Reynolds said could be shortened by the study of antique statues and the great Italian paintings. But though the young student was to study these models, he was recommended to examine them analytically, and warned not to copy them mechanically. One was to study the conceptions behind the works of art, not the particular touches on the canvas or marble. In this way, through the effort to re-travel the road of invention that the Greek or Italian had himself travelled, Reynolds believed that the young artist could become an original master and not a servile imitator. It is obvious how constantly Reynolds indicated the literary, scholarly, or analytical approach to painting, rather than the simple craftsman's approach. Now although Reynolds erected a kind of Platonic idealism for his theory of nature, he resorts to a Lockian empiricism in explaining the psychological preference for different types of beauty. "Though habit or custom cannot be said to be the cause of beauty," he writes, "it is certainly the cause of our liking it." [114] If we compare one species with another, they are equally beautiful. Preference

RELATIVITY OF TASTE NOT INCOMPATIBLE WITH RULES.

---

[111] *Ibid.*, Vol. II, p. 130.
[112] *Ibid.*, Vol. II, p. 128.
[113] *Loc. cit.*
[114] *Ibid.*, Vol. II, p. 133.

is given from custom or some association of ideas; in creatures of the same species beauty is the medium or center of all its various forms. Thus he says a goddess of beauty painted by a negress would have thick lips, because custom and habit make any particular group like what it is most accustomed to.[115] Reynolds has a metaphor to illuminate his doctrine of preference on the basis of association of ideas. He says that a pendulum, however many points it crosses outside the center, in each of its swings hits the central point. This central point across which the pendulum swings represents the esthetic habit built up through repeated experience.[116]

GENIUS ABOVE, NOT AGAINST RULES.

There is one other respect in which Reynolds modifies his insistence on obedience to the rules. Those who have great genius or have disciplined themselves by long and careful training may leave the rules behind. Or rather, the rules of men of genius are above the ordinary reach, "either such as they discover by their own peculiar observations, or of such a nice texture as not easily to admit being expressed in words." [117] "Could we teach taste and genius by rules," he says, "they would no longer be taste and genius." [118] One sees in these developments of Reynolds' thought, —in his psychological explanation of esthetic choice, and in his acknowledgment of the region beyond the rules—the more than merely conventional character of his Neo-Classic thought.

SUPPLEMENTARY READING

Allen and Clark, *Literary Criticism from Dryden to Croce*, New York, 1940.

Bosanquet, *History of Aesthetic*, pp. 202–209.

Laurence Binyon, "English Poetry in Relation to Painting and the Other Arts," 1918, in *Proceedings of the British Academy*, Vol. VIII.

Durham, ed., *Critical Essays of the Eighteenth Century*, New Haven, 1915.

---

[115] Reynolds, *op. cit.*, Vol. II, p. 134.
[116] *Ibid.*, Vol. II, p. 132.
[117] *Ibid.*, Vol. I, p. 387.
[118] *Ibid.*, Vol. I, p. 332.

Hibben, *The Philosophy of the Enlightenment*, New York, 1910.

E. F. Carritt, *The Theory of Beauty*, 4th ed., London, 1928, Ch. IV.

H. A. Ladd, *With Eyes of the Past*, New York, 1928.

Elizabeth Manwaring, *Italian Landscape in Eighteenth Century England*, New York, 1925.

S. H. Monk, *The Sublime*, New York, 1935.

Draper, *Eighteenth Century English Aesthetics: a Bibliography*, Heidelberg, 1931.

Leslie Stephen, *History of English Thought in the Eighteenth Century*, New York, 1876.

Leslie Stephen, *English Literature and Society in the Eighteenth Century*, London, 1910.

Mirabent, *L'Estetica Inglesa del Siglo XVIII*, Barcelona, 1937.

Saintsbury, *History of Criticism*, Vol. II, Bk. VI, Ch. I.

Venturi, *History of Art Criticism*, Ch. VI.

CHAPTER IX

The Eighteenth Century in Italy and France

FOR THE philosophy of the imagination, the grand event in Southern Europe in the early eighteenth century was the appearance in 1725 of Giambattista Vico's *New Science*. The central esthetic idea of the *New Science* is that the poet's imagination is the natural expression of humanity's childhood and that the mind of childhood, with its spontaneity and concreteness, must be understood and respected for itself alone. Vico's esthetic insight, however, that fiction and myth are the natural and proper language of the ingenuous spirit, a language not to be judged by irrelevant logical standards, was the striking climax of a long succession of real but less bold and thorough defenses of the imagination. For the cause of the heart and the fancy had its minority leaders throughout the age of reason. As early as 1575 the Spanish writer, Juan Huarte, declared in his *Trial of Wits* that "he who would set up for a topping poet must take leave of all the sciences relating to [understanding]." [1] For there is a great contrariety between what makes a poet and what makes a logician. There is not required the same "heat, dryness, and moisture" for the two sorts of wits. History supports the distinction. "Democritus arrived at so great a perfection of understanding in his old age that he entirely lost his imagination." [2] In the first quarter of the seventeenth century Bacon had said that the musician who makes an excellent air, like the painter who "makes a better face than ever was," does it not by rules but "by a kind of felicity," and

[1] Juan Huarte, *Examen De Ingenios*, capitulo IX. (In *Biblioteca de Autores Espanoles, obras escogidas De Filosofos*, Madrid, 1929, Vol. 65, p. 442.)
[2] *Loc. cit.*

that Dürer was a fool for trying to find a mathematical law upon which to rest his designs.[3] Even before him Castelvetro had said that the purpose of poetry was to please the mob and cater to the pleasure-loving instinct.[4] Bruno had declared that the only rule for poetry was the singing of the poet;[5] and Pallavicino in his *Del Bene* of 1644 cut the bonds between any sort of truth and poetry by saying that sweet dreams, sumptuous imagery, and lively fancies existed in poetry for their own sakes.[6]

The Italian Giovanni Vincenzo Gravina (1664–1718) was a modern radical both for literary criticism and for esthetics. He was the first European literary critic, we are told, fully and completely to repudiate blind adherence to Aristotle and to try out the Cartesian method in its relation to works of imagination.[7] His importance for esthetic beginnings is his treatment of imagination. He dwells on the force and frequency of imagery in the lives of the masses of people. 'Vulgar minds' cannot grasp universal truths directly, and they live a prey to their passions.[8] For example, a man filled with ambition or possessed by lust is practically insane, for these passions fill his soul to the exclusion of all ordering and controlling ideas.[9] The poet must work in this inflammable material of passions and images and convert it to good ends. How, then, can he work wisely? He can simulate the laws of God and man in his own characteristic material, and he can so subtly compose and enhance the matter through novelties and marvels that this wholesome content instead of malignant ideas shall wholly occupy the mind. Availing himself of the power of passion and imagery to hold fast the attention, the poet can by deliberate patterning annex to the given virtue of poetry the borrowed one of pious

GRAVINA: MORAL BEARING OF IMAGINATION.

---

[3] *The Works of Francis Bacon*, ed. Spedding, Ellis, and Heath, 15 Vols., London, 1857–59, Vol. XII, p. 226.

[4] Castelvetro, *Poetica d'Aristotele*, p. 679.

[5] Giordano Bruno, *The Heroic Enthusiasts*, "A Discourse of Poets." (Eng. trans. in Library of the World's Best Literature, ed. Charles Dudley Warner, New York, 1897, Vol. V, p. 2617ff.)

[6] Croce, *Aesthetic*, London, 1909, p. 267.

[7] J. G. Robertson, *Studies in the Genesis of Romantic Theory in the Eighteenth Century*, Cambridge, 1923, p. 24.

[8] Gravina, *Della Ragion Poetica*, ed. Natali, Lanciano, 1933, p. 62.

[9] *Ibid.*, p. 52.

and truthful teaching.[10] The skilful use of the imagination then will be successful both for the cause of the highest interests of man and for the peculiar exhibition of poetry's powers. Poetry is a good delirium that drives out bad delirium.[11]

ESTHETIC DISTANCE
AND THE CYCLE OF
TASTE.

How in this view of imagination did Gravina suggest but not adequately carry out a true view of poetical imagery? The most interesting development under his hands of the idea of poetical imagery is that imitation cannot be effective unless it distances the object and makes an attack upon the beholder's attention. We notice but little what is too close to us or too familiar. The good magician's siege of the imagination must therefore make use of elements that will cause the mind to take notice, to bend back, and react.[12] To devise spells of this character the poet must at once be inspired by the eternal idea of beauty, mother and fountain of all fair forms, and yet adapt his work, disregarding hard and fast rules, to the changing needs of the moving times. These references by Gravina to the psychological phenomenon of interest and the historical phenomenon of changing taste are modern. But the general notion of poetry's power to use beneficent passion for the expulsion of malignant is as old as Aristotle himself. And Gravina always thus thinks of imagination as at worst evil and at best a means to intellectual and moral ends. In this he belongs not to the modern era, but to the main medieval-renaissance tradition.

MURATORI: IMAG-
INATION AS SELEC-
TIVE TACTFUL
JUDGMENT.

A more interesting and vivid description of the ways of the poetical imagination is given by Ludovico Antonio Muratori (1672–1750) in his *Perfetta Poesia*. The wares, he says, that the senses import through their five gateways are spread out as at a fair for the imagination to select from. In order to give a pleasing appearance of truth to her images—which is her chief end—the faculty of imagination, fertile and alert, selects those on display that are distant in time and place, of unusual minuteness, and of unusual pattern, as in figures of speech. This part of the poet's equipment, the "gardener in him who perfects the flowers," must be balanced by a judicial faculty, which should be "king of his

[10] Gravina, *op. cit.*, p. 70.
[11] *Ibid.*, p. 61.
[12] *Ibid.*, p. 72.

soul." The judgment does not apply universal truths to the particular case, but judges which are fit among the individuals themselves, thus being like tact rather than like the Cartesian 'reason. The laws of judgment are infinite in number, because the circumstances among which she must decide are infinite; and her study is always of particular and individual examples. It is what makes us choose the discreet and becoming; it is "the Light that discovers to us, according to the circumstances, those extremes between which beauty lies." [13] Thus, as Gravina perceived that true taste must change with the changing times, Muratori perceived its relativity to circumstance. But Muratori, like Gravina, thought of imagination as servant of the moral and intellectual powers of man. Like a medieval mystic, he taught that incorporeal beauty is apprehended by the intellect, and that the conveyance of light and charm of ultimate truth must determine proper qualities of style.[14]

Instead of such glimmerings of a new way of thought as are found in the men just discussed, in Giambattista Vico (1668-1744) we have the insight of a "bold and revolutionary spirit." The essence of his discovery is that imagination is not a daughter or servant or minister to anything else, but is good in and of itself. This good character is learned through history. For there is a rationalistic fallacy, as there is a pathetic fallacy. The rationalistic fallacy consists in imputing to simple human creatures the same analytical powers as are enjoyed by the sophisticated observers of simplicity. Most learned writers on manners, morals, law, and ancient happenings have been guilty of this fallacy. Let a well-founded idea of the history of man, framed in the history of the world, correct this mistake in method. Right method in science means to start interpreting at the beginning.[15] Conceive the universe as an unfolding process. Then watch civilization break into being, and once born, march. Let human ways begin, under the

VICO FREES IMAGI-
NATION; MODERN
GENETIC METHOD.

---

[13] Carritt, *Philosophies of Beauty*, p. 64. Ludovico Antonio Muratori, *The Perfection of Italian Poetry.*

[14] *Ibid.*, pp. 60–64.

[15] *La Scienza Nuova*, giusta l'edizione del 1744 a cura di Fausto Nicolini, (Scrittori d'Italia) Vol. I, p. 123; Bk. I, Ch. IV.

ordinances of God, with the experiences of the rough wild men
who peopled the earth after Noah's flood. New science may take
its point of departure instead of in the Bible, with the stones thrown
by Deucalion, the seeds of Cadmus, the oak-sprung race mentioned by Vergil. Or if the accounts of primitive beings inhabiting
the earth be taken from the philosophers instead of the classical
poets, new science sets out from the frogs of Epicurus, the cicadas
of Hobbes, the men "simple and stupid" of Grotius, or the creatures
thrown into the world without succor or concern of God, told
of by Pufendorf.[16]

IMAGINATION AS
FIRST CHARACTER-
ISTICALLY HUMAN
BEHAVIOR.

The divine environment crashed into the gross sensuality of
these first giant-men and awakened them from animality into humanity. Thunder and lightning smote and blinded their heavy
senses. They feared, admired; and at a stroke were initiated into
racial manhood. The first psychological condition after animal
sensing is that of the imagination. The giants could only fancy the
thunder and lightning as a fearful sign-language,[17] a gesture or
word of another giant like themselves, but much grander. So
poetical wisdom created a theology. A class of priests arose who
could interpret the signs of the terrible divinities. Shame and an
intimation of an immortal life followed the lively sense of a sky
alive with gods and a watching Providence. This ensemble of
ancient beliefs about the gods is at once poetry, religion, and a
crude metaphysics. But its special psychological character is its
imaginative corporeality, the lack of abstract ideas and all rational
criticism.[18] It was born out of the collective sense of a people
who had God's spirit immanent, but needed an external stimulus
to call this forth.

HOMER WAS
GREECE.

Because Vico was led to believe that man's history runs through
a cycle, as God's continual creative act makes fact, and that the
first stage of the cycle was the stage of the gigantesque or heroic
imagination, he took Homer for the name of a collective point of
view. Homer, he says, is the ideal character of the Greek people
telling the story of their career and singing their national songs.

---

[16] *Loc. cit.*
[17] *Ibid.*, Vol. I, pp. 147–48; Bk. II, Sec. I, Ch. I.
[18] *Ibid.*, Vol. I, p. 148; Bk. II, Sec. I, Ch. I.

Homer was young like the Iliad and old like the Odyssey. He was the lover of force, pride, and generosity in Achilles, of prudence in Odysseus, because he was all that the Greek peoples were. As the picturing imagination of racial childhood, he was the founder of Greek civilization, the father of all other poets, and the source of the various philosophies of Greece.[19]

The strength and weakness of Vico's position lie near together. It was a great thing to have made the province of the poetical function coequal with that of the intellect by 1721, and to have identified it with myth-making and with primitive language. But his enthusiasm over his new discovery carried him little beyond aphoristic assertions of these differences and identities. Thus his view bears largely a negative aspect. Philosophy is truer, the more universal; poetry more certain, the more individual. "The studies of Metaphysics and Poetry are in natural opposition one to the other; for the former purges the mind of childish prejudice and the latter immerses and drowns it in the same; the former offers resistance to the judgment of the senses, while the latter makes this its chief rule; the former debilitates, the latter strengthens, imagination: the former prides itself in not turning spirit into body, the latter does its utmost to give a body to spirit: hence the thoughts of the former must necessarily be abstract, while the concepts of the latter show best when most clothed with matter: to sum up, the former strives that the learned may know the truth of things stripped of all passion: the latter that the vulgar may act truly by means of intense excitement of the senses. . . . Hence from all time, in all languages known to man, never has there been a strong man equally great as metaphysician and poet: such a poet as Homer, father and prince of poetry." [20]

VICO'S FRESH IN-
SIGHT NO REAL
SYNTHESIS.

Between Muratori's *Perfetta Poesia* in 1706 and the first sketch of Vico's ideas in 1721, two treatises appeared in France demanding our attention: Condillac's *Essay on the Origin of Human Knowledge* (1716) and Dubos' *Critical Reflections on Poetry and*

CONDILLAC: ART
AND COMMUNICA-
TION COEXTENSIVE
AT ROOT.

---

[19] *Ibid.*, Vol. II, pp. 8–9; Bk. III, Sec. I, Ch. I; Vol. II, pp. 34–39; Bk. III, Sec. II, Ch. I.
[20] *Scienza Nuova*, Vol. I, Bk. III, Ch. 26. Quoted by Croce, *op. cit.*, pp. 220, 221.

Painting (1719). The first developed a theory of the origin of language strikingly similar to that of Vico; the other with a less self-conscious break with the past and with a less sharp cutting between the poetical function and the other forms of the spirit, founded a logically developed and rich doctrine of the arts, taking as basis not the imagination, but emotion, the other faculty which from Plato down had been linked with the special work of poetry.

Condillac was stimulated to find the origin of language and knowledge by reading Locke,[21] as Vico was influenced by Bacon to find individual experiences rather than general ideas at the basis of knowledge. The first attempts at communication Condillac believed were integral dances. Such pantomimes were the nearest possible reinstatements of the whole scene through the language of gesture. For example, if a primitive man wished to describe some one in fear, he would imitate the sounds and actions of the fearing man, and bring the original fact as a whole before the eyes. But this heavy mode of description and communication had soon to be shortened as intelligence advanced. So the language of words arose out of the original total mimicry by a second degree of imitation. Certain phases of the original could be reinstated through the sole medium of the sounds of voice. But the words thus framed would be picturesque, redundant, and pregnant with the liveliness and full-bodiedness of the original. The arts of dance, music, painting, and drama arose out of these fumblings as a way to report a happening or express a feeling—fumblings which requisitioned at first all the bodily parts, the mouth and throat for making sounds, and legs and arms for mimicking. But a dance of steps arose by refinement out of the dance of total gesture, and music and drama arose by abstracting from the first aping groans, the more pleasing relations of accent and rhythm. Painting arose out of mimicry through picture-writing.[22]

DUBOS: ART NA-
TURE'S SELFHOOD
MADE VISIBLE.

Dubos took motion instead of picturing as the characteristic element of the arts. Plato had condemned poetry because its pictures were too faint and remote from the original, and also be-

---

[21] E. B. de Condillac, *Essai sur l'Origine des Connaissances Humaines*, Paris, 1798, p. 175.

[22] *Ibid.*, pp. 257ff.

cause it stirred up too much emotion.[23] Dubos took up the second half of poetry's original shame, the kinship with passion, and claimed that the passions connected with true poetry and painting are not only necessary effects of them, but that their power to touch and move is a biological virtue.[24] In this use of the wholesome motion induced by poetry to regulate destructive and animal motion, Dubos was in a sense only taking a leaf out of the book of Plato's immediate follower, Aristotle, who said that poetry is made of motion and so has peculiar kinship with our feelings, and has the power to purge our pity and fear. Dubos explicitly refers to this Aristotelian doctrine.[25] But there is a new cast in Dubos's thoughts that links him as much with the scientific age to come (*e.g.*, with Taine) as to classical times, to Aristotle and the Aristotelian Lessing. For Dubos the primary characteristic of human nature is motion. The mind's primary motions are the needs and feelings and senses. Our feelings are so intimately ourselves that we hold to them in spite of rational opposition. We can be argued out of our theories but not out of our affective set.[26] And yet if an appeal is made to our feelings, nothing is more remarkable than the ready response. It takes but a little thing to move the human heart, if an emotional stimulus is supplied. This tenacious hold upon us and yet swift shifting of our emotional life comes from the first need of man. This first need is to escape boredom.[27] The most powerful and elemental of our instincts leads us to a career of passions and affections, and the thirst for excitement and danger is only this primary need running free and unchecked.[28]

Man being so made, art is his remedy and protection. Art must be made moving in order to reach and touch the human nature that must always be moving. The essence of art then is founded on the essence of man. "One merits the name of poet by rendering the

ART MUST MOVE BY ITS TRUTH.

[23] L'Abbé Dubos, *Reflexions Critiques sur la Poésie et sur la Peinture*, 2 Vols., Paris, 1719, Vol. I, Part I, Sec. 5.

[24] *Ibid.*, Vol. I, Part I, Secs. 1, 3.

[25] *Ibid.*, Vol. I, Part I, Sec. 7.

[26] *Ibid.*, Vol. I, Part I, Sec. 4.

[27] *Ibid.*, Vol. I, Part I, Sec. 1. Cf. Voltaire: "All kinds of art are good except the boring kind."

[28] *Ibid.*, Vol. I, Part I, Secs. 1, 3, 5, 40, 50.

action of which one treats capable of moving." [29] It is also because art exists to move us that the public is a better judge of art than specialists in artistic technique. A sixth sense in us answers by a reflex movement and without deliberation to the touching imitation of natural objects. People call this sense 'sentiment' or 'the heart'; and it is just for this response to beautiful forms that the heart is made. "If a man lacks this he cannot be communicated with through art any more than a blind man can be shown sights." [30] Not only this; but the greatest applause actually goes to the painter or poet who moves us to the point of grieving us. From this primary truth about art's relation to emotion important corollaries follow.

First, the subject is more important than skill of execution, although this is truer of poetry than painting, and although the management of the style must be governed by the emotional end of all art. Pleasure and not conformity to rule, in other words, is the first consideration. Wonder must coöperate with probability. But points of artistry are in all cases second to shrewd choice of subject-matter, because our experience in witnessing art is a copy of our experience in witnessing the reality, and on this fact the primary effect depends.[31] Other things being equal, tragedy is more moving than comedy, because actual tragic events surpass in this respect the comic surface of life.[32] For this reason again a naturalistic style is preferable to allegorical embellishment. Dubos suggests that Rubens' painting of the *accouchement* of Marie de Medici would have been more effective if instead of the allegorical figure of Genius near the bed, the painter had introduced portraits of actual women of the period.[33] Corneille, again, excels in the natural words put into Caesar's mouth at the death of Pompey, whereas he is weak in his allegorical prologues. Because "it is in proportion to the verisimilitude that we are seduced," [34] tragedies

---

[29] L'Abbé Dubos, *op. cit.*, Vol. I, p. 199. Part I, Sec. 24.
[30] *Ibid.*, Vol. II, p. 308. Part II, Sec. 22.
[31] *Ibid.*, Vol. I, Part I, Secs. 10, 11.
[32] *Ibid.*, Vol. I, Part I, Sec. 7.
[33] *Ibid.*, Vol. I, p. 177. Part I, Sec. 24.
[34] *Ibid.*, Vol. I, p. 176.

must take their subjects from antiquity, that the effect of what
is grave and venerable in the action may be assisted; and comedies
must take their subjects from the present, because it is easier to
satirize manners that we witness daily than those remote. On this
ground again one may praise modern opera. Lulli conveys the actual
sentiments of men through his regulation of tones and rhythms.

Though truth to life is indispensable for the emotional power
of art, this truth cannot produce its peculiarly artistic effect if it
is not experienced as weaker than the corresponding real emotion.
Qualitatively, the function of art is to touch and move; but quantitatively, the effect must be mild. The feigning of art gives us
change and excitement without inconvenient consequences: adventure without danger, motion without weariness. For the only
difference between the motive power of art and of its original is
the lesser force of art. The weakness of art is its excellence, always
providing the emotional value is present. The crux of the artist's
problem then is to supply interesting material that will without
fail interest, touch, and move the beholder, and yet that will make
the motions salutary instead of harmful. It is then as important
to feel the artificiality of a work of art as to feel its lifelikeness.
We require naturalism but not illusionism. When we go to the
theatre, one hundred things remind us what we are and where we
are; so 'good sense' enables us to keep our head and avoid being
carried away by enthusiasm even while we are undergoing a treatment of our emotions through emotion.[35]

In order to produce the kind of art that shall move and yet heal,
a genius is required that ferments readily, and yet mirrors faithfully.[36] When poets speak of a "divinity that animates their breasts"
and makes them sing, they are referring through a figure of speech
to a happy combination within themselves of a blood which boils
abundantly near the springs of the imagination in the brain, and
a fortunate disposition of the organs of the brain itself such that
the images that seethe up so freely may be clarified and shown
faithful to fact. But "there is a genius of ages and nations which
makes them by nature do well and easily certain things which

ESTHETIC DISTANCE
AND ART AS BALM.

NATURE AND NUR-
TURE OF GENIUS.

---

[35] *Ibid.*, Vol. I, Part I, Sec. 44.
[36] *Ibid.*, Vol. II, Part II, Sec. 2.

others could not do even with effort." [37] The favorable time and place for genius is also partly a matter of physical conditions, as well as of patronage and public appreciations. A genius must not only have a bubbling spring and a clear mirror in his own breast but he must breathe a certain sort of air. Soul depends upon blood; blood depends upon air; and air depends on exhalations from the earth. So artistic genius is a kind of spiritual crop and is helped or hindered by time and place, as the same seeds planted in the soil one season will do better than in another, or in a fertile soil will prosper more than when dropped on stony ground. Our minds record the state of the atmosphere, said Dubos, almost as exactly as thermometers and barometers. In general the great artists of all kinds appear at the same hour in the history of the world, *i.e.* when conditions conspire to favor their genius. And yet one may say that though cold and heat act on the vital spirits of both painter and poet, "Poetry does not fear the cold as much as painting." [38]

In his observations on the influence of climate and epoch on the appearance of artistic genius, Dubos in a degree anticipates the main idea of Madame de Staël, Stendhal, and Hippolyte Taine. In his discussion of the differences between poetry and painting, he links with Shaftesbury and Lessing. "Poetry can lead up to an act; painting must take it in an instant." [39] Therefore the painter is limited to the representation of such sentiments as find immediate natural expression in an attitude or action. Succession through time gives the poet other advantages besides that of building up an action or a character; he can cover over minor defects by the fading of the old and the impact of the new image. Moreover, the successive attack with new passionate weapons through a period of time gives the poet the power to touch and move his audience strongly, even though at any given instant the impression he can make is weaker than that of the painter. For the painter uses signs that are more natural, more like the original, and in so far forth more quickly emotive. Also the painter has the advantage over the

[37] L'Abbé Dubos, *op. cit.*, Vol. II, p. 11. Part II, Sec. 1.
[38] *Ibid.*, Vol. II, p. 140. Part II, Sec. 13.
[39] *Ibid.*, Vol. I, p. 79. Part I, Sec. 13.

poet that he addresses the sense of sight which holds empire over all the other senses.

Closeness to nature because art must move—this central thought in Dubos persists and grows in the reflections on art in France. In 1746 Batteux issued a book in which he announced that he had reduced all the arts to a single principle. And what then was this principle? It was "imitation of nature," [40] and much in the sense of Dubos. What Dubos puts second, approaching it through the psychological law that art must move, Batteux puts first. At a first look the definition of art as imitation of nature seems far from the treatment of its emotional value. But, says Batteux, there are two fundamental ways in which the spirit of man may relate itself to nature. He may consider nature as an independent being. Then he is pure intelligence. Or he may consider the same nature not supposing it independent, but regarding it in its concernment with us. Then he is a man of taste, and his concern with nature is not through intelligence but sentiment. But when nature is imitated without subtracting its human implications, nature becomes "fine nature," "because it is at once perfect in itself and has more connection with our own perfection, advantage, interest. Hence (here he meets Dubos) it pleases, moves, touches." [41] We can go farther. Taste is not a clear mirror, but is built on self-love. Therefore art must depict objects close to us—a dog rather than a rock—and most of all it must present the passions of the human heart and flatter our weakness.

In the end Batteux's phrase, "imitation of nature," offered as a master-key for the interpretation of art, becomes a dead blank that opens nothing. For not only for art is nature contracted into beautiful, interesting, and perfect nature—the nature that human beings care for; but at will it is expanded into the total possibilities deducible from the elements of nature. "Genius, like the earth, can produce nothing of which it has not received the seeds." [42] It has no other forms with which it can work than those that the

IMITATION OF NATURE AS EMBODIMENT OF SENTIMENT.

---

[40] Batteux, *Les Beaux Arts Réduits à un Même Principe*, Paris, 1746, pp. xxii, xxiii.

[41] Batteux, *Principes de la Littérature*, 5 Vols., Paris, 1764, Vol. I, p. 84.

[42] *Ibid.*, Vol. I, p. 16.

universe supplies to it. But Nature is all that we can easily conceive as possible, not only the existing physical, moral, and political
worlds, but the historic, fabulous, and ideal worlds. Batteux
stretches nature further still. Since it is the function of art to
transplant seeds found in nature to foreign fields, *viz.* the artificial
media of art, the imitation is not real but apparent, and poetry is
a perpetual lie, which has all the characters of truth. The query
arises in one's mind: Why did Batteux write about art, the imitation of nature, if art seems in no way restricted to such a business
as the words would suggest? He answers this partially, when he
says that 'imitation' is a more inclusive term than the other three
which have been used to express the nature of poetry: versification,
fiction, enthusiasm. But the course of his argument would seem
to show that near his heart was the idea that art ought to be natural
in the sense that it ought not to do violence to common human
sentiment.

DIDEROT: BEAUTY
AS RELATION

If one derives one's conception of Diderot's (1713–1784) theory
of beauty from the long article entitled 'Beau' [43] which he wrote
for the *Encyclopedia* of which he was chief editor, one sees at first
but little connection with the characteristic and growing conviction in France that it is the chief business of art to touch and move,
and to do this by getting close to 'nature.' For he defines beauty
cryptically and vaguely as 'relations.' Yet a search through Diderot's critical treatises for light on this abstract esthetic discussion
proves that his purpose was nothing else than to give solid philosophical ground to the view less well developed and carried less
far by Dubos and Batteux that the arts must engage with our sentiments by becoming natural. Before Diderot makes the baffling
assertion that Beauty "lies only in the notion of *rapports*" [44] he
briefly summarizes other theories of the beautiful which he thinks
worthy of notice.

All historical treatments, however, in Diderot's opinion, lacked
one thing: there was no attempt to tell the *origin* of the ideas of
connection, order, and symmetry in which beauty was said to
consist. Diderot occupies himself at once with this problem of

---

[43] *Œuvres Complètes de Diderot*, 20 Vols., Paris, 1876, Vol. X, pp. 5-42.
[44] *Ibid.*, Vol. X, p. 26.

origins. He says that our esthetic experience begins, like all other experience, with sense perception. These initial sense-impressions, or motor stimuli, are combined and related by us sometimes with satisfactory and sometimes with unsatisfactory results. Again, at the basis of our experience are certain primitive needs, and we devise tools and mechanisms to meet these needs. Now when the relationships that we contrive, and the tools that we design meet with our approval, we name them beautiful. "So our needs and the most immediate exercise of our faculties teach us notions of order, arrangement, symmetry, mechanism, proportion, unity. . . . These notions are experimental like all the others; [they] come from the same source as those of existence, number, length, depth." [45]

Hutcheson and his group were wrong, says Diderot, to separate a mysterious inner sense, which necessarily receives impressions of beauty, from the reflective faculty, which gradually elaborates our concrete ideas of harmony and symmetry. For esthetic experience belongs to no sacrosanct sixth sense, but stems pragmatically from the same simple seeds as any skill or knowledge. And it as naturally takes on critical and reflective elements. The ideas of order, unity, symmetry, and proportion "are as positive, as distinct, as clear, as real, as those of length, breadth, and thickness, quantity and number." As they arise from our needs and experiences . . . , however high, however variable, they are always "mental abstractions," mental constructs. [46]

INNER SENSE AND THE MIND.

As science and taste begin according to an identical pattern, so they run in closely parallel lines all the way. The poet must be a philosopher, Diderot says. He must be deeply versed in the ways of the spirit and the lights and shades, goods and evils of human society. [47] Not only must he be profoundly instructed in individual and social moral philosophy, but he must be logical. "The poet who feigns, and the philosopher who reasons, are equally, and in the same sense, logical or illogical, for to be logical and to be aware of the necessary chain of phenomena is the same thing. This

TASTE, LIKE KNOWLEDGE, IS VERIDICAL.

---

[45] *Ibid.*, Vol. X, pp. 24, 25.
[46] *Ibid.*, Vol. X, p. 25.
[47] *Ibid.*, Vol. VII, p. 309.

suffices, it seems to me, to show the analogy between fiction and truth, and to characterize poet and philosopher." [48] Diderot, like most philosophers of his time and earlier, makes little difference between the good and the beautiful. But Diderot also brings the beautiful and the true thus into close proximity. The philosopher, committed to the representation of the truth, traces the connections he actually finds in things; the poet makes a beginning in nature, and then traces, by an act of scientific imagination, a connection that might be found in things.

HOW IS ART VERIDI-
CAL, TASTE DIF-
FERENT FROM
KNOWLEDGE?

Two questions arise now concerning Diderot's esthetic theory: (1) How may one apply this universal pattern of the origin and growth of experience to the special case of the arts? (2) Since the likeness between growth in taste and growth in scientific or philosophical knowledge is so great, in what does one find the distinguishing mark of taste that will fix the esthetic species within the whole genus? Both of these queries move in the same direction. They demand a more concrete definition of beauty than the all-inclusive word 'relation.' Diderot seems to have chosen this elastic term partly in reaction against earlier estheticians, who, he felt, had omitted some factor. He wished to choose a term broad enough to include, first, the relationship of pleasure and admiration which arises between the observer and the object; secondly, the various types of relationship, those of means to end, of mathematical ratio and proportion, sign to thing signified within the object; and thirdly, those relationships that are not narrowly esthetic but are expressive of kindred human values, for example, the moral relationships. Where then, should a word be found wide enough for all these states and conditions, except the simple word 'relationship'? But Diderot seems also to have chosen his all-inclusive term in order to emphasize the infinitely conditional character of the esthetic experience. A relation Diderot defines as a mental operation through which a being or quality involves another being or quality.[49] There are thirteen different possibilities of such involvement. Examples would be variation in interest, passion, ignorance, prejudice, custom, manners, climate. For example, a color may

[48] *Œuvres Complètes de Diderot,* Vol. VII, p. 334.
[49] *Ibid.,* Vol. X, p. 31.

become displeasing because experience has associated it for a particular observer with the garb of the peasant. In addition to the diversity of relationships on the subject side, there is a complication on the 'real' or objective side. For example, size as a factor in beauty must be taken in relation to the natural kind or the age. A beautiful child must be tiny; a beautiful man, tall; a woman less tall.

But how the definition applies and how the general pattern UNIFORMITY AND works for esthetics are most clearly seen from two examples. In DIVERSITY IN MU-SICAL TASTE. an elementary treatise on music [50] Diderot illustrates his theory that taste consists in the perception and complication of relations.

National taste in music varies widely, for example, as between Italy and France. In spite of this diversity, there is an examinable uniformity in the phenomenon of musical appreciation. The simplest relations in music are the most universally appreciated, and of all relations the simplest is equality, which gives the octave. But the fifth and third follow closely in pleasantness. The vibrations of high notes are more rapid than those of low, and relations among them are easier to grasp. Musicians have been secretly guided by this truth and have therefore allowed quick succession among high notes and have sustained the lower.

Pythagoras founded this universal science upon which music depends by analyzing out of nature herself the mathematical abstract uniformities at the base of our primary preference for simple chords. But Pythagoras studied only 'real' musical beauty, and neglected that 'relative beauty' which has to do with the way the ear receives the impulsions from the sounding lyre. To study the reactions of the human organism to music Diderot assumes an ideal listener, well instructed and with sound organs of perception. For musical beauty is conditioned on the side of the observer by the state of the sense-organ, of the retained image and its transmission to the mind, of the mind itself at the moment when it receives this image, and of the judgment. The ideal listener will have a maximum capacity to seize and combine in a short period of time complicated relationships of pitch, intensity, and timbre, that result from the extent, number and form of the ether-vibra-

[50] *Ibid.*, Vol. IX, pp. 83–131.

tions coming to him. A peasant, even with a naturally good ear, cannot take in and place mentally in order the ensemble of a flute duo, the separate parts of which, being simple enough for his apprehension, may have enchanted him. Experience and training are necessary to judge the relations of sounds to each other, because the shape of a tone varies as it is held, and thus creates perplexity as to its relation to the surrounding tones.

SCULPTURE IDEAL
IN FORM, INDIVID-
UAL IN CONTENT.

In this way Diderot suggests what he means by musical beauty as constituted by 'relationships.' In the "Essay on Dramatic Poesy," the theme turns on sculpture. Diderot imagines a student eager to get exact definitions of truth, goodness, and beauty. He, like the student of musical beauty, is struck at the outset by the bewildering variety of opinion and feeling. How can he discover any central standard when men differ in physical make-up, in mind and imagination, in habit, education, environment, and when even within themselves there is perpetual growth and decay? He is told to follow the example of painters and sculptors, who have not made a chimerical ideal man—the white-washed reflex of general thought —but who have modified their ideal according to circumstances, and have made a man appropriate to his state and condition. "Study bows down the man of letters. Exercise strengthens the carriage and raises the head of the soldier. The bent man disposes his members otherwise than the erect man. Such are the observations which, multiplied to infinity, train the sculptor, and teach him to alter, strengthen, weaken, disfigure, from the state of nature to such another state as pleases him.

EMOTIONAL COM-
PONENT OF TASTE
DIVIDES IT FROM
KNOWLEDGE.

"It is the study of passions, customs, characters, usages which will teach the painter of men to alter his model and to reduce it from the condition of man to that of a good or bad, tranquil or angry man.

"It is thus that from a single simulacrum [pattern] there will emanate an infinite variety of different representations." [51]

From these two illustrations it becomes fairly clear what Diderot means by beauty as relation and by taste as the perception of relations. But one still wishes to isolate the element which makes

---

[51] *Œuvres Complètes de Diderot*, Vol. VII, pp. 393, 394.

esthetic relativity different from scientific relativity. Diderot furnishes the required mark when he says, "The beautiful is nothing but the true, brought into relief by circumstances which are possible, but also rare and marvellous." [52] For beauty, however close to the intimate order and connection of actual events, must touch and move. "To keep to the middle path—that is the way of happiness; to throw oneself into extremes—that, the rule of the poet. One ought not to make poetry out of one's life. Heroes, romantic lovers, great patriots, inflexible magistrates, apostles of religion, philosophers though the heavens fall—all these rare and divine fools make poetry in their lives at the cost of their happiness. They furnish after death the material for great pictures." [53] Constantly Diderot's critical approbation is given to the writers and painters who touch and move. Richardson "raises the spirit and touches the soul." [54] Deshaye, "the first painter of the nation . . . attaches and touches you by his scene: it is grand, pathetic, and violent." [55] The pathetic canvases of Greuze have the power to fashion morality through paint.[56] Neither nature nor the art that imitates it, says Diderot, has anything to say to a cold heart. Rules of composition are well enough; but an inspiration, an effective idea is the prime requisite. The first question is: "Do you know how to invent those terrible and voluptuous songs which even as they astonish or charm my ear carry love or terror to the bottom of my heart, dissolve my sense or convulse my entrails?" [57]

Diderot exhorted the young art-students of Paris to leave the tiresome hide-bound professors of the Academy and the insipid models there, and to go to school to the market-place, the garden, and the public-house. If they would learn the true outward expression of piety or contrition, let them linger at Chartres; if the form and motions of anger, let them observe a street-quarrel. If they would acquire a vital sense of the law of variety and contrast—something quite different from a rule about them—let the student

ARTIST LEARNS FROM NATURE RATHER THAN RULE.

---

[52] *Ibid.*, Vol. XII, p. 125.
[53] *Ibid.*, Vol. XI, p. 124.
[54] *Ibid.*, Vol. V, p. 212.
[55] *Ibid.*, Vol. X, p. 122.
[56] *Ibid.*, Vol. X, p. 207.
[57] *Ibid.*, Vol. XI, p. 312.

note the living individuality of the monks in the long rows of stalls in the cathedrals, who, despite identical garb, identical function, identical architectural frame, never look quite alike.[58] His opposition to rules was positive and thorough. In his theory of drama this independence of the traditional rules, and this appeal directly to nature, meant the defense of the newly appearing drama of manners, the serious comedy. He believed that drama should exhibit not types of characters, nor the well known fables, but men in their peculiar conditions and situations; not heroes and sublime reversals of fortune, but private virtues and domestic life.

Diderot appealed to the slogan 'imitation of nature' as Batteux had done. He even said, "Nature never does anything wrong." [59] There are doubtless acceptable proportions for works of art, but the thing to be emphasized is that such proportions cannot hold a minute against the despotism of nature, and that particular circumstances necessitate the sacrifice of these proportions in a hundred different ways. "I have never heard a figure called badly drawn when it showed clearly in its external organization age, habit, or facility for fulfilling the daily functions. These are those functions which determine both the entire grandeur of the figure, and the true proportion of each member and their ensemble: It is from this source (the revelation of age, habit, and function) that I see issue the child, the adult, the old man, the savage, the policeman, the magistrate, the soldier and the porter." [60]

And it was from the minute observation of the moment of the day, the season, climate, situation, state of the weather, position of the light, that the painter is to learn how to give the effective tone of light to his work—directions that might have been deduced from conversations with Constable. Thus the nature of beauty and the taste of the observer were both according to Diderot to be built up out of infinite sensitive explorations into Nature's own courses, exactly as his own critical method he professed to derive from such painstaking detailed listening to facts. "I have allowed time for the impression to arrive and enter. I have opened my soul to effects.

---

[58] *Œuvres Complètes de Diderot*, Vol. X, pp. 465, 466.
[59] *Ibid.*, Vol. X, p. 461.
[60] *Ibid.*, Vol. X, p. 463.

I have let myself be penetrated by them. I have collected the word of the old man and the thought of the child, the judgment of the man of letters, the word of the man of the world, and the statements of the people; and if I happen to have wounded an artist, it is often with weapons that he himself has sharpened. I have questioned him, and I have learned what is meant by the finesse of design and truth to nature." [61]

If in Diderot the cryptic synonym of beauty—'relation'—has to be interpreted by help from his declarations in favor of imitation of nature in music, drama, and painting, in Jean-Jacques Rousseau (1712–78) the same urge toward natural feeling in art was present, clear and intense, and not veiled in any cryptic abstract definition. Rousseau built up no system of beauty. His only interest for esthetics is in the extreme emphasis he gave to the new meaning of 'nature' as the model for art. Without ceasing he fought what he thought the artificiality and corruption of French taste, whether in dress, or the stage, or music. But his ideas were first the cry of a reformer, and second a theory. They can be best illustrated by his dispute with Rameau over French versus Italian music. Rousseau, always the partizan of the 'heart,' praised Italian music as the direct expression of the simple passions of a people who as a race let their feelings show in the tones of their voices, and who then transposed the natural music of their voices into their lyrical opera.[62] And he denied the possibility of a genuine French music [63] —and thought even a satisfactory poetry difficult to obtain in French—because the spoken French language which according to him was the necessary basis of their melodies was too monotonous and intellectual. Musical harmony, he taught, is independent of the accent and rhythm of a national speech; but the effect of harmony is only physical and a slow chorale merely sensuous: it acts on the sensorium like an abstract color scheme, and does not touch the emotions. The air is what finally matters. It is analogous to the action or story of a play, and gives unity and meaning to the whole. To be sure, he taught that harmony enters into the

FOR ROUSSEAU NATURE IS FEELING, NOT KNOWING.

---

[61] *Ibid.*, Vol. X, p. 233.
[62] *Œuvres*, Paris, 1839, Vol. VI, p. 150. "Lettre sur la Musique Française."
[63] *Ibid.*, Vol. VI, p. 153.

subject and is the basis of the scale on which the melody is formed; but these were illogical concessions. He also recanted his whole attack on French music twenty years after he wrote his *Letter on French Music* (1753).

SUPPLEMENTARY READING

H. P. Adams, *The Life and Writings of Giambattista Vico*, London, 1935.
Irving Babbitt, *Rousseau and Romanticism*, Boston and New York, 1919. (Valuable for bibliography.)
Croce, *Aesthetic*, Part II, Ch. V.
Francesco De Sanctis, *History of Italian Literature*, New York, 1931.
Havelock Ellis, *The New Spirit*, Modern Library, "Diderot."
Robert Flint, *Vico*, Edinburgh, 1884.
John Morley, *Diderot and the Encyclopaedists*, London, 1886.
J. G. Robertson, *The Genesis of Romantic Theory*, Cambridge, 1923, Chs. II, III, VIII.
Saintsbury, *History of Criticism*, Bk. VI, Chs. II, III.
Venturi, *History of Art Criticism*, Ch. VI.

CHAPTER X

German Rationalism and the New Art Criticism

THE HONOR allotted to Alexander Gottlieb Baumgarten (1714–1762), the founder of German esthetics, has traditionally been grudging. He named the science of esthetics, and givers of names, from Adam down, have been celebrated as a species of sage. But names are not things. Herder, it is true, extolled Baumgarten's definition of a poem as the best that had ever been framed.[1] But most writers have rated Baumgarten's contribution as nominal rather than substantial. They have been of the opinion that a strain of reflection wasted away and came to its end in his dry rationalistic discourses rather than that he brought the thing itself, esthetics, to the birth. And Herder, one may remark, may easily have projected some of the brilliant color of his own imagination upon the five Latin words that he admired: *Oratio sensitiva perfecta est poema.* (A poem is a perfect sensuous utterance.) [2] Recent studies have, however, put Baumgarten's labors in a fresh light.[3] Not a ceremony of christening, not even an inspired definition, is now seen as his contribution to esthetics, but the recognition of the intellectual problem involved in a distinct sphere of esthetics. His philosophical grandfather, Leibniz, the great German rationalist, had by far the

BAUMGARTEN NAMED ESTHETICS, SET ITS CHIEF PSYCHOLOGICAL PROBLEM.

---

[1] *Herders Sämtliche Werke*, ed. Bernard Suphan, 33 Vols., Berlin, 1877–1889. Vol. IV, p. 132.

[2] *Meditationes Philosophicae de Nonnullis ad Poema Pertinentibus*, §9.

[3] Alfred Baeumler, *Kants Kritik der Urteilskraft*, Vol. I, Halle, 1923.

Hans Georg Peters, *Die Ästhetik Alexander Gottlieb Baumgartens und ihre Beziehungen zum Ethischen*, Berlin, 1934.

Albert Riemann, *Die Ästhetik Alexander Gottlieb Baumgartens*, Halle, 1928.

more powerful and comprehensive mind, and Leibniz defined concepts, such as *individuality* and *petites perceptions* (half-conscious
adumbrations), which were indispensable for the work that Baumgarten was to do. But Leibniz could not or did not, by virtue of
the important esthetic concepts, isolate an esthetic region. Baumgarten's philosophical father, the schoolmaster Wolff, gave his successor little more than the pedant's method and care. What Baumgarten did was to claim the rights of an independent science for
the theory of the imagination, for that class of things represented
by the title of his early thesis, *Some Matters Pertaining to Poems*
(1735) and, in the second place, to suggest that his recognition of
the science of esthetics was an event of prime importance for the
human spirit.

The event in Baumgarten's work that was important for the
human spirit was the claim of dignity for what had been thought
common. In his response to the fourth objection to his new science,
he used words exactly modelled on those famous ones used by
Terence in defense of the new comedy of manners: "I think nothing human alien to me." "It can be objected to our science," Baumgarten writes, "that it is beneath the dignity of philosophers, and
that deliverances of the senses, fancies, fables, and stirrings of the
passions are below the philosophical horizon. I answer: A philosopher is a man among men. Indeed he does not think alien to himself so great a portion of human knowledge." [4] In this fine assertion
of the free and broad humanity of the true philosopher Baumgarten
furnished the text not only for the philosophy but for the art
criticism and culture that was to develop in the next fifty years in
Germany. There had to be at that historical moment an element
of apology and extenuation in Baumgarten's tone because of the
novelty of his position. "The opposition claims," he wrote in
response to the fifth objection to the theses of his *Aesthetica*, "that
the confusion of esthetic experience is the mother of error; but I
answer that one cannot suddenly leap from darkness to the light
of noon. In the same way one must pass from the darkness of
un-knowingness to distinct thought through the kind offices of

---

[4] *Aesthetica*, Frankfurt a. O., Vol. I, 1750, §6.

the confused but vivid imagery of the poets." [5] Baumgarten was
no Romantic or prophet, assigning to the poet insight into the
eternal. He was a devotee of the slow processes of reason. What
reason showed him was that there is a specific and honorable kind
of order and perfection, as also a separate field, in poetry and the
like; that this order and perfection may be less glorious than the
virtues of reason, but that they are *sui generis*, that they require
interpretation by an independent discipline, that they can be methodically connected into a logical whole which is entitled to a
freehold in the general community of philosophy. Philosophers in
other countries in the early eighteenth century, Vico and Burke,
Dubos and Hutcheson, were noticing and affirming the imagination
and the sense of beauty. But it was left to the German to do the
German thing. Baumgarten organized the undeveloped acknowl-
edgments into a carefully elaborated system that could sustain
intellectually the *aperçus* of the less thorough philosophers and the
critics, and could point the way through the century toward Kant's
Critique of Judgment, which was to crown its end. Not only did
his system underlie later intellectual construction concerning
beauty. It can be and has been said that German esthetics prepared
the way for the great age of German poetry and drama: the flowering of a national German literature.

Baumgarten had a definite sense of the twofold nature of his
task. He saw that (*a*) the arts have a material which is unique and
precisely not intellectual; and (*b*) the arts have values, or, as he
said, a 'perfection' which is not reducible to any other kind of
perfection, and which is not intellectual though parallel to reasonable perfection. He had first to mark off his territory. The mind
has an upper and lower level. The 'upper apprehension' is the
faculty of distinct and adequate thinking. It is what produces
science and philosophy. The logically precise ideas appropriate
to science do not suit poetry. The stuff of poetry evidently must
be drawn from below. Baumgarten illustrates the necessity of the
separation of spheres by an experiment in wrongly oriented
poetry.[6] A philosophically educated man, and one not utterly lost

ESTHETICS MUST
NOT CONFUSE
TASTE WITH OTHER
JUDGMENTS.

---

[5] *Ibid.*, §7.
[6] *Philosophical Meditations*, §14. Quoted by Riemann, *op. cit.*, p. 19.

to the meaning of poetry, will not be able to let this pass as poetry, whatever attention may have been given to verse form:

> Refute do they, who demonstrate that others err;
> No one refutes, unless a proof has shown
> The error of another. Whose task it is to prove
> Must needs be logic-skilled; and so whoe'er refutes,
> Unversed in logic, plain it is, refutes amiss.

Here the garb of metre quarrels absurdly with the content; there is a jumble of genres. The wares of poetry are not mathematical or quasi-mathematical proofs, definitions, quiddities, entities, or tables.

THE "LOWER" MIND IS IMAGINATIVE.

Baumgarten declares that the fine arts belong to the lower apprehension, the region of often vivid, but always confused, that is, unanalyzed, imagery. He lists point by point the materials of poetry that are available in the reservoir of the lower half of the mind. Individual things, because they are wholly unique and determinate, and also those classes of things which are nearest the single example, are right stuff. On the other hand science and logic, organs of the upper mind, deal in universals. Lists of particular items, such as the catalogue of ships in Homer's *Iliad*, Book II, carry out the very principle of poetry, and those paltry little poets who turn up their nose at this type of thing are wide of the mark.[7] From Horace and Tibullus and Persius Baumgarten fetches illustrations to show what proper poetry is made of. Horace substituted "Olympian dust" for "sports-field," "palm" for "reward of victory," the concrete for the abstract.[8] Examples are more poetical than general truths. Campanella, for instance, called a fever the battle between the human spirit and disease.

REASONABLE CLARITY AND SHARPNESS IS NECESSARY.

Within the soul, the changes that go on and are felt as particular sensations, or as the emotions of pleasure and pain, serve the poet's ends. An image bathed in passion is more poetical than a simple image. As one descends into the depths of the soul one finds presages and dreams, dim forebodings of the future, and the phantasms of sleep. These vague dark modes of feeling threaten to disappear

---

[7] *Philosophical Meditations*, §19. Trans. Riemann, op. cit., p. 111.
[8] *Ibid.*, §20. Trans. Riemann, *loc. cit.*

into Cimmerian darkness. Baumgarten warns against the uncommunicability of dark mutterings and movings. "Dark images do not contain as many images of characters as are needed for recognizing the thing again and distinguishing it from others. . . . There are therefore more parts that can be communicated in sensitive speech when there is clarity, than when there is darkness. Therefore a poem is more perfect whose images are clear than whose images are dark." [9]

Fictions are also poetical material. An artist may resolve his representations of the given world into elements, recombine them into fresh forms, and use them to good advantage in poetry, provided only he steer clear of combining elements that contradict each other. This rule gives range to the poet's fancy with but little barrier to his freedom. Still Baumgarten teaches that the artist is wisest who imitates nature, not indulging rashly in complexes built up on the fashion of a different world, 'heterocosmically.' The familiar slogan of the times, Art is the imitation of nature, here fits neatly into the logic of Baumgarten's argument. In the existent world there is the greatest possible variety of forms that can coexist without contradiction. Like Leibniz, but for another reason, Baumgarten declared this the best of all possible worlds. Let the artist imitate nature, the nature of this real world, for by so doing he also emulates the ideal.

NATURE THE RICH-EST MODEL; CON-TAINS THE IDEAL.

But why the ideal? Why should an artist seek as model that which contains the maximum variety that avoids contradiction? With this query we press in toward Baumgarten's conception of the perfection or intrinsic value of poetry. Though a poet must avoid the kind of clarity which comes from intellectual discrimination and definition, he must on the other hand diligently seek what Baumgarten calls "extensive clarity." Extensive clarity is quantitative richness of imagery. "A sensuous discourse is perfect in proportion as its component parts arouse many sensuous ideas." [10] So long as the rushing fullness of detail does not baffle the mind's power to seize, the more individual elements are compressed in a given moment, the better. The "shining and glory," *"nitor et*

"EXTENSIVE CLAR-ITY."

---

[9] *Ibid.*, §13. Trans. Riemann, *op. cit.*, p. 108.
[10] *Ibid.*, §8. Trans. Riemann, *op. cit.*, p. 106.

splendor," of a poem depend on this extensive clarity. The crowding and rushing must not make a mere vibrant mist; vividness and richness require a maximum of marks and notes.

ART'S PECULIAR
UNITY AND ORDER.
Besides richness Baumgarten indicates various types of order as contributing to the perfection of poetry. For the highly individual content of poetry must be made ready for absorption by the lower apprehension. And now we come to the crux of the interpretation of Baumgarten: deciding on the basis of his handling of order whether he has anything vitally new to say or not. His types of order are analogous to those discovered by reason, but are not themselves intellectual connections. Baumgarten is thus trying to keep his kingdom of rushing, clear confusions still separate from the kingdom of logical inferences and mathematically distinct definitions. He says that a poet comprehends morality in a way distinct from the philosopher, and a shepherd looks at an eclipse with eyes unlike those of the astronomer.[11] What then are the equivalents in esthetic knowledge for the types of order reason discovers? Perfection, abstractly defined, is unity in variety. Now if Baumgarten meant that beauty is nothing more, after all, than a vague way of grasping this unity in variety which is better apprehended by the clear understanding, then he does not really mark off his field nor clinch his independent esthetic perfection. There are several types of poetical order, he says: that which is parallel to the deduction of conclusions from a premise; that which binds similar to similar; and that which history furnishes. As poetical arrangements of matter, these are unclear imitations of the order reason establishes. If a chain of reasoning is felt rather than understood, then, there is the value of art: if the relation of like to like is seized by a happy inspiration and crystallized in a metaphor, rather than supported by analysis, then wit is at work; if historical connections such as memory furnishes are grasped as wholes and not examined carefully link by link, then the poetical rather than the historical imagination is concerned.

What then has Baumgarten succeeded in doing? Are these structural frames specifically esthetic, or are they the left-overs

---

[11] *Aesthetica,* §§425, 429. Cited by Croce, *Aesthetic,* p. 216.

cast off by reason, which has better work to do? The answer seems to be that Baumgarten is trying to keep the type of order of which he is speaking as art's peculiar domain. The unity required is not a false intellectual unity, but a function of the togetherness of emotional and pictured units. The confused parts consent together and form a unity when the "ratio that determines perfection" dominates; and the required ratio is not a point-for-point correspondence with things as in intellectual truth, but a ratio that yields the right amount of "richness, magnitude, life, clarity, certainty, and poetical truth." [12] Baumgarten's meaning develops toward his later period in the recognition of the esthetic linkages and attributes of the confused thoughts themselves. Beauty is "phenomenal perfection," he taught. He assumes indeed a kind of correspondence between the poetical thoughts and the things to which they refer: a relationship of probability. Poetry must not fly off into insubstantial Utopian dreams. But the chief rule of lucid method in composing poems is so to make images and passionate elements succeed each other that the richness, the extensive clarity, will constantly increase. [13] The theme—the consenting together of words and phrasing and ideas—ideally admits an effect of a maximum number of impressions.

The Swiss esthetician J. G. Sulzer (1720–1779) in his compendious and influential *Allgemeine Theorie der Schönen Künste* (1771–1774) described, as did Baumgarten, the esthetic idea as less distinct than the cognitive. Yet with him, this difference is based not upon the nature of the object contemplated but upon the act of contemplation. The same object may be perceived either as a distinct idea or as a 'sensation' (Empfindung) according to the effect it has upon our sensibility. The sight of a jewel, *e.g.*, affects the dealer and the amateur differently. The first will concentrate on the distinct details which constitute its commercial value. The second, content with a total impression of the object, will dwell on the delight aroused in him by symmetry of form and soft lustre. The idea of the latter is less rich in distinctive marks but richer in "partial ideas" dimly conveyed by the whole object. Enjoying

SULZER ON ESTHETIC ATTITUDE AND EMOTION.

---

[12] *Ibid.*, §22. "Copiousness is the nobility and sure light of moving truth."
[13] *Philosophical Meditations*, §13. Trans. Riemann, p. 108.

this sensuous richness he cannot but enjoy simultaneously his own sensations and feelings attaching to them. His soul is thus stirred to its very depths. In the act of cognition, our attention is entirely absorbed by the object; in esthetic experience we are aware of the object as well as of the state of our mind and the play of our psychic energies. Thus the perception of beauty connects perception and ideation with emotion and volition.

Sulzer set forth clearly the emotional factors in art. He saw that the arts, in representing visible and tangible objects, reflect also states of mind. Music, for example, gives expression to passions.[14] Furthermore, esthetic life appeared to him as a means of safeguarding the unity of human nature. "The uncultivated man is merely coarse sensuousness craving animal life; the man whom the Stoics wished to form but were never able to form, would be mere reason, solely a knower, never an agent. But the character which the fine arts have molded, strikes a mean between the two; his sensuousness consists in a refined sensibility that makes man fit for moral life." [15] This passage clearly anticipates Schiller's doctrine of 'esthetic education.'

MENDELSSOHN: ART AS INTEGRATOR OF THE SOUL.

Moses Mendelssohn's (1729–1786) views on esthetics moved in the same direction. Taking a less rationalistic view of the psychic facts than former psychologists, he pointed to a "triple source of pleasure": (*a*) uniformity in variety (or beauty), (*b*) agreement in variety (or rational perfection), and (*c*) improved condition of the bodily state (or sensuousness). The apprehension of the first perfection was attributed by him to a special "faculty of approbation." [16] Like Sulzer Mendelssohn foreshadows Schiller's ideas. According to him art, in exercising the intermediate faculty of the soul, helps to convert moral principles into natural inclination, establishing a harmonious coöperation of the energies of the soul.[17]

---

[14] R. Sommer, *Grundzüge einer Geschichte der deutschen Psychologie und Ästhetik*, 1892, p. 201f.

[15] Sulzer, *Allgemeine Theorie der schönen Künste*, II, 252. Art, furthering a moral end, assumes also a rôle in social and political life. This aspect is emphasized by another writer of the Baumgarten school, Karl Heinrich Heydenreich, *System der Ästhetik*, Vol. I, 1790.

[16] *Briefe über die Empfindungen*, 1755, Letter 4.

[17] R. Sommer, *op. cit.*, p. 120.

The psychological triad, implied in Sulzer's theory and proposed by Mendelssohn, was carefully elaborated and definitely introduced into psychology by J. N. Tetens (1736–1807). He distinguished three faculties: reason, feeling, and will—a division that Kant adopted and the influence of which is still to be felt in the Post-Kantian systems. However dubious in itself, it stood when first proposed for the acknowledgment of beauty as an irreducible phenomenon.

The Dutch philosopher Franz Hemsterhuis (1720–1790) cannot be reckoned among Baumgarten's followers, though his theory points in the same direction. For him also beauty is a mediator. But the extremes are mediated in a very different way. In his theory of knowledge, he is an adherent of Grotius and the English empiricists. All our knowledge, he believes, springs from sense-perception. But he endows man with an 'internal sense' which directs our striving towards the total and indivisible One. Man is placed between the sensuous flux and the immutable Platonic entity, and through the enjoyment of beauty he becomes aware of both the privilege and the limitation of this peculiar position. Beauty appeals to our senses and therefore cannot convey the spiritual light that flows from the super-sensuous source of existence. But it succeeds in translating the message from above into the broken language of the senses. By quantitative wealth it makes up for the eternal lack in substance. It substitutes an accumulation of impressions for the intuition we are forever denied. Thus Hemsterhuis arrives at his famous definition. Beauty, it reads, is "that element in an object which affords the largest number of ideas in the shortest time." [18]

HEMSTERHUIS: "INTERNAL SENSE."

A vast literature sprang up in the wake of Baumgarten's esthetic. J. Elias Schlegel,[19] Johann August Eberhard,[20] and Johann Joachim Eschenburg [21] may be mentioned as belonging to the most popular

---

[18] *Œuvres*, ed. Meyboom, 1846–50, 3 Vols. Vol. I, pp. 14–18, 24, 66 ("Lettre sur la sculpture"; "Lettre sur les désirs"). Cf. Max Schasler, *Kritische Geschichte der Ästhetik*, 1872, I, 329ff.

[19] *Von der Nachahmung*, 1742.

[20] *Theorie der schönen Künste und Wissenschaften*, 1783.

[21] *Entwurf einer Theorie und Literatur der schönen Wissenschaften*, 1783.

writers of this group. But side by side with this fundamental
philosophical movement another movement was going on in Germany, better known to the student of the general history of culture.
This was a new orientation of taste and a new canon of criticism.
The naïve grandeur of Greek art and poetry, the works of Milton
and Shakespeare, were being felt as embodied refutations of the
severe rules of Boileau and Racine. Art was attaining a dignity of
its own, not borrowed from philosophy. The controversy between
J. Ch. Gottsched (1700–1776), strict adherent of the classical
rules, and the Swiss critics J. C. Bodmer (1698–1783) and J. C.
Breitinger (1701–1776) centered around the idea of poetic invention. The Swiss defended the rights of the imagination. The poet,
they contended, is entitled to transform bare reality by an act,
called by Breitinger *abstractio imaginationis*. This act as distinguished from the *abstractio rationis* discerns the "possible worlds"
hidden in the actual world of our experience. Here the influence
of Leibniz on criticism appears, as it has already appeared in the
thought of Baumgarten. Crude reality becomes elevated to the
supernatural and the miraculous.[22] The immediate purpose of this
doctrine was doubtless to justify Milton as the great poet of
Protestantism. But the full breadth of the new movement first
shows in the writings of the two great critics, Winckelmann and
Lessing.

NEW INTEREST IN   Although Lessing's most famous work, the *Laocoön* (1766),
GREECE.   had as its immediate occasion the desire to refute a statement of
Winckelmann's in which he depreciated the method of Vergil in
comparison with that of the sculptor of the Laocoön group, the
spirits of the two great German art critics of the eighteenth century
had more likenesses than differences. They both eagerly desired
to reform the national taste by carrying attention straight back to
the Greek well-head. Though it was to immediate contact with
the classical originals—the careful study of Aristotle or the minute
observation of the remains of classical sculpture in Rome—that they
looked for national esthetic salvation, what they expected from
this contact was such a freshening of feeling and purifying of taste

---

[22] Cf. Bodmer, *Abhandlung vom Wunderbaren*, 1740.

as Diderot and Rousseau were appealing for in France with their slogan: 'Back to nature.' They not only condemned as false the second or third-hand treatment, through scholiasts or engravings, of classical style, but they felt disgust in general with the old-fashioned 'wig and pigtail' manner, the violence and exaggeration on the one hand of the baroque buildings, and the sophistication, unnaturalness, and small prettiness of French courtly taste in painting and landscaping. How back to the classical originals meant back to nature for Winckelmann can be illustrated by the similarity between his reaction to Pigalle and that of Rousseau. Winckelmann is dumbfounded that a sculptor who had studied in Rome could descend to such impure sensuality: "A Venus at Potsdam by Pigalle is represented in a sentiment which forces the liquor to flow out at both sides of her mouth, seemingly gasping for breath; for she was intended to pant with lust; yet, by all that's desperate! was this very Pigalle several years entertained at Rome to study the antique." [23] Rousseau is if anything more outraged by the prostitution of Pigalle's powers: "And you, rival of Praxiteles and Phidias, you whose chisel the ancients might have employed to make gods that would have condoned to us their idolatry; inimitable Pigalle, your hand must be persuaded either to sell apish grotesques or else remain idle." [24]

That Greek ideal of beauty resting on the attributes of majesty and repose which Winckelmann opposed to the current love of exaggeration and involution, he drew from long close observation of the sculptural remains at Rome. He reached Rome, having longed for a sight of it as a devout pilgrim does for his holy city, the same year that archaeological researches were begun at Pompeii (1755), and he himself wrote scholarly reports of the Herculaneum discoveries. The first systematic *History of Ancient Art* (1764) is from his hand. But in this zeal to touch and see the classical statues themselves instead of trusting to second-hand reports, Winckelmann is rather the culmination of a long-ripening

---

[23] *Reflections on the Painting and Sculpture of the Greeks: with Instructions for the Connoisseur, and an Essay on Grace in Works of Art*, trans. Fuseli, London, 1765, pp. 278, 279.

[24] *Ibid.*, p. 278, footnote.

interest in classical archaeology than a pioneer. Even in the fifteenth century two Italians, Poggio Bracciolini and Ciriaco of Ancona, had commenced to collect objects and copy inscriptions. However, widespread and persistent interest did not arrive until a century before Winckelmann's time. Two Englishmen, Thomas Howard of Arundel and George Villiers, Duke of Buckingham, were rivals in collecting monuments of Greek art from the Turkish dominions (c. 1620–1630). Soon after this it became the fashion for English gentlemen to bring home from Greece and the islands such fragments of architecture and sculpture as they could move, to adorn their country-houses. Then began with the Frenchman Jacques Carrey the careful drawing of sculpture and architecture from the existent monuments where they were. The work of James Stewart, a poor fan painter who became enthusiastic over classical remains, and Nicholas Revett, on the *Antiquities of Athens*, was made possible financially and in every way furthered by the English *Dilettanti Society*, founded in 1734 to promote the study of ancient art. This Society fitted out an expedition to take up the work of Stewart and Revett in the same year that Winckelmann published his *History of Ancient Art*. From the point of view of archaeological study, then, Winckelmann's work represents the flowering and generalizing of a lively interest that had been growing for some years in England, France, and Germany.[25] Organizing into a new unity the materials furnished by philologists, antiquarians, writers of *Lives,* and moralists interested in earlier forms of civilization, Winckelmann laid the foundations of a modern scientific History of Art. Almost a century was to elapse before the study of post-Greek art, in the works of Karl Schnaase and Jakob Burckhardt, reached the level of Winckelmann's work.

WINCKELMANN: THE SERENE PERFECTION OF GREEK BEAUTY.

What then was the new esthetic ideal which Winckelmann extracted and held up for admiration out of the ancient statues? The highest beauty, he says, is embodied in the human figure. The artist analyzes the body of man as a philosopher analyzes the modes of spirit. The beauty of the human figure consists in the harmony of its various parts and the design of its relations through a func-

---

[25] Lionel Cust, *History of the Society of Dilettanti*, London, 1914, Ch. IV; K. Justi, *Winckelmann und seine Zeitgenossen*, 2nd ed., 1898.

tional elliptical line. This elliptical line is both uniform and various; for " 'Tis not in the power of Algebra to determine which line, more or less elliptic, forms the divers parts of the system into beauty—but the ancients knew it; I attest their works, from the gods down to their vases." [26] The ancients knew, then, 'the line of beauty,' and they arranged drapery, cut features, disposed limits in a way that incarnated beautiful form. The total impression, Winckelmann was never weary of saying, is nobly simple and full of quiet dignity. "As water

> That least of foreign principles partakes is best

so Grace is perfect when most simple, when freest from finery, constraint, and affected wit." [27] "The attitude and gestures of antique figures are such as those have, who, conscious of merit, claim attention as their due, when appearing among men of sense." [28] Their blood is clear and pure, their spirits settled. "In the countenances of antique figures joy bursts not into laughter. . . . Through the face of a Bacchanal peeps only the dawn of luxury. In sorrow and anguish they resemble the sea, whose bottom is calm, whilst the surface raves." [29] Again: "The gestures of the hands of antique figures and their attitudes in general are those of people that think themselves alone and unobserved." [30] The drapery of the ancient statues is light and quietly folded, for the "gods . . . are represented as the inhabitants of sacred places, the dwellings of silent awe." It would not be becoming for their garments to be "sport for the winds" or as waving flags. [31] This ideal of reserve and harmonious stillness Winckelmann at all points contrasts with restlessness and the boiling passionateness of the art he saw popular around him. He said that modern taste finds a quiet attitude insipid, and so must force the heads of statues around as if the characters represented had been suddenly dazzled by lightning. The gestures

---

[26] Winckelmann, *op. cit.*, p. 259.
[27] *Ibid.*, p. 273.
[28] *Ibid.*, p. 276.
[29] *Ibid.*, pp. 277, 278.
[30] *Ibid.*, p. 280.
[31] *Ibid.*, pp. 281, 282.

in vogue were those of "a young preacher, piping-hot from the college," [32] and graces were decked out as if in birthday robes. 'Grace' never visited Bernini even in his dreams, said Winckelmann, and Michelangelo, who started the pure style of Raphael on its downward course, was so charmed by "mazy learning," that he abandoned grace and decency.[33] Thus in his lifelong and loving study of statues and paintings in Rome, Winckelmann evolved the ideal of serenity and control that has spelled 'Greek' to us until quite recently.

EVOLUTION OF STYLES AND ENVIRONMENTAL INFLUENCES. Winckelmann treated the course of ancient art as a biological phenomenon which gradually comes to maturity, passes through several phases, and then decays. Though much that Winckelmann records in his history is no longer valid, because his material included no authentic examples of the earlier periods of Greek art, he is yet permanently important because he introduced the concept of the evolution of styles, and also because he communicated his ideal and knowledge and enthusiasm to the greater ones who came after him: Goethe and Schiller, Schelling and Hegel. "The history of art aims at expounding," he said, "its origin, growth, change and fall, together with the diverse styles of peoples, ages, and artists, and at demonstrating this as far as possible from the extant works of antiquity." [34] In tracing this living development, Winckelmann took into account the effects of climate and political and social conditions. It was the fashion already in England to connect the esthetic ideas of sublimity and grandeur with the political ideal of liberty. So when Winckelmann writes that freedom, the mother of great events, planted lofty dispositions in the Greeks, just as the prospect of the immeasurable surface of the sea enlarges our gaze, he might have taken his start from Addison's "A spacious horizon is an image of liberty," or from Shaftesbury's linkage of the rising taste in Britain and her generous devotion to the cause of liberty. The idea of the relation of climate to genius was also in the air. Dubos set the style and French writers carried it on until it reached a climax in Taine.

---

[32] *Winckelmann, op. cit.,* p. 280.

[33] *Ibid.,* pp. 284, 285.

[34] *Geschichte der Kunst des Altertums,* Vienna, 1934, p. 9.

Winckelmann recognized four stages in Greek art after the first formless beginning. First, archaic Greek art up to the time of Phidias was hard and powerful in its drawing, often full of minute precise detail, and devoid of grace.[35] The second period included for Winckelmann Phidias and Scopas and was called by him "the lofty or grand style." This he regarded as the highest manifestation of the Greek plastic genius, but he did not assign to it the epithet "beautiful." He said its characteristics were lofty simplicity and unity.[36] The corresponding period in Italian painting was for him that of Raphael. The third period was represented for him by Praxiteles, and was characterized by the softer qualities of beauty and grace.[37] The parallel Italian painter was Guido Reni. The fourth period was that of the imitators, and it is eclectic and trifling.[38] He who follows, said Winckelmann, must always be behind.

POWER, MAJESTY, BEAUTY, PRETTINESS.

The conception of beauty given by Winckelmann in separate essays and in individual statements in his history conflicts in a measure with the richer and more tolerant ideal that spreads itself out in the course of the history as a whole. His inconsistencies in the use of terms show not only his scorn for system-mongering and the way of the scribe, but the ferment in his own mind working with the precise degrees of excellence and appropriate epithets to apply to different kinds of classical production. These tensions were doubtless an index of the pioneering and living quality of his works. Though he called the third period 'beautiful,' his sympathy was obviously with the second period which he called 'lofty,' but described by verbal contradiction as aiming at 'true beauty.' In the works of this lofty second period, the age of Phidias, there was, he found, a minimum of expression of mental passion. And yet he wavers between the idea that these statues are without expression—without flavor like pure water—and the conception that they express the greatest emotions of all, tranquillity and power, but with great reserve. At times he seems to hold up

THE IDEAL AND THE CHARACTERISTIC.

---

[35] *Geschichte*, p. 215.
[36] *Ibid.*, p. 217.
[37] *Ibid.*, p. 219.
[38] *Ibid.*, pp. 225, 226.

for our admiration an almost uninteresting placidity, a symphony in lines and masses without soul, but at other times he insists that beauty without expression is characterless. Too much expression he felt pushed creation over into deformity. On the other hand, the lack of it took away beauty. It was a potent esthetic drug requiring nice administration.[39] Two ideals then passed and re-passed before Winckelmann's eyes without ever being brought into consistent relation with each other. In so far as an artist seeks beauty, he must subordinate characteristic and individual features, details of the body, and definite expression of feeling. On the other hand, the artistic ideal includes the ideal state of soul—greatness and tranquillity—and a state of soul is naturally imitated and ex-pressed in movements of the face and posture of the body.

LESSING: THE DO-MAINS OF POETRY AND VISUAL ART.
It was with this vexing problem of the rival claims of formal beauty not confused by interference with the claims of any spiritual ideal, and those of the expression of emotion, that Lessing (1729–1781) dealt in the *Laocoön*, his famous essay on the limits of poetry and painting, 'the organon of esthetic cultivation.' He like Winckelmann wanted to settle certain concrete esthetic questions by clearing away all obstructions between his mind and the testi-mony of antiquity. Esthetic opinions were running in grooves—French grooves which confined and distorted ancient thought. Lessing wished to mount to the free-running original streams, and sharply re-examine such catch-phrases as: 'As painting, so poetry,' in those clear waters. The specific occasion of the *Laocoön* was a declaration in an early writing of Winckelmann's that the reason why the Laocoön statue refrains from shrieks while Vergil's Laocoön cries out is the superior noble restraint and simplicity of the Greek genius over the Latin. Lessing admitted that the facts were as Winckelmann reported. This has since been proved, with access to the actual sculpture, not to be the case. But Lessing in-sisted upon a different explanation of the supposed fact. He claimed that the Greeks, as well as the Latins, following the urgings of mother nature herself, allowed vehement expression of emotion for godlike character. He cited in proof of his contention that

---

[39] Bosanquet, *op. cit.*, pp. 247–50.

Homer's wounded heroes frequently fell with cries to the ground; that Venus, when merely scratched, shrieked aloud giving suffering its due; that even "the iron Mars, when he feels the lance of Diomedes, shrieks so horribly that his cries are like those of ten thousand furious warriors." [40]

Since, then, it is not the Greek genius that is opposed to violent expression of emotion, one must find some other ground for the toning down of passion in the Laocoön group. Lessing found that ground in the requirements of plastic beauty.[41] He said that in the Laocoön "the master aimed at the highest beauty compatible with the adopted circumstances of bodily pain," [42] and so he softened the shriek into a sigh. An artist of this type can only represent a single moment of an action, and this single moment lasts forever in its impression upon the spectator.[43] Therefore the extremity and development of emotional situations must not be put into marble. On the other hand a poet, who is not compelled to concentrate his picture into the space of a single moment, may "take up every action of his hero at its source, and pursue it to its issue, through all possible variations" [44] and to any extremity.

Lessing finally passes from the discussion of the distinction between poetry and sculpture in the specific instance to what he believes to be the irrefragable demonstration of their distinction upon ultimate principles. He says, I should like to base my demonstration on its ultimate logical ground. A sign should always be adapted to that of which it is the sign. Painting uses one class of signs; poetry another. Painting uses shapes and colors in space; poetry uses sounds, joined together in time. Pictorial signs are, therefore, adapted exclusively to spatially coexistent elements, in other words, to physical bodies; poetical signs, on the other hand, are adapted to objective situations in which there is movement through time, in other words, to actions.[45]

MEDIUMS MUST NOT TRESPASS.

---

[40] *Lessings Sämtliche Schriften*, 16 Vols., Stuttgart, 1893, Vol. IX, p. 8. "Laocoön." Eng. trans. London, 1914, p. 9.
[41] *Ibid.*, Vol. IX, p. 14; trans. pp. 14, 15.
[42] *Ibid.*, Vol. IX, p. 17; trans. p. 17.
[43] *Ibid.*, Vol. IX, p. 19; trans. p. 19.
[44] *Ibid.*, Vol. IX, p. 22; trans. p. 23.
[45] *Ibid.*, Vol. IX, pp. 94, 95; trans. 91, 92.

Yet pictorial signs may indirectly suggest action; and poetical signs may indirectly represent bodies. For bodies, the proper object of painting, endure and change in time. A painter may choose to depict a body in its capacity as the center of an action, that is, as it appears to sum up its own previous history and foreshadow what is still to come. The law of painting deducible from these truths is that a painter must depict the pregnant moment of an action, as it shines through bodily form. A parallel truth applies to poetry. Bodies are the proper material of poetry in so far as they carry the action progressing through time. Therefore a poet should describe bodies only in so far as they apply to the action, and economically, in the most vivid way possible. A single epithet should serve.[46]

Lessing gives many effective illustrations of the principles thus laid down.[47] He shows convincingly that an elaborate description point by point of an Alpine gentian does not appeal to our sensibilities, and then he shows by appeal to Homer how a great poet may expand and enrich his account of an object not by using inappropriate pictorial epithets, but by dynamic devices. Homer makes Helen's beauty living to us not by enumerating the charms of her eyes and forehead and hair, but by reminding us of the overwhelming effect of the ensemble of her beauties upon the Trojan elders. And there is another possibility for a poet beside suggestion of effect. A great poet may emulate Homer in presenting such an object as a ship or a shield through the story of its making. It is much more effective to carry back Agamemnon's scepter to the workshop of the gods and watch it grow than merely to list the sum of its beauties when finished. Homer converts a tedious painting of a body into a vivid picture of an action, says Lessing. Having separated the art of words thus sharply from the formative and plastic arts, Lessing slightly softens the distinction. Painting and poetry, he says, are not so much perfectly exclusive of each other as friendly neighbors. Raphael's drapery, though an example from spatial art, reveals the influence of the person's last act, the efficient cause in the movements of the limb of the

---

[46] *Loc. cit.*

[47] *Op. cit.*, Vol. IX, pp. 95–108; trans. 92–104.

apparent effect in the fall and swell of the garment. Thus the idea of the 'pregnant moment' gives poetry and painting a small area of coincidence.

In his concept of the pregnant moment Lessing had been antici- LESSING DEVEL-
pated by Shaftesbury, who had made a definite problem of it in OPED FRAGMEN-
the case of the representation of the 'Choice of Hercules.' Hercules TARY SOURCES.
being accosted at the cross-roads by Virtue and Vice, each presenting to him the advantages of her own line of life, what moment
in the encounter is the perfect one for the painter to choose?
Shall it be the one when Hercules is first greeted, when he is disputing, when Virtue is gaining in her hold over Hercules, or after
his struggle? Shall it show Hercules surprised, interested, agonized,
or departing? Shaftesbury says that the moment of agonized but
triumphant pondering, veering toward resolution and yet showing
traces of what has preceded, as presaging the life to come full of
toil and hardship, is the cross-section of the total action suitable for
the painter's brush.[48] Lessing was a great admirer of Diderot, and
one finds in Diderot's early letter on deaf mutes (1751) another
almost exact anticipation of one of Lessing's important passages.
Why should a subject appropriate to one art be absurd in another,
he asks. An example is brought from Vergil. The poet represents
Neptune in the act of raising his head above a storm at sea. Could
a painter do the same? No; because a body partially immersed in
water is made ugly by the refraction of the rays of light. The
question is tested by another instance from Ariosto. The enumeration of Alcina's 'points' does not communicate to the reader her
beauty. But let her walk. Let me follow her stride and carriage
as she moves, and I fill in with my imagination all I care to know
of her points. To do more than this in poetry is to confuse the
functions of poetry and painting, says Diderot. A still further
example is the story of the giant Polyphemus grinding the bones
of a companion of Ulysses between his teeth—bearable in poetry,
but unthinkable as a subject for painting.

But it was perhaps less by carrying on fragmentary suggestions
than by combatting a powerful contemporary tendency in poetical

---

[48] Shaftesbury, *Characteristics*, ed. Robertson, 2 Vols., London, 1900, Vol. I,
pp. 34–39.

writing that Lessing was primarily moved to compose his *Laocoön*.
It was the fashion in both England and France in Lessing's century
to explain the classic poets through art-relics: for example, Addison's *Dialogues on the Usefulness of Ancient Medals especially
in relation to the Greek and Latin Poets* (1702), and Spence's
Polymetis (1747). Lessing was inclined to make a distinction
rather than to forward this assimilation. And he not only aimed
to distinguish the arts from each other upon a fundamental philosophical principle, but he was arguing at the same time against the
popular opinion that painting is a greater art than poetry, because
wider in its range. Poetry, he said, can include in its materials not
only such circumstances as are good and beautiful, but also hideous
and horrible, because poetry unfolds its scroll slowly. We can bear
as foils or as passing impressions unpleasant sensations when we
repudiate them in a fixed static work of art. He stretched the
possibilities of poetry still wider than this. He thought even disgusting and loathsome elements could be effectively introduced
by a cautious hand as accents in poetry. He instanced the indication of the blood and sweat on Hector's body as it was dragged
around the walls of Troy.

Lessing's exquisite little essay, "How the Ancients Represented
Death," at once elaborates the theme of the *Laocoön*, being virtually an elaboration of a foot-note to the eleventh chapter of that
book, and also sets in relief Lessing's scholarly precision, his reliance
on truth to ancient fact, as the ground of his theories. In his *Pictures Drawn from the Iliad and Odyssey of Homer and the Aeneid
of Vergil* (Paris, 1757), Count Caylus had raised the problem of
how 'sleep' should be represented in illustrating the Homeric passage in which the dead body of Sarpedon is carried by 'sleep' and
'death.' Caylus thought a contradiction existed between the appropriate emblem of a poppy-wreath for sleep and the repulsive
form of a dead body. Lessing replied, proving it by examples, that
the ancient way of representing death was not by a skeleton or
repulsive form, but by a youthful genius, sometimes winged, carrying a reversed torch—the twin-brother of sleep. "To none does this
shape seem sorrowful." [49]

---

[49] Lessing, *op. cit.*, Vol. XI (1895), p. 1. Quoted from Bellori.

Lessing's important work on dramatic theory, the *Hamburg*
Dramaturgy, interests us because of its treatment of two problems:
(1) on what basis can a modern national drama be developed?
(2) how much authority has Aristotle's *Poetics* for the direction
of such a movement, and what exactly did Aristotle mean by his
various generalizations on the causes and effects and nature of
good drama? A second motive besides his admiration of the Greeks
controlled Lessing's theory of the drama: his Gallophobia. "His
heart was set on proving Shakespeare and not Racine to be correct
according to Sophocles and Aristotle." [50] It was indeed one of the
paradoxes of his complex esthetic doctrine that he wished to make
the great English drama which he admired and which was irregular and in one sense of the word romantic coincide with the classical dicta of Aristotle; whereas he lost no opportunity to accuse
Corneille, who definitely and consciously founded his ideas and his
plays upon Aristotle, of misunderstanding the true spirit of the
Greek authority.

Corneille had insisted on the exact observance of the so-called
three Aristotelian unities: place, time, and cause. Lessing said
that there was in Aristotle and therefore in any good play only one
important unity—that of action, and that the suggestions about
limitations of place and time were incidental to the peculiar conditions of Greek staging and composition. Corneille said that the
Aristotelian hero should be either a very good or a very bad man.
Lessing said that it was heathenish as well as unaristotelian for a
good character in a play to be made to suffer through no fault of
his own. Corneille had interpreted the 'probability and necessity'
in action, upon which Aristotle insisted, as meaning such a connection of events as can be accepted by us as probable because of our
familiarity with history and tradition. For example, Clytemnestra's
murder of Agamemnon is not probable, but we accept it as such,
because of the habit created in our minds by the well-known story.
Lessing, on the other hand, interprets the Aristotelian probability as
meaning the exhibition of a strict causal nexus. There must be no
accidental deaths; no deaths, he says humorously, "from the fifth
act," but only such as are obviously the results of previous cir-

---

[50] Bosanquet, *op. cit.*, p. 231.

cumstances.[51] The rise of passion must swell and grow clearly and plausibly before our eyes, not be simply described. The character imputed to persons must be vindicated by what we see them do, and not by what we are told they are.[52] Aristotelian probability, Lessing thought, involved the impossibility of a true Christian tragedy. "The unchangeable meekness of a true Christian is quite untheatrical." [53] Corneille was explicit in requiring a moral range for drama. He said that unless there is a good moral, the majority of people are not pleased, and therefore Horace's teaching that a poem must profit is a just emendation on Aristotle. Lessing believed in the uplifting effect of drama, but he thought the emphasis given to a moral by Corneille and by Gottsched ridiculous. One of the most interesting divergences of interpretation between Lessing and Corneille is in regard to the famous catharsis doctrine. Corneille said that according to Aristotle a tragedy should cause in the spectator either the emotion of pity or the emotion of fear, and that to be purified meant to be deterred from performing an act similar to the one witnessed. Lessing believed that the emotions Aristotle had in mind were not pity or terror, but a union of pity and fear, by which he implied that the true Aristotelian fear was an awed sense of some dreadful thing that might happen to us and which, because of its felt imminence in our own case, arouses compassion as it befalls others. He widened the meaning of fear to something approaching 'cosmic shudder,' that is, to a lively sense of that awe-inspiring constitution of things which suspends the sword of destiny over us all.[54]

We have seen how Winckelmann and Lessing brought about a thoroughgoing critical revolution. This esthetic revolution however was conservative: the classicist canon was overthrown in favor of a classicism refreshed by contact with the Greek originals. This voluntary submission to the ancient authorities was a joyous act of self-liberation. Yet it was only natural that the

---

[51] Lessing, *op. cit.*, Vol. IX, p. 190.

[52] *Ibid.*, Vol. IX, p. 219.

[53] *Ibid.*, Vol. IX, p. 189. Eng. trans. in *European Theories of the Drama*, ed. Clark, New York, 1930, p. 258.

[54] *Ibid.*, Vol. X, p. 123.

inner drive of the esthetic revolution should not allow it to halt at the revitalized classicism of Winckelmann and Lessing. To radical minds this was not yet release from the fetters of dogma, against which the generation of the mid-century began the movement called "Storm and Stress." This movement demanded originality rather than correctness and elegance, richness and intensity of feeling rather than adherence to rules. In overstepping rules genius fulfills a higher law and gives the utterance of nature herself. This current of ideas was to run underground during Goethe's and Schiller's classicism until it reappeared with Schlegel, Novalis, and their circle.

In Wilhelm Heinse (1746–1804) the pagan naturalism of the Italian renaissance revived. For him, beauty was natural perfection. Since he denied any reality beside or above nature, this value was absolute and supreme. One of his recently published fragments reads: "Good and useful and advantageous mean the same; good is a perfectly relative conception and nothing is good in and for itself. Beautiful however is everything in nature if it is what it ought to be according to its kind and purpose. A lion is beautiful though not useful to man." [55] Heinse did not shrink from admiring even Nero's or Cesare Borgia's crimes, provided they betrayed the fierce vigor of untrammeled nature. Reason is treated scornfully. Anxious above all to understand the essential unity of the human being, body and mind, Heinse conceived of it as an instrument of life that reaches perfection in beauty. "All beauty springs from life." [56] It is with the senses that we visualize beautiful objects. Yet no sense is an isolated function: in the pleasures of the eye and the ear our whole organism is involved. Similarly, beautiful form is the concrete appearance of a thing in all its richness, not the pale idealization of reality which Winckelmann likened to clear colorless water. "Every form is individual, and there is no abstract form; a merely ideal human figure is not to be conceived, either of man, woman or child." [57] The denial of abstract esthetic

HEINSE'S NATURALISM; AUTOCHTHONOUS ART.

---

[55] W. Brecht, *Heinse und der ästhetische Immoralismus. Zur Geschichte der italienischen Renaissance in Deutschland*, 1911, p. 39.

[56] *Gesammelte Werke*, herausgegeben v. Leitzmann, VII, 115.

[57] *Ibid.*, p. 493.

form implies the appreciation of the varying geographical and historical factors that condition esthetic creation: "Every race, every
climate has its characteristic beauty, its own food and drink." [58]
Consequently there is no sense in going back to the Greeks. Their
life has passed away, and with it their art also. Since life alone
yields life, we must go back to nature. Thus the project of a national art arises: "Let every artist work for the people among whom
fate has thrown him and with whom he has passed his youth; let
him endeavor to touch their hearts and fill them with pleasure and
delight; to maintain, intensify and ennoble their joy and well-being;
to help them weep when they weep. What is antiquity or posterity to us? The former has disappeared, and these youngsters
will have first to take our places before they are able to judge us." [59]

BEAUTY SPRINGS
FROM SENSE AND
SEX.
 When we turn from Baumgarten and his followers to Heinse,
we leave a lecture-room to attend a Bacchanalia. The cautious admission of a sensuous perfection in ideas had given way to the
proclamation of sensuality as supreme esthetic value. In the enjoyment of carnal pleasure life, the fount of all beauty, reasserts
and propagates itself. Thus, according to Heinse, esthetic enjoyment is largely due to sexuality. "Painting and sculpture," he said
bluntly, "serve first of all lust." While attributing a more intellectual character to poetry and music, he calls the fine arts "Phrynes
of the eye." [60] With him the sexual interpretation of art was not
cynical nor did it smack of obsession with the physiological aspects
of sex. It rested upon a pagan deification of nature. Heinse's pagan
sensibility helped to instill in German esthetics a fresh feeling for
elemental esthetic qualities. His descriptions of pictures and statues
betrayed that firm hold on the visible and palpable appearance so
rare in contemporary life. It was his mission to champion those
primitive powers that always feed esthetic pleasure and to remind
his sophisticated and rationalistic age of the animal charm of a
healthy creature. A genuine vision is communicated by his poetry

---

[58] *Briefe aus der Düsseldorfer Gemäldegalerie* (1776–1777). *Kritisch herausgegeben und eingeleitet* v. A. Winkler, 2. Aufl. 1914, p. 123.
 [59] *Ibid.*, p. 123.
 [60] *Werke*, VIII, 487; another attempt to derive esthetic approval from sexual
pleasure was made by Ernst Platner, *Neue Anthropologie*, 1790, §814.

and criticism: a scene of glowing colors, under the Italian sun, where bodies display the splendor of their naked limbs in a dionysian dance, and nymphs gambol with fauns in olive groves.

The opposite esthetic ideal was espoused by J. G. Hamann (1730–1788), the "Magus of the North" as his contemporaries called him. Common to both was the emphasis laid on the senses. But Hamann did not, like Heinse, cherish the senses for their own sake. For him the senses are carriers of divine truth, and this in an even more marvellous, more direct manner than abstract thought. His religion is an esthetic creed: "My whole Christianity," he confesses, "is a taste for tokens"—and this means for esthetic symbols.[61] It is however equally true to say that esthetic was reduced by Hamann to a commentary on the mysteries of Theophany and Incarnation. Dwelling on St. Paul's: "now we see through a glass, darkly, but then face to face," [62] he took the soul's eye in this life to be represented less by pure reason than by "senses and passions." These understood nothing but images, and "in images resides the whole wealth of human knowledge and happiness." [63]

HAMANN: SENSE AS EPIPHANY.

By his own confession Hamann had no natural liking for works of art, and he was absolutely lacking in a sense of form and proportion. His own literary productions are chaotic aggregates of learned digressions, far-fetched allusions, quaint and picturesque similes, emphatic exclamations mingled with flashes of genius—an unpalatable mixture out of which a few scattered remarks, unforgettable in their purity and simple grandeur, shine forth. In fact, language was the only esthetic medium which aroused in him a genuine and deeply felt response. From this feeling for language, he derived his half religious, half esthetic interpretation of the world. According to him, the whole creation is Word, communication of a meaning by images. It is the creature's answer to the Creator's "Speak that I may see you!" [64] But this language requires translation to become intelligible. Not the learned and the clever are best

TRUE POETRY IS THE "NOBLE SAVAGE" OF DISCOURSE.

---

[61] *Schriften*, herausgegeben von F. Roth and G. A. Wiener, 8 Theile, 1841–1843, V, 278.

[62] *Cor.* I, 13, 12.

[63] *Schriften*, II, 258 (Aesthetica in Nuce).

[64] *Ibid.*, p. 261f.

fitted to render "the language of the angels," but the undefiled, those who speak like children with primeval simplicity, ignoring the artifices of refined rhythm and exquisite imagery. The humblest garb is best fitted to clothe the divine truth which condescends to take mortal shape. Hence Hamann preferred the archaic simplicity of the Pentateuch and the vulgar Greek of the New Testament to the majesty of the tragic iambus and the eloquence of the classic orators. All these ideas and preoccupations are implied in the statement that "Poetry is the mother-tongue of the human race." [65]

Hamann's esthetic doctrine is, on the whole, a Christian and Protestant re-interpretation in the spirit of the Age of Rousseau of the neo-Platonic idea of poetic inspiration. He revived some ideas from Vico's *Scienza Nuova*, which he never read, and foreshadowed certain doctrines of the Romanticists, who hardly deigned even to notice him. In the progress of esthetic thought a man far superior to him in literary ability, intellectual discipline, and esthetic sensibility became his heir and successor, J. G. Herder (1744–1803).

HERDER: THEORY NOT BEAUTIFUL NOR ART CLEARLY LOGICAL.

There is something in Herder's nature that led a modern critic to take him for the living model of Goethe's Faust.[66] His is Faust's passionate craving for truth and the tragic struggle of opposing forces within. As esthetician and critic, he began his career by advocating the most modern and radical ideas. His attack on the current notion of the "fine Arts and Sciences" definitely disposed of a confusion which had hampered the progress of esthetics and had thwarted to some extent the better intentions of Baumgarten's school. The study of beautiful objects, Herder maintained, has no better claim to the title of "beautiful" than the study of square or oblong figures has to be called square or oblong. A sharp distinction must be made between the "esthetic event" and "esthetic discernment." Esthetics, "the most rigorous philosophizing about a worthy and very difficult subject," cannot acquiesce in the use of "confused ideas." But as little "does it wish to rectify and to solve

---

[65] *Schriften*, II, p. 258. Cf. Rudolf Unger, *Hamann und die Aufklärung. Studien zur Vorgeschichte des romantischen Geistes im 18. Jahrhundert*, 1911.
[66] Guenther Jacoby, *Herder als Faust. Eine Untersuchung*, 1911.

this confusion so that, in the future, we are to feel beauty distinctly and not confusedly." [67]

Thus was formulated with unerring sureness the program of the scientific discipline of esthetics. Herder went on to assign the new science a place within the field of Anthropology. Anthropology conceives its subject as essentially one, as the indivisible compound of the body and mind, of the senses and the intellect. Itself a living whole it is brought into being and kept alive by a larger whole, Nature. In accordance with such metaphysical assumptions the further development of Herder's esthetic notions pointed in a sensualistic and physiological direction. He held the three chief senses: sight, hearing, and touch, to be the instruments with which we feel beauty. Each of these senses has its own domain in art and its specific requirements and rules. Hence the uncertainty in judging the three corresponding kinds of art, painting, music, and sculpture, is mainly due to a confusion of the respective criteria. Sculpture for example is generally judged by the eye instead of by touch.

THE TRINITY OF ESTHETIC SENSE.

These empirical inquiries were intended to form together an "esthetic phenomenology," but Herder himself did not furnish more than the outlines of this theory. He even dropped a part of it altogether. The idea that sculptural beauty is to be sensed by touch disappeared from his writings. But apart from their intrinsic value Herder's ideas express a new esthetic practice. Among German critics Herder was the first great master of the complete esthetic sensibility. As critic of Shakespeare, as discoverer of folk-poetry, as translator and interpreter of foreign verse, he opened up a new epoch in German intellectual life. A standard of appreciation, based through an esthetic phenomenology upon the study of human nature, may justly claim universal validity. It enables us "to appreciate Beauty untrammeled by any national or personal tastes, wherever it is to be found, in all periods, and in all nations, and in all arts, and in all the varieties of taste; separated from all ingredients foreign to it, to respond to it everywhere and to feel it in its unalloyed purity. Happy the man who responds to it in

---

[67] *Viertes kritisches Wäldchen, Sämtliche Werke*, ed. B. Suphan, IV, 25.

this way! He is the one initiated into the mysteries of the Muses, and into all ages, and into all memories, and into all works: the sphere of his taste is infinite like the history of mankind: the circumference encircles all centuries and productions, and He and Beauty stand in the center." [68]

THE UNITY OF MAN AND OF HIS WORKS.

Herder's esthetic phenomenology finally leads back to its starting-point: the knowledge of Man. Herder was not content merely to admire the abundance of beauty in the poetry and art of all centuries and ages. He regarded this rich offering as a great document of Mankind. Listening to the folk-songs of many languages, he discerned the "voices of the peoples." Artistic taste, unlimited in its capacity of enjoying and sympathizing, revealed to him the meaning of history. The finest output of these reflections was not the promised analysis of the single senses but the *Contributions to a Philosophy of the History of Mankind.*[69] The cultivation of taste demanded by his phenomenology was not conceived as the philosopher's or philologist's special endowment. It is grounded in Man's inmost nature, in his "humanity." The perfect esthetic sensibility is the "blossom" of a sympathetic and well-balanced soul. Is this idealist conclusion in keeping with the sensualistic basis of Herder's doctrine?

TWO SOLUTIONS OF DUALITY OF NATURE AND SPIRIT.

Herder's sensualism should not be judged by its face value. It is much nearer to Hamann's than to Heinse's ideas. Not the sensuous appearance as such attracted Herder but its symbolic value. His doctrine, in spite of its sensualistic vein, centered around the problem of expression. He was at heart a believer in Spirit. At the same time he was filled with veneration for Nature—a natural cosmos self-sufficiently moving in its own sphere and endowed with a perfection all its own. To reconcile these opposed tendencies, Herder implanted a striving after a union with the Spirit in the very core of Nature. The problem of this union was approached by him in a twofold way. First he proposed a dynamic solution, interpreting Nature as a process of evolution, ascending through various stages up to the lucidity and perfection of pure Spirit. Herder's exposition of this idea remained a rough sketch, the vision

---

[68] *Viertes kritisches Wäldchen,* p. 41.

[69] *Ideen zu einer Philosophie der Geschichte der Menschheit,* 1784–1791.

of a dreamer. The second, "static" solution led him to the fundamental conceptions of his esthetics.

Spirit, he argued, is not only nature's aim—it is present in nature, visible, audible, and tangible in the esthetic experience. He contemplated Nature with the eye of a rapturous lover and at the same time as a physiognomist. Passionately he captured every single trait offered to his senses. But he was equally eager to discover a hidden meaning in and to coördinate a spiritual significance with each observed feature. His first publication deals with the question whether "a fair body is the messenger of a fair soul." [70] In nearly all his works the problem of the relationship between thought and expression, inward life and outward representation recurs. The same query gives rise to his doctrine of the *Origin of Language*.[71] The moan of the suffering animal and Philoctetes' pathetic eloquence illustrate the same phenomenon at different stages. For Herder's polar philosophy, expression is an inscrutable mystery as well as the paramount justification of his outlook. It calls attention to the disparateness of meaning and sign, and at the same time testifies to their intelligible relation, without which human intercourse would be impossible. Herder then found the most pregnant form of expression the work of art. Here idea and representation are inseparable, indissolubly united. "When I am not simply out to write my ideas but to speak to the other's soul so that he feels them and responds to them—then the true expression is inseparable from the thought." [72] In this "free expression" idea is related to form not as body to covering, but as soul to body.[73]

It is in the light of this theory of expression that we must understand Herder's phenomenology of the senses. His point of view may be described as 'ecstatic sensualism.' It is cognate to the theory of the mystic who 'tastes' God. While allowing to the senses more than most thinkers before him, he rejoiced in the thought that God reveals Himself even in the sphere farthest from His spiritual es-

NATURE AS AVATAR.

---

[70] *Ist die Schönheit des Körpers ein Bote von der Schönheit der Seele?*, 1766, *Werke*, I, 43ff.

[71] *Über den Ursprung der Sprache*, 1772, *Werke*, V, 1ff.

[72] *Über die neuere deutsche Literatur*, 1767, *Werke*, I, 395.

[73] *Ibid.*, p. 394.

sence. Works of art spoke to him in a twofold language. They
revealed to him the inmost thought of the artist, and through him,
of ages and peoples. At the same time they showed him, though
dimly in enigmatic signs, the foot-prints of "God's walk through
history." [74]

Herder found still another means of bridging the gulf between
God who is Spirit and self-sufficient Nature. He adopted an "esthetic Platonism," the counterpart of his "ecstatic sensualism." In
Greek sculpture, in his opinion, there is a visible and tangible embodiment of an absolute, timeless revelation of humanity. Thus
Hamann's follower, the admirer of ancient oriental poetry and the
bold advocate of the senses, takes sides with Winckelmann's rigid
dogmatism.[75] This clash of views corresponds to a similar tension
within his conception of humanity. His sympathetic insight into
everything human on the one hand, and his idea of a harmonious
perfection of the mental and the physical on the other, are confused rather than synthesized by his ideal of humanity.

HERDER A BRIL-
LIANT PIONEER BUT
LESS THAN COM-
PLETE.

Herder lacked the analytic power required to overcome the
conflict of his views or to conceive properly his own historical
rôle. He was the prophet who saw the promised land but failed
to recognize it. The daring pioneer turned into a bitter *laudator
temporis acti*. He unhappily combined the final exposition of his
esthetic ideas (in *Calligone. On the Agreeable and the Beautiful*) [76]
with an unjust and bitter criticism of Kant's *Critique of Judgment*.
The pivot of the controversy is the problem of the "agreeable."
Herder did not deny that the two words "agreeable" and "beautiful" actually refer to different objects. Yet he was terrified and
repelled by the rigidity with which the distinction was drawn by
Kant. He feared that the sharp line might tear asunder the phenomenon of artistic expression. For him, whose philosophy hinged
around the idea of expression, a vital interest was at stake. An absolute diversity was affirmed where in reality a gradual transition
takes place. Unfortunately he was not aware that Kant dissected
with a view to achieving a new synthesis. Thus he failed to un-

---

[74] *Werke*, XIII, 9.
[75] *Plastik*, 1778, *Werke*, VIII, 1ff.
[76] *Kalligone. Vom Angenehmen und Schönen*, 1800, *Werke*, XXII, 1ff.

derstand the meaning of the criticized doctrine. On the whole, Herder's esthetics suffered from an abundance of only partially reconcilable views and the absence of logical stringency. He was great as a pioneer, but not great enough silently to tolerate the carrying out by others of what he had begun.

Attention to the creative activity of the artist increased with the gradual release of esthetics from Wolffian rationalism. This development was furthered by the influence of English critics, and Edward Young's *Conjectures on Original Composition* (1774) in particular was frequently echoed by German writers. The doctrine of "genius" became an invariable topic in works on esthetics. A decisive step forward was taken in a small volume entitled *On the Creative Imitation of the Beautiful,*[77] by Karl Philipp Moritz (1757–1793), who was Goethe's friend and companion during the Italian journey. For the first time, a German writer definitely assumed the point of view of the artist who wishes to understand the operation of the creative energies in himself. Man, according to Moritz, is a microcosm—the Universe on a small scale. Effectiveness is given to this congruity of Man with the Universe by two complementary faculties: the "formative" and "sensitive" powers (Bildungskraft, Empfindungskraft), the first being related to the second as activity to passivity, male to female. Both powers which are in fact only two different modes of one fundamental activity have a biological basis in "the finer tissue of our organism."[78] They are both directed toward the harmonious organization of the Universe. The "sensitive power" receives its impress, the "formative power" reproduces its structure. In the artist's imagination a perfect balance of these energies is present. Owing to this harmonious disposition the artist, while imitating single beautiful objects, impresses upon his creation the image of the universe. Thus every work of art represents as it were Man's badge of citizenship in the Universe.

Moritz's essay, though over-concise, is full of surprises: the concentration on the problem of artistic creation; the imaginative

MORITZ: ARTISTIC CREATION AN ANALOGY TO BIO-LOGICAL.

INFLUENCE OF GOETHE.

[77] *Über die bildende Nachahmung des Schönen*, 1788, re-edited by S. Auerbach, *Deutsche Literaturdenkmale*, Vol. 31, 1888.
[78] *Op. cit.*, p. 21.

metaphysics combining physiological views with Pythagorean cosmology, and the assignment of the apprehension of the universe not to reason but to an esthetic faculty. Apparently he reached his metaphysics by way of generalizing esthetic conceptions. What fresh impulse inspired these ideas? Moritz had brought home his manuscript from Italy. There he had learned to see art and nature with Goethe's eyes. His essay is a portrait of Goethe, conceived by a speculative mind and translated into an abstract terminology. It heralded an epoch of German esthetics ruled not so much by Goethe's ideas as by Goethe's personality. On him, the greatest creative mind of German history, a theory of artistic creation was to be modelled.

SUPPLEMENTARY READING

Bosanquet, *History of Aesthetic*, pp. 182–88, 210–48.
Croce, *Aesthetic*, Part II, Ch. VI.
Saintsbury, *History of Criticism*, Vol. III, Bk. VII, Ch. V.
Venturi, *History of Art Criticism*, Ch. VI.

CHAPTER XI

Classical German Esthetics: Kant, Goethe, Humboldt, Schiller

KANT spoke the first rational word on esthetics." [1] This opin- HOW ORIGINALion expressed by Hegel of the importance of Immanuel Kant WAS KANT'S ES-(1724–1804) is only a terser statement of the opinion of Schelling, THETICS?
who expressed the hope that "time the mother of all development"
would finally bring to maturity "those seeds of great disclosures
. . . which Kant has sown in his immortal work." [2] But it has
lately been the fashion to question both the primacy and the pre-
eminent rationality of Kant's discoveries. It has not been difficult to
turn up a large number of anticipations both of Kant's actual phrases
and of some of his ideas. As these evidences of lack of absolute
originality on Kant's part have accumulated, writers have increasingly thrown back the "first rational word" toward Hutcheson,
Addison, Baumgarten, Vico, or Muratori. "If some carpers have
thought," says a recent writer, "that what Kant did to Hume's
epistemology, was to systematize rather than to annihilate, there
would be more truth in holding that Kant's philosophy of beauty
owes nearly everything but its systematic form to English writers." [3] "There are few original ideas in Kant's esthetic," he says
again. "He has systematized and hardened distinctions, and opposi-

---

[1] *Sämtliche Werke*, 25 Vols., Stuttgart, 1927ff., Vol. 19, p. 601. "Geschichte
der Philosophie," III, 3, B, 3, a.
[2] Manuscript translation of Schelling's *Dogmatism and Criticism*, kindly loaned
by Professor Fritz Marti.
[3] *The Monist*, 1925, Vol. XXXV, The Open Court Publishing Company,
Chicago, E. F. Carritt, "The Sources and Effects in England of Kant's Philosophy
of Beauty," pp. 315, 323.

tions current in English for the preceding eighty years, and this exaggeration results in a *reductio ad absurdum*." We can indeed take piecemeal most of the topics treated by Kant and match his statements with earlier ones by other people. For instance, Kant made the imagination a mediator between the other two principal faculties of the mind, sense-perception and reason. Lord Kames had said that the science of criticism, that is, the theory of the arts, is a middle link between feeling and reason. Addison had said that the pleasures of the imagination were less refined than those of understanding and less gross than those of sense.[4] Muratori, the Italian Baroque critic, had focussed his attention on the function of the esthetic imagination in its capacity as the harmonious union of the understanding and the imagination in general.[5] Again, Kant placed great emphasis on the disinterestedness of esthetic pleasure. This was a commonplace in Shaftesbury, Hutcheson, and Lord Kames. Commonplace also was Kant's doctrine of the immediacy and non-intellectual character of judgments of taste. Lord Kames says that there is a rule for taste, a subjective one, so that, though there is no disputing, there is good and bad taste. Kant used almost these words. Kant's distinction between pure and relative beauty, or intrinsic and extrinsic beauty, was one which he could easily have brought into his work from almost any of the contemporary British writers—Hutcheson, Berkeley, Kames, Hume, or Addison. There is a striking echo of Addison in Kant's treatment of the sublime. Addison says that nothing is so pleasing to our imagination as to enlarge itself by degrees, and compares the body of a man successively to the earth, the sun, the solar system, space.[6] Kant makes the same observation using the same progression. Kant uses precisely the illustrations of sublimity—St. Peter's at Rome and the pyramids—that were mentioned by Lord Kames, although to mention works of art as examples of sublimity contradicted the thesis Kant had just laid down that only nature is sublime. Kant's whole theory of sublimity was influenced by Burke, who speaks of "that state of the soul, in which all its motions are suspended, with some

---

[4] Addison, *The Spectator*, 8 Vols., London, 1898, Vol. VI, p. 57, No. 411.
[5] Carritt, *Philosophies of Beauty*, p. 63.
[6] *Spectator*, 420.

degree of horror," when describing our experience of the sublime.[7] This idea appears in Kant under the form of a momentary check to our vital powers. Beside the separate items which Kant owed to the psychological school of esthetics, mainly the British writers, he owed to Baumgarten, whose metaphysics he used as a manual in teaching, familiarity with the rational approach. The conceptions of confused knowledge and perfection, around which Baumgarten's esthetic theory revolves, Kant painstakingly discusses.

But one notes these debts of Kant to former writers rather to be rid of the reckoning than to make progress with Kant's own theory. The important thing in Kant is not his debts, but his originality. We quoted the recent opinion that Kant added little to former writings except "systematic form." But what a systematic form was that! With a little dramatic emphasis one might say that Kant and the idea of system are interchangeable terms: so that to leave him originality at this point is to leave him originality in all. Kant's mere system was in germ this world-shattering thing: the proof that esthetic enjoyment, while retaining its unique and characteristic quality (a-moral, a-logical, a-real), is more serious and philosophical than physical science. More so, because while Kant's first effort was to demonstrate the necessary presuppositions of physical science, his effort to demonstrate the philosophical presuppositions of taste, though following the same method, included all the work that had gone before and so aimed to crown his total intellectual structure.

HIS SYSTEM THE NOVELTY.

So much we can say by way of anticipating the meaning of his achievement for esthetics. To state the steps in that achievement is very difficult because the argument moves in the thinnest intellectual air, the most fragile medium of abstract implications. Having spent his life in trying to establish better than any predecessor the exact place in our total body of knowledge of mathematics and physics, ethics and religion, he spends his late years in trying to do the same for our feeling for beauty, and he finds this faculty the most delicately suspended of all and the most baffling and least under-

REJECTION OF EARLIER METHODS.

---

[7] *Philosophical Inquiry*, Part II, Sec. I.

stood. In his first Introduction to the *Critique of Judgment* he
sets out the reasons why the methods of the earlier writers on
taste seemed to him unsatisfactory. He specifically criticizes the
method both of the psychological estheticians, such as Burke and
Addison, and that of Baumgarten. Neither does justice to the
individual physiognomy of esthetic experience, he felt. Neither
bases taste on a philosophical foundation that can withstand assault.

Those who, like Baumgarten, make taste a confused knowledge
of perfection, do not stick to the concerns of esthetics. For the
mere fact of confusion in our knowledge has nothing to do with
its reference to pleasing form. "Few people indeed, including
philosophers, have a clear conception of what is right." [8] Clearness
of knowledge differs from confusion only quantitatively, and is the
result of more concentration of attention. Therefore a position
on this quantitative scale cannot constitute the distinguishing attribute of a kind of judgment. Then again, perfection has nothing
to do with esthetics; for perfection may mean (*a*) the unity of a
manifold, totality, and the fact that a thing is complete does not
mean that it is beautiful; or (*b*) that a thing fulfills a purpose.
Again the fulfilment of purpose need not have any concern with
beauty. All the elements then in Baumgarten's treatment of esthetic
are beside the point. [9]

Nor is the psychological school in a better case. A judgment
of taste sets itself up as universally valid, Kant says. No psychological explanation of origin can explain or justify that claim.
"Esthetic judgments of reflection . . . judgments of taste . . .
do not say, this is how men do judge, but rather this is how men
should judge. The former would have made them a problem for
empirical psychology to explain, but the latter indicates that they
have for themselves a principle *a priori*." [10] It is an "obvious ab-
surdity," Kant says, "to deduce from the fact that every man
judges in a certain manner . . . that he ought so to judge."

---

[8] *Immanuel Kants Werke*, ed. Cassirer, 11 Vols., Berlin, 1922, Vol. V, p. 207
(trans. Kabir, *On Philosophy in General*, Calcutta University Press, 1935, p. 47).
[9] *Ibid.*, V, 296–98 (*Kant's Kritik of Judgment*, trans. Bernard, London, 1892,
pp. 77–80) Part I, Div. I, #15.
[10] *Ibid.*, V, 219; Kabir 65, 66.

Psychology can be useful to esthetics at certain points. It can investigate "why the judgment of beauty has been wanting in development, under some conditions of place and society," and "through what causes it has been able to develop into luxury." He refers to the hundreds of sham psychologists who multiply causes and explanations at will, "who profess to know how to specify the cause of each affection or movement of the mind, occasioned by plays, poetic representations and natural objects. They give the name philosophy to this play of their wit." [11] Of Burke's *Essay on the Beautiful and the Sublime* he says that its obvious purpose of mere observation and collection of data, without pretension to apprehension, is all such psychology can hope to attain. For "empirical psychology will hardly ever be able to claim the rank of a philosophical science." [12] There is a contradiction on his view between pointing out the empirical origin and fulfilling the intent of esthetic experience. That is, if you can point to empirical origin, by that token you preclude the necessity in the judgment. "The reflective judgments demand a laborious investigation in order to guard against their being wholly limited to the empirical in respect of their principles, and thus destroying their claim to universal validity." [13] Kant never found any satisfying necessity in the immediacy of the operations of the sense organs, external and internal, in the animal frame, as Hutcheson and Kames did. This kind of necessity seemed to Kant to have no real binding power. He wanted an *a priori* condition. An *a priori* condition was what Hutcheson and Kames did not want.

In order to understand the idea of system upon which Kant founded his philosophical esthetics, we must approach it in two ways. In the first place, we must observe what system was for him wherever it operated; for Kant was ambitious to support his treatment of taste by the same kind of irrefragable logic as he believed he had discovered for science and morals. In the second place we must note that the demand for system was more exacting in esthetics than elsewhere because, as he found when the problem of esthetics

---

[11] *Ibid.*, V, 218; Kabir 64, 65.
[12] *Loc. cit.*
[13] *Ibid.*, V, 221; Kabir 70.

finally matured in his mind near the end of his life, its solution was
to constitute the system of systems.

IS AN ESTHETIC
SYSTEM POSSIBLE? In 1769, while Kant was composing his *Critique of Pure Reason*,
he doubted the possibility of making esthetics such a solid systematic structure as he was at the time making of the theory of
knowledge. He writes that Baumgarten's attempt to base taste on
reason is hopeless because taste is always empirical.[14] At this period
of his development, then, Kant would have been willing to agree
with Burke that in so far as we have a standard of taste, that
standard is no more than the actual agreement of many men on
questions of poetry and painting. In such an agreement, there is
no system in Kant's rigorous use of that term. In the second edition
of his *Critique of Pure Reason* (1787) Kant modified the reference
to Baumgarten's attempt and said that taste is "in its main sources"
empirical.[15] In the same year Kant wrote to his friend Reinhold
that the general scheme of his Critiques had become confirmed in
his mind by the discovery of a new department of knowledge
which has *a priori* principles. This new department of knowledge,
he said, was the department of esthetics, which he was now ready,
not to base on reason in the sense of Baumgarten, but to base on
a priori principles in his own unique sense.[16] Three years after this
letter to Reinhold he published his *Critique of the Power of Judgment* (1790). In it there is indeed a system, a scheme of reasoning
which removed his characteristic point of view by nothing less than
a world from those esthetic essays which followed Locke's historical plain method and which had given the model for his own
early and unimportant *Observations on the Feeling of the Sublime
and the Beautiful* (1764).

KANT'S TRANSCEN-
DENTAL METHOD
AND THE FIRST
TWO CRITIQUES. What was the method which Kant finally became convinced he
could legitimately apply to taste as he had applied it in other fields?
In some ways Kant's so-called transcendental method, the hall-
mark of his systems, resembles the method of an eclecticism. That

---

[14] *Immanuel Kants Werke*, III, 56; *Critique of Pure Reason*, trans. N. K.
Smith, London, 1933, p. 66, footnote.

[15] *Loc. cit.*

[16] *Werke*, IX, 345; cf. Caird, *The Critical Philosophy of Immanuel Kant*,
2 Vols., Glasgow, 1909, Vol. II, pp. 376, 377.

is, Kant tried to include on the one side, the valuable elements from the Lockian school which emphasized the importance of sense perception and experience of the real world, and asserted that the mind at the beginning is a blank sheet of paper upon which the impressions coming in through the various senses write; and on the other side, the main concern of the rationalists, that knowledge, however it starts, must be certain and demonstrable in order to deserve the name of knowledge. But Kant's method was actually less eclectic than it was irenic. He did not superficially recognize an element of truth on both sides and in an external way tie them together in a loose doctrinal fabric, but he tried to find the common ground which lay unacknowledged beneath the differences of the two schools and so to prepare the way for an enduring intellectual peace. He said indeed that sense experience gives the filling of knowledge (this was Locke's contribution) and reason gives the form of knowledge, the categories or organizing principles (and this was from Leibniz). But his solution of the problem went deeper. In his effort at conciliation he asked a new kind of question, forged a new tool of approach so that it would be appropriate to say that he granted nothing to the contending parties, but did all himself. He asked not so much what fraction of the whole of knowledge comes from sense and what from reason, as what is implied, or postulated, in the mere presence of our actual knowledges. We have geometry and we have physics; nobody doubts that these are existing systems of knowledge. Kant inquires: What in general about the nature of the world and our mind is implied in the existence of these bodies of knowledge? To put it in other words, the inquiry is: Something being given (sciences or the moral order or the world of beauty) what are the necessary presuppositions which the very possibility of its existence forces us to admit?

In pressing backward in a complex analysis to find the ultimate presuppositions of knowledge, Kant proves the *a priori* character, first, of space and time as the necessary conditions of our orderly sensuous observation; then of causality as the necessary presupposition of all our scientific organization of the facts of experience; then of a functional unity of consciousness, an 'I think,' which is not a soul substance, but a necessary hypothesis of all knowledge.

Josiah Royce called these formal principles which Kant thus isolated the mind's 'sanity' in its dealings with the world.[17] If these synthetic activities, or these aspects of human sanity, are necessary postulates of our undoubted knowledge, Kant would claim that he was entitled to call them *a priori* and necessary, and not merely customary and natural, as would Hume.

Kant uses the same transcendental method in tracing the necessary conditions of the moral life. Man's sense of duty, the *datum* to be explained, implies, Kant believes, the freedom to carry out the dictate which the sense of duty categorically utters. Otherwise this feeling of obligation would be senseless—insane. But a being who is free to do what his conscience commands is not a link in a causal chain; he is something that can cause itself. He is self-legislative. Now because the idea of cause turned out to be the most important formal principle in the field of scientific knowledge for Kant, and because on the other hand the denial of such causation in the interests of human freedom is the most important idea in the moral world, these two spheres, that of knowledge, and that of morality, issue at the end of Kant's first analyses in strictly separated parts of the philosophical universe.

THE BRIDGE BE-
TWEEN THE
WORLDS.

By thus suggesting the character of Kant's method in his first two *Critiques* we have achieved two ends. We have found the model that he wished to follow in his esthetic analysis and also the pressing problem which the termination of his previous analyses left for an analysis of taste to solve. In the second and final introduction to his *Critique of the Power of Judgment* Kant strikingly expresses his feeling of the need for a conciliation of his two earlier systems. Nature and Freedom, he writes, are separated by a gulf that one cannot see across.[18] There is apparently no passage possible from the one to the other. They are like two mutually impenetrable spheres. Having made the separation thus absolute, Kant begins gradually to peer across the gulf, throw a bridge across the impassable cleft, and bring the two imperial spheres into communion with each other. But he keeps this linking very delicate. It is valid only in the realm of thought. This is what he says:

[17] Royce, *The Spirit of Modern Philosophy*, Boston, 1928, p. 128.
[18] Kant, *op. cit.*, V, 244; Bernard 12, 13. Introduction #2.

Morality *ought* to have an influence on the real world. Freedom *ought not* to be an empty ideal. It ought to be a fact. Therefore, unless we are to despair of all the leadings of our sanity, we must assume a general harmony between what the moral world requires and what the factual world can produce. "There must, therefore, be a ground of the *unity* of the supersensible which lies at the basis of Nature with that which the conception of freedom practically contains." [19] This ground of the unity is, he says, merely something we cannot help thinking about, when we inquire into the relations of morality and the common world. It is not anything we can definitely envisage, or scientifically expound. It must be—that is all. Otherwise we would go mad.

But the question arises for us whether Kant has the right to bind together two worlds for which he has with such difficulty won scientific bases by dint of an act of radical separation. The coercive power, the *a priori* validity and certainty, of the principles of space, time, and causality could be claimed by Kant for the worlds of common sense and science because these worlds were admitted by him to be only phenomena. Man's organizing faculties, the schemas and terms of his physical sciences apply, in other words, only to what *appears* to him, leaving the question of things-in-themselves out of account. On the other hand, the postulates of the moral law *never* apply in the factual world because their reference is ideal, and not real. Moralists talk about 'oughts,' and not about what is. The success of Kant's argument, then, seems to depend on the degree to which he keeps the world of nature and the world of freedom apart. And yet, as he starts his *Critique of Judgment*, he seems inconsistently to be acknowledging a logical obligation to bring together logically the realms which his logic had required him to separate. Are we to say that with the development of his esthetic theory, his earlier doctrines crumble? It is clear that Kant does not believe that there is any essential contradiction between the statements of his new Critique and the earlier findings. On the contrary, he says: "The critical examination of the ground for this edifice [the esthetic edifice] must have

[19] *Loc. cit.*

been previously carried down to the very depths of the foundation of the faculty of principles, independent of experience, lest in some quarter it might give way, and sinking, inevitably bring with it the ruin of all." [20]

It is true that Kant emphasized the restriction of morality and science to prevent their interference with each other, and to insure ultimate peace between them. It is true also that a gulf appears to gape between them, but the new Critique, destined to function as a mediator and a bridge, involves less inconsistency with the earlier point of view than at first appears. There were feelers put out, even in the first *Critique* dealing with Pure Reason, which Kant found it now possible to pick up, strengthen, and attach to more definite conclusions. While a reinterpretation of his system certainly occurs through the medium of his writing on esthetics, there is no recantation. Delicate suggestive minor themes become major motives; analogies and equations are discovered, where formerly there was a blank, and a positive and constructive attitude seems to supplant one of negation and restriction.

Some of the minor themes in the earlier work, if attentively considered, may be seen as preparing the way for the new Critique. The principal minor motive is the treatment of the regulative use of the Ideas of Reason in the last part of *The Critique of Pure Reason*. Kant had been proving that the intellect is not justified in asserting dogmatically any of the traditional absolutes: God, the soul, and the universe as a single Whole. There is no way, he had claimed, by means of which such ultimate conceptions can be logically demonstrated in the sense that causal connections in the physical world and mathematical sequences can be demonstrated. But such "Ideas, although transcendent for our faculty of theoretical cognition, are not redundant. . . . They lead understanding in its study of nature according to a principle of completeness . . . and so promote the ultimate aim of all knowledge." [21] "I may have sufficient grounds to assume in a relative point of view what I have no right to assume absolutely." [22] One may paraphrase his

---

[20] Kant, *op. cit.*, V, 236, 237; Bernard, 3. Preface.

[21] *Ibid.*, V, 235, 236; Bernard, 2.

[22] *Ibid.*, III, 461; quoted by Caird, *op. cit.*, II, 127. "Kritik of Pure Reason."

train of thought thus: Although I cannot dogmatically assert that there is a God or a soul, or a universe, since my understanding in its limited capacity has to creep from point to point and part to part, I can help myself in my legitimate and natural functions, by proceeding on the assumption of an Intelligent Being behind the world, and of an harmonious wholeness both in nature and in myself. In other words I can use the Ideas of Reason 'heuristically' though not 'ostensively'; as experiments but not as dogmas. That is, these hypotheses, adopted for the time being, teach us nothing positive about the world, but create favorable conditions under which we may move forward in our investigation of the world. We may suppose, for instance, that objects "in their detail are not infinitely varied, but have a certain similarity and continuity through all their difference, which makes it possible for the intellect to get a hold on them." Dialectic shows us "that reason in its regulative use gives rise to certain principles of investigation—homogeneity, specification, and continuity." [23] The subordination of species to genus, the assumption of an infinitely shaded continuum of forms, and of some degree of likeness in all things that cohabit the same world, help to make nature comprehensible. "Particular empirical laws are not isolated and disparate, but connected and in relation." [24] To use principles of connection beyond the point where we clearly see our way is doubtless taking an intellectual risk, but we are pragmatically justified in following such guiding threads in the twilight of our attempt to give order to experience. Only by use of them can we make any progress beyond a certain point in the employment of our understanding. Besides admitting the desirability of a pragmatic use of complete wholes for reason, Kant asserts our right to use the absolute 'kingdom of ends' which we inhabit as moral beings as a type or analogue of the 'kingdom of nature.'

These tentative softenings of the hard outline of the original metaphysical structure become firm parts of the new framework. The assumption of complete wholes harmoniously ordered and

---

[23] Caird, *op. cit.*, II, 381; *Werke*, V, 248–55; Bernard, 16–26. Introduction, ##4, 5.

[24] Kant, *op. cit.*, V, 252; Bernard, 22. Introduction #5.

designed, and of a proportion or binding analogy between the noumenal and phènomenal worlds, take on slightly new shapes, and involve a new terminology in the *Critique of Judgment,* but are in essence the old ideas revived and enlarged. Kant was now seeking the formal principles of a definite sphere, the esthetic, instead of a hazardous projection of our intellectual faculty. He wished on independent grounds to discover if possible *a priori* principles of taste. The desired *a priori* principle turns out to be that of design or system, the very one which was so cautiously utilized by the intellect. The coincidence seemed to be of happy augury for the validity of the principle of taste. That which was found to be regulative now becomes constitutive within set limits. There is also the happy augury of a *rapprochement* of the two spheres. Since the esthetic sphere turns up as a middle sphere, the application of moral principles to the world of nature—before only a pious wish—now has a solid bridge to walk on. It is also a happy chance to find the esthetic sphere fitting exactly into a gap in the philosophical system. All the parts of the picture suddenly take on more vivid meaning through the slipping into place of lost pieces.

We must inquire further what is meant by saying that *The Critique of Judgment* occupies a position between the already existing Critiques. In part it means for Kant something very pedantic. In the traditional psychology which Kant used, three faculties were given: understanding, judgment, and reason, corresponding to the functions of cognition, the feeling of pleasure and pain, and desire or will. Again, these three faculties and functions, Kant thought, correspond to the three propositions of a syllogism: the understanding gives the major premise, the judgment the minor premise, and the reason the conclusion. Kant's schematizing habits were reassured by the coincidence of the persistent presence of this middle term in all these schemes. The middle term, representative of the dialectical triads, seemed to be asking to be given its proper *Critique.*

JUDGMENT, DETER-
MINANT AND RE-
FLECTIVE.

The 'judgment' then is a connecting link in the mind, a sort of intellectual *liaison* officer. Kant distinguished two ways in which the judgment performs its task of binding together. It may either start from the more general laws laid down by the reason and then drop to the detail, or it may move in the other direction, and begin with particular cases and work upward toward a law for them. Kant calls the first a determining or determinant judgment, the second reflective. This latter bends back, in other words, in its search for a general form. "Judgment in general is the faculty of thinking the particular as contained in the universal." [25] It is with the judgment of the reflective type that taste is concerned. The problem is: How and where can taste—a liking of this and that—find a general law? Not from experience, because experience gives no 'ought.'

Kant's answer is that the principle of adaptation or design is DESIGN. what we require. Design, or as he calls it, subjective purposiveness or finality is that delicate and suspended bond which implies the suitability of nature to us, that man's mind and nature in her detailed content appear to have been made for each other, that the pieces of the epic picture-puzzle do fit together. But in this idea of fitting together there is no implication that an Architect preestablished the harmony. Rather the idea implies the experiment of thinking as if there had been some such thoughtful prearrangement, at the same time withholding any belief in one. Meaningfulness is imputed in order to attain intelligibility. The question: What is the unitary meaning or purpose of this situation before me? is assumed to be a sensible question to ask. Kant says various maxims constantly crop up that illustrate how inevitably our mind likes to work on this pattern. For example, we say, "Nature takes the shortest way." [26] That sounds reasonable, and we often venture to trust it as if it were a certain law in things, but it is not. It is simply expressive of the design-seeking, pattern-loving habit of the reflective judgment.

But all this sounds like a repetition of the analysis of the regulative use of Reason. Indeed it is. Just as the reason trusting to an ultimate harmony in the nature of things which it cannot prove builds up systems of speculation, even theology, so the reflective judgment believing in a harmony which it cannot prove refers what

---

[25] Kant, *op. cit.,* V, 248; Bernard, 16. Introduction #4.
[26] *Ibid.,* V, 251; Bernard, 20. Introduction #V.

it sees and hears to a welcome feeling of successful adaptation of the parts in what is given in perception.

Although an esthetic principle of design works in us on the occasion of seeing a beautiful flower or beautiful bird, the principle does not apply directly to the flower or bird out there in the world. The harmony on such an occasion is really in us, although we have a tendency to impute it to the object. As Kant puts it, the *a priori* principle of the reflective judgment is always subjective. All the other *a priori* principles—space, time, cause—enter into the substance of nature. But the principle of design is a name for the pleasure *we feel*. It is not a name for anything external to us. To analyze it further, then, one must press back upon one's own experience of pleasure and discover more specifically the traits of a pleasure that deserves the name of reflective judgment. We sometimes feel a pleasure which is disinterested, untainted by any selfish concern. Usually pleasure presupposes a desire, an appetite, a want. But the appetites man shares with the animal world, and the vital urges in the animal world, are explained by the responses of the animal organism to the environment. A man's wants, in so far as he is an animal, are natural causes, and produce natural inevitable effects. The satisfaction in that case is not a free pleasure. Pleasure obtained from eating when we are hungry is a part of a chain of causes and effects. Pleasure from the sense of form—in the pleasant ritual of a meal—might be construed as disinterested pleasure or free delight in form. The pleasure connected with lust is animal and therefore interested. The pleasure in the contemplation of the rhythms and texture of a beautiful body on the contrary would be free. Kant says that disinterested pleasure, "free favor," [27] is indifferent to the real existence of a thing; whereas interested desire craves possession and consumption. He illustrates the distinction by reference to the social views of Rousseau. He might agree with Rousseau that it was wicked for the world to indulge in the luxury of beautiful buildings and pictures and statues; and yet he might take esthetic pleasure in those same objects, because his esthetic attitude has nothing to do with existence in time and space.

---

[27] Kant, *op. cit.*, V, 279; Bernard, 54. Part I, Div. I, #5.

It has to do only with the way a pattern suits our sensibilities.[28] "The judgment of taste is merely *contemplative*." [29] The pleasure that we feel in the shape of a Greek vase, for example, should not be caused by a desire for the vase, but by the mental activity, the stimulating and exhilarating play of our mental faculties in the presence of the vase. "One possessed by longing or appetite is incapable of judging beauty." [30]

The involutions of Kant's thought show in the statement that a judgment upon an object of our delight may be 'disinterested' but withal very interesting; *i.e.*, taste relies upon no interest, but produces one. His meaning is that we are not externally compelled by pressures and urges in our bodily nature while feeling beauty. But he wishes to guard against the inference that disinterestedness, freedom, contemplation, should be terms implying coldness or a merely intellectual attitude toward beauty. We take an interest, but we are not driven by interests. We take an interest when the conditions of esthetic satisfaction being fulfilled, we try to prolong that satisfaction and reinforce the harmonizing activity.

The disinterestedness of esthetic pleasure entails a second property. The exclusion of all reference to private advantage or personal connection with what gives pleasure justifies us in asserting that the pleasure applies to everybody equally. What applies to nobody in particular may be said to apply to everybody in general. That is at least one of the ways by which Kant moves from the first property of esthetic judgment to the second. The first eliminates all private points of view. The second affirms the public reference. An object that pleases me esthetically pleases me impersonally, and what pleases me impersonally, pleases me as a member of humanity, and not as a unique individual. Therefore Kant believes himself entitled to describe the esthetic judgment as universal and necessary. We demand of all men that they agree

---

[28] Kant's objection to the connection between interest and pleasure in esthetic experience could be the basic text for Galsworthy's satire on Soames Forsyte. Soames' delight in his gallery of pictures was the pleasure of a possessor; his gallery enhanced his pride as a man of property. Had the same pictures belonged to somebody else, the interest would have failed.

[29] *Ibid.*, V, 278; Bernard, 53. Part I, Div. I, #5.

[30] *Ibid.*, V, 273; Bernard, 47. Part I, Div. I, #2.

with us, when we esteem something beautiful. Yet we cannot point out to other men the exact reason why they should agree with us.

There seems at first to be here the eliciting of a something out of a nothing. Kant seems to say: because no particularity, no reference to a personal situation, therefore universality. But he supplements this argument by another more positive one. Although the purity of the esthetic state of mind requires absence of any owner's pride or reformer's iconoclasm, the same purity requires the presence of a definite state of affairs in the subject's mental machinery. Though seeming to be judging about a thing outside himself, he must be really judging about himself. The authority for the assertion of the universal validity of esthetic pleasure inheres in a soul-state which we have a right to presuppose in all men under given conditions. This subjective condition is the harmonious interplay of reason and sense-perception. This harmonious interplay we are logically bound to assume as existent whenever there is a feeling in us favorable to the progress of our knowledge. One might call it a vague intimation of an understanding yet to come. Thus though we are not compelled by logical premises to pronounce a thing beautiful, we are compelled by the forebodings of reason so to judge it.

The sense of beauty is the light shadow cast by the peaceful coöperation of all the parties to the fact of knowledge. This shadow falls on the whole scientific enterprise. Science marches. It could not march, if the world and our thoughts did not coöperate. If the universe were as mad as in our nightmare speculations we sometimes fancy, or in bitter despair we affirm, then our thoughts, trying to sew together molecule and molecule, cell and cell, symptom and disease, would bound back against us in derision. But knowledge grows from more to more. And the mental reflex of this happy state of affairs is the feeling of pleasure we experience, especially when in the presence of a field of nature presenting itself as artificially orderly. The judgment of taste, then, which directs this pure pleasure, puts forth a claim to universal assent; calls on others to participate, not in the knowledge of an object, but in a feeling of pleasure auspicious for knowledge that is referred to an object. The organ of esthetic feeling Kant calls the common sense. The *sensus communis* is the perception or inward reflection of the coöperation of sense and reason in man. It is a kind of sympathy.[31] For it involves the confluence of the feeling of any one man with the feeling of all.

The third distinct property which Kant analyzes out of the judgment of taste is "purposiveness without purpose." [32] This property follows very quickly from the properties already expounded. He means by his paradoxical phrase that those things that please us esthetically have the look of being designed to fit our needs and desires, yet that there is no rational basis for supposing any actually designing intelligence that produced the object for the apparent end. We may not call an object which pleases us because of its fitness to a namable end, whether practical or moral, a beautiful object. Beauty is absolute, not instrumental. Kant here would go directly contrary to Ruskin when Ruskin makes the beauty of a church proportional to its utility as a roof, or the beauty of a goblet proportional to its utility as a drinking vessel. The feeling of adaptation must be present, Kant believes, but not to anything except the happy play of our faculties. What is the purely esthetic value of a church or a cup for Kant? Not in the one case that there is protection from the elements and suitability for divine worship, nor in the other case that there is facility for drinking, but in both cases that there is a semblance or form happily constructed to make our faculties play—things easy to look at that make us want to keep on looking, because they meet the needs of our looking-apparatus in some way we cannot understand.

NON-PURPOSIVE PURPOSE.

These three characteristics of the esthetic judgment support Kant's distinction between pure and adherent beauty. Pure beauty, Kant says, is that in which we have no definite knowledge of purpose or use. Greek decorative designs, foliations for margins and on wall-paper, musical fantasies, pantomimes, dances, any kind of arabesque in any medium, such natural beauty as we find in flowers, shells, crystals, illustrate the free type.[33] In these cases, we

PURE AND ADHERENT BEAUTY.

---

[31] Kant, *op. cit.*, V, 367; Bernard, 170. Part I, Div. I, #40.

[32] *Ibid.*, V, 290, 291; Bernard, 69, 70. Part I, Div. I, #11.

[33] *Ibid.*, V, 299; Bernard, 81. Part I, Div. I, #16.

respond immediately to the agreeable design. We do not need to be botanists, Kant says, in order to have a full appreciation of the loveliness of rose or iris.[34] In fact he would go further. He is of the opinion that scientific consciousness of the functions of the parts of a flower would militate against pure sense of beauty. The scientist does not respond as such to the purposiveness without purpose of what he contemplates, but to the fitness to a known end. Kant realizes how thin in the last resort this forces pure beauty to be. And so he adds a class of beauties which he calls adherent. In this are such objects as houses, palaces, arsenals, churches, summer-houses, in which appreciation of design mingles with awareness of the end to be subserved. Then the two satisfactions, that of our pure sense of form, and that of practical intelligence, coalesce in a single experience. Though there is here loss in purity, there is gain in richness. Kant admits greater magnitude and importance in those experiences where we are aware at once of the form and the content, the form as a harmonious design, and the content as an apt instrument for some recognized good.

For Kant the highest case of adherent beauty is ideal beauty. Men and women may have only adherent beauty, because, Kant believes, in admiring their form we can never abstract from the idea of their use and type.[35] A beautiful woman can never be mere linear rhythm; she must always strike us as excellently adapted to the function of a woman in order to appeal to us as beautiful. In other words, the ideal of humanity is present in human beauty. Kant says we arrive at this type by a double process: first, an average or norm of any human group is obtained by eliminating specific peculiarities. Thus we get a kind of composite photograph. But superimposed on this normal beauty of a type, there must be for ideal beauty the suggestion of fitness for the moral destiny. A man looks like a man in the first place because he resembles his fellows biologically; but in the second or higher sense because he looks as though he could admirably accomplish the peculiarly human duties—service to humanity, the maintenance of good faith, the enlargement of the amount of goodness in the

---

[34] *Loc. cit.*

[35] *Ibid.,* V, 299, 300; Bernard, 82. Part I, Div. I, #16.

world. Although this kind of beauty consists in fully half of the
rejected idea of 'perfection'—that perfection which reason ap-
preciates—Kant here draws it back into the esthetic picture for the
sake of the completeness of the satisfaction of man's desire for
harmony. Adherent beauty, at its highest point, includes even a
moral significance.[36]

The analysis of ideal beauty is not the only instance in which
Kant makes the esthetic judgment lean toward the moral judgment.
He originally divides esthetic judgments into those of beauty and
sublimity, and this division corresponds to a tension in the esthetic
experience. In so far as the esthetic judgment predicates beauty, it
is pulled toward intellectual cognition; in so far as it predicates
sublimity, it tends to be drawn out of the center in the direction
of the supersensible sphere of morality. In the case of the judgment
of the sublime, it is much easier to understand Kant's characterizations of the esthetic experience as subjective, and as hinting, without
fully revealing, man's relation to an absolute whole.

The process of the judgment of the sublime has for Kant two THE SUBLIME.
phases: the first is the failure of human sensibility in the presence
of the size or might of nature.[37] The stars of the heavens or the
sands of the seashore in their infinity overpass the human mind's
power to get a single articulate impression of their number and
extent. Or a storm at sea or torrent of falling water stuns the
human imagination by a force which seems incommensurable with
the utmost extent of the force of the human body. Thus "a
sensible object . . . may by its magnitude strain and tax our
imagination till it fails." [38] This brings on the second phase of the
feeling for the sublime. The conquered imagination "in its effort
to widen itself falls back upon itself." [39] In other words, the experience of sublimity issues in a recoil from the impression of
natural grandeur upon the moral dignity of man, which is greater
than any number or power in nature. There is first a check, then

---

[36] *Ibid.*, V, 303; Bernard, 86. Part I, Div. I, #17.
[37] *Ibid.*, V, 323; Bernard, 111, 112. Part I, Div. I, #26.
[38] Quoted by Caird, *op. cit.*, II, 403; *Werke*, V, 323; Bernard, 112. Part I,
Div. I, #26.
[39] *Loc. cit.*

an overflow in the welcome sense of the supersensuous dignity and
vocation of man. There is first the suspension, then the release,
in the expansion of soul that comes with the passage to the moral
attitude. "The feeling of the sublime in nature is respect for our
own destination, which by a certain subreption we attribute to an
Object of nature."[40] The unreflective tendency of our minds is
to call the ocean or the starry heavens sublime, but the true inward
meaning of our instinct is respect for a spiritual being who can remain
cool and even be uplifted in admiration in the presence of natural
existences that on the merely physical plane reduce him to the in-
significance of a mite on a cheese. Thus again we see that Kant
slips almost insensibly from the esthetic sphere, which by hypothesis
he makes utterly unique, into the moral sphere. The experience of
the sublime, we might almost say, is an intimation of morality. It
is morality rejected from beauty, returning by the back door and
moving toward its earlier primacy.

In comparison with the experience of beauty, the feeling for the
sublime turns toward the subject rather than the object; suggests
motion rather than rest; quantity rather than quality; and uses formless material out of which to build what pleases instead of harmoniously designed patterns. According as sublimity refers for Kant
to size or power, it is called by him the mathematical or the
dynamical sublime. The mathematical sublime is our experience
of the object which we cannot measure. The pyramids of Egypt,
Saint Peter's at Rome, and the systems of the Milky Way exhaust
our powers of counting.[41] We instinctively use an anthropomorphic
unit or measurement. But with reference to these enormous
stretches, the repetition of the unit would have to be carried on
to an extent that would be futile. More significant is the dynamic
sublime, which is the presentation of the force which again makes
futile measurements in anthropomorphic terms. It is essential for
the esthetic experience of the sublime that there should be an absence
of fear before these great and mighty objects. Fear introduces a
physical interest which is always for Kant inappropriate in esthetic
experience. "He who fears can form no judgment about the Sublime

---

[40] Kant, op. cit., V, 329; Bernard, 119. Part I, Div. I, #27.
[41] Ibid., V, 323, 328; Bernard, 112, 118. Part I, Div. I, #26.

in nature; just as he who is seduced by inclination and appetite can form no judgment about the Beautiful." [42]

In our discussions of Kant's definition of ideal beauty and sublimity, we have noticed how a moral interest creeps in. Near the end of the *Critique of Esthetic Judgment* Kant makes a separate topic of the relation of taste to morals.[43] He says that an esthetic idea can serve as a moral symbol. He distinguishes a schema from a symbol. A schema is a diagram which helps the mind to grasp a meaning which can never be literally given in sense perception, but which can correspond, point for point, with such a picture. A symbol, on the other hand, though an analogue, resembles what it symbolizes only in the plan of its organization. An organism symbolizes a constitutional government; a machine, a despotism. | ART AS MORAL SYMBOL.

Kant occupies himself not only with the products and appreciation of esthetic form, but with the power that creates them. Genius, he says, is Nature working as reason in man.[44] It is a talent for producing that for which no rule can be given. What it brings forth must in a sense seem like a natural growth. There must be no labored effort, no academic form betraying it. Artistic genius is specifically distinguishable from what may be acquired by industry backed up by imitation. In thus emphasizing the aspect of spontaneous generation in genius, Kant agrees with all the creative artists who have found it impossible to give an intellectual description of the mode of creating beauty, and have found no comparison better than that of gestation. Kant says that Homer and Wieland could not have shown how their ideas entered and assembled themselves in their brain, for the very good reason that they did not themselves know, and so could not teach others. One thinks of Lessing's phrase, 'the living jet of inspiration,' that he, a mere man of talent working by rule, lacked. Thus is art for Kant negatively distinguished from science, for which rules can be given. Kant believed that anyone could succeed in science with sufficient labor. So would Newton be distinguished from Mozart. The rules for scientific procedure are open to the daylight, and available to any- | CREATIVE SPONTANEITY.

---

[42] *Ibid.*, V, 332; Bernard, 124. Part I, Div. I, #28.
[43] *Ibid.*, V, 428–31; Bernard, 248–52. Part I, Div. I, #59.
[44] *Ibid.*, V, 393; Bernard, 203. Part I, Div. I, #49.

one. The ways of the artist are obscure, enigmatic to most men—often to himself.

GENIUS IS NATURE
WORKING AS REA-
SON IN MAN.

A positive condition of creative genius is the presence of *Geist*, soul. By this Kant means native fecundity, a sort of richness of mind, favorable to germination, and to the production perhaps even of erratic and obscure offshoots, but for want of which nothing original can be done in art. The waywardness of the working of *Geist* is imitated by second-class men, but the imitation always leaves tell-tale traces. Though lesser men go wrong when they try to mimic the idiosyncrasies of genius, such aspirants rightly perceive that a general rule for production can be shaped out of the works of genius. Genius follows no rules, but furnishes a model, from which rules can be made. It is the work of taste to clip the eccentricities from the rich full production of genius and to make a more harmonious and suitable model than genius itself can achieve.[45]

Genius is also defined by Kant as the faculty of Esthetic Ideas.[46] By esthetic ideas, he means pictures to which no intellectual idea is adequate. There are images possible to genius which lie beyond the

---

[45] The history of the idea of genius has been made the subject of numerous recent studies. Originally the word designated a demon or demonic being like Socrates' inner voice. After the belief in demons had faded, probably as late as about the middle of the sixteenth century, the term in its modern sense began to spread. (Cf. Edgar Zilsel, *Die Entstehung des Geniebegriffs*, 1926, p. 296.) It became now equivalent to *ingenium* and was wedded to the Platonic theory of inspiration. This combination of ideas played a prominent rôle in eighteenth century esthetics. Especially in England the conception of genius was used as a weapon in the attacks levelled against classicism and esthetic rules. Divine inspiration was opposed to rational legislation. This pre-romantic English irrationalism, culminating in Young's *Conjectures on Original Composition*, deeply impressed the German writers. (Hermann Wolf, *Versuch einer Geschichte des Geniebegriffs in der deutschen Ästhetik des 18. Jahrhunderts;* Vol. I, *Von Gottsched bis Lessing*, 1923; Hans Thüme, "Beiträge zur Geschichte des Geniebegriffs in England," in: *Studien zur Englischen Philologie*, Heft LXXI.) But the idea of creative genius, if taken as the basis of esthetics, is obviously subversive of all theory. So a fumbling after a synthesis of the polar ideas of inspiration and rules began. This process was brought to fulfilment by Kant's formula: genius is the talent "through which Nature gives the rule to Art." In post-Kantian speculation the problem assumed a new aspect: the professed aim was now to draw up an esthetic theory which reflected the experience of genius, in other words, to rationalize inspiration.

[46] *Werke*, V, 389ff., Bernard, 197ff. Part I, Div. I, §49.

limits of abstract thought; such are the myths of Plato, in which the soul figures as a charioteer managing diverse steeds, and the images of the *Divine Comedy* of Dante, in which rainbows and roses, rivers of blood and lakes of ice give the sense of heaven and hell better than rational discourse.

Kant hoped to rescue philosophy from endless debates and to set it squarely on the road of steady progress. Actually he brought about a revolutionary movement of thought that soon overstepped the limits he had set. This is also true of his esthetics. The harmony between reason and the nature of things which he believed we sense in esthetic pleasure was for him not susceptible of discursive exposition, and his philosophy pointed to it only from afar. His followers desired to penetrate to the hidden source of an ultimate metaphysical unity and there to locate the very center of their theoretical scheme. As a result of this desire of his followers, Kant's idea of purposiveness was swelled beyond its true limits. Kant in his *Critique of Judgment* treats beauty and organic nature as parallel phenomena. Instead of feeling a 'purposiveness without purpose' in the subjective apprehension of things, we may, by virtue of reasoning, attribute an inherent objective purpose to the things themselves. We may conceive nature as if it were designed in accordance with ends. To allot its place to such a teleology of nature and to define its limited validity is the purpose of Part II of the third *Critique*. In it the heuristic idea of a great system of purposes of nature is unfolded. Within this frame, Kant says, "also the beauty of nature . . . can be regarded as a kind of objective purposiveness of nature. . . . We can regard it as a favor which nature has felt for us, that in addition to what is useful it has so profusely dispensed beauty and charm; and we can therefore love it . . . and feel ourselves ennobled by such regard; just as if nature had established and adorned its splendid theatre precisely with this view." [47] Such sentences moved Goethe to whole-hearted assent. But Goethe, the Romanticists, and Schelling, taking up the idea of a close kinship between organic nature and art, cared little for the restrictions which Kant had imposed on his thesis. From Kant's

---

[47] *Ibid.*, pp. 286f., Part II, §67.

point of view they were impelled by a legitimate admiration for
Nature's apparent purposiveness to allow themselves to rise
"through misunderstanding . . . to the height of fanaticism." [48]

SINGULARITY OF
GOETHE'S POSITION.   The place of Johann Wolfgang Goethe (1749–1832) in the
development of German esthetics may be illustrated by a simile.
Let us imagine a geometrical ornament with a figure in the center:
this middle figure is framed by an analogous band at the periphery.
Cut out the center—and there will be still balance and sequence in
what remains. Yet the new whole will impress us as somehow
empty and defective. Similarly a straight line of thought leads from
Kant to Schiller, the Romanticists, Schelling, and Hegel. To draw
it accurately we need not even mention Goethe. Yet such an historical picture would leave us with the impression that German
esthetics, however admirable and profound, was on the whole a
wayward adventure, a colorful speculative mirage. In dealing with
Goethe, we feel under our feet the firm ground of reality. From
speculative flight we return to experience, though not to the experience of everybody. Experience has hardly ever been interpreted by
as great a genius. Hardly ever has a human eye been wider open
to reality.

The singularity of Goethe's position makes it difficult to appraise
his contribution at its true value. The German thinkers around him
came to the beautiful, the realm of the visible and audible, from
the transcendent and invisible. They found it a tremendous effort
to reach the sensuous appearance of beauty, and the happy attainment of this end was for them the supreme test of their speculative
enterprise. Solger declared beauty to be a paradox because it united
the infinite life of the Idea with finite existence. This is only the
extreme expression of a conviction underlying German esthetics
as a whole. For Goethe, on the contrary, beauty was the most
natural thing in the world. His mind, imperturbably clear and
sovereign, was at home in the world of appearance. He was a
native of his fellow-countrymen's promised land. Still the realm
of the transcendental was not unknown to him. He believed in the
"inscrutable" that encompasses the sphere of our experience; he

---

[48] *Op. cit.,* p. 264, Part II, §62.

taught men "to revere it quietly"; he pointed out its vestiges in nature around us and, in his Orphic poetry, he grants us a glimpse of the mystery. But the attempt to unveil it by speculation violated, it seemed to him, the sacred bounds of human competence. "About the Absolute in the theoretical sense," he wrote with implicit reference to Post-Kantian speculation, "I dare not talk; yet I maintain that he who has recognized it in appearance and keeps his eye constantly fixed on it, will derive a great benefit from it." [49] The emphasis, in this sentence, is on the word "appearance." [50]

It is a marked feature of German philosophy since Kant that it does not accept reality as an unquestioned datum but tries to find its origin in the cognitive process. Again Goethe's outlook is exactly in counterpoise with this 'subjective' approach. The secret of his achievements, he explains, is that he has never thought about thinking.[51] Pious and grateful acceptance characterizes his attitude towards the world, and intuition (*Anschauung*) is his means of taking possession of it. Very different from the introspective "intellectual intuition" (*intellectuelle Anschauung*) in Fichte and Schelling, the Goethean *Anschauung* is entirely absorbed in the object; it is a faithful visualizing of the world. Goethe alone among modern thinkers is capable of adopting the language of the great Pre-Socratics; for like them he viewed reality as a cosmos. One of his Heraclitean fragments reads: "For the gods taught us how to imitate their own work; yet we know only what we do, ignorant of that which we imitate." [52] Again Goethe stresses the limits of our power without casting a doubt on the reality of that prototypical sphere which he symbolically denotes by "the gods." "We know

---

[49] "Maximen und Reflexionen über Literatur und Ethik," *Werke, Grossherzogin Sophie Ausgabe*, XXXXII, 142.

[50] Wilhelm Dilthey characterized the working of Goethe's mind as "intuitive thinking (*anschauliches Denken*) constantly animated by a feeling of the unity of the universe." "Goethe und die dichterische Phantasie," in *Das Erlebnis und die Dichtung*, 6th ed., 1919, p. 249.

[51] "Zahme Xenien," 7. Series:
> "Wie hast du's denn so weit gebracht?
> Sie sagen, du habest es gut vollbracht!
> Mein Kind, ich habe es klug gemacht.
> Ich habe nie über das Denken gedacht."

[52] "Aus Makariens Archiv," *Grossherzogin Sophie Ausgabe*, XXXXII, 185.

only what we do," that is, the limits of our knowledge are determined by the limits of our activity. There is no act of pure
contemplation beyond our practical life, revealing Being as such.
Even the pure visualizing, practiced and exalted by Goethe, is a
mode of activity, the assimilation and appropriation of reality by
the subject.[53]

GOETHE BOTH A
SUBJECT FOR ES-
THETICS AND A
TEACHER OF IT.

The uniqueness of Goethe's place consists further in that he
occurs in the history of esthetics in two capacities: as a subject and
as an agent. He taught what art is by his poetical work and by
his personality even more effectively than by his theoretical assertions. In his person, people felt, the creative imagination itself dwelt
among them and estheticians looked upon the working of his spirit
as on the living model from which they abstracted their theories.
But they viewed creative imagination not as the mere play of a
natural force to be analyzed like any other phenomenon in nature.
Their search for a definition of beauty was bound up with the
quest for a beautiful life. Now in Goethe's person this ideal, or
at any rate one aspect of it, appeared to have become flesh and
blood. The crucial question, with both esthetic and ethic relevance,
was how to unite the intellectual and the sensuous part of human
nature into a harmonious whole. Nature herself seemed to have
solved this problem by bringing forth the perfectly well-built and
healthy constitution of this man. He expressed the animal element
of human existence with so unimpeachable a grace that he makes
us forget the boldness of his language. Then again, even when
speaking of the mysteries of the world as a poet and seer, he loses
nothing of his simple and modest humanity. It has often been remarked that the search of the German thinkers after the truth in
beauty involved a religious aim. Goethe was destined to become
the object of this intellectual worship.

The distinction between Goethe the subject of esthetic analysis
and Goethe the teacher of esthetics, however important, does not
involve divergent intellectual bases. The reason for this is that
Goethe's theory consists largely of self-explication. He never

---

[53] When Novalis characterized Goethe as a "practical poet," he had in mind
this pragmatic trait of his nature; *Schriften*, ed. Paul Kluckhohn, 1928, 4 Vols.,
II, 404.

uttered his ideas on general esthetic topics in a systematic form; and the numerous and momentous sayings which he pronounced on various occasions constitute a part of what he himself called a confession. Confession, however, with Goethe does not mean the revelation of his intimate self, but rather the reflection of that process in which his self extends and transforms itself into a world. Goethe's confessions express the growth of his wisdom. Accordingly his esthetic thought is neither a detached analysis of the object nor the introspective mirroring of the individual self.[54] It is a reflection accompanying and furthering artistic creation. As the goal of this reflection is to raise the creative act to a higher level of validity, it reveals primarily the universal features of the imaginative process. Thus, while presenting true knowledge, it remains nevertheless self-revelation. That is to say, it reveals the individual Goethe engaged in the process of *Bildung*, self-formation. The genuine Platonic idea of "fashioning oneself"—a metaphor taken from sculpture—revives in the German poet.[55] Through *Bildung* man comes to inhabit a sphere within which moral excellence, complete rationality, and esthetic activity combine to form, the sphere of the "universally human." Again this "universally human," humanity in man, is not a transcendent idea nor an abstract law. Its embodiment in personality is both a gift and an achievement. No ardent effort, no earnest striving can do more than evolve the "coined form" that Nature has stamped upon each of us.

There is still another aspect of Goethe's uniqueness. From the very beginning of its development in Baumgarten, or, to go still further back, from its beginnings in early Greek philosophy, esthetic thought had either subordinated art to philosophy or classed both together. This analogy contained the germs of an ancient rivalry which was to become more and more the force behind the new developments. The keener the struggle in grasping for the

HARMONY OF INTELLECT AND IMAGINATION IN GOETHE.

---

[54] Charles du Bos, in "Aperçus sur Goethe" (*Approximations*, 5ième série, 1932, p. 175ff.), characterizes the poet as an "anti-introspective genius." The author derived valuable information from this fine and profound study. Nowhere else has he found a more adequate analysis of the specifically Goethean outlook on life.

[55] Plato, *Republic*, 500 d.

Absolute in Post-Kantian philosophy, the more conspicuous becomes this competition. Goethe is outside and above such conflict. In him the antagonism of the rival powers is appeased and supplanted by a fruitful coöperation. Occasionally, it is true, he uses harsh and scornful words in his references to philosophy. But then his target is rather a special type of philosophy, that modern school of thought which teaches man to shut himself up in his own mind and to ferret out the nature of its secret operations.[56] Moreover these outbreaks are matched by no less unfriendly remarks against poetry, uttered in the period when Goethe's interest in natural science was dominant. In the deeper layers of Goethe's mind there is perfect harmony, even coincidence of the creative and the cognitive faculty. In one of his most important documents of self-revelation, Goethe said, speaking of himself in the third person: "A poet's ever active impulse toward shaping (*poetischer Bildungstrieb*) working progressively both inwardly and outwardly, forms the center and the basis of his existence." [57] The word *poetisch* in Goethe's saying must be assigned that full meaning which brings to mind the original sense of ποιεῖν, to make, to create. Now this formative or creative striving which Goethe discovers at the very heart of his existence is neither an artistic nor a theoretical faculty. It is both. It is even more than this, for it embraces the whole sphere of conduct. It denotes all that human activity which elicits order out of chaos, which discovers or produces form, law, connection, meaning. If a world is reality perfectly appropriated by man, then this elemental striving may be termed cosmogonic nisus or instinct of world-creation.

It would be a mistake narrowly to characterize the above sentence as 'idealistic.' Goethe likens the subject modelling his world to a flame devouring the wick.[58] Again he tells us he always believed the world to be more ingenious than his own genius.[59] There

---

[56] "Der Sammler und die Seinigen," 2. Brief, *Werke, Jubiläumsausgabe*, XXXIII, 141.

[57] "Fragment," 1797, *Propyläenausgabe*, XI, 451.

[58] Conversation with Riemer, *Goethe's Gespräche, Gesamtausgabe*, ed. Freiherr von Biedermann, 5 Vols., 1909–11, I, 255.

[59] Cf. Charles du Bos, *op. cit.*, p. 289.

is not pure spontaneity and creative impulse on the one side, and pure passivity on the other. Whenever genuine production takes place, whenever there is a leap forward through human achievement, an individual must have encountered something akin to himself. We may desiderate such an encounter and make ourselves ready for it. Since, however, the event itself cannot be willed or calculated in advance, creation belongs to the super-human sphere of the demonic.

The creative impulse may be put to work in the sphere of knowledge. So Goethe studied the nature of colors, made important discoveries in the field of anatomy, and contributed to discussions of meteorological problems. In all these endeavors nature was for him the revelation of a continuous and visible order. His aim was to throw this order into prominence, to make it, so to speak, more visible. At the same time he was eager not to overstep the boundaries of this visible world—the world to which our sense-organs joyfully respond and which can be reproduced by artistic imagination. Therefore he rejected Newton's theory of optics as failing to take into account the immediate effect of colors in our perception. For the same reason he loathed telescopes and microscopes—artifices which distort the natural perspective of experience as conditioned by the human organism. And where others would have posited an idea or an abstract law to explain a series of phenomena, Goethe tried to get hold of an "original phenomenon" (*Urphänomen*), the crystallization of the lawful order in a single visible thing. So the passage say from a meteorological investigation of the nature of granite to poetry was for him a passage from one extreme to the other, from the study of the most static to that of the most volatile object in nature. But this change, in Goethe's mind, was the shifting from one object to another (both objects, after all, being mutually related as parts of one and the same world) rather than a radical change of procedure and outlook. The artist, no less than the meteorologist and the botanist, is a student of nature intent upon revealing truth that eludes the superficial observer.

IMAGINATION ANTICIPATES REALITY. THE ARTIST MASTER AND SLAVE OF NATURE.

Merck had early divined the nature of Goethe's genius. He said to him these perspicacious words: "Your tendency, your invincible bent is to confer a poetical shape on reality; others seek to realize the so-called poetical, the imaginative, and this leads to nothing but nonsense." [60] Goethe accepted this diagnosis. About half a century later he said to Eckermann: "All my poems are occasional poems, they are stimulated by reality and rooted in it. I do not think much of poems taken out of the air. . . . Nature shall yield the subject, the topics to be expounded, the very nucleus; yet to mold out of this a beautiful, animated whole is the poet's business." [61] On the basis of these principles Goethe advised Eckermann and others how to proceed in their poetical endeavors. These poetical lessons of the old master, invariably inculcating a minute study of nature, should be taken in their context, that is, in relation to the purpose of the master and the character of the pupil. They do not contain ultimate truth about poetry, nor do they reflect Goethe's own practice. A remark concerning his own experience reveals a deeper knowledge. "I wrote my *Götz von Berlichingen*," he said, "as a young man of twenty-two, and ten years later I marvelled at the truth of my representation. As a matter of fact I had not experienced or seen anything of the sort, and consequently I must have possessed the knowledge of manifold human conditions by anticipation." [62] Then Goethe adds these even more notable words: "When afterwards I actually found that the world is such as I by myself had imagined it to be, it became a nuisance to me and the pleasure I took in depicting it was gone. Indeed, I dare say: had I postponed the representation of the world until I knew it, my representation would have turned into persiflage."

Time and again the idea has emerged that poetry is an anticipation of rational knowledge. The remark just quoted, based on a wider experience than any other student of this problem may boast of, testifies to its truth. Yet for Goethe himself this is only a partial truth. The phases of his life are marked by alternating passages from poetry to science and from science to poetry. And every time the revival of poetic creation discloses a new sphere of

---

[60] Johann Heinrich Merck, *Schriften und Briefwechsel*, in Auswahl herausgegeben von K. Wolff, 2 Vols. 1909, I, 10.

[61] *Gespräche mit Eckermann*, September 18, 1823.

[62] *Ibid.*, February 26, 1824.

insight, anticipates an unexplored realm of truth. In another conversation with Eckermann he discusses the inconsistent treatment
of light in a landscape of Rubens: the figure shadows cast backward into the picture, and the tree shadows cast forward toward the
spectator. Goethe justifies this inconsistency by appealing to the
specific laws of imagination. "If imagination did not give birth to
things which for ever will remain enigmatic to reason, then imagination would be altogether but of small account." [63] Combining the
idea of anticipation and that of the supremacy of imagination,
Goethe's point of view may be paraphrased as follows. Poetry,
and art in general, is anticipation. As such it may be partly superseded by rational experience. But in its very essence a work of art
anticipates that which eternally eludes verification through experience. Hence the artist may be said to be at once the slave and the
master of nature. He cannot change the details, for example the
anatomic structure of an animal body, without destroying the
particular character of nature. But the whole which he desires to
create is not found in nature. It springs from the artist's spirit;
or rather it is due to a "fructifying breath" blowing on him from
Divinity.[64] So the freedom of imagination is not arbitrariness.
Guided by inspiration it anticipates a stratum of reality with which
we are for ever denied communion in terms of ordinary knowledge.

The creative process, then, for Goethe develops as a play of
action and counter-action between nature and the artist. In this
emulation both competitors are finally victorious. The artist surpasses nature and attains to the Divine or, as Goethe likes to say,
the Demonic. But if only his art is great and pure, his work stands
revealed as a "second nature" rather than as a super-sensuous oblit-
eration of nature.[65] Twice Goethe has described the phases of this
emulation as a dialectical progress. It is characteristic of the practical element in Goethe's esthetic thought that these two analyses
refer to painting instead of to poetry. In a field where his genius
refused to lead him to an easy victory, auxiliary reflection sprang
up the more abundantly. The first treatment of the subject bears

THE CREATIVE EM-
ULATION OF ARTIST
AND NATURE.

[63] *Ibid.*, July 5, 1827.
[64] *Ibid.*, April 18, 1827.
[65] *Ibid.*, February 26, 1831.

the title "Simple Imitation of Nature, Manner, Style." [66] In the
first stage, the artist faithfully devotes himself to the rendering
of nature. A high perfection can be reached on this level, and
such humble but fruitful tasks may be best performed by a calm
and loyal though somewhat limited mind. A bolder spirit will find
out that many details must be sacrificed to render more visible the
predominant features, and so progress to a second phase. He chafes
at merely spelling out nature's message. To express its meaning he
invents an artistic language of his own. Since, however, this language is bound to reflect his personal outlook, there will be as
many languages as artists. This "easier method" of expressive representation is called 'manner' (*Manier*) by Goethe, taking the word
in "a high and respectable sense." Yet the more freely the artist
uses the self-invented abbreviations of reality, the farther he drifts
away from nature. At last his language may become a meaningless routine. A return to nature only can save him and finally
raise him to the peak of perfection, to style. Style again results
from the study of nature. However it is based not on the perception of the object presented to our senses, but on the very fundamentals of knowledge, on "the essence of things, in so far as we
are granted the recognition of it in visible and palpable shapes." [67]

The parallel exposition, in the paper "The Collector and His
Friends," analyzes the single creative act. The initial stage, the
modest representations of the single object or the individual being,
is felt to be unsatisfactory. The artist then proceeds to take a bird's
eye view of a whole series of kindred beings, studies both their likenesses and their dissimilarities and ultimately arrives at the conception of the genus. But the generic idea impresses his mind as lifeless.
The sculptor for example who molds an eagle will not be content
with representing him as "the eagle as such." He must confer upon
him that divine quality which makes him worthy of sitting on
Zeus' sceptre. With the attainment of the Divine a third and, it
might be assumed, the supreme stage of the artistic process is
reached. But this time Goethe feels that the development has as yet

---

[66] "Einfache Nachahmung der Natur, Manier, Stil," *Jubiläumsausgabe*, XXXIII, 54ff.

[67] *Ibid.*, p. 57.

not come full circle. Grasping the ideal, he says, man is lifted above himself. But he is unable to persist for long in the state of adoration. Longingly he glances backward and downward, recalling his early affection for the individual. At the same time he is unwilling to give up the higher meaning and to return into the narrowness of his former outlook. While he lingers, baffled and uneasy, Beauty appears and happily solves the riddle. She unites the apparently incompatible elements. She fills the notion with life and warmth and softens the ideal and meaningful by endowing it with grace, thus bringing it nearer to us. "A beautiful work of art has completed the circle; it is again a kind of individual which we embrace with affection, which we may appropriate." [68]

Beauty is here introduced as an event, a happening as incalcu- LOVE CREATES
lable as inspiration. Yet it is not an event isolated from the context BEAUTY.
of our life. The search for the nature of beauty culminates and ends in a praise of the divine power of Love—Love, that great artificer who eternalizes the image of the beloved by creating it afresh every moment. Goethe has expressed all these ideas through the person of a young philosopher, unmistakably a portrait of Schiller. At this point of the discussion, he rids his hero of his opponent, a stolid defender of Hirt's idea of the characteristic as the supreme value in art.[69] Thus gracefully knitting together doctrine and poetry, Goethe offers his philosopher an opportunity to declare his love to the charming Juliet. As in Plato's *Banquet* Love is the power guiding the soul upward beyond the realm of nature. In Plato Eros leads the soul to the colorless and shapeless 'beautiful in itself.' For Goethe, however, as for Heraclitus, the upward and the downward path are one. Love lifts us above life; then, engendering beauty, it ties us all the more closely to life. It initiates us into the mystery of "Die and become!"

The outlines, then, of Goethe's esthetics may be sketched in a few summarizing sentences. Wisdom fixes and guards limits. Love, lending wings to imagination, leads it first to transcend these

---

[68] "Der Sammler und die Seinigen," 6. Brief, *Jubiläumsausgabe*, XXXIII, 179.
[69] Cf. Ludwig Hirt, "Über das Kunstschöne," *Horen*, 1797. Subsequently Hirt's term "characteristic" was adopted by Friedrich Schlegel and used for the definition of the romantic ideal. Cf. p. 380.

limits by anticipation, then to acquiesce within the limitation and to generate beauty. In Greek life Goethe found the wisdom to which he himself was aspiring, in Greek art a perfection teaching him how to express his own vision of beauty. The story of a passionate love—the Helena Interlude in *Faust* II—is the adequate poetic symbol of his loyalty to the Greek ideal. If such veneration and such love form the basis of classicism, then Goethe was indeed a classicist. Goethe himself, rejecting a narrow conception of classicism, said: "Who must take ratio (the measurable) from Antiquity, should not bear us a grudge, because we wish to take the immeasurable from Antiquity." [70]

HUMBOLDT'S ES-
THETICS PART OF A
UNIVERSAL AN-
THROPOLOGY.

To a large extent the esthetic writings of Wilhelm von Humboldt (1767–1835) are homage paid to Goethe's creative genius. He proposed a definition of the epic—and this definition was based on a poem of Goethe. He expounded his views on the laws of poetic creation—and again what he did was to portray Goethe's procedure as learned from the master's pronouncements or abstracted from his creations.

Humboldt's esthetic inquiries were only a part, and not even the most important part, of a plan of wider scope—a universal "Anthropology." This anthropology, like that outlined by Herder, was to combine extensive empirical observations with a regulating norm. It aimed at the representation of a 'human ideal,' reached not by abstract argument but by comparative study of the actual variety of human characters, habits of life and thought, institutions, and inventions. Humboldt assumed that human life naturally tends towards a uniform ideal. The existence of multiple human types and races, he held, is not an accidental fact but is required by the ideal itself. Nothing short of this tremendous wealth of varied forms was needed to express fully the nature of Man. The best approach, in Humboldt's opinion, to an anthropology of universal scope is the study of the systems of signs arising out of human intercourse. These signs are the most adequate expression of man's profoundest interests, bringing to light the uniformity as well as the variety of human nature. Thus the idea of an anthro-

---

[70] "Maximen und Reflexionen über Kunst," *Jubiläumsausgabe*, XXXV, 328.

pology led to a "universal symbolism." [71] An analysis of various systems of signs was proposed, all of them pointing, in the last analysis, "from a given finite to a never perfectly known infinite." [72] In executing this gigantic plan Humboldt developed his "universal science of language." His esthetic doctrine sprang from the same context of ideas. Within the scheme of his anthropology, art appeared the most human of human creations, manifesting with utmost clarity man's place in the universe: "As in mankind natural necessity is wedded to liberty, so we see in beauty matter coupled with form." [73] Consequently "art is to be ranked not with the mechanical and subordinate activities which only prepare us for our true destiny, but with the supreme and most sublime ones by which we immediately fulfill it." [74] An original meaning attached itself to these general statements from their connection with the analysis of creative imagination in the essay "On Hermann and Dorothea."

Humboldt defined art as "the ability to make imagination productive in accordance with laws." [75] The laws of imagination derive from Nature to which it is intimately related. Another definition reads: "Art is the representation of Nature through imagination." [76] Representation differs from imitation taken as a mimicking of given objects: "Art consists in the destruction of Nature as reality and her reconstruction as product of the imaginative power." [77] Nature, here, is obviously a metaphysical conception, and imagination is credited with the power of revealing the ways of Nature, inscrutable to reason. We may remember Moritz's analogous theory of a dual psychic faculty and Goethe's idea of a "second nature" created by the artist. [78]

---

[71] Eduard Spranger, *W. von Humboldt und die Humanitätsidee*, 1909, p. 327.

[72] *Briefwechsel W. v. Humboldt und F. H. Jacobi*, ed. A. Leitzmann, 1892, pp. 77f.

[73] *Gesammelte Werke herausgegeben von der Preussischen Akademie; 1. Abt.* herausgeg. v. A. Leitzmann, 7 Vols., 1904–1908, I, 351.

[74] *Ibid.*, II, 129.

[75] *Ibid.*, III, 12f.

[76] *Ibid.*, II, 133.

[77] *Ibid.*, VII, 2.

[78] "Zu Diderot's Versuch über die Malerei" (Propyläen), *Werke, Jubiläumsausgabe*, XXXV, 215.

Humboldt based his "esthetic metaphysics" upon a description of the creative act and of esthetic appreciation. In the initial stage of creation, the artist comes in contact with some beautiful object. This object engages and increasingly absorbs his attention, until he feels the fervent desire to grant existence to something similar to it. He wishes to form an image endowed with that magic power which holds him spellbound. Thus his sole aim will be to reproduce faithfully what has so deeply interested him, and to give the image the highest possible degree of likeness. Inadvertently however, the very ideal of fidelity to the model leads him to abstract from its appearance. Eager to imitate the essence, he feels compelled to move farther and farther from that compound of accidental features falsely honored with the name of reality. He then transforms the object in order to preserve its nature. At last he recognizes that by all his concern for truthful imitation, he involuntarily created his own image. The contemplator of this image has to tread in the artist's footsteps. The listener to poetry, like the poet himself, has his eyes fixed upon the represented subject. "He takes an interest in it, but slowly and gradually; yet every moment the warmth with which he embraces it increases, until at last it reaches the supreme degree of intimacy; he believes he lives only outside his own being and in the object, until he notices at last with joyful astonishment that a great change has taken place in himself through the object, shaking his mind to its innermost core and lifting it to an ideal sphere." [79] Meanwhile, the poem itself seems to have been similarly changed. "We cease to see only Hermann and Dorothea, we discern in them the greatness of man and of woman, animated by the deepest human feelings and guided by supreme human energies." [80]

The description of the creative and reproductive process yields three esthetic laws or, as Humboldt puts it, three degrees of objectivity: "determinate objectivity" corresponding to the initial attachment to an experienced object, "lively sensuous representation" resulting from the artist's growing intimacy with the appearance of his object, and finally "objective structure based on laws"

---

[79] *Werke*, II, 170f.
[80] *Ibid.*, II, 188.

(*gegenständliche Gesetzmässigkeit*). Only in the last stage the integration of the object, its amalgamation with the artist's imaginative life, is fully achieved. These laws furnish special rules when applied to the separate arts. Humboldt confined himself to the epic. He defined it as the poetic representation of a plot by narration such that, not designed to arouse one and only one definite sensation, it creates in our mind a state of most intense and comprehensive contemplation.[81] Thus the epic poem fulfils in even a higher degree than either the lyric or the drama the purpose common to all poetry, of "affording mankind complete self-expression." [82]

In his analysis of the creative process, Humboldt described the artist's activity as closely related to man's pursuance of his supreme end. It is "the greatest and most difficult business," "man's final destiny," "to connect in the most intimate way the outer world around him and himself, to take the world in first as an alien object, and then return it as an assimilated object bearing the marks of free creation." This may be what the artist does in his way and with his instruments: "The material offered to him by observation is organized by him so as to yield an ideal form conceived by imagination, and the surrounding universe appears to him as nothing else than an altogether individual, living, harmonious whole of multifarious forms, limited nowhere, dependent on nothing, subsisting entirely for itself. Thus he has transferred his inmost and best nature into the world and made it over to a being with which he is able to commune." [83] These assertions may be understood to mean that the "anthropomorphic world" created by the artist exists only in man's imagination. Humboldt's later esthetic reflections more and more preclude this subjective interpretation. He emphasized increasingly the metaphysical element of his doctrine. The world of forms visualized by the artist appeared now as the basis of reality. We said earlier that for Humboldt "art is the most human of all human creations"; to this may now be added, it is also the most adequate symbol of the deity.[84]

---

[81] *Ibid.*, II, 241.
[82] *Ibid.*, II, 273.
[83] *Ibid.*, II, 142.
[84] *Ibid.*, III, 146.

SCHILLER THE
MORALIST SYMPA-
THETIC TO KANT,
SCHILLER THE POET
CRITICAL.

Within the development of German thought Goethe's vision of the world formed a cosmos of its own. Humboldt rendered the important service of expressing this Goethean substance in the philosophical idiom of the time. But it was left to Friedrich Schiller (1759–1805) really to fuse Goethe's unique intuition with the powerful current of philosophical thought initiated by Kant. And from this fusion a whole new philosophical scheme was to spring. In Hegel the fusion is complete. In his system, we may say, Goethe's spirit is omnipresent. So Schiller's contribution marks a turning-point in the history of both German esthetics and German philosophy in general.

First of all Schiller was a Kantian in the strict technical sense of the word. He raised the problem of esthetics in terms of the transcendental method. The main difficulty is, he wrote to his friend Körner, "to establish a conception of beauty in an objective form and to legitimate it wholly *a priori* by deduction from the nature of reason. Experience should thoroughly verify this conception which, however, does not need such testimony for its validity." [85] A great poet adopting Kant's rigorously abstract philosophy and on this basis elaborating an original theory of beauty—this is a surprising sight. Goethe, we feel, would sooner have become a Minister of State and an author of petty ordonnances than submit his natural language to the foreign rule of Kantian terminology. Both the fact and method of Schiller's philosophical labor require an explanation.

Kant's moralism, the root of his dualistic conception of the world, appealed to a kindred element in Schiller's nature. The clash between the moral idea and the powers of "hunger and lust" ruling this world of ours is the recurrent theme of his dramatic poetry. In Schiller's case this tension was interwoven with an antagonism of the bent toward abstraction versus the gift for imagery. He belonged to the type of the orator-poet. The wealth of imagery and music latent in his language needed, so to speak, the awakening breath of thought to make them live. By his dynamic moralism Schiller was destined to become Kant's pupil, by the

---

[85] January 25, 1893, *Schillers Briefwechsel mit Körner*, 2d ed., Karl Goedeke, 2 Vols., II, 5.

antagonism in his talent to become his critic. In the functioning of his intellectual life abstract reasoning played a rôle exactly the reverse of that of reflection in Goethe's creative process. For Goethe reflection stemmed from a surplus of conscious energy. It was creation carried beyond the limits of poetical representation. Schiller, on the contrary, arrived at poetry through philosophical thought. For him philosophy was a means of freeing himself for creation. It was with him a matter of conscience not to set about his poetical work before having obtained a clear idea of the 'significance' of which his poetry was to carry the weight. Goethe knew from the very outset "what he was doing," Schiller did not.

To say that Schiller used philosophy to rid himself of philosophy sounds like playing with words. Yet such is the simple truth. The precise meaning of the paradox is to be learned from Schiller's criticism of Kant's esthetics. While accepting Kant's method he declared himself dissatisfied with Kant's definition of beauty. The "subjective conception" of beauty, he thought, must be supplanted by an objective one. With a view to such a revision of Kant's doctrine he proposed in the so-called "Kallias Letters" his own definition: "Beauty is freedom in appearance." [86] The progress of this definition (and of its modification in the Letters on Esthetic Education) towards objectivity consists in the substitution of genuine manifestation for symbolic pointing. The real is revealed instead of lying underneath as an inscrutable base. Only half aware of the far-reaching consequences of his innovation, Schiller put in the place of Kant's vision of reality a poetical reality, or more precisely a reality fitted for poetical representation. Once this goal was reached, Schiller turned away from speculation and devoted his all to poetical creation.

THE SYNTHETIC FUNCTION OF SCHILLER'S THEORY.

Kant's vision of reality (this is implied in the foregoing assertion) was especially unfitted for furnishing subject-matter to poetry. Greek philosophy did away with the tragic conception of man by banning passion and exalting the ideal of self-control. Kant's philosophy did the same in an even higher degree. For him man as a moral being is a citizen of two worlds. In moral action

---

[86] *Ibid.*, II, 14.

the world of Reason intervenes in the causal chains of the world
of appearance. But this intervention, which reveals the distinctively
human in man, is hidden from the observer who clings to appearances, that is, from the poet. Respect for the law, the only impulse
prompting a good action according to Kant, is wholly severed from
the common affections and passions. But the poet cannot admit
any such severance and rupture in human nature. For him man may
be a disintegrated and rebellious unity, but must remain a unity.
His world may be threatened with disruption and ruin by inherent tensions, but it must be one world. Schiller the moralist
was attracted by Kant's dualistic system. Schiller the poet had to
regain the unity of human nature and of the human world. But it
was not in Schiller's nature simply to throw away Kantianism and
philosophy. He had to achieve the conquest of the realm of poetry
by philosophy and so to outstrip Kant by Kant's own instruments.
Accordingly only on the surface was the issue between these two
an esthetic one. Actually the discussion hinged upon a moral and
metaphysical problem. Having expounded the dualistic conception of man derived from Kant, Schiller exclaims: "How then shall
we re-establish the unity of human nature, a unity that appears
completely destroyed by this primitive and radical opposition?" [87]

Now the pledge of this unity was present to Schiller in a living
person and a great historical phenomenon: in Goethe and the
Greeks. In the letter that opens the famous correspondence between Goethe and Schiller, Schiller portrays the newly gained
friend as a preëminently intuitive genius. The intellect, guided
by imagination, reveals the world as one and human nature as an
original unity. This Goethean unity was Schiller's ideal. His own
starting-point in dualistic speculation hinted at a want. I float, he
writes, "like one with two natures between ideas and perceptions." [88] His thinking is an oscillation between these two poles:
between dualism as the spring and monism as the terminus of his
speculation. In his own opinion Goethe's standpoint was higher,
or at any rate more appropriate to poetical creation. Yet his atti-

---

[87] "Letters upon the Aesthetical Education of Man," Letter 13, in: *Essays
Aesthetical and Philosophical*, newly translated, London, 1906, p. 63.
[88] August 31, 1794.

tude toward Goethe was not the deference of the inferior genius to his better. Their friendship was one of equals. Schiller was proudly conscious that the passionate striving after a final unity (a process which involved an intellectual and moral as well as an artistic development) endowed his work with a greatness of its own.

In Schiller's bipolar philosophical scheme the one pole which was conceived partly as the contrast to his own nature, partly as a supreme end to strive for, is shown under different aspects and embodiments. From a moral point of view it is represented by Schiller's idea of the "beautiful soul." In a man who deserves this name, duty and natural instinct work in perfect accord.[89] The harmony of reason and imagination, or esthetic perfection, took shape in Greek Antiquity. And in Goethe these two aspects interpenetrate. As a contemporary Goethe's person and work assume an even higher significance for Schiller. By his very existence he proves that it is not a hopeless undertaking for a citizen of the modern world to strive after harmony. This peculiar constellation of ideas drove Schiller to write his essay on *Naïve and Sentimental Poetry* (1795). In it the desire of placing his ideal within in his philosophical cosmos is combined with a defense of his own way of poetizing.

"ALL POETS ARE NATURE OR SEEK NATURE."

All poets, says Schiller, either are nature, or seek nature. Naïve poetry imitates by clear-cut individual pictures the ideal of humanity as given to it without effort. The capacity of the naïve poet is a first jet of inspiration; there is no thought nor correction; all is accomplished by immediate happy feeling in the presence of a benign nature, by a rejoicing in a oneness with it. The vision is unclouded and clear-cut; the images of the naïve poet are the direct simple discourse of the keen and pleased observer. The sentimental poets of modern times have lost the happy state of union with a favoring world, and they look back with yearning on a different age. This breeds the reflecting and idealizing habit. They sigh for what they have not. And the consciousness of their lack leads them to reëstablish the lost union as Idea. In the dawn of humanity

---

[89] "On Grace and Dignity," *op. cit.*, p. 203.

there is a perfect accord between the imagination and the understanding; sensations and sentiments spring from necessity and
thoughts from reality. But with civilization this primeval harmony
ceases. The power of the Ancients consisted in compressing their
objects into the finite; and the Moderns excel in the art of the
infinite.

The contrast in spirit between the two types of poetry can best
be shown by an example. Schiller contrasts the inspiration that
filled the soul of Homer when he depicted his divine cowherd giving
hospitality to Ulysses, and that which agitated the world of the
young Werther when he read the Odyssey on issuing from an
assembly in which he had found only tedium. "The feeling we
experience for nature resembles that of a sick man for health." [90]
He also illustrates the contrast by confessing his own early distaste
for Shakespeare. Brought up in an age essentially sentimental, that
is, in a time when the reader was encouraged to look behind the
work for the artist, "to meet his heart, to reflect with him on his
theme, in a word, to see the object in the subject," he felt that
Shakespeare was heartless because he could not discover a separate
personality behind. "Like the Deity behind the universe, the naïve
poet hides himself behind his work; he is himself his work, and his
work is himself." [91]

What Schiller asserts with reference to the naïve forms of life
and expression in general applies especially to the Greeks: "They
are what we were, what we must be again some day. . . . We perceive eternally in them that which we have not, but which we are
continually forced to strive after; that which we can never reach,
but which we can hope to approach by an infinite progress." [92]
Friedrich Schlegel was to derive from these sentences his philosophical scheme of world history and the idea of romantic poetry as
'progressive universal poetry' (*progressive Universalpoesie*). For
Schiller however the distinction of the two types, though applicable
to history, primarily denotes a psychological rather than a historical
antagonism. True genius, he says, is guided only by nature and
instinct. Therefore it is of necessity naïve or it is not genius. [93]

---

[90] *Op. cit.*, p. 280.
[91] *Ibid.*, p. 281f.

[92] *Ibid.*, p. 264f.
[93] *Ibid.*, p. 272.

Shakespeare, and above all Goethe, are examples of the naïve genius in modern times. Schiller admits that poets of this order are scarcely any longer in their place in this artificial age. But whenever they appear, "the seal of empire is stamped on their brow." [94]

Schiller's chief theoretical work, and one of the classic texts of German esthetic literature, is the *Letters upon the Aesthetical Education of Man* (1793–94). The tendencies of his thinking here reach their consummation. Schiller 'justifies' artistic beauty in a double sense of the word: he deduces the idea of art from a conception of reason and man, and he assigns to it a purpose within practical life. This practical and speculative justification of art involves the absorption of the Goethean vision of reality in Kantian philosophy. Schiller leads us from a dual conception of the world to a union that rises triumphantly above all cleavages and dissonances and makes us forget that the origin is a metaphysical antagonism. This speculative ascent, regarded as a link in the evolution of ideas, prepares a new type of speculation fully developed by Schelling and Hegel. Considered as an autobiographical document, it marks Schiller's progress from philosophy to poetical creation. THE CORRUPTION OF MANKIND AND THE PROBLEM OF AN ESTHETIC EDUCATION.

In this mature essay the starting-point is no longer an abstract dilemma but rather a pressing moral and intellectual need, the experiencing of the actual events of the time. He begins with a dramatic picture of the moral status of contemporary man, conceived within the frame of his impression of the French revolution. Mankind then seemed on the verge of overthrowing the primitive political machinery based on force which served merely to preserve the race. The age of the new state, organ of human freedom, seemed to dawn. But man failed to live up to the demands of this great hour, revealing instead the depth of modern depravity in its twin forms: brutality and effeminacy. It became obvious that contemporary man is morally unworthy of political freedom. But how is it possible to raise man and to educate him for his royal task of self-rule, so long as the essentially immoral condition of unfreedom lasts? Thus on the level of political thinking the problem necessarily is circular.

---

[94] *Ibid.*, p. 284.

To discover the remedy we must study more closely the nature and causes of the illness. It was, Schiller says, culture itself that inoculated society with the germs of disease. The refined diversification of functions in social life, though promoting the ends of society as a whole, threatens the single soul with disintegration. "With us there is a sharp separation of the sciences, a strict sundering of ranks and occupations, a rupture between state and church, laws and customs; enjoyment is separated from labor, means from end, effort from reward." [95] Man has in these latter days of the efficient division of labor lost his internal totality. "Man himself, eternally chained down to a little fragment of the whole, only forms a kind of fragment; having nothing in his ears but the monotonous sound of the perpetually revolving wheel, he never develops the harmony of his being; and instead of imprinting the soul of humanity on his being, he ends by being nothing more than the impress of the craft to which he devotes himself, of the science that he cultivates This very paltry and partial relation, linking the isolated members to the whole, does not depend on forms that are given spontaneously; for how could a complicated machine which shuns the light, confide itself to the free will of man?" [96]

Greek life furnishes the foil of the gloomy picture of modern civilization. "In Greek culture . . . the senses and the spirit had no distinctly separated property. . . . Poetry had not as yet become the adversary of wit, nor had speculation abused itself by passing into quibbling. . . . An all-uniting nature imparted its forms to the Greeks and all-dividing understanding gives our forms to us." [97] In other words, happy circumstances, natural conditions of time and place and climate favored Greece toward that happy issue of harmony of faculties that for the modern man is a laborious achievement. Every god embodied the totality of human nature. Wholeness and harmony of human attributes was implied in the Greek notion of divinity.

Schiller's criticism of his age has its roots in a dissatisfaction of the critic with himself. The short-comings which he detects in

---

[95] Letter 6, *op. cit.*, p. 38f.
[96] *Ibid.*, p. 39.
[97] *Ibid.*, p. 37f.

life around him point to the problem with which he himself labors. This becomes obvious, when he traces the disintegration of modern civilization back to its source in philosophical thought. He writes: "The speculative mind, pursuing inviolable goods and rights in the sphere of ideas, must needs have become a stranger to the world of sense and have lost sight of matter for the sake of form." [98] No doubt these remarks allude to Kant's philosophy and to Schiller's own Kantianism. Modern culture, Schiller thinks, must heal the wounds which it has inflicted. This demand, applied to the deepest layer of cultural life, to the practice of philosophy, reads: speculation with its own instruments must overcome the self-created dualism. The hiatus in life, as we shall soon see, is to be bridged by art. Correspondingly the philosopher's contribution to the work of unification and salvation consists in thinking, art. For Schiller himself the fulfilment of the latter task was preliminary to entering upon his specific office: to educate through art.

The idea of beauty as a mediator between form and matter, reason and sense was already present in Kant's *Critique of Judgment*. But within the confines of Kant's system the development of this conception was restricted by the character of the fundamental dualism. To posit for example a balance between form and matter would be senseless, because a balance can only exist between forces of equal right; and matter is nothing but a limit in Kant's scheme of thought. It exists only by virtue of form. Therefore in the "Kallias Letters" Schiller had striven in vain to express in Kant's language his conception of beauty as "freedom in appearance." This definition implied the idea of a form which succeeds, after a hard struggle, in subduing matter—a thoroughly non-Kantian idea. Before writing his Letters on Esthetic Education Schiller became acquainted with Fichte's publications. Here he found a clue for his difficulties and the *Letters* are Fichtean rather than Kantian in method.

Two impulsions, Schiller says, compose the essence of human nature and constitute his world: the sensuous instinct (*Stofftrieb*) and the formal instinct (*Formtrieb*). The first determines man as

THE PLAY-DRIVE RESPONSIBLE FOR ARTISTIC CREATIVENESS.

---

[98] *Ibid.,* p. 41.

a finite being confined to a limited space and placed in time. The second impulsion issues from his free and rational nature and tends to impose law and order upon the diversity of impressions furnished by the sensuous instinct. As man is both matter and spirit, it is his task to keep these two coördinate instincts in balance. To secure this balance as the truly human state of the human being, Schiller introduces a third 'drive,' the play-impulse which constitutes beauty and art.

At a first glance the term 'play' in this connection may surprise and baffle the reader, the more so, because the whole discussion moves somewhat ambiguously on the border-line between trans-cendental analysis in Fichte's style and an empirical anthropology. The idea of play does not, as later in Spencer, merely form the contrast to the life-preserving activities. Rather it implies a double negation. A play or game is conducted in accordance with rules. But these rules are a free creation. They are prescribed neither by natural necessity (the sensuous instinct) nor by moral law (the formal instinct). They exhibit perfect lawfulness. But at the same time they suspend the never ceasing conflict between the law of nature and the law of reason, between force and liberty. The result is a phenomenon mediating between Appearance and Free-dom—freedom in appearance according to the formula of the "Kallias Letters."

The prerogative example of the appearance of freedom in beauty always remained to Schiller's mind the Greek genius. "It is neither grace nor is it dignity which speaks from the glorious face of the *Juno Ludovici;* it is neither of these, for it is both at once. While the female god challenges our veneration, the godlike woman at the same time kindles our love. But while in ecstasy we give ourselves up to the heavenly beauty, the heavenly repose awes us back. The whole form rests and dwells in itself—a fully complete creation in itself—and as if she were out of space, without advance or re-sistance; it shows no force contending with force, no opening through which time could break in. Irresistibly carried away and attracted by her womanly charm, kept off at a distance by her godly dignity, we also find ourselves at length in the state of the greatest repose, and the result is a wonderful impression, for which the understanding has no idea and language no name." [99]

The object of the sensuous instinct is Life, a concept that denotes here all material existence that is presented to our senses; the object of the formal instinct is shape or Form in the widest acceptation. Hence beauty, as the object of the play-instinct, may be characterized by the name of 'living form.' [100] As however no' real creation will ever perfectly conform to the ideal requirements, beauty met in experience will always belong to one of two types. The type of 'gentle beauty' will arise when that softening and moderating effect prevails which keeps the two basic impulsions within their bounds. To stimulate them the opposite type called 'energetic beauty' is required. According to the frame of mind to which they are applied, they may either help to overcome a weakness or, on the contrary, increase a deficiency and one-sidedness of character. [101] Only the true artist, who is the son and not the creature of his epoch, will know the need of his fellow-creatures and mete them out their wholesome dose. The artist, on the other hand, who is lacking in such wisdom, will add to the existing corruption.

Owing to the duality of impulsions in his make-up man has to face a choice. He must choose whether he wishes to put his trust in the formal instinct and live a free life; or whether he will allow himself to be overpowered by the passivity of his sensuous nature. The state of mind of a man who confronts this choice but who has as yet not chosen may be imagined in two different ways. It is either the merely negative indifference of the mind comparable to a blank tablet. Or, on the other hand, we may, as it were, live in suspense, wide awake to all the implications of the choice before us, perfect master of both our passive and active powers, ready to turn with equal ease either to the gay or grave, to rest or movement, to abstract thinking or intuition. "This high indifference and freedom of mind, united with power and elasticity, is the disposition in which a true work of art ought to dismiss us, and there is no better test of true esthetic excellence." [102] Thus finally we have

---

[99] Letter 15, p. 72.
[100] Letter 15, p. 68.
[101] Letter 16, p. 73ff.
[102] Letter 22, p. 90.

arrived at the idea of passage or transition sought for from the outset of the investigation. The problem of how man can be guided from slavery to freedom, from animal existence to moral life, is solved: "There is no other way of making a reasonable being out of a sensuous man than by making him first esthetic." [103]

AN ESTHETIC IDEAL OF HUMAN PERFECTION.

However, Schiller proved more than he set out to prove. That state of energetic aloofness and readiness created by the intuition of beauty is not really, or at any rate is not exclusively, moral indifference. On its face-value it is a transitory moment in the passage from sensuous to rational life. Accordingly beauty seems merely an instrument of moral progress that may later be dispensed with. Yet the drift of Schiller's argument urges upon us a different interpretation. The transitory moment of neutral preparedness, as a balance and harmony of powers, is in itself a consummation. Man, Schiller says, is completely a man only when he plays; and he adds that the whole edifice of both esthetic art and art of life must be made to rest on this principle.[104] If a balance between the two basic impulsions is the most human state of a man, what further kind of perfection can he crave or reach without endangering his humanity? We may imagine a purely moral attitude which results from the unquestioned predominance of the 'formal instinct.' But this condition, as it involves the crippling of one half of humanity, would compare unfavorably with the esthetic state. So we conclude that this esthetic equipoise, a "self-limitation out of inner power and wealth," is in the last analysis not the indifference preceding moral decision but rather the result of a choice and representation of a supreme value. Schiller, coming from Kant's dualistic moralism, chooses a new ideal of humanity. This choice is bound up with a synthesis of Kant's transcendental method and the Greek or Goethean vision of man and the cosmos. It was left to Schelling and Hegel to draw out the philosophical implications of Schiller's enterprise. Schiller himself was content with having defined his own position as an artist. Is poetry futile in the hour of great moral and political decisions? He was now able to answer this question by an unambiguous No.

---

[103] Letter 23, p. 93.
[104] Letter 15, p. 71.

The upshot of Schiller's essay stands in still another way at variance with the problem raised in the first letters. The way Schiller opens his argument leads us to look forward to a magnificent prospect in the epilogue. We expect art to be celebrated as the true liberator of mankind, paving the way to a free and dignified life for the whole human race. In fact the following generation of romantic and idealistic thinkers reared their visionary buildings on the foundations laid by Schiller. They prophesied the fusion of poetry and philosophy and a life in accordance with their joint creation. As befits the typical exponent of classic style, Schiller was more sceptical and realistic. He asks at the end of his exposition: "Does such a state of beauty in appearance exist, and where?" And he answers: "It must be in every finely harmonized soul; but as a fact only in select circles, like the pure ideal of the church and state—in circles where manners are formed . . . by the very beauty of nature; where a man passes through all sorts of complications in all simplicity and innocence, neither forced to trench on another's freedom to preserve his own, nor to show grace at the cost of dignity." There is an element of resignation in this conclusion. But it is, so to speak, a creative resignation. What appears a renunciation on the level of philosophy, is at the same time a stimulant of poetical creation.

SUPPLEMENTARY READING

E. F. Carritt, "The Sources and Effects in England of Kant's Philosophy of Beauty," *Monist*, 35 (1925), pp. 315–28.

E. F. Carritt, *The Theory of Beauty*, Ch. V.

Victor Basch, *Essai Critique sur l'Esthétique de Kant*, Paris, 1927.

R. A. C. Macmillan, *The Crowning Phase of the Critical Philosophy*, London, 1912.

J. C. Meredith, *Kant's Critique of Aesthetic Judgment*, Oxford, 1911. (Introductory essays.)

E. Caird, *The Critical Philosophy of Immanuel Kant*, 2 Vols., Glasgow, 1889, Vol. II.

George Santayana, *Three Philosophical Poets: Lucretius, Dante, and Goethe*.

Thomas Carlyle, *Essays on Goethe*, 1828–32.

Thomas Carlyle, *Life of Schiller, Comprehending an Examination of His Works*, 1846.

Ernst Cassirer, *Idee und Gestalt. Fünf Aufsätze*, 1921.

Venturi, *History of Art Criticism*, Ch. VIII.

Bosanquet, *History of Aesthetic*, Ch. X.

CHAPTER XII

German Romanticism

THE GENERATION that entered the arena at the beginning of the nineteenth century was brought up on the poetry and esthetic ideas of Goethe and his contemporaries. This early experience left an indelible mark on the minds of those born about 1770. They either fervently admired or violently repudiated what had been achieved. But even by their criticism they betrayed how much they were indebted to their predecessors. In general the conviction was in the air that a gigantic work, carrying with it the reform of art and of life itself, had been planned and started, but that at a decisive stage the workmen had shrunk back from their own project and had thus failed to finish their edifice. Therefore it fell to the younger men to proceed unswervingly on their way, drawing conclusions from their elders' premises.

Though often boldly original, they may properly be called heirs and successors, just as the thinkers of the earlier stage were essentially pioneers, in spite of their many borrowings from English and French thought. It is this peculiar historical position which accounts for the perfection as well as for the shortcomings of Romantic esthetics. Assisted by a refined sensibility and a natural liberty of mind, the Romantic thinkers ingeniously worked upon the fundamental ideas handed down to them and applied them to new experiences. Owing, however, to a lack of elemental experience revealing life as it is outside literature and art, they lost grip on reality, confusing the poet's dream, the moralist's ideal, and the metaphysician's intuition.

Taking the achievements of the generation of 1770 as a whole and including the idealist philosophers (who should not be reckoned

371

as Romanticists) we perceive certain general distinctive features. In the first place, there was a strong demand for a controlling higher unity. Kant had only cautiously hinted at an 'unknown ground'— a basis common to the practical and theoretical reason. His romantic and idealistic followers, not content with a mere inkling of the Absolute, wished to grasp it and to explain how it discloses its nature in the hierarchy of beings. A highly intensified metaphysical rationalism resulted from this new ideal. In the second place, art, especially poetry, was taken to be the supreme fact. Though not the Absolute itself, it was the privileged form in which the Absolute was supposed to reveal itself. A poetical interpretation of all philosophical problems sprang from this assumption. Though idealism did not necessarily imply the romantic exaltation of art, Novalis' and Schlegel's romanticism did imply idealistic metaphysics. Idealism furnished an apt instrument for elaborating the worship of art into a system. The brilliant rather than solid products of this synthesis fall short of the self-consistency of the idealist systems, and words borrowed from Fichte and Schelling assumed a slightly different shade of meaning when pronounced by Novalis or Friedrich Schlegel. But even so, the alliance between the philosopher of the new type and the romantic magician was a natural one. Both desired to grasp the Absolute and 'construe the universe.' 'Measure and harmony,' 'simplicity and still greatness,' resignation—these were the catchwords of the Classic. An enthusiastic ἓν καὶ πᾶν gave voice to the longing of the younger generation.

WACKENRODER'S GOSPEL: ART IS RELIGIOUS SERVICE.   Youthfulness is the very nature of the romantic aspiration. German romanticism, similar in this respect to that of Shelley, was adolescent. The movement begins with a typical document of puberty, *The Heartfelt Outpouring of an Art-loving Monk* (1797). Its author, Wilhelm Heinrich Wackenroder (1773–98), died at the age of twenty-five soon after the publication of his book. In these papers, he artlessly relates the lives of artists and anecdotes illustrating their work. Albrecht Dürer, little esteemed at the time, is celebrated as the master of a truly German art as it was in the good old days: sturdy, honest, and profound in all its simplicity. This sentimental nationalism is inoffensive and liberal. In a vision Wackenroder sees Dürer and the 'divine' Raphael standing hand in hand and contemplating in friendly silence their juxtaposed pictures.[1] Wackenroder as a theorist wished to feel, not to reason. Belief in a system seemed to him worse than superstition. Art, he believed, issues from the depths of a heart undefiled and fervently devoted to God. It is religious service, the artist God's humble servant, his work communion with his Maker. Depicting the things of this world he follows in devout love the vestiges of the Creator's workmanship, visible in the blade of grass as well as in the structure of the universe. This esthetic gospel was preached with the accents of a gentle and almost bashful sincerity. It is 'unmanly' in the highest degree. But the limited and undeveloped truth which these papers contain could hardly be presented more adequately. To unfold the truth—and also the error—of the romantic position was left to others.

"Poetry is a genuine absolute reality. This is the gist of my philosophy. The more poetical the more true." [2] Acknowledgment of poetry as 'supreme fact' cannot be expressed more strongly than by this fragment from Novalis (the pen-name of Friedrich von Hardenberg, 1772–1801). His paradoxical saying was not meant to apply to all poetry but to the spirit or essence of poetry and the hoped-for purity of it in future achievement. He spoke of poetry as it actually is, as it ought to be, and as it will be, thus combining the claims of the metaphysician who defines the essence, of the poet who reveals his poetical ideal, and of the prophet who foretells a future development. Novalis' Utopian poetry is identical with philosophy. Both poetry and philosophy furnish a representation of the mind, "the inner universe in its totality." [3] Another fragment says: "The distinction between poet and thinker is merely apparent and to the disadvantage of both. It is symptomatic of a morbid constitution." [4] All the fine arts share in the philosophical dignity of poetry. They all help to realize the "Kingdom of Spirit."

NOVALIS: MYSTIC IDENTIFICATIONS AND THE MAGIC UNIVERSE.

---

[1] *Herzensergiessungen eines kunstliebenden Klosterbruders, Werke und Briefe,* ed. F. von der Leyen, 1910, 2 Vols., I, 62.

[2] *Schriften,* herausgegeben von Paul Kluckhohn, 4 Vols., 1928. "Neue Fragmentensammlungen," 1798, II, 411.

[3] *Ibid.,* "Neue Fragmentensammlungen," 1798, II, 363, 367.

[4] *Ibid.,* "Brouillon 1798–99," III, 137.

Music is nothing but a perfect form of hearing; painting a "perfection of seeing." [5] We remember that Schiller regarded artistic play as a harmonious employment and balance of the soul's active and passive energies. Novalis, in the last citation, goes further, actually identifying activity and passivity, productivity and receptivity. The artist's mind, surrendering itself to the universe, rouses in it a full capacity for rendering itself both visible and audible. Beauty, according to the classic interpretation, establishes a balance between sense and intellect which preserves their independence. In the ecstatic experience of the Romantic thinkers this distinction of the two spheres disappeared altogether. Perfection of visibility came to mean the transfiguration and spiritualization of appearance, the absorption of terrestrial dawn into mystical daylight. Whenever it happens that the distinction between poetry and philosophy is revived, this works to the disadvantage of philosophy. Sometimes philosophy is treated as the hand-maid of poetry, its function being to explain what poetry is, *viz.* "One and All." [6] Then again it ministers to poetry as forerunner and herald. Philosophy gives law and order to life. Then poetry teaches us to embrace this law with joy. In assimilating philosophy to poetry, Novalis returned in a curious inverted way to the old rationalistic esthetics of the eighteenth century and acknowledged Baumgarten's definition of beauty as true. [7] In the age of reason, Baumgarten had modestly advocated the appreciation of poetical values by stressing their kinship to rational perfection. In the later epoch, when poetry had reached independence and authority, the romantic poet-philosopher subjected reason to poetry.

The romanticist was not content to synthesize poetry and philosophy alone. Life itself was summoned to enter that magic circle which transformed everything into poetry. He conceived morality as an art; [8] he demanded that even processes of industry

---

[5] *Schriften*, "Neue Fragmentensammlungen," II, 360.
[6] *Ibid.*, II, 375.
[7] *Ibid.*, "Brouillon 1798–99," III, 240.
[8] *Ibid.*, "Neue Fragmentensammlungen," II, 363.

should be "poetically" carried through.[9] He foretold a universal human society which should be bound together by poetry, as the 'household' (*Haushalt*) of the universe is ruled by its spell.[10] According to the classical doctrine, esthetic joy and appreciation constitute a middle state of mind between subjection to a foreign command and self-indulgence in a purely inner life. Removing the barrier separating pressure from without and spontaneous impulse, Novalis no longer discriminated between objective reason ruling the universe and the imaginative sense that the poet confers upon his creations. The assertion of poetry as cosmic power followed naturally. The real world and the world of imagination were blended into one dreamlike realm of shadows. This hybrid world, far from being irrational, shows a high degree of systematic order. It binds together the remotest phenomena into an organic whole like a work of art. But at the same time, it lacks all those features that make reality real. This magic universe is presided over by the creative mind—a replica of Fichte's demiurgic self. But in Fichte's idealism, the absolute self building up reality by gradually limiting itself was clearly distinguished from the individual self. Novalis deliberately confounded the two, producing thus the fantastic imagery of his enchanted universe.

Novalis' doctrine, in spite of its paradoxical conclusions, contains an element of truth. We can imagine a poet who, in the hour of inspiration, turns from poetic creation to a philosophical interpretation of his own state of mind. It is exactly this that Novalis did. What was thus exposed to the light of consciousness was neither the process of poetical creation nor the growth of philosophical intuition but a dreamlike vision prior to both, and containing elements of both. This vision shared in the imaginative freedom of art as well as in the rationality of metaphysics. Not content with the poet's unconscious wisdom, Novalis longed for greater clarity of understanding. At the same time he shrank from the hardship and labor that reality lays upon the philosopher. He lingered thus before an alternative which he refused to acknowledge. With perfect candor he relates to us his experiences in an

THE DREAM-LIFE AS SOURCE OF INSPIRATION.

[9] *Ibid.*, "Fragmente der letzten Jahre," III, 298.
[10] *Ibid.*, "Die Christenheit oder Europa," II, 82ff.

intermediate sphere, where no one else could have lived and breathed, even for the short space of time that was granted to Novalis.

The subconscious sphere, upon which Novalis drew, reveals itself in dream-life. For the common sense of waking life, dreaming is an evasion of reality, beautiful or horrid, refreshing or depressing, but at any rate isolated from everyday life. This is not so for the romanticist. He will not interpret dreams in terms of waking life but life in terms of dream-experience, convinced that it reveals a profounder stratum of universal existence. In this way a highly sophisticated system of thought links with ancient religious ideas. The romantic dreamer, listening attentively to the confused murmur that rises inwardly in him in the stillness of the night, discerns prophetic voices. His poetry then becomes a means for insuring a local habitation to the floating images and emotions of his dreams. The truths realized in subconsciousness, unattainable by ordinary experience, not to be uttered in common language, are brought to life by the magic word. It is well known that when we dream, even the most familiar things take on a tinge of utter strangeness. This is precisely the effect which romantic poetry wishes to catch. "The art of estranging in a pleasant manner, of making an object appear alien and yet familiar and attractive—this is romantic poetry," says Novalis.[11] Another of his sayings reads: "Our life is not a dream, but it should become one and it is likely to attain this end."[12] The romantic poets discovering the purely musical values of language conferred upon words a magic fascination hostile to logical precision. They knew that the dream can only be evoked, not described. Ludwig Tieck developed the notion that poetry is verbal music,[13] and Jean Paul, expert and theorist of dream life, wrote: "The dream is to poetry the vale of Tempe and its motherland,"[14] and he called dreams

---

[11] *Schriften*, "Fragmente der letzten Jahre," III, 348.

[12] *Ibid.*, II, 98; cf. Albert Béguin, *L'âme romantique et le rêve. Essai sur le romantism allemand et la poésie française*, 2 Vols., 1937, II, 93ff.

[13] *Phantasien über die Kunst, für Freunde der Kunst* herausgegeben von Ludwig Tieck, 1799; ed. Jacob Minor in *Deutsche Nationalliteratur*, Vol. 145, p. 88.

[14] "Über die natürliche Magie der Einbildungskraft" in *Leben des Quintus Fixlein, Sämtliche Werke*, G. Reimer, 1840, 33 Vols., III, 235f.

"involuntary poetry." [15] The observation of dreams led him to emphasize the passive attitude of the poet toward his vision: "The true poet while writing is only the hearer, not the master of his characters, that is, he does not patch up their dialogue according to a standard painfully acquired from psychology but he intuits them as living in a dream, and then he listens to them." [16]

A playful enjoyment of unreality is the subtlest among the refinements of social life. Thus the romantic disintegration of reality inspired the ironical and enthusiastic conversations, letters, pamphlets, and poetical productions of a circle that made Jena a center of German literary life. Novalis, its youthful prophet, moving in his own solitary sphere, did not allow himself to be fully drawn into this witty and fanciful community. But his friend Friedrich Schlegel (1772–1828) was destined to become its head. No less eccentric and radical in his views than Novalis, he was more keenly conscious of his idiosyncrasies. Novalis lived entirely in his magic universe. Schlegel, aware of and yet scorning the real world, gave license to a 'divine insolence.' At the same time, the realistic component of his nature enabled him to give a more substantial content to the romantic doctrine by bringing it into contact with historical facts. Though ironically disguised as a mock prophet, he was actually an eminent critic of poetry. His program of the romantic movement as given in his early aphorisms pretended to usher in a new era. If, however, we strip these false pretensions of their trappings, we discern a genuine vision of art and its history. This is Schlegel's essential contribution to esthetics: he introduced the notion that art, and especially poetry, does not move through history as through an indifferent medium which only superficially affects its modes of expression, but that its very essence is involved in the process of evolution. Thus he became the precursor of Hegel and his philosophy of art.

This disproportion between what Schlegel pretended to do and what he actually did is particularly obvious in his "Discourse on Mythology." If we think only of the author's claim, we are

THE ROMANTIC SECT AND FRIEDRICH SCHLEGEL'S ESTHETIC PROPHECY.

---

[15] "Über das Träumen, bei Gelegenheit eines Aufsatzes darüber von Dr. Viktor" in *Briefe und bevorstehender Lebenslauf, Werke* XIII, 262.

[16] "Blicke in die Traumwelt," in *Museum* XI, *Werke* XXVII, 181f.

tempted to pronounce his enterprise a hopeless failure. Schlegel triumphantly acclaimed the advent of a new mythology. He believed he could read unmistakable omens in the poetry and above all in the physics of his time, and he assumed the task of helping on what was to be. It is easy for us to see that his prophecy was misguided. The would-be seer ignored the conditions that must underlie the arrival of a myth. At the same time his error contained a vestige of truth. Myth really is the fount of artistic creation. The researches of nineteenth century philologists, who were largely inspired by romantic ideas, have shown how pregnant was Schlegel's insight. Moreover, Schlegel's statements included a criticism of classical German poetry which was probably justified. In their uncertainty about proper subjects these poets had often made unfortunate experiments. Even Schlegel's claim to be a prophet has something in it. Auguste Comte's plan to institute a new cult for a new society, Hölderlin's groping after a synthesis of Christianity and Greek paganism, Nietzsche's attempt to erect Zarathustra's image as the central figure of a new belief, Wagner's revival of the Germanic myth, and finally the religious pretensions of the totalitarian states, might all be interpreted as his prophecies in some sense fulfilled. There was a demand for an interpretation of life, satisfactory to the emotional and imaginative faculties and freed from the suzerainty of reason. It is interesting to note that this new disintegrating impulse emerged in the field of esthetic experience. Schlegel's doctrine, however wrong, was wrong in a typical way. Its strained esthetic rationalism paved the way for modern irrationalism.

IRONY—THE FREE-   The reflections on mythology are only one aspect of Schlegel's
DOM OF THE RO-   esthetic program. On the whole this consists of a statement of the
MANTIC MIND.   meaning of romantic poetry, and Novalis shared in this part of the work. The mystic fusions which enabled Novalis to conceive his esthetic Utopia are used by Schlegel for the same purpose. But it was Schlegel who invented the suggestive slogans and furnished the final definitions. He coined the notion of irony under which caption he placed the romantic, what is romantic being at the same time what is highest in poetry. Schlegel was as much indebted to Fichte as to Novalis. In fact, his conception of irony is the esthetic

version of Fichte's moral dynamism. In an infinite progress, Fichte's 'self' transcends the stations of its self-limitation. Correspondingly, the ironic subject, never acquiescing in a definite shape, enjoys infinite freedom in ascending from one form to another. The end, however, of the first process is reality, the second dissolves reality and makes it over to an "artistically arranged chaos, the charming symmetry of contradictions, the marvellous eternal alternation of enthusiasm and irony." [17] Irony is thus the self-consciousness of the creative mind which, not fettered by a single form, plays with all in sovereign liberty. At the same time, it expresses the psychological fact of the self-consciousness that shuns creation and takes to the contemplation of its own abortive activity.

'Insolence' and 'cynicism,' practical applications of the romantic irony, were expressions of literary libertinism rather than of a metaphysical experience. The essential function of irony, in Schlegel's doctrine, was to make clear the program of the school. In his mind, this program was linked with an interpretation of the history of poetry. He tried to show that the form of poetry which he advocated was esthetically superior to earlier forms, and that it was conditioned by the historical development of art from the Greeks on. The forward look of Romanticism was bound to clash with the older 'classicist' esthetics which made the past perfection of Greek art an eternal pattern. Schlegel, loyally preserving this venerable dogma, as a romanticist made it lead to conclusions which altogether reversed its original intention.

At first sight, Schlegel's early criticism [18] seems to reassert the absolute superiority of Greek art. The author acknowledged Hellenism as the model of beauty and embodiment of esthetic law. Applying this unique perfection as a measure to modern, that is, post-classic art, he declared he had discovered a chaos of attempts testifying to an enormous expenditure of effort but never beauty. These assertions, though more classicist than classicism itself, were

THE CLASSIC AND THE ROMANTIC IDEAL RECONCILED WITHIN PHILOSOPHY OF HISTORY.

---

[17] *Seine prosaischen Jugendschriften,* herausgegeben von Jacob Minor, 1882, 2 Vols., II, 361.

[18] *Die Griechen und Römer. Historische und kritische Versuche über das klassische Altertum,* 1797.

intended to premise a 'glorious justification' of modern art; and this
historical justification contained in its turn the outlines of the
romantic program.

Like Winckelmann Schlegel regarded Greek art as the result
of a happy natural disposition. The Greeks, he said, lived in a state
of nature. For them intellect and instinct were in perfect harmony,
but instinct dominated. Thus the beauty of their creations appeared
as the reflex of their rôle in the drama of world history. They
produced beauty because in the evolution of the life of mankind
they represented the age of youthful beauty. But if age and art
must always correspond it is unfair to assess modern art with a
measuring-rod taken from the ancients. The peoples of the Christian era would have to produce an art of their own, in accordance
with their specific historical function. The old harmony would
go; a long and painful striving follow after, until finally Greek
perfection would come again on a new rational plane. The esthetic
measure appropriate to a life that consists essentially in the effort
to reach a far-off ideal is 'esthetic energy' instead of beauty, and
the products of energetic art are 'characteristic' instead of 'beautiful.' In the last resort, the standard for both Greek and modern
art is the same. But the embodiment of the identical ideal in the
former is naïve and direct, in the latter an energetic attempt guided
by reflective anticipation. Greek art is finite fulfilment, modern
art infinite approximation.

Schlegel himself acknowledged that his duality of classic and
characteristic (or romantic) art is a parallel to Schiller's distinction
of naïve and sentimental poetry. Yet the two conceptions differ
in that Schiller stated two essentially timeless categories; whereas
Schlegel's antithesis is of historical as well as of systematic significance. In both cases, the principle of the distinction is somewhat
ambiguous. Schiller had to admit that the 'sentimental' poet is a
poet only in so far as he is also naïve. Similarly, Schlegel's modern
or romantic poetry is poetry only in proportion as it shares in the
principle of classic art; it is as yet incomplete. Schlegel, shifting
from the interpretation of history to prediction of the future,
proclaimed the coming of a synthesis of poetry and science, the
joint triumph of the imagination and the intelligence, functions

to be reunited after a separation of two thousand years. This program proved useful in justifying certain peculiarities of romantic art. Both its lack of proportion and structure and the abundance of reflections and 'arabesques' could be explained by reference to the new ideal. The typical romantic creations—Novalis' *Heinrich von Ofterdingen*, Tieck's plays, or Arnim's novels—seem imperfect if they are considered as wholes and subjected to classic standards. To appreciate their value, we are requested to understand them as approximations to an ideal too sublime for full realization.

In many cases Schlegel's doctrine helped to justify the unjustifiable. But on the whole his bold construction had the merit of suspending the application of the classic norm to the works of the Christian era. Thus he successfully led the way for that expansion of esthetic appreciation characteristic of the nineteenth century. The immediate fruit of this revolution toward liberalism was the perception of the beauty of medieval art, Dante's *Commedia*, Shakespeare's tragedies, and Calderon's plays. That idea of a 'world literature,' sponsored by Herder and Goethe, was carried forward and enriched by new investigations and translations. Friedrich's brother August Wilhelm Schlegel (1767–1845), eminent critic and translator, systematized and popularized the new esthetic ideas.[19] Schleiermacher presented the scheme for the organization of the translation of all outstanding documents of the poetic spirit. Shakespeare's plays were made available in the classic German version. The touching simplicity of the old popular songs was rediscovered and savored. Along with all this, esthetics, as the theory of artistic creation and appreciation, had to face an entirely new problem. It was no longer possible to look upon Greek art as the timeless law-book of esthetic perfection. The philosopher could no longer transcribe into theory what Phidias had wrought in marble, Homer and Sophocles in Greek verse, and Raphael in frescos. Henceforth esthetic theorists had to take into account the whole diversity of artistic creation in all times and countries.

---

[19] A. W. Schlegel, *Vorlesungen über schöne Literatur und Kunst*, ed. J. Minor (*Deutsche Literaturdenkmale des 18. und 19. Jahrhunderts*, H. 17–19), 1884.

It is difficult to place correctly the esthetic work of Jean Paul (Jean Paul Friedrich Richter, 1763–1825). Is the doctrine expounded in his *Esthetics* [20] essentially romantic? There is much to be said for this view. He openly takes sides with the new school of poetry and philosophy. He makes use of Schelling's philosophical terms, and he devotes considerable space to setting forth the ideal of romantic beauty, which he regards as the natural outcome of Christianity and defines as "the Beautiful without limitation." [21] He emphasizes the essentially romantic character of the novel and there is no doubt that he reckons his own creations among romantic models. Yet he was no partisan, or at least no partisan of the romantic school proper.

Through the literary circle of Jena, the word 'romantic' had taken on a double meaning. In the wider sense, it described a tendency of modern art, exhibited with the utmost clarity in Dante, Shakespeare, and in some, at least, of Goethe's works, and directed toward an absolute but as yet unattained ideal. Only if we accept this use of the word, as Jean Paul himself did, may we class his esthetics as romantic. According to the more precise meaning of the word as denoting the creations of a clearly defined literary group, Jean Paul both is, and is not, romantic. He sympathized with the romanticists, but he disliked them too. He heartily greeted the bolder flights of imagination upon which they ventured; he shared their taste for the miraculous and for the dreaminess of moonlit scenery, enchanted gardens, and fabulous countries. But his sense of decency was shocked by their libertinism, and he was aware of the weakness of their creative powers. Under the heading 'Schlegeliana' he noted: "Poetic inclination does not make poetry nor conscience a saint. For both, beyond this a native gift is required." [22] In his esthetics the congenial description of the romantic type of poetry is balanced by no less sympathetic chapters on "Classic Beauty," which exhibit the author as a staunch believer in Winckelmann's classicist gospel. He praises the Greeks who knew "how to

---

[20] *Vorschule der Ästhetik*, first edition, 1804. The title of the book is misleading in so far as it deals almost exclusively with the theory of poetry.

[21] *Op. cit.*, §22, *Werke* XVIII, 96.

[22] E. Berend, *Jean Pauls Ästhetik*, 1909, p. 47.

make their bodies alive and spirited and to give their spirits a bodily habitation," [23] who shaped in marble images of gods and men indulging "in the *far niente* of eternity," [24] and who endowed poetry with objectivity, ideality, cheerful repose, and moral grace. No wonder that the arch-romanticist Tieck, feeling his friend to be not altogether his ally, declared himself dissatisfied with the *Vorschule*.

Jean Paul's esthetic writings cannot be classified with categories borrowed from the literary disputes of his epoch. He combines the traits of thought of the man of the eighteenth century with romantic imagination, a German Richardson fleeing from his sentimentality into glowing visions of supernatural worlds. This impartiality, on which he justly prided himself, corresponded to a conflict deeply rooted in his own nature. Owing to the continued striving for a state at least resembling harmony in himself, he became an equitable umpire in the disputes around him. This inner process left its mark on the very structure of his esthetic theory. It led him into a dialectic process and at the same time filled him with the spirit of a transcendent metaphysics. As a thinker he was always concerned with two opposite tendencies, as a believer with a world beyond this world. He considered his *Vorschule* the counterpart of his novel *Titan*, and both as evidence of his craving for inner harmony—in fact as 'Anti-Titans.' They proved, he thought, that the rational and plastic energies of his mind had got the better of the Titanic extravagance of his imagination.

We can trace the results of the basic conflict on three planes of his esthetic doctrine: in the dialectical discussion of esthetic creation, in the doctrine of poetic genius, and in the analysis of humor.

Jean Paul described esthetic creation as a 'beautiful imitation of nature,' regarding 'beautiful' as synonymous with 'spiritual.' The object of imitation is not the outward aspect of Nature with all its common casual detail, but its inner structure. This is the spirit and even the letter of Goethe's esthetic creed. But it is expounded in a very original way. Jean Paul distinguishes between

THE POET—INTERPRETER OF THE UNIVERSE.

---

[23] *Vorschule*, §17, *Werke* XVIII, 79.
[24] *Ibid.*, §19, p. 83.

materialists and nihilists. The materialist, unaware of Nature's universal features, treats it as a compound of particular objects presented to our senses. He has the 'dust of the ground' but he lacks 'the breath of life' to breathe into the nostrils of his creatures. Conversely, the nihilist possesses the animating spirit, but as he lacks solid matter, he enthrones a void instead of a substantial creation, filling the boundless space of inner life with diffuse imagery or indulging in the purely negative and critical activity of the mind. Deprived of matter, the control of universal ideas avails him nothing. Like a flame without fuel, his mind consumes the objects on which it fastens, reducing them to nothing. Both the materialist and the nihilist are denied the secret of form. It is the privilege of the creative imagination to combine opposed energies, and to establish a happy harmony in which particular and universal are wedded. It is creative imagination that makes the poet.

Like the preceding esthetic doctrines in Germany, Jean Paul's poetics is based on a theory of poetic genius. The poet is nothing but the true man—*homo maxime homo*—and, at the same time, the true interpreter of life and the universe. Every human being bears in himself all the various forms of humanity, all its possible characters, and the individual character is merely the 'creative choice' made between the infinity of worlds, the transition from infinite liberty to finite appearance.[25] "A genius is different only in that in him the universe of human powers and characters stands revealed like an image in high relief on a clear day, while in others the image lies unlit and corresponds to his own world like a sunken work. Humanity gains consciousness and speech through the poet; that is why he so easily arouses them in others." [26] Compared with poetry, all rational statements are one-sided and therefore threaten our liberty: "A single human being who pronounces a judgment on the world, gives us his particular world, a world diminished and broken up instead of a living and vigorous one, like a total without the items. That is why poetry is indispensable: because it presents to the mind only the world which is spiritually re-born, and because it does not enforce an arbitrary construction. Through

---

[25] *Vorschule*, §56, p. 243f.
[26] *Ibid.*, §56, p. 245.

the poet humanity addresses humanity only, not one man the
other." [27] Its polarity is an essential feature of the moral world:
"The most definite and best characters of a poet are, therefore,
two old and cherished ideals born with his own self, the ideal
poles of his acting nature, the sunken and raised sides of his humanity. Every poet gives birth to his own angel and his own devil;
the profusion or dearth of creatures between these two poles
determines his greatness or his deficiency." [28] Yet the poet's chief
merit is the representation of noble characters: "Great poets, if
they have the key to both, should more often open the door to
heaven than to hell. To bequeath to humanity a morally ideal
character, a saint, deserves canonization." [29] In the present age—
"a period in which religion, the state, and morals fade into obliv-
ion" [30]—the only remaining hope for their elevation is in science
and poetry. "The latter is the stronger."

Friedrich Schlegel, opposing the classical program, had attempted an esthetic justification of the characteristic. Jean Paul,
joining with the classicists, contended that poetry, ushering us
into the realm of intellectual necessity, has to reject the incidental
traits of a portrait, that is, individuality. Poetry must rise to the
species which represents mankind as a whole. In order to point
out that this generality is not incompatible with vital determination,
Jean Paul employs once more (as he did to explain the relation of
poetic genius to man as such) an idea taken from Leibniz. Like
the monad, each character somehow contains all characters, the
totality of human faculties and dispositions linked together in
proportions that vary infinitely. The poet is more typically human
than other men. This is why he can penetrate the rule controlling
the weaving together of particular and general features. Steering
a mean course between the abstract model of the species and the
casual image of the individual man, he is able to construe the
"symbolic individuality." [31]

---

[27] *Ibid.*, §69, p. 297.

[28] *Ibid.*, §57, p. 249.

[29] *Ibid.*, §58, p. 257.

[30] *Ibid.*, "Kantate-Vorlesung über poetische Poesie," XIX, 142.

[31] *Ibid.*, §59, XVIII, 259ff.

There are, however, some elements in Jean Paul's doctrine that are utterly different in spirit from classic esthetics. A gloss of Christian transcendence spreads over his fundamental metaphysical conceptions and even over his psychological observations. Goethe wished to train the artist's eye through careful study of organic nature; Jean Paul attributed to him the mysterious power of piercing the surface of things and discovering a hidden reality. His conception of the world is rather Platonic than Aristotelian. Like the Swiss critics in the middle of the eighteenth century, he defended the validity of the 'miraculous,' not as an astonishing event in the visible world but as the sudden disclosure of unfathomable depths of soul. The agency that sets in motion the poet's creative imagination is, according to Jean Paul, a supernatural instinct or a bent, a 'sense of the future.' "This instinct of the mind that perpetually anticipates and postulates its subjects without regard to time, since they are located beyond all time, enables one, by merely pronouncing the words 'terrestrial,' 'worldly,' 'temporal,' to understand them; for only this instinct is capable of giving them meaning through their opposites." [32] It sheds a light through the soul, and this marks a momentary victory of the divine in its internecine warfare against earthly things and our natural instincts. Because of the inner illumination, the poetic genius sees all things in their essential oneness. His imagination soars as high above the inferior concerns of life as does the "Spirit of Morality." Thus he is able "to paint on the veil of eternity the spectacle of the future" and to present in his art the "magic mirror of the time that is not." [33]

In Jean Paul's world finite things, depicted with all a primitive's patient care, are set off against the background of infinity. Poor little schoolmaster Wutz, a character in one of his novels, contains within himself dreams of wisdom and eternity, endowing his humble and shabby figure with dignity like the golden background in a medieval picture. This is the reason why much room is given in Jean Paul's novels and in the discussion of his *Vorschule* to the ridiculous as "infinite unreason, presented to the senses," [34] to wit,

---

[32] *Vorschule*, §13, p. 61f.
[33] *Ibid.*, "Kantate-Vorlesung," XIX, 141.
[34] *Ibid.*, §28, XVIII, 122f.

defined as "sensuous sagacity," [35] and to satire, irony, and humor. Humor, a crucial conception for him, is the reverse of the sublime. The sublime arises when the infinite appears in our finite world overwhelming our senses with its immeasurable magnitude; conversely, if we measure the infinite with the finite, the effect is humorous. "If man, like ancient theology, glances down from the world beyond on the terrestrial world, the latter looks small and vain; if he measures the infinite world with the small one, as humor does, connecting them with each other, then laughter arises wherein is sorrow and greatness." [36] Hence Humor, though "treading in the low buskin of comedy," carries the tragic mask in her hand. Indeed, the finest humorous creations are the work of a melancholy people, the Spaniards. Differing in this from parody and irony, humor annihilates not the single object but finiteness as such, setting it in opposition to the idea. "For humor there exists neither single follies nor single fools, but only foolishness and a crazy world; it does not emphasize some particular foolery but it lowers the great so as to place it side by side with the small, it lifts the small to associate it with the great, thus exterminating both because, confronted with the infinite, all is levelled to nothing." [37] Obviously this definition of humor comes close to the earlier descriptions of poetic imagination as guided by a 'supernatural instinct.' We may conclude that the humorist and novelist Jean Paul has dictated to the esthetic thinker. A similar observation holds good for his theory of the novel. The novel, regarded as a typically romantic form of expression, is the paramount poetic genus, combining the characteristics of both epic and drama, and bearing, as Herder had already remarked, a profound likeness to the dream.[38] The question arises whether Jean Paul's self-portrayal impeaches the validity of his doctrines. The objection would be justified if Jean Paul were not actually a true poet, and therefore, as the model and subject of an esthetic study, a symbolic individual.

---

[35] *Ibid.*, §43, p. 199.
[36] *Ibid.*, §33, p. 147.
[37] *Ibid.*, §32, p. 142.
[38] *Ibid.*, §70, p. 298.

The true poet is sage and prophet. This was the belief underlying the romantic identification of poetry and art in general,
poetry and philosophy, poetry and politics, dream and reality.
This basic claim was challenged by Sören Kierkegaard (1813–55).
He declared: poetry and wisdom (the only true wisdom which
is in the Gospel) are incompatible. To be a poet we must renounce
becoming what we are aspiring to become. This renunciation is
despair; and out of this despair springs the burning desire which
engenders poetry. Thus the delight in poetry, however rapturous
and profound, is born out of desolation. "The poet is the child
of eternity—but without the earnest of eternity." [39] In Kierkegaard's
theory the romantic dreamer awakes and deliberately destroys his
dream by analysis.

SUPPLEMENTARY READING

Irving Babbitt, *Rousseau and Romanticism*, 1919.
Oskar Walzel, *German Romanticism*, trans. from the fifth edition, 1932.
R. M. Wernaer, *Romanticism and the Romantic School in Germany*,
1910.
R. F. Egan, *The Genesis of the Theory of 'Art for Art's Sake' in Ger-
many and England*, Smith College Studies in Modern Language,
II, 4, and V, 3, 1921–24.
Georg Brandes, *Main Currents in Nineteenth Century Literature*, Vol.
2: "The Romantic School in Germany" (1873), trans. 1902.

[39] *Christliche Reden*, German translation, Jena, 1929, p. 292.

CHAPTER XIII

Romantic Ideas and Social Programs in England and America

THE BEGINNING SITUATION REVERSED.

IT IS no mere literary coincidence that in 1790 William Blake repeated almost exactly what Heraclitus had said in the fifth century before Christ. It is rather the sign of a reinstated situation. At the moment when the science of esthetics was coming to birth Heraclitus the philosopher had complained of the ignorance of the poet. The foolish poet prays for the cessation of strife because he does not know strife's deep meaning, Heraclitus declared. But, he added, without the opposition of sex there could be no creature born into the world.[1] In the opening 'argument' of *The Marriage of Heaven and Hell* Blake reiterates, as if even after thousands of years it were not too late to vindicate the deep wisdom of poets, the cosmic importance of opposites, the doctrine which Heraclitus had announced to confound the poets. "Without Contraries is no progression. Attraction and Repulsion, Reason and Energy, Love and Hate, are necessary to Human existence."[2] There are many places where Blake asserts the necessity of cosmic opposition, as when he says that the two classes of men, the producers and devourers, are always upon earth; that they should be enemies, and that whoever tries to reconcile them destroys existence;[3] or as when he asserts that Hell revives when Heaven begins.[4] But while both Heraclitus and Blake proclaimed that the war of op-

---

[1] Diels, 22 A, 22.
[2] *Poetical Works*, ed. Ellis, London, 1906, Vol. I, p. 240.
[3] *Ibid.*, I, 249.
[4] *Ibid.*, I, 240.

posites is father of all and king of all, and while both used this
truth as touch-stone for the wisdom of poets and philosophers,
Heraclitus proved by it that philosophers are wise and poets fool-
·ish, and Blake offered himself as a philosopher, however much
he might also be a poet. Thus in the latter half of the eighteenth
century, when the heralding beams of Romanticism were beginning to light up the horizon of English poetry and speculation,
the ancient quarrel of philosophers and poets was revived in all its
early vigor and with the picturesqueness of a pioneering imagination. Blake indeed referred to himself as "the voice of one crying
in the wilderness." [5] But the situation out of which the quarrel
and its esthetic treatment arose was the reverse of its ancient
prototype. In ancient Greece the poets had been for centuries the
accepted teachers of men, the revered sages. The philosopher had
then had to establish the claims of reason and order and science
in an open clash with poetical prophets and seers. But Blake was
an early lonely champion of prophecy and vision in a period when
reason and nature as known to the senses had been for two centuries the synonym of wisdom.

Everybody acknowledges Blake as an early romanticist in
England but at the same time treats him as something of a solitary.
He was so. But in his claim that the poet is the true wise man
Blake simply gives with singing resonance the key for the 'prefaces'
and 'defences' and philosophical essays of a whole line of poet-
prophets in England and America. These romanticists belong in
esthetics by virtue of their reassertion of the poet's claim to intellectual insight and because of their counter-blasts to the Lockians,
Cartesians, and Newtonians. Blake announces the new 'glad day'
of a released imagination in a language as strange to the ordinary
reader as Arabic, and with an arsenal of symbols drawn from
Swedenborg, Jakob Boehme, Paracelsus, and the Hebrew prophets.
The painful effort of making sense out of his words and ideas
heightens the impression of the distance between him and the other
romanticists. When, however, his esthetic ideas are collected for
and in themselves, they proclaim a scheme of creation and salva-

---

[5] *Poetical Works*, I, 212.

tion and a vision of beauty not very remote from those of other militant inspired mystics.

In the early 'Argument' from which we have already quoted, and in the seven succeeding 'Principles,' Blake asserts the primacy of 'the poetic genius.' All men and all religions, he says, have this one source. This Poetic Genius is also named the Spirit of Prophecy. The individual coloring of the religions of different nations comes from the way a particular nation receives the spirit of prophecy. Not only religious faiths but philosophical schools derive from this primordial source. They are offshoots of that Genius or Spirit that was in the beginning. Philosophy as we know it in systems is not philosophy in its full strength but adapted to the weakness of individuals.[6] In a 'memorable fancy' Blake reports dining with Isaiah and Ezekiel and having table-talk regarding the grounds of truth. Isaiah explains his criterion of the knowledge of God as not common sense-perception, but "firm persuasion." Blake inquires whether "a firm persuasion that a thing is so," makes it so. Isaiah then replies: "All poets believe that it does, and in ages of imagination this firm persuasion removed mountains; but many are not capable of firm persuasion of anything."[7] Isaiah proceeds to describe the all-conquering faith of the Jews in Poetic Genius as First Principle, King David's adherence to this principle, and his conviction that through it he conquered enemies and governed kingdoms. Blake, so he relates, first wondered and then was convinced. "Imagination is Eternity," on this view;[8] it is the body of the Savior as He exists in our minds and takes shape to our inner eye. Thus Blake associates the discernment of truth with the visions of the old Hebrew prophets and with religious revelation generally.

The poetic genius as diviner has his own peculiar object and his own peculiar organ in Blake's theory. His object is the Infinite —the Infinite which for him that knows is the true nature of all common things: of a knot in a piece of wood, of a grain of sand, of a wild flower, of "every Bird that cuts the airy way." He who

---

[6] *Ibid.*, I, 212–13.

[7] *Ibid.*, I, 246.

[8] *Ibid.*, I, 221.

sees the Infinite in all things, sees God.[9] This Blake lays down as a principle; he also puts it into the mouth of Isaiah: "I saw no God, nor heard any, in a finite organical perception; but my senses discovered the infinite in everything." [10] This Infinite which unfolds itself at the heart of all things is offset by 'the bounded' and 'ratios.' Here we have an ancient Greek opposition between the bounded and the unbounded revived, but preference given, not as with the classical Greeks, to what has limits, but as with all the romantically-minded and mystics, to what has nothing to check its power or compete with its all-inclusive reality. Blake associates the bounded with machines, and the unbounded with life. "This bounded is loathed by its possessor. The same dull round, even of a universe, would soon become a mill with complicated wheels." [11] With the attribute of Infinity in the Poet's object goes also the attribute of unity. His vision catches the eternal brotherhood of humanity and of all created things. Or to put it otherwise, he who sees God in all things sees the Divine Image in the forms of Mercy, Pity, Peace, and Love, which are the feelings that create a harmony out of the manifold existence.

THE POET AS SEER.   The organ of the Poet for Blake is spiritual sensation. This faculty is distinguished both from reason which yields only the 'ratios' of things to each other, and from the various compound senses. It is a kind of cleansed sensing or a clairvoyant capacity. From his childhood, when he saw the branches of trees occupied by perching angelic beings, throughout his life Blake had in high degree the power to see the absent as if present. And be believed that all truth-seekers should cultivate this ability: they should exercise their imaginations to the point of vision. Both schools of philosophy that had flourished during the seventeenth and eighteenth centuries would stand condemned by this standard. The Empiricists who stemmed from Bacon and Locke trusted the first deliverances of the ordinary senses as the foundations of knowledge; and Descartes and his successors classed imagination with error and rational deduction with truth. Blake shares with the Em-

---

[9] *Poetical Works*, I, 215.
[10] *Ibid.*, I, 246.
[11] *Ibid.*, I, 215.

piricists the appeal to perception and disbelief in systematic deduction; and with the Romanticists skepticism concerning the infallibility of the ordinary bodily inlets. Blake states his own 'epistemology' with almost cryptic terseness in an early manifesto. "Man's perceptions are not bound by organs of perception; he perceives more than sense (though ever so acute) can discover. . . . Man by his reasoning power can only compare and judge of what he has already perceived." [12] Imagination, then, is for Blake 'spiritual sensation.' It is God in Man intuiting the fitting object of Divine Vision. Blake puts it thus: "God becomes as we are, that we may be as He is." [13]

The Agent, Object, and Instrument of truth are all transformed then by Blake into what belongs to the Poet and the Genius. At the same time, all the excellences, whether of art, morals, or intellect, change from neo-classic moderation and order into types of extravagance, flux, and emanation. Beauty he defines as exuberance; [14] "the way to wisdom is through Excess"; [15] delight becomes energy. His philosophy like his favorite plastic design is one of fiery force, of rushing and floating and tension. "The cistern contains, the fountain overflows." [16] "Prudence," he says, "is a rich, ugly old maid courted by Incapacity"; [17] and number, weight, and measure, which for classic St. Augustine were the very essence of Divine Beauty become with Blake the emblems of death.[18] The classics he makes the source of desolation and war,[19] or again "Mathematic Form," [20] with which he contrasts the "Living Form" of the Gothic. Aristotle's rules for the unity and characterization of poems, which had been the backbone of the Neo-Classic creed, he definitely repudiates. He demands life and energy in a work of art; a torso, he says, can exhibit unity. "Unity and Morality

BLAKE'S DY-
NAMISM.

---

[12] *Ibid.*, I, 213–14.
[13] *Ibid.*, I, 214. Quoted from Athanasius.
[14] *Ibid.*, I, 245.
[15] *Ibid.*, I, 242.
[16] *Ibid.*, I, 243.
[17] *Ibid.*, I, 242.
[18] *Loc. cit.*
[19] *Ibid.*, I, 217.
[20] *Loc. cit.*

are secondary considerations, and belong to Philosophy and not to Poetry." [21] He has no more use for the eighteenth century creed of painting as given in Reynold's *Discourses* than for Aristotle and Horace. Enthusiasm rather than reason, any vividly outlined form rather than one central grand style, the particular rather than the general, are held up for praise, and so the issue is radically stated.

WORDSWORTH: POET IN DIRECT TOUCH WITH TRUTH.

If Blake was the Baptist, making straight the way for English Romanticism, Wordsworth in the various editions of the Preface to the *Lyrical Ballads*, his philosophical poetry, and in his association with Coleridge, may be fairly called the Messiah himself of that movement. The difference between the two seems at first too great to allow them to be related as announcer and announced. What can Blake's queer verbal coinages—Urizen, Ahamia, Luvah, Tharmas, Palamabrom—and his mystical clairvoyance substituting another world for the common one have to do with Wordsworth's realism, naturalism, and good sense? Blake himself expressed the difference in a marginal note to Wordsworth's poems. "Natural objects always did, and now do weaken, deaden, and obliterate imagination in me." [22] Blake saw floating forms, flames, and eerily twisted roots where Wordsworth looking steadily at his object saw London in the light of dawn, a cuckoo, a host of daffodils waving in the breeze, or humble folk in the business of rustic life. But both men trusted the poet's imagination as the vessel of wisdom, and repudiated the parcelling out of the intellect by geometric rules, [23] and the "False secondary power by which we multiply distinctions." [24] Both believed fervently in the myth-making poet's capacity through his vision to reveal ultimate truth, and distrusted the divisions and concatenations of dry system-makers. Both believed in experimental truth; that is, the truth that is felt and proved by the sensitive human soul, and chiefly by the poet's soul. The watch-words of the eighteenth century: taste, rules, forms, were discarded by both. This is the prime matter for the

---

[21] *Poetical Works*, I, 216.
[22] Burdett, *William Blake*, New York, 1926, p. 171.
[23] *Prelude*, Text of 1850, Bk. II, 203–4.
[24] *Ibid.*, Bk. II, 216–17.

esthetician, not the secondary question of how this philosophical truth finds its language and imagery. In various memorable passages Wordsworth assimilated the first principle of Romanticism: that the poet is prophet and sage, to its second: that poetical truth is truth of feeling. For example: "Poetry is the most philosophic of all writing: . . . its object is truth, not individual and local, but general, and operative; not standing upon external testimony, but carried alive into the heart by passion; truth which is its own testimony. . . . Poetry is the image of man and nature. . . . Poetry is the breath and finer spirit of all knowledge; it is the impassioned expression which is in the countenance of all science. . . . Poetry is the first and last of all knowledge—it is as immortal as the heart of man." [25] Thus Wordsworth puts his definition of the Poet in the "Preface." In the *Prelude* are records of the same conviction regarding the poet's high mission of revealing the ultimate nature of things. He, Wordsworth the poet, treads holy ground; he speaks "no dream, but things oracular"; [26] he has an "animating faith" that "Poets, even as Prophets" are bound together in "a mighty scheme of truth." [27] His endowment is "Heaven's gift"; by it he has an insight into things unseen before, and cherishes a hope that he may accomplish a work rivalling in its creative and enduring power, Nature's own. [28] If thus much binds Wordsworth and Blake together and makes them brothers in Romanticism, they differ in their theories of the object and instrument of poetic revelation. For Blake's symbolic and fantastic universe seen in telepathic vision Wordsworth substitutes the permanent reals and relations of nature and humanity. He states his purpose in writing the *Lyrical Ballads* as the pleasurable presentation of the primary laws of our nature, its essential passions, the elementary and more durable feelings, important moral relations. As some philosophical outlook informed much of the poetry of this period, so a metaphysics lies at the basis of Words-

FEELING.

---

[25] *Prose Works*, ed. Knight, 2 Vols., London, 1896, Vol. I, pp. 59, 60, 62. "The Preface to Lyrical Ballads."

[26] *Prelude*, Bk. XIII, 252–53.

[27] *Ibid.*, Bk. XIII, 300–2.

[28] *Ibid.*, Bk. XIII, 304–12.

worth's "Preface." Platonism is clearly present in it, but from nearer
to his life-experience comes the English Associationism of David
Hartley. This rather than Cabalism or Swedenborgianism supplied him with his broad intellectual scheme. In other words,
Wordsworth wished to be philosophical in his poetry; he wished
even to choose a diction and a style that he could properly call
philosophical. But he usually sought a philosophy not too far
from familiar modes of thinking and speaking. Such a common-
sensible basis appeared to him to give the dignity, reality, and
permanence he coveted for poetry. His fundamental good sense
reacted against the gaudiness and inanity, capriciousness and
arbitrariness of the thought and poetical style of certain contemporary German writers and of artificial Neo-Classicism. He determined upon a higher degree of simplicity and nearness to "plain-
living people" than the poet of the rejected schools manifested.
Seeking the reality behind the false glitter and show of life, he
thought the likely place for it was "humble and rustic life." From
"mouths of men obscure and lowly," [29] from "nature yoked with
toil," [30] he learned what is the essence of passion, its sincere verbal
expression, what are the natural linkages of our elementary feelings,
and how nature and man are intertwined. Sailors, shepherds,
wanderers, and afflicted mothers and children were his teachers
and his subjects.

Wordsworth said that what pertained to man was "the main
region of his song." [31] In the proof, humble humanity was his
topic; but man's ways and nature's ways were so mutually dependent for him that we cannot put nature even second to man
in his philosophy. One reason he assigned for choosing to write
of simple folk was the incorporation of the passions of such people
with the beautiful and permanent forms of nature. He usually remains conscious of the distinction between the external world
and the inner world of feelings; yet at the same time so lively for
him is the interchange of influence that again and again he seems
on the point of merging the two worlds—organic and inorganic

---

[29] *Prelude*, Bk. XIII, 182.
[30] *Ibid.*, Bk. XIII, 175–76.
[31] Prospectus to *The Recluse*.

—in one pulsing, breathing cosmos. This mystic consummation can be found in his writings at times; for example, in the well known passage:

> A motion and a spirit that impels
> All thinking things, all objects of all thought,
> 　And rolls through all things.[32]

In a less familiar fragment Wordsworth's acknowledgment of the identity of all things in God would be hardly distinguishable from Blake's: "God becomes as we are that we may be as He is."

> . . . One interior life
> That lives in all things . . . ,
> In which all beings live with God, themselves
> Are God, Existing in the mighty whole
> As indistinguishable as the cloudless East
> At noon is from the cloudless West, when all
> The hemisphere is one cerulean blue.[33]

A mediating genius frequent in romantic and mystical minds notes the "affinities in objects where no brotherhood exists to passive minds." [34] Wordsworth's mental habit is here rooted "in the great social principle of life" that coerces "all things into sympathy." [35] He drank his visionary power, he confesses to us, from such experiences as standing in the darkness of the night alone listening to the oncoming of a storm.[36] He sums up the effects of sun and moon, spring and autumn, mountain cataract and valley upon him:

> Thus while the days flew by and years passed on
> From nature and her overflowing soul,
> I had received so much that all my thoughts
> Were steeped in feeling.[37]

---

[32] *Tintern Abbey*, 102–4.
[33] *The Prelude*, ed. de Selincourt, notes, pp. 512–13.
[34] *Ibid.*, Bk. II, 384–86.
[35] *Ibid.*, Bk. II, 389–90.
[36] *Ibid.*, Bk. II, 304–10.
[37] *Ibid.*, Bk. II, 396–99.

Sometimes he was more conscious of what his feeling gave to nature: "An auxiliar light" could come from his mind and lend splendor to the setting sun.[38] Sometimes for him the forms of nature seemed to have their own inherent passions; sometimes their forms were what human passion gave them.[39]

BALANCE OF FEEL-
ING AND THOUGHT.
    In this preoccupation with the relation of man to the external world, this advancing and retreating on the degree and nature of the bond that unites them; once again in the relating of the whole philosophical problem to the function of imagination, one recognizes the contemporary of Kant and the meditative soul who had often discussed Kant's philosophy with his closest friend, Coleridge. To say that the Poet "considers man and nature as essentially adapted to each other," [40] is to speak a Kantian language. For a Romantic poet, Wordsworth on the whole retained a balanced view of the relation of the mind to nature and of the psychological structure of the creative activity of the artist. He has no doctrine of a sense above sense as had Blake, but a theory of feeling in equipoise with thought. "A poet," he says, "rejoices more than other men in the spirit of life that is in him." [41] But a poet's more "lively sensibility," "enthusiasm," and "tenderness" are reined in by a superior capacity for tracing connections and singling out essential meanings.[42] The half of Wordsworth's definition of good poetry most often quoted: "The spontaneous overflow of powerful feelings," is misleading without the other half: "Poems to which any value can be attached were never produced on any variety of subjects, but by a man who . . . had thought long and deeply." The passion at the spring of lyricism, he said, must be recollected in tranquillity.[43] The solitude that Wordsworth loved, and the sublime features of the landscape, mountains, and waters to which his spirit answered, gave movement and tune to his soul's ponderings, and also the note of rarity and novelty,

---

[38] *Prelude*, Bk. II, 368-70.
[39] *Ibid.*, Bk. XIII, 289-91.
[40] *Prose Works*, Vol. I, p. 61.
[41] *Ibid.*, Vol. I, p. 58.
[42] *Ibid.*, Vol. I, pp. 57, 58.
[43] *Ibid.*, Vol. I, p. 68.

so that in his actual poetical achievement he became one of the great leaders of British romanticism. But these influences at the same time, through polarity of virtue, quieted the motion and song within him and conduced to meditation. In comparison with the more ardent and fanciful members of the Romantic movement, Wordsworth stands apart as a representative of British stability and conservatism. Although he was the founder of a new school of poetry, his words in their wide, sanely-argued setting seem consistent with the sober rational humanity of Reynolds or Locke. He was carried away for a brief time with the strong wind of the French Revolution. But he soon drew back from this "juvenile error" and indeed always from what appealed to him as extravagance or heresy. A poet was a teacher in his eyes and he said that he sometimes interpreted his own mission as instruction. Wordsworth unquestionably illustrates the competition between poets and philosophers for the chief place in the "palace of wisdom"; but the tension in Wordsworth's case is slight. By virtue of unadorned diction and universal sympathies he hoped to be reckoned, though a poet, a "man speaking to men." One might add that so much criticism, experience, and reason lie in his work that he could have claimed almost as well to be a philosopher speaking to, as well as competing with, other philosophers.

In 1816 Coleridge wrote to a friend: "I am convinced that a true system of Philosophy—the Science of Life—is *best* taught in Poetry." [44] What the words 'poetry' and 'philosophy' mean in the mouths of the Romantic poets depends of course upon the context in their minds at the moment of speaking, upon the philosopher that stands to them as model of philosophizing, and upon their definition of poetry, whether allegory, lyrical emanation, or instruction. We have just allowed the poet Wordsworth a place close to the philosophers. Coleridge would have freely granted this to his friend: "I think Wordsworth possessed more of the genius of a great philosophic poet than any man I ever knew, or, as I believe has existed in England since Milton." [45] Coleridge would have assimilated the two functions to each other in his

COLERIDGE: POET AND PHILOSOPHER, BUT NOT PHILOSOPHER-POET.

[44] *Unpublished Letters*, ed. E. L. Griggs, London, 1932, Vol. II, p. 190.
[45] *Table Talk*, July 21, 1932.

own case in a somewhat different way. In the context just given
he refers to "my system of philosophy." His own "system of
philosophy" included a larger share of logic and of reasoning on
abstract principles and relations than did any other English Romanticist's thought. But if a philosopher must be a philosopher *qua*
poet, then Coleridge is a moon to Wordsworth's sun. *Qua* poet
Coleridge could create a strange new realm better than Wordsworth; he was apter in laying on the modifying colors of the
imagination. But he was not that indissoluble fusion of thinker
and singer which could produce

> . . . a linked lay of Truth,
> Of Truth profound, a sweet continuous lay.[46]

On the other hand his greater gift for metaphysics and his capacity
to participate in the contemporary philosophical Copernican Revolution enabled him to delve for "seminal principles" when Wordsworth was limited to grounding the distinction between mental
powers on mere effects and products. The mass of Coleridge's
prose writings lies in the field of applied esthetics, literary criticism;
but he carried his critical perceptions back to their roots in Being
as few critics have done.

IDEALISM WITH
KANTIAN BASE.
The ingredients of Coleridge's power as a theorist of art were
partly temperament and childish experience and partly the intellectual influences of reading and study. He had a bent for the
Vast, which he associated with talks with his father about the
universe of stars, and a love of the Great and the whole, which he
linked with the tales of wonder and imagination.[47] An appetite
thus engendered was fed by congenial readings in Plotinus, Iam-
blichus, and Jakob Boehme. Acquaintance with German Romantic literature, a visit to Germany, and then serious study of
Kant and Schelling gave certain terms and frames, but still more,
welcome corroboration to his idealistic vision of the universe and
his theory of the function of art. Kant, he said in an oft-quoted
testimony, laid hold on him as "with a giant's hand." [48] What-

---

[46] *To William Wordsworth,*   58, 59.
[47] Letter to Thomas Poole, Oct. 16, 1797.
[48] *Biographia Literaria,* Ch. IX, ed. Shawcross, Vol. I, p. 99.

ever philosophy can be learned comes from him,[49] he said. But Schelling's contribution to Coleridge's esthetics is scarcely less notable. The lecture: "On Poesy or Art" (1818) closely parallels and in part reproduces Schelling.

Coleridge declared that Kant's distinction between Reason, which is concerned with wholes and ultimate values, and Understanding, which can only trace the connections from point to point in a limited sphere, is the ground-work of all speculation.[50] However, Kant, the cautious and critical, did not sufficiently extend the creative faculty of the mind or expatiate long enough among *noumena*, to satisfy the expansive and inspired Coleridge. Coleridge would not even accept Kant's own declarations of his modest intentions, but believed that behind the symbol of his literal statement lay some transcendent leaning.[51] The road led straight for all pure Romanticists from nature and phenomena to the Absolute. Coleridge saw a "genial coincidence" between his own views and those of Schelling, who travelled the straight road. He also praised Fichte's teaching that in the beginning was an Act. This exaltation of an Act above things and substances, he said, put the keystone to the metaphysical arch, and allowed metaphysics to have its "spring and principle within itself." [52]

Within a freely interpreted and mystically consummated Kantianism Coleridge then found the clue to the labyrinth of mental functions, including the poet's creative imagination, and to an enlightened literary criticism. No psychology which explained the force and life of mind by a texture of processes or by the relation of stimulus and response between man and nature could content him. Early in life he, like Wordsworth, found Hartley's system of associationism ingenious and applicable to numerous mental phenomena. But Coleridge came definitely to reject Hartley. The ultimate effect of associationism, he concluded, was the reduction of acts of will and thought to blind chance and dead mechanism. The soul is a cause and essence, not a condition, he

---

[49] Letter to J. Gooden, Jan. 14, 1820.
[50] *The Friend*, 1863, Vol. XI, p. 243.
[51] *Biographia Literaria*, Ch. IX, Vol. I, pp. 100–101.
[52] *Ibid.*, p. 101.

insisted; and the events within the world of soul are emanations of energy and not configurations in time and space. Hartley had made of the soul an *ens logicum*, a something-nothing.[53]

FEELING SHAPED INTO IDEA.

Already in an early fragment written for a proposed Encyclopedia Coleridge had tried to place the Fine Arts and particularly Poetry on the map of Being and Knowledge. For the distinction of the encyclopedia was to be its methodical, reasoned, logical character. The place of arts and sciences was to be determined as a true philosophy should dictate. The dynamic unity of the Fine Arts he placed, as Kant did, in a middle position between the examples of Spirit's self-relation in the pure sciences and the examples of mentally instituted order in the physical world. The Fine Arts have *a priori* laws of taste, and so illustrate mind's self-determination. But they also are concerned with the external facts of sound and color. But in the end this compromise between mind and matter, this half-way station between spirit and sense, hardly did justice to the protoplastic unity and the echo of Divinity which Coleridge guarded for Poesy—Poesy, the type of all art because it implies *making* and not mere disposition or arrangement of parts, end and means indissolubly joined and not externally collocated. "Certainly," he said, "the Fine Arts belong to the outward world, for they all operate by the images of sight and sound, and other sensible impressions; and without a delicate tact for these, no man ever was, or could be, either Musician or a Poet; . . . but as certainly he must always be a poor and unsuccessful cultivator of the Arts if he is not impelled first by a mighty, inward power, a feeling, *quod nequeo monstrare, et sentio tantum;* nor can he make great advances in his Art, if, in the course of his progress, the obscure impulse does not gradually become a bright, and clear, and living Idea!"[54] "It has escaped some critics," he says in the same context, "that in the Fine Arts the Mental initiative must proceed from within." Where the name poetry is really deserved, the physical medium is relatively insignificant. It is the idea that counts. Witness in music our revulsion to the encroachment of the glass or steel—the body of the sound—upon the spiritual law of music,

---

[53] *Biog. Lit.*, Ch. VII, Vol. I, pp. 80–88.
[54] *Treatise on Method*, ed. Snyder, London, 1934, p. 63.

that is the mathematical proportion that obtains between the notes.[55]

What does Coleridge mean by the bright, clear, and living Idea which must be the presiding genius of a successful artist? By Idea he means a Platonic Idea, or Kant's Idea of Reason, a true archetype and well-spring of being. A poet governed by the Idea has genuine imagination; the others have fancy only. Coleridge's most significant use of his philosophical equipment and temperament was in the development of this fundamental esthetic distinction and in his application of it to Shakespeare versus the minor lights of poetry, the tinklers. The fancy for Coleridge was the artistic faculty that simply rearranges a given material. It "has no other counters to play with but fixities and definites." All imagination, on the other hand, was for him a "living Power and prime Agent . . . a repetition in the finite mind of the eternal act of creation in the infinite I AM." [56] Artistic imagination is a variant of this universal human faculty of origination. As it inspires the artist, it enables him to diffuse, dissolve, and dissipate in order to re-create.

To try to explain Shakespeare by the laws of association or by finding a recipe for him, by tallying his reading with his output,[57] or by "measuring and spanning him muscle by muscle" [58] was, according to Coleridge, to fail as a critic through the employment of pre-Kantian or sub-transcendental tools. Shakespeare's gift for creating dramatic characters followed from his possession of an Idea of humanity, a knowledge of the universal tendencies of all men incarnated in the perfect individuality of separate persons. His power in presenting passion had the same philosophical root of Idea, a universal specifying itself through tones and conditions. Coleridge praised the saying of Schlegel that Shakespeare lays open to us in a single word a whole series of preceding conditions. Shakespeare gives us, says Coleridge, the "history of minds." He

---

[55] MS. Fragment, British Museum, Egerton 2800, 64, quoted by Snyder, *op. cit.*, p. 85.

[56] *Biog. Lit.*, Ch. XIII, Vol. I, p. 202.

[57] *Treatise on Method*, p. 62.

[58] *Ibid.*, p. 32.

"contemplated *Ideas*, in which alone are involved conditions and consequences *ad infinitum*." [59]

The Whole before the part; the end before the means; the feeling or instinct before the idea: these principles of order furnish the main body of Coleridge's esthetics and "restoration of literary criticism." The senses are informed from the mind and not the mind from the senses. [60] The purpose or end of a poet must be grasped before his technique is judged. Shakespeare appeared "irregular and wild" to Neo-Classic critics because they interpolated their own literary ideals between Shakespeare and his work. [61] The end summing up the whole—for Coleridge always a precondition of the particular means used by an artist—is normally felt and striven after by a vague appetency of mind before it is understood. Feeling is primary; intellection secondary. Poetry is grandest when a sublime feeling of the unimaginable takes the place of a mere image; where there is not a distinct form, but a strong working of the mind. [62] Not only does feeling give the keynote and presage the whole, afford the grandest parts, and symbolize the dominance of heart over head, but feeling, running like a breeze among the particulars of experience, binds them into a unified reasonable system and so accomplishes the work that the mechanism of association was supposed by earlier philosophers to do. [63]

ADVANCE BUT NO SYSTEM.

What one comes to with Coleridge is that his own feelings and instincts, his own ideal presagings both in the theory of beauty and of art were right. They were clearly placed with the esthetic opinion that was to be instead of with that which was outworn. His fragmentary and abstract restatements of Kant and Neo-Platonism do not, however, carry the subject forward nor round out a system. His lack of ability to carry through an enterprise shows here as in his poetry.

---

[59] *Treatise on Method*, pp. 27-31.
[60] *Table Talk*, July 21, 1832.
[61] *Coleridge on Logic and Learning*, ed. Snyder, New Haven, 1922, p. 110.
[62] T. M. Raysor, *Coleridge's Shakespearean Criticism*, London, 1930, Vol. II, p. 38.
[63] Letter to Southey, Aug. 7, 1803.

Shelley's *Defence of Poetry* (1821) is a true descendant of the royal line of such Defences, Sir Philip Sidney's being perhaps the most famous among those in the English language. The immediate occasion of Shelley's eloquent panegyric was Sir Thomas Peacock's sneer at poetry as a mental rattle and aimless mockery. But these relations of Shelley's work are less important for esthetics than the illustrious exhibition it gives of the Romantic faith in the poet as prophet. The enthusiastic praise of the poet as wisest, noblest, most beneficent, and most intuitive of men is passed along a whole rainbow of beautiful phrasings. A poet essentially combines and unites the characters of both legislator and prophet.[64] "A poet participates in the eternal, the infinite, and the one."[65] "Shakespeare, Dante, and Milton . . . are philosophers of the very loftiest power."[66] "Poets are the hierophants of an unapprehended inspiration."[67] "Poets are the unacknowledged legislators of the world."[68] Only God and the Poet deserve the name of creator, he says, quoting Tasso.[69] "A poet, as he is the author to others of the highest wisdom, pleasure, virtue, and glory, so he ought personally to be the happiest, the best, the wisest, and the most illustrious of men . . . ; the greatest poets have been men of the most spotless virtue, of the most consummate prudence." As poets, so poetry. "All high poetry is infinite. . . . A great poem is a fountain for ever overflowing with the waters of wisdom and delight."[70] "A poem is the very image of life expressed in its eternal truth."[71] "Poetry is the record of the best and happiest moments of the happiest and best minds."[72] "Poetry lifts the veil from the hidden beauty of the world."[73] "Poetry strengthens the faculty which is the organ of the moral nature of man."[74] "Poetry

---

[64] *Works*, ed. Forman, 8 Vols., London, 1880, Vol. VII, p. 104.
[65] *Loc. cit.*
[66] *Ibid.*, p. 108.
[67] *Ibid.*, p. 144.
[68] *Loc. cit.*
[69] *Ibid.*, p. 140.
[70] *Ibid.*, pp. 129, 130.
[71] *Ibid.*, p. 108.
[72] *Ibid.*, p. 138.
[73] *Ibid.*, p. 111.
[74] *Ibid.*, pp. 111, 112.

is indeed something divine. It is at once the centre and circumference of knowledge; it is that which comprehends all science, and that to which all science must be referred. It is at the same time the root and blossom of all other systems of thought." [75]

In all these utterances there is Romanticism's true note of wide faith in poetry's powers. And coupled with them there is the usual condemnation of the deadness and dryness of calculation. However much Blake, Wordsworth, Coleridge, and Shelley differ in the special paths of their thought, they all think of imagination and its offspring poetry as a living tree, as full of seed and fruit, and on the other hand of calculation and reason in the narrow sense as cold blight or "rattling twigs and sprays in winter." Utilitarianism and prudence are Mammon over against Poetry, which stands for God. [76]

KEATS' PSYCHOL-
OGY OF CREATION.
In opposition to all this enlargement and exaltation of the poet's function, John Keats (put in here as foil to the main line of Romantic esthetes) trims its wings and deflates its body. Not but what he tries his hand for a moment now and then, poet though he is, at a philosophical scheme of salvation, and perhaps yields more acute suggestions per minute than the more self-confident Wordsworth: the 'giant' by whose side he stands to show how tall he is. [77] But how little he agrees in defining the poet as a teacher and sage, the following vivid characterization bears witness: "As to the poetical Character itself (I mean that sort, of which, if I am anything, I am a member; that sort distinguished from the Wordsworthian, or egotistical Sublime; which is a thing per se, and stands alone), it is not itself—it has no self—it is everything and nothing—it has no character—it enjoys light and shade; it lives in gusto, be it fair or foul, high or low, rich or poor, mean or elevated—it has as much delight in conceiving an Iago as an Imogen. What shocks the virtuous philosopher delights the chameleon poet. It does no harm from its relish of the dark side of things, any more than from its taste for the bright one, because they both end in speculation. A poet is the most unpoetical of anything in

---

[75] *Works*, Vol. VII, p. 136.
[76] *Loc. cit.*
[77] *Letters*, ed. Colvin, pp. 105–108, May 3, 1818, to J. H. Reynolds.

existence, because he has no Identity—He is continually in for and filling some other body. The Sun,—the Moon,—the Sea and men and women who are creatures of impulse, are poetical, and have about them an unchangeable attribute; the poet has none, no identity—He is certainly the most unpoetical of all God's creatures —If then he has no self, and if I am a poet, where is the wonder that I should say I would write no more? Might I not at very instant have been cogitating on the Characters of Saturn and Ops? It is a wretched thing to confess; but it is a very fact, that not one word I ever utter can be taken for granted as an opinion growing out of my identical Nature—how can it when I have no Nature? When I am in a room with people, if I ever am free from speculating on creations of my own brain, then, not myself goes home to myself, but the identity of everyone in the room begins to press upon me, so that I am in a very little time annihilated—" [78]

The poet then for the heretic Keats was that very passive Aeolian lyre over which impressions are driven as if by a wind and upon which melody is played, the instrument unwitting and without volition, which Shelley had said he was not. Shelley, insisting on the poet's participation in the intellectual and political achievements of men, could not abandon a poet to such bare impressibility. But Keats cleared poetry of moral responsibility, as he cut away the poet himself from the legislator and the philosopher. For himself, he never quite knew, he said, the bearings of his assertions. But what thus from the logical and moral point of view might be wandering, might seem from the esthetic point of view very fine. "Though a quarrel in the Streets is a thing to be hated, the energies displayed in it are fine; the commonest Man shows a grace in his quarrel." So "the alertness of a Stoat or the anxiety of a Deer" may be beautiful to witness. [79]

In Thomas Carlyle's (1795–1881) doctrine of the poet as Hero, we have the right Romantic dye again. The poet for Carlyle was one of those powerful personalities who dare to think and to act independently and who are moved by a vision of reality, in whom, therefore, the hope of the world lies. The poet's heroic quality

CARLYLE: POET AS HERO, SEER, SINGER.

---

[78] *Ibid.*, pp. 184–85.
[79] *Letters*, p. 237, Sept. 18, 1819, to George and Georgiana Keats.

consists in his vision of the Ideal which is everywhere present in
the actual, but not discerned by common men. The poet is a
prophet, a seer. In addition to his "clear, deep-seeing eye," [80] he
must have a warm heart. But his primary character is the gift
to see the mystery and the infinity in all that is, "to live in the
very fact of things." [81] Through his works he offers symbols of
the Godlike and the Infinite.

Besides the seeing eye and warm heart he must have the singing voice. "All deep things," Carlyle says, "are Song"—the rest,
"wrappages and hulls!" [82] The Ideal to which the poet's eye penetrates converts into melody. "The *word* that will describe the
thing follows of itself from such clear intense sight of the thing." [83]
For Carlyle the music of verse is no added grace. In the great
poet's fancy the very essence of the thing turns into music; for
penetrating vision and passionate sincerity naturally express themselves in rhythmic chants.

The universality and truth of a poet make him kin to all men.
"A vein of poetry exists in the heart of all men. . . . We are all
poets when we *read* a poem well." [84] The Hero-poet has *more* of
the specific element, that is all. "I confess," says Carlyle, "I have
no notion of a truly great man that could not be *all* sorts of men." [85]

In his distinguishing degree, to be sure, he stands apart from
other men. But on this high level he joins the other Heroes—the
religious, military, and legislative Heroes. Carlyle claims that it
is primarily the sphere into which circumstance throws a Hero
that determines his kind. Petrarch and Boccaccio were good diplo-
mats; Napoleon had in him the potentiality of words instead of
battles; Shakespeare could have dealt "right strokes" at Agincourt,
instead of giving it to us in verse.

Like most romanticists, Carlyle is more bent on breaking down
distinctions than in discovering and defining differences. He does,

[80] *Works*, 30 Vols., London, 1896–1899, Vol. V, p. 79. *Heroes and Hero-
Worship*.
[81] *Ibid.*, Vol. V, p. 81.
[82] *Ibid.*, Vol. V, p. 83.
[83] *Ibid.*, Vol. V, p. 104.
[84] *Ibid.*, Vol. V, p. 82.
[85] *Ibid.*, Vol. V, p. 78.

however, briefly distinguish the moral from the esthetic hero. The first emphasizes what men must do; the second what men must love. Carlyle follows Goethe, his acknowledged master, in making the Beautiful, "the true Beautiful," [86] higher than and inclusive of the Good. Following Goethe, again, he interprets the show of things as God's living garment.

Speaking in New York in 1843 on New England, Ralph Waldo Emerson (1803–1882), the American Transcendentalist, said that the influence of Wordsworth, Coleridge, and Carlyle, had been more readily received in the United States than in their own country.[87] The "new love of the vast," he says, which the Germans always feel, but which the Romantic writers introduced into England, finds in America a most congenial soil.[88] He claims a deeper ethical interest for the Romanticism of the New World. In Emerson's own writings an utter directness, a bold curtness even, of speech, imparts a note of the virgin wilderness to the familiar expression of eternal mysticism. His preoccupation with the particular flowers and trees, birds and hills that he saw around Concord gives the reader a reviving sense of new possibilities in the worn theme of the poet as prophet, the universally circulating divinity, occult correspondences, the infinite dignity and powers of the human spirit, and the primacy of the imagination. One might well borrow a phrase from Emerson's spiritual kinsman, Wordsworth, and say that the fresh quality of Romanticism as it appears in Emerson comes from his looking steadily at the American object. Not but what the philosophy is traditional mysticism; but it reads like a new legend in this expositor. He himself says: "The thoughts are few, the forms many." [89]

Emerson insists then, like the others we have considered, on the wide and deep powers of vision in the poet. "The birth of a poet is the principal event in chronology." [90] The poet is a

EMERSON: NEW
WORLD MYSTIC.

---

[86] *Ibid.*, Vol. V, p. 81.
[87] *Works*, Centenary ed., Vol. XII, p. 472, note to Dial paper "Thoughts on Modern Literature."
[88] *Ibid.*, p. 318.
[89] *Ibid.*, Vol. VIII, p. 18, "Poetry and Imagination."
[90] *Ibid.*, Vol. III, p. 11, "The Poet."

"winged,[91] an eternal" man.[92] Among partial men, he stands out
as complete.[93] He is the Sayer and the Namer of things, because
his power to express his impressions is equal to his sensitiveness in
receiving them. He belongs in the company of heroes and sages.
The three types of men fulfill the Trinity of sublime vocations:
acting, thinking, speaking. Yet of the three, the poet is the greatest.
The others furnish him with materials; he is the designer and
architect.[94] He is a prophet: "The signs and credentials of the
poet are that he announces that which no man foretold." [95] He
has "an ulterior intellectual perception" and can bind together
the broken fragments of evil or superficial sensing. "The poet . . .
reattaches things to nature and the whole." [96]

MORAL STRICTNESS.　　　In discussing the literature and spirit of his time Emerson reported that "the very child in the nursery prattles mysticism." [97]
It is not to be wondered at then that hymns to the Infinite, the
all-pervading Unity, the Ideal, the deep secrets of the Universe
which the poet tells through symbols, living Nature, the healer and
inspirer of souls are Emerson's constant theme. But, as he himself
prepared us for finding, there is a New England moral strictness in
his rendering that is often absent in European analogies. Emerson
admired Goethe, but he denied him a place among the highest
singers because of his lack of the moral sentiment.[98] He composed
for Goethe a self-vindication as "keen beholder of life" with its
evil as well as good. There speaks the mystic who is also a New
Englander: "Yes, O Goethe, but the ideal is truer than the actual.
That is ephemeral, but this changes not. . . . Nature is moral.
. . . We are never lifted above ourselves, we are not transported
out of the dominion of the senses, or cheered with an infinite
tenderness, or armed with a grand trust [by your poetical realism]."

　　　"Goethe, then must be set down as the poet of the Actual, not

---

[91] *Works*, Vol. III, p. 12.
[92] *Ibid.,* p. 9.
[93] *Ibid.*, p. 5.
[94] *Ibid.*, pp. 7, 8.
[95] *Ibid.*, p. 8.
[96] *Ibid.*, p. 18.
[97] *Ibid.*, Vol. XII, p. 318.
[98] *Ibid.*, p. 328.

of the Ideal; of this world, and not of religion and hope . . . the poet of prose, and not of poetry . . . the Muse never essays those thunder-tones which cause to vibrate the sun and the moon, which dissipate by dreadful melody all this iron network of circumstance, and abolish the old heavens and the old earth before the free will or Godhead of man. That Goethe had not a moral perception proportionate to his other powers is not, then, merely a circumstance, as might relate of a man that he had or had not the sense of tune or an eye for colors, but it is the cardinal fact of health or disease; since lacking this he failed in the high sense to be a creator, . . . a Redeemer of the human mind." [99]

But it is also a differentia of Emerson's outlook that both in HOMELINESS. his definition of the poet and of beauty he required a first firm layer of homeliness. In words of one syllable and of common household use he describes the perception of matter as the indispensable basis of the very imagination which finally soars so high: This common sense is "the cradle, . . . the go-cart of the human child. We must learn the homely laws of fire and water; we must feed, wash, plant, build. These are . . . first in the order of Nature." [100] At this early point in the treatment of the imagination he is able to talk of "the common sense which does not meddle with the absolute." [101]

Beauty itself has for Emerson a parallel lowly concrete basis: men leading horses to water, farmers sowing seed, the smith at the forge, "barrows, trays and pans." He singles out for comment forms that have pleased his own eyes, such as the swaying of crowds of yellow butterflies over masses of blue pickerel-weed in a brook basin. He observed the daily and seasonal clock of natural appearance, much as did Constable. Although he had warm appreciation of the great examples of Italian art, he always preferred to artificial things the "cup and cover" of earth and sky.

To connect the grace and charm of simple things in nature and PLATONIC LADDER. of man's use with the last attained vision of cosmic Beauty, Emerson, following his great master Plato, raises a ladder with successive

---

[99] *Ibid.*, pp. 331–32.
[100] *Ibid.*, Vol. VIII, p. 3.
[101] *Loc. cit.*

rungs representing the soul's esthetic education. "There is a climbing scale of culture, from the first agreeable sensation which a sparkling gem or a scarlet stain affords the eye, up through fair outlines and details of the landscape, features of the human face and form, signs and tokens of thought and character in manners, up to the ineffable mysteries of the intellect. Wherever we begin, thither our steps tend: an ascent from the joy of a horse in his trappings, up to the perception of Newton that the globe on which we ride is only a larger apple falling from a larger tree; up to the perception of Plato that globe and universe are rude and early expressions of an all-dissolving Unity."

The levels which Emerson establishes have a tendency to multiply and break down as distinct stages. For finally it is to the notion of the mobility of beauty, its expressiveness and pervasiveness through the universe, that the great American returns. Beauty like Venus is the child of foam; is not "stark or bounded"; streams with life; shows most clearly in transitions from one form to another, and in the rhythm of successive balancings, as in the dance, waves, and bird flight. "To this streaming or flowing belongs the beauty that all circular movement has; as the circulation of waters, the circulation of the blood, the periodical motion of planets, the annual wave of vegetation, the action and reaction of nature."

Besides his scale of beauty Emerson enumerates "a few of its qualities": [102] simplicity, economy, fitness, universality, moderation, permanence, and the tendency to ascend. His exposition of these qualities as indeed of all his esthetic notions is informal and literary rather than scientific.

RUSKIN: ROMANTI-
CIST WITH A PRAC-
TICAL PROGRAM.

In acknowledging his indebtednesses in *Modern Painters* John Ruskin (1819–1900) mentions both Wordsworth and Carlyle, but he emphasizes the debt to Carlyle saying that he, Ruskin, had read and studied his friend's works so much that he found himself constantly falling into his actual phrases.[103] It is obvious to the merest skimmer of Ruskin's writings that on the doctrine of artist as prophet

---

[102] *Works*, "Thoughts on Modern Literature," Vol. VI, 306, 289, 293.

[103] Part IV, Appendix III, "Plagiarism"; *The Works of John Ruskin* (Library Edition), ed. E. T. Cook and Alexander Wedderburn, 39 Vols., London, 1903–1912, Vol. V, p. 427.

and teacher, Ruskin stands in the very heart of Romanticism. He writes in italics as a "precious conclusion" of his reflection on art that "greatness in art . . . is . . . *the expression of a mind of a God-made* great man." [104] In grading human beings according to their emotional capacities, he puts highest those who are "submitted to influences stronger than they," and who are in a state of prophetic inspiration.[105] Still in the end it is another side of Romanticism which we feel to be strongest in Ruskin. The second half of his working life was devoted to political-economic questions. Instead of ascending more and more into the clouds and dispersing his feeling more and more into the Unity that binds all things together, Ruskin with increasing years planted his feet more solidly upon the implications of the gross facts of dollars and cents as they are related to the production and distribution of art. His thought was opposed to that of the reigning School of Manchester. Still he must be put with the Romanticists who had a practical program, who bound art to social conditions and moral states. Wordsworth, Carlyle, even Blake, were mightily moved by the French Revolution and what it implied concerning liberty and the common man. Such an interest in the wide human implications of art is the primary fact about Ruskin. Late in life he declared that the clearest truth he had learned in thirty years was that the faculty for art can neither be cultivated nor exercised in isolation, that on the contrary, it is "but . . . a visible sign of national virtue." [106] Because he persistently and eloquently linked art with the life of the workman and with social and political virtues and vices, his theory has been held aloft as a conspicuous example of the moral fallacy in esthetics. It is truer to see in it the refusal to abstract art from art's conditions. Ruskin encountered the moral and economic implications of art in his searching inquiry into its causes in human producers, its effect in the prevailing temper of a society, and its object in the laws and essences of the world.

Though Ruskin must be grouped with the late romantic writers ART AND MORALS. on art, particularly with the religious socialists of art, the shape

---

[104] *Modern Painters*, Part IV, Ch. X, §22; Vol. V, p. 189.
[105] *Ibid.*, IV, XII, 9; V, 209.
[106] "The Relation of National Ethics to National Arts"; XIX, 164.

of his thought was peculiarly original. John Stuart Mill said of him that, barring his own group, Ruskin was the only original British thinker of his day, a day characterized largely by commentators and imitators.[107] Not only did Ruskin react against the popular school of taste in his time, but he supported his own novel outlook by drawing in unprecedented fashion on the words of the Bible and the saints. His ideas moreover were infinitely graded and interlaced, defying simple apprehension, and witnessing to strong individual bents and unusual home-discipline. In stating his own opinion as to the determinant forces on his life he emphasized two: love of beauty and love of justice.[108] Part of his history is the story of the tension of these two forces. As he asked himself early in life whether it was right for him to devote energy to the arts while innumerable souls were going to hell through failure of human exertion on their behalf, so late in life he asked himself whether it was right to scrutinize clouds and shells while the tides were floating by full of corpses.[109] But in the last analysis the two instincts were, in Ruskin, but phases of one. Indeed he himself declared that the lessons in justice of *Stones of Venice* were but the expansion of a slight theme in *Modern Painters*, which is a series of lessons in natural beauty.[110] The love of beauty meant finally for him the love of the Creator of beauty and involved veneration of God's attributes in his works: infinity, unity, repose, symmetry, purity, moderation—what he summarized as "typical beauty." [111] But God's attributes are moral attributes and require for their appreciation a moral habit of mind.

IMPORTANCE OF INSTINCT AND EMOTION.

The psychological basis of art for Ruskin was instinct. The greater emphasis on the instinctive origin of art—that it cannot be taught nor learned as a set of rules—differentiates his late from his early writing. Art can be fed or starved, guided or neglected, but it cannot be generated in schools. It must exist as feeling and appetite first. In Ruskin, the person, such an instinct underlay

---

[107] E. T. Cook, *The Life of John Ruskin*, 2d ed., 2 Vols., London, 1912, Vol. II, p. 550.

[108] Intended *Preface for Proserpina; XXXV, 628.

[109] *Fors Clavigera*, Letter 72; XXVIII, 757.

[110] *The Stones of Venice*, VI, II; X, 207; Intro., xlvii.

[111] *Modern Painters*, III, V–XI; IV, 76–141.

all his intellectual concern with art. "There is the strong instinct in me which I cannot analyse, to draw and describe the things I love," he wrote to his father at the age of thirty-three; "not for reputation, nor for the good of others, nor for my own advantage, but a sort of instinct like that for eating and drinking." [112] But earlier than his desire to "eat up into his mind" all St. Mark's and all Verona was the appetite in him for the primary beauty of nature. As a young man he would lie on the grass and draw the blades as they grew, "until every square foot of meadow, or mossy bank, became an infinite picture and possession" [113] to him. Natural sensitiveness to gracious form and color in meadows and mountains was early fostered in Ruskin by travel among the Alps.

Irresistible propension then is for Ruskin the beginning of art. In the case of great men this propension is something they cannot help saying or doing. Ruskin often describes it in terms of emotion: affection, love, praise, kindness, tenderness. Whatever his word, he means that an artist's chief mark is his involuntary movement toward an object of interest and desire. To Ruskin as for any good Romanticist the lack of some dynamic feeling for beauty is the one absolute lack. In his estimate of carving, it was not blunt or coarse carving that he rated lowest. "It is *cold* cutting—that look of equal trouble everywhere—the smooth, diffused tranquillity of heartless pains—the regularity of a plough in a level field." [114] And so of painting: "Only that picture is noble, which is painted in love of the reality." [115] Self-conscious thought he believed a danger to the creative genius. Love must be allowed to do its own proper work without too much self-consciousness. "The only true test of good or bad is, ultimately, strength of affection." [116] This true test Ruskin applied to Turner, his protégé and perduring theme. Turner's greatness, he said, depends on the largeness of his sympathy. A less great man casts his eye on his subject unfeelingly. And egotistic pleasure, a narrow and superficial fancy, the utilitarian

[112] June 2, 1852; cited by E. T. Cook, *op. cit.*, I, 263.
[113] Note-books of the year 1847–48; *ibid.*, I, 218.
[114] *The Seven Lamps of Architecture*, V, 21; VIII, 214.
[115] "Laws of Fésole," XV, 354.
[116] *Modern Painters*, V, II; VI, 47.

philosophy of Ruskin's day, results he thought in cleverness, not in art.

As Aristotle taught that the raw material of the impulses must be formed by education into right habits, so Ruskin taught that the raw material of love of beauty must be molded into a right artistic habit—the habit of rightly seeing. There is, he says, even in the feelings of those who naturally love beauty much imperfection, inconsistency, and positive error, unless the enjoyment be regulated. His words are almost a literal quotation from Plato's *Laws* and Aristotle's *Politics:* "There is a right and wrong way in liking and disliking; . . . even the most instinctive inclinations . . . are governable, and . . . it is a kind of duty to direct them rightly." [117]

Habit and discipline, then, supervene upon affection and impulse and change sensuous concern into steady and energetic contemplation. *Aesthesis*—the work of the eye—is brought along until it becomes *Theoria*—a spiritual beholding through the instrument of the eye. But all the way it is vision with which art is concerned. "The greatest thing a human being ever does in this world is to *see* something, and tell what it *saw* in a plain way." [118] Artists then are exact and comprehensive visualizers. They have practiced exact seeing until they have formed a noble habit which works in them effortlessly. "All the great men *see* what they paint before they paint it,—see it in a perfectly passive manner,—cannot help seeing it if they would; . . . vision it is, of one kind or another,—the whole scene, character, or incident passing before them as in second sight, whether they will or no, and requiring them to paint it as they see it; they not daring under the might of its presence, to alter one jot or tittle of it as they write it down or paint it down." [119] The virtue of the graphic artist is for Ruskin this adherence to the vision. "It is always wrong to draw what you don't see." [120]

As the basis of Turner's excellence was for Ruskin his larger sympathy, so the superstructure of his quality was his better seeing. The imaginative truth-telling of Turner, a truth-telling in

---

[117] *Stones of Venice*, II, 3; IX, 62, note.
[118] *Modern Painters*, IV, XVI, 28; V, 333.
[119] *Ibid.*, IV, VII, 5; V, 114.
[120] *Ibid.*, V, II, 2; VI, 27.

which "the vanity and individualism of the man himself are crushed and he becomes a mere instrument or mirror for the reflection to others of . . . truth" is superior to maps and charts and scientific truth generally. Ruskin cites Turner's *Nottingham* as a case in which a seeing artist boldly contradicts the ordinary expectation of the uncultivated eye. The uncultivated eye, concerned with what its owner tells it it ought to see, looks for a "mockery of the reality" in a reflection in water. But Turner paints in his reflection an "entirely new picture, with all its tones and arrangements altered," [121] a manner of representing which not only is more faithful to the fact, but conveys a sense of the watery medium by which the reflection is received. In his treatment of Turnerian light, Ruskin proves by the experiment of comparing colors reflected on white paper with their daylight tones that, in spite of the opinion to the contrary, "Turner, . . . and he alone, of all men, *ever painted Nature in her own colors.*" He claims that if we try to match colors on a paper in the open air with the colors of things in the landscape as exactly as "a lady would match the colors of two pieces of a dress," we shall find that shadows of trees that we had thought dark green or black are actually pale violet and purple, that lights we had supposed green are intensely yellow, brown or golden, and that our result corresponds with Turner's method.[122]

Ruskin argues that the artist not only sees accurately the particular object he sees, but discerns the relative values in what he sees. He grasps the essence or law in what he beholds. In the sense that the great painter or carver sets down the principal facts in their presiding function, he reveals the universal laws of nature and the principal uses of concrete things. For example: "The essence of a wind mill, as distinguished from all other mills, is, that it should turn round and be a spinning thing, ready always to face the wind; as light, therefore, as possible, and as vibratory; . . . Turner [marked] this great fact of windmill nature; how high he has set it; how slenderly he has supported it." [123] The masterly PENETRATIVE IM-
AGINATION.

---

[121] *Ibid.*, Part II, Sec. V, Ch. V, §9; III, 543.
[122] *Ibid.*, V, III, 9; VI, 55.
[123] *Ibid.*, V, I, 10; VI, 16.

carver of the grotesque, Ruskin says, may be rough and untutored in his mode of carving, but his work will nevertheless have profound relations with the true: "He may not be able to carve plumes or scales well; but his creatures will bite and fly, for all that." [124] He isolates and records the principal facts.

This excellent seeing capacity Ruskin calls the penetrative imagination, and here again Ruskin is moving with the broad stream of Romanticism. The "penetrating, possession-taking power of the imagination," he says, is "the very life of the man, considered as a *seeing* creature." [125] For the ultimate "play and power of imagination depend altogether on our being able to forget ourselves and enter like possessing spirits into the bodies of things about us." [126] In *Modern Painters*, Ruskin distinguished this imaginative vision of the heart and inner nature not only from the blindness of the unimaginative, but also from the cool externality of fancy. "The fancy sees the outside, and is able to give a portrait of the outside, clear, brilliant, and full of detail." [127] He also distinguishes between rational and orderly perception of the real power and character of things from morbid or passionate perception. The latter is subject to what Ruskin calls the "pathetic fallacy." [128] Under the influence of beclouding and dazzling emotion we may make the foam cruel and the wind lazy. He always extolls loving truth as the basis of art, but in his late *Pleasures of England* he repudiated his early distinction and named the term fancy as meaning for him all 'inventive vision.'

Although the imagination lifted thus to its highest power always sees things as they are, it sees them when and where they are not; it sees moreover with that "inward eye" which "forever delights to dwell on that which is not tangibly present." So Dante sees the Centaur Chiron "trot visibly across his brain" and so the author of the Apocalypse saw heaven, and so those nations which add an idol-making instinct to the simpler mimetic instinct "bring the

---

[124] *Stones of Venice*, III, 48; XI, 169.
[125] *Modern Painters*, IV, X, 8; V, 177.
[126] *Ibid.*, Part III, Sec. II, Ch. III, §31; IV, 287.
[127] *Ibid.*, §7; IV, 253.
[128] *Ibid.*, Part III (*passim*); V, 201ff.

immortals out of the recesses of the clouds, and make them Penates; and bring the dead from darkness and make them Lares." [129]

Seeing then becomes definiteness and scope of envisaging power for Ruskin. He treats the artist as receiving the impress with peculiar tenderness and delicacy of all living forms, so that even what appears from his hand later in the shape of abstract ornamentation, gets its quality and beauty from what was seen. Thus what analysts take as beauty of abstract contour or relation, expressible most readily in geometrical terms, derives its validity from the seeing eye, from Nature's forms. "All beautiful lines are adaptations of those which are commonest in external creation." [130] "The Romanesque arch is beautiful as an abstract line. Its type is . . . the apparent vault of heaven, and horizon of the earth. The cylindrical pillar is always beautiful, for God has so moulded the stem of every tree that is pleasant to the eyes. The pointed arch is beautiful; it is the termination of every leaf that shakes in summer wind." [131] The egg and dart pattern is beautiful because the form is familiar in the "soft housing of the bird's nest." [132] The harmonies of line which Ruskin admired in the tomb of Ilaria [133] he saw as copies in the world of art of the laws of the river's wave, the aspen branch, and the star's rising and falling.

METAPHYSICAL, RELIGIOUS BEARING OF VISION.

Because sympathetic vision ripens into insight into the law and structure of the universe, its fulfilment is akin to religious contemplation. Though the artist is always a see-er and an interpreter of nature, he sees in common things "parables of deep things, and analogies of divinity." [134] So had said Carlyle, and the whole procession of the believers in Wonder. The phenomena of imagination are due finally for Ruskin to the presence of the Divine Spirit in everything, a Spirit recognized, praised, and worshipped through art by the highest order of minds.

Ruskin has often been accused of teaching the crude doctrine

---

[129] *Aratra Pentelici*, §33; XX, 223.
[130] *Elements of Drawing*, Lecture II; XV, 91ff.
[131] *Seven Lamps*, IV, 2; VIII, 144.
[132] *Ibid.*, IV, 5; VIII, 144.
[133] Cook, *op. cit.*, Vol. I, p. 178.
[134] W. G. Collingwood, *The Art Teaching of John Ruskin*, London, 1891, p. 133.

that art is imitation of nature. After the analysis through which we have put his conception of vision and imagination, we are prepared to understand how to take Ruskin's declaration that art must paint stern fact. When he says that "the object of the great Resemblant Arts is, and always has been, to resemble; and to resemble as closely as possible," and that "a good landscape [should] . . . set the scene before you in its reality; . . . make you . . . think the clouds are flying, and the streams foaming," and that "the best sculptor . . . make[s] stillness look like breathing, and marble look like flesh," [135] he means that the artist must have an outward-turning eye and interest, must care for the real world around him, and that out of the infinitely rich range in nature must select sensitively the classes of truths that will harmonize best together, and best communicate to a second beholder the vital and universal facts of the visible kingdom. He was opposing the egotistic dilletantism of the contemporary English gentleman-connoisseur, who only cared enough for art to have his portrait painted. He was opposing also the contemporary school of taste, a taste which he felt encouraged artificial technique and uncontrolled fancy. Art has little to do with luxury or pleasure, the "tickling and fanning of the soul's sleep."

ART AS NATIONAL COMPLEXION.   In deepening, as he believed, the meaning of art Ruskin investigated not only its spring in instinct and its object in natural law, but its social and economic conditioning. His primary love of justice was never far away when he was dealing with the facts of esthetic experience. Art being, he said, the formative and directive action of a spirit, the deed is dependent on the doer. And the doer is inevitably influenced by the esthetic climate in which he works. "The beginning of art *is in getting our country clean and our people beautiful.*" [136] Ruskin believed that the flourishing of the machine-age, the practical worship as he put it of the Goddess of Getting-on or Britannia of the Market [137] kept many people slaves and made the country unbeautiful. For machinery in place of hand-labor prevents the expression of the whole man—inventive

---

[135] *Aratra Pentelici,* §122; XX, 282.
[136] *Lectures on Art,* §116; XX, 282.
[137] *Crown of Wild Olive,* II, 73; XVIII, 448.

power, affections, strength—in his output. Also the indirect results of machinery, its smoke and dirt, its cutting with arbitrary lines and dull colors the natural grace and brightness of the landscape, deprive those born with talent for truthful representation with the necessary sensuous nutriment.

Ruskin centered both his rendering of the history of art and of the immediate art-task around his belief that "the art of any country *is the exponent of its social and political virtues, . . .* [that] you can have noble art only from noble persons, associated under laws fitted to their time and circumstances." [138] Genius and a favoring social soil have only coexisted in certain periods of the world's history: notably the Greek, Tuscan, and Venetian periods. Even these great periods were not equal in greatness. "The Greek school of sculpture is formed during, and in consequence of, the national effort to discover the nature of justice; the Tuscan, during, and in consequence of the national effort to discover the nature of justification." [139] "Every nation's vice, or virtue, is written in its art," he says again: "the soldiership of early Greece; the sensuality of late Italy; the visionary religion of Tuscany; the splendid human energy of Venice." Ruskin said that England's virtue of "enduring and patient courage" is expressed in her iron-work; but her jealousy in the riveting of her armor. [140]

The linking of art with the general state of culture began for Ruskin in his earliest work of any pretension: *Introduction to the Poetry of Architecture; or, The Architecture of the Nations of Europe considered in its Association with Natural Scenery and National Character*, by Kataphusin. This work was the 'prelude' to his *Seven Lamps of Architecture* and *Stones of Venice*, in which the early modest study of Alpine cottages and the significance of chimneys grew into an analysis of the noble characteristics of Gothic, as savageness representing love of liberty; variety showing love of novelty; naturalism, showing love of the facts of nature; rigidity, expressing energy; and redundance, showing generosity; and the contrasted analysis of Renaissance art, as showing love of

---

[138] *Lectures on Art*, I, §27; XX, 39.
[139] *Aratra Pentelici*, Lecture II, §40; XX, 228.
[140] *The Crown of Wild Olive*, Lecture II, "Traffic"; XVIII, 437, 438, 439–40.

luxury and sensuality. More and more Ruskin tended to concentrate his esthetic interests upon the moral and economic and social implications of art and to preach to Englishmen that beauty presupposed justice, modesty, honesty, cleanliness, contentment. "Keep the temper of the people stern and manly; make their association grave, courteous, and for worthy objects; occupy them in just deeds; and their tongue must needs be a grand one." [141]

It was through his master Ruskin,[142] William Morris affirmed, that he learned to give form to that discontent which was one of the ruling passions of his life. The discontent was partly with the rapacity and cruelty but even more with the vulgarity of the Whig "civilization" in the midst of which he lived. This civilization, it seemed to him, had "turn[ed] history into inconsequent nonsense," and had made it culminate in a counting-house and cinder-heap; he found it sordid, aimless, and ugly.[143]

The chief misdeeds of the contemporary lords of society in England Morris believed to be the separation of work from joy, and of art from craft and from its social and individual roots. With the zeal of a confessed Socialist, he cried out against the sharp division of rich from poor and of employer from employee. *"It is right and necessary,"* he said, *"that all men should have work to do which shall be worth doing, and be of itself pleasant to do; and which should be done under such conditions as would make it neither over-wearisome nor over-anxious."* [144]

When there is joy in work, as there should be for everyone, we then by that very fact have art. For art, according to Morris's definition, is "man's expression of his joy in labour." [145] Thus Morris's views not only of the rights of the common people and of the essence and circumstances of labor, but also of art ran counter to the prevailing conceptions. He rejected the placing of art in the class of luxuries and the removal of it from use and common things.

---

[141] "The Relation of National Ethics to National Arts"; XIX, 174.
[142] "How I Became a Socialist," *The Collected Works of William Morris,* 24 Vols., London, 1910–1915, Vol. XXIII, p. 279.
[143] *Ibid.,* XXIII, 280.
[144] "Art and Socialism," XXIII, 194.
[145] "Art under Plutocracy," XXIII, 173.

We ought not to be content, he said, to be "publicly poor while some of us are privately rich." [146] Public wealth meant for him no task performed without the solace and illumination of imagination, and even the great arts pursued and appreciated by human beings who knew the feel and obligation of physical work. Esthetic activity, he insisted, embraces everything from the cathedral to the porridge-pot. The real scope of art goes beyond the Arts to "the shapes and colours of all household goods, . . . the arrangement of the fields for tillage and pasture, the management of towns and . . . highways . . .; the aspect of all the externals of our life." [147] Drawing a line between the crafts and arts has been a misfortune both for society and art, he taught. When the crafts or lesser arts of making clothes and dishes, floor-coverings and wall-coverings, carts, gates, fences, and boats are divorced from the greater, the latter become "nothing but dull adjuncts to unmeaning pomp, or ingenious toys for a few rich and idle men." [148] What Morris preached as theory, he performed as practice. He revived the old Eastern art of dyeing with natural dyes, of weaving with a hand-loom, of printing with beautiful type on fine paper.

But though Morris insisted on the enhancement of the worth of daily labor by the encouragement of the free play of imagination, that there may be ornament and decoration where there is utility, he laid down the supplementary requirement that ornament should have relation to nature and use. "Nothing," he said, "can be a work of art which is not useful, *i.e.*, minister to the body when well under the command of the mind, or which does not amuse, soothe, or elevate the mind in a healthy state." [149] Ornament and decoration while glorifying use and nature are to be continuous with it. For example, in choosing building-materials, whether stone, wood, or brick, one is to think not alone of the sheer nobility of the medium but of the suitability to place and condition. Again, lovely art is not bound down to the forms of nature, but it should, he felt, "remind us of the outward face of the earth." Art should remind

[146] "Address to Birmingham Students," Vol. XXII, p. 422.
[147] "Art under Plutocracy," Vol. XXIII, p. 165.
[148] "The Lesser Arts," Vol. XXII, p. 4.
[149] *Ibid.*, p. 23.

us of the outward surface of the earth and of the "innocent love of animals," not in the spirit of science which binds us down to "hard facts and the troubles of life," but in a way to give ease and rest.[150]

MEDIEVALISM. Morris believed that in European history the Middle Ages exemplified better than any other historical period that fusion of art with life, freedom of the craftsman, and social neighborliness and simplicity, which he advocated. He was not, however, as is sometimes thought, blind to the weaknesses of that stage of civilization. "I quite admit," he says, "that the oppression and violence of the Middle Ages had its effect on the art of those days; its shortcomings are traceable to them; . . . and for that reason I say that when we shake off the present oppression [this was written in 1886] we may expect the art of the days of real freedom to rise above that of those violent days. But I do say that it was possible then to have social, organic, hopeful, progressive art; whereas now such poor scraps of it as are left are the result of individual and wasteful struggle, are retrospective and pessimistic." [151] It was part of Morris's admiration for the Middle Ages that he should make architecture "the mistress-art which includes and consummates all other arts: for the sake of which, or as element in which, most of those other arts exist." This appreciation of the art and spirit of the Middle Ages had been for a whole century part of the new Romantic creed. In 1762 in his *Letters on Chivalry*, Richard Hurd had already not only claimed a place for the Gothic style coördinate with the Greek but for the purpose of poetry had declared Gothic manners superior.[152] The youthful Goethe in an enthusiastic paper *Of German Architecture* (1772) had celebrated the beauty of Strassburg Cathedral. Then the Nazarene painters had come with their worship of the so-called primitive masters; also the brothers Boisseree, who had planned the restoration of Cologne Cathedral and had initiated the Schlegels and their friends into the knowledge of Gothic art; and again in France Chateaubriand and Victor Hugo had recaptured the spirit of the great Christian past.

It is characteristic however of the Romantic spirit to connect

---

[150] "Some Hints on Pattern-Designing," Vol. XXII, p. 177.
[151] "The Aims of Art," Vol. XXIII, pp. 89, 91.
[152] Letter IX.

dreams of the past with Utopian hopes and schemes for the future. This combination of the romantic glorification of bygone days and a program for the England of the future was present in Morris. In the New World across the sea it was natural that an enthusiasm for a popular art—an art looking ahead and honestly expressive of the lives and ambitions of the proletariat and of pioneering heroes—should come into being.

The attempt to define the peculiar esthetic task of the United States was made by Walt Whitman in 1871 in his *Democratic Vistas*. He styled himself "primitive surveyor" [153] and devout believer in America. The theory of his esthetic essays is that, though literature has certain universal and abiding characteristics "irrespective of climate or date," its "inspiration and throbbing blood" [154] must always come from the social and material conditions in which it arises. The moving power, the home-touch, is the result of the "autochthonic lights and shades, flavors, fondnesses, aversions, specific incidents, illustrations out of his [the author's] own nationality, geography, surroundings, antecedents." [155] Like the "untellable look" of a human face, a literary soul distils out of a people's history and material circumstances. Literature is a nation's soul, Whitman said. It is both the greatest of the arts and of the modes of national expression.

In urging that America accept the challenge of its material and technical greatness and put itself into form by creating a characteristic literature, Whitman broadly contrasts the upholstered second-hand culture still in his time favored by American parlor professors with the qualities that spring from the soil. He writes of the "ultramarine, full-dress formulas" of feudal and ecclesiastical regimes [156]—love, war, and heroes—"refinement and delicatesse"— "exiles and exotics" in the United States of his time. [157] The proper American qualities are youth, "healthy rudeness," adventure, boldness, oceanic, even cosmic breadth, faith in the average man—

WHITMAN: SEC-OND-HAND ART WORTHLESS.

---

[153] *Democratic Vistas and Other Papers*, London, 1888, p. 40.
[154] *Ibid.*, pp. 63, 74.
[155] *Ibid.*, p. 63.
[156] *Ibid.*, p. 52.
[157] *Ibid.*, pp. 41, 42.

clerk, farmer, and mechanic; in a word, belief in the "all-levelling aggregate of democracy," [158] and "healthy average personalism." [159] He thought of these qualities as pervasive like the physical elements, massive like American methods of production, and far-stretching like the American prairies.

With the idea of democracy Whitman linked the concept of science as a suitable stock source for the new poetry. [160] He believed that poets should sing, not only of their own country, but also of their own century. In his *Leaves of Grass* he exemplified his esthetic theory.

Akin to Ruskin and Morris in his insistence upon the inseparability of social experience and esthetic expression, Whitman also suggests in his ideas the primitivism of the romantics and the Utopian programs of the positivists. Like an American Comte, Whitman divided the philosophical history of the United States into three stages: (1) its period of asserting and establishing political independence and equality for all men; (2) its period of epoch-making expansion, material prosperity, and technical progress. The third is the one yet to be: the period in which the gigantic body and political and economic chaos of the United States are to be shaped into the greatest artistic cosmos yet known to the world by idealistic, devout, archetypal men of letters. [161]

SUPPLEMENTARY READING

Arthur Symons, *The Romantic Movement in English Poetry*, New York, 1909.
A. E. Powell, *The Romantic Theory of Poetry*, New York, 1926.
S. F. Damon, *William Blake, His Philosophy and Symbols*, New York, 1924.
J. C. Bailey, *Walt Whitman*, New York, 1926.
André Maurois, *Ariel; The Life of Shelley*, New York, 1924.
Louis Cazamian, *Carlyle*, New York, 1932.

---

[158] *Democratic Vistas and Other Papers*, p. 52.
[159] *Ibid.*, p. 42.
[160] *My Book and I*, p. 88.
[161] *Democratic Vistas*, pp. 61, 62.

O. W. Firkins, *Ralph Waldo Emerson.*
S. F. Gingerich, *Essays in the Romantic Poets*, New York, 1929.
J. H. Muirhead, *Coleridge as Philosopher*, New York and London, 1930.
Saintsbury, *History of Criticism*, Vol. III, Bk. VIII, Ch. I.
W. A. Knight, *Six Lectures on Some Nineteenth Century Artists, English and French*, Chicago, 1909, Ch. III on Ruskin.
Venturi, *History of Art Criticism*, Ch. VII.

CHAPTER XIV

Absolute Idealism: Fichte, Schelling, Hegel

ESTHETICS AS CEN-
TER OF PHILOSOPH-
ICAL DEVELOP-
MENT. **F**OR THE first time in the history of European thought esthetics, within German Idealism, became the pivot of a philosophical movement. How did this novel thing come to pass and what was its meaning?

Kant assigned to the human subject a creative power. But he carefully limited the sway of the human intellect over its objects to the sphere of 'mere appearance.' His followers, chafing at Kant's restrictions, took a great step beyond. They developed a theory of absolute creativeness. They hoped to discover in the human mind the formative drive which builds up reality, or to comprehend reality as a creation of the mind. The thinkers who engaged in this enterprise looked upon the artist as the exemplar of a human creator. The poet or the sculptor gives birth to a world of his own. His capacity for creation, the idealist argued, may be understood to hint at a creative process, hidden from our everyday observation in the depths of the mind. Man, as an artist, can become the creator of an imaginary world only because, as an intelligence, he partakes of that universal life which gives rise to the real world. So the idea of artistic imagination as developed by Kant opened a path for a new type of bold speculation. An esthetic notion took the lead in metaphysics; and esthetics, in its turn, was remolded from the point of view of idealist metaphysics.

Idealist philosophy and artistic romanticism belong together. The philosopher endeavored to integrate in his own work the artist's creative imagination. He was eager to be both philosopher and more than philosopher. The romantic artist, on the other hand, enlarged his consciousness so as to embrace philosophical insight.

He aspired to the rank of seer, philosopher-poet. Each encroached upon the other's domain and they came to an understanding on the basis of this mutual violation of their frontiers. Whenever we hear the idealist asserting that poetry reveals the working of the world-ground, we have to understand 'romantic poetry,' or poetry romantically interpreted. Only with this proviso in mind can we appraise his assertion at its true value.

Speaking of a violation of boundaries we do not intend to express a censure. The violation, dangerous though it was, sprang as a necessary result from a situation in which philosophy and art found themselves; and it is inseparable from the peculiar greatness of the two movements. Philosophy, supported in the Pre-Kantian epoch by a theological framework, had now to stand on its own ground. The poets of the younger generation were involved in a similar plight. To them the great achievements of the preceding generation were a powerful stimulant. But this legacy conveyed no tradition to develop, yielded no esthetic code to guide their steps. Both philosopher and poet had to redefine the meaning of their labor. The mutual infringement in which their joint efforts issued indicated a crisis in the intelléctual life. What might appear a wilful confusion was actually a search for new limits.

The procedure intended to reveal the creative operations of the mind was termed 'transcendental method.' Thus Fichte's dictum, that art has "to make over the transcendental standpoint into a universal one," [1] unmistakably points to the trend of the general development. But Fichte did not care, and was hardly able, to follow up and amplify his remark. The single philosophical act, by which the creative life is grasped, was called 'intellectual intuition.' The next step to be taken was to elucidate the interrelation between the basic philosophical act, intellectual intuition, and the basic esthetic act, esthetic intuition. But this could not be done on the plane of speculation which Fichte's *Wissenschaftslehre* had reached. For him the single acts of intellectual intuition marked the steps in an endless approximation to a total vision of reality. Hence they stand in contrast to the esthetic act which offers a total whole as

INTELLECTUAL AND ESTHETIC IN-TUITION.

---

[1] *Das System der Sittenlehre nach den Principien der Wissenschaftslehre,* 1798, §31 (Sämtliche Werke, ed., J. H. Fichte, IV, 353ff.).

present fulfillment. Friedrich Wilhelm Joseph Schelling (1775–1854) suggested a peculiar solution of the problem. In his system of 1800, which is still close to Kant and Fichte, he construes philosophical cognition as a gradual overcoming of the duality of subject and object. As the consummation of this process he erects the picture of art—of a romantic super-art, the ocean into which all streams of intellectual development, philosophy, science, religion, and political life, are destined to flow. Esthetic intuition, he declares, "is intellectual intuition turned objective." [2]

ESTHETICS WITHIN SCHELLING'S SYSTEM OF 'ABSOLUTE IDEALISM.'

It is, however, doubtful whether the new position really solves the problem at hand. It seems as if the philosopher confines his work to the forecourt of metaphysics, leaving to the artist or super-artist the unveiling of the source of reality. Schelling soon regretted his romantic abandonment of philosophy in favor of a Utopian art. He now took his stand exactly where he had previously located the universal art of the future. At the same time the idea of an infinite approximation to a total synthesis was abandoned. Philosophical thought does not approach the Absolute without ever attaining its goal. The Absolute, present from the outset, gradually reveals itself in the cognitive process. The structural outlines of the new system are much the same as those of the earlier. Faithful to the threefold division derived from Kant's three Critiques, Schelling distinguished a triad of Ideas: truth, goodness, and beauty.[3] Since truth involves necessity and goodness involves liberty, the synthetic function assigned to beauty is defined as the "indifference of necessity and liberty." [4] Yet this gives rise to a puzzling problem. As truth is embodied in knowledge, goodness in the virtuous life, so beauty, synthesizing these one-sided activities, should find its appropriate realization in art. Thus the supremacy of art seems to be secured once more at the expense of philosophy. For philosophy, as a form of knowledge, will presumably be classed with truth and necessity on a lower level of reality. But then a philosophy of art becomes in-

---

[2] *System des Transcendentalen Idealismus*, 6. Hauptabschnitt §2 (Sämtliche Werke, ed. K. F. A. Schelling, III, 624).

[3] *Philosophie der Kunst*, Lectures presented 1802–1803, §16 (Werke V, 382).

[4] *Ibid.*, p. 383.

conceivable. How could the inferior manifestation of the Absolute comprehend its more complete expression? Schelling meets this objection by attributing to philosophy a unique position: "As God resides above and embraces the Ideas of truth, goodness, and beauty, so does philosophy. Philosophy deals solely with neither truth, morality, nor beauty alone, but with what is common to them all, deriving them from a single well-head." [5] Philosophy is both science and more than science: within it truth, goodness, and beauty, and consequently science, virtue, and art, interpenetrate. This all-embracing philosophy is not poetry, but it is analogous to a work of art. "The universe," asserted Schelling, "is God in the form of the absolute work of art and in eternal beauty," [6] and he regarded world history as "a great poem the achievement of which the universal Spirit meditates." Even the romantic idea of a final transfiguration of reality is preserved in the expectation of the moment when the "great poem" shall be finished and the successive phases in the modern world transmuted into simultaneity. [7]

At the basis of Schelling's Idealism is an identification of contraries: a "point of indifference" of all antagonisms and contradictions both of life and science is posited. [8] The potencies marking the diversity of subject matter and the steps of philosophical research are neither independent sections nor parts of absolute reality nor do they give rise to independent disciplines. Each of them is virtually the whole of reality viewed from a certain angle, or presenting a specific aspect of its indivisible nature. This structure of the Absolute is reflected in the mutual relationship between the different studies in the sphere of knowledge. Philosophy is as indivisible as reality. "Accordingly," Schelling said, "I do not first construe art as art, as this particular phenomenon, but I construe the universe in the form of art; and philosophy of art is science of the universe in the potency of art." [9] This procedure is intended to guarantee the scientific character of esthetics. In accordance with

ART MANIFESTS ETERNAL FORMS WITHIN THE 'REFLECTED' WORLD.

---

[5] *Ibid.*, p. 382.
[6] *Ibid.*, §21, p. 385.
[7] *Ibid.*, §42, p. 445.
[8] *Ibid.*, Einleitung, p. 365.
[9] *Ibid.*, p. 368.

its inherent laws, the realm of art has to be built up by the philosopher as an organic whole analogous to nature; [10] and this method
of *a priori* construction does not even stop short of individual works
and artists. Homer, Dante, and Shakespeare are deduced as parts of
a speculative system.[11]

The essence of art is defined by its relation to philosophy.
The philosopher concerns himself with Ideas, that is, with 'eternal
conceptions' reflecting in the ideal sphere the 'potencies' of the
Absolute. Art, too, represents Ideas, Ideas however 'grown
objective.' In other words, art manifests the Infinite not through
'prototypes' but through 'reflected images.'

As art represents the ideal models, of which things are but defective reproductions, it portrays the 'intellectual world' within
the 'reflected,' that is, factual world. Music for example is the
proto-typical rhythm of the Universe. The shapes of sculpture are
the prototypes of organic nature. Homer's epic is the Identity itself
through which history is based upon the Absolute; and every picture
discloses the intellectual world.[12] Thus art builds up the counterpart and illustration of philosophical truth. As it represents Ideas
which, as 'eternal conceptions,' reside in God, God is "the immediate cause of all art." [13] Artistic creation is due to the "eternal
Idea of man in God, who is linked up and united with the soul." [14]
This presence of divinity in man is 'genius,' the gift that enables
the individual to translate the ideal world into objectivity.[15]

AFFINITY OF ART
AND ORGANIC NA-
TURE.

There is close kinship between the realms of organic nature and
art as defined by Schelling. Philosophy is related to art within the
ideal world as reason to organism within the real world. "As reason
immediately becomes objective only in the organism, and as the
eternal intellectual Ideas turn objective as souls of organic bodies,
so philosophy becomes immediately objective through art, and the
Ideas of philosophy grow objective as the souls of real objects." [16]

---

[10] *Philosophie der Kunst*, §21, p. 375.
[11] *Ibid.*, p. 363.
[12] *Ibid.*, p. 369.
[13] *Ibid.*, §23, p. 386.
[14] *Ibid.*, §62, p. 458f.
[15] *Ibid.*, §63, p. 460.
[16] *Ibid.*, §17, p. 383.

Art and organic nature occupy strictly analogous places at different levels of the system. The organism exhibits the synthesis of conscious and unconscious activity, or of liberty and necessity, *before* their separation by the human mind; art reunites them *after* their separation in the sphere of conscious life.[17] Hence the sculptor or the painter who represents nature has to undo in his own mind the separation effected by human consciousness. He reverts to a subconscious stratum where man and nature are one. His relation to the outer aspect of the natural world will pass through two phases. First he will withdraw from nature in order to free himself from what is mere outcome, shell, lifeless surface. Thus he rises to the creative energy which he discovers in his own mind. Only in the last stage of accomplishment will he return to nature. Thus he will fulfill his true task which is "to imitate the spirit of nature which, working in the core of things, speaks by form and shape as if by symbols."[18]

Schelling's system is articulated by the successive preponderance now of the ideal, now of the real factor. Accordingly a system of the arts is constructed by means of repeated twofold divisions that issue in a third, which is the synthesis. The basic distinction divides the figurative arts, exponents of the real series, from the arts of the word, representative of the ideal side. The application of the same design yields, on the real side, music set over against painting, and finally sculpture, their synthesis. In the sphere of ideality, the lyric is described as the "incorporation of the infinite in the finite, that is in the particular," the epic as the "representation of the finite in (or its subsumption under) the infinite, that is the general," drama as the perfect union of the particular and the general or the real and the ideal.[19]

SCHELLING'S SYSTEM OF ARTS.

"The same unifications which, regarded in themselves, are Ideas, that is images of divinity, are gods, when looked upon as real."[20] We should expect this definition to define works of art rather than

GREEK MYTHOLOGY AS ARTISTIC CREATION. IT REVEALS PHILOSOPHY OF NATURE.

---

[17] *Ibid.*, §18, p. 384.
[18] *Über das Verhältnis der bildenden Künste zu der Natur. Rede gehalten am 12. Oktober 1807*, translated by A. Johnson, 1845, pp. 9f.
[19] *Philosophie der Kunst*, Einleitung, pp. 370f.
[20] *Ibid.*, §28, p. 390.

gods, and we cannot but wonder for what purpose a plurality of divine beings is introduced into an esthetic inquiry. As a matter of fact these gods are conceived essentially as esthetic creations. They are the material of artistic production and the total representation of them is mythology.[21] Mythology, subjected to the supreme law of beauty,[22] is visible only to the imagination.[23] 'Gods' and 'mythology' signify Greek gods and Greek mythology. As such they constitute the historical counterpart of the timeless system of the arts. Like the realm of art, Greek mythology is held to disclose in sensuous form the whole wealth of speculative wisdom. Disregarding his own warning not to force upon "these delicate creations of fancy" an alien rational context, Schelling goes so far as to identify Jupiter with the 'point of absolute indifference,' Apollo with the ideal world, Vulcan with the formative principle embodied in iron, Neptune with water—the formless principle.[24] Thus Winckelmann's classicist dogma, claiming timeless validity for Greek art, is reinforced by a revival of the polytheistic creed. And this in its turn is understood to consist in the imaginative deification of natural potencies as discovered by speculation. A Greek statue of the classical period is revered not alone as a document of absolute beauty. It is believed to reveal both a real God and an aspect of the universe.

SPECULATIVE HISTORY OF ART.

Granting this makes it difficult to account for the continued existence of art in the modern world. Schelling solved the problem by devising a plan of universal history. The representation of the Absolute in the form of particularity (with a perfect indifference of the general and the particular) is possible only in symbol.[25] Greek art is the paragon of symbolic expression. The same 'point of indifference' however can be reached also in the sphere of universality. A new era of world history was needed to develop this alternative: "Whereas the requirement fulfilled by Greek mythology was the representation of the Infinite in the Finite and consequently sym-

---

[21] *Philosophie der Kunst*, Einleitung, p. 370.
[22] *Ibid.*, §32, p. 397.
[23] *Ibid.*, §31, p. 395.
[24] *Ibid.*, §35, p. 402.
[25] *Ibid.*, p. 406.

bolism, the opposite demand was at the basis of Christianity: to absorb the Finite into the Infinite and to transform it into an allegory of Infinity." [26] Greek paganism and Christian faith are wedded together in a revelation of God in history. The days of Greece, when gods joined in the life of mortals, appear to hold the promise of a future state of still greater blessedness. "It is as if Christ, the Infinite embodied in Finitude, offering itself in human shape to God, were bringing the old epoch to a close. He is only there to mark a limit as the last God. After Him comes the Spirit, the ideal principle, the ruling soul of the modern world." [27] Under the rule of the Spirit the symbols are supplanted by symbolic actions,[28] and the church as the catholic organization of these actions becomes the all-comprehensive work of art.[29] The universe, instead of being visible as Nature, reveals itself as history and Divine Providence.

Yet this character of the modern age does not involve the extinction of artistic, that is, symbolic expression. The tomorrow of Schelling's prophecies is the return of the ancient world transfigured and elevated to the spirituality of our own era. The philosophy of nature is called upon to stand by in readiness to provide fresh symbols for the mythology that is to be. "Whereas in the mythology of the first kind (the Greek) the gods of nature transformed themselves into gods of history, so in the other kind the Gods of History must transform themselves into Gods of Nature." [30] As long as the circle of this development is not yet complete, every artistic creation is to be regarded as the anticipation of future accomplishment. For the time being a great poet must be content with testifying of a world in its becoming, and this world, however dimly and fragmentarily perceived, furnishes him the matter out of which he moulds his own mythology. Therefore his works will be stamped with originality as with the hall-mark of our age.[31]

---

[26] *Ibid.*, §42, p. 430.
[27] *Ibid.*, p. 432.
[28] *Ibid.*, p. 433.
[29] *Ibid.*, §54, p. 455.
[30] *Ibid.*, §61, p. 457.
[31] *Ibid* §42, p. 445.

Schelling asserts that the contrasts which arise from the dependence of art upon time, are, like time itself, of a purely accidental and formal kind.[32] But actually he develops his historical scheme of symbolic and allegorical expression in a strict analogy to the timeless system of art. To make sense out of this contradiction, we have to define the temporal place of Schelling's philosophy within universal history as outlined by himself. On the one hand his doctrine anticipates the future of mystic simultaneity. In Absolute Idealism the circle of evolution is closed and time ceases to be. On the other hand, since this final synthesis is described as future, the philosophizing mind must take its stand in the temporal movement towards a far-off end, and thus remain subject to the sway of time. On this point, the Kantian-Fichtean notion of an infinite progress persists in Schelling's system. It anticipates in a pseudo-prophetic and half-poetic vision a crowning fulfilment beyond the bounds of rational comprehension.

This combination of conflicting views is reflected in Schelling's esthetics. While locating the organism of art within a realm of timeless Forms, it mediates, in the form of a speculative history of art, between the supratemporal Absolute and the philosophizing mind which moves within the historical process. The two aspects are not truly reconciled. The problem of the metaphysical significance of art, powerfully stirred by Schelling, did not come to rest in his system. The way lay open for a new attempt at synthesis.[33]

HEGEL'S DIALECTI-
CAL RECONCILIA-
TION OF CON-
TRASTS.

The system of Georg Friedrich Wilhelm Hegel (1770–1831) is the document of a great act of reconciliation. In the 'harmony of discords' achieved by his dialectic the antagonisms of previous controversies persist. But the conflicting views no longer appear to be exclusive of one another. Embraced in a comprehensive whole they become complementary aspects of the total truth, con-

---

[32] *Philosophie der Kunst*, Einleitung, p. 372; cf. J. Gibelin, *L'Esthétique de Schelling d'après la philosophie de l'art*, 1934.

[33] Influenced by Schelling is Karl Christian Friedrich Krause (1779–1829), author of a system expressed in an abstruse terminology. His posthumous works: *Abriss der Ästhetik oder Philosophie des Schönen und der Kunst*, ed. J. Leutbecher, 1837; *Vorlesungen über die Philosophie des Schönen und der schönen Kunst*, 1882.

tradictions within a process that moves perpetually through contradictions and solves them all. Thus his mature doctrine is, so to speak, transparent. The record of past struggles shows through the palimpsest that is the harmonious and final document. In the first part of the Berlin Lectures, there is a careful discussion of general problems. What is beauty? What is the meaning of art? What is the correct scientific approach to these problems? Weighing one definition after another and so leading up to his own, Hegel by implication recapitulates the eventful history of esthetics since Baumgarten. The effort of rescuing the conception of art from a too narrow rationalistic interpretation, the struggle for a rigorous observance of the uniqueness and autonomy of art (an idea which was to rank art with the highest of spiritual activities and indicate its place and function in cultural life)—all this recurs in Hegel's Lectures. Then there was the other great matter of previous debates: Winckelmann's Greek ideal against the romantic idea of Christian art. The second part of Hegel's esthetics dealing with the Ideal both reflects and liquidates this controversy. He holds firmly to the classicist faith but endorses at the same time some of the more moderate claims of romanticism and realism. Finally the idea of the contrast of Greek and Modern style, worked out by Schiller and Friedrich Schlegel, had brought into esthetics an historic element that was subversive of its systematic character. Schelling had tried in vain to integrate history in system. Such wavering to and fro comes to an end in Hegel's system. For him history and system are two aspects of the same dialectical process. So the history of art, and the system of arts, are clearly distinguished and at the same time made mutually dependent.

In Hegel's system dialectic, the living thought, is substituted for life. The problem is: how can art be located in the speculative system? When Classicists and Romanticists came to close quarters over the problem of an esthetic standard, they were both concerned with finding a way which might lead art toward a future perfection. What matters for Hegel is chiefly the allotment of an appropriate place to both classic and romantic art in his survey of the universal development of art. In Friedrich Schlegel and Schelling, the philosophy of history was a hybrid product, half report of the past, half prophecy of a Utopian achievement. For Hegel, Idea is no longer anticipation of the possible. Spirit is wholly immersed in reality, materialized in history; and such history, at any rate as history of art, has no future. Considered in its relation to earlier thought, Hegel's esthetic is, and is intended to be, consummation. There is no want in his perfect cosmos of art and, as a consequence, no striving after new aims. Art is viewed as a phenomenon of the past.[34]

NATURE CREEPS UP
TOWARD BEAUTY,
BUT ONLY ART
ACHIEVES IT.

Turning now to a closer examination of the Berlin Lectures we find Hegel defining art as the presentation of the Ideal. Philosophy must follow and interpret this presentation. The Ideal is his technical term for the Absolute as art yields it: it is the animating Spirit of things manifested to sense. When and how does this occur? Never adequately in nature. For when the Absolute becomes present to sense it must show the freedom and power of self-motion, the infinite differentiation, yet harmony and stability of the Whole of Things. Nature as she ascends from crystal to man increasingly exhibits these characters, but never in a degree and combination sufficient for true beauty. The Ideal must endow its sense-appearance with the marks of reason, and reason, moreover, expressing itself at every point and in self-initiated movement. A piece of metal, representative of the mineral kingdom, is an "indifferent equilibrium of identical qualities." [35] Here there is lacking the richness and mobility of the Absolute. The solar system is too loose an organization, its unity too little dispatched into the parts to exhibit reason's full force. Plants are rooted to the soil and so far immobile. In the animal kingdom Spirit struggles with the tight bands of nature toward free self-shaping. But the coverings of animals are often more like the heavy dull rinds of vegetables—scales or fur—than of a substance that lets the light of Spirit shine through. In so far as the organs and limbs of animals are variously adapted to specific functions, yet all centered around the purpose of the body as a whole; and

---

[34] Cf. Helmut Kuhn, *Die Vollendung der klassischen deutschen Ästhetik durch Hegel* (in *Die Kulturfunktion der Kunst*, Vol. II), 1931.

[35] Hegel, *Philosophy of Fine Art*, trans. F. P. B. Osmaston, 4 Vols., London, 1920, Vol. I, p. 161. Part I, Ch. II, A, 1, a.

also, in so far as, like birds, they can express through song an inner feeling, animals begin to manifest the central attributes of reason, and so to be beautiful. Man, as the highest animal, is not only intellectually the crown of nature but also nature's most beautiful product. This is because the marks of reason are more evident in him. He is more independent of his environment, thus meeting the requirement of self-contained unity and harmony. He has speech as well as song among his gifts, and so is more rationally expressive. And his inward vitality, the energy of the spirit in him, shines through his thin and ruddy skin.[36] Man's body, compared with the other objects in the natural world, is, so to speak, all alive with the Idea. He begins therefore to convey to a beholder the nature of the Ideal, for reason shapes and illumines, binds, and differentiates all the parts of him. Yet even man falls short. His limitations, his fragmentariness in time and space are plainly visible and betoken his inability to convey the meaning of an Absolute.

It is in art rather than in nature that the Ideal must be found. For art is nature twice-begotten, nature born again in the inventions of genius. In the passage through the medium of a poet's brain, the prose of reality and the brutishness of raw nature take on the plasticity and harmony of Spirit. The world of art, Hegel says, is initiated in a sacrament or baptism which symbolizes the art-objects' participation in the free self-awareness of the human self-consciousness.[37] Indeed the artist's own mind in its act of creation possesses something god-like in its strength. That art is Ideal means then that its source in the poetic imagination insures its exaltation above the crude and common given fact.[38]

Nature offers then a scale rising toward beauty but does not achieve beauty. Hegel shows in an analogous way that the formal attributes of symmetry and balance qualify rather than constitute beauty.[39] He exhibits these also in an ascending scale, showing how they climb toward fuller harmony and richer expressive-

THE FORMAL PRIN-CIPLES QUALIFY RATHER THAN CON-STITUTE BEAUTY.

---

[36] *Ibid.*, Vol. I, p. 200. Part I, Ch. 2, Sec. C, 1, b.
[37] *Ibid.*, Vol. I, p. 39. Introduction III, 1, c.
[38] *Ibid.*, Vol. I, pp. 220, 221.
[39] *Ibid.*, Vol. I, pp. 184–96. Part I, Ch. 2, B.

ness as they increasingly conform to the definition of the Ideal. *All* formal principles of beauty are variants of unity in difference. But unity in difference comes closer to the requirements of Appearing Totality when the differentiation is marked and abundant and the energy at the center more commanding. Least expressive of the ideal is bare repetition, as in a succession of columns. Symmetry of parts balanced around a center contains more matter of interest. Still higher is lawfulness, or a conformity to rule, which involves the combination of unlike parts into a single whole as in the ellipse or parabola, a serpentine form, or the combination of the inner and outer curves of the human arm. Higher than rule comes harmony, which is the bonding together of unlike series, as colors with shapes, sounds with movements. This unity is stronger because the difference is so. Hegel adds to this ascending series of formal principles one that stands slightly apart, the unity of sensuous materials: the purity of the blue of the heavens, the translucence of the atmosphere, pure vowel sounds, cleanliness of a well-drawn straight line, primary tints. These please us, he claims, because of the simplicity and purity of the medium.

THE BEST MATE-
RIAL FOR ART: THE
DIVINE IN HUMAN
SHAPE.

After testing all the phases of nature and of form in their relation to beauty and showing that they converge for their fulfillment and correction upon his own conception of beauty—the revelation of the Ideal in sensuous form—Hegel takes up the more particular statement of the nature of this Ideal itself. What state of affairs, human and extra-human, makes the best material for an artistic whole? Man himself, though the most beautiful of nature's products because he manifests in the highest degree freedom and intelligence, harmony and variety, yet falls short of a complete realization of these qualities. Beauty in itself requires the divine. But the divine for art is different from the divine for thought. Art demands that condition of divinity in which organic shape, presence to sense, is at its maximum.[40] When the Divine Substance breaks itself up into a multiplicity of independent gods, that is, in religion at the stage of Greek polytheism, the needs of artistic representation are best served. For in the Greek gods, the

---

[40] Hegel, *op. cit.,* Vol. I, p. 237. Part I, Ch. 3, B, 1, 2.

natural entity, the human body, which almost meets art's demands, is refined and exalted into complete fitness. The Greek gods have bodies, and so a means of showing their souls; but they are wiser and more powerful than men; and this superior state of spirit is revealed in forms free from disfigurement and limitation. God as revealed in the incarnate Christ also fits the requirements of art. As Greek gods are the chief material of the greatest sculpture and poetry, so the history of the Christian God-man is the favorite subject in the great period of painting.

We recognize here the outlines of Hölderlin's and Schelling's prophetic vision of world history without their expectation of a future synthesis and with a more realistic statement. Man as an independent product of Nature, Hegel argues, does not meet the requirements either of Divinity or of art. But if man's greatness is enhanced by the conditions of his environment, and if he is stretched to a stature of more than ordinary power or virtue, if, in a word, he becomes heroic or coöperates with the environment so as to make together with it a noble harmony, the resulting situation is deiform. There are certain historical epochs, certain world-situations, then, that are appropriate to art even on Hegel's exacting conception of it. The heroic age in which a single person assumes the duties of a whole society, personally rights its wrongs and embodies its ideas, is an example.[41] Orestes and Hercules drew up into their persons the substance of their clan or nation. There is something generic about them; and yet this larger whole is compressed into an individual's shape and history. The modern counterpart of the mythical hero is the leader of a revolt, or a champion of the oppressed, such as Charles Moor, or the embodiment of an ideal, as Don Quixote. In contrast with situations such as these, the well-regulated state of today, in which the individual becomes an adjusted member of the social organism, with no heroic responsibilities on his own shoulders, is prosaic. Princes, splendid robbers, and heroes, who make and execute the law in their own persons, are the right stuff for epic and drama.

The Ideal of Beauty exhibits first of all an aspect of calm

---

[41] *Ibid.*, Vol. I, p. 249. Part I, Ch. 3, II, 1, *aa.*

majesty or beatific enjoyment, a "deedless and infinite self-repose" as in certain statues of Hercules "taking a rest"; but the Ideal shows also development and activity, as when Christ is represented in his suffering and death. Besides these exemplifications of grand Ideality, Hegel instances the translation of common life as in Dutch painting. Dutch "interiors" strike one at first as too pedestrian for Hegel's requirements. But he interprets the general substance of their pictures as a "staunch sense of citizenship, . . . passionate love of enterprise, sterling self-consciousness, careful, clean, and dainty mode of life, liveliness and lustiness." [42]

Genius, the human power to make the Ideal actual, Hegel describes as the native, inborn "lust of work . . . and an imperative impulse akin to any other natural want to give artistic form to . . . emotional and imaginative life." [43] The artistic imagination was for him no inward fancy, no power that feeds on its own subjective dreams. Rather it involves observation, memory, and wide experience of the world. [44] So Schelling had taught that genius must submit itself at first to exact rendering of the separate individual things, with their precise limits and characters, that make up the least "spiritual" level of nature, before passing to the projection of feeling and charm upon these phenomena.

ORIENTAL SYMBOLISM THE FORECOURT OF ART.

The second part of the *Aesthetics* is devoted to a detailed description of the way in which the Ideal evolves. Hegel is adapting here his ideas on "absolute art," expounded in the *Phenomenology*, to the theme and the systematic structure of his lectures. In symbolic art, particularly in Egyptian architecture, the Ideal, the perfect union of significance and form, is feeling its way uncertainly toward expression; in classic art, particularly in Greek sculpture, the poise and harmony of the Ideal are at home and at the zenith of their power; in romantic art, particularly in modern music, the Ideal has declined by becoming over-self-conscious, too subjective and spiritual. This is, on the whole, Friedrich Schlegel's scheme of the world's history, curtailed by the removal of the program of future perfection. Romantic eschatology is absorbed in history.

---

[42] Hegel, *op. cit.*, Vol. I, pp. 229, 230. Part I, Ch. 3, A, 2, c.
[43] *Ibid.*, Vol. I, p. 388. Part I, Ch. 3, C, 1, b.
[44] *Ibid.*, Vol. I, pp. 381, 382. Part I, Ch. 3, C, 1, a.

Hegel's idea of the symbol is a direct descendant of the old esthetic notion of the sublime assimilated to an historical trend of thought. In the symbolic as well as in the sublime there is a disproportion between content and form. Symbolism is "the fore-court of art." [45] In it the sensuous show and the divine content do not perfectly match. Matter serves rather as the environment of Spirit than as its plastic incarnation.

Ambiguity, uncanniness, sublimity are all characteristic qualities of symbolic art, for always there is the lack of poise and easy self-assertion in it. Indeed, Hegel calls the tombs and sphinxes of Egypt, with their cryptic problematic character, the very symbol of symbolism.[46] For Egypt is "the nation Art claims for herself." [47] By saying this Hegel does not mean that art on his view reaches its highest point in Egyptian architecture but that the function of art is first consciously realized in Egypt. In her tombs and pyramids there is a plastic adumbration of the root-idea of all true religion, that the death of the natural form is the condition of the life of the spirit. The Pyramids, as the impressive monuments of dead kings, are "enormous crystals which secrete an Inward within them." [48] And yet being symbols only, they remain "full of mystery and silence" and "without music and motion." [49]

The sublimity of Hebrew poetry is another example of symbolism. The disproportion between content and form here lies in the unsuccessful straining of words and metaphors in the Psalms to communicate the aloofness and abstract unity of the One True God. The Hebrews taught that God is too high and great ever to dwell essentially in any finite thing. Yet poetry cannot be except through defined images and signs. Therefore the impossible is attempted, and the straining of the poet to do what is beyond human power results in a characteristic kind of symbolic art. Here Hegel leaves behind him the conception of sublimity characteristic of Kant and taken over from the English school, that

---

[45] *Ibid.*, Vol. II, p. 23.
[46] *Ibid.*, Vol. II, p. 83. Part II, Ch. 1, C, 3, c.
[47] *Ibid.*, Vol. II, p. 75. Part II, Ch. 1, C.
[48] *Ibid.*, Vol. II, p. 77. Part II, Ch. 1, C, 7, c.
[49] *Ibid.*, Vol. II, p. 75.

sublimity is constituted on the objective side by vast size or power
of mountains or storms. God alone, for Hegel, is sublime; and
Hebrew poetry is the one authentic expression of the sublime.[50]

Hegel describes a final form of symbolic art as the fable, inclusive of parable, riddle, metaphor, allegory, and descriptive and
didactic poems.[51] These all make a deliberate but unsuccessful attempt to inclose a definite thought within the circle of an image.
The meaning-side in every case over-balances and remains external
to the image. In the earlier forms of symbolic art, the still unconscious process of the World-Spirit labored toward artistic
utterance. But in the moment of its dissolution symbolism realizes
its own peculiar function and industriously fits sign to thing signified by conscious contrivance. But in the very over-charging
of the reflective and comparing element, Spirit fails once more to
generate a perfect vehicle.

PERFECTION
REACHED IN CLAS-
SIC ART.

In symbolic art the artist is always searching for a material
form that will express his meaning without remainder. He never
finds it. The classic artist finds what he is seeking in the natural
human body. The perfect fitness of man's body to express man's
soul, for example, the depth of meaning in a serious glance from the
eyes, makes the style which chooses the human body as its principal
thematic material art's zenith. "More beautiful art than this can
neither exist now nor hereafter." [52] Spirit, the ultimate meaning of
things, has in man's body its ultimate vehicle, and man's body is
Spirit manifest. So far as Spirit can work through art, man's shape
must be its mode of self-declaration.

The Greeks grasped this philosophical truth and uttered it to
the senses in their statues of the gods. The air of serenity and
happy repose that envelops these stone and bronze deities is the
emotional seal on the wisdom of their art. The Greek sculptor not
only *found* in nature the shape he needed, but he *made* this found
form into something consonant with itself but more universal,
more harmonious and sublime, more nearly in unison with the ideal
of beauty and divinity. So the human form, through the power of

---

[50] Hegel, *op. cit.*, Vol. II, pp. 85–89. Part II, Ch. 2.
[51] *Ibid.*, Vol. II, pp. 113–66. Part II, Ch. 3.
[52] *Ibid.*, Vol. II, p. 283.

the poetry of the Greek sculptors, became the inhabitant of Olympus. Because this humanity exalted to divinity has many sides, not one god but a circle of gods was brought into being. Zeus, holding dominion over gods and men, Apollo, lord of light and knowledge, Ares, spirit of war, Hephaestus, divine craftsman, Dionysus, Demeter, Hera, each had his or her sphere. Thus the Absolute Spirit was individualized. But in this too great individuality of the gods there were the seeds of the dissolution of classicism. Anthropomorphism makes perfect art, but it menaces and shackles philosophy and religion. Spirit has to go beyond the stage of presenting itself to itself in material form, in order to think and feel itself. But when it thinks or feels itself, there must be more complexity and depth of meaning than the visible Pantheon can figure. There must be the stern necessity of an ultimate logic. The gods of Greece formed an aggregate, not a necessary totality, not the iron chain of a dialectic. Therefore their independence, shape, and freedom, so happy a condition for art, dissatisfied even their human makers after a while. Man cannot finally rest in any object which does not unfold the last heights and depths of spirit. Spirit must suffer and die. The beautiful house of clay must yield to the truth of sacrifice. The gods of the Greeks were not after all absolute or in the ultimate sense spiritual. Fate was above them. Man's intrigues engaged them. They were unfeeling in their eternal bliss. So a stage of satire, congenial to the Roman spirit, illumined the inadequacy of the Greek conception. This prosaic art and the historical events that initiated Christianity pointed the way toward romantic art.

With the passing of the classic phase of culture, the supreme suitability of art as a medium of human expression passes also. The World-Spirit in its progress waxes more reflective and religious, and less inclined to content itself with the kind of satisfaction associated with the body, however superb the line and bearing of the body may be. The very gods of Greece as sculptured in the Hellenistic period modulate the divine substance into mental nuance, and illustrate the lesser ideals of grace and charm rather than the grander ones of nobility and calm. As art fines away and rarefies its theme actual men also appear in Greece and then in

ART ECLIPSED BY CHRISTIAN SPIRITUALISM. ROMANTIC ART AND ITS DISINTEGRATION IN ROMANTIC IRONY.

Rome—Socrates and the Stoics, for example—who are animated by an unworldly faith and a reliance on individual righteousness alien to the psycho-physical balance of the palmy days of art. Morality and religion have come into their own and displace beauty as a primary value. Morality, Hegel says, is essentially intellectual. Its full meaning cannot be translated into sensuous terms. The Christian religion teaches that the very substance of God became an historical man, and entered into the full gamut of the sufferings of a real human being. The imagery, the half-make-believe realm of art, is not sufficiently in earnest, nor sufficiently capable of complete contradiction to express this new religious truth easily. The plastic imagination did not invent the Christian scheme: God made flesh, born of woman, living in Galilee, rising from the tomb; and art cannot at once and easily throw these ideas into plastic form.[53] Thus art stands down, and faith mounts up. For the world is now ready to focus its attention on inward spiritual depths and strains, the law of conscience and the greatness of sacrifice. The supreme Christian truth is that the death of the body conditions the resurrection of the soul. But a truth so ascetic is incompatible with the genius of art: art which always gives soul its body.

That art yields to faith does not mean, however, that art does not in some wise live on. It simply means that art is no longer the supreme natural expression of the cultural outlook, and that in her future history, she must bend herself to a new mode congenial to the new human ideal. Music is the particular art that suits the romantic Christian mood best; and the concept that threads its way in and out of all the romantic manifestations is that of Christian love. Modern painting, the first of the romantic arts, repeats infinitely the chosen theme in its representations of the life of Christ and Mary, the Holy Family, the acts and sufferings of the saints and martyrs. Love is the agreement of Spirit with itself, as beauty is the agreement of Spirit with a physical incarnation. In music and poetry the infinite melody and meaning utter in the last resort this reconciliation of the soul with the soul's demands

---

[53] Hegel, *op. cit.*, Vol. II, p. 265. Subsection II, Ch. 3, 2, a.

upon itself; its going out and its return. Even in tragedy, the consummate form of poetry, the initial conflict of forces is re- solved and a higher acquiescence in the unity behind the conflict suggested. As Schelling had already said: "the beholder is over- taken by the certainty that all antithesis is but apparent—that love is the bond of all being." [54]

But the romantic spirit has its secular aspect. For example in chivalry, the desire for personal distinction and the love of a lady or the sentiments of honor and loyalty furnish romantic themes, but on a lower key than the Gospels. When romanticism abandons its attachment to religion, it starts on a downward road. The realistic representation in plays and novels of powerful characters who seek private ends, as Macbeth sought the throne and Othello the satisfaction of his consuming jealousy, can only be kept on a level worthy of art by the rare genius of a Shakespeare. It is religion and morals that normally furnish private individuals with aims fit to dignify their lives. Usually stories of characters who confess no allegiance to divinity are prosaic. The imitation of commonplace reality marks the fading away of the art-conscious- ness into the light of common day.

The last phase of all in the romantic sphere is that of humor. By humor Hegel means romantic irony. It implied for him the artist's repudiation of control and his sublimely egoistic sporting with all aims and ideals, possessions and aspirations, traditions and customs. A genius confident enough in the power of his art, and sufficiently independent of all normal claims, thus cuts the last thread that binds content to form, soul to body. "Humor can dissolve and make pliable to itself every form of stable definition." It implies the "perversion and overthrow of all that is objectively solid in reality; it works through the wit and play of wholly personal points of view, and if carried to an extreme amounts to the triumph of the creative power of the artist's soul over every content and every form." [55]

In the second part of his system Hegel proposes to show how the World-Spirit in its historical evolution lives through three

THE SYSTEM OF ARTS CORRESPONDS TO THE HISTORY OF ART.

---

[54] Schelling, *The Plastic Arts and Nature*, trans. Johnson, London, 1844, p. 24.
[55] Hegel, *op. cit.*, Vol. II, p. 386. Subsection III, Ch. 3, 3, b.

essential moods, and that to each of these moods a particular art in
a particular epoch has been most congenial. In the third part,
he analyzes each of the great arts as the development of a special
sensuous medium and shows that, this being its character, it was
chosen by the World-Spirit at a particular point of world-history.

Architecture Hegel regards as the heaviest and, intellectually
speaking, the dumbest of the arts. Although it aims at both utility
and beauty, in its beginnings in Syria, Babylonia, and Egypt, there
was little immediate practical purpose involved. A mass of stone
or brick was set up to convey a general thought: to symbolize the
generative organs, the sun's rays, or the new social solidarity of
many peoples. No immanent artistic laws were observed in the
building of the towers and obelisks; rather the foreign laws of
geometry and mechanics. Hegel believes that architecture, because
of its own choice of medium and mode of expression belongs to
the age of symbolism. Before there were houses and churches
and tombs fit to be called architecture, there were these mounds
and spires, which the people instinctively employed as a crude first
language of their emotions. This fumbling for a vehicle of a
vague meaning is the symbolic tendency. Men felt the surge of
enigmas within them; and they uttered these enigmas in their
forests of gigantic columns or huge pyramids and sphinxes; they
wrote them in hieroglyphics on a wall. But as architecture developed, its utility became more apparent. In the classic period
men made temples and houses, circuses and amphitheatres, whereas
in the last period of the symbolic age they had only attained ↩
the making of tombs. The chief Greek building is the temple, and
its purpose is to shelter a god. The art of sculpture which on the
symbolic plane is fused with architecture, separates itself here,
and constructs a center and justification for the whole edifice.
But though architecture has advanced, its function is less pure and
independent. It wants to be a symbol; and when it becomes the
house for a divine image, sculpture has taken over the main work
of conveying an idea, and architecture has accepted the office of
hand-maiden. Christian architecture is the union of the symbol
and the utility. The Gothic cathedral is a church, the house of
a God. But its whole design means religion. Instead of the cheer-

ful porch of a Greek temple, the Gothic cathedral combines the dark brooding interior which conduces to the spiritual moods of self-examination and exaltation with the infinite up-shooting of its spires and vaults. It symbolizes the aspiration toward the Infinite God of the Christian religion. But Gothic architecture is still farther removed from conformity to the bare definition of the meaning of architecture: the use of solid matter for the adumbration of a vague meaning. In Gothic architecture the solidity of the matter begins to melt. Thin points, and walls subtilized by windows, and the disdainful disregard of the natural tendency of matter to press downward, metamorphose the temple into a strange kind of music. So Schelling had said: Architecture is frozen music.

Sculpture resembles architecture in its use of three-dimensional solid matter. It differs in the clarity and spirituality of the idea it wills to deposit in stone. The idea expressed in a building is vague; but the communication of a statue is clear and unambiguous. In man's shape the soul is as it were poured over his whole body; it makes him stand erect, as master of nature and determiner of his own fortunes. "Stansion is an act of will—possesses a spiritual significance, just as we are accustomed to say of an essentially free and independent man who keeps his opinions, views, principles, and aims unaffected by others, that he stands on his own feet." [56] At the same time the soul vitalizes the surface and all the members, so that there is the impression of energetic freedom. The face of a man reflects the soul even more. Even the drapery of a Greek statue suits the demand of ideal art; for its folds add grace and harmony to the total form. The genius of sculpture, then, choosing hard real matter, bronze, stone, gold, or wood, for its medium, and expressing a divine but embodied spirit, corresponds to the Greek genius. The middle point in the system of the arts is the proper mate of the middle point in the evolution of Spirit. As the Greeks were the people most gifted artistically, so sculpture is the most beautiful art.

In painting, the first of the three romantic arts, the burden

---

[56] Hegel, *op. cit.*, Vol. III, p. 157. Subsection II, Ch. 2, 2, b.

of real, three-dimensional space is gone, and an ideal space takes its place. Light, 'spirit visible,' which offers no resistance and carries no weight, takes its place.[57] But what painting loses of material reality, it gains, through the ethereality of its medium, in power of representation. Though the painter cannot make an image of a god with full verisimilitude on the surface of a canvas, he gains the whole world, all objects, actions, emotions, and relations, for his province. The semblance of all solid things, their distances from and relations to each other, can be given through the modes of light in color and chiaroscuro. Thus by limitation of medium a gain in expressive capacity is won. In place of the Pantheon of Greek gods, painting chooses to portray the intimate history of the God whose essence is spirit and love, and whose kingdom is within the heart. Certain situations in the Biblical stories are most appropriate for rendering in paint: Christ in the passion-scenes, and in his childhood, and the tenderness of Mary's love.[58] In such scenes the intensity and intimacy of the Christian spirit are best illustrated. Sculpture chooses to express the main substance of a god, avoiding historical details; painting chooses precisely those moments of divine life which carry divinity farthest into tragedy and emotion. No aloofness here, but the community of God with man's soul. The coincidence of what painting can do best with what the Christian spirit desires to express is plain. But painting's universality admits landscape-painting, realistic portraits, and genre subjects. "Whatever can find a place in the human heart, as emotion, idea, and purpose, whatever it is capable of actually shaping —all such diversity may form part of the varied presentations of painting. The entire world of particular existence, from the most exalted embodiment of mind to the most insignificant natural fact, finds a place here." [59]

Music is the central embodiment of the romantic spirit. For music goes farther than painting in refusing to labor with the heavy weight of the material world to create its expressions. Space is no longer merely contracted from three dimensions to two, but dis-

---

[57] Hegel, *op. cit.*, Vol. III, p. 237. Subsection III, Ch. 1, 1, b.

[58] *Ibid.*, Vol. III, pp. 255–57. Subsection III, Ch. 7, 2, a.

[59] *Ibid.*, Vol. I, p. 118. Introduction, V, 4, c.

appears entirely, and the vibration of string or membrane is substituted for a solid existent.[60] Moreover the sense of hearing is more ideal than the sense of sight,[61] because in listening to music, we do not contemplate an object over against ourselves, but seem somehow to be following the very movement of the soul itself.[62] Or better, the observer in this case fuses with the object; the emotion in the melody is accepted as the emotion of the soul. There is a further respect in which music is ideal. The melody is not all there at once, but is a moving point. For the grasp of the melody as a whole, memory must help. Most of what is accepted as the beauty of the music is the dead vibration held in the recollection and there fused by an act of mental synthesis with what is actually beating upon the ear. The very existence of music is therefore spiritual. But it is the emotional spirit rather than the thinking mind that is embodied. In making soul intelligible to soul, music does not symbolize general concepts nor duplicate within, the outer spatial juxtaposition of things perceived. Out of inweaved motion and a texture of tones, it obliges feeling and sympathy to take on form; it creates a living being within the central current of the soul.[63]

The art of poetry, to which Hegel devotes one fourth of the whole space of his lectures, is not so much the culminating romantic art—though it is this—but the universal art. Essentially spiritual, it is less vaguely so than music, and resumes, though not in actual matter, the plastic clarity of sculpture. "The art of poetry celebrates its epochs of brilliancy and bloom among all nations and in all ages. . . . It embraces the collective Spirit of mankind, and it is differentiated through every kind of variation." [64] It is an art both of space and time; for it works in images, which are quasi-spatial entities, carved and definite; but it also recounts the history of men and peoples through time.[65] Its universal

POETRY—THE UNI-
VERSAL ART.

---

[60] *Ibid.*, Vol. III, pp. 340, 341. Subsection III, Ch. 2, Introduction.
[61] *Ibid.*, Vol. III, p. 341.
[62] *Ibid.*, Vol. III, p. 343.
[63] *Ibid.*, Vol. III, p. 358. Subsection III, Ch. 2, Introduction, 1, b.
[64] *Ibid.*, Vol. IV, p. 27. Subsection III, Ch. 3, Introduction I, 1, b.
[65] *Ibid.*, Vol. IV, p. 5.

capacity enables it to embody spiritual meanings at once clearly and fluidly. It can unfold the conditions of events and the conflicts of passions, as well as carve a character or a scene in sharp relief. When Homer describes the shield of Achilles, he competes in poetry with sculpture; but when he relates the changes in the wrath of Achilles, he follows the emotions of an inner self, musician-like. The medium of poetry is the image, not sound, as in music; and an image is halfway between a body and a thought. But the poetical image is a halfway house facing toward thought and philosophy; and turning its back on art. On Hegel's view the musical element in poetry is negligible. The meaning of a word is all that really matters, not its sound.

Poetry expresses itself in three forms: the epic, lyric, and drama. The epic is the most objective and comprehensive of the poetical forms; the lyric, the least. In the epic, we have the mirror of the original spirit of a folk, a kind of bible or saga. The heroes do not stand out as independent individuals focussing the reader's interest on their particular acts and fortunes, but fuse with the background of their nation's history and their local surroundings. The wrath of Achilles is significant chiefly as the hazard of the Greek forces in their war with Troy. Moreover in the *Iliad* the character of souls is reflected in the inanimate objects that they make or possess: swords, ships, goblets, tents, shields. The form of the epic is loose and tranquil, as suits its large, varied, and objective theme.

The poetical pendulum swings to the opposite extreme in the intensity of the lyric. Here the singer withdraws from the substantial background of the land and epoch that sustain him and give him support and occasions; and accents the utter loneliness, the absolute uniqueness of his feelings. He gives his heart away to the world. Thus the content of lyrics should be slight. Goethe, Hegel says, was one of the most successful of lyric poets because he could discover material for a song in the slightest incidents of his life.

Drama combines the personal interest of the lyric with a treatment of the ethical and social substance behind persons. Like classic sculpture, dramatic tragedy represents eternal forces, but sculpture represents these in their blessedness and tranquillity. Tragedy represents them in violent collision, and using human heroes to fight for the domination of one institutional value rather than another: the family rather than the state; the father's claims versus the mother's. Hegel believed that Sophocles' *Antigone* represented better than any other play what a tragedy signifies. Antigone's pious loyalty to brother and family comes in fatal conflict with the law of the land. Both the law of the state and family piety are positive and just claims on the loyalty of individuals; and when these two forces contradict each other, a tension arises which can only be loosened by the sacrifice of the life of an individual. There is violence done the harmony of all forces in the Absolute Spirit over all, if an individual espouses one single force, one particular ethical purpose to the exclusion of others. Since the very essence of art demands harmony in the end, the conflict of tragedy must not be its final moment. There must be a reconciliation, and a suggestion of calm after storm. But this peace is bought at the price of the complete annihilation of the individual as such. It hints the more massive substantiality of ideal beings.

Reconciliation of contradictions is the essence of Hegel's doctrine. But this doctrine itself resulted from a choice between two rival forms of reconciliation. From the outset it entailed the refutation of the poet's claim to be able to bring about the consummate synthesis. Must we conclude that there is a tension not integrated in dialectic? Is the ancient quarrel between philosophy and poetry understood and finished or is it rather perpetuated by Hegel's esthetics? To decide this question we use the phenomenon of the tragic as a touch-stone. For in the idea of mankind disunited and broken by conflicting tendencies is found the basic experience common to philosopher and poet. It is the stuff they are working on to achieve their respective forms of harmony. Now Hegel is surely correct in assuming that tragedy, like any other form of poetry, cannot end on a discordant note. Its dissonances, however radical, must be resolved into harmony. But Hegel, in his analysis of poetry, is too prone to seek this ultimate harmony on the level of intellectual consciousness. Dealing with

LIMITS OF THE DIALECTICAL REC-ONCILIATION.

poetry, he says, we have come "dangerously near to saying good-bye to art." [66] In fact he treats poetry almost as if it were versified philosophy. So he is barred from a genuine understanding of the greatest tragic genius of modern times, Shakespeare. He describes the type of the tragic hero in Shakespeare as "the individual walled up in himself." In Hegel's world, where all blessedness flows from participation in the total Life, this definition describes a state of utter desolation, a wretched and benighted soul. Upon one occasion, when he had listened to Tieck reading *Othello*, Hegel broke out with the words: "How torn must have been this man —Shakespeare—in his inner life to represent things in this way!" [67] The tragedian among Hegel's followers, Friedrich Hebbel (1813–63), set himself to reverse Hegel's position and to vindicate poetry. Art, he declared, cannot be outstripped by philosophy but rather is its realization. Tragedy alone—the intellectual sort of tragedy typified in Hebbel's own dramas—adequately represents the ultimate antinomies of reality. [68] Henrik Ibsen's conception of poetry as 'criticism of life' unmistakably derives from these post-Hegelian notions.

In one way or another Hegel's adherents felt that the harmony of his system was too easily obtained and that they had to assume the rôle of an *advocatus diaboli*. So Karl Rosenkranz (1805–79) brought into relief the esthetic relevance of the ugly as the 'self-destruction of the beautiful.' [69] Max Schasler (1819–1903) joined in his views. [70] Arnold Ruge's esthetic treatise centers round the idea of the comic. [71] They all conceived of their innovations as a

---

[66] Hegel, *op. cit.*, Vol. IV, p. 8.

[67] Wilhelm Waetzoldt, *Hebbel und die Philosophie seiner Zeit*, Dissertation, 1903, p. 40.

[68] *Tagebücher*, herausgegeben von R. M. Werner (Säkular-Ausgabe der Werke), II, 422f.; III, 5; IV, 173. "Vorwort zur 'Maria Magdalena,'" 1844, Säkular-Ausgabe, 1904, XI, 40.

[69] *Ästhetik des Hässlichen*, 1835.

[70] *Kritische Geschichte der Ästhetik. Grundlegung für die Ästhetik als Philosophie des Schönen und der Kunst*, 2 Vols., 1872.

[71] *Neue Vorschule zur Ästhetik. Das Komische, mit einem komischen Anhang*, 1837. Further Hegelian writers: H. G. Hotho, editor of Hegel's esthetic lectures and author of *Vorstudien für Kunst und Leben*, 1835, and Kuno Fischer, celebrated historian of philosophy, who wrote *Diotima. Die Idee des Schönen*, 1849.

development of Hegel's own ideas. Actually they touched upon a vital principle and prepared a radical criticism of the dialectical system.[72]

SUPPLEMENTARY READING

J. S. Kedney, *Hegel's Aesthetics. A Critical Exposition*, 1885.
A. C. Bradley, "Hegel's Theory of Tragedy," in *Oxford Lectures on Poetry*, 1909, pp. 69–95.
Bernard Bosanquet, *A History of Aesthetics*, 1892, Ch. XII.

---

[72] Cf. Ch. XVII.

CHAPTER XV

Dualistic Idealism: Solger, Schleiermacher, Schopenhauer

ART, THROUGH
IRONY, REVEALS
IDEAL WORLD.

THE ESTHETICS of Karl Wilhelm Friedrich Solger (1780–1819) strays markedly from the main current of the post-Kantian development. Fichte, Schelling, and above all Hegel, trying to overcome Kant's dualism by a monistic metaphysics, concerned themselves principally with the universe as a process embodying and disclosing the Absolute. Solger, no less metaphysical in his outlook but with a more static vision of the world, retained a dualism which he shared with the pronouncedly Christian minds of his age.[1] Among estheticians, Jean Paul stands closest to him. Strictly guarding its quality of transcendence, he allows his Idea to break through into experience only by momentary flashes. And art is, for him, the chief carrier of these intermittent revelations. A passage in one of his letters to his friend Tieck reads: "I believe on the strength of sure experience that in the world of our day a glimpse upward at a higher world may be best elicited from man by art, and that it is art which first introduces him into the core of things."[2]

Art, Solger claims, imitates God's creative work. But like all other earthly things, beauty is vanity before the true majesty of God. This is why melancholy hovers over all fair things.[3] Solger agrees with the other idealists in asserting that Beauty re-affirms the finitude and specifically human character of our existence.

---

[1] Cf. Maurice Boucher, K. W. F. Solger. Esthétique et philosophie de la présence, 1934.

[2] Nachgelassene Schriften und Briefwechsel, 1826, 2 Vols., I, 316.

[3] Vorlesungen über Ästhetik, herausgegeben von K. W. L. Heyse, 1829, p. 252.

From the point of view of moral or religious or philosophical experience our bodily constitution may be considered a fetter restricting the blessed life of the Idea. Art alone is human throughout. "In Man, conception and existence, soul and body are united; they interpenetrate completely; hence Man participates preëminently in beauty." [4] Solger, like Schelling, does not even shrink from interpreting God's incarnation in Christ in the light of these propositions as an allegorical fact. But for Solger this is only one side of esthetic theory, and the less characteristic one. Beauty, while proving by transitory revelations the congruity of Idea and Appearance, discloses at the same time the total heterogeneity of the two realms. The Idea, taking on the shape of an object in our world, steps into the place of the world, dissolving its complexus of particular and universal factors. Thus even in the crowning stage of the dialectical development, beauty keeps a touch of the paradoxical. But this paradox as the hall-mark of human finitude neither admits of nor requires further explanation. Through beauty, an object belonging to our world definitely confounds the common human presumption of self-sufficiency. By the consecration through genius of a single visible or audible form, a doom is pronounced on the whole visible and audible realm. The state of mind, in which this basic experience occurs, is Irony. "The spirit of the artist must concentrate all tendencies into one all-comprehensive gaze, and this gaze, superior to everything and destroying everything, is called irony." [5] "No work of art can come into being without this irony which, together with enthusiasm, constitutes the center of all artistic activity. It is the frame of mind, whereby we notice that reality embodies the Idea but is vain in and by itself, and that it returns to truth only by dissolving into Idea. . . . Irony recognizes the nothingness not of single characters but of the whole human condition just where it is highest and noblest; it recognizes that this is nothing compared with the divine Idea." [6]

---

[4] *Ibid.,* p. 78.
[5] *Erwin. Vier Gespräche über das Schöne und die Kunst,* 1815. *Neuausgabe* 1907, p. 279.
[6] *Vorlesungen,* p. 125.

Schelling's monistic idealism, transforming the Universe into a work of art, nearly obliterated the border-line separating art from reality. Solger's system preserves by its crowning conception the peculiar character of esthetic illusion. Unless irony reduces the world to empty semblance, no artistic transmutation of Idea into reality is conceivable. "If the artist gave himself up to the presence of the Idea in reality, art would cease to be, and a kind of fanaticism, a superstition would replace it which believes it finds in beautiful objects fixed conceptions under sensuous form." Irony teaches the artist that his work is symbol. Since the Idea when entering reality is bound to assume the form of "fixed conceptions," its unlimited freedom must be redeemed by the ironical dissolution of the finite world.[7] At the same time, irony as the mood in which "the immediate presence of the divine" is revealed by "the disappearance of our reality" sets art in the very core of human existence. It is with regard to irony as 'the perfect fruit of the artistic understanding' that Solger asserts: "Our present real existence, recognized and experienced in its essence, is art." [8]

SOLGER'S 'IRONY' NOT IDENTICAL WITH ROMANTIC IRONY.

After all this it is clear that Solger's conception of irony has but little in common with Romantic irony. For Solger, irony reasserts the transcendental character of the Idea, momentarily suspended by the presence of the Idea in a finite object. It thus converts into a proof of the vanity of this world what was regarded by the other idealists as the badge of its inherent divinity. For the Romanticist, irony signified the freedom of the individual subject who, because he set all bounds, assumed the right of overstepping and playing with them. He thus confused the spheres of subjective and objective existence, of the finite world and the transcendent Idea. The transcending movement started by Solger's dialectic terminates in God; the transgressive movement of Romantic irony terminates where it started: in the arbitrary self-enjoyment of the individual subject. From Solger's standpoint of irony "even the highest exists for us only in a limited, finite shape." "Everything whereby we hope to pass beyond human

---

[7] *Vorlesungen*, pp. 199f.
[8] *Nachgelassene Schriften*, II, 515.

ends is vain and empty illusion." [9] There is no room in Solger's philosophy for the megalomania of the self-sufficient individual as conceived by Friedrich Schlegel. On questions of taste this theory will not support the romantic loosening of the severe classic form into fantastic or witty play. The serenity of Homer's epic furnished Solger his favorite example of irony. This irony is necessarily coupled with enthusiasm—the feeling of the annihilation of the visible world with the awareness of the divine presence in an object of this world. [10] Yet though Solger did not sympathize with Schlegel's ideas, his philosophy certainly is closely related to the romantic religious feeling. It is, within the field of esthetics, the clearest evidence of a revival of the spirit of mystic transcendence. Solger writes: "Mysticism, looking toward reality, is the mother of irony; looking towards the eternal world, it is the child of enthusiasm or inspiration." [11]

Friedrich Daniel Ernst Schleiermacher (1768–1834), like Schelling, Solger, and Hegel, considers a system of Forms or Platonic Ideas the essence of reality. This system, innate in the human spirit, is called into activity by contact with the outer world. Among the activities assuring us that the real and the ideal worlds, the universe and the mind, spring from the same root, art occupies a prominent place. Imitating the prototypes of perceived objects, the artist develops germs inherent in his own mind. Since he is concerned with the ultimate ground of reality (the ground from which the prototypical forms derive) his works contain both truth and moral goodness. But truth and goodness in art, alienated from their original context, are reduced to their semblance. [12] There is, however, no reason to speak disparagingly of 'mere semblance,' as opposed to truth. The esthetic semblance of truth is still truth, though disguised as illusory appearance. The artist creates only isolated images, and so has to suppress the links re-

SCHLEIERMACHER'S "VIA MEDIA" BETWEEN CONSTRUCTION AND EXPERIENCE.

---

[9] *Ibid.*, II, 514f.

[10] *Vorlesungen*, p. 198.

[11] *Nachgelassene Schriften*, I, 689.

[12] *Ästhetik*, nach den bisher unveröffentlichenten Urschriften zum ersten Male herausgegeben von Rudolf Odebrecht, 1931, p. 118. We shall refer constantly to this recent edition, which is much preferable to the older edited by S. Lommatzsch (*Werke*, 3. Abteilung, Vol. VII).

lating the reproduced object to others. Thus renouncing the claim to cognitive truth, he finds himself richly rewarded: the isolated image proves to be a symbol of the Absolute.[13]

This nucleus of idealist convictions, exposed as it is in Schleiermacher to a specific intellectual climate, develops in a peculiar way and leads to original conclusions and observations. His dialectic, combining the advantages of the constructive and empirical method, is the art of limiting, at each step, the amount of irrationality introduced. He puts before himself a whole range of experienced facts. This empirical mass is a complex of identities and variants. Taking a tentative definition of an identical element he applies it to the factual multitude before him. In the case of esthetics, the facts are furnished by the arts and the like. The question is: Does the proposed definition of art really cover the range of relevant experiences? If the definition proves inadequate, either the provisional arrangement of the facts must be altered so as to conform to the general concept—perhaps by a fresh cracking up of a block of facts—or the fault is charged to the proposed definition. It applies perhaps only to certain arts, say to mimic art and music, and must be broadened. With this method, even an initial failure in definition may prove useful. Perhaps the first definition, though too narrow, points to a natural division within the subject under consideration, and indicates the direction in which the dialectical analysis must be continued. Thus, through reiterated adjustments of definitions and of experienced facts, the internal structure of a certain domain of knowledge is revealed.

FIRST DEFINITION:
ART IS EXPRESSION.

To define art means to determine its place within the whole of human activity. Man is acted upon by the surrounding world and in turn reacts upon the world. Thus an unceasing oscillation takes place, a wavering to and fro between human mind, the 'ideal factor,' and world, the 'real factor.' This interaction aims at gradually surmounting the opposition and achieving a synthesis dominated by identity. The goal is reached in either of two ways. Man may receive and assimilate the world. This is the way of knowledge. Or the inward life may be projected into the outside

---

[13] *Ästhetik*, p. 119.

world. This second mode, called 'organizing activity,' belongs to ethics. The doctrine of art falls under ethics. It therefore remains to define artistic creation as a specific form of 'organization' at large.[14]

The first approach to this definition is the distinction between the identity of human nature and the uniqueness of the person. These two components combine in such a way that in some acts the identical factor prevails, in others the variant or individual element. Let this distinction now be applied to the organizing activity. In the mechanical products of craftsmanship the identical is the predominant component. Hence the assignment of art to the individual factor.

This placing of art—within organizing activity when dominated by the uniqueness of the person—may be made more specific by reference to feeling. Through feeling we become aware of our own personality and its status. Thus art is to be classed with the phenomena of expression. We may imagine a series of ordinary experiences through which an emotion is given outward form, visible or audible representation: attitudes, gestures, exclamations. All these modes of utterance fulfill the conditions of the definition and still are not art. Rather we face in them that artless expression which consists "in the immediate identity of emotion and utterance." [15] To ennoble this immediate expression and transform it into art, a second factor beside emotion is required. Schleiermacher designates it *Besonnenheit*, deliberation or illumination, as we may render this untranslatable term. 'Illumination' checks the eruptions of emotional life, transfiguring them and impressing upon them the mark of prototypical form: measure and harmony. Thus the crude agitation of the body takes on rhythm, and develops into an orderly sequence of attitudes controlled by a new type of consciousness—and the dance is born. In a similar way, the cry of passion or delight is modulated and purified, so as to set free and develop the harmonious sound of the human voice. It assumes rhythm and melodious order and the song as artistic creation arises.

Creative contemplation originating in illumination does not

---

[14] *Ibid.*, pp. 23f.
[15] *Ibid.*, p. 31.

seize upon any emotion indiscriminately. There can be no mechanical separation of forming energy from plastic emotional substratum in the life of the mind. All components, acted upon and reacting, are closely woven together into the tissue of inner experience. The impetuous current of passionate feeling, hemmed in and staved off by the inhibiting energy of light and yielding to its formative power, is no longer the same as before. Ceasing to pursue its special ends, the emotion rouses and exalts our whole being. It then deserves the more appropriate name of 'enthusiasm.' Thus the final definition of art may be "identity of enthusiasm and illumination." In this synthesis, the parts are so assigned to the combining factors that illumination contributes the 'prototype,' while enthusiasm represents the uniqueness of the person. The creative individual, externalizing what is most intimate in himself, finds himself wedded to the Idea—ground of all reality.

SECOND DEFINI-
TION: ART AN IM-
AGINATIVE PLAY.
But our labor of definition is not yet complete. In the light of the full stretch of esthetic experience, our definition will not do. No doubt it applies to those arts which can easily be viewed as the development of a natural gesture-language: the dance, music, and the histrionic. But the figurative arts do not fit in. The ties binding a picture or a building to our feelings are less visible. A world of objective forms is unfolded before us, either representing natural objects, or creating, like architecture, useful structures without any natural model. These types appeal to our intellectual and imaginative faculties rather than to our emotions. Every attempt at classifying such fine arts under the proposed formula is frustrated.

In a fresh approach, we trace the origin of art (remembering the fundamental bi-partition of human activities held by Schleiermacher) to the cognitive life instead of to the faculty of 'organization.' Our first move is to draw a distinction between two types of creation through ideas. In knowledge we build up a universe which is one and the same forever and for everyone. This identical world is expounded in assertions of universal validity. But there is still another way of combining ideas into a well-ordered whole —through imagination. Imagination initiates a free play of ideas. The creations of this faculty do not claim universal validity;

they exhibit a personal version of super-personal reality. Thus we arrive at a theory of art which is applicable to sculpture and painting and, perhaps, also to architecture. But again there is failure to cover the full compass of artistic creation. Instead of one definition of art we arrive at two supplementary ones, each corresponding to a specific mental impulse. We rejoice in some beautiful sight. Later, in a separate act, we express our joy in an exclamation. The second element is developed by actors, dancers, and musicians into their expressive performances. The first act is at the basis of painting, sculpture, and architecture. These two mental elements are distinct though connected with each other, and the one name of art seems to cover two different phenomena.

The final stage of the dialectic shows that the two definitions of art describe two aspects of one fact. Emotion as expressed in the medium of bodily movement seemed to be a passive state, a mere reaction to some stimulus from outside. In order to correct this misleading impression, we must reconsider the concept of emotion or feeling. At the basis of artistic expression lies not the emotional response in its isolation but an accumulation of feelings embodied in what Schleiermacher calls '*Stimmung*.' *Stimmung*, mental tone, related to single emotions and feelings somewhat as a musical key is to its single notes, is the emotional basis of the person and as such is bound up with the free activity of the mind. The passive emotions as expressed in art are based, in the last analysis, on a profounder layer of our personality; not on the mere condition of being affected, but on the willingness to be moved. Only if we understand feeling in the comprehensive sense of 'tone' can we see how emotion is fitted to rise to enthusiasm and to combine with 'inner illumination' for the sake of artistic creation. UNITY OF THE TWO PROPOSED DEFINITIONS.

Thus a first barrier separating the expressive from the representational arts is removed. Their essential unity is brought fully to light by reflection on the close relationship between imagination and feeling. The free activity of ideas in imagination plays an intimate individual variation on the theme of the common world. The spring of this imaginative activity, which leads the artist to stress certain features of reality at the expense of others, is again his spiritual tone or temper. Thus we arrive at the conclusion that the imaginative play of ideas in the fine arts expresses feeling just as, on the other hand, the expressive forms of the mimic arts involve the free activity of imagination. The definition of art as the expression of an emotional tone originating in the unification of enthusiasm and illumination is universal and applies to all arts. What first seemed to threaten the unity of art is now revealed as a distinctive mark dividing the realm of arts into two hemispheres. This distinction is as follows: Music and mimes borrow their expressiveness from the immediacy of feeling, the fine arts and the arts of speech, from the manner in which the emotional tone acts upon the free play of ideas.[16]

Having thus re-established the essential unity of art, Schleiermacher can assign to it a place and function in human life. Joining the chorus of ancient thinkers, he asserts 'purification of the passions' to be the purpose of art. The artist, wedding the eruptive force of emotion to mental enlightenment makes the perfection of measure shine forth in his creations. Thus "the unmeasured disappears more and more in life and measure increasingly permeates everything." [17]

SCHOPENHAUER'S
METAPHYSICAL
PARADOX: BLIND
STRIVING SUP-
PLANTS REASON.

On first sight, Arthur Schopenhauer (1788–1860) seems to be merely another member of the group of those thinkers who, like Solger and Schleiermacher, developed a metaphysics out of Kant's transcendental theory, but preserved the dualistic conception of the world. The essence, then, of Schopenhauer's metaphysics appears to rest upon the sharp demarcation between the phenomenal and noumenal worlds, which Kant had made and which Hegel had obliterated. Science and common observation, Schopenhauer taught, give us the phenomenal world only. But the idea of 'phenomenal' had assumed a different meaning with Schopenhauer. Much against both the spirit and the letter of Kant's philosophy, he understood the knowing subject in the Transcendental Logic to mean the individual subject with his equipment of human sense-organs. Thus he arrived at a phenomenalism which is nearer to Berkeley's than to Kant's doctrine. He writes: "What we know is not a sun and earth, but an eye that sees the sun and a hand that

---

[16] *Ästhetik*, p. 52.
[17] *Ibid.*, p. 287.

feels an earth." The relativity of all known objects to an individual knower makes them ideas rather than independent beings. "All that exists for knowledge is only an object in relation to a subject, the perception of a perceiver, in a word, *idea*." [18] Science introduces exact order into the world of common sense-perception by using the forms of time, space, and causality. But science only does more precisely what common observation already does; and science also therefore only knows a relative, phenomenal world. Our common mode of seeing, and the scientific mode, assume the distinctness of individual things, for time dates, and space places things outside of each other; it is also naïvely realistic. But though this prepares things for the action of our will, it conceals them 'by a triple veil' from our true vision.

Behind the world of mere appearance looms the noumenal world. 'Noumenal,' derived from the Greek word νοῦς (Reason), means 'rational,' and the thinkers before Schopenhauer had respected this original sense of the term. Defying tradition and language, Schopenhauer ordained that, from now on, it had to mean the opposite. According to him, the real is not Reason but Unreason, an irrational force, a blind nisus. Schopenhauer calls it Will; but as it is devoid of sense and aim, it hardly deserves this name nor that of desire. Every attempt at definition must fail, because it is essentially not an idea but the negation of an idea. It is Reason deprived of all its positive characteristics save its metaphysical function and its dynamic power. There is a last source of all sense, but this source, we are told, is senseless. Rational order, through the human brain, springs from disorder, or, more exactly, from some dynamic substance negatively defined by the absence of intellect and purpose. A bold paradox is at the bottom of Schopenhauer's metaphysics. He occupies and claims as his own the whole edifice of traditional Platonism. But he removes the spring that sets all to working, the heart, as it were, of the living body of metaphysics. Instead of supplanting it with some other vital principle, he exalts the void which he created by his operation.

---

[18] *The World as Will and Idea,* trans. Haldane and Kemp, 7th ed., Vol. I, p. 3.

HEDONISTIC PESSI-
MISM.

If the world is at bottom a striving, an eternal unsatisfied hunger, then it is also evil. Schopenhauer's metaphysics involves a pessimistic outlook on human life. Pleasure, he asserts, signifies no positive state or quality. It is to be prized merely as a suspense of pain. This hedonistic pessimism maintains to a certain extent a traditional doctrine, but turns its positive into a negative. If we strike a balance between pleasure and pain in sensuous enjoyment, the result is zero. The pleasure of eating, for example, is paid for in advance by its necessary condition, an equal amount of displeasure, that is of hunger. Such calculation is a common-place since Socrates. But it is matched in Plato, Aristotle, and their modern followers by the conception of a higher and truly positive enjoyment, granted to us in the contemplation of the rational structure of the world. But since Schopenhauer denies the rationality of the world, he must deny the positive character of pleasure. Precisely here, where he breaks away from tradition, he claims conformity with it by citing Aristotle as his witness. He writes: "As the supreme rule of all practical wisdom I regard a statement, incidentally pronounced by Aristotle in the Nichomachean Ethics: 'A man of practical wisdom pursues what is free from pain, not what is pleasant!' " [19] But Aristotle actually refers to this saying only as to one of the objectionable opinions which "some people" hold; whereas he himself, in the true spirit of Platonism, is convinced of the existence of pleasures "that involve no pain or appetite, for example, those of contemplation." [20]

SALVATION
THROUGH PLA-
TONIC-ESTHETIC
CONTEMPLATION.

Schopenhauer maintained the idea of contemplation, though he repudiated both its positive value and its appropriate object. But as the irrational Will is unfit to assume the rôle of the contemplated object, the Platonic Idea is called to the rescue, interpreted by Schopenhauer as stages of the objectivation of the Will. The kingdom of nature is a hierarchy, beginning with inorganic matter, stones, and earth, and ascending through the plant and animal world to man. Each level of the Will's expressiveness is represented by a Platonic Idea. Stones and plants are the utterances

---

[19] *Aphorismen zur Lebensweisheit*, Ch. V (*Sämtliche Werke, herausgeg. von* Frauenstaedt, V, 430); cf. *Ethica Nicomachea*, 1152b, 16.
[20] *Ibid.*, 1152b, 36.

of world-desire at a particular stage of clarity or unclearness. They are the shape of the success of the eternal nisus at some point of pause.

What this paradoxical combination of an irrational Will with Platonic Ideas means is revealed in the third book of Schopenhauer's chief work. The solution shows that his philosophy, even in a higher degree than Schelling's doctrine at any of its phases, deserves the name of an "esthetic metaphysics." Schopenhauer asks: ". . . What kind of knowledge is concerned with . . . the *Ideas*, which are direct objectivity of the thing-in-itself, the will? We answer, *Art*."[21] Esthetics is not only a part of Schopenhauer's metaphysical doctrine. This doctrine itself is based upon the idea of esthetic contemplation. Schopenhauer often emphasizes his voluntarism as a distinctive feature of his philosophy. But none of the intellectualists of the Kantian school proposed so downright an intellectual interpretation of art as Schopenhauer did. For him art is the highest achievement of the human intellect and the supreme form of knowledge. Its only source, he writes, "is the knowledge of Ideas; its only aim the communication of this knowledge."[22]

The pure will-less subject of such knowledge, gifted with a clear vision of the world, is genius; and this word denotes for Schopenhauer indiscriminately the great artist and the speculative philosopher of the Platonic type. We may infer from this that he considered his own metaphysics an artistic creation. At any rate, genius, according to Schopenhauer, is preëminent capacity for the contemplation of Ideas. One thing represents a thousand for him; it breaks its apparent bounds and rejoins its primeval matrix. As a spectator of life, he attains to a temporary freedom from pain. "It is the painless state which Epicurus prized as the highest good and as the state of the gods; for we are for the moment set free from the miserable striving of the will; we keep the Sabbath of the penal servitude of willing; the wheel of Ixion stands still."[23]

Thus the kind of knowledge that science yields is different in

---

[21] *The World as Will and Idea*, I, 238f.

[22] *Ibid.*, I, 239.

[23] *Ibid.*, I, 254.

purpose and scope from the intuitions of art. Science works in the service of our common desires, and arranges causal sequences so that we may have what we want in the immediate future. But genius is half-mad. Ignoring the relation of an object to its past history or its future probable consequences, it pierces to the eternal character of it, and so is romantic and impractical. "To the ordinary man his faculty of knowledge is a lamp to lighten his path; to the man of genius, it is the sun which reveals the world." [24] A portrait-painter should see in a face not its utility or social status, but its metaphysics. If the artistic sun-like way of looking at things is inconvenient in the common paths of life, it compensates for this disadvantage by transporting its subject beyond the strains and stresses of restless striving. Man as practical is "never done wanting"; man as artist is the serene spectator. The artist, having cast off the chains of desire, is blessedly peaceful; he is freed from individuality and the pain that proceeds from it.

SYSTEM OF ARTS REFLECTS HIERARCHY OF IDEAS.
    The artistic genius then sees eternity. But he sees it at some given moment of its unrolling, one facet of its self-revelation. Schopenhauer erects a theory of the particular arts on the basis of the stages of Will-Objectification. According to this theory every art must be understood as the product of forces; and its grade of excellence corresponds to the stage of advancement of will—the crude heaviness or fine spirituality—of the force at work. Architecture is, in this sense, the lowest of the arts. Its function is to bring to distinctness the relation of gravity to rigidity. The conflict between heavy matter which wills to fall toward the earth and the will of a rigid column, buttress, or arch, which opposes the earthward tendency of stone and brick, is the problem which architecture must solve and must declare. In order to exhibit the war of opposing forces, a building must conduct the forces, as it were, by a circuitous route. Gravity must be held back from its simple purpose of descent, and rigidity must be given burdens to bear. The roof is kept from the ground by columns, and the arches must sustain the weight of their own outward thrust and pressure. Moreover, a physical material must be employed in beautiful

---

[24] *The World as Will and Idea*, I, 243.

buildings which appears to be what it actually is. For the external texture of the material is relatively unimportant; it is what the material can do as the incarnation of a force that matters for art. Stone can do certain things, and it must be required to exhibit these potencies. Something made to look like stone cannot do the same work except by a *tour de force,* and the discovery of a contradiction between what the elements of a structure seem to do, and what they actually do, destroys the esthetic pleasure of contemplation. Schopenhauer believed that Greek architecture excelled in doing what architecture is supposed to do, because in a Greek temple the relation of burden and carrier in the columns and architrave is the chief theme. In Gothic architecture the adventitious beauty of sculpture is imported into architecture, because the architectural problem *per se* has not been sufficiently isolated and emphasized.[25]

Schopenhauer inconsistently asserts that it is the function of architecture to demonstrate the nature of light as well as of qualities so different from light as heaviness and rigidity. For a building acquires a "double beauty in full sunshine, with the blue sky behind it," he says. And there is a distinct beauty given to buildings by moonlight and in the various kinds and degrees of light. Inside a building "the light is intercepted, confined, and reflected by the great opaque, sharply outlined, and variously formed masses of stone."[26] This is an interesting and valid observation, but one feels that it flows from Schopenhauer's general delight in "light, the most joy-giving of all things" rather than from the logic of his system.

The outline of his system does demand the next step, however, for Schopenhauer sketches in a hypothetical art, which the ascending scale of the forces of nature calls for, but which yet does not exist. This is an art of water, analogous to architecture, the art of earth. The relation of fluidity to rigidity should be consciously portrayed by designed water-falls and cataracts, still lake-surfaces, and arranged brooks.[27]

---

[25] *Ibid.,* I, 276–82.

[26] *Ibid.,* I, 279.

[27] *Ibid.,* I, 282.

The Eternal Idea of Plant is the material of landscape gardening and landscape painting. Here the ideal is to arrange the individual plant forms so with regard to each other that plant as a whole species, a combination of stillness and the power of growth, shall shine forth.[28] Animal-essence is revealed both through painting and sculpture. But animals have only the beauty of type, not that of individuality. The tiger or elephant or horse should be carved as the active representative of a species. Only the animal man adds to his generic character individuality.[29] Great sculpture, then, seizes upon some definite aspect of the idea of humanity, and sets it forth. So the statues of Hercules, Apollo, Bacchus, Antinous, Silenus, and the Faun, added together, give the dynamic meaning of man in entirety.[30] As man is the culmination of the evolution of nature, so the representation of man is the highest artistic task. "No object transports us so quickly into pure esthetic contemplation as the most beautiful human countenance and form." [31] The drapery in a statue must be used not to cover up the human form, but to expound and enhance its main outlines.[32] The greater versatility of painting allows this art to carry the exposition of man's nature into greater detail: to "exhibit man in his psychological permutations." Though a situation full of picturesque detail for drawing out the possibilities of man's reactions is desirable, no individual man nor single historical event is ever intended by a genuine work of art. Pictures of Moses found in the bulrushes by the King of Egypt's daughter really intend to portray the relationship of any lady, as such, to a foundling.[33] And as chess is the same whether played with wooden or golden pieces, so humanity is the same whether displayed by the Dutch in a tavern-brawl, or by the English in Parliament.[34] Art, by its very nature, appeals to will-less and unhistorical contemplation.

Poetry is the richest and highest of the arts. Even more than

---

[28] *Loc. cit.*
[29] *Ibid.,* I, 285.
[30] *Ibid.,* I, 291.
[31] *Ibid.,* I, 285.
[32] *Ibid.,* I, 296.
[33] *Ibid.,* I, 299.
[34] *Ibid.,* I, 298.

painting it can depict man in his relationships and entanglements.[35] In tragedy impediments are put in the way of man's direct will-tendencies and thus the resource and strength of the human will are set in a bright light.[36] As in architecture the down-pressing of a beam or the up-thrusting of a column can be shown raised to a higher power by conflict with obstacles, so on a more spiritual plane in poetical tragedy. There are three tragic methods: (1) through an excessively evil person; (2) catastrophe through fate or chance; or (3) through the complications of ordinary life.[37] Tragedy performs the useful human service of opening a window into the ultimately evil nature of existence. The art of tragedy, in a word, justifies the philosophy of pessimism; but being an art, it is cut free from reference to the will and so brings on a mood of resignation.

The art of music is not for Schopenhauer coördinate with the others, but is both their crown and sum. All the other arts select for embodiment only one Platonic Idea, one stage of the Will's objectification. Music, on the contrary, gives voice to the full compass of the Will itself and therefore to all the steps of Nature's process. "The other arts speak only of Shadows, it speaks of the Will itself." [38] "The composer reveals the inner nature of the world, and expresses the deepest wisdom in a language which his reason does not understand; as a person under the influence of mesmerism tells things of which he has no conception when he awakes." [39] Leibniz had said that music is the blind practice of mathematics. Schopenhauer objects to the association of music with a science so intellectual and abstract as mathematics. He amends Leibniz's epigram to read: Music is the blind practice of metaphysics—unconscious philosophizing. As the world in its entirety is a precipitate of the Will, music is an alternative precipitate. In fact, Schopenhauer attributes to music an even greater expressiveness of the ultimate meaning of things than the history

MUSIC REVEALS WILL ITSELF.

---

[35] *Ibid.*, I, 315ff.
[36] *Ibid.*, I, 327.
[37] *Ibid.*, I, 328, 329.
[38] *Ibid.*, I, 336.
[39] *Ibid.*, I, 342.

of actual events. For it reveals the secret history of motives and aspirations, all that penumbra of actual existence which is included under the vague terms 'feeling' and 'emotion.'

Schopenhauer not only claims that music is in general a copy of the Will; but he divides up the elements of musical form and associates these with regions of the world. The lowest voice in harmony corresponds to the crude mass of the planet, the tenor to crystals, the alto to animals, and the melody of the highest part to the rational life of man.[40] "The melody has a before and after, significant intentional direction from beginning to end." In this rational superiority to the flux of time, in the more articulate utterance of its voice, it symbolizes, then, man himself.

ESTHETICISM AN-
TICIPATED.

For a long time unread and unknown, Schopenhauer became at the end of the century the most popular and influential of writers. Even in authors, like Gautier or Flaubert, who probably never set eyes on one of his books, we may fancy we feel a kindred spirit. Schopenhauer was the first to embody an attitude which afterwards became more and more typical of the educated and well-to-do. In a readable and even attractive form, he expounded a system of 'estheticism.' The pessimistic philosopher carries over the idea of contemplation from philosophy into art, offering, under the form of a refined idea of esthetic pleasure, a welcome substitute for the *vita contemplativa.* Through Schopenhauer's philosophy, contemplation survives the belief in its original object, that is, in Reason as the ground of reality.

SUPPLEMENTARY READING

André Fauconnet, *L'esthétique de Schopenhauer*, 1913.
L. D. Green, "Schopenhauer and Music," *Musical Quarterly*, 1930.
Benedetto Croce, *Aesthetics*, trans. by Douglas Ainslie, 2d ed., 1922, pp. 312-23. On Schleiermacher.

---

[40] *The World as Will and Idea*, I, 333ff.

CHAPTER XVI

Society and the Artist

SOCIAL forms and intellectual needs had undergone a profound change by the end of the eighteenth century, and it fell
to the esthetic doctrine of the nineteenth century to assign art its
place in a new world. In Germany, where social and economic
progress was hampered by the political calamity of the disrupted
empire, analysts thought of the coming era in terms of metaphysics. For them Kant had definitely destroyed the ancient rational
knowledge of the Universe and of God, and they were concerned
to build it up again in an altered form. The study of art was used
for this purpose; and the new metaphysical concepts in their turn
were put to work for a better understanding of art. In any case
the field within which beauty was supposed to lie was determined
by the great facts of the human soul, the life of mankind in the
world's history, the universe, and a supernatural Being.

The peoples to the west of Germany, on the other hand, experienced the advent of the modern world in a more concrete way.
They raised its problems primarily in terms of human society. The
English and French students of art asked: What is the legitimate
place and purpose of art in social life? In France, where, after
fearful revolutionary convulsions, the structure of society had to
be rebuilt from the bottom, the problem was felt in its utmost
poignancy. The more practical spirit of the English handled the
problems in a way that secured the artist greater influence over the
communal life. The artist naturally answered the too impetuous
claims of society by a fierce assertion of the uniqueness and self-
sufficiency of art. Yet it is significant that in doing so he did not as
a rule resort to solitary vision as the source of his independence.

473

He rather preferred to justify his seclusion by putting forward the imperative requirements of artistic craftsmanship. That is, he stressed that side of his work which is common to all productive labor in society.

FRENCH IDEALISM UNDER GERMAN INFLUENCE.   German metaphysical esthetics soon spread westward over the frontier. In the wake of the pioneering work of Madame de Staël and above all of Victor Cousin (1792–1867), an idealist school of esthetic thought was born in France, carried forward by Cousin's disciple Théodore Jouffroy (1796–1842) and brought to its culmination by the writings of Jean-Charles Lévêque (1818–1900) and Victor de Laprade (1812–1883). Their ideas are largely borrowed from German sources, yet the spirit in which they are thought out and applied bears witness to the interests prevailing in French intellectual life. Cousin, author of an essay *On the True, the Beautiful, the Good*,[1] assures his fellow countrymen who are always naturally distrustful of German philosophical abstruseness, that his spiritualism is a reasonable and moderate one, which keeps clear of any kind of "chimeric and dangerous mysticism." [2] In the attention given to the social problems of art, these idealists, Cousin and his followers, hardly fall behind their positivistic antagonists. Their ideas on the metaphysics of beauty exhibit no marked originality. Cousin, combining his somewhat vague Platonism with ideas derived from French eighteenth century moralists, emphasizes the ethical implications of his concept of beauty, and in doing so he verges on looseness in his use of terms. In a formula that reminds us of Shaftesbury he defines the purpose of art as the "expression of moral beauty with the help of physical beauty." [3] Closer to German philosophy is the fervently religious speculation of the great Catholic writer H. F. R. de Lamennais (1782–1854). He believes that art is a manifestation of the same innate metaphysical power which issues in the closely related modes: religion, morals, and science.[4] Charles Lévêque furnishes in his treatise *The Science of Beauty* the best example of a definition conceived in the

---

[1] *Du Vrai, du Beau, du Bien*, 1937.
[2] *Ibid.*, p. 141.
[3] *Ibid.*, p. 188.
[4] *De l'art et du beau*, 1841, p. 10.

spirit of German Platonism. "The beautiful," he asserts, "is in all possible cases a force or soul acting with all its power and in conformity with order, that is, in such a way as to fulfill its law." [5] Later we learn that the individual force or soul, the cause of beauty, is determined in its creative activity by its "generic ideal." [6] This dynamic idealism leads the author to suggest the analogy between artistic creation and the formation of character by self-education. He who is not born an artist should, "in accordance with Plotinus' magnificent expression carve out ceaselessly his own statue after the image of ideal beauty." [7]

But whatever their classical or German kinships, the problem of the social conditions and social purpose of art was constantly present to the mind of these writers. Cousin has a keen appreciation of the influence on art of the various factors which later were described as constituting the 'milieu.' Jouffroy, adopting Cousin's definition of beauty as a type of order, concludes that artistic style depends on the different meanings attributed to 'order' at different historical periods. It is again Lévêque who brings a strain of ideas to its fullest expression. It is not the solitary individual, he teaches, who strives after the realization of the ideal by acts and works of art. The power of the ideal emanates from the agent, pervading and imperceptibly moulding those who live in contact with him. Thus the artist is bound to transform the community of which he is a member. But the relationship between artist and society is reciprocal. The artist takes from contemporary society the ideas which raise him to an ideal sphere. On this point Lévêque expresses himself in words worthy of Ruskin. "There is no great art," he writes, "without great doctrines, and, let us add immediately, without great doctrines that have passed over into acts, that have turned into living beauty and been realized in the conduct of individuals. . . ." Consequently if the artist fails to achieve beauty, the blame does not lie with him alone. He has to draw upon the surrounding world. "There is a living model which, incessantly and every-

---

[5] *La Science du beau, ses principes, ses applications, son histoire*, 1862, 2 Vols., I, 368.

[6] *Ibid.*, II, 559.

[7] *Ibid.*, I, 115f.

where, poses before the artist's eyes, in the salon, in the theatre, in the church, in the street; this living model is everyman. Haunted by this vision, or rather finding it always before him, how could the artist escape it, or how could he entirely forget it when he is in his studio?" [8] This idea of Lévêque's recurs almost literally in Taine's remarks on the 'model character.' But while the Positivist feels it his vocation to hail the modern age and to fight for its ideals, the idealist assumes a more critical attitude. Laprade questions whether the Positivistic idea of progress is relevant to art as it is to science and technique. The rapid perfection and vulgarization of technique may as well subject art to mere industry.[9]

SAINT-SIMON: THE ARTIST IN THE TRIUMVIRATE OF REFORM.
    A frankly and thoroughly 'modern' philosophy was created by the Positivistic movement. The doctrine taught by the Comte de Saint-Simon (1760–1825) and his disciples shows this philosophy in the stage of its childhood. They had the courage to plan what, at first sight, seemed fantastic: to bring about a collaboration of modern science and Christian charity. It was their desire to help the poor and to rescue a suffering class from the plight into which the economic system and modern working conditions had plunged it. They hoped to carry through the reform by a change "from above," allotting to the scholar the task of drawing up the scientific design of the novel "social machine" and to carry it out in collaboration with the industrialist. Finally the artist was called upon to join this reforming staff as the third member of a modern triumvirate. He is, they argued, in control of the souls. The reformer must try to win him over to his plans and to put his spell in the service of the good cause. The artist will be richly rewarded for his assistance, for there is, in the opinion of the Utopian philosophers, no nobler and more inspiring aim imaginable than to fill the heart with enthusiasm for a just and happy ordering of human life.[10] A certain hesitation is noticeable in the attitude of the Saint-Simonist group towards art. Art was regarded by its members alternately as a product of society, conditioned by its

---

[8] *La Science du beau, ses principes, ses applications, son histoire*, II, 314.
[9] *Essais de Critique idealiste*, 1882, pp. 72ff.
[10] *Œuvres de Saint-Simon et d'Enfantin*, Vol. XXXIX, Olinde Rodrigues, "L'Artist, le Savant et l'Industriel," p. 212.

actual state, and again as an instrument to raise it to a higher level. In his later years Saint-Simon declared that all artistic creation should be suspended until there was completed the building of the future society. Then a finer and purer art would grow up as the spontaneous expression of a just and well ordered life. It would have been surprising if a doctrine entirely preoccupied with the idea of the world as it ought to be should have contributed much to our knowledge of a creative activity which, on the whole, teaches us to delight in the world as it is. The works or utterances on art by the socialist reformers, as for example Pierre-Joseph Proudhon's (1809–1865) treatise on art,[11] were often lacking in familiarity with their subject.

Saint-Simon's lofty aspirations were translated into philosophical terms and developed into a system by Auguste Comte (1789–1857). In his doctrine the breach with the theological and metaphysical tradition becomes decisive and irretrievable. The concept of the world is reduced to that of an infinite complex of 'positive' facts. With the levelling down of the hierarchical structure of the ancient universe to coördinate given facts the privileged position of philosophy disappears. There is only one method by which the facts must be investigated, classified, and subjected to empirical rules. How do scattered facts come to crystallize finally in a system? For a system it was that Comte hoped to extract out of his multiple data. This question was not raised explicitly. But well aware of the incompleteness of a merely factual world, Comte supplemented his view by a theory of human activity. Human acts, as dependent upon our will, do not fall under the conception of fact. The facts themselves, when seized upon by human activity and subordinated to rational ends, assume a different aspect: they become the means of which the agent avails himself for the fulfilment of his purposes. In other words, the facts, established and connected into a theoretical whole by science, turn into instruments within the practical context of technique. Science and technique, factuality and instrumentality, are interrelated by a knowledge which is essentially foresight.

COMTE: ART IS CONDITIONED BY THE PRESENT AND PREPARES THE FUTURE SOCIETY.

---

[11] *Du principe de l'art et de sa destination sociale*, 1865.

Accordingly, art is visualized from a dual point of view. Art is, first of all, a fact or a context of facts. As such, it is like other human accomplishments dependent upon the state of society. The study of it requires the same impartiality as befits the astronomer. But there is, in the second place, another aspect of art: it is a means of helping on the advent of a perfect social order. Inspiring himself with the great idea of Man, master over nature and his own life, the artist is stirred to contribute to the realization of this ideal. The mental faculty on which he acts is an intermediary between the intellectual and the moral faculties and therefore the appropriate medium through which to lead from insight to action. There is no better way to influence both intellect and moral attitude than to train the intermediate sensibility which is closely connected with both.[12]

We may venture the equation: Hegel is to Schelling as Comte to Saint-Simon. The idea of a future state of the world was a vision for Schelling as it was a Utopian project with Saint-Simon. For both Hegel and Comte it assumed the new aspect of a result, that is, the product of an historical development, and both were led to demonstrate their point by means of a philosophy of history. Man, according to positivistic views, was not from the beginning what, through the course of a long and eventful development, he is going to become: lord of the globe and creator of a harmonious social life. In tracing the advance of mankind through history from the earliest times, Comte assumes two main epochs, the age of theology and that of metaphysics, the transition from the first to the second leading through two intermediate stages: fetishism and polytheism. Fetishism which "immediately conferred upon all external bodies our fundamental feelings of life"[13] witnessed the flourishing of the mimic arts and of dancing. The triumph of sentiment over animal instinct, characteristic of the epoch, was symbolized by these performances. In the following phase, the age of Greek polytheism, sentiment in its turn was outstripped by the imagination. This psychic change was accompanied by an

---

[12] *Cours de Philosophie Positive*, 2d ed., Paris, 1864, V, 107.
[13] *Ibid.*, V, 101.

unparalleled efflorescence of the fine arts. Favored by the existence of a stable and homogeneous society, the art of that time wielded a power over the human mind which it lost soon afterwards and has never recovered.[14] Hegel's view, on this point, was similar, though more consistent. According to him, the dominant position of art in life was a thing of the past. Comte claimed a continuous progressive development of the esthetic faculties and predicted a future art worthy of a liberated humanity and great enough to overshadow antiquity.

Passing to a further phase of this movement, we encounter an enhanced attention to the work of art itself. In Comte's doctrine two rival ideas concurred: on the one hand the idea of fact and science, on the other, the idea of action. The latter, 'activist' component is now either whittled down to a vague aspiration or dropped altogether. Hippolyte Taine (1828–1893), the outstanding exponent of this second group of positivists, tells his hearers: "My sole duty is to offer you facts and show how these facts are produced." [15] And his translator writes in the preface to the *Philosophy of Art:* "These lectures consist of an application of the experimental method to art, in the same manner as it is applied to the sciences. Whatever utility the system possesses is due to this principle." [16] This statement, however erroneous, faithfully renders Taine's own belief. Considered as a fact, a work of art is related to, and conditioned by, other facts. This is obviously true. But Taine goes a step further, urging that the work of art is a product of its environment and nothing else. And this is more than Taine, or any other philosopher, is able to prove. We have, writes Taine, "to lay down this rule: that, in order to comprehend a work of art, an artist or a group of artists, we must clearly comprehend the general social and intellectual condition of the times to which they belong. Herein is to be found the final explanation; herein resides the primitive cause determining all that follows it." [17] The favorite analogy which this naturalist philosopher uses in order to

TAINE: ART IS A PRODUCT OF ITS ENVIRONMENT.

---

[14] *Ibid.,* V, 114.
[15] *The Philosophy of Art.* Translated by John Durand, 1873, p. 37.
[16] *Ibid.,* p. 5.
[17] *Ibid.,* p. 28.

explain art, is offered by botany. Again and again he impresses upon us the idea that a poem or a statue is comparable to a plant. As the plant is determined by climate and the quality of the soil, so is the poem by a certain "moral temperature." [18] As all kinds of seeds are carried over the globe by changing winds, so we may assume that all types of talent are permanently present in an approximately constant proportion throughout all epochs of history and among all peoples. Hence the selective power, exercised in vegetative life by climate and soil, falls in artistic life to "moral temperature." Let us admit with the author that nearly the same number of melancholy and joyous temperaments are encountered among the artistic talents of all times. Suppose, furthermore, a mood of melancholy to prevail in the public life of a certain period. Nothing more natural than that, under such circumstances, every outburst of cheerfulness should either pass unheeded or meet with disapproval, whereas the gloomy talent, encouraged by the sadness around, will take its chance. A crop of melancholy and tragic creations is the inevitable result. Taine was too well acquainted with the history of art not to feel how unsatisfactory this explanation was. He, therefore, tried to support his view by another argument. The same principle of selection, he holds, that makes a choice among available talents, favors "a group of sentiments, aptitudes, and needs," and these, when concentrated in one person and powerfully displayed by him, constitute the *representative man*, that is to say, a model character to whom his contemporaries award all their admiration and all their sympathy. There is, for example, in Greece "the naked youth of fine race and accomplished in all bodily exercise." [19] The artists, concludes Taine, "either represent this character, or address themselves to it." [20]

A "final explanation" surely must point out what art, or a work of art, really and in itself, is. No inquiry into the conditions determining its origin and development can ever furnish such a defining concept. In fact, Taine himself thinks it necessary to tell what art in itself is, and he devotes the first section of his treatise to

---

[18] *The Philosophy of Art*, p. 103.
[19] *Ibid.*, p. 182.
[20] *Ibid.*, p. 183.

this task. But these initial definitions have nothing whatever to do with the "final explanation" in sociological terms. They draw on the much despised traditional and even idealist esthetics. No sociology was needed to discover that art has to represent 'the essential character' of its object.

In the meantime the naturalistic movement in art had arisen. Courbet's exhibition of his pictures was the first signal. A few years later, in 1856, the publication of Gustave Flaubert's novel *Madame Bovary*, much to the author's surprise and annoyance, raised a storm of excitement; men felt that the code of a new type of artistic creation was drawn up. The advocates of "Realism," as the new style was termed, were busy developing their revolutionary views into a doctrine and this gave birth to "naturalistic esthetics." [21] To a certain extent this esthetic was a translation of positivistic views from the language of the sociologist into that of the artist. The positivistic philosopher raised mankind to the rank of true agent and vehicle of philosophical thinking. In this he claimed to be no more than the spokesman of his time. Modern artists chimed in with similar declarations. Jules Antoine Castagnary (1830–1888), friend of Courbet and eloquent codifier of the principles of the new school, writes: "Our painter will thus be of our own time, live our life with our costumes and our ideas. The feelings which society and the objective spectacle will give him—he will render in images in which we shall recognize ourselves and our surroundings." [22] Courbet himself exclaims hyberbolically: "To make verses is unfair; to speak in a fashion different from all the world, that is an aristocratic pose." [23] Just as for the positivist all imaginable objects are simply phenomena, facts of equal right and dignity, so the artist adopts a similar impartiality of outlook. One of Courbet's contemporary biographers says with some exaggeration: "His reform pertained to little more than the selection of subjects, which he admitted indiscriminately to the honors of

NATURALISM— THE NEW DEMO- CRATIC ART.

---

[21] This current of thought recently found its competent historian in René König, *Die naturalistische Ästhetik in Frankreich und ihre Auflösung. Ein Beitrag zur systemwissenschaftlichen Betrachtung der Künstlerästhetik*, 1931.

[22] *La Philosophie du salon de 1857*, 1858, p. 188.

[23] Gros-Kost, *Courbet, souvenirs intimes*, 1880, p. 31.

his 'democratic' brush." [24] "Scrupulous imitation of nature," "study after nature," the "signature of nature itself"—these were the catchwords upon which the changes were rung and which the critics and artists preached. "Nature as it is, even if ill-washed, that was what he wanted. Nothing was repugnant to him if true, were it even a default," writes another critic with regard to Courbet.[25] Constable's saying that the artist facing nature has to forget he ever saw a picture roused a multiplied echo.[26] Since the artist claims to be concerned with truth and truth alone, he must look upon himself as a scientist. The confusion of art and science, previously spread by the Romanticists, now reappears, with no better arguments, though in a somewhat different key. This time the leading part in the forced union falls to science. Both poets and painters wage a war against imagination in the interests of reality. Allowance must be made, it is true, for a certain amount of subjectivity arising from the artist's temperament. But the natural feature that escapes one artist will be only the better exhibited by another, and all artists taken together will reveal in the end all truth. "The sole true landscape-painter," writes Castagnary, "is mankind." [27] Together with the idea of artistic selection and of the "essential character," to put it in Taine's terminology, the old conception of beauty as a value of timeless validity is thrown overboard. Castagnary declares it to be an abstract idea covering different phenomena, the phenomena varying with the social conditions and even from individual to individual.[28] Each time ('time' being a collective subject consisting of the contemporary members of society) has to settle for itself the concrete meaning it wishes to attach to the abstract term beauty.

THE ARTIST COMES HOME TO EARTH. ZOLA: THE POET AS EXPERIMENTALIST.   Positivism and artistic realism belong together. Comte's doctrine was based upon the denial of a world beyond this world. The downfall of the ancient transcendental creed associated with a thousand years of Christian otherworldliness led artists toward

---

[24] Comte H. d'Ideville, *Gustave Courbet, Notes et documents sur sa vie et son œuvre*, Paris, 1878, pp. 107f.

[25] Gros-Kost, *op. cit.*, p. 77.

[26] König, *op. cit.*, p. 24.

[27] *Loc. cit.*, p. 52.

[28] *Ibid.*, pp. 102ff.

this present world. The earth was to mean more to them than it ever had to their forefathers: it was to be also heaven and hell. As they found themselves deprived of the invisible world, they clung the more passionately to the visible one. "The naturalistic school," wrote Castagnary, "is desirous to capture the forms of the visible world." [29] The idea of minutely imitating nature may easily be ridiculed as a gross esthetic error. In this case it was more: it was the expression of a fresh and as yet untested love.

Naturalistic esthetics culminates in Émile Zola's (1840–1902) theoretical essays. The modern artist, in his opinion, is less concerned with the human individual than with the social organism, the latter bearing a close resemblance to the organic body in nature. The work of the novelist is that of a scientific sociologist and psychologist. His main object is truth. Like a scholar he works under the guidance of a preconceived hypothesis and applies the rules derived from it to a selected case. [30] The result will be "a corner of nature seen through a temperament." [31] Yet this intervention of personality in the artist does not mean arbitrariness. His views, if artistically valuable, contain suggestions for future investigation and verification. So he becomes a scientific pioneer opening new ways to knowledge. Like the worker in a laboratory, the artist determines his initial conditions and starting-points. After having thus released the action, he assumes the rôle of mere observer. An analysis carried through in this fashion serves a supreme practical purpose. No work can be imagined which is nobler or of wider scope than that which teaches us how to become "master of good and evil, how to rule life, how to rule society. . . ." [32]

Fortunately the artist Zola is wiser than the theorist. The artistic naturalism of the author of *La faute de l'abbé Mouret*, a late document of romantic nature-worship, strikes its roots deeper into reality than his dogma can penetrate. Zola hints at the meaning of his naturalism when he least thinks of theorizing. Putting his ideas into the mouth of his hero, he writes: "Oh good Earth, take me,

---

[29] *Ibid.*, p. 105.
[30] *Le Roman Expérimental*, 5e éd., Paris, 1881, p. 49.
[31] *Ibid.*, p. 111.
[32] *Ibid.*, p. 24.

thou that art the common mother, the sole source of life, thou the eternal, immortal, where the soul of the world circles, that sap penetrating down to the stones and turning the trees into our tall brothers. . . . Thou alone shalt be in my work as primeval force, means and aim at once, the immense ark, wherein all things are animated by the breath of all beings!"

Jean-Marie Guyau (1854–1888), who quotes these words,[33] attempted to overcome the one-sidedness of both naturalistic and idealistic esthetics by showing that their common root is to be found in a broader conception of reality. There will always be two types of the artist: the artist who, like Zola, craves union with the earth, and the other who dreams of ascending to heaven. But on a philosophical examination, these apparently opposite conceptions prove to be aspects of a single truth. The pronouncedly realistic work may, in spite of its subservience to nature, fail to understand the language of real things. This, however, is the only justification of realism: that all things speak and that it is worth while listening to them. The idealist, on the other hand, remains faithful to truth only if the possible, at which he aims, stands revealed as the real rising to a higher stage of its development.[34]

Guyau's own theory may be regarded as a unification of the two currents of naturalist and idealist thought in a romantic metaphysics of Life. He defines art as "a methodical whole of means chosen to create that general and harmonious stimulation of conscious life which constitutes the feeling of beauty." [35] This feeling of beauty is explained by what may be termed an "introjection" of the idea of social order, "the higher form of the sentiment of solidarity and unity in harmony; it is the consciousness of a society in our individual life." [36] In a similar way the esthetic phenomenon of expression becomes an expansion of sympathy beyond the bounds of human companionship.[37] But the notion of society depends on the more comprehensive idea of life. "The principle

---

[33] *L'art au point de vue sociologique*, 6e éd., 1903, p. 78.
[34] *Ibid.*, p. 75.
[35] *Ibid.*, p. 16.
[36] *Ibid.*, p. 10.
[37] *Ibid.*, p. 15.

of art is . . . life itself. . . . The highest aim of art is, after all, to make the human heart throb, and, as the heart is the very center of life, art must find itself interlaced with the whole moral and material existence of mankind." [38]

The sociological thinkers of the Saint-Simonist and positivist school in France voiced the moral demands of the new society. Pointing to suffering and striving humanity, to the masses collecting in the industrial centers and longing for intellectual guidance and happiness, they said to the artist: This is our world and yours, and there is no other beside it. Help us to save mankind and to build up a noble and free life. This ideal appeal was enforced by brutal pressure. Those who did not shape their utterance to the configuration of modern mass civilization with its capitalistic patron as well as its under dog were threatened with starvation. Victor Hugo's novel *Les Misérables* shows the poet's compliance with both the moral and the material demand. It presents social aspirations in the garb of the "industrialized" sensational novel introduced by Eugène Sue. Thus the seamy side of the requirement became visible. The artist, accepting the leadership of the masses, was on the way to become their obedient servant. How were art and beauty to survive under the terrible pressure of a mankind estranged from the esthetic tradition either by a hard life or by the greedy pursuit of wealth? The force of this question was deeply felt by a group of artists and writers, who decided to make a firm stand against the adulteration of art by the modern world. They set out to defend uncompromisingly art's aloofness and purity. This movement, known under the slogan "art for art's sake," originated in France. Gustave Flaubert (1821–1880), Théophile Gautier (1811–1872), Edmond and Jules de Goncourt (1822–1896, 1833–1878), and Baudelaire (1821–1867) were its acknowledged leaders. It was represented in England by Walter Pater [39] (1834–1894) and

ART FOR ART'S SAKE MOVEMENT—DISILLUSIONED ROMANTICISM.

---

[38] *Problèmes de l'Esthétique contemporaine*, 10e éd., 1921, pp. vii f.

[39] The question as to when the slogan "art for art's sake" first appeared has been recently elucidated by Rose J. Egan (*The Origin of the Theory "Art for Art's Sake."* Smith College Studies in Modern Languages, Vol. 2, No. 4, Vol. 5, No. 3). Apart from this minor problem Miss Egan's thesis is that the doctrine of "art for art's sake" is not an original creation of the group of French writers generally credited with it, but that it pre-existed in German philosophy and

Oscar Wilde (1856–1900); and the American Edgar Allan Poe (1809–1849), whose life ended before the movement developed, may be regarded as its pioneer. These men are bound together partly by intimate friendship, partly by mutual admiration, above all by a common outlook on life and art which, though expounded by none of them in systematic form, is remarkably consistent. Compared with the clear outlines of this system, the variations due to personal and national temperament and character, however considerable in themselves, are of small account. As to the historical affiliation of the movement, it was undoubtedly a continuation of Romanticism. Friedrich Schlegel's doctrine contains the germs of its ideology, and Heinrich Heine, living in Paris as a refugee, imparted the romantic gospel of the freedom of art. The members of the movement carried on the romantic vision of beauty in the face of an avowedly hostile world. They were disillusioned Romanticists.

WORSHIP OF
BEAUTY.

While the industrialization of the civilized world proceeded rapidly and inexorably, these guardians of the romantic legacy turned their back on the loathsome spectacle. They kindle in the privacy of their studies and esoteric circles an impassioned worship of beauty. This creed is expressed sometimes in the ancient language of Platonism. Like Walter Pater's Marius the Epicurean, they profess to be of the number of those who must be "made perfect by the love of visible beauty." [40] More frequently they speak in the poignant accents of sensuous passion. Gautier, through a character in his novel, confesses: "I have coveted Beauty, nescient of what I desired. That is like gazing at the sun without eyelashes, like touching a flame. I suffer horribly. Not to be able to become like this perfection, not to pass over into it and take it in, to have no means of rendering it and making others feel it." [41] Raised to

---

criticism. As far as the conception of an "autonomous" art is concerned this derivation is certainly correct. But the development of this principle in Winckelmann, Goethe, or Schlegel on the one hand, and in Flaubert or Wilde on the other, is utterly different. So it seems advisable to abide by the traditional view concerning the beginning of the movement. An inquiry into the historical roots of any phenomenon is easily tempted into a derivation *ab ovo*.

[40] *The Renaissance*, Modern Library, p. 26.
[41] *Mademoiselle de Maupin*, p. 37.

superhuman heights by frantic veneration, beauty assumes an aspect of terrible majesty, or of malicious and gloomy splendor like an idol in some barbarian cult. "Whether thou comest from Satan or from God, what does it matter?" asks Baudelaire in his *Hymn to Beauty.*[42]

Beauty is a supreme and absolute value. This simple idea gives rise to two different schemes of thought. In the first of these schemes, in 'practical estheticism,' the idea of the supremacy of beauty is adopted in an unrestricted sense. Life has to be beautiful, and all its other values, goodness, truth, honesty, and wisdom, are either comprised in the esthetic consummation or subordinated to it. None of the writers of the art for art's sake movement fully developed this idea or tried to embody it in his own life. None felt both the grandeur and misery of the 'esthetic life' as deeply as Kierkegaard or Nietzsche did. But they all somehow visualized it as a possibility. It fascinated them, even if they rejected it. Walter Pater improvises nineteenth-century Epicureanism: a world formed by the interaction of atoms culminates in the most refined and vivid experience, the sensation of beauty. "For our chance lies . . . in getting as many pulsations as possible into the given time." [43] Flaubert finds a striking image: the fools are those who, on the shore of life, set about counting the grains of sand. This is the race of philosophers, gloomily enthusiastic, who need conclusions and search a goal. "Do you know what we are to do on the gravel? Kneel down or take a walk. Go and take a walk!" [44] Oscar Wilde, with a keener appreciation of the moral implications of an esthetic life, invents the elegant teacher of corruption. His Lord Henry preaches the gospel of "life treated artistically": every mode of conduct, even crime, is regarded as "a method of procuring sensations." "Live!", he exclaims, "Live the wonderful life that is in you! Let nothing be lost upon you. Be always searching for new sensations. Be afraid of nothing!" [45] The idea, on which

PRACTICAL ESTHETICISM.

---

[42] *Fleurs du Mal*, "Hymne à la Beauté," XII.
[43] *The Renaissance*, "Conclusion."
[44] Flaubert, *Correspondence*, III, 120.
[45] *The Writings of Oscar Wilde*, New York, 1931, 5 Vols.; Vol. 3, *Dorian Gray*, pp. 388, 386, 47.

Thomas de Quincey in the essay on "Murder considered as one of the Fine Arts" had humorously played, was on the verge of being taken seriously. Nothing short of crime seemed exciting enough to quench the thirst for untried emotions. Wilde is as little Dorian Gray as Walter Pater is Marius the Epicurean. But though not identical with this fictitious creation he yields foolishly to the temptation of the imagined ideal. In *De Profundis* he relates with a few strokes the story of his downfall. First he boasts of his former gifts and achievements: "I treated art as the supreme reality and life as a mere mode of fiction." Then, as if unaware of the connection between this confusion and the ensuing catastrophe, he goes on: "But I let myself be lured into long spells of senseless and sensual ease. I amused myself with being a flaneur, a dandy, a man of fashion. . . . Tired of being on the heights, I deliberately went to the depths in search for new sensation." [46] Compared with this disastrous experiment, the dandyism of Barbey d'Aurevilly, Théodore de Banville, Baudelaire, and Whistler is no more than the innocuous approximation to an idea. The dandy understood exquisite dress as a symbol of the aristocrat in the age of democracy. Proud, fiercely independent, he avoids disdainfully any contact with vulgar things. Not necessarily an artist himself, he is devoted to beauty and gifted with artistic delicacy. However, a life guided solely by beauty proves impracticable. It resists, by its very nature, theoretical systematization: Philosophical ideas are appreciated only in so far as they "may help us to gather up what might otherwise pass unregarded by us," as instruments to rouse, to startle the human spirit to a life of vivid sensibility. [47]

ART FOR BEAUTY'S SAKE AND THE 'DOUBLE LIFE' OF THE ARTIST.
Estheticism really comes to terms with life only by shifting from a general practical philosophy to what may be called "artistic estheticism," the philosophy of artists for their own use. The basic principle is now modified and restricted by an addition: In art, it reads, (and this means: not in life as such) beauty is a supreme and absolute value. Life is no longer subjected to beauty, but within life an autonomous dominion is claimed for art. Art, with its specific value, exists for its own sake. It fulfills its purpose

---

[46] *The Writings of Oscar Wilde*, IV, 29.
[47] Pater, *loc. cit.*

by being beautiful. "We believe," writes Gautier in the preface in which he introduced himself as editor of the periodical *L'Artiste*,[48] "in the autonomy of art; for us art is not a means but the goal; an artist who pursues an object other than the beautiful is not an artist in our opinion." "As a rule," says the same author, "a thing that becomes useful ceases to be beautiful." [49] Never was more fervent service devoted to art than by these defenders of its unalloyed purity. They shrank from no privations or sacrifices; no labor was deemed too strenuous in the service of this great mistress, who, in her turn, was "selfishly occupied with her own perfection." [50] "The more experience in art I acquire, the more this art becomes a torture to me. . . . Few men, I believe, will have suffered more from literature than I," confesses Flaubert.[51] A similar anxiety, but mixed with rejoicing, is revealed in Baudelaire's "Prayer": "Oh Lord, grant me the favor of creating some beautiful verses which shall prove to myself that I am not the last of men, that I am not inferior to those whom I despise." [52] Oscar Wilde, disgraced, condemned, locked up in jail, turns in his deep distress to art as to his savior: "If I can produce only one beautiful work of art I shall be able to rob malice of its venom, and cowardice of its sneer, and to pluck out the tongue of scorn by the roots." [53] Artistic beauty, exalted to heaven in the presence of an unsympathetic public, is bought at the price of utter isolation. This is the meaning of "autonomous art." In his "Ten o'clock Lecture" (1888) Whistler says: "The master stands in no relation to the moment at which he occurs—a monument of isolation—hinting at sadness—having no part in the progress of his fellow-men." [54] According to Wilde, the "first condition of creation is that the critic should be able to recognize that the sphere of Art and the sphere of Ethics are absolutely distinct and separate." [55]

---

[48] December 14, 1856.
[49] *Préface des Premières Poésies,* 1832.
[50] J. A. McNeill Whistler, *The Gentle Art of Making Enemies,* 1924, p. 136.
[51] *Correspondence,* III, 154.
[52] *Petits Poèmes en prose: À une heure du matin.*
[53] *De Profundis,* Works, IV, p. 41.
[54] J. A. McNeill Whistler, *op. cit.,* p. 155.
[55] *The Critic as Artist, Writings,* V, 210.

Life however is essentially one. To be truly one is, according to Plato, the basis of human happiness. The involuntary grace of a simple and heartfelt song, childlike play, and humorous laughter—all this is excluded from the kingdom of the new art. Its beauty, like that of an archaic goddess, is enthroned in stern majesty, and accustomed to receive strange and terrible offerings. Since art, divorced from life, does not cease to be part of life, the artist has to lead two lives. The visualizer of a beauty hitherto unknown, rapturously lifted above the needs of this frail body and feeding upon glowing visions, drags on, at the same time, the drab, monotonous, laborious, respectable life of the much despised bourgeois. Flaubert notes: "I maintain, and this should be a practical dogma of the artistic life, that one has to divide one's existence into two parts: to live as a bourgeois and to think as a demi-god. The satisfactions of the body and those of the brain have nothing in common with each other." [56] This twofold life benefits both the artist's art and the artist's person. The passions and affections, denied full expression in life, flow into the work. At the same time, the escape from life into art is the self-preservation of a soul too delicately sensitive. "You will paint wine, love, women, fame, provided, my dear fellow, you are neither drunk nor in love, neither a husband nor a swordsman. Mingling with life, one is unable to see it well; it makes one suffer too much, or rejoice too much." [57] Flaubert lived up to these words, enduring a lifelong monastic seclusion in a small provincial town. The Romanticist, wavering to and fro between contempt for the world and the enthusiastic hope of assimilating it to his own heart, had considered himself the most fascinating subject of his art. Now the artist's person, unworthy instrument of his artistic achievements, appears as merely another specimen of an alienated reality. "A great poet," says Wilde through Lord Henry, "is the most unpoetical of all creatures." [58] The artist will continue to live an emotional and affective life, but it will be banished into the depths of his being. In Flaubert's words: "Each of us has in his heart a royal chamber; I have walled it up, but it is not destroyed." [59]

---

[56] *Correspondence*, II, 259.   [58] *Writings*, III, 105.
[57] *Ibid.*, II, 23.   [59] *Correspondence*, III, 258.

The artist, exiled, as it were, from his own self, feels separated by a gulf from the world around him, from his public. He pours the full measure of scorn over the bourgeois, that is, the non-artist, and he does so in the very books which he hopes to have bought and read by his victims. Of course he will not admit that he is guilty of this contradiction. He will protest that the artists write "for their equals," or at least, as Barbey d'Aurevilly adds hesitatingly, "for those who understand them." [60] It is significant that the adherents of the school failed as playwrights; the art that requires the immediate response of a broader public was beyond their reach. The bourgeois society took its revenge for the abuse inflicted upon it by relishing its own scornful portrait as a new seasoning. Art for art's sake became a luxury for the benefit of the leisured and well-to-do, for those who could afford to lead a "second life" devoted to idleness. The movement in France matched the society of the second empire. It thrived on a prosperous bourgeois class, which had been freed from political responsibility by a liberal dictatorship. When the army surrendered at Sedan and the enemy advanced towards Paris, the hour of French estheticism had struck. A terrible reality swept away the artifice of a 'double life.'

The emancipation of art from life puts its stamp both on the artistic form itself and on the life in which the form originates. *De nobis ipsis silemus* is the motto inscribed on the creations of these esthetes. Musset who simply expressed what passed through his mind in a flowing, rather loose, and often careless diction is surely condemned. The artist of the new type like the scientist fixes a cold calm gaze on his object. Again and again recurs the idea of science as the model of the modern artist. On this point the art of art's sake movement and artistic naturalism overlap. Flaubert advises: "Try to cling to science, to pure science; love facts for their own sake; study ideas as the naturalists study gnats." [61] This is spoken in full earnest. Flaubert himself went to Egypt to study the scenery for his novel *Salammbô*. He plunges

THE IDEAL OF CLARITY AND OBJECTIVITY.

---

[60] Préface to *Une vieille Maîtresse.*

[61] A. Cassagne, *La théorie de l'art pour l'art en France chez les derniers romantiques et les premiers réalistes*, 1906, p. 271.

into psychiatric studies while writing his *Saint Antoine,* and later on he acquires a scientific knowledge of hysteria and insanity.[62] We find a similar scientific curiosity in Poe, the Goncourts, and Leconte de Lisle. Walter Pater writes: "The literary artist is of necessity a scholar," [63] and Flaubert's friend Bouilhet, in his scientific scrupulousness, goes to the length of taking lessons in Chinese.[64] This does not mean, however, that these men believe in all ways in science. Their leaning toward scientific minuteness even goes together, as in Flaubert, with contempt for scientific results. Scientific methods are adopted only in so far as they serve an artistic purpose. Again, logical clarity is appreciated not for its own sake but with a view to its effect on the human sensibility. Pater speaks of "a poetic beauty in mere clearness of thought, the actually esthetic charm of a cold austerity of mind: as if the kinship of that to the clearness of physical light were something more than a figure of speech." [65] This intellectual clearness marked the new art off from most of the romantic creations and reminds us of the classical style. In science the impartial attitude of the student is prized not for its own sake but for its results. If the artist assumes a similar attitude, he seeks the intrinsic value. The aloofness and non-attachment of the observer is enjoyed as an esthetic charm. In but very few cases do the realistic descriptions of the esthetes spring from real sympathy with the object. As a rule, these artists feel nature, facts, every-day reality as something foreign, hostile, or even mean and despicable. "People believe," writes Flaubert with reference to *Madame Bovary,* "I am taken with the real, whereas I detest it." [66] The beauty of the Alps makes no impression on his mind, and Baudelaire, most akin to him in his attitude toward nature, wishes the meadows painted in red, the rivers golden yellow, the trees blue. In its native hues nature strikes him as monotonous and boring.[67] Wilde feels the same way: "My own

---

[62] *Correspondence,* III, 207.
[63] *Appreciations,* 1922, p. 12.
[64] Cassagne, *op. cit.,* p. 377.
[65] *Marius the Epicurean,* p. 102.
[66] *Correspondence,* III, 85.
[67] Jules Levallois, *Mémoires d'un critique,* p. 95.

experience is that the more we study art, the less we care for nature. What art really reveals to us, is nature's lack of design, her curious crudities, her extraordinary monotony, her absolutely unfinished condition." [68]

Picturing reality with a cold minute attention to details, the artist asserts his own superiority over the impact of strange, bewildering, fascinating, or disgusting impressions. Representing them, he wards them off, and he combines them in an image which he keeps at some distance from his own spontaneous reactions. This ideal of an objective image, established as it were outside the cloudy and agitated atmosphere of inner life in the neutral dominion of form, color, and light, is more easily attained by painting and sculpture than by poetry. Hence the Goncourts praise the profession of the painter, Gautier regrets having relinquished his first vocation which was painting, and Baudelaire draws his inspirations not from the poets but from Rubens, Leonardo da Vinci, Rembrandt, Michelangelo, Puget, Watteau, Goya, and Delacroix. [69] The coldness of the objective image is not absence of expression but the expression of the artist's own coolness, his perfect self-possession. The more exciting the represented subject is in itself, either in its sensuous charm or passionate appeal, its violence or cruelty, the more impressive is the disdainful serenity of the artistic report. The face of a man in whose mind desire and fear, passion and horror are raging but who subdues these feelings by a powerful effort of will, may be more expressive than that of a person who yields to the impulses of his nature. It is the former type of expression which the modern artist adopts as congenial. But as the suppression of feeling requires a strenuous effort, his art is grave and somber. Each work is the monument of a victory won after painful struggle. As a dual life is behind the work, the work shows, so to speak, two faces. One face expresses proud and triumphant cheerfulness, the manly clearness of the philosopher. The other is sorrowful and distorted like a tragic mask. The artist who

---

[68] "Decay of Lying," in *Intentions and the Soul of Man, Writings*, V, p. 3. Cf. J. A. McNeill Whistler, *The Gentle Art of Making Enemies*, 1924, p. 143: "Nature is usually wrong."

[69] Cassagne, *op. cit.*, p. 366.

wishes to conceal his feelings finds himself in a paradoxical situation. Hiding himself, he gives himself away. For he expresses not only his feelings but also the reluctance and shame which the exhibition of his inner life causes in him. When the painter Feydeau lost his wife, Flaubert expressed his sympathy, and at the same time, his congratulations. "You will paint fine pictures and you will be able to make excellent studies. But the price is high. The bourgeois hardly suspect that we serve them our heart. The race of gladiators is not extinct; each artist is one. He amuses the public with his agonies." [70]

POE: RATIONALITY
OF THE 'PURE ART.'

The art advocated and produced by this movement is more rational than art ever was, while at the same time more irrational. Reason and passion, intellect and sensuality are not here mediated by infinite transitions as in classic art, but forced together and joined in a mystic marriage. The artistic workman proceeds in the full light of his rational consciousness, closely watching and controlling every step. But the clearness thus created is not open daylight but a search-light throwing into sharp prominence the elaborate design of a façade. As the main body of the building looms behind in impenetrable darkness, the effect produced is uncanny. Reading a poem like "The Raven" we become slightly intoxicated; we feel invaded by a sensuous horror of loneliness and by an unfathomable melancholy. But Poe, in the famous essay *The Philosophy of Composition*, shows us the *modus operandi* by which these verses were put together. The poem might have been a clock. As he starts on his work, the artist selects an effect which he wishes to produce, and his art consists in finding out and applying the proper means to this end. The initial consideration, reports Poe, was that of extent,[71] and he decided upon about one hundred lines. Only a brief poem, not passing beyond the limits of a single sitting, can, in his opinion, be enjoyed as a beautiful sensuous whole. The essence of beauty is "the intense and pure elevation of soul" which it engenders,[72] and to gain this effect is the artist's sole concern. Poetry as the art of words is "the Rhythmical Creation

---

[70] *Correspondence*, III, 170.
[71] *Complete Works*, ed. by J. A. Harrison, Vols. XIV–XV, p. 196.
[72] *Ibid.*, p. 197.

of Beauty. Its sole arbiter is taste. With the Intellect or with the Conscience, it has only collateral relations." [73] Thus the determination of the length of the poem follows from a reflection on the nature of art and beauty.

Going on in his analysis of "The Raven," Poe tries to demonstrate "that no one point in its composition is referable either to accident or intuition—that the work proceeded, step by step, to its completion with the precision and rigid consequence of a mathematical problem." [74] Having in mind the general desirable effect, he chooses for his manifestation of beauty the most efficient tone, and this, he thinks, is sadness. The idea that the poet expresses a state of his own mind is out of the question. The expressed melancholy is a means calculated to produce a certain effect and nothing else. And the death of a woman, combining the idea of beauty with that of mortality, is introduced, as it appears to be the most melancholy and the most poetic topic in the world. Following up his induction, the poet searches for some artistic 'piquancy,' and finally he comes upon an old and universally employed device, the refrain. He decides to improve upon it and to make the most of the monotonous recurrence of a few fascinating sounds. The spell-binding "nevermore" occurs to him, and this leads with logical stringency to the conception of a Raven—the bird of ill omen—to the invention of an appropriate locale, to the careful elaboration of the climax preparing the dénouement. With reference to the choice of the rhythm, Poe tells us that his first object (as usual) was originality. This originality has nothing to do with the expression of personal feelings. It consists chiefly in the avoidance of outworn and ordinary forms. "In general, to be found, it must be elaborately sought, and although a positive merit of the highest class, demands in its attainment less of invention than of negation." [75] Baudelaire, for whom Poe's theory is a revelation paving the way for his own great art, admires especially this idea of an acquired originality. [76] The striving after 'nov-

---

[73] "The Poetic Principle," *loc. cit.*, p. 275.

[74] *Ibid.*, p. 195.

[75] *Ibid.*, p. 203.

[76] Cassagne, *op. cit.*, p. 303.

elty of beauty' is the refined form of the 'search for new sensations.' [77]

Poe taught how to handle a thoroughly irrational subject-matter in a highly rational fashion. His theory half reveals and half
disguises a sensuous mysticism. True art, he writes, conveys no
mere appreciation of the beauty before us, but it is "a wild effort
to reach the beauty above." [78] The 'beauty above' is reminiscent of
Platonism. But the expression 'wild effort,' much out of tune in
this connection, makes us doubt whether the aspiration is more
than "a sensuous longing posing as spirituality." [79]

ART DIVORCED
FROM NATURE.

The effortless streaming forth of harmonious language, much
admired in Musset and Lamartine, is supplanted in the new rational
art by an elaborate method of composition. Every clause is chis-
elled with infinite care. Guy de Maupassant describes Flaubert's
manner of composition thus: "Possessed of an absolute belief that
there exists but one way of expressing one thing, one word to call
it by, one adjective to qualify, one verb to animate it, he gave himself to superhuman labor for the discovery, in every phrase, of
that word, that verb, that epithet." [80] The outcome is inevitably
the precious and choice expression. Walter Pater, himself a master
of the precious style, likes to compare literary composition with
metal-work. Describing Flavian's concern for the purity and power
of his native Latin he writes: "He would make of it a serious study,
weighing the precise power of every phrase and word, as though it
were precious metal, disentangling the later associations and going
back to the original and native sense of each,—restoring to full
significance all its wealth of latent figurative expression, reviving
its outworn or tarnished images." [81]

The 'precious' style tends to become artificial. It then banishes
nature as vulgar, abominable, mean. "The beautiful is always
bizarre," claims Baudelaire. [82] The emperor Algabal, in one of

---

[77] Cf. Paul Valéry, *Variété*, II, pp. 162ff.
[78] *Op. cit:*, p. 274.
[79] Norman Foerster, *American Criticism*, 1928, p. 50.
[80] Quoted by Walter Pater, *Appreciations*, p. 29.
[81] *Ibid.*, p. 79.
[82] Cassagne, *op. cit.*, p. 316.

Stefan George's early books, builds a wholly artificial world: artificial sky, rivers, and meadows; but he is unable to grow in his enchanted garden "the dark flower of life." Nature in order to be recognized as beautiful has to borrow from art. "A thing characteristic of our being," remarks Goncourt, "is to see nothing in nature that is not a remembrance and recollection of art." Art furnishes the prototype of things, nature their pale effigy: "Before the canvas of a good landscape painter I feel more in the country than in the open field or in the middle of a forest." [83] Art feeds upon art, refining on the traditional procedures, multiplying, combining, and developing the well-tested devices. Creation then is practical criticism. In one of his essays Wilde, reviving an idea of Friedrich Schlegel's, points out that the critic is the true artist. The work of art, he thinks, has to be generated by an immaculate conception, undefiled by contact with crude reality. Not only is this inbred art assumed to revolve in its own sphere like the Aristotelian god; it is also destined to become a *primum mobile*, the moving force of life. Gilbert, in Wilde's *The Critic as Artist*, prophesies: "I am certain that, as civilization progresses and we become more highly organized, the elect spirits of each age, the critical and cultured spirits, will grow less and less interested in actual life, and will seek to gain their impressions almost entirely from what art has touched." [84] "The proper school to learn art," Wilde maintains, "is not Life but Art," [85] and he amuses himself with turning upside down time-honored esthetic truths. Life, he says, "imitates Art far more than Art imitates Life," and "external Nature also imitates Art." [86] "Where, if not from the Impressionists, do we get those wonderful brown fogs that come creeping down our streets, blurring the gas-lamps and changing the houses into monstrous shadows?" [87]

The objection frequently raised against these writers that they cared too much for form and too little for ideas is regularly met

---

[83] *Ibid.*, p. 325.
[84] *Writings*, V, p. 175.
[85] "The Decay of Lying," *loc. cit.*, p. 27.
[86] *Ibid.*, p. 56.
[87] *Ibid.*, p. 41.

by the contention that this very distinction is senseless. Or they
said like Baudelaire: "Idea and Form are two beings joined into
one." [88] Now there is so much confusion in the current opposition
of form to idea, form to subject, form to content, that it is difficult to see what either criticism or justification really means. To
make sense of the discussion and to see what the reproach of
'formalism' amounts to, we may adopt a distinction suggested by
A. C. Bradley in his lecture on *Poetry for Poetry's Sake*.[89] Bradley
calls "substance" the figures, scenes, events forming a part of the
poem; and "subject" the corresponding figures, scenes, events existing outside the poem in myth, folklore, or oral report. So the
"Fall of Man" as dogma or symbolic story is the subject of Milton's
Paradise Lost, but it is not identical with its substance, the poetically transformed story as told by the poet. Now, if "idea" (idée)
in our discussion signifies substance, Flaubert and Baudelaire are
right. Substance and form are aspects of an indivisible unity and
the reproach of formalism is senseless. But the criticism may aim
at an objectionable attitude of the poet towards the "subject" of
his creations, at his contempt of reality outside the poem—and then
it does not miss its target. Flaubert dreams of writing a book "on
nothing." [90] As this proves impossible, the artificial subject is preferred to the natural, the strange to the familiar, the violent to the
moderate. The idea of originality, that is of rareness, rules the
selection. Fastidious taste requires always spicier dishes. So come
exoticisms both of space and time. Oriental life and primitive war-
rior tribes offer more colorful images than does industrial Europe.
These highly civilized writers of the old world take a strange delight in pure vitality, or in what they take to be such, in a mixture
of greatness of soul and cruelty, fierceness and self-sacrifice, generosity and sensuality. As he entered Jaffa, Flaubert relates, he
scented "at the same time the odor of lemon-trees and of carrion.
. . . Don't you sense that this poetry is perfect and that this
is the great synthesis?" [91] Exoticism of the mind is perversity: the

---

[88] Cassagne, *op. cit.*, p. 439, cf. p. 137.
[89] *Oxford Lectures on Poetry*, 1920, pp. 3ff.
[90] *Correspondence*, II, 86.
[91] *Ibid.*, 183.

enjoyment of the gruesome or of the disgusting, the glorification of the evil done for evil's sake. While among these writers ordinary vice is repudiated as a kind of deformity, the Satanic receives poetic oblations. With the diabolic goes the 'macabre,' "that species of almost insane preoccupation with the materialities of our mouldering flesh, that luxury of disgust on corruption." [92]

Surveying modern estheticism as a whole, we distinguish three closely interrelated systems: the system of a life ruled solely by esthetic value ('practical estheticism'), the system of an art separated from life and occupied exclusively with the creation of beauty, finally the system of the artist's life—the living source of this kind of creation. The last mentioned is a revival of the Platonic and Christian idea of the contemplative life. "To us," writes Oscar Wilde, "the *Bios Theoretikos* is the true ideal. From the high tower of thought we can look out at the world. Calm, and self-centered, and complete, the esthetic critic contemplates life, and no arrow drawn at a venture can pierce between the joints of his harness. He at least is safe. He has discovered how to live." [93] Retire from active life, contemplate, look on life from above, climb a tower! This is the advice invariably given by Flaubert to all his friends. The unbeliever turns preacher and holds out the promise of salvation: "You will be like Moses, descending from Sinai. He had rays round his face, because he had seen God." [94] Yet the contemplation of the Platonic philosopher revealed the beauty and goodness of the cosmos. Returning from his visionary exaltation, he was able to trace the divine vestiges in imperfect matter. The elevation of his modern follower is, by confession, a flight from the burden of existence, and the object of his contemplation is nothingness, forgetfulness. "Life is such a hideous thing that the only means of bearing it is: to avoid it," reads another passage in the letter just quoted. No qualms of conscience! the nihilist's sermon goes on. Impotent for evil or for good as we are, to feel guilty is sheer vanity. A saying of Gautier echoes Gorgias: "Nothing is good for anything and, first of all, there is

NIHILISTIC IMPLICATIONS. ON THE THRESHOLD OF CHRISTIANITY.

---

[92] Walter Pater, *Marius the Epicurean*, p. 49.
[93] *The Critic as Artist, Writings*, V, 194.
[94] *Correspondence*, III, 119.

nothing. Yet every thing happens! But that makes no difference." [95] Thus the movement of art for art's sake ends in a blank
and radical negation of life, not because of the whims of its disciples but because of a logical development of its philosophy. In this
context the much praised contemplation is not a beatific vision, a
source of life, but a strong narcotic, a draught of Lethe. After the
ecstasy is over the devotees awake worn and broken, and ordinary
drugs may have to supplement the spiritual intoxication. One
feels tempted to ask whether this nihilism is genuine. We may suspect that this too is a last desperate means of quenching the thirst
for 'new sensations.' Is there anything solid and durable left in
this universal dissolution of the fundamentals, any basic belief, any
unbroken conviction? Flaubert, who justly prided himself on his
veracity, seems to suggest an answer to this question in one of his
letters: "Last year when I told you about my idea of entering a
monastery, that was the old leaven which rose in me. A moment
comes when one feels the need of making oneself suffer, of hating
one's flesh, of throwing mud into one's face, so hideous it seems.
Without the love of form, I should perhaps have become a great
mystic. . . ." [96]

The idea of a 'double life' was developed for the sake of beauty.
Yet this life was ugly—a broken and disunited thing. So we return
to our starting-point, the idea of a life governed by beauty. Is it
not possible to devote a whole life to esthetic enjoyment, but an
enjoyment free from that pernicious striving after 'novel moods'
which, because boundless, leads again to ugliness? Perhaps we may
call to the rescue that ancient wisdom that teaches us "with a sense
of economy, with a jealous estimate of gain and loss, to use life
not as a means to some problematic end, but, as far as might be,
from dying hour to dying hour, an end in itself—a kind of music,
all sufficing to the duly trained ear." This was Walter Pater's idea,
and it was embodied by him in his Marius the Epicurean. There
is, however, some ailing breach, some deep-lying deficiency even
in such a melodious life. It is imprisoned in the world of predomi-
nantly esthetic values. Cecilia and Cornelius, both Christians, move

---

[95] Cassagne, op. cit., p. 336.
[96] Correspondence, II, 192.

outside, beyond reach; with them dwell hope, faith, and love. But through a lifelong education of his receptive powers Marius has "prepared himself towards possible further revelation some day—towards some ampler vision, which should take up into itself and explain this world's delightful shows, as the scattered fragments of a poetry, till then but half understood, might be taken up into the text of a lost epic, recovered at last." [97] In Marius estheticism transcends itself. So his last action—a decision against himself, in favor of Cornelius—shows him on the border-line. His supreme sacrifice, from the point of view of his old world, is ambiguous: half act of friendship, half fatigue of the soul. But to a more generous view, it may be interpreted as martyrdom. [98]

The doctrines taught and the works created in France and England awakened a strange response in the east of the European continent. Leo Nikolayvitch Tolstoy (1828–1910) raised his voice to protest and to preach repentance. Your theory, he declared, expresses the views of a degenerate ruling class. Your art, catering to the perverted appetites of the well-to-do, is artificial, obscure, involved, affected. He pointed to the models of true art, understood by all, speaking the simple language of the human heart, to Homer, to the epic of Genesis, the Gospels, folk-legends, fairy-tales, and folk-songs. We will listen respectfully to this angry sermon. Nobody could speak more competently on epic greatness than the author of *War and Peace*. But we are bound to remark that Tolstoy's own conception of art, as an activity "having for its purpose the transmission to others of the highest and best feelings," [99] was inadequate. Nor can we admit that Tolstoy's criticism of the Art for Art's sake Movement was equitable. Not the whim of effete and fastidious esthetes had manoeuvred the theory of art into dangerously radical views. These views honestly expressed the plight of the artist in the modern world, and they resulted from a passionate quest of a way out. Baudelaire, the poet of decadence, was also a great religious poet. The members of the movement

TOLSTOY'S PROTEST AGAINST DECADENT ART.

---

[97] *Op. cit.*, pp. 379f.

[98] *Ibid.*, p. 384.

[99] Tolstoy, *What is Art?* Translated by Aylmer Maude, Centenary Edition, 1929, p. 143; cf. the definition, p. 123.

deified beauty and thus became guilty of idolatry. But there was true service in their idolatry. Once the vision of the scale of values was obscured, their error was not only pardonable, it was a stage within a wholesome crisis. It led back, tortuous and bewildering though the road was, to those feelings which Tolstoy called "the highest and best."

SUPPLEMENTARY READING

H. A. Needham, *Le développement de l'esthétique sociologique en France et en Angleterre au XIX. siècle*, 1926.

R. F. Egan, *The Genesis of the Theory of 'Art for Art's Sake' in Germany and England*, Smith College Studies in Modern Languages, II, 4, and V, 3, 1921–24.

G. E. B. Saintsbury, *History of Criticism and Literary Taste in Europe*, Vol. 3, "Modern Criticism," 1904, pp. 544–52 (on Walter Pater).

CHAPTER XVII

Metaphysics in a Crisis

G ERMAN idealist esthetics had soared so high that it was evidently impossible to persist in so bold a flight. It was time to find a way back to the fertile plains of experience. The generation which followed Schelling, Hegel, and Solger came home to earth. A great hunger for concreteness, reality, and active life stirred into being. The philosopher, bent on coming to terms with reality, carried within him the lingering vision of the kingdom of Ideas. Was he able to recognize the vestiges of this visionary world in the new environment? Could he remain faithful to the past while serving the present? Or did he look back on the idealistic phase as on a rapturous dream which leaves the dreamer exhausted and weakened at heart?

Post-classical esthetics does not furnish us with an unequivocal answer. If, with our question in mind, we view the work of Friedrich Theodor Vischer (1807–87), the most typical exponent of this period, we shall be baffled rather than enlightened. Is the outcome of his endeavors adjustment or disintegration, reconstruction or dissolution? Perhaps it is an ambiguity inherent in his thought that makes us hesitate before this alternative.

Vischer's difficulties were those of the heir and successor, of the *Epigone*, to use a significant term introduced at that time by Immermann. A normal development would lead from tentative essays to a comprehensive doctrine. But Hegel's belated disciple begins with an elaborate system providing an answer to every imaginable esthetic problem, and ends with essays in which he modestly and searchingly gropes after the solutions to a few fundamental questions.

The *Esthetics*,[1] which laid the foundation of Vischer's fame, is frightening both by its bulk—six enormous tomes—and by the scholastic form of its presentation. The thought is pressed into the strait-jacket of infinite divisions, subdivisions, sub-subdivisions, propositions, notes, and corollaries. The author himself was the first to feel scared and bewildered by this unmanageable apparatus. He implored his friends to put aside system and proposition and to read the application of the doctrine in the notes. It is unnecessary to give a detailed account of the system. It is frankly Hegelian. In the notes, the freshness and somewhat rugged vigor of Vischer's mind happily manifests itself. He sifts and organizes a vast esthetic experience with the help of an insight gained chiefly from the German classics. At the same time, the spirit of a new age shines forth in the concrete parts of Vischer's work.

Vischer and his friends rebelled against the spirit of retrospective aloofness in Hegel. Hegel understood the evolution of art in terms of the past; Vischer, returning to Schiller's and Schelling's views, in terms of the future. He proclaimed a coming synthesis of modern tendencies and classic ideals. He feared that an art modelled on Winckelmann's ideas might create a "false esthetic idealism," masking under the smooth surface of harmonious forms the sufferings and struggles of mankind. Even Goethe's and Schiller's poetry, though he cherished and admired it, seemed to him guilty of this classicist fault. The first of poets, in his opinion, was Shakespeare. He described the poetic ideal of the future as "Shakespeare's style, purified by a true and free appropriation of Antiquity."[2] His advice to modern poets was to find subjects worthy of their art in their own time, celebrating the heroic struggle of peoples for liberty and nationhood instead of fostering outworn individualistic ideals.

THE NOTION OF CHANCE BREAKS UP IDEALISM. Such heresy seems to lie merely on the surface. Actually it betrayed a new attitude which could not but affect the very fundamentals of the Hegelian doctrine. Vischer adopted Hegel's system but he did not share his belief. Hegel believed in the Idea as 'one and all': formative cause determining the species as well as 'principle

---

[1] *Ästhetik oder Wissenschaft des Schönen, zum Gebrauch für Vorlesungen,* 1847-57; 2d edition, 1922-23.   [2] *Op. cit.,* VI, 311, §908.

of individualization,' energy of progress and *vis inertiae* hindering or steadying the progressive drive. For Vischer the Idea is permanently struggling against alien influences which together form the 'Kingdom of Chance.' "All life, all history, all movement of Spirit in every sphere make up essentially the history of the annihilation and assimilation of chance." [3] In the Beautiful alone the impress of restive energy is preserved. Only here chance is organized, not exterminated. An object in nature, *e.g.* a lion, is beautiful on account of its conforming to esthetic laws in spite of (or owing to) the fortuitous factors that influenced its formation. They prevent it from becoming a pure type, a mere embodiment of the idea of 'carnivorous animal.'

Vischer believed that his theory of chance filled a gap in Hegel's doctrine. Actually, it negated Hegel's idealism. An Idea limited from outside, by the operation of an alien matter, runs counter to the spirit and the letter of the dialectic. Thus it testifies to Vischer's intellectual sincerity that he gradually liberated himself from a doctrine which he had never fully assimilated. From idealism he turned to a metaphysically tinged positivism. [4] He now substituted for Idea the vague expression 'content of life.' "A simple object of the senses," he said, "awakens a definite presentment of an all-pervading and ruling energy otherwise not attainable to perception but only to reason and belief." [5] Along with the Hegelian notion of "Idea" the doctrine of consecutive stages of consciousness also disappeared from his later writings. It gave way to that of a mere coördination of esthetic and intellectual intuition: "There are two methods of ideation (*Denken*): by words and notions, and by forms; there are two ways of deciphering the Universe: by letters and by images." [6]

---

[3] *Loc. cit.,* §41.

[4] The development of Karl Köstlin moved in the same direction. His Hegelianism is documented in the section on music which he contributed to Vischer's *Ästhetik*. In his later publications the psychological method is combined with views akin to Formalism (*Über den Schönheitsbegriff*, 1878, *Prolegomena zur Ästhetik*, Tübinger Universitätsschriften, 1889).

[5] *Das Schöne und die Kunst. Zur Einführung in die Ästhetik*. Vorträge herausgegeben von Robert Vischer, 1898, p. 143.

[6] "Das Symbol" (1887), *Kritische Gänge*, edited by Robert Vischer, 2d ed., 5 Vols., 1920–22, IV, 432ff.

Idea, in Vischer's earlier work, was conceived as spiritual energy organizing and animating beautiful objects. When doubt had undermined his belief in ideal entities, a new way of accounting for esthetic facts was required. The beautiful animal or beautiful landscape affects our sensibility as though it were itself animated by the feelings it awakens. This fact, once a welcome verification of his metaphysical convictions, had now become a mystery to Vischer. The depersonalization of the world rendered the personifying effect of esthetic experience a pressing problem. How can an object, belonging to non-human reality, become the carrier of human expression? Since objective reality, deprived of its divine substance, no longer yielded an explanation, the analyst had to turn from the objective world to the working of the mind. The theory of '*Einfühlung*' (empathy), suggested by his son Robert Vischer, was called upon to supply a new solution.

ART AS SUBSTITUTE FOR KNOWLEDGE AND FAITH.

The positivism of the disillusioned idealist had reduced the spirited Hegelian universe to an aggregate of facts. Had it not, at the same time, debased Beauty to the meaningless play of a hidden mental mechanism? Vischer was anxious to avoid this inference. Therefore, he retained the Hegelian Idea in so far as it assigned to art a high rank in life, and termed it Universe or universal Harmony. The mind dimly shadows forth in esthetic pleasure the unity of Spirit and Nature. This "truth of truths" is held to be the basis of esthetic illusion.[7] As however the idea of this Unity is now reduced to a hypothesis, or even to a mere emotional postulate, beauty takes on a new meaning. Its work is to gloss over insoluble contradictions and to console us for the irremediable misery of our existence.[8] Rational metaphysics is superseded by a vague metaphysical belief, reminiscent of Schopenhauer's irrational 'Worldground' rather than of Hegel's Spirit. Like many of his contemporaries, Matthew Arnold in England, Ernest Renan in France, D. F. Strauss and F. A. Lange in Germany, and like the adherents of Art for Art's sake, Vischer came to regard beauty and art as a substitute for metaphysics and religion.

---

[7] *Das Schöne und die Kunst*, p. 163.

[8] Ewald Volhard, *Zwischen Hegel und Nietzsche. Der Ästhetiker F. T. Vischer*, 1932, pp. 147ff.

Vischer is an idealist without idealistic faith. His theory of humor best reveals this contradiction in his outlook on life. "The comic," he wrote, "is based upon this contrast: the same being, Man, whose head reaches up into the sphere of Spirit, stands, at the same time. with both feet on the ground, deeply attached to Mother Earth. The comic is: Man taken by surprise" (*"der ertappte Mensch"*).[9] The esthetician Vischer never took his stand wholeheartedly in the one hemisphere or the other. While a denizen of Hegel's spiritual realm, he was tricked by *die Tücke des Objects* (the perversity of inanimate objects)—a reminder that the spirit dwells in matter. Later, after his conversion to more 'earthy' views, he still could not help pondering wistfully over vestiges of an absolute Truth. 'Tragic' is perhaps too eulogistic an epithet for this conflict. The melancholy humor of Vischer's autobiographical novel *Auch Einer* best expresses a dilemma which, after all, is a very human one.

The rational, which for Hegel was identical with the real, was limited in Vischer's thought by the irrational principle of chance; in the 'theistic' school by the super-rational power of God. For Christian Hermann Weisse (1801–66) Idea was not reality itself but the logical framework and the *"conditio sine qua non* of reality."[10] A timeless order of inexorable laws governs the region of logical knowledge. But we are not wholly enslaved by this fatal necessity. Opening itself to the infinite wealth of concrete phenomena, the mind perceives in beauty the emblem of liberty engraved by God upon His creation.[11] From this metaphysical meaning inherent in beauty there follow its peculiar characteristics: the infinite range of its diverse shapes, which elude systematization, its microcosmic structure, and its irrationality, which precludes the determining of pleasurable ratios and abstract esthetic norms. No

HERMANN WEISSE'S THEISTIC ESTHETICS.

---

[9] "Über Zynismus und sein bedingtes Recht" (1879), *Kritische Gänge*, V, 448.

[10] *System der Ästhetik als Wissenschaft von der Idee der Schönheit, in drei Büchern*, 1830; 2 Vols., I, p. 7 footnote. Further exponents of the "theistic school": Karl Friedrich Eusebius Trahndorff (1782–1863), *Ästhetik oder Lehre von Weltanschauung und Kunst*, 2 Vols., 1827, and Moritz Carrière (1817–95), *Die Kunst im Zusammenhang der Kulturentwicklung und die Idee der Menschheit*, 5 Vols., 1863–73.

[11] *System der Ästhetik*, I, 99.

rule can exhaust the "inward infinity of existence" of esthetic appearance.[12]

Hermann Lotze (1817–81), the last great exponent of German philosophical Idealism, utilized Weisse's suggestions for his own systematic building. Unlike Vischer, Lotze was sympathetic from the first to the claims of modern naturalism and empiricism, and he endeavored to discern and assimilate what was sound in their arguments. Thus his system bore the stamp of compromise —but of an honorable compromise. He did not abandon any vital principle. Notwithstanding his sympathy with the new empirical methods in psychology and physiology, he unswervingly upheld his idealist conviction that "the living Spirit alone truly is, and there is nothing before it and outside it." [13]

HERMANN LOTZE:
FEELING AS BASIS
OF THE ESTHETIC
PHENOMENON.

The faculty, which is responsible for the esthetic experience, is feeling; and feeling is an awareness of our inner condition as determined by impressions from without.[14] These two assertions are at the basis of Lotze's esthetic doctrine. Like every theory which emphasizes the emotional component of esthetic life, it impresses upon beauty the mark of subjectivity. The truly beautiful, Lotze maintains, "is not elsewhere than in the emotion of the enjoying spirit." The 'feeling spirit' conditions beauty not only by apprehending it; it gives birth to beauty by coming in touch with the object.[15] Yet though originating in the subject, beauty is not foreign to the object. The inwardly felt pleasure does not arise at random but responds to cognate things in the outer world. Hence we have a right to conclude that the cause of our pleasure resides in the object. But we have no right to add "in the object alone." [16] The "great fact" which is at the basis of esthetic enjoyment is the "fitting together" of subject and object—the fact that world and mind are made for each other, the world to stir the soul to its depths, setting its energies into harmonious play; the mind, to

---

[12] *System der Ästhetik*, I, p. 130.
[13] *Mikrokosmos*, 3. Auflage, III, 548.
[14] *Geschichte der Ästhetik in Deutschland*, 1868, p. 261.
[15] "Über den Begriff der Schönheit," *Göttinger Studien*, 1845, 2. Abteilung, p. 70.
[16] *Geschichte der Ästhetik*, p. 65.

respond with joyful acceptance to the appearance offered to the senses.[17] In esthetic pleasures we feel that we are at home in the universe.

What are the features of reality that move the mind to give its assent to things by appreciating them as beautiful? And upon what inner motions is this appreciation based? Lotze distinguished three kinds of susceptibility to outer stimuli, and accordingly three conditions or layers of beauty: (*a*) "sensuous agreeableness" (*das Angenehme der Sinnlichkeit*), (*b*) "the pleasures of conscious process" (*das Wohlgefällige der Vorstellung*), and (*c*) "reflective beauty" (*das Schöne der Reflexion*). BODY, SOUL, AND SPIRIT AND THE THREE CORRESPONDING LAYERS OF SENSIBILITY.

(*a*) If the impressions received through eye and ear agree with the fabric and purpose of our senses, their functioning is stimulated and their enhanced activity gives us a feeling of well-being. The reference of this feeling to its outer cause is expressed by the predicate 'agreeable'—a predicate which, according to Lotze, is subsumed under the beautiful rather than differentiated from it.

(*b*) The next stratum of sensibility comprises the 'pleasures of conscious process,' in which sensations are endorsed and assimilated by an intellectual apparatus. This mechanism carries with it memories of earlier perceptions, distributed and ordered into temporal, spatial, and logical groups and series. This process of ideation follows mechanical laws grounded in the structure of the human intellect. Now among the sequences of sensations there will be some which run counter to the habitual course of our ideas and hamper the smooth and orderly action of our ideational life. There will be other groups and configurations which either by steady and rhythmic progress or harmonious spatial distribution or other qualities of a similar kind will quicken the functioning of the inner system. It is the outer structures of the latter type, creating, in the words of Kant, "a harmonious play of our faculties," which are the source of the 'pleasures of conscious process.' [18]

(*c*) Man however is not merely the locus of the action and reaction of ideas ruled by a mechanical law. He can combine single ideas into a total view of the universe and into a just appreciation of

---

[17] *Ibid.*, p. 67.
[18] *Ibid.*, p. 262.

the good. This activity also is subject to laws, but laws that are convictions concerning the nature of what may be and what ought to be. "We propose to call 'reflective beauty' that which is in keeping with these convictions and stimulates the mental activity growing out of them." [19] This third form of pleasure belongs to the spirit, the first to the body, and the second to the soul. All three are fused in the genuine esthetic emotion in which our whole being is involved.

HUMAN NATURE IN ITS ENTIRETY INVOLVED IN ESTHETIC ENJOYMENT.

The highest stratum of sensibility is not the outcome of the two lower strata, but contains them. Esthetic science has to demonstrate "that all esthetic interest which we take in apparently pure formal proportions is entirely based upon the fact that these are the natural forms which the highest assumes for the sake of its own content. The higher type of beauty does not please as a happy combination of simple beautiful elements but the elements please as parts of the total beauty of which they remind us." [20] Therefore beauty eludes all calculations.[21] The esthetic quality of certain ratios, types of connection, and modes of temporal order depends, in the last resort, on the value which we grant them,[22] and this act of valuation holds the very core of the moral personality. Moreover, all perceived forms are modified by recollection.[23] "I remember a bizarre expression of Köstlin's: the straight line, he says, is the symbol of all [moral] straightness. He is right. The esthetic impression made by a line is not really based upon the fact that it is the shortest distance between two points . . . but is due to the moral idea of fidelity and truthfulness which bestows a meaning first on the abstract notion of consistency and later also on its visible representation by straightness in space. Furthermore, if complication, tension, and resolution, if surprise and contrast, possess esthetic value, this value derives, in a similar way, from the fact that all these forms of behavior and action are elements in a world-order which provides, by its structure, the formal conditions necessary for the universal realization of the good. . . . Only a plan (drafted

---

[19] *Geschichte der Ästhetik,* pp. 262f.

[20] *Ibid.,* p. 265.

[21] "Über den Begriff der Schönheit," *loc. cit.,* p. 88.

[22] *Ibid.,* p. 74.

[23] *Ibid.,* p. 77.

in monumental style) of the moral world in its totality would suffice to bring out the derivative value of these forms of being and action." [24] This idea of derivation is typical of idealism. But Lotze objects to 'traditional' idealism in that it cares exclusively for the 'beauty of reflection,' and contemptuously overlooks the two lower forms. [25]

The experience of beauty testifies to the harmony of Man and World, to their being made for each other (*Füreinandersein*). Yet this harmony is only the reflection of a still deeper lying consonance. The threefold articulation of sensibility reflects an analogous structure of the universe. Thus an additional element of meaning accrues to beauty.

HARMONY OF MAN AND WORLD MANIFESTED THROUGH ART.

Lotze distinguishes three realms of reality: (1) "The realm of universal laws which impress themselves upon us as of binding force with an absolute necessity, which rule all that is real, but which on account of this very universality produce of themselves nothing definite whatever." (2) "The realm of real substances and forces," which are not necessary but exist in fact, and which create the manifold forms of reality according to the laws of the first realm. (3) A universal plan, according to which the real substances are brought under the universal laws in such a way as to serve a supreme good, in the realization of which the purpose of the Universe is fulfilled. [26]

To our ordinary conception of the world these three principles spring from different sources quite independent of each other. But we cannot rest content with a triad of independent realms. We are bound to seek for a single supreme principle. It may be said that the problem of this basic unity has never been solved and never will be solved. "Between cognition, however, which fruitlessly seeks complete insight into this connection, and conduct, which just as imperfectly endeavors to bring about a unity of all that is real with its purposes—and, therefore, between the realm of the true and the good—feeling intervenes as the effect of beauty in

---

[24] *Geschichte der Ästhetik*, pp. 323f.

[25] *Ibid.*, pp. 264f.

[26] *Outlines of Aesthetics*, dictated portions of the Lectures of Lotze, translated by G. T. Ladd, 1886, §8.

a peculiar manner; not indeed so as to furnish any theoretical insight or practical realization of a solution of these contradictions, but yet so as to obtain in the intuition of the beautiful an immediate certainty and assurance of the existence of such a solution. We can therefore designate beauty . . . as the appearance to immediate intuition of a unity amongst those three powers which our cognition is unable completely to unite." [27]

The duality of method in Lotze corresponds to the two hinges on which his doctrine turns: the notion of human personality and that of a supreme Being. Man enjoying beauty communes with God; this idea is combined in Lotze with an unprejudiced recognition of the physiological and psychological components of esthetic pleasure. All idealist philosophy is animated by the impulse to bridge the gulf between the two poles of reality in an act of pure contemplation which makes man "similar to God within the bounds of possibility." This impulse is weakened in Lotze's system. By asserting that the problem of a supreme principle, from which the three 'realms of reality' derive, remains impregnable to reason, he introduces an element of resignation. But the loss in metaphysical impetus involves a gain in esthetic insight. For what, after all, does a picture or a poem, however beautiful and moving, mean to a man who is permitted to behold the spectacle of the Universe? The ingredient of scepticism in Lotze's philosophy—whether it be a sign of weakness or of wisdom—allows the philosopher to dwell more patiently upon a phenomenon which, for him too, is a mere simile—a simile pregnant, however, with a meaning beyond rational comprehension.

IDEALISTIC POST-LUDE: E. VON HARTMANN.

Eduard von Hartmann (1842–1906), the last German of this generation to present a metaphysical system, knew how to adapt his untimely doctrine to modern conditions. He was an industrious and occasionally brilliant eclectic. Wedding Schelling's and Hegel's absolute idealism to Schopenhauer's pessimistic voluntarism, he declared that the "world-ground" called by him the "Unconscious," possesses both the absolute Idea and the blind Will as attributes.[28]

---

[27] *Outlines of Aesthetics*, §9.

[28] *Philosophie des Schönen. Zweiter systematischer Teil der Ästhetik. Ausgewählte Werke*, 2d ed., IV, 472.

But he allowed neither his eclectic metaphysics nor his Hegelian conception of beauty to interfere with the psychological investigations which fill the main part of his esthetic treatise. With Hartmann metaphysics is on the verge of becoming both innocuous and useless.

The idealist esthetician was primarily concerned with the meta- physical significance of art. Reacting against this school, Herbart and his followers concentrated on the formal structure of the beautiful object. With their sober and empirical method they paved the way for the psychological and scientific esthetics of our own day. On the other hand, their opposition to idealism lies merely on the surface. On a closer examination Formalism appears to be a peculiar type of idealism, deriving partly from Leibniz and eighteenth century rationalism, partly from the anti-metaphysical element in Kant's philosophy. Both schools believe in a system of timeless Forms, but they differ in the meaning assigned to 'form.'

HERBART: BEAUTY IS FORM.

What is the 'meaning' of beauty? The idealist replies that it points, in a symbolic way, to God or to the harmonious order of the universe. This answer is rejected by Johann Friedrich Herbart (1776–1841). Beauty, he maintains, signifies nothing but what it is—beauty. By appropriate observation a certain quality of given things is discerned and we respond to it, immediately and involuntarily, by a judgment expressing either approval or disapproval: "This is beautiful"; or else: "This is ugly." It would be of no use to embark on an enquiry into the reasons for such judgment. The first thing for esthetics to do is to endorse these judgments as they actually take place and to ask with what type of given objects they are associated. Furthermore, what specific differentiations of reality correspond to the positive and negative valuation?

Herbart prepares an answer to these questions by making a distinction between simple elements (the 'content' of experience) and their relations (the form of experience). The entirely simple, in his opinion, is esthetically neutral, neither pleasing nor distasteful.[29] Hence esthetics is exclusively concerned with relations.[30]

---

[29] *Lehrbuch zur Einleitung in die Philosophie*, 1813–37, *Sämtliche Werke*, ed. Karl Kehrbach, IV, 119ff. In this and the following quotations from Herbart we use E. F. Carritt's English rendering (*Philosophies of Beauty*, 1931, pp. 153ff.).

[30] *Allgemeine Praktische Philosophie, Werke* II, 345.

Esthetic experience consists in the complete comprehension of a given set of relations, upon which the esthetic judgment follows automatically.

What kind of relation does Herbart have in mind and how is it that the proposed study of these relations must proceed? Herbart never developed his suggestions into a comprehensive theory of art. His illustrations were almost entirely taken from music. He summons us, for example, to consider a third or fifth or any interval and to ask in which of its components its esthetic value resides. "Obviously neither of the single tones whose relation composes the interval has by itself, in the least degree, that character which attaches to it when they sound together." Consequently those judgments which are commonly conceived under the name of taste, "are the results of the perfect apprehension of relations formed by a complexity of elements." "Esthetic philosophy, as the establishment of esthetic principles, would properly be bound not to define, demonstrate, or deduce, nor even to distinguish species of art or argue about existing works, but rather to put us in possession of all the single relations, however many they be, which in a complete apprehension of anything produce approval or distaste." Appraised by such a standard, nearly the whole previous work in this field appears to be done in vain: "Might we venture to say that the musical discipline which bears the strange name of figured bass is the only real example so far existing of genuine esthetics?" [31]

A FORMALISTIC EX-
PLANATION OF
MUSICAL BEAUTY.
A conclusion could be drawn from these propositions to the effect that esthetic study must be confined to some sort of selection and classification; the whole field of esthetic experience has to be searched for relations, indefinite in number, of variable elements. This procedure would be completed, if the empirical accumulation should finally yield a series of mathematically definable ratios. The question as to the reason *why* certain relations are approved as beautiful has to be dismissed as unanswerable.

Herbart's own practice, however, is less narrow than his program. He is not content with stating observed relations but tries to give, at any rate with music, a kind of causal explanation of the

---

[31] *Allgemeine Praktische Philosophie, Werke* II, p. 344.

occurrence of beauty, that is, of consonant intervals. As a psychologist he conceives the process of conscious life as a combination of elements or elemental ideas acting upon one another according to the rules of a psychic statics and mechanics. Applying this to music, he assumes that every heard tone is represented, in our consciousness, by an elemental idea. Owing to the unity of our consciousness, no two sensations can be present simultaneously without affecting each other. In so far as they are equal, they tend to combine into one single sensation, while any difference keeps them apart. Owing to a clear disparity, which, however, does not exclude some measure of equality, the so-called harmonious tones accompany each other without mutual interference—a fact to which our taste responds by spontaneous approval. In the relationship of other tones the discrepancy is counterpoised by an equally strong similarity, with the result that an irreconcilable struggle arises between the tendencies toward unification and opposition. The contest becomes audible as dissonance.[32]

A number of followers gathered round Herbart, among them Adolf Zeising,[33] a former Hegelian who proclaimed the 'Golden Section' as the clue to the esthetic riddle, and Wilhelm Unger, who tried to establish a theory of the dissonant and consonant relations of colors.[34] Finally Robert Zimmermann (1824–1898) developed Herbart's suggestions into a comprehensive system. But he bought scope at the price of definiteness. Doubtless it is possible to find formal relations and ratios in the ideas and imagery of a poem and thus to subject it to formal analysis. But such analyses cannot teach anything concerning the essence of poetry. Formalist doctrine, when forced to cover the whole field of artistic experience, first evades the issue, and then becomes meaningless. The proposition: "Predominant identity in the content of the formal components creates harmony, predominant disparity, disharmony," [35] is a mere

---

[32] *Psychologische Bemerkungen zur Tonlehre, Werke,* III, 96ff.; *Psychologische Untersuchungen, Werke,* XI, 45ff.

[33] *Neue Lehre von den Proportionen des menschlichen Körpers,* 1854; *Ästhetische Forschungen,* 1855; *Der goldne Schnitt,* 1884.

[34] *Die bildende Kunst,* 1858.

[35] *Allgemeine Ästhetik als Formwissenschaft,* 1865, Vol. I, §102.

truism so long as the exact meaning of 'predominant' remains undefined. Another thesis reads: "The large beside the small pleases, the small beside the large displeases."[36] This is less commonplace, but hardly accurate.

THE FORMALISTIC SCHOOL.

There was merit in directing attention to a measurable component of the esthetic object. But as the Formalists expelled sentiment as irrelevant, they crippled the esthetic experience. Ruling out metaphysical interpretation, they failed to see in art more than an intellectual amusement. Their doctrine ignored both meaning and sensuous quality as esthetic factors and thereby neglected the supreme rule: a work of art is an indivisible unity. Zimmermann for example declared that neither metre nor melodiousness of language could be an integral part of a poem as an esthetic whole.[37] He thus leaves us with the impression that he misconceived form as an outer adornment of some pre-existing subject.

CRISIS OF IDEALIST METAPHYSICS CULMINATES IN NIETZSCHE.

The decay of German Idealism was symptomatic of a profound transformation going on in European society as a whole. A crisis in the faith of the modern world loomed ahead, scarcely hidden behind the idealist façade of Victorian civilization and openly revealed by the German "*Realpolitik.*" The question was whether mankind, plunged in the adventure of a new age and exposed to conditions hitherto unheard of, could continue to cling to its ingrained modes of transcendental thinking.

Friedrich Wilhelm Nietzsche (1844–1900) tried to solve the burning question of his time by a stern denial of all elements of

---

[36] *Allgemeine Ästhetik als Formwissenschaft*, Vol. I, §92.

[37] *Ibid.*, §73. Mention may be made of some further writers who shared Herbart's anti-idealistic attitude. Bernard Bolzano (1781–1848), outstanding logician, synthesized Baumgarten's esthetic and ideas borrowed from Kant. According to him, that object is beautiful which is grasped neither too easily nor by the laborious effort of clear thinking and which allows us to guess, at a first glance, those qualities of the object which a subsequent examination might fully reveal. From this anticipation we derive a pleasant though obscure awareness of the power of our cognitive faculties (*Über den Begriff des Schönen. Eine philosophische Abhandlung*, 1843, p. 30; cf. *Über die Einheit der schönen Künste. Eine ästhetische Abhandlung*, 1843). Adolf Trendelenburg (1802–1872), prominent interpreter of Aristotle and logician, sketched an eclectic theory of art (*Niobe, oder über das Schöne und Erhabene*, 1846). J. H. von Kirchmann (1802–1884), while freely drawing on idealist esthetics, tried to supplant the idealist basis by an uninspired sensationalism and so-called realism (*Ästhetik auf realistischer Grundlage*, 2 Vols., 1868).

otherworldliness. The universe as he conceived it was wholly 'natural,' self-sufficient, enclosed in itself, unrestricted and unsupported by any transcendent power, source of its own perfection. As such it embodied new and higher values, a sanctity and a nobility unknown to the past. One suspects, however, in all the predicates by which Nietzsche confers greatness upon his natural universe, their veiled descent from the very tradition which they are meant to supplant. The finite cosmos is declared to be eternal. But does not the idea of eternity clearly bear the marks of the 'outworn' theological superstition? And is not even the idea of 'Being' an illusory remnant of the repudiated transcendental ontology? Thus Nietzsche's philosophy, drawing up positions and then destroying them, takes on the aspect of the suicidal struggle of a great mind against its own aspirations. Combating what he thinks to be the powers of decadence, Nietzsche's attack is directed against himself. The 'Will to Power' and the 'Eternal Recurrence' express a desperate optimism.[38] The first signifies the sinister determination to *will* in the face of the absence of any reasonable end; the second quenches the thirst for eternity in an image of life reminiscent of Sisyphean toil. The Promethean defiance is relieved by the dream of a life spirited and light like a dance; or by the vision of flawless and mature perfection, effortless and forgetful of pain and toil, evoking the image of a Mediterranean bay or the great calm and lucidity of halcyon days.

ART AS FLOWERING OF LIFE.

The ambiguity of Nietzsche's position recurs in his esthetic. He greets the artist as his natural ally and then again he treats him as the corruptor of philosophical integrity. It is, indeed, the artist in himself who is behind both his exaltation and his reproach. Nietzsche is strongly opposed to traditional esthetics. He charges it with adopting exclusively the position of the contemplator of art and with misinterpreting esthetic contemplation as a method of detaching the mind from this world of ours. Art, he holds, is essentially "affirmation, benediction, deification of existence." [39] A

---

[38] Karl Löwith, *Nietzsches Philosophie der ewigen Wiederkunft des Gleichen,* 1935.

[39] *Werke,* Grossoktav-Ausgabe, 16 Vols., VII, 407ff.; XIII, 100; XIV, 134f.

pessimistic art is a contradiction. "But Zola? the Goncourts? The objects which they show are ugly. Yet the reason why they show them is because they rejoice in the ugly. . . ." [40] "In the main," he writes, "I agree with the artists more than with all philosophers up to now: they did not lose the great track where life advances, they were fond of the things of 'this world'—they were fond of their senses." [41] The philosopher keen on proving the unique glory of the finite world finds the artist concerned to do the same.

The creative center of the terrestrial and natural universe is 'life.' Confounding the broader meaning of the term with the narrower one connected with sex, birth, growth, and movement among plants and animals, Nietzsche develops the conception of an "affirmative" and worldly art into the program of a "biological esthetics." It would be more accurate to call it "pseudo-biological"; for even his markedly physiological propositions carry with them connotations which belie the professed naturalist creed. "What, for our instinct, is esthetically repellent, has proved to Man, in the course of a very long experience, to be harmful, dangerous, unreliable. The spontaneously speaking esthetic instinct (*e.g.* of disgust) contains a *judgment*. In that respect the beautiful falls under the generic category of biological values such as useful, wholesome, augmentative of life; yet in such a way that a quantity of stimuli which are associated with and remind us remotely of useful objects and states, awaken in us the sentiment of beauty, that is of an increase of the feeling of power." [42] The last clause distinctly points to a range of ideas beyond "naturalism" or "biologism." Art, Nietzsche says, "is a stimulating of animal energies by images and desires of an enhanced life." [43] The idea of an "enhanced life" suggests far better things than an augmentation of animal vigor: it conveys implicitly Nietzsche's program of "the transvaluation of all values."

ANTI-ROMANTIC   Although Nietzsche regards art as an expression of life, he is
ART AS IDEAL.   far from considering it as "natural" in the sense of an effortless

---

[40] *Werke*, XVI, 247.
[41] *Ibid.*, XVI, 246.
[42] *Ibid.*, XVI, 230.
[43] *Ibid.*, XIV, 229f.

utterance of inner motions comparable to the song of birds. Beauty, he holds, is only to be achieved by an act of self-assertion which arranges, transfigures, and overrules reality in order to make it appear beautiful, that is, adapted to human needs. Our judgment of beauty lends the object "a charm which is entirely foreign to the nature of the object. To apprehend an object as beautiful means to apprehend it falsely." [44] This is meant as a radical refutation of the classical principle that "only the true is beautiful." But the inferences drawn from this revolutionary proposition are much in the spirit of the classical tradition. The forcible transformation of given reality into beauty has to be matched by the severe discipline to which the artist subjects his natural propensities, bents, and feelings. Nietzsche repudiated both the cult of originality as a value in itself and the lax romantic ideal of spontaneous and uncontrolled creation. The 'classic' or 'grand' style of which Nietzsche dreams is characterized by "coldness, lucidity, and rigidity." Its further qualities are logical consistency, enjoyment of the intellectual, terseness, and hatred of "sentiment," "*Gemüt*," "*esprit*," hatred of the multifarious, the uncertain, and the vaguely intimating as well as of the brief, pointed, pretty, and benign. Classic style implies that the abundance of life is mastered by measure based upon "the calm of a powerful soul which moves slowly and repudiates the all too lively. The element of generality, the law, is revered and emphasized." "This style has in common with great passion that it disdains to please, that it forgets to persuade. . . . To become master of the chaos that one is, to compel one's chaos to assume form, to become logical, simple, unambiguous, mathematics, *law*—that is here the great ambition." [45] Nietzsche knows that this high form cannot be prescribed and willed but that it will shine forth when the artist carries greatness within himself. [46] Having reached this point of consummation, he does everything by necessity, and only then he enjoys to the full his liberty and creative authority. [47]

---

[44] *Ibid.*, XVI, 231f.
[45] *Ibid.*, XVI, 264f.
[46] *Ibid.*, XII, 182.
[47] *Ibid.*, XV, 47.

The judgment of beauty, as we saw, has no foundation whatsoever in the quality of real objects. Accordingly a state of exaltation is required to lift us above the sober rational assessment of given reality. To the idealist this conception offered no difficulty because his whole doctrine was based on the idea of transcendence. Nietzsche, however, had to resort to what may be styled an "immanent transcendence." He conceived a state of mind which caused life to transcend itself while yet remaining within its own sphere. In the famous essay on *The Birth of Tragedy*, he describes the initial stage of artistic creation as an intoxication, a holy drunkenness, "*Rausch*." Overwhelmed, stunned, and inspired by an explosion of his vital energies, the artist becomes possessed with Dionysian madness; the "eternal lust for becoming" breaks forth. The ordinary bounds and limits of existence are annihilated and consciousness, filled with a mixture of horror and joy, is submerged in the eternal flux of things, carrying with it both creation and destruction. Then, at a second stage, a dreamlike Apollonian vision of life disengages itself from the orgiastic excitement, related to the Dionysian rapture as is Being to the flux of Becoming, or as light is to darkness. In a luminous symbolic dream-picture, it redeems the primordial pain of Dionysian ecstasy and reinstates appearance ordered according to eternal laws.

The Dionysian enchantment, Nietzsche writes, "is the prerequisite of all dramatic art. In this enchantment the Dionysian reveller sees himself as a satyr, and as a satyr he in turn beholds the god, that is, in his transformation he sees a new vision outside himself as the Apollonian consummation of his state. With this new vision the drama is complete." "According to this view, we must understand Greek tragedy as the Dionysian chorus, which always disburdens itself anew in an Apollonian world of pictures. The choric parts, therefore, with which tragedy is interlaced, are in a manner the mother-womb of the entire so-called dialogue, that is, of the whole stage-world of the drama proper." [48] Subsequently, after relinquishing the Schopenhauerian metaphysic of the early essay, *The Birth of Tragedy*, he generalized his observations so as

---

[48] *The Complete Works*, ed. by Oscar Levy, III, 68.

to provide a basis for a psychology of art. Dream, he asserts, foreshadows esthetic vision, intoxication, esthetic orgy. A corresponding division of all arts follows. Actor, dancer, musician, and lyric poet, as exponents of Dionysian art, are set over against the Apollonian artists, the painter, sculptor, and epic poet. Architecture is held to elude this distinction; it reveals the creative act of will-power in its purity.

Through an act of ecstatic self-transcendence, the artist gains ART AS ESCAPE from crude reality his vision of beauty. To this power of trans- FROM REALITY. figuration mankind owes infinite gratitude. Only as an esthetic phenomenon is existence bearable: "we have art in order that we may not perish through truth." [49] Yet this idea of a beneficently delusive power reveals the ambiguity inherent in Nietzsche's esthetic doctrine. The noblest qualities which he bestows on his "superman" are courage and integrity. The superman feels strong enough to confront truth face to face. He disdains to seek refuge in a world beyond, or to deceive himself by a flattering picture of this world. But does not the artist do precisely these despicable things? Since artistic beauty excludes truth, the artist is surely exposed to the reproach of falsehood. "Many lies are told by the poets." This old Greek saying is now revived in Nietzsche's thought, turning his praise into insult. He charges the artists with cowardice: they always needed a shelter, an established authority; "they were at all times the servants of a moral system, a philosophy, or a religion." [50] The creator of beauty, hailed first as a champion of the new values, finds himself convicted of the same crime of which the Christian and the metaphysician were accused. He too prepares an escape from this world and its cruel truth. There is a gulf between reality and the artistic imagination: "Neither had Homer portrayed Achilles nor Goethe Faust, if Homer had been Achilles, or Goethe Faust." [51] Nietzsche's blow, aimed at a revered object, hits his own work. He was haunted by a fear lest his own glorification of the world might prove an esthetic vision, a hopeless evasion of paralyzing knowledge; lest he be doomed to be "only poet, only

---

[49] *Werke*, XVI, 248.
[50] *Ibid.*, VII, 405; XV, 489.
[51] *Ibid.*, VII, 404.

fool." The "old quarrel of philosophy and poetry" was kindled afresh.

HEALTHY AND DE-
CADENT ART.

All attempts at reconciling the positive and the negative aspects of Nietzsche's evaluation of art must fail. There is, however, a limited sphere within which he reaches a synthesis. He projected the contradictions into life itself as its inherent dialectic. Life, being all-comprehensive, cannot be endangered or corrupted from without. It generates its own negation: sickness, decay, and death or, in psychological terms, resentment, hatred, and self-denial. Applying this to art, we have to distinguish between two opposite types of creation: "Regarding all esthetic values I am now availing myself of this capital distinction: I ask in every case 'Is it hunger that has become creative or is it not rather abundance?' In Goethe for instance the creative power is due to affluence, in Flaubert and Pascal to hatred. When Pascal wrote poetry, he tortured himself." [52] The 'decadent art,' result of a resentful denial of life, is described by Nietzsche as the "romantic" counterpart of the "grand" or "classic" style. Taking a secret revenge on mankind for his own shortcomings, the romanticist instills his poisonous pessimism into his hearer's mind. His art, lacking in serenity and measure, captures the senses with a profusion of effective details and an exhibition of uncontrolled passion. For Nietzsche, Richard Wagner's music is the prototype of this romantic caricature of Dionysian ecstasy.

Decadence is the natural decline as well as the corruption of life. Hence the theory of two contrary types of art carries with it the idea of an historical "life-cycle." Classic art stands for the ripeness of life. It dissolves, through a natural process, into decadent or 'baroque' art. The single arts show an affinity to the stages of the cyclic process, architecture to primeval forms of civilization, music, to its consummation. [53]

The criterion of health does not really solve the problem of the positive and the negative evaluation of art. Its application will always be open to doubt. Even the idyllic serenity of a classic poem like Goethe's *Hermann und Dorothea* may mean that the artist

[52] *Werke*, V, 326.
[53] *Ibid.*, XVI, 264.

prepares an escape for himself by idealizing realities. On the other hand, Swift's cruel picture of the animal-men in the *Houyhnhnms* may flow from a pure but disappointed love of mankind. If, however, handled by a master of appreciation, the criterion may do the wholesome work of a surgeon's knife—the purpose for which Nietzsche intended it.

The crisis of metaphysics culminated in Nietzsche. The secularized Christianity of the nineteenth century, a joint creation of Romanticism and Idealism, was undermined by his criticism. But the strategy of his anti-romantic campaign was largely of romantic origin. We may speak of a self-destruction of romanticism. This critical work was offset by a last self-assertion of romanticism in the theoretical writings of Richard Wagner (1805–64).[54] His basic ideas—of 'folk' as the force conditioning artistic creation, of myth as the matrix of poetry, and the proclamation of the 'universal art-work' as the consummation of all creative efforts—revived romantic tenets. The old doctrine has gained little by its incorporation in the program of a great opera composer. Nietzsche, first a believer, developed his teaching as an apostate of the Wagnerian gospel. The truth, in the Wagner-Nietzsche controversy, was on the side of the critic. There is no salvation in the return to the romantic dreamland.

WAGNER: RE-AS-SERTION OF THE ROMANTIC.

SUPPLEMENTARY READING

Ewald Volhard, *Zwischen Hegel und Nietzsche. Der Ästhetiker F. T. Vischer*, 1932.

L. W. Flaccus, *Artists and Thinkers*, 1916.

H. R. Marshall, "Some Modern Aestheticians," *Mind*, 1920, pp. 458–71 (on Lotze).

A. Matagrin, *Essai sur l'esthétique de Lotze*, 1901.

Bernard Bosanquet, *A History of Aesthetic*, 1892, Chs. XIII and XIV.

---

[54] *Prose Works*, translated by W. A. Ellis, 1892.

CHAPTER XVIII

Esthetics in the Age of Science

ESTHETICS 'FROM
BELOW.'

ABOUT 1870 the speculative school seemed dead. The proclamations of the new scientific method were usually combined with epitaphs on the old. This was especially true in Germany, where most had been done and, as people now felt, there had been most sin in the field of pure thought. A German writer, Ernst Grosse (1862–1927), commented on the downfall of the old philosophical systems in the following typical passage: "If we measure them by the strict standard of science, we shall have to admit that they deserved their fate. We may admire their brilliancy, but we cannot on that account fail to see that the foundation of facts was not sufficient for these tottering constructions. . . . The philosophy of art of the Hegelians and the Herbartians has today only a historical interest." [1] Then comes a no less typical enunciation of the modern scientific tendency: "The science of art is in the same position as all the other sciences that depend on observation . . . the truth finally emerges out of the patient comparison of numerous and various facts." [2] To these writers the immense labor of centuries seemed almost entirely wasted. It must be conceded, continued the spokesman of the new time, that "we have no right to boast of a science of art." [3] We have to heed the lesson taught by the bankruptcy of the former investigations and set about rebuilding the relinquished edifice in a humbler fashion. To understand art in its highest manifestations is a noble but far-off end. First we must examine the elements and "not attempt to

---

[1] *The Beginnings of Art*, 1897, p. 3.
[2] *Ibid.*, p. 25.
[3] *Ibid.*, p. 5.

explain the more complicated forms till we have informed our-selves concerning the nature and condition of these simple ones." [4] The old philosophical method, claimed Gustav Theodor Fechner (1834–1887), the pioneer of experimental esthetics, moves "from above," from the universals downward to the particulars. This was Schelling's, Hegel's, and even Kant's approach. Since however we do not believe any longer that we possess a reliable system, it is wise for us to choose the opposite way and build esthetics "from below." We have to start with facts and then rise, cautiously and gradually, to generalizations. [5]

From these few leading principles follow the characteristics of the scientific school—its assets as well as its shortcomings. The empirical procedure involved a close collaboration with neighboring studies, and a broader knowledge of related facts accrued to the stock of traditional ideas. Physiology, [6] biology, [7] psychiatry, [8] sociology, [9] and ethnology [10] furnished new material for elucidation and comparison. The field of research extended itself both in time and space. A growing interest in the primitive stages of art on the one hand, in the highly refined creations of the far East on the other, did away with a great many cherished prejudices. Among them there was the classicist dogma based on the belief in the unique validity of the Greek canon. The appreciation of multifa-

---

[4] *Ibid.*, pp. 18f.

[5] *Vorschule der Ästhetik*, 2 Theile, 1876, Preface.

[6] Georg Hirth, *Physiologie der Kunst*, 1885; Francis Galton, *Hereditary Genius: An Inquiry into Its Laws and Consequences*, 1896.

[7] Colin A. Scott, "Sex and Art," *The American Journal of Psychology*, 1896, VII, pp. 153ff.

[8] Cesare Lombroso, *Genio e follia*, 1877, *L'Uomo di genio*, 1888, *Nuovi studi sul genio*, 1902.

[9] J. M. Baldwin, *The Mental Development in the Race and in the Child*, 1895; *Social and Ethical Interpretations in Mental Development*, 1897; F. H. Giddings, *The Principles of Sociology. An Analysis of the Phenomena of Association and of Social Organization*, 1896; T. Ribot, *L'imagination créatrice*, 1900; Gabriél Tarde, *Les lois de l'imitation*, 2d ed., 1895; Gabriél Séailles, *L'origine et les destinés de l'art*, 1886; Georges Sorel, *La valeur sociale de l'art*, 1901.

[10] H. Balfour, *The Evolution of Decorative Art*, 1893; John Lubbock (Lord Avebury), *The Origin of Civilisation and the Primitive Condition of Man*, 1870; A. C. Haddon, *The Decorative Art of British New Guinea*, 1894, *Evolution of Art*, 1895; Ernst Grosse, *The Beginnings of Art*, trans., 1897.

rious artistic forms dealt a blow also to the naturalistic theory of imitation. Its idealist counterpart—the view that the artist imitates the idea or essence of an object—was also undermined. Another dogma which science encountered was that "autonomous art"— art for art's sake—is the normal manifestation of the creative energies of men. Ethnological and sociological studies showed that the contrary is true. Art in the epochs of its vigorous flowering is usually subservient to other interests. The alleged autonomy, on the other hand, appears to be itself conditioned by the social status of some concerned class—for instance by the precarious freedom of the Humanist in the Renaissance or by the relative independence of the bourgeois artist in the nineteenth century.

UNITY OF ESTHETIC THREATENED.

There was, however, some danger in the new close association of art and reality at large. It sometimes seemed as if the boundaries marking off art as art might vanish altogether. For example, the adherents of Spencer's play theory were inclined to forget that art, however intimately connected with play, is after all more than a game. Other scholars were tempted by their bias toward the so-called "primitive" into expecting more esthetic enlightenment from some crude totem image than from Raphael's *Sistine Madonna*. A prerequisite of esthetics, according to older views, was a highly developed artistic sensibility in the student. Now, an esthetician of this type incurred the reproach of lacking in scientific sobriety. Grant Allen (1848–1899) confesses in the Preface to his *Physiological Aesthetics:* "I am not myself an excessive devotee of fine art in any form. But, on the whole, I count this as gain . . . because . . . the worshipper of art is liable to bring with him into the consideration of the simplest elements of beauty those enthusiastic feelings which are aroused in him by its highest developments. Moreover, such a person will probably regard with contempt every species of esthetic emotion except those most elevated ones which are capable of edifying his own fastidious and educated taste." [11] "Psychology without psyche" had been the judgment passed on the psychology of the positivists. An unfriendly reader of Grant Allen's preface might feel tempted to add: "Science of

[11] *Op. cit.,* pp. viiif.

beauty without sense of beauty." The more esthetics adapted itself to lecture-room and laboratory, the farther it seemed to move
from the artist's studio. The spirit of Wilhelm Wundt's psychology
somehow seemed incompatible with a developed esthetic sensibility.

The philosopher was dislodged from his chair as a teacher of
esthetics. But who was to replace him? The psychologist, the
sociologist, or the historian of art? There are a great number of
equally competent applicants. The new scientific tendency created
many sciences of beauty instead of one, psychological esthetics,
ethnological esthetics, and the like. The disintegration of the study
was in rapid progress. It was arrested only at the end of the period
under consideration, when the growing wealth of findings and
tendencies was newly hedged in by the elastic and liberal conception of "Esthetics and general Science of Art" proposed by Max
Dessoir.

The firm decision to dispense with metaphysical hypotheses A METAPHYSICAL
did not stop altogether the use of general ideas. The question en- RESIDUE.
countered at the very threshold of empirical research—the question what are the 'elements' of the esthetic phenomenon—was not
to be settled by observation. So the older currents of thought
persisted, though transformed and duly adapted to the new intellectual conditions. Their principles were attenuated and reduced either to working hypotheses or to assumptions catering to
emotional needs of non-empirical parentage. And these alternative
types of general assertions were not always clearly held apart. In
the idea, taught by Spencer, Grosse, and others, that esthetic pleasure breeds feelings of human fellowship, the social enthusiasm of the
early Positivists survived. Fechner, in the very book that laid the
foundations of experimental method in esthetics, asserted that
beauty, in the last analysis, derives from God. The theological
bent of German esthetics survives here like a vestigial organ which
has become useless because of changed conditions of life.[12] Johannes
Volkelt is eager to reassure readers regarding the metaphysics which
he annexed to his esthetics of the tragic, though it was little more
than an innocent ornament. "I wish to note," he writes, "that the

---

[12] *Vorschule der Ästhetik*, I, 17.

theory of the tragic is absolutely separated from and independent of the exposition of the last section, which is devoted to the metaphysics of the tragic." [13]

Earlier German esthetics had defined beauty by showing its place and function within a mental cosmos. This same tendency, weaned from its metaphysical aspirations, now gave rise to a doctrine of the mental elements of beauty. Such a doctrine was Fechner's psychological esthetics. French and English scholars had given particular attention to the rôle of art in social life and social progress. The continuation of this trend of thought produced the evolutionist school of scientific esthetics. The farther the psychologists of Fechner's type on the one hand and the evolutionists on the other advanced, the more the two schools began to fuse.

FECHNER'S EXPERI-
MENTAL METHOD.
The book generally considered to mark the beginning of the new science is Fechner's *Vorschule der Ästhetik,* published in 1876 and preceded in 1871 by an address of the same author on *Experimental Esthetics.* [14] The *Vorschule* is a collection of essays loosely strung together rather than a systematic treatise. A system requires as its basis a definition of beauty. But a scientific treatment, in Fechner's opinion, is but little interested in finding a universal formula—a task that baffled all the former speculative efforts. Beauty is only a name roughly denoting the subject-matter of esthetics and as such is applicable to "everything with the property of arousing pleasure directly and immediately, and not only on reflection or because of consequences." [15] It is this type of pleasure (and corresponding displeasure) with which the analyst is concerned. This is the firm ground on which he may safely settle to work. For the "esthetic feelings," as modifications of pleasure and pain as such, are primary and simple qualities of the soul. Like gold among the physical elements, these psychic atoms may be blended with other elements. But even so they remain what they are and withstand any attempt at dissolution. This admitted, the

---

[13] *Ästhetik des Tragischen,* 1897, p. v.
[14] *Zur experimentellen Ästhetik. Abhandlungen der sächsischen Gesellschaft der Wissensch.* Math. Physical. Klasse 9, 556ff.
[15] *Vorschule,* I, p. 15.

problem, stated in scientific terms, is this: What objects please and what displease? And why do these please while others displease? A correct answer must indicate the law that rules the causal relationship between outer object as cause and pleasure as effect. And such a law must be verified experimentally in exactly the same way as a law discovered by the physicist in the field of the motion of bodies.

The general idea of a scientific esthetics lightly drawn in the preliminary definitions took fuller shape for Fechner in a long series of "esthetic principles." Most of these, however, are broadly psychological rather than specifically esthetic.[16] They outline a psychology of mental activity in general and bear on esthetic problems only in an indirect way. Of unquestionable esthetic relevance are the three "supreme formal principles": (*a*) unified connection of the manifold, (*b*) consistency, agreement, or truth and, finally, (*c*) clearness. This central part of Fechner's esthetic doctrine is also its most traditional component. Though provided with a couple of novel terms we walk the well-trodden way of a formal theory of beauty.

For Fechner, as for many of his contemporaries, the experiment was the badge of scientific exactness. It was unfortunate that precisely his "formal principles" largely escaped direct experimental verification. But an indirect approach to exact demonstration of their validity still seemed possible. Fechner proposed to settle the question as to whether there are any esthetically preferable ratios of dimension and division and what these normal or elemental ratios are. Time and again, speculative minds had busied themselves to develop a mystical mathematics of beauty.[17] By subjecting the question to an unprejudiced and strictly scientific examination, Fechner opened a new epoch of esthetic research.

---

[16] *Ibid.*, I, 51.

[17] *Elementarbeiträge zur Bestimmung des Naturgesetzes der Gestaltung und des Widerstandes und Anwendung dieser Beiträge auf Natur und alte Kunstgestaltung* von F. G. Roeber, mit 6 lith. Tafeln, 1861. Further publications of this type are quoted and discussed by Fechner, *Zur experimentalen Ästhetik*, pp. 593ff. and 567; cf. the Bibliography in Charles Lalo, *L'esthétique expérimentale contemporaine*, 1908, and J. Larguier des Bancels "L'esthétique expérimentale," *L'Année Psychologique*, 1900, pp. 148ff.

Fechner distinguished three experimental methods. The first was the method of selection of which more will be said immediately. The second was the method of construction. This may be illustrated by the so-called "inquiry into the letter 'i.' " Four vertical lines of different length are drawn on a paper and the subjects are directed to put a dot over each at the distance that seems most suitable to them. The results show that the average distance chosen increases with the length of the line. The third method consists in the measuring of manufactured objects used in daily life. Fechner measured visiting-cards and books chosen at random and stated that a high percentage yielded the ratio of the Golden Section (with a marked straying from this rule in the case of learned books which are generally more oblong, and of children's books which are broader).[18] He also inaugurated a statistical study of the dimensions of pictures, but attributed little esthetic relevance to the results thus obtained.[19]

The method most practiced by Fechner was that of choice or selection. The best known experiment of this type is concerned with mathematically defined ratios. Fechner prepared ten rectangles of white paste-board of equal areas (64 square centimeters), varying in form from a square to an oblong of 5:2. These were spread at random over a black table. The subjects, chosen from the educated class but without reference to artistic training, were directed to point out the most pleasant and the most unpleasant of these figures. The judgments of preference and of exclusion were noted respectively in special columns of a table, each with a full number (1) if the judgment was given unhesitatingly, with a fraction (1/2 or 1/3) if the subject—doubtless hampered by the abstractness of the conditions—lingered between figures.

The result of this experiment seemed to support the view that there exist "ratios possessing in themselves a specific esthetic value." [20] The majority of rejections fell definitely at the extremes, the square and the oblong at the other end of the scale, while the

---

[18] *Vorschule*, Ch. 44.

[19] *Ibid.*, pp. 273, 314; cf. Lalo, pp. 57ff.

[20] Lightner Witmer, "Zur experimentellen Asthetik einfacher räumlicher Formverhältnisse," *Philosophische Studien*, 1893, p. 209.

rectangle with the ratio 34:21, that is, the Golden Section, received by far the largest number of approving votes.

Fechner's experiments roused a world-wide interest. Two Americans, Lightner Witmer and Edgar Pierce,[21] refined and developed his procedure. Analogous investigations were undertaken on the field of color impression by D. R. Major,[22] Jonas Cohn, and others.[23] The exultation over the new findings was, however, slightly impaired by certain misgivings. Even in the markedly successful experiments some unexplained accompanying circumstances often made the result imperfect. In Fechner's experiment with the ten rectangles the subjects usually lingered for a considerable time over their choice. Moreover the inspection of the table obtained by Fechner in this experiment reveals a fact at variance with the general results. The square carried not only more votes of rejection than the figure following it but also more votes of preference. Thus the curve illustrating the gradual decrease of displeasure runs smoothly to its lowest point at the Golden Section, whereas the corresponding curve of increasing pleasure is broken. It drops immediately after the square and then climbs steadily to its culminating point. Fechner attributed this anomaly to an intellectual prejudice. Some of the subjects may have thought that a perfectly regular figure like the square should not pass without due acknowledgment of merit. This explanation may be correct. But it implies a doubt which, once admitted, may carry with it a much more dangerous criticism of the results as a whole. If alien influences affected the outcome in one case, why not in the majority of cases? May one not suspect that the regularity of the curve expresses a psychological fact which has nothing to do with

---

[21] "Aesthetic of Simple Forms," *The Psychological Review*, I, 1894, pp. 483–95, III, 1896, pp. 270–85.

[22] "On the Affective Tone of Simple Sense-Impressions," *The American Journal of Psychology*, 1895, VII, pp. 57–77.

[23] Jonas Cohn, "Experimentelle Untersuchungen über die Gefühlsbetonung der Farben, Helligkeiten und ihrer Combinationen," *Philosophische Studien*, 1894, X; "Gefühlston und Sättigung der Farben," *ibid.*, 1900, XV, pp. 279ff. Experiments of this type were also carried through by J. M. Baldwin (*Mental Development in the Child and in the Race*, 1895, pp. 39, 50ff.), E. S. Baker (*Univ. of Toronto Studies, Psychol. Series*, Vol. II), and A. Kirschmann (*Philosoph. Studien*, Vol. VII).

esthetic laws? Rectangles of the type chosen by Fechner are commonly associated with our recollections of pictures, mirrors, and related objects. So the judgments might simply reflect an attachment to the form of the familiar; and the customary shape of the recollected objects may in its turn be determined by an historical development, national character, fashion, etc. The form of pictures preferred by Chinese and Japanese artists—long and narrow—is, according to Fechner's table, extremely unpleasant.

The slightness of the emotional reaction gives rise to another objection. How can these hardly noticeable feelings contribute in any considerable degree to the exuberant delight often awakened by works of art? Fechner met this doubt by his principle of "esthetic help." The emotional effect, resulting from the co-operation of various elements, surpasses the sum of these elements. But does not this very principle involve the admission of the fact that these elements are mere auxiliary factors rather than elements proper, that is, original sources of esthetic enjoyment? The abstractness of laboratory conditions again becomes obvious.

INTERPRETATION OF THE EXPERIMENTAL FINDINGS CONTROVERSIAL.

Apart from the question of the validity of the results of the experiments there is the further problem of their meaning. On this point the opinion of the experimentalists themselves differed widely. Wilhelm Wundt (1832–1920) believed that when we feel pleased by an exemplification of the Golden Section we actually are aware of the mathematical relationship. A ratio in which the whole is to its larger part (or major) as the larger to the smaller (or minor) is felt to be a means of unifying with the least possible effort the greatest possible multiplicity. Thus esthetic pleasure appears as the result of mental economy. Oswald Külpe (1862–1915) tried to support this view by reference to Weber's Law.[24] According to him, the equality of the differences (in the relation between minor and major on the one hand, major and whole line on the other) is neither too easily discerned nor so near to the limits of perceptibility as to escape attention. Hence the perception of this equality causes esthetic pleasure similar to that aroused by symmetry. The Golden Section is, as it were,

---

[24] *Grundriss der Psychologie auf experimenteller Grundlage*, 1893, p. 261.

"a symmetry of a higher order." R. P. Angier [25] and Witmer [26] contended that an esthetic efficacy of the mathematical relationship as such is out of the question. The latter assumed that there is only one basic principle: unity in variety. In symmetry the first element, unity (or the factor of esthetic equality) predominates, in the Golden Section variety, or the factor of esthetic contrast, plays the leading part. Hence the Golden Section is the right mean between excess and lack of diversity. Witmer himself recognized that this statement hardly deserved the name of an explanation. [27] A physiological interpretation, referring to the most easily performed eye-movements, was suggested by Edgar Pierce and others, and was widely accepted, especially by French psychologists. But recent research has shown the weakness of this hypothesis. [28]

Fechner's experiments were hampered by the fact that our optical perceptions are always interwoven with images of external objects or actions. We may define a curve by a mathematic formula. But how could we test experimentally its power of evoking the image say of a human figure? The case is different with music. Here the sensations of tone as such are the material of the art. "In this sense it is clear that music has a more immediate connection with pure sensation than any other of the fine arts, and, consequently, that the theory of the sensation of hearing is destined to play a much more important part in musical esthetics, than, for example, the theory of *chiaroscuro* or of perspective in painting." [29] Hence an especially fruitful use of the experimental method was made in the field of the theory of music, and these inquiries were brought to fulfilment by Hermann Helmholtz's (1821–1894) famous work *On the Sensations of Tone*. This great scholar is con-

HELMHOLTZ'S PHYSIOLOGICAL THEORY OF MUSIC.

---

[25] "The Aesthetics of Equal Division," *Psychological Review*, Monograph Supplements, 1903, IV, pp. 541ff.

[26] Witmer, *op. cit.*, pp. 261ff.

[27] *Ibid.*, pp. 261ff.

[28] Sir William Mitchell, *Structure and Growth of the Mind*, p. 501; cf. C. W. Valentine, *An Introduction to the Experimental Psychology of Beauty*, London, pp. 44ff.

[29] Hermann L. F. Helmholtz, *On the Sensations of Tone as a Physiological Basis for the Theory of Music*. Translated by Alexander J. Ellis, 1930, p. 3.

cerned mainly with the physiological basis of music and with the psychological basis only indirectly. This restriction is decisive as far as the method of investigation is concerned, but is almost negligible for the interpretation of the meaning of the results. Helmholtz shared with Fechner the conviction (shattered only recently) that there is a strict coördination between psychic elements or elementary ideas on the one hand and stimuli in the perceiving organ or physiological events on the other. A perfect psychology, in Fechner's sense, involves a physiology of the senses and *vice versa*.

Helmholtz's problem was proposed by Pythagoras about 2500 years ago: "Why is consonance determined by the ratios of small whole numbers?"[30] Pythagoras' answer looked for explanation to the structure of the cosmos: "Everything is Number and Harmony." Leonard Euler (1707–1783) supplanted the idea of cosmos with the modern notion of Reason.[31] The soul is pleased when it easily detects a certain amount of perfection or rational order. Now it is very easy to discover the ratio of small whole numbers. Then the Italian violinist Tartini (1692–1770)[32] and two French scholars, Jean-Philippe Rameau (1685–1764)[33] and Jean d'Alembert (1717–1783),[34] opened the third stage of this development by advancing views taken from physiology. As the successor of Cosmos and Reason, the structure of the inner ear, more particularly the fibres in the organ of Corti, is regarded by Helmholtz as the true source of acoustic harmony. This is his answer to the Pythagorean question: "The ear resolves all complex sounds into pendular oscillations, according to the law of sympathetic vibration, and it regards as harmonious only such excitements of the nerves as continue without disturbance."[35] Harmony then is a continuous sensation, disharmony an intermittent one. Like his precursors, Helmholtz tries to show that the laws of musical

---

[30] Helmholtz, *op. cit.*, p. 229.

[31] *Ibid.*, p. 230. Leonard Euler, *Tentamen novae theoriae Musicae*, Petropoli, 1739.

[32] *Trattato di Musica secondo la vera scienza dell' armonia.* Padova, 1751.

[33] *Traité de l'harmonie réduite à des principes naturels*, 1721.

[34] *Élements de Musique, suivant les principes de M. Rameau*, Lyon, 1762.

[35] Helmholtz, *op. cit.*, p. 229.

harmony are prescribed *by nature*. Yet he restricts the bearing of his causal explanation by saying "that the System of Scales, Modes and Harmonic Tissues does not rest solely upon unalterable natural laws, but is also, at least partly, the result of esthetical principles which have already changed, and will further change, with the progressive development of humanity." [36]

A long and heated discussion followed the publication of Helmholtz's work.[37] It was almost universally admitted that his theory succeeds in explaining the occurrence of harsh, disharmonious beats in the consciousness. But does it yield a convincing explanation of the musical effect and value of the harmonies? The equation, continuity=harmony, seems to stand at variance with musical experience.

Helmholtz was not, and did not pretend to be, a philosopher, and his ideas on the bearing of his propositions were but little developed. Fechner, on the contrary, was conscious of being the heir of a great philosophical tradition and even his experimentation is controlled by his philosophical criticism. He foresaw and discussed nearly all the objections which were to be raised later on against the experimental method. The chief point for attack in a philosophical discussion of this method was apparently to be the idea of element. It might be maintained that the elements or elementary forms, with which the experimental method is exclusively concerned, never actually occur as isolated data.[38] Fechner did not believe that this statement, though correct in itself, invalidated his investigations. He replied: an esthetic experience, though a compound of elements, is usually dominated by a single form, as is a musical composition by a *Leitmotiv*, or a picture by some compositional scheme. Furthermore, a work of art, more than any other object in our experience, is an isolated whole. The frame separating a picture from the surrounding world and cutting off alien influences is the clearest symbol of this fact. Finally, the mode of combining several elementary forms may in its turn become a subject of refined experimental investigations. Presumably

THE 'ASSOCIATIVE FACTOR' IN FECHNER. LIMITATION OF HIS DOCTRINE.

---

[36] *Ibid.*, p. 235.
[37] Cf. Lalo, *Esquisse d'une esthétique musicale scientifique*, 1908, pp. 90ff.
[38] Cf. Katherine Gilbert, *Studies in Recent Aesthetic*, 1927, pp. 13ff.

the esthetically pleasing forms will retain their value as "esthetic centers" even when united into a complex whole. The further objection, that the variety of gifts and dispositions in the subjects may vitiate the results, appears to Fechner to carry less weight. Such differences can be tested by experiment and statistics and, by means of this procedure, the inevitable variations will finally yield an average value.[39]

The chief difficulty under discussion is, however, not removed by referring to the combinations of simple elements. There are components in the esthetic object of an altogether different origin and character, such as expression and meaning. Contemplating some picture, we do not see merely a compound of particles of yellow, golden, and green color united into a certain shape, but we see a lemon. That is, the primary impressions are the carrier of a meaning. Owing, furthermore, to the connotations bound up with this particular fruit, its smell *e.g.* and the country of its origin, an expression may be embodied in the visual image. The lemon evokes the remembrance of a sky of dazzling blue, of dark foliage, of the charm of an Italian landscape. It has, to put in Fechner's own words, "mental color." [40] The old difficulty, with which Kant struggled and which led him to distinguish between pure and adherent beauty, recurs here in the very stronghold of experimental esthetics.

To incorporate the ingredient of meaning and expression in his doctrine, Fechner resorted to the idea of association as developed by English empiricism. He inserted into his list of "principles" the "principle of association." This coördination is, however, misleading. Fechner himself recognized clearly that the "associative factor" is of an entirely different nature from the other principles classed together as forming the "direct factor" of esthetic pleasure.[41] The latter has its source in immediate experience, the former principally in memory. Creative imagination becomes in this new doctrine simply associative energy. It is the power of awakening recollections sunk into subconsciousness and blended there with the store of latent ideas.

---

[39] Cf. Fechner, *op. cit.*, I, pp. 187ff.   [41] *Ibid.*, I, pp. 157ff.
[40] *Ibid.*, I, p. 89.

Instead of completing the doctrine, the introduction of thè associative factor brings into relief an irremediable defect. The problem under consideration is not to be solved by an addition to the theory of elements but only by its revision. The pleasure aroused by a simple form, for instance by a circle, is not a sum: the pleasure taken in the mathematical figure plus expressive value attributed to it by association. As object of esthetic contemplation the circle is no longer the bare mathematical figure. Its roundness pleases because it is tinged, from the very outset, with specific expression attaching to things which are closed in themselves, swinging round their own axis, self-sufficient. This expressiveness is not logically definable. It informs none the less the contemplated figure in a very distinct fashion. From Fechner's point of view, this phenomenon is unaccountable. Another school of thought, proposing the psychology of empathy (*Einfühlung*), was needed to supplement the one-sidedness of the psychology of elements.

Empathy means the projection of human feelings, emotions, EMPATHY. and attitudes into inanimate objects. The fact itself was already familiar to Aristotle who deals with it in connection with the problem of the metaphor.[42] The modern term *Einfühlung* was first used by Robert Vischer.[43] His suggestions were taken up and developed in Germany by Theodor Lipps,[44] and Johannes Volkelt,[45] and Karl Groos,[46] in France by Victor Basch,[47] in England by Vernon Lee.

Homer calls Sysiphus' stone rolling incessantly back to the plain 'shameless.' This is an illustration used by Aristotle. "The moon doth with delight Look round her when the heavens are

---

[42] *Rhetoric*, III, 2 (1411b, 34).

[43] *Das optische Formgefühl. Ein Beitrag zur Ästhetik*, 1873; reprinted in *Drei Abhandlungen zum ästhetischen Formproblem*, 1927, pp. 1–44.

[44] *Ästhetische Faktoren der Raumanschauung*, 1891, *Raumästhetik und geometrisch-optische Täuschungen*, 1897, *Ästhetik*, 2 Vols. 1903–06, 2d ed., 1914–20, "Ästhetik" in *Kultur der Gegenwart*, I, 6, 1905.

[45] *Der Symbolbegriff in der neuesten Ästhetik*, 1876; *System der Ästhetik*, 3 Vols., 1905–14.

[46] *Einleitung in die Ästhetik*, 1892; *Der ästhetische Genuss*, 1902.

[47] *Essai critique sur l'esthétique de Kant*, 1896.

bare." The moon, in this line of Wordsworth, lives a life of her own like an animated being, enjoying in human fashion the survey of earthly things, and the question where she takes this life from, is forgotten. In a similar way we speak of a rising mountain, of raging waves, or of a melancholy evening sky. This animation of the surrounding world extends from elementary kinesthetic sensations up to our most delicate feelings and our loftiest thoughts.

The phenomenon under consideration stretches farther than esthetics. Social intercourse as a whole is based on the understanding of expressive attitudes, gestures, and words. Myth and religious symbol are vehicles of expression. The empathy theorists were not blind to these facts. But the animation of the lifeless, they believed, attains to consummation in the esthetic act. A sympathetic generosity, prompting us to lend a human soul to inanimate objects and to unite us with the universe, accounts for the depth and power of the esthetic enjoyment. Thus the idea of sympathy as developed by Lord Kames and other eighteenth century writers re-entered the esthetic discussion. Victor Basch rendered the term *Einfühlung* by 'sympathetic symbolism' or 'symbolic sympathy.'

There is a tacit presupposition underlying the arguments of the empathy psychologists. Experience appeared to them to offer facts and objects originally alien to man. Hence the occurrence of anything like expression, a human feature in non-human reality, was to be marvelled at, and the hypothesis of a hidden psychic mechanism was needed to account for it. This hypothetical act, occult in itself though manifest by its result, was called 'empathy.' An emotional state is infused into and merged with some object, so as to penetrate and mold it to its own image. All this goes on in subconsciousness. The conscious self, knowing nothing of this loan made to the external thing, encounters the manifestation of itself without necessarily recognizing it. We find things talking to us in our own language and we are unaware that their voice is merely the echo of our own. On the other hand, the responsive power in the object may persist after we become conscious of this fact. It is the latter possibility on which art rests. Art is the persistence of illusion in a disillusioned world. Wordsworth pictures daffodils and waves "dancing in glee." Yet he does not expect us to ascribe in full earnest any mood to waves and flowers; or if he did so, this wish would have nothing to do with the beauty of his verse. Reality may be dumb, unfeeling, utterly estranged from us. Yet we are in possession of a device which re-awakens it to temporary life and responsiveness, and the psychological mechanism which works this transformation is designated 'empathy.'

Fechner and the formalists were unable to recognize fully the import of the problem of artistic expression. The empathy school, on the other hand, is almost wholly preoccupied with this phenomenon. Expression is placed in the center of esthetics, all its implications are followed up, and a minute and comprehensive account given of its different modes. But is the problem under analysis really solved by the hypothesis? The act of projection is by its own nature unobservable. It is moreover unique in kind and no analogous process throwing light upon it is available. The question naturally occurred whether empathy might be understood as a variety of association. Most writers rejected this explanation. We do not see first some external form, and then associate it with an emotional content. Percept and emotion, the object perceived and the feeling expressed by it, constitute an indivisible unity. It is as though our feeling had crystallized and taken shape in an appearance of the outer world. When we contemplate Michelangelo's Moses, the posture of his mighty figure and the turning of his head do not convey the idea of a frame of mind as a secondary accompaniment. The wrath of the prophet is actually "seen with" (*mitgesehen*) a gesture which otherwise would be unintelligible.[48] Thus empathy is held to be an entirely original act, essentially independent of the association of ideas and rooted deeply in the structure of the human mind.[49]

But these statements leave the chief question unanswered. The act of empathy is not performed at random. Certain emotions attach themselves to certain forms and gestures according to strict rules. There is in some cases, especially in the sentimental anima-

OBJECTIONS AGAINST EMPATHY DOCTRINE.

---

[48] Volkelt, *System der Ästhetik*, I, 145ff.
[49] Lipps, *Ästhetik*, I, 112ff.

tion of nature, a large margin for arbitrary connection. The same configuration of clouds may impress one person as dramatic and threatening, another as joyfully triumphant. But the understanding of works of art is possible only if there exists a lawful relationship, linking percept with emotion. So the real enigma lies in the expressiveness of inanimate objects, rhythms, sounds, and visible forms in artistic representation. Relying on what law can the artist expect to arouse by his creation the same feelings which he conferred upon it by his creative act? Is the assumption of an unobservable act such as empathy any more warranted than the other hypothesis of an actually animated universe? The germs of the doctrine of empathy are found in romanticism, especially in Novalis' Magic Idealism, and it almost necessarily leads back to its romantic origin. We remember a saying of the German mystical writer who relates how, according to Swedenborg, delicate affinities establish themselves between the "orderly soul" and her outer dwelling-place—"until at last, in the entire expressiveness of what is outward, there is for her, to speak properly, between outward and inward, no longer any distinction at all." [50] If we wish to avoid such a conclusion, a revision of the very basis of the doctrine is needed.

DARWIN: BEAUTY A FACTOR IN SEXUAL SELECTION.

The quest of elementary facts, turning to the genetically primitive instead of to psychic elements, is the mainspring of the evolutionist movement led by Darwin and Spencer. Charles Darwin (1809–1882) in *The Descent of Man* directs attention to beauty as an important factor in sexual selection. The sense of beauty is not peculiar to man. "When we behold male birds elaborately displaying their plumes and splendid colors before the females, . . . it is impossible to doubt that the females admire the beauty of their male partners." [51] He points out striking parallels between natural sex colors in animals and the artificial ornaments of the human body. His observations on the field of ethnology finally led him to state again the truth of a principle,

---

[50] Quoted from Pater, *Marius*, p. 274. Cf. P. Stern, *Einfühlung und Assoziation in der neueren Ästhetik*, in "Beiträge zur Ästhetik," ed. Lipps and Werner, Vol. V, 1898, pp. 1ff.; Valentine Feldman, *L'esthétique française contemporaine*, 1936, pp. 6f.
[51] Part I, Ch. 2.

long ago insisted on by Alexander von Humboldt: "Man admires and often tries to exaggerate whatever character nature may have given him." [52]

Darwin's hint concerning a community of taste uniting animals and men was taken up by Grant Allen and others and developed into a genetic theory. They regarded art as the most sublime expression of an instinct, deeply rooted in animal nature. This current of thought was both enriched and forced into a new direction by Herbert Spencer (1820–1903). Like Darwin, Spencer seeks an explanation of art not in art itself but in a larger context. This more comprehensive reality presents itself to him not as mere animal nature but as a compound of nature and society. Physiology and sociology interpenetrate in his doctrine. These are the surroundings into which he transplants the play hypothesis borrowed from Schiller (referred to by Spencer as a German author whose name he did not remember). [53]

EVOLUTIONISM AND SPENCER'S PLAY THEORY.

In the great organisms of nature and human society, each functional part and each structural feature is determined by its peculiar utility. All our bodily powers and mental faculties, the instincts and appetites as well as the highest feelings subserve either the preservation of the individual or the maintenance of the species. There are only two activities which are exceptions to this rule and they belong together by their very exemption from the dominion of necessity: art and play. [54] It is true that activities of these orders may bring the ulterior benefit of increased power in the faculties exercised. But they have this indirect effect in common with the primary actions of the same faculties. Art and play are, as it were, the luxury of life. The individual, pausing from his attendance on the serious business of his existence, is allowed to enjoy the abundance of his energies. Taking 'play' for the general term denoting this type of useless exercise of energy, we may classify art as a kind of play.

Spencer's theory furnished an excellent though somewhat one-sided explanation of play. But it certainly did not explain art.

---

[52] *Personal Narrative*, Eng. trans., Vol. IV, 518.
[53] *The Principles of Psychology*, 1870–1872, Vol. II, Part IX, §533.
[54] *Ibid.*, §533.

To say that art is a kind of play is simply a confusion. Spencer himself occasionally seemed to have forgotten his own doctrine. His analyses of music and of beauty in men move along very different lines of thought.[55] But the decay of philosophy in Spencer's time had enlarged the credulity of his contemporaries. His thesis had a markedly scientific air about it, and thus was very successful. Grant Allen, a model disciple of his, systematized, interpolated, and completed Spencer's sketch. He is responsible for the much quoted formula: "The esthetically beautiful is that which affords the maximum of stimulation with the minimum of fatigue or waste." [56] This physiological corollary to the play theory, dubbed 'the economic principle,' stimulated various experimental studies. The eye movement theory mentioned above is a typical instance.[57] In England Alexander Bain [58] and James Sully [59] gave their votes to the play theory. It was widely accepted in France. Guyau [60] and Séailles [61] re-interpreted it in the light of their romantic conception of life, and Basch assimilated it to his idealist version of the empathy doctrine. A similar fusion was brought about by the German Karl Groos, whose books, *The Play of Animals* (1898) and *The Play of Man* (1901), were rightly admired as standard works on the subject. Hugo Riemann [62] utilized the idea of the

---

[55] "On the Origin and Function of Music," in *Essays on Education and Kindred Subjects*. Everyman's Library, pp. 328ff.; "The Purpose of Art," in *Facts and Comments*, pp. 31ff.; "Personal Beauty," in *Essays: Moral, Political, and Aesthetic*, pp. 149ff.

[56] *Physiological Aesthetics*, 1877, p. 39.

[57] The physiological reactions to esthetic impressions were experimentally investigated by Charles Féré, *Sensation et Mouvement*, 1887.

[58] *Mental and Moral Science*, 1872, Vol. I, p. 290; cf. *Education as a Science*, 1879.

[59] *The Human Mind. A Textbook of Psychology*, 1892, Vol. II, pp. 134ff.

[60] Cf. Ch. XVI.

[61] *L'origine et les destinés de l'art*, 1886, p. 18; cf. the survey and classification of the various play theories in P. A. Lascaris, *L'éducation esthétique de l'enfant*, 1928. The publications of the Spencer School are enumerated and discussed by A. Needham, *Le développement de l'esthétique sociologique en France et en Angleterre au XIXe siècle*, 1926, pp. 277ff.

[62] *Musikalische Logik*, 1873; *Grundlinien der Musikästhetik*, 1887. Later Riemann freed himself from the positivistic outlook; cf. "Ideen zu einer Lehre von den Tonvorstellungen," in *Jahrbuch der Musikbibliothek Peters*, 1916, pp. 1ff.

play-impulse in his theory of music, and Konrad Lange [63] developed it into a psychology of art. The play, he taught, which is at the very core of art and the true source of esthetic pleasure, is a deliberate and conscious self-deception, or, more accurately, an oscillation between the bent to sustain the illusion and the opposite tendency aiming at disillusionment. The observation of childish play furnishes a clue to the esthetic enjoyment of grown-ups. Little ones looking at picture books anticipate the idea of painting, and sculpture is a refined form of playing with dolls. Can we overlook the ultimate identity of toy-shop and art-gallery? This is what Spencer's play leads to when treated earnestly and thoroughly.

The various tendencies of the time come to an understanding in Yrjö Hirn's *Origins of Art* (1900). Ideas borrowed from German psychology, English and French sociology, ethnology, and physiology are here skilfully combined. The medium in which these heterogeneous ingredients fuse is supplied by Nietzsche's conception of Dionysian trance. The author is critical of the play theory as a merely negative explanation. Art, he thinks, has to serve a twofold purpose. It makes us enjoy that rich and complete sensation of life for which we strive the more eagerly the greater our vitality. And at the same time we find in art deliverance from the oppression of overstrung feeling. Like Dionysus "art moves among men, ennobling their joy and blunting the edge of their sufferings." [64]

Both psychologists and evolutionists treated esthetics as a natural science. There was, however, an undercurrent of thought opposed to this tendency. It was carried on by writers on art of various provenience, by critics, historians, connoisseurs, artists, in a word, by people whose ideas sprang from their intimate relation to art rather than from the philosophical discussions of the first half of the century, or the scientific spirit of the second. Following up this thread, we may go back as far as to Carl Friedrich von Rumohr (1785–1843), the founder of philological method

THE ESTHETICS OF THE ARTIST AND THE CRITIC: (*a*) RUMOHR AND SEMPER

---

[63] *Die bewusste Selbsttäuschung als Kern des Künstlerischen Genusses*, 1895; *Das Wesen der Kunst*, 1901.

[64] *Loc. cit.*, p. 110.

in the history of art.[65] He repudiated both Winckelmann's classicism and Wackenroder's romanticism as an intrusion of literature and literary ways of thought in the field of art. His own theory, strictly opposed to Hegel's idealist doctrine, stressed the importance of craftsmanship and technique. The finest 'conception' (*Auffassung*), he contended, is worthless without an adequate 'representation' (*Darstellung*) in a determinate material. Another exponent of the realistic countermove against esthetic idealism was the architect Gottfried Semper (1803–1879).[66] In his theoretical work, remarkable both for depth of thought and scope of learning, there are interwoven a number of ideas of which it is difficult to determine the common source and precise relation. There is first, as the background of his more specific theories, the ancient conception of the work of art as a microcosm. But this idea leads Semper to original conclusions. The three formal elements in beauty, he holds, are symmetry, proportion, and orientation, and these correspond to three levels of organization in nature, illustrated respectively in the snow-crystal, plant, and animal. There is, furthermore, the thesis that architecture, the mother of all figurative arts, has been developed out of elements prepared by the craft of the weaver, the potter, the wood-carver, and the metalworker, and that these 'minor arts,' in their turn, are derived from textile work. When man recognized that he was naked and learned to make clothes to hide, to protect, and to adorn his body, the foundations of the arts were laid. This genetic hypothesis he finally combines with the view that form in the applied arts is determined by material, purpose, and technique.[67] The latter assertion went

---

[65] *Italienische Forschungen*, 1827–32, 2 Vols., Chs. 1–2, cf. Wilhelm Waetzoldt, *Deutsche Kunsthistoriker*, Vol. I: "Von Sandrart bis Rumohr," 1921.

[66] His uncompleted chief work: *Der Stil in den technischen und tektonischen Künsten, oder Praktische Ästhetik*, 2 Vols., 1860–63, 2d ed., 1878. A draft of his doctrine in *Über die formelle Gesetzmässigkeit des Schmucks und dessen Bedeutung als Kunstsymbol*, 1856, reprinted in *Kleine Schriften*, ed. by Manfred and Hans Semper, 1884, pp. 304ff. Cf. the excellent analysis of Semper's views in Herman Nohl, *Die ästhetische Wirklichkeit*, 1935, pp. 184ff.

[67] This view was anticipated by Padre Carlo Lodoli (1690–1761) and others. Cf. Julius Schlosser, *Die Kunstliteratur. Ein Handbuch zur Quellenkunde der neueren Kunstgeschichte*, 1924, pp. 578ff.

down in history as esthetic materialism—a misnomer when applied to Semper's doctrine as a whole.

A second group of writers, more or less loosely connected with (*b*) HANSLICK Herbart's school, emphasized the importance of form as the essence of art. But unlike Herbart and his immediate followers, they were not concerned with rejecting an outworn metaphysical interpretation of art. They raised their voice against an abuse in art itself —an abuse supported, it is true, by an erroneous theory. The work of art is what it is through itself, through its appearance as a sensuous self-contained whole, and not through a message which it conveys, a story which it relates, or a mood which it imparts. This insistence on form was not amiss in an epoch in which Alma-Tadema won fame as a great painter and program music grew up luxuriantly. In a situation somewhat analogous to that which gave rise to the art for art's sake movement it was meritorious to vindicate an uncompromising conception of the purity of art.

Music was defined by Eduard Hanslick (1825–1904) as "moving figures of sound." [68] There is no subject or content separable from the musical expression and denotable in words. Even the word 'expression' has to be used with a proviso. Music, Hanslick declared, presents a dynamic pattern of sentiment but it is unable to express determinate feelings such as love, joy, sorrow, or longing. A similar segregation of non-artistic elements from pure form was achieved by Konrad Fiedler (1841–95) for painting. [69] He (*c*) FIEDLER AND assigned to the painter a domain of his own—the infinite kingdom STEVENSON of the visible, a pre-logical sphere of colors, forms, light, and shadow. The true painter is a man who knows how to see, undisturbed by the interference of rational knowledge and practical valuation. His creation is nothing but the development of a primeval faculty of vision. R. A. M. Stevenson, who held similar views, quoted in support of his theory a saying of the French

---

[68] *Vom Musikalisch-Schönen. Ein Beitrag zur Revision der Ästhetik der Tonkunst*, 3d ed., 1865, p. 45.
[69] *Über den Ursprung der künstlerischen Tätigkeit*, 1887. Re-edited in *Schriften über Kunst*, herausgegeben von Hermann Konnerth, 2 Vols., 1913–14. Cf. Hermann Konnerth, *Die Kunsttheorie Konrad Fiedler's. Eine Darlegung der Gesetzlichkeit der bildenden Kunst*, 1909.

painter, Léon Pelouse, to the effect that "the gift of the naturalist lay in the power of recreating the eye of childhood." [70] Clive Bell and Roger Fry are the rightful heirs of these theorists in our own time.

Adolf Hildebrand (1847–1921) applied Fiedler's theory with some modifications to sculpture, the art of which he himself was a master.[71] In Heinrich Wölfflin (1864–   ) the same influence was wedded to Jacob Burckhardt's refined method of esthetic analysis. His studies on the development of painting from the early Renaissance to Baroque led Wölfflin to abstract a series of polar 'forms of vision' such as linear–picturesque, plane–spatial depth, closed form–open form, variety–uniformity, absolute clearness–relative clearness.[72]

The attempt to single out formal patterns of universal applicability is typical of classicism. Wölfflin's set of types of vision is more pliable and of less practical value than the classification of styles and means of expression drawn up by Raphael Mengs and Heinrich Meyer. Yet the eighteenth century academics and the modern historian of art belong in the same family. Thus it is not surprising that an alternative type of interpretation, intended to overcome the one-sidedness of the formal analysis, was offered by an anti-classicist. Alois Riegl (1858–1905) called attention to the peculiar excellence of the post-classic Roman art.[73] We speak disparagingly of this epoch as degenerate, he argued, because our own taste is framed upon classic models. Unwittingly we expect the late Roman artist to pursue the esthetic ideal on which we have been brought up and we censure him for missing it. But we had better ask whether the artist really willed this type of perfection. He may have aimed at a different mode of expression, and his specific aim may have required new forms of representation. A

---

[70] *Velasquez*, 1899, reprinted 1914, p. 115.

[71] *Das Problem der Form in der bildenden Kunst*, 1893, 4th ed., 1903.

[72] *Kunstgeschichtliche Grundbegriffe. Das Problem der Stilentwicklung in der neueren Kunst*, 1915, 6th ed., 1923.

[73] *Spätrömische Kunstindustrie*, 1901, new edition 1927; cf. Erwin Panofsky, "Der Begriff des Kunstwollens," *Zeitschrift für Ästhetik und allgemeine Kunstwissenschaft*, 1920, XIV, pp. 321ff.; Edgar Wind, "Zur Systematik der künstlerischen Probleme," *ibid.*, 1925, XVIII, pp. 438ff.

new 'will to art' (*Kunstwollen*) may have been at work. This idea of 'will to art,' a modern replica of Friedrich Schlegel's 'esthetic energy,' is a tool to free the analyst from the classic dogma or any other esthetic bias; and it provides a clue for the understanding of any style alien to that of our own time. It denotes the universality of the artistic striving while leaving full scope to the infinite variety of styles and ideals.

A gulf seems to separate the scientifically minded psychologist or the evolutionist and adherent of the play theory on the one hand, and the German esthetes from Rumohr down to Riegl and Wölfflin on the other. Yet they belong together as complementary figures. The members of the second group are intimately acquainted with art. But the development of their ideas does not keep pace with their sensibility. They are fascinated by their own theses, ignorant of both the history and the implications of the conceptions they use. Arbitrariness and lack of balance disfigure their views. Fiedler's theory of 'pure visibility' is not free from some romantic mystification, and Riegl's 'will to art' leaves us in doubt as to whether we have to do with a psychological hypothesis or with a rudimentary metaphysics. The shortcomings of these writers are those of the highly cultured amateur, whereas the weakness of the scientific school is typical of the specialist of little developed esthetic sensibility. Both were children of the age of ignorance and vast information. Both had lost contact with the esthetic knowledge of the past. This knowledge, imperfect and inconsistent though it was in many respects, had evolved within a total view of life and world. Owing to this framework a philosophical sense of proportion had developed, forestalling waywardness and gross deviations. Is it possible to recapture this enfeebled sense? Can we restore the pattern of the mind within which art holds its proper place and rank, neither idolized nor slighted, related to what is greatest in human life, but not arrogating to itself a false predominance? .

An awareness of the dangers and the needs of the situation was to grow out of a fresh contact with the life and thought of the past. It partly resulted from, and issued in, studies delineating the history of esthetics. It is fully alive in two thinkers who may be

SCIENTIST AND ESTHETE AS COMPETITORS IN ESTHETICS.

A RETURN TO HISTORY: BOSANQUET AND DILTHEY.

mentioned here as the last important exponents of nineteenth century esthetics, Bernard Bosanquet (1848–1923) and Wilhelm Dilthey (1833–1911). Bosanquet, a member of the English Hegelian school, did not forge a doctrine destined to impress its mark on a future development. But the virtues of his teaching shone the brighter as they were almost absent in the contemporary investigations considered above. The avoidance of one-sidedness, a hospitable totality without loss of rigor, is the main characteristic in his writings. Criticizing the doctrine of empathy, an instance of a one-sided view, he avowed distrust of "all highly specialized explanations." For him the creative imagination is not "a sort of separate faculty," but "precisely the mind at work"; [74] and the creative imagination he resets in a total view of the world as having a pervading life. This life pulsates most palpably in the historical process, and Bosanquet's theory is saturated with history, from which it is a kind of effluence.

A theory which is not an airy superstructure above the infinite wealth of the historical life but rather its extract and outgrowth —this was also the ideal pursued by Dilthey. The universal matrix in which the creative gift of the artist originates, he taught, is 'the acquired context of inner life.' This whole, latent in every individual, is fully active only in the highest achievements of mankind. In the genius it determines and directs the elementary ideas and acts, conferring upon them a more than temporary meaning and stamping them with the impress of its totality. This dynamic pattern of life is not to be grasped by an enumeration of elements of pleasure, nor can it be construed by deduction. A new method of analysis, Dilthey believed, has to reveal the universal human nature within the perpetual flux of history. Dilthey never fully and satisfactorily developed his idea of an analytical method. He bequeathed to us the draft of a doctrine and an appeal to our own philosophizing powers rather than a philosophy. [75]

The Neo-Hegelian Bosanquet and Dilthey, the representative

---

[74] *Three Lectures on Aesthetic*, 1915, pp. 21f.

[75] "Die Einbildungskraft des Dichters. Bausteine für eine Poetik," 1887, *Schriften*, VI, pp. 103ff., "Die drei Epochen der modernen Ästhetik und ihre heutige Aufgabe," 1892, *Schriften*, VI, pp. 242ff.

of a modern 'philosophy of life,' belonged to widely different camps. But both had gained a profounder insight through the study of history. Their breadth of view was the antidote against the departmentalization of esthetic thought in their time. While around them the specialists, prompted by some particular knowledge and a general ignorance, fabricated all too many theses and doctrines, they cultivated that *docta ignorantia* which keeps the mind open to a comprehensive knowledge.

SUPPLEMENTARY READING

Earl of Listowel, *A Critical History of Modern Aesthetics*, 1933.
C. W. Valentine, *An Introduction to the Experimental Psychology of Beauty*, 1913.
M. M. Rader, *A Modern Book of Esthetics;* an anthology with introduction and notes, 1935.
Katherine Gilbert, *Studies in Recent Aesthetic*, 1927.
Max Dessoir, "Aesthetics and the Philosophy of Art in Contemporary Germany," *Monist*, Vol. 36, 1926, pp. 299–310.
Lionello Venturi, *History of Art Criticism*, trans. by Charles Marriott, 1936, Ch. 11.
H. R. Marshall, "Some Modern Aestheticians," *Mind*, 1920, pp. 458–71.

CHAPTER XIX

Twentieth-Century Directions

CROCE FREES ART
FROM CONFUSING
ADHESIONS BY
DEFINING IT AS
LYRICAL INTUITION.
BENEDETTO CROCE's (1866–1952) theory that art is lyrical intuition was the reigning esthetic at the turn of the century and for at least twenty-five years afterward. His trenchant negations, setting off the peculiar value of art from things conventionally confused with it and from foreign intrusions, and his positive conception of the poetical imagination seemed at last to compress all esthetics into a nutshell. [1] Croce defines art with simple brevity: it is the expression of sentiment, a pure but vital act of the imagination. Imaginative in essence, it shares imagination's primal innocence. As the most elementary kind of human language, it gives form to the passions, attractions, and revulsions of youth taking the world freshly. It articulates the formless flux of raw experience. Not being bound to represent things as they are nor to edify, art is not concerned with truth or morality, or for that matter with any laws, rules, or conventions. As pure function, it is man's passage out of infantile babbling and reacting into the ways of clear speech.

---

[1] *Aesthetica in Nuce* is the title of the Italian form (1946) of the article "Aesthetics" written by Croce for the 14th edition of the *Encyclopedia Britannica*. It is one of the best sources for a conspectus of his esthetics. An excellent general view is also given in *Breviario di estetica*, Bari, G. Laterza e figli, 5th edition, 1938 (English trans., 1st ed., Douglas Ainslie, *Essence of Aesthetic*, London, Heinemann, 1921). For more extensive study, *Estetica come scienza dell'espressione e linguistica generale*, Laterza, 6th ed., 1928 (Eng. trans., Ainslie, *Aesthetic as science of expression and general linguistic*, London, Macmillan and Co., 1909); *Problemi di estetica e contributi alla storia dell'estetica italiana*, Laterza, 2nd ed., 1923; *La Poesia*, Laterza, 1937.

The primal innocence of art can be demonstrated on a Crocean chart of being. Being is mind or spirit for Croce, because mind's nature, it seems to him, is understood through our several basic ways of grasping what is, both what is around and within us. Now the eye may see more quickly on a chart what a logical sorting out of basic ways implies: that a single shaping act necessarily comes before the scientific weaving together of individuals into systems; and that knowing things, whether individual or general, must precede doing something about them. 'Being' in its four grades, then, in logical order and with, in each case, its appropriate conception and discipline is as follows:

	General Function	Specific Function	Determining Concept	Ordering Science
1.	Theory (Individual)	Imagination	The Beautiful	Esthetics
2.	Theory (General)	Reason	The True	Logic
3.	Practice (Individual)	Desire	The Useful	Economics
4.	Practice (General)	Will	The Good	Ethics

If this be accepted as the philosophical picture of the way the most general kinds of things are, it is obvious why art as art must be free from scientific, economic, or moral adhesions. First and without prejudice must occur a knowing of things that hang together as 'ones' for humanity to operate on. These units are beautiful because they are passions brought to expressive shape. This elementary creation of order is the beginning for esthetics.

Yet though the imagination is primal shaping, it has nevertheless something under it and informing it. As a human function, the imagination presupposes the dim ferment and push of feeling; as a grade of being, imagining is a recurring moment of mastery molding the material that the spiraling dialectic of history has accumulated. The world's poets illustrate this. In any particular age they are both unaffirming inventors of new forms (being on the level

of primal innocence), and at the same time members of an ageing
humanity that has put away in its storehouse of unconscious wisdom
long centuries of moral and scientific reflection. Feeling or accumulated historical experience cannot count as a distinct grade of
spiritual being because it is subconscious. But its energy and color
are what make the characteristic content of first apprehensions.
The concept of 'feeling' as vague subterranean matter fills a place
in Croce's whole picture which many critics have missed; it gives
content to form and character to intuitions; it is the massive background and potentiality of knowledge and action.

There are many corollaries and critical implications of this
'esthetics in a nutshell,' but its kernel has been given. A recent
Italian writer, G. M. Tagliabue, who credits Croce with fifty years
of dominance in Italian reflection on art, says that for Croce defining of art is nothing but placing art. Having placed art in one of
four mental frames, Croce, he says, had essentially completed his
system, laid the basis for all his criticism, asserted art's autonomy and purity. "The innumerable ways Croce has used in approaching works of art have always been one single way: that of
defending its autonomy, in other words, of defining its position." [2]

THIS VIEW GAINS
AND HOLDS WIDE
ACCEPTANCE.

What Tagliabue finds over-simple, many theorists have found
triumphantly right, "the one thing necessary for the proper conduct of the criticism of works of Poetry." [3] Lionello Venturi, a
leading Italian art critic, uses Croce's general definition of art as
the postulate of his own criticism and of his evaluation of other
critical writing. [4] An important American literary critic, J. E.
Spingarn, wrote in 1911 that the Crocean identification of poetry
with an individual act of vision had suddenly cleared criticism of
its dead lumber and weeds. [5] He then proceeds to detail in paragraph after paragraph what the old false notions were. "We have

---

[2] G. M. Tagliabue, *Il Concetto dello Stile*, Milano, 1951, p. 50.

[3] J. A. Smith, *The Nature of Art*, London, Oxford University Press, 1924,
p. 14.

[4] L. Venturi, *History of Art Criticism*, trans. Marriott, New York, E. P. Dut-
ton and Co., 1936, "Introduction."

[5] "The New Criticism," in *The New Criticism, An Anthology of Modern
Aesthetics and Literary Criticism*, ed. E. B. Burgum, New York, Prentice-Hall,
1930, pp. 14ff.

done with all the old Rules," he says; we have done with the genres, or 'kinds'; with the comic, the tragic, the sublime, and an army of vague abstractions; with theories of style and rhetoric; with all moral judgment of art as art; with the confusion between the drama and the theatre; separation of technique from art; history of artistic themes; the treatment of art as social or cultural document; the rupture between genius and taste. From these many good riddances a well-known English follower of Croce, Edgar F. Carritt, selected one for special praise: "Nothing has so stultified criticism and appreciation as the supposed necessity of first determining the genus and species of a beauty. To ask in face of a work of art whether it is a religious painting or a portrait, a problem play or a melodrama, post-cubist or pre-futurist, is as ingenuous a confession of aesthetic bankruptcy as to demand its title or its subject." [6] Though Carritt thinks of himself as on the whole a Crocean, and approves concentration by the lover of beauty on the single act of beholding what is individual, he has queried this simplification at one point: the theory of the ridiculous. The perception of the comic, he suggests, is not immediate intuition of an individual, but redemption into individual form of what is threatening to be esthetic failure. [7] A second consideration has helped to convince Carritt of the essential rightness of Croce's esthetics: the convergence, as he believes, of philosophies of beauty through the ages toward the view first unambiguously announced by Croce. In 1931 he published a source book of esthetic theory "from Socrates to Robert Bridges," [8] and in 1932 on the basis of his historical research says of Croceanism in *What Is Beauty?*: ". . . this is no new view, and indeed . . . one reason which commends it to me is the great mass of evidence in its favour given by artists and thinkers before it had been distinctly formulated." [9]

That part of Croce's simplification which has probably roused more objection than any other is his denial of the physical reality

AFTERMATH OF CROCE'S SIMPLIFICATION: HAS HE PURIFIED ART AT THE EXPENSE OF THE ART-OBJECT'S PHYSICAL REALITY?

---

[6] *The Theory of Beauty*, London, Methuen, 1914, pp. 204-205.

[7] *Ibid.*, "The Ridiculous," Appendix 2.

[8] *Philosophies of Beauty, From Socrates to Robert Bridges, Being the Sources of Aesthetic Theory*, Oxford, The Clarendon Press, 1931.

[9] Oxford, Clarendon Press, 1932, p. 87.

of the art-work. This not only makes impossible the classification of the arts in terms of media, but it leaves out of sight the degree of control often given in the development of, say, an individual carving by the texture and habit of stone or of a painting by the load of paint on the brush. The material worked *on*, works *with* the imagination, is the retort to Croce's "lean idealism." [10] Samuel Alexander in his *Beauty and Other Forms of Value* is troubled by Croce's error or obscurity on this point. Croce "inverts the plain order of facts,"[11] Alexander complains; he makes the physical world secondary, instead of the primary matrix of life and human achievement. Now in defense of Croce it must be said that he allows incorporation in medium as a practical convenience and for the preservation of the image. But he contends that physical science tells what matter is and that physical science's methods and materials are inappropriate in esthetic analysis.

But it was not Croce's idealism nor his rejection of analysis and classification that ended his reign. It was history itself, the history that is always in motion and brings new problems and manners into the foreground for reflective philosophy to deal with. In a sense Croce left behind is Croce vindicated, for he himself defines philosophy as history thought about. He teaches that the problems of philosophy cannot be predetermined by the principles of a system, but that what comes up from day to day in work or reflection or social intercourse is the perpetually renewed material for meditation. The real problems are not fixed by a professor in a schoolroom, but arise as the historical process changes things and ties new knots for man's ingenuity to cope with. This is a realism and an empiricism that Croce may claim.

COLLINGWOOD, AT FIRST A CROCEAN, TURNS TO AN INTERPRETATION OF ART'S NEW WAYS.

Yet it was precisely renewed material for meditation that moved R. G. Collingwood (1889-1943), who had written his early *Outline of a Philosophy of Art* under Croce's banner, to enroll elsewhere when he wrote *The Principles of Art* in 1937. He now wished to do "penance for youthful follies," and meet squarely new occasions. For esthetic theory, he affirms in the preface to the new book, is not the contemplation of "eternal verities concerning

---

[10] Bernard Bosanquet, "Croce's Aesthetic," *Mind*, XXXIX, pp. 214, 215.
[11] London, Macmillan and Co., 1933, pp. 57, 133.

the nature of an eternal object called Art . . . [but] the solution of certain problems arising out of the situation in which artists find themselves here and now." [12] He had written this new book in the belief, he adds, that all he had put down would bear on the condition of art in England in 1937; and in the hope that artists and lovers of art would find his words useful. The book begins, to be sure, with the familiar basic Crocean question: What is art?, a question answered much as Croce would answer it, that is, by the assertion: Art is imaginative activity. Yet, however many echoes of the old Italian idealism still sound from Collingwood's pages, such as: Art is not for sensuous pleasure; not technique; not representation; he has only taken up his pen again, he says flatly, because around him there is a new poetry and a new way of painting that calls for an equally new way of ideas. However ambiguous Croce may be in relation to empiricism, Collingwood allied himself with it. He is convinced that his own freshly minted thoughts can sharpen judgment on the new practice. On page 3 he is already saying that a philosophical esthetician must be able to "adjudge the merits" of James Joyce, T. S. Eliot, Edith Sitwell, or Gertrude Stein. And his book not only ends with an application to *The Waste Land* but fulfills itself so. Readers who want to understand what art is when it is not amusement or magic but the expression of feeling in the language of the imagination may learn from consideration of that poem, Collingwood says. *The Waste Land* expresses for him a decayed civilization "where the wholesome flowing water of emotion, which alone fertilizes all human activity, has dried up . . . and the only emotion left is fear." [13] The 'expression,' then, is not of any personal urge in the artist, but of what the artist has had the gift to become aware of and the sensitiveness to be burdened by in the world of which he forms a part. He is the one who is able to utter what everybody senses or feels but cannot find words for. His 'virtue' or 'excellence' lies in incorruptibility of imagination. The fleeting flashes of man's elementary life take care of themselves. Their expression is automatic: the cry, shudder, or slap. But human self-consciousness can achieve awareness of what goes on in

"THE WASTE LAND," OUR AGE'S HEALING REVELATION.

---

[12] Oxford, Clarendon Press, 1938, p. vi.
[13] *Ibid.*, p. 335.

these flashes of sentience and can 'own' or 'disown' them, control or not control them. Art is the combined respect for their given burden or content and the rendering of them communicable. The artist catches their primitive savor and makes it human and intelligible to others. Art's 'truth' is the faithful transcription of the sense of surrounding events and transactions, and the compacting and welding of these transient essences into individual and relatively stable images.

This man gifted to speak the truth of imagination Collingwood calls a prophet. Prophecy in this context has nothing to do with the future or with religion. It is the revelation of unknown but socially important secrets: the lifting of subterranean currents and menaces into the light of knowledge. T. S. Eliot is a prophet for Collingwood in that he tells this age about its hidden cancer and dim dread, and gives it the poetry of self-knowledge as medicine.

However Crocean in original inspiration, then, Collingwood's last word takes a different direction. Croce had tended to lift the esthetic image free from all compromising entanglements. The Crocean-taught critic normally finished his task when he pronounced an act of imagination just that: *viz.*, a case of imagination. Collingwood's last pages operating from outside pure imagination and in obedience to the life of history warn his contemporaries to receive the medicine offered by the poet-prophet.

SANTAYANA, COMPLEMENT TO CROCE, MAKES ART SPRING FROM PHYSICAL NATURE AND ACCIDENT BUT AT TIMES ASCEND TO SYMBOLIC WISDOM.

Comparable in importance to Croce in the first part of the twentieth century is George Santayana (1863-1952). Croce is an idealist, Santayana a materialist. On a first look it would seem that these two have nothing in common. Indeed, in 1903 Santayana reviewed Croce's *Estetica come scienza dell' espressione e linguistica generale*, speaking of its barren and futile transcendentalism, tightrope artificiality, and formal truism. [14] Certainly their ways of developing their esthetic theories diverged widely and they favored contrasting terms and emphases. Yet viewing the two in perspective and seeing the total shapes of their philosophies, one remarks that Croce's ideal transcendentalism is kept from barrenness by a vast use of the particularity of history; and that Santayana

---

[14] *Journal of Comparative Literature*, I (April 1903), 191-195.

supplemented his materialism by a doctrine of essences more ethe-real than anything in Croce.

Santayana's esthetic was sketched in early, and did not so much change as the years went by as acquire "buttresses and supports" with the growth of his philosophy of nature and of essence. He was willing to say in 1939 that the humanism of his *The Sense of Beauty* and *Reason in Art* remained standing for him.[15] What was that humanism? On the whole it was a theory of values that centered around man's desiring. All good is good for Santayana because human nature makes it so. In the end no other justification can be found for the worth assigned to knowledge, religion, and the arts than the vital impulses that reach out for these satisfactions. Esthetic goods though usually thought more subjective are no more hu-manly-centered than are science and justice, goods of the intellec-tual and moral spheres. Beauty is, however, marked off from the other kinds in being immediate, positive, and intrinsic. Moral values first appear as prohibitions, and science is a texture of relations. Santayana's realm of beauty has many mansions, for his tempera-ment is tolerant and imaginative. Heresy in esthetics, he says, is orthodoxy. Yet he has and shows his preferences. He praises the serene and disciplined arts of Greece and he lights up with love the charms of sense. He has himself summed up the breadth of his taste in his retrospective "Apologia pro Mente Sua" in 1940: ". . . nor has my love of the beautiful ever found its chief sustenance in the arts. If art *transports*, if it liberates the mind and heart, I prize it; but nature and reflection do so more often and with greater authority. If ever I have been captivated it has been by beautiful places, beautiful manners, and beautiful institutions: whence my admiration for Greece and for England and my pleasure in youth-ful, sporting, ingenuous America."[16]

Esthetics for Santayana must discuss the origin, place, cause, elements, and scope of beauty. In his treatment of these things the materialistic basis of his philosophy is evident. Croce rejected the

---

[15] "A General Confession," in *The Philosophy of George Santayana* (*The Library of Living Philosophers*, Vol. II), ed. P. A. Schilpp, Evanston, North-western University Press, 1940, p. 23.

[16] *Ibid.*, p. 501.

physical fact of the medium of art; but Santayana writes: "The Parthenon not in marble, the king's crown not of gold, and the stars not of fire, would be feeble and prosaic things."[17] And when he is reporting the constitution of beautiful objects, he shows how many carnal aspects of man's nature are projected to give us pleasure: sex, breathing, drowsiness, the varieties of sensing. Of sex he says that no mechanism could have been contrived more able to suffuse the world with the deepest meaning and beauty; of breathing, that the esthetic categories of exquisiteness and awe stem from actual recurrent sensations in the throat and lungs.[18] Just as a material base is in Santayana's view indispensable for beauty, so the happy accidents in nature's evolution often initiate an art. "If [a man] happens by a twist of the hand" [19]—he will say in indicating how decorative art may have come to be; or "if the way in which idle sounds run together should matter . . . much . . ." [20] the seed of music may have been sown. The ferment of nature breeds what it will breed, the highest as well as the lowest. Once in a while chance produces a poised shape, a figment, that gives the fumbling, groping psyche delightful pause. Man picks up the luck and goes on with an art.[21] It is necessary, then, to trace the casual causes and physical origin of various types of beauty. But form in art, types of organization, the various balances of the one and many in a structure are more important than the material base for Santayana. And most important of all is the scope of an artist's vision. Imagination and intuition, mounted on natural beginnings, may rise to the full height of most profound wisdom. "The distinction of a poet . . . can be measured by nothing . . . so well," Santayana says, "as by the diameter of the world in which he lives." [22] In so far as philosophy is not the rational tracing of relations, but speculation, and in so far as poetry has power to grasp an immense sweep

---

[17] *The Sense of Beauty*, New York, Charles Scribner's Sons, 1896, p. 78.

[18] *Ibid.*, p. 56.

[19] *The Life of Reason, Reason in Art*, New York, Charles Scribner's Sons, 1917, pp. 118, 119.

[20] *Ibid.*, p. 45.

[21] *Ibid.*, p. 16.

[22] "The Elements of Poetry," *Interpretations of Poetry and Religion*, New York, Charles Scribner's Sons, 1900, p. 275.

of things and happenings, the two fall together for him. He interprets three philosophical poets: Lucretius, Dante, Goethe. Lucretius sang the birth and change of all things, atoms and the void, nature's drifts, incidents, and products; Dante, the hierarchy of good and evil and the meaning of salvation and damnation; Goethe, the varied pleasures and emptiness of a life of romantic impulse.[23] In a very early essay[24] Santayana presented Christian dogma as the poetic symbol of human destiny. His esthetic intuition universalized the significance of the atonement and of future rewards and punishments by detaching these moral ideas from factual history. The divine-human on the cross stands for the tragic suffering that meets man everywhere and at all times; heaven and hell, for the importance of the act of choice and the infinity of its inevitable consequences.

By lifting Christian dogma into the realm of poetic symbols, Santayana not only removed from religion the heavy burden of blind fact and fanatical faith, but allied himself in principle with those estheticians who recognize the importance of symbolism. Around 1925 the concept of symbol began to be central. Definitions of art as intuition-expression or as imagination, or of beauty as objectified pleasure, yielded to discussions of the implications for art of man's peculiar and marvelous power of forming symbols and signs. This movement has been many-sided, associated now with anthropology and humane scholarship, now with mathematical logic or logical positivism, and again with psychology, or once more with religion. That the science of signs and symbols began to form these alliances, and often to borrow thence a method and a frame, whereas Santayana's symbolism had grown up freely within his own individual way of looking at things, is part of the more self-conscious and perhaps pedantic way in esthetics lately.

Though specialization was imminent, a broad base for the many-sided discussion was laid by Ernst Cassirer (1874-1945) in his *Philosophie der Symbolischen Formen.*[25] Many of his articles and

ABOUT 1925 BEGINS THE DOMINANCE OF THEORIES OF THE SYMBOL.

ERNST CASSIRER, A PIONEER.

---

[23] *Three Philosophical Poets*, London, Humphrey Milford, 1910.

[24] "The Poetry of Christian Dogma," *Interpretations of Poetry and Religion*, pp. 76-117.

[25] Berlin, Bruno Cassirer, 1923-1931; Books I, II, III.

treatises, both earlier and later, supplemented this. Now a believer in the primary place of symbols in the life of man can be neither an idealist in the Crocean sense nor a materialist in Santayana's sense, but lives largely in an 'in-between realm' of distanced images and deposited meanings. Symbols are, it is true, more ideal than material and Cassirer thought of himself as an idealist in the line of Kant. But he made it clear in discussing the crucial role of symbol-creation in the functioning of man that symbols are by no means only in man's head, but belong to the "persistent, continuously expanding and refined art of the detour," [26] by which man can pause in his organic traffic with his environment and store and stabilize his experience in unique mid-way carriers. The faculty of symbol-formation, rather than reason, is, for this school of thought, what makes man man. Art, being symbolization at its height, is what makes man most man.

A symbol for Cassirer is not only an ideal object half-way between man and his world and binding the two. It is also a busy messenger running back and forth between the two with the office of conciliation. It is always ambiguous because of its polarity, which nevertheless it constantly overcomes by active and accumulative interpretative potency. It is the chief tool by which man cuts himself free from nature and instates himself in the universe of intelligible forms and functions. "The beautiful," says Cassirer, "is essentially and necessarily symbol because . . . it is cleft inwardly; because it is always and everywhere both one and double. In this split, in this attachment to the sensuous, and in this rising above the sensuous, it . . . expresses the tension which runs through the world of our consciousness . . . and [the] basic polarity of Being itself." [27] The best illustration for Cassirer of this symbolic process is the poetical work of Goethe, and within Goethe's work, the *Pandora*. As a poem the *Pandora* floats on the surface of sensuous show, but as meaning, it all at once draws into the range of

---

　　[26] " 'Spirit' and 'Life' in Contemporary Philosophy," in *The Philosophy of Ernst Cassirer*, ed. P. A. Schilpp (*The Library of Living Philosophers*, Vol. VI), Evanston, The Northwestern University Press, 1949, p. 870.
　　[27] "Das Symbolproblem und seine Stellung im System der Philosophie," *Zeitschrift für Ästhetik und Allgemeine Kunstwissenschaft*, XXI, 296.

man's apprehension the way primitive manual skill calls for the light of science, and shows how science is incomplete without practical application in social life; and how the human hope of progress must be balanced by acceptance of the inevitability of passage and decay for all things sprung from Nature. Thus a total vision of the limits and potentialities of human life is caught in the poem's crystal of physical sound.

Cassirer's doctrine of symbolic form is one of the determining influences in the impressive output of the Warburg Institute. [28] The very first article published by its *Journal* was Jacques Maritain's "Sign and Symbol," and the aim professed in the Foreword of the *Journal* was the exploration of "the working of symbols—the signs and images created by ancient, and employed by modern generations, as instruments both of enlightenment and of superstition." Maritain's point of view is Neo-Thomist. He not only insists on the miraculous change effected in the Eucharist, but distinguishes the various uses and contexts of sign-employment generally. He says that in our present 'solar' or 'logical' state of culture, artistic and poetical symbols are speculative signs because they manifest a reality beyond themselves, practical signs because they embody an order or appeal, magical because they bewitch, and inverted because they reveal the state of the artist's soul and his social situation. CONTRIBUTIONS TO THE THEORY OF SYMBOLS BY THE WARBURG INSTITUTE.

Erwin Panofsky, author of the second article published in the *Journal*, "The Early History of Man in a Series of Paintings by Piero di Cosimo," is one of the main members of the Warburg group, and his point of view concerning artistic symbolism is closer to Cassirer's and more typical of the whole school of writers than is Maritain's. Panofsky identifies the symbolic function of a picture with its fourth and deepest layer of meaning, and explicitly links his statement with Cassirer's theory. On the surface or first level, says Panofsky, a picture shows recognizable objects and events; next, below this, one reads off the style in which artistic convention required objects to be painted in a particular period; on

---

[28] 23 German and 14 English volumes of studies begun in 1922; 9 volumes of lectures; and the *Journal of the Warburg* [later *Warburg and Courtauld*] *Institute* (1937–).

the third level one finds types or allegorical figures, Melancholy, Eros, or St. Paul; and on the fourth is the intrinsic, philosophical significance, "where the total habits of the time bear subtle witness to themselves." In order to understand these total habits, the art-historian must be a learned humanist, searching for light on the symbolism of his picture through "as many documents of civilization historically related to that work . . . as he can master, of documents bearing witness to the political, poetical, religious, philosophical, and social tendencies of the personality, period, or country under investigation." [29]

One of the best illustrations of Cassirer's concept of the symbol as utilized by the Warburg group is Panofsky's study *Die Perspektive als Symbolische Form.* [30] Here Panofsky traces the handling of perspective from classical times to the present and relates the ordering of space to the characteristic world-view of the time. In classic times, the 'intrinsic meaning' of setting many bodies loosely and casually in the picture-space is to be discovered in the philosophy of Democritus. For Democritus all Being is an aggregate of atoms and a void loosely related, like the objects in the picture's space. The inconsistent impressionism of Hellenistic landscape gets meaning from the contemporary inconclusive Pyrrhonic scepticism; the succession of roofings and canopies in Gothic architecture goes with St. Thomas's doctrine of space as a nest of forms, with a divine outer body sheltering all; Piero della Francesca's mathematical perspective system in the Renaissance is to be ultimately seen in the light of the rising mathematical rationalism in philosophy; Rembrandt's distortion of space symbolizes the modern rise of subjectivism; and non-Euclidean pan-geometry is behind Abstractionist and Suprematist painting.

Thus committed to the prime importance of symbolic meaning the Warburg scholars have defended the controversial 'literary' approach to the visual arts. In the early Christian sarcophagi they see not masses and lines alone but what the history of religion discloses: the Christian faith at grips with the beliefs of Paganism and

---

[29] *Studies in Iconology*, New York, Oxford University Press, 1939, p. 16.
[30] *Vorträge der Bibliothek Warburg*, 1924-1925, pp. 258-330.

Judaism; in Velasquez's portraits, the whole ethos of the Catholic Spanish Court; [31] in the portraits of Gainsborough, the plain naturalism of Hume. [32]

The doctrine of signs and symbols has been freshly applied to music by Susanne Langer in *Philosophy in a New Key*. Though Mrs. Langer refers to Cassirer as "that pioneer of the philosophy of symbolism," she expresses primary indebtedness to the "sage" Alfred North Whitehead, pioneer in contemporary mathematical logic. [33] From this science she would seem to have received her chief methodical direction; inspired by logic is her distinction between types and intentions of languages; terms that are functions of systems; operation with mediators; precise orientation; cautious movement in argument.

SUSANNE LANGER'S THEORY OF THE SYMBOLISM OF MUSIC: UNCONSUMMATED SYMBOL OF THE INNER LIFE.

Mrs. Langer agrees with most competent musicians in denying artistic significance to the composer's personal history or to the emotional effects on listeners. The meaning of music as art is not to be found in these casually related psychological events. But she is equally opposed to the "nonsense" of saying that music has no meaning but itself. She places music, like myth, in that obscure middle realm between immediate biological experience of the human animal and the thinner air of reason. It belongs to the stage when the soul of man is beginning to refer impressions beyond themselves, to stabilize his feelings and his images, and forge tools with which to master the dizzying flux around him. Both in myth-making and in music-making Mrs. Langer declares unfinished the act of distinguishing product from process in meaning. She therefore calls music an "unconsummated symbol." It stands, she claims, for the rise, fall, and iridescent interplay of feelings—not the composer's, but universal man's. The flowing process of feeling is ordered by musical intelligence into a tonal pattern. But the translation of process into form itself grows, shifts its plane, and proliferates. "Music," she says, ". . . is a form that is capable of conno-

---

[31] Rudolf Wittkower, *The Warburg Institute Annual Report, 1947-1948*, "Appendix," Fritz Saxl, 1890-1948, p. 17.

[32] Edgar Wind, "Humanitätsidee und Heroisiertes Porträt in der Englischen Kultur des 18 Jahrhunderts," *Vorträge*, 1930-1931, pp. 156-229.

[33] Cambridge, The Harvard University Press, 1942, Preface, p. ix.

tation, and the meanings to which it is amenable are articulations of emotive, vital, sentient experiences. But its import is never fixed. . . . We are elaborating a symbolism of such vitality that it harbors its principle of development in its own elementary forms as a really good symbolism is apt to do." [34] In summary she says: "Music is our myth of the inner life—a young, vital, and meaningful myth, of recent inspiration and still in its 'vegetative growth'." [35]

SEMANTIC
ANALYSIS OF
I. A. RICHARDS:
EVOCATIVE
FUNCTION OF
POETICAL SIGNS,
PROJECTILE
ADJECTIVES.

We said that the now dominant science of signs and symbols is many-sided. Besides the anthropological and logical approaches we have been noting, there are those of 'semanticists' and 'semioticians' whose goal is a positive science allied with psychology. The best known of these attempts and that most used by critics of literature [36] and the arts is the one initiated by Charles Ogden and I. A. Richards in the publication of *The Meaning of Meaning.* [37] As scientists, semanticists break down the meaning situation into its factors and variable functions, and insist on verification of interpretation by reference to tangible fact. The meaning situation for them consists of three elements: the subject using the sign; the object referred to; and the sign itself, carrier of the reference. The main functions of 'meaning' are four: description of the object; expression of feeling about the object; of attitude toward a listener; and of practical end to be achieved by what is spoken. For art, the usual emphasis of language is the second: the expression of the author's feeling about his material. But in discourse with an esthetic

---

[34] *Ibid.*, p. 240.

[35] *Ibid.*, p. 245.

[36] The "new" (since c. 1920) literary criticism shares much with the semantic movement here noticed both in problem and in recognizing the primary position of I. A. Richards. Each gives to the term 'meaning' a new emphasis and sophistication. But the new critics as yet lack any unifying philosophy though they seek both a theory of being and of knowledge as related to poetry. With the help of the new psychology, of logical distinctions, and of acute sensibility they analyze the multiple significance, the formal pattern of poems new and old, and the intricacies of poetical experience. Common critical terms used technically by them are: metaphor, structure, texture, tension, irony, ambiguity, paradox. Among the critics are, in addition to Richards: R. Blackmur, C. Brooks, J. C. Ransom, A. Tate, R. P. Warren, Y. Winters.

[37] First edition, New York, Harcourt Brace, 1923; begun in 1910, parts published in periodicals in 1920-1923.

color, this meaning is frequently mingled with other functions, particularly with a tone taken toward the audience. Thus poetry is thought of as mainly, though not purely, an evocative use of signs. "Many, if not most, of the statements in poetry are there *as means* to the manipulation and expression of feelings and attitudes, not as contributions to any body of any doctrine whatsoever." [38] Now one of the main devices used by poets in their function of evocation is metaphor. Richards calls metaphorical adjectives esthetic or 'projectile' adjectives, because while belonging strictly with the feelings of the speaker they are often erroneously projected by him on to the object or state-of-affairs referred to. This displacement gives rise to a series of ambiguities. For example, 'pleasant' usually stays fairly well set in the speaker's own attitude, being equal to: 'It pleases me'; but 'pretty' gets out into the middle between subject and object; and 'beautiful' tends to join the object end of the situation.

Observation of the place and weight of ambiguities in 'aesthetic' adjectives moved William Empson, a follower of Richards, to write *Seven Types of Ambiguity*. Here the stages of increasing logical disorder in poetry are linked with increasingly intense metaphorical language, and also with the ever more dramatic division in the torn spirit of the poet himself. Empson follows the logic of the poetical sign from easy two-way faceting in a simple metaphor, through pun and allegory, to a broadening and deepening of reference, querying, artificiality, and problem-raising, until the climax is reached in the expression of schizophrenia. [39]

EMPSON ON AMBIGUITY.

Pluralism, whether in the structure of the metaphor, or as the true philosophy of definition, is a first principle in scientific semanticism. Pluralism's relevance for the interpretation of critical terms is illustrated by the sixteen distinct definitions of 'the beautiful' listed and briefly oriented in *The Foundations of Aesthetics* by Charles Ogden, I. A. Richards, and James Wood. [40] The original preface claims novelty of method for *The Foundations* in its toler-

ESTHETIC PLURALISM IN SEMANTICS.

---

[38] I. A. Richards, *Practical Criticism*, New York, Harcourt Brace and Company, 1929, p. 186.
[39] Norfolk, Connecticut, New Directions, 1947, pp. 245, 275, 282, 286.
[40] New York, International Publishers, 1925.

ance: "verbal conflicts are avoided," and distinction rather than opposition of theories is presented, each theory being allowed its separate sphere of validity. For example, one may identify 'the beautiful' with an intrinsic property of an object, with the expression of genius, with objectified imitation, with revelation of a higher truth, with self-projection, with play, or (and this is the one the authors prefer) synaesthesis, *i.e.*, the capacity to produce harmony and equilibrium in the varied and sometimes contrary impulses of the beholder. Though reasons are given for preferring the final definition (it is better to be fully alive than partially alive), the postulate of the *Foundations* is esthetic pluralism, *i.e.*, one is entitled to find esthetic excellence wherever one's own thought leads.

The semanticists, then, seek logical clarity and public assent regarding definitions of critical terms in the arts, by placing every definition in its proper relation to the intention and background of the definer. Analysis of the various frames of reference should end, they claim, the long and futile war of words. [41]

THE RATIONAL AND LOGICAL OUTSIDE SEMANTICS.

Semanticism has become an influential school of thought with leaders, adherents, and a program. There are, however, writers on esthetics not thus attached who share the semantic emphasis on logic and rational analysis but develop their thought more freely. For instance, D. W. Prall [42] examines the basic orders in nature which "frame" the qualities of color and sound; C. J. Ducasse [43] defines esthetics as the science of the definition of critical terms; R. W. Church [44] inquires into the meaning of the term 'beauty' and defends intellectual criticism. Also in harmony with the logical and scientific trend in esthetics, but carrying it toward abstract rigor, is the group of mathematical studies: essays on *Dynamic*

---

[41] Currently a widely read writer on semantics as science. is Charles W. Morris. See his *Foundations of the Theory of Signs (International Encyclopedia of Unified Science*, Vol. I, No. 2), Chicago, University of Chicago Press, 1938. A briefer and more popular statement of his views is to be found in *The Kenyon Review*, I (Autumn 1939), 409-423: "Science, Art and Technology."

[42] *Aesthetic Judgment*, New York, Thomas Y. Crowell Co., 1929; *Aesthetic Analysis*, New York, Thomas Y. Crowell Co., 1936.

[43] *Philosophy of Art*, New York, Dial Press, 1929.

[44] *An Essay in Critical Appreciation*, London, G. Allen and Unwin, Ltd., 1938.

Symmetry by Jay Hambidge, [45] George Birkhoff's *Aesthetic Measure,* [46] and Matila Ghyka's *The Geometry of Art and Life.* [47]

Proceeding to another aspect of the esthetic concern with symbols, we find its most popular application uses psychoanalysis. The treatment of obscure subconscious symbols by Freud, Jung, Adler, and kindred thinkers has claimed the orderliness of analytical science and has won also the popular fascination that comes with morbidity and the occult. It draws both those interested in causes and in wonders. Thus it has from opposite quarters entered strongly into the common climate of explanation and reference. Psychoanalysis appears sometimes as one tool in the logical semanticism we have just been noting, although Freud directs attention below the rational level. In the course of his short discussion of the seventh type of ambiguity Empson refers to Freud three times. [48] Freud's theories throw light for him on the hidden grounds for the employment of opposites. The conjunction of God and dung in Crashaw's poetry, for example, may be interpreted as the mark of a deepseated childish conflict. One may almost say that there is hardly an esthetic theory in our day that has not been influenced in some degree by the Freudian approach. Because psychoanalysis was originally cure of sick souls, it is concerned with particular cases and veers toward the eccentric. For example, Freud suggests that the famous elusive smile of Leonardo's Mona Lisa refers to intense erotic relations of tenderness between a sensitive illegitimate child and a lonely deserted mother; also to a vulture-fantasy in a dream of childhood. Literature even more than painting has been subject to psychiatric scrutiny: for example, *Hamlet* and *Faust.*

POPULARITY OF INTERPRETATION THROUGH PSYCHOANALYTICAL SYMBOLS.

Though the interpretation of art and artists thus tends to be converted into the biography of the mentally abnormal, this school of thought has developed a more general theory of the way deepseated blocks and the biological crises confer a pattern on poetry and on the other arts. Its adherents describe typical mechanisms of behavior. Taking as her basis Jung's doctrine of "the collective un-

BODKIN ON ARCHETYPES

---

[45] New Haven, Yale University Press, 1920.
[46] Cambridge, Mass., Harvard University Press, 1933.
[47] New York, Sheed and Ward, 1946.
[48] *Op. cit.,* pp. 194, 223, 226.

conscious" and the principal epochs of its career, Maud Bodkin [49] has elaborated a theory of archetypes in poetry. The guilt-haunted wanderings, the terror-hued descents of heroes into caverns and the menacing of dragons, the fountains of youth and gardens of love are all in some way masks of generic man's fear of falling and of darkness, and of consolation and resurrection. Water stands for drowning and for healing: the engulfing flood and the fountain of life and baptism. Air, wind, and breeze stand for life; the motions of the individual psyche for power. The violent human crises of birth, sex, acceptance of parents, and self-discovery are the inner-meaning, according to this approach, of most great drama; and all Greek art can be discerned dimly in the symbol of the Sphinx.

NAHM ON PRESUPPOSITIONS.
A more philosophical employment of symbols for esthetic theory, though one using psychoanalysis and anthropology, is made by Milton Nahm in his *Aesthetic Experience and Its Presuppositions*. [50] The work of art, Nahm says, is a symbol of feeling-tension on two levels: It refers in a backward-looking phase to the instincts of the race (generic Epimethean emotion): ancient habits of the chase, erotic passion, and will to be leader and master. These broad animal instincts are specified and narrowed when man achieves the faculty of thought. Then the leader of the pack becomes the Divine Father; and the light of spring and noon, the fiery chariot of Apollo or the nimbus of a god. For Nahm these older and newer conditions of feeling unite in an artist to precipitate the creative, forward-looking phase of feeling. So the Promethean moment of art-activity rises on top of the Epimethean and gives courage and exaltation to the poet. The meaning of a work of art is ultimately its force for the creation of human creators.

THE NEO-THOMIST ROOTS SYMBOLIC FUNCTION IN DIVINE ACTIVITY;
Those who write on esthetic symbolism from a religious point of view ground artistic quality in divinity, and this is still another kind of esthetic concern with symbols. What is beautiful is the language of the Perfect conveyed through human organs of speech. Neo-Thomists inevitably render, in contemporary idiom, St. Thomas's doctrine that Beauty comes from integrity, proportion,

---

[49] *Archetypal Patterns in Poetry: Psychological Studies of Imagination*, London, Oxford University Press, 1934.
[50] New York, Harper, 1946.

and splendor. These qualities, we are taught, come in the last resort from an encounter deep in the artist's engendering faculty with the All-Creative Divine Presence. God fertilizes the artist's genius in 'the dark night of his soul'; kindles the elements in his receptacle; and when the incubation is over, the artist communicates to the world the symbol of the vision of his brooding-time. The condition of poetizing, says Jacques Maritain, [51] is the interior silence, a recoil from the senses upon the center of the self and a long germinating slumber. The collected and stored energies continue to operate in the poet's dreams. They engage, there, with the wider spirit that moves through all things. In this way the inspiration of the poet reveals its identity with the Prime Craftsman, the Architect of the World. [52]

Not confined to Thomistic inspiration, but with a parallel orientation, is Ananda Coomaraswamy's theory of art as religious, or better, as metaphysical symbol. His view, enriched by learning that stretched from ancient Hindu to American Shaker sources, is a doctrine of universal correspondences. The beauty of art, he declares, is to remind rather than to delight, and esthetic savor fulfills its function when it becomes a support for contemplation. The 'esthetic shock' of the loveliness of the dew drop, for example, should pass into an awareness of the transitoriness of all living things. For Coomaraswamy the current emphasis on esthetic surfaces, on formal elements in abstraction from 'literary' meaning, and on 'function' without consideration of religious symbolism, is provincial—"bourgeoisie fantasy." [53]

THE ORIENTAL IN METAPHYSICAL CORRESPONDENCES.

Twentieth-century directions in esthetics, we have claimed, have become more than any other one thing semantic directions. But theories of signs and symbols have, as we have noted, joined or utilized now one science and now another to make a total method and view, have been now literary or speculative, now positivistic,

---

[51] *Situation de la Poésie*, Paris, Desclée de Brouwer et cie, 1939. See K. Gilbert, "Recent Catholic Views on Art and Poetry," *The Journal of Philosophy*, XXXIX (November 19, 1942), pp. 654-661.

[52] Cf. Dorothy Sayers, "Toward a Christian Aesthetic," *Unpopular Opinions*, New York, Harcourt, Brace and Co., 1947, pp. 30-47.

[53] *Why Exhibit Works of Art*, London, Luzac and Co., 1943, p. 95.

now rational, and now instinctive in tendency. Some of these sciences and tendencies that have been allied with semantics have also developed in other ways without much reference to semantics. Psychology, for instance, has been interested in art independently of Freudian symbolism; social and historical studies have made art or taste their object without research on icons; and the special approaches of phenomenology and existentialism have not been without esthetic concern. It is obvious that the varied wealth of recent studies can only be briefly suggested in such a summarizing chapter as the present one.

FROM DOCTRINE OF SYMBOLS TO VARIOUS PSYCHOLOGICAL TRENDS.

First, certain psychological expositions and explorations other than the Freudian. One of the earliest was Richard Müller-Freienfels' *Psychologie der Kunst*. This cultivated humanist had been a student of William James and shared James's belief in the mind as a goal-seeking structure developing on the basis of biological need. This emphasis on the mind as an organic whole and on all mental experiences as attitudes or strivings may be illustrated from his account of the creativity of the artist. An artist's creative power, says Müller-Freienfels, belongs to his inmost essence, and is no later-acquired dexterity. The best single name for his power is imagination (*Phantasie*), but this is not an eccentric command of unrealities, nor indeed anything separate from representative human behavior. The artist is not a special type of man, but has a high degree of sensitivity and ability to express and give articulate form to deeply imprinted experiences. Edgar Allan Poe was not an artist because he dreamed strange dreams, but because he unfolded at a deeper level the visions of many and rendered the type plastic. [54] Both in his psychology of art itself and in his *The Evolution of Modern Psychology* [55] Müller-Freienfels shows appreciation of and ability to draw from many approaches: psychopathology, psychoanalysis, Gestalt psychology, comparative and socio-psychology, characterology, and philosophical backgrounds, such as Bergson's theory of memory and duration.

---

[54] *Psychologie der Kunst*, Dritte Auflage, Leipzig, Berlin, B. G. Teubner, 1923, Band II, 26.
[55] Trans. W. B. Wolfe, New Haven, Yale University Press, 1935.

The theory of artistic creativity put forward by Samuel Alexan- INSTINCT THE
der is closely associated with the hormic and social psychology of BASIS OF ARTIST'S
William MacDougall. Alexander was convinced that the right way CREATIVE POWER.
to explain the artist's creative process was to survey, as a naturalist,
the various animal and human impulses. From these he selected as
the true biological spring of art the constructive impulse. Bees construct hives; beavers their mound homes. And similarly man makes
art, excited into productivity by the delightfulness of some sensed
matter. He goes on from instinct to craft, for he foresees the good
end he works to attain. But to be a fine artist, he must rise to the
third stage in which he makes a thing for the sake of its intrinsic
beauty in contemplation. [56] Another esthetician, Swedish by birth,
but closely sympathetic with the psychology of MacDougall and
the esthetic method of Alexander, is Helge Lundholm. Lundholm,
however, develops the esthetic productivity out of the instinct of
curiosity instead of out of the impulse to construct. [57]

The psychology of Gestalt (form, configuration) associated THE GOOD GESTALT
in recent years with the names of Wertheimer, Wolfgang Köhler, IS THE
Koffka, and Arnheim offers still another esthetic theory. This PHYSIOGNOMY OF
theory is based on wide experimentation concerning the elements A WHOLE.
of good shape and why man is attracted to it. Man likes shape—so
the theory goes—because nature likes shape. Man merely follows
nature's lead in preferring forms economically built and easy to
appropriate. Shapeliness, with its sub-characters of balance, rhythm,
design, and hierarchical organization, is welcome because nature
must produce her forms efficiently or lose her pains. Now efficiency is economy, and economy is grace, and grace is pleasant.
When an artist shapes his material, we learn, he does not select from
nature's confused offerings what he as a superior intelligence finds
good; nor does he impose order on a given chaos. He goes the
easiest way that succeeds, as the crystal crystallizes and the cat co-
ordinates. The imagination of the artist, again, is not a function distinct in kind from ordinary perception, but only more self-con-

---

[56] *Beauty and Other Forms of Value,* London, Macmillan and Company,
1933, Chapter II.
[57] *The Aesthetic Sentiment,* Cambridge, Mass., Sci-Art Publishers, 1941,
p. 169.

scious and emphatic. Common perception strives toward organic integration in itself and in its environment from the beginnings of sentience. The pattern produced is the best possible permitted by circumstances. Beauty, or the sum of esthetic character, becomes, then, in this theory the physiognomy of a whole; for it is wholes, not isolated points, that succeed in evolution and in human experience. [58]

But the physiognomies of art-shapes vary in their drawing power, just as human faces charm, some more, some less. In the official language of Gestalt certain object-wholes require the response of the spectator more than others. The ego and its object are together in a field and the tension between the poles is stronger or weaker, according to the strength of the 'requirement' and the resistance to or compliance with it. A good work of art has a high degree of requiring quality; the fit spectator meets the requirement 'purely.' And every great artist responds 'purely' to the configuration of the presentment. That is why he is an artist: his vision is clear. But certain configurations pull harder and reach down in their drawing-act to profounder levels of the ego than others; and reciprocally, some personalities resist the call of important form more than others; and among those who resist some succeed more quickly or for longer periods in attaining reconciliation with that part of their world that is addressing them and demanding incarnation in art. On this basis three types of artistic personality may be distinguished: (1) the sympathetic or well-adjusted, such as Mozart and Raphael; (2) the demonic-balanced, such as Goethe and Leonardo; and (3) the demonic-anarchical, such as Baudelaire and Beethoven. [59]

VARIETY OF
ARTISTIC TEMPERA-
MENTS; CLASSIFI-
CATIONS OF EVANS
AND READ,
FOLLOWING JUNG
AND DILTHEY.

The psychological interest in distinguishing types of artists developed after Wilhelm Dilthey's striking essay correlating types of men with species of world-view. [60] His follower, Eduard Spranger, made a more concrete and widely applicable analysis in

---

[58] Kurt Koffka, in *Art;* a Bryn Mawr symposium, Bryn Mawr, Pa., Bryn Mawr College, 1940, pp. 254-256.

[59] *Ibid.*

[60] "Weltanchauung und Analyse des Menschen seit Renaissance und Reformation," Berlin, 1925.

his *Types of Men: the Psychology and Ethics of Personality.*[61] Recently, in 1939, Joan Evans, the art-scholar, turned aside from her medieval researches to publish a "brief study of psychological types in their relation to the visual arts."[62] She was aware of the whole historical background of typology, but leaned immediately on Carl Jung's *Psychological Types* (1921). She distinguished four, splitting Jung's introvert and extravert in two: (1) slow extraverts, who love power and have a strong sense of fact and produce an art dramatic, geometrical, technically powerful, as Michelangelo; (2) quick extraverts, who favor sensual beauty, sentiment, and religious ecstasy, as Botticelli; (3) quick introverts, who liberate what is significant from what is not, and have an instinct for rhythmical relations, as Piero della Francesca; and (4) slow introverts, who are calm, veering toward melancholy, and favor repose, frontality, and simple reasonableness, as Hugo van der Goes.

Also reflecting Jung's distinction of types, but controlled as well by Edward Bullough's work and Jaensch's researches on eidetic imagery, is a set suggested by Herbert Read. Though Read checked his results by general theories, he actually found his way to his groups through sorting thousands of children's drawings. He thus deduced eight kinds of artistic temperament. "The child as such does not exist," he says, "and any uniform education based on such a mythical figure is merely a rack on which the all too plastic mind of the individual is distorted."[63] The eight types are mere emphases in disposition, and not mutually exclusive. They represent, however, distinctions both in mode of apprehension and expression. The eight are: (1) Organic (fusion with object, and sympathy with groups in relation, as growing trees); (2) Impressionist (records sensations produced by objects; preference for characteristic detail); (3) Rhythmical (makes a pattern out of repeated motifs); (4) Structural (favors stylization to the point of a geometrical formula; (5) Enumerative (painstaking recorder); (6) Haptic (expresses tactual sensations); (7) Decorative (makes

HERBERT READ ON IMPORTANCE OF ART FOR SOCIETY. NEED TO RECOVER TRUST OF FEELING AND INTUITION.

---

[61] Berlin, 1914, 1919. Authorized trans. 5th German ed., Paul J. W. Pigors, Halle, M. Niemeyer, 1928.

[62] *Taste and Temperament*, London, Jonathan Cape, 1939.

[63] *Education through Art*, London, Faber and Faber, 1943.

a gay pattern in two dimensions); (8) Imaginative (elaborates a fanciful theme often from literary sources).

Herbert Read develops his theory of artistic types among children as a necessary part of his essay on *Education through Art;* and his care for the importance of art belongs in its turn to his enduring concern that society should understand and cherish what artists can do. We pass with Read to contemporary interest in the social implications of art. "When we are no longer children, we are already dead," Read affirms; and he finds us so today. If civilization is to continue, a new way of life must be found. He insists not only that art is the most important element in a child's education, but that commercial manufacture is made vicious through indifference to the arts of design, and that the health of society—interpersonal as well as international—requires harmonizing and vivifying influences. Art must be reinstated in the common life out of which it arose and for whose beneficent course it is the chief hope.

SUPPORT OF BERGSON AND WHITEHEAD.

Herbert Read traces our fatal loss of childlike simplicity in part to distrust of intuition. For four centuries we have been building our practice on mathematical reason and accumulations of positive fact. This has induced habit efficient, strong, competitive, and cold; but it has robbed us of feeling and *The Innocent Eye.* [64] Read recommends to us the recovery of feeling and intuition, as all readers of his works know, on the basis of his personal experience and temperament. But he can claim also the ultimate support of the philosophy of Bergson. The kernel of Bergson's teaching is that there are basically two approaches to reality made by man: one is scientific, and it simplifies and canalizes the rich, varied stream of reality in order to act on it for practical human ends; the other is rare, penetrating, and subtle. The latter is the insight of artists, saints, and all spiritual inventors, who by-pass science, by-pass practical advantage and control, and go to the depths of individuals: individual rhythms in nature and individual qualities in men. Belonging with the inventive intuition is the gift of contagion. The artist, seeing freshly, communicates powerfully. Bergson believes that the first approach has monopolized men's attention for too long, and that

---

[64] The title of Herbert Read's autobiography in the American edition: New York, Henry Holt and Company, 1947.

integrity, sympathy, and sanity will only return when the artist's mode of vision and sympathy is given its due importance in human affairs. The kinship with Read's outlook is obvious. Indeed, he says that only in Bergson, among the philosophers of the past, has he found a "wisdom," "objective theories," and a "definition of art" which he could accept. [65] In 1924 Read edited the *Speculations* of T. E. Hulme, and this collection of "essays on humanism and the philosophy of art" includes one entitled "Bergson's Theory of Art."

Professor Alfred North Whitehead also urges the importance for contemporary life of supplementing logic with esthetic intuition. Whitehead has already been mentioned as the pioneer mathematical logician who influenced Susanne Langer's theory of symbolism. Now Bergson has often been classed as an irrationalist; no one could so classify Whitehead. And yet Whitehead speaks explicitly of the unfortunate effect on the "aesthetic needs of civilized society" of scientific domination, and of analysis as "eviscerating." Almost as if he were Bergson or for the moment Read, he says: "The soul cries aloud for release into change. It suffers the agonies of claustrophobia. The transitions of humor, wit, irreverence, play, sleep, and—above all—of art are necessary for it. Great art is the arrangement of the environment so as to provide for the soul vivid, but transient, values." He goes on to say that the values are also permanent and disciplinary, and that it is scarcely possible to exaggerate their importance in an age which threatens to go down in its materialism and mechanism. [66]

At the opposite pole from metaphysicians Bergson and Whitehead, city-planners and architects of the new school have also been concerned with the social implications of art. Without lacking philosophy these men have had a hand and a craft that could manipulate detail. For they are fitted to organize traffic, materials, techniques, economy as well as to envisage the comprehensive ideal of the integrated human being in well-designed surroundings. They

THE NEW ARCHITECTS AND DESIGNERS HAVE A THEORY OF COMMUNAL HUMAN VALUES.

---

[65] "The Present Philosophy of Art," *Art Now*, London, Faber and Faber, 1936, pp. 53-56.

[66] *Science and the Modern World*, New York, The Macmillan Company, 1925, pp. 290-292.

work and write under the general postulate that man's ethic makes
his shell, and his shell largely influences his ethic. Lewis Mumford
1895–   ), follower of Patrick Geddes, and author of a notable
series of volumes on the culture of cities, the connection between
technical invention and civilization and the human values involved, [67] furnishes an array of historical illustrations of the thesis.
The early New England village is a prime example, he shows, of a
community kept small enough and so organized physically and
spiritually that all the inhabitants could participate effectively in
the common business: a plot of land in the center reserved for the
common use; about it grouped the places housing community interests: meeting-house, school, and town-hall; land for private cultivation divided fairly. [68] Over against such an organic group of
buildings and lands informed by such a spirit is Greater New York,
a sprawling mammoth, where the greed of the speculator has in-
flated the price of land beyond reason and justice, and where the
resulting skyscrapers for big business at the center deprive "of dignity the human beings who walk in their shadows." [69]

LEWIS MUMFORD'S
ORGANIC SOCIAL
PHILOSOPHY
BALANCED BY
RESPECT FOR
THE INDIVIDUAL.

Like Herbert Read, Lewis Mumford has studied community-
design not as a science alone, but as part of morals. Building and
cities are for the good of man; mechanical invention and city-plan-
ning must serve human vitality, tolerance, freedom, and religious
self-transcendence. Mechanical ingenuity and city expansion are
desirable only when they facilitate mutual understanding and the
fruitful enjoyment of leisure; not when allied with quantitative
production and congestion or with military power. Mumford's eye
is on the whole man in the whole place; his is an organic social philosophy. But though his attention has been largely on community
designs, he never forgets the permanent need for private cells for

---

[67] *Sticks and Stones, a Study of American Architecture and Civilization*,
New York, Boni and Liveright, 1924; *The Brown Decades*, New York, Harcourt
Brace and Co., 1931; *Technics and Civilization*, New York, Harcourt Brace and
Co., 1934; *The Culture of Cities*, New York, Harcourt Brace and Co., 1938;
The South in Architecture, New York, Harcourt Brace and Co., 1941; *City De-
velopment*, New York, Harcourt Brace and Co., 1945.
[68] *Sticks and Stones*, p. 23.
[69] *Ibid.*, p. 175.

meditation and enclosed gardens for refreshment. [70] The universal language of classicism in architecture must be balanced for him by respect for the uniqueness of the neighborhood and the locality. [71]

For the last quarter century architectural design has been distinguished among the arts for the amount and quality of reflection devoted to it. Siegfried Giedion, for example, has issued monumental studies, technical and historical, on the sensitive relation of building and town-planning to the changing concepts of space and time from Florence in 1400 to Rockefeller City today, and again on the way household equipment from locks to bath-tubs has become mechanized and how this has affected human living. [72] Dean Richard Hudnut published, in 1949, a kind of architect's philosophy in his *Architecture and the Spirit of Man*. [73] Members of the Bauhaus group, with Walter Gropius at their head, and Moholy-Nagy as leader in experiment and literate defence, have revived the old conception of architecture as the mistress-art, but in a manner congenial to the twentieth century. In fact, architects have recently so busied themselves with their art's wider implications and relations that at least one of their number has suggested that they need once more to 'mind their own last.' [74]

Social philosophy and humanism characterize the interpretation of art by John Dewey and his associates. Dewey's own appearance as a thinker focussing on the meaning of art came late in his career. He had already published his views on logic as experiment and practical instrument, on education for democracy, and on ethics as theory of the good for individuals in relation to their social context. The basis for an esthetics was thus familiar ground. Art for Dewey is experience; experience is biological interplay, doing and under-

JOHN DEWEY'S SOCIAL PHILOSOPHY FLOWERS IN ESTHETICS.

---

[70] *The Culture of Cities*, pp. 28-29; *City Development*, p. 185; *Town Planning Review*, April 1949, p. 14.

[71] The necessary supplementation of the two for America is the theme of *The South in Architecture*.

[72] *Space, Time, and Architecture, the Growth of a New Tradition*, Cambridge, Mass., Harvard University Press, 1941; *Mechanization Takes Command, a contribution to anonymous history*, New York, Oxford University Press, 1948.

[73] Cambridge, Mass., Harvard University Press.

[74] John Summerson, *Heavenly Mansions, and Other Essays on Architecture*, London, The Cresset Press, 1949, p. 197.

going. In the experience which is art, the rhythm of intaking and outgoing is "lifted high above the threshold of attention and made manifest for itself." Though Dewey published *Art as Experience* in 1934, [75] he had long been associated with the art-connoisseur and collector Albert C. Barnes, [76] and as Educational Director of the Barnes Foundation had published a series of articles in its Journal. Here he had said that art and labor, art and nature, above all art and normal human experience must not be abstracted from each other. "Art is not something apart, not something for the few, but something which should give the final touch of meaning, of consummation, to all the activities of life." [77]

ACHIEVEMENTS OF HIS FOLLOWERS.

Though Dewey's personal output in esthetics was late and small, the expression of his philosophical position, social, empirical, and scientific, through friends and disciples who were interested in esthetics, has been very large. Irwin Edman, [78] by his literary felicity and the insights of a cultured human being, has won a wide public hearing for the general attitude; Lawrence Buermeyer gave in 1924 a clear and patient analysis of *The Aesthetic Experience;*[79] more recently Bertram Morris has done an analogous thing for *The Aesthetic Process;* [80] Van Meter Ames has applied the method to the *Aesthetics of the Novel* [81] and to *André Gide.* [82] Horace Kallen in his two-volume history of the relation of *Art and Freedom* [83] makes Dewey's concept of art as the liberating and consummatory aspect of experience the touchstone and climax of the right placing of the artist in society through the ages. Thomas Munro is a follower of Dewey who has written extensively and with detailed analysis on the application of the *Scientific Method in Esthetics.* [84]

---

[75] New York, Minton, Balch and Co.
[76] Author of *The Art in Painting,* New York, Harcourt, Brace and Co. 1928.
[77] Dedication Address, Barnes Foundation, May 1925, pp. 5-6.
[78] *Arts and the Man,* New York, W. W. Norton, 1939.
[79] Merion, Pa., Barnes Foundation.
[80] Evanston, Northwestern University Press, 1943.
[81] Chicago, University of Chicago Press, 1928.
[82] New York, New Directions, 1947.
[83] New York, Duell, Sloan and Pearce, 1942.
[84] New York, W. W. Norton, 1928.

His recent extensive volume *The Arts and Their Interrelations*[85] shows his analytical engine at work on the problem of the title. He lays before the reader all the significant definitions of art and the classifications of them in their interplay, not failing to include recent or minor additions to the world of art, such as the 'film.' *Art and the Social Order*, a relativistic and scientific discussion, with Dewey's general orientation, was published by D. W. Gotschalk in 1947.[86] Gotschalk defines art in order to set himself this main question: "What is the importance of the arts for social life, especially in the twentieth century?" He considers both central and peripheral values: development of maturity and dignity in human beings is central; service to medicine, recreation, education, religion, commerce, commemoration, and physical convenience is peripheral.

Also very much interested in the social implications of art as scientifically determined is Charles Lalo, president of the *Société Française d'Esthétique*, and author of a half-dozen works in the field.[87] Lalo is a relativist and positivist in philosophy, and has special competence in music among the arts. It is natural that he should conceive all works of art, therefore, on the analogy of musical structure. Every work of art, he says, is a combination of the polyphonic type, a structure made pregnant by a process of counterpointing one structure against structures on other planes within the whole. His relativism leads Lalo to a sustained examination of the effect on art of the erotic impulse, religious repression or stimulation, technical discoveries, fashion, fame, and economic changes.

LALO'S RELATIVISTIC ESTHETICS IS SOCIAL AND MODELLED ON MUSICAL POLYPHONY.

Investigation of taste and esthetic orientation in past centuries has been hardly less active than the interest in art's social significance. Perhaps this is not due to intellectual curiosity alone but in part to a prophetic feeling that history rather than psychology or

MANY HISTORICAL RESEARCHES AND TRANSLATIONS; FEWER GENERAL SYSTEMS.

---

[85] New York, Liberal Arts Press, 1949.
[86] Chicago, University of Chicago Press.
[87] Among them: *Introduction à l'esthétique*, Paris, 1912; *L'art et la vie sociale*, Paris, 1921; *L'art et la morale*, Paris, 1922; *La beauté et l'instinct sexuel*, Paris, O. Doin, 1922; *La faillite de la beauté* (with Anne-Marie Lalo), Paris, 1923; *L'expression de la vie dans l'art*, Paris, F. Alcan, 1933; *Éléments d'une esthétique musicale scientifique*, Paris, J. Vrin, 1939.

anthropology is to be the dominant discipline of the future. Only a few examples of historical monographs, translations, and articles can be listed here; among histories of taste, general or special: *Cycles of Taste* [88] and *The History of Taste* [89] by Frank P. Chambers; *Tides in English Taste, 1619-1800* by Beverly Sprague Allen; [90] "The Mona Lisa in the History of Taste" [91] by George Boas. Mr. Boas' essay exemplifies his well-known relativistic and historical attitude in criticism. Studies of past esthetic theory have been numerous: *Études d'esthétique médiévale* by Edgar de Bruyne; [92] *L'esthétique de Calvin* by Leon Wencelius; [93] *The Aesthetic Theory of Thomas Hobbes* by Clarence A. Thorpe; [94] *The Sublime: A Study of Critical Theories in Eighteenth-Century England* by Samuel H. Monk, [95] also his supplementary study, "A Grace Beyond the Reach of Art"; [96] *L'Esthétique de la Grâce* by Raymond Bayer, [97] a massive collection of studies with emphasis on Leonardo da Vinci's theory of grace and of light; *Die Vollendung der Klassischen Kunst bei Hegel* by Helmut Kuhn; [98] and a special issue of *The Journal of Aesthetics and Art Criticism* [99] devoted to the meaning of the baroque style as exhibited in various arts. Among translations with introductions may be noted: *The New Science of Giambattista Vico* by Thomas Bergin and Max Fisch, [100] and *Kant's Critique of Judgment* by H. W. Cassirer. [101]

Since the mood of the twentieth century is empirical, pluralistic, and specific rather than sweeping and speculative, it has produced more studies of special problems than comprehensive surveys

---

[88] Cambridge, Mass., Harvard University Press, 1928.
[89] New York, Columbia University Press, 1938.
[90] Cambridge, Mass., Harvard University Press, 1937.
[91] *Journal of the History of Ideas*, I (1940).
[92] Brugge, "De Tempel," 1946.
[93] Paris, Les Belles Lettres, 1937.
[94] Ann Arbor, University of Michigan Press, 1940.
[95] New York, Modern Language Association, 1935.
[96] *The Journal of the History of Ideas*, V, 131.
[97] Paris, Félix Alcan, 1933.
[98] Berlin, 1931.
[99] Volume II (December 1946).
[100] Ithaca, Cornell University Press, 1948.
[101] London, Methuen and Co., 1938.

or systems. Yet esthetics has occupied certain of the philosophers who see all things in relation. The race of speculative philosophers never dies. Volumes of a systematic character have been addressed sometimes to advanced students and independent scholars and sometimes to those being given a first broad look at the field. For illustration attention may be called to an early and a recent example of work of this comprehensive type. In 1906 (second edition 1923) Max Dessoir, now chiefly associated in our minds with his editorship of the *Zeitschrift für Ästhetik und Allgemeine Kunstwissenschaft* and his organization of international congresses for esthetics, published his treatise: *Ästhetik und Allgemeine Kunstwissenschaft*. His primary motive was the long-needed distinguishing of esthetics from the general science of art, and the orderly and patient exposition of the problems of each. Esthetics, he claims, investigates taste and those agreeable impressions regularly conditioned by the harmonious structure and "envelope" of objects in nature, life, and art. An esthetic experience is a welcome intuition the necessary grounds of which may be traced in the objective counterpart. The discipline of esthetics is controlled by the concept of the beautiful, while the arts arise not from pleasant feelings linked with beauty, nor from the play-impulse, but from the impulse to make form (*Gestalt*). The general science of the arts, in distinction from esthetics, seeks to determine the complex origin, essence, value, and interrelations of the arts. It is peculiar to the artistic creator that he generates a form as a whole in his own psyche, and feels the thrust toward making this form a real object, when stimulated by an external occasion. The arts may be divided into the two great classes of figurative (two- and three-dimensional) and musical (mimicry, music proper, and poetry). Dessoir, following Schiller, makes the spiritual function of art the welding of the sensuous and spiritual sides of man.

Recently Stephen Pepper has published three works of wide scope: *Aesthetic Quality*, [102] *Principles of Art Appreciation*, [103] and *The Basis of Criticism in the Arts*. [104] Pepper himself describes his

---

[102] Boston, Charles Scribner's Sons, 1938.
[103] New York, Harcourt Brace and Co., 1949.
[104] Cambridge, Mass., Harvard University Press, 1945.

Basis as a prolongation of evidence into the esthetic fields of the material gathered for his more general *World Hypotheses.* A critic, he says, usually will assume "some tentative organization of the totality of evidence." [105] This tentative totality will be one or more of four doctrines of universal order: the mechanistic, contextual, organistic, or formistic. Pepper attributes the mechanistic hypothesis to Santayana, though he points out that Santayana's esthetics spilled over its limits. The mechanistic hypothesis emphasizes the location of the sense of beauty in the body's reactions, and turns around the experience of pleasure-pain. The contextual hypothesis does not locate beauty in bodily sensation but in the general situation. Values gathered thence into a work of art are creatively and cumulatively intuited, and yield an experience of intense and profound quality, rather than of measurable pleasure. The organistic basis of criticism places esthetic value in "integration of feeling about a perceptive center such as a work of art." The fourth or formistic basis exalts the normal and the universal; the balanced and the typical.

In addition to these two examples and to those already mentioned in connection with special trends or interests, the following general treatments may be listed: *Beauty, A Philosophical Interpretation of Art and the Imaginative Life* by Helen H. Parkhurst, [106] a sensitive work, with a slightly mystical cast; *The Principles of Aesthetics* [107] and *The Analysis of Art* by De Witt H. Parker; [108] *Art and Beauty* by Max Schoen; [109] *The Spirit and Substance of Art* by Louis William Flaccus, [110] all being readable and useful texts for undergraduate students. An original but abstruse work, developing thoughtfully a system of esthetic categories, is *The Aesthetic Object* by E. Jordan. [111]

---

[105] *Ibid.,* p. 32
[106] New York, Harcourt, Brace and Co., 1930.
[107] Boston, Silver, Burdett and Co., 1920.
[108] New Haven, Yale University Press, 1926.
[109] New York, Macmillan Co., 1932.
[110] New York, F. S. Crofts and Co., 1941 (3rd edition).
[111] Bloomington, Ind., The Principia Press, 1937.

An ambitiously comprehensive but not speculative treatment of the arts is Theodore Greene's *The Arts and the Art of Criticism.*[112] He diagrams and describes the matter, form, and content of the six major arts: music, dance, architecture, sculpture, painting, literature, making subdivisions and cross-references until the whole world of the arts stands finely articulated before the reader. The meticulousness of his division of categories may be illustrated by the kinds of matter he distinguishes in music: (1) the primary raw material of qualified sound; (2) the secondary raw material of emotions and strivings that may realize expression in pure music, of perceptual events in program music, and of literary language in songs; (3) the primary artistic medium of tonalities with their "intricate grammar and syntax"; and (4) the secondary artistic medium of universalized emotions or external happenings. Greene crosses the path of the semanticist by discussing the nature of meaning and the possibility of 'truth' in the arts. He argues that there is truth specific to art, the expression of an "insight which, though original in the sense that the artist was the first to achieve it, must be such that others, following in his footsteps, can more or less closely approximate to it." John Hespers has also defended in *Meaning and Truth in the Arts* [113] a special kind of "truth-to" for art as distinguished from "truth-about" in science.

The importance of Moritz Geiger's phenomenological esthetic lies rather in its depth than in its breadth. [114] The method involves the intuiting of the essential worth and structure of an art-object. Such an intuiting, which yields an essence, is a patient and disciplined contemplation undertaken by the person, the 'I' in its completeness and most profound seriousness. This deep-lying self penetrates to the law of the relevant art-form by analyzing and assimilating the individual. One case, known through and through, teaches man what no statistics nor accumulation of points could show. Geiger distinguishes sharply between the pleasure-accompaniment of amusement and the joy-characteristic of the authentic

PHENOMENOLOG-
ICAL ESTHETICS OF
MORITZ GEIGER.

---

[112] Princeton, Princeton University Press, 1940.
[113] Chapel Hill, University of North Carolina Press, 1946.
[114] *Zugänge zur Ästhetik*, Leipzig, Der Neue Geist Verlag, 1928.

entering into art. Pleasure goes with temporal occurrences that merely mark the biological adjustment of the psyche to its environment. Joy in art, in contrast, belongs to the permanent worth-engagement of the person. It is, indeed, a measure of a man's humanity, as is his religious engagement, his sense of deep social responsibility, and his scientific acumen. Geiger describes the essence intuited by the ego as combining the qualities of the Platonic Form and the dynamic object-aspect of the Hegelian *Geist.*

STUDIES IN RECENT ESTHETICS.

    The varying direction of esthetic reflection in recent years has been the subject of several books with diverse approaches: *Studies in Recent Aesthetic* [115] and *Aesthetic Studies* [116] by Katharine Gilbert; *A Critical History of Modern Aesthetics* by the Earl of Listowel; [117] *A Modern Book of Esthetics*, edited by Melvin Rader; [118] and *New Bearings in Esthetics and Art Criticism* by Bernard C. Heyl. [119] Naturally, restricted expositions such as these give only a token of the multiplied interests and inquiries into details of the last half-century. A completer sense of the variety may be

JOURNALS.

obtained from a look through the tables of contents of the two main journals of the period: *the Zeitschrift für Ästhetik und Allgemeine Kunstwissenschaft*, running from 1906 to 1939, and edited by Max Dessoir; and the American *Journal of Aesthetics and Art Criticism*, begun in 1941 and going on actively at present. The American *Journal* has been edited since 1945 by Thomas Munro. The first name in the German table of contents is that of the famous German empathist, Theodor Lipps, "On 'aesthetic mechanics'," and the last that of Richard Müller-Freienfels, on "Cognition of art and understanding of art." One thousand nine hundred eleven articles are listed. Everything from Japanese lacquer to general systems of esthetics is purveyed. Sample titles from the American *Journal* are "The System of the Arts" by Helmut Kuhn; "Gestalt and Art" by

---

[115] Chapel Hill, University of North Carolina Press, 1927.
[116] Durham, Duke University Press, 1952.
[117] London, G. Allen and Unwin, 1933.
[118] New York, Henry Holt, 1935.
[119] London, Oxford University Press, 1943.

Rudolph Arnheim; "Some Aspects of St. Augustine's Philosophy of Beauty" by Emmanuel Chapman; and "Psychological Aspects in the Practice and Teaching of Creative Dance" by Franciska Boas.

Tools for the esthetician have been prepared by bibliographers and dictionary-makers: *A Bibliography of Aesthetics and of the Philosophy of the Fine Arts*, edited by William A. Hammond; [120] *A Bibliography of Psychological and Experimental Aesthetics, 1864-1937*, edited by A. R. Chandler and E. N. Barnhart; [121] *Encyclopedia of the Arts*, edited by Dagobert D. Runes and Harry G. Schrickel; [122] *Dictionary of World Literature*, edited by Joseph T. Shipley. [123] Responsibility for a selective current bibliography in esthetics and related fields was assumed in 1945 by Helmut Hungerland, associate editor of the *Journal of Aesthetics and Art Criticism;* the first bibliography was published in the December 1945 issue, and sections have appeared in the issues for June 1949, June 1950, September 1950, and June 1951. The bibliography is carefully classified by the arts and includes a German and a Polish section.

---

[120] New York, Longmans, Green and Co., 1933.
[121] Berkeley, California, University of California Press, 1938.
[122] New York, The Philosophical Library, 1946.
[123] New York, The Philosophical Library, 1943.

INDEX

Absolute Idealism, 430-436
absolute and relative beauty, 242
Absolute, the, and appearance, 345; and
common sense, 411; manifested in art,
372; symbolized in art, 460
abstract forms yield pure pleasure, 38
abstractio imaginationis, 298
Achilles, 46, 175, 521
action, indispensable in tragedy, 70; in
poetry and visual art, 305-306
activity, continuous and uniform, accompanied by pleasure, 75
actor, art of, classed with dance and
music, 462; true, must be fictitious
character, 126
actors, number of, 97
Addison, J., 233, 237-239, 250, 253, 302,
308, 321-322, 324
adherent and pure beauty, 322, 337-338,
536
Adler, A., 567
admiration, 223
adventure without danger, 277
Aeneas, 122, 181
Aeschines, 97-98
Aeschylus, 97
Africanus, 98
Agatharcus, 31
ages of man, characterized, 93
'agreeable' and 'beautiful,' meaning of
terms, 318
agreeableness, a riddle, 192; sensuous,
509
Alberti, L. B., 163, 166-167, 170-171, 177,
184-185, 187, 189, 192
Albertus Magnus, 129, 141
Alcamenes, 34
d'Alembert, J., 534
Alexander, S., 554, 571

allegory, all-inclusive, 150; cultivation
of, by Stoics, 95; in *Divine Comedy*,
149; makes best poetry, 205; in painting, 562, 565; too cold, 276; veil of
truth, 165
Allen, B. S., 580
Allen, G., 526-527, 541-542
Alma-Tadema, 545
ambiguity in poetry, 565, 567
ambition, explains esthetic expansive-
ness, 255; and sublimity, 254
America, esthetic task of, 425-426
Ames, Van Meter, 578
Amor, used as religious type, 149
anagogical meaning of *Divine Comedy*,
149
analogies, cosmic, 117; of divinity in
art, 419
analogy of Pythagoras, 259
analysis of art, 16
anatomy and art, 178
Angier, R. P., 533
animal form, 107; perfect, as standard
for art, 64, 69, 188
Anschauung (intuition), 345-346
anthropology, 315, 354-355, 568, 580
anthropomorphism, 5, 7, 357; favors art,
445
anticipation, imaginative, 350-351, 354
anticipatory character of modern art,
435
Antigonus, 98
Antiphanes, 30
Antiquity, as standard, 354
Apelles of Kos, 90, 107
aperçus on art, 89
Apollo, 51, 434, 445, 470, 568
Apollodorus, 29, 99
Apollonian form, 520-521